International Marketing

Analysis and strategy

Fourth edition

Sak Onkvisit and John J. Shaw

Routledge
Taylor & Francis Group

NEW YORK AND LONDON

First edition published by Charles Merrill in 1989
Second edition published by Macmillan in 1993
Third edition published by Prentice-Hall in 1997

Fourth edition 2004
Simultaneously published in the UK, USA and Canada
by Routledge
29 West 35th Street, New York, NY 10001

and by Routledge
11 New Fetter Lane, London EC4P 4EE

Routledge is an imprint of the Taylor & Francis Group

© 2004 Sak Onkvisit and John J. Shaw

Typeset in Perpetua and Bell Gothic by Florence Production Ltd, Stoodleigh, Devon

Printed in the United Kingdom by the Alden Group, Oxford

British Library Cataloguing in Publication Data
A catalogue record for this book is available from the British Library

Library of Congress Cataloging in Publication Data
Onkvisit, Sak.
    International marketing : analysis and strategy / by Sak Onkvisit and
    John J. Shaw. – 4th ed.
        p. cm.
    Includes bibliographical references and indexes.
    1. Export marketing. 2. Export marketing – Management.
    I. Shaw, John J.   II. Title.
      HF1416.O55 2004
      658.8'4 – dc22   2003023746

ISBN 0–415–31132–2 (hbk)
ISBN 0–415–31133–0 (pbk)

To my family and the memory of my grandparents and Lawrence X. Tarpey, Sr.
and
Ann and Jonathan and the memory of Rebecca

Contents

CONTENTS

CONTENTS

Illustrations

FIGURES

TABLES

EXHIBITS

CULTURAL DIMENSIONS

MARKETING ETHICS

MARKETING STRATEGIES

IT'S THE LAW

Preface

UNIVERSITIES IN THE NEW MILLENNIUM AND INTERNATIONAL EDUCATION

Policy makers (executives and government leaders), educators, and students alike have a basic obligation to take advantage of the opportunities to learn and transmit the knowledge of the world. International experiences are not luxuries. Without the comprehension of global issues, education is not complete.

International marketing is not a subset or special case of domestic marketing. While a person should benefit from an observation of marketing in another culture, the greater benefit is derived from one's better understanding of oneself in the process.

To both the universities and students, global – not national – orientation is essential. Universities in this millennium should strive to offer international education, and to differentiate between business techniques that are universal and those that are unique to a particular country or region.

UNIVERSALITY OF MARKETING: INTERNATIONAL OR PAROCHIAL?

Marketing, just like medicine and engineering, is a universal discipline of study. As such, the marketing discipline provides insights for the understanding of the business process anywhere – irrespective of national borders. Ideally, due to its universal nature, that is how marketing should be taught.

In a perfect world, there should be nothing international or domestic about the discipline of marketing, since all international and domestic activities are supposed to be naturally and seamlessly integrated. Any marketing concepts and theories should thus be covered as global activities that are applicable everywhere regardless of the national context. As an example, the essence of the concept of market segmentation may be first described in a universal way and then applied in the context of, say, Japan or Spain – with any countries being interchangeable. As a consequence, such courses as consumer behavior, marketing research, and advertising should be taught as discipline-based courses by having the international nature fully woven or incorporated into all courses. If that were the case, international courses and international textbooks would be redundant and unnecessary.

Unfortunately, because of the dominance of American textbooks (and European textbooks to a lesser extent), marketing has always been taught from either the US or European perspective. In response, the AACSB International and the efmd have urged the business schools to incorporate the international dimension into the curriculum.

A conventional approach employed by business schools all over the world is to offer a few international courses (e.g., international business, international marketing, international finance). This approach splits international marketing from domestic marketing and implies that the international aspect of marketing is distinct and different from the national (usually American or European) dimension of marketing activities. This artificial dichotomy may do more harm than good.

The blunt truth is that, unless and until business schools are willing to truly reorient their academic approaches and strategies by teaching marketing as a universal discipline, scholars, practitioners, and students will need to adopt the second best approach by offering a course of "international" marketing. Toward this end, it is critical that a textbook covers international marketing in the most rigorous way.

THE MOST AUTHORITATIVE TEXTBOOK

Marketing, as a discipline of study as well as in practice, is dynamic, exciting, rigorous, and challenging. Our approach in this text reflects this belief. The fourth edition of *International Marketing: Analysis and Strategy* has been written for the purpose of educating future executives to meet international challenges. Designed for marketing majors and MBA students, it provides solid foundations that are useful for explanation, prediction, and control of international business activities. Due to its depth and breadth, the text is suitable for any international marketing (and perhaps international business) courses at both undergraduate and graduate levels. We are hopeful that you will find this textbook to be one of the most, if not *the* most, authoritative in a number of ways – international perspective, comprehensiveness, substance, and rigor.

Global perspective

Our attempt is to present the concepts and practices of international marketing in the most universal and authoritative way. Certainly, this text recognizes the economic and political significance of the USA, the European Union, and Japan. As a result, there is a significant and appropriate coverage of the triad. On the other hand, the textbook also pays attention to the importance of the emerging markets.

Unlike some standard (i.e., national) marketing textbooks that merely insert foreign examples, this textbook aims to be internationally relevant by using the global perspective. All regions of the world are covered, and their cultural and business practices are considered. There is a serious attempt to make the treatment of the subjects as international as possible.

In terms of international adoption, this textbook is one of the most successful ever. We sincerely appreciate the confidence of the instructors and students from all parts of the world. The textbook has been adopted in the USA, the UK, Australia, India, and so on, thus confirming the international focus of the text.

Rigor

One misconception often held by casual observers is that international business is not a rigorous field of study. Perhaps the most significant contributing factor to this unkind assessment is the failure of most textbooks to adequately provide scholarly substance. Many well-known texts provide only a "soft" coverage of international marketing by basically reporting *anecdotes* rather than scientific facts. From the academic standpoint, anecdotes are never adequate to prove the validity of a proposition. To compound the problem, such textbooks employ a simplistic approach that focuses mainly on cultural differences rather than on decision making.

In reality, international marketing is a solid discipline that is just as rigorous as such courses as consumer behavior, marketing research, and marketing management. Reflecting the reality, this text has made a serious attempt to use the theoretical and empirical evidence to offer marketing insights as related to actual applications. It should appeal to the instructor or student who wants *substance* and is tired of the simplistic and repetitive approach employed by most other texts. The text is for the reader who prefers a *rigorous* treatment of the subject as well as an integration of theories, applications, and managerial implications. The approach is analytical and managerial rather than merely descriptive.

Because of the textbook's rigor and sophistication, coupled with its strong application focus, the text has been used at all education levels – undergraduate, MBA, and Ph.D.

Comprehensiveness: breadth and depth

The fourth edition provides solid foundations – strategically and theoretically. In terms of breadth and depth of coverage, this text is the most complete and authoritative one. This text is more comprehensive than the others in treating in depth a number of relevant and significant topics. There are chapters on marketing barriers, financing, foreign exchange, consumer behavior, branding and packaging, and physical distribution. There are two chapters for each of the four Ps of marketing. Discussed in detail are financial strategies, analysis and management of political risks, bribery, jurisdiction, counterfeiting, gray marketing, subcultures, services, foreign trade zones, representation agreements, dumping, and countertrade.

An examination of the index should quickly reveal that the coverage of the text is far superior to that of the other standard texts. The *company and trademark index* shows that the text is highly applications-oriented and that it extensively covers real-world practices. The *country index*, in contrast, clearly demonstrates the global perspective of the text. The *subject index*, on the other hand, lists all the critical topics, including the latest developments. Finally, the *name index* and *end notes* leave no doubt as to the inadequacy of the other popular texts in terms of theoretical and empirical substance.

A high degree of teaching/learning flexibility is possible because the materials found in the text stress decision making. As such, they are thought-provoking and may be used for a variety of assignments, classroom discussions, term papers, and exams.

The best conceptual framework and theoretical coverage

Most well-known texts use a descriptive approach which merely reports isolated incidents based more on casual and personal observation than on rigorous investigation. Naturally, the descriptive materials can become obsolete very quickly. This simplistic approach does not serve the instructor and students well. A competent textbook should not be basically a compilation of anecdotes (i.e., newspaper and magazine examples). Clearly, there must be a conceptual/theoretical framework to understand international marketing problems and guide marketing decisions.

The first edition of *International Marketing: Analysis and Strategy* broke new ground by providing fundamental principles and a theoretical framework to understand international activities and/or pursue a managerial career in international marketing. The approach has been very well received and widely praised because it fulfills a real need. The fourth edition continues this leading edge.

The text is highly distinctive in that it is essentially the only text that seriously uses scholarly sources to provide theoretical explanation and empirical evidence to support the actual practices. The leading international journals (i.e., *Journal of International Business Studies* and *Journal of World Business*) are the major sources of information. At the same time, we also rely on several other well-known international marketing journals (e.g., *International Marketing Review*, *European Journal of Marketing*).

To have a complete understanding, we have considered other marketing sources as well. In particular, we rely on the two most influential sources: *Journal of Marketing* and *Journal of Marketing Research*. In addition, the two major advertising journals (i.e., *Journal of Advertising Research* and *Journal of Advertising*) provide information on international advertising practices.

There is no other international marketing book which comes close to the fourth edition of *International Marketing: Analysis and Strategy* in terms of scholarly substance. Unlike other texts which still discuss the traditional concepts in a static manner, this text offers the latest findings which show the advancement of those concepts. Students will greatly benefit from this higher level of sophistication.

Strong application

In spite of its strong theoretical foundations, this text does not describe international marketing concepts only in abstract terms. Actually, the text is highly applications-oriented. A great deal of effort has been spent on meaningfully integrating the theoretical foundations, empirical evidence, and actual business practices.

The fourth edition of *International Marketing: Analysis and Strategy* is superior to other texts in terms of application. Like others, we rely heavily on such leading business publications as *Business Week*, the *Wall Street Journal*, the *Asian Wall Street Journal*, and the *Financial Times*. This coverage is very extensive and second to none.

Unlike others, we also rely on the most authoritative US government publications such as *Export America*. At the international level, readers will benefit from the publications of the International Monetary Fund — *IMF Survey* and *Finance & Development*.

In addition, industry-specific publications such as *PROMO* are used to report the stories about international promotional activities and foreign exchange activities.

The fourth edition is very user-friendly. First, the "marketing illustration" section begins each chapter. Second, its unique feature is a collection of interesting advertisements to illustrate international marketing activities. Third, the text includes discussion assignments and minicases to stimulate discussion.

To further emphasize the real-world applications, the fourth edition includes another innovative feature. There are boxes of marketing illustrations included in each chapter. These boxes contain the "Marketing strategy," "It's the law," "Marketing ethics," and "Cultural dimension" illustrations. These real-world examples illustrate the effects of the legal, ethical, and cultural dimensions on the one hand and the good and poor strategies of business firms on the other.

In sum, the fourth edition employs a pragmatic approach by emphasizing actual applications in the real-world marketplace. It uses numerous leading business publications extensively for pragmatism.

Revision

We do not believe that the revision of any textbook should merely update the business examples or that it should list only new references for decorative reasons. Unlike consumer behavior texts which report the latest theoretical developments and empirical findings, international marketing texts have a tendency to report the latest anecdotes. Most international marketing texts contain references or footnotes that are mainly magazine and newspaper articles. When theoretical and empirical sources are used at all, they are not really part of the text discussion. A brief sentence in the text portion is not going to describe the content of a reference, thus doing students a great disservice.

Unlike other books, this text incorporates the latest scholarly works into the text materials so as to reflect the latest progress of academic works. At the same time, it reports the latest practice in the real world. The references used are the latest available, with about 50 percent of the sources of information being from the 2000s.

LEARNING AIDS

The fourth edition gives the instructor a great deal of flexibility. Each chapter includes discussion assignments, minicases, and cases. As a result, the instructor and students are not restricted to only review questions. They can select from numerous assignments for active classroom discussion and class projects. The fourth edition has added several new cases and minicases. In addition, there is an abundance of chapter-opening vignettes, advertisements, exhibits, tables, and other illustrations that highlight the discussion and show how the business concepts are used in practice.

Each chapter includes a number of pedagogical aids. The questions at the end of each chapter ask students to review or explain the concepts. In addition, discussion assignments and minicases require students to apply what they have learned in actual situations. In order to further stimulate ideas and debate so that students can become actively involved in applying the concepts, there are cases of varying length for each chapter. These cases were written specifically to address concepts and issues introduced in the chapter.

A unique feature of the book is the inclusion of two simulation games: one involving culture and another focusing on foreign exchange. These games are easy to follow; they do not require the use of a computer. They teach students about common international marketing problems. Although the games can begin at almost any point during the first half of the semester, they should be started early enough in order to maximize the potential benefits. Students should find them interesting and challenging.

In terms of research opportunities, the text suggests research topics and avenues. This will greatly aid the reader who wants to pursue research on a particular topic. Students and instructors can expect up-to-date and extensive coverage of the literature which may be useful for research purposes.

Because the instructor's manual is an important teaching tool, the task of writing it was not relegated to an outside party. Instead, the manual accompanying the text was completely written by us to ensure the quality and relevance of the materials. The instructor is encouraged to contact us for any additional teaching materials which we may have available.

READER RESOURCES

In addition to the learning tools included in this textbook, there is a website which provides additional material for readers of this book (http://www.Routledge.com/textbooks/0415311330). Designed for both lecturers and students, this additional learning resource includes extra material for study, as well as downloadable presentation visuals and extra teaching materials not contained in the student text version.

ACKNOWLEDGMENTS

It is a pleasure to acknowledge the contribution of many individuals. First, we are grateful for the support, assistance, and encouragement of the instructors, students, and users of the textbook. We would like to thank a number of people who have given us kind encouragement and useful feedback. Second, we want to thank our colleagues who have written cases for this book. Next, for those reviewers who have given us their useful and insightful comments, we are thankful. We would like to express our appreciation for the support of Routledge and all those who are involved in the preparation and production of this textbook. In particular, we thank Francesca Poynter and Rachel Crookes for their encouragement and patience. Their assistance is certainly valuable.

We are indebted to a number of companies and organizations for their permission to use their advertisements and materials. Such materials provide valuable information. In particular, we would like to thank Asia Pacific Advertising Festival (and Vinit Suraphongchai and Vinai Uesrivong of Plannova) for providing us with the 2003 AdFest video CDs and other information. Material from the 2003 AdFest video CDs are made available to the instructors who adopt this textbook, courtesy of AdFest and its support of education. AdFest is the largest advertising contest in Asia. These video CDs are available from the authors; please email onkvis_s@cob.sjsu.edu for more details.

Writing a textbook is a major undertaking. The reward is not monetary. The true reward is the kind comments received from the students and adopters of the book. We sincerely hope that this textbook has played a meaningful role in advancing this important discipline of study.

Chapter 1

Nature of international marketing

Challenges and opportunities

We are citizens of the world – and citizens of every city and village where we do business.

Douglas N. Daft, Chairman and CEO, The Coca-Cola Company

CHAPTER OUTLINE

- Process of international marketing
- International dimensions of marketing
- Domestic marketing vs. international marketing
- The applicability of marketing
- Multinational corporations (MNCs)
  - ☐ Pros and cons
  - ☐ Multinationality and market performance
  - ☐ Characteristics of MNCs
- The process of internationalization
- Benefits of international marketing
  - ☐ Survival and growth
  - ☐ Sales and profits
  - ☐ Diversification
  - ☐ Inflation and price moderation
  - ☐ Employment
  - ☐ Standards of living
  - ☐ Understanding of marketing process
- Conclusion
- Case 1.1 Sony: the sound of entertainment

PURPOSE OF CHAPTER

This chapter addresses the who, what, why, and how of international marketing by giving an overview of the nature of international business. The discussion begins with an examination of how marketing in general is defined and how that definition works for international marketing. The chapter examines the criteria that determine when a company has successfully transformed itself into a multinational firm. To dispel some popularly held misconceptions, there is an explicit treatment of the benefits of international trade.

MARKETING ILLUSTRATION   NESTLÉ: A "GLOCAL" COMPANY

Henri Nestlé founded Nestlé SA in 1867 to market his baby formula. The Swiss-based Nestlé is the world's largest food and beverage company, with $71 billion in annual sales and almost 230,000 employees around the world. It markets some 8000 brands that include instant coffee (first produced by the company's scientists in 1938). The company has more than 500 factories in more than eighty countries. Remarkably, its products are sold in every country in the world, including in North Korea. During the past two decades, the company spent $40 billion to acquire Friskies in 1985, saucemaker Buitoni in 1988, and Perrier in 1992. Recently, the company acquired Ralston Purina Co., North America's leading pet-food manufacturer, for $11 billion.

Nestlé's strategic goal involves a transformation of far-flung operations into a single global entity. To increase its efficiency and competitiveness while adding value to its products, Nestlé has consolidated its production and marketing activities. Countries are grouped or regrouped according to close geographic links and similar consumption behavior. For example, Thailand, Vietnam, Myanmar, and Cambodia comprise one Indochina sub-region market. The other groups include India and Pakistan, Singapore and Malaysia, and Australia and New Zealand. This strategy aims to develop brands and products on a regional basis so as to create a larger critical mass.

Nestlé's CEO, Peter Brabeck-Letmathe, certainly reflects Nestlé's international mentality. This native of Austria started his first foreign assignment in Chile. Subsequently, he was a manager in Venezuela and Ecuador. At home with his Chilean wife and children, he speaks Spanish. In addition, he speaks French, Italian, Portuguese, and English.

As a multinational corporation, Nestlé crosses cultural borders. It understands that food is and has always been a local product. A Bavarian soup will not appeal to noodle lovers in Taiwan. As a result, the company has been practicing a balancing act by trying to simultaneously achieve economies of scale and yet cater to a variety of cultural preferences. In effect, Nestlé is a "glocal" company that thinks global but acts local.

The Nestlé case exemplifies the importance of international marketing and the desirability of transforming a national company into a multinational firm. In one of its advertisements Nestlé mentions that Switzerland's lack of natural resources forces the company to depend on trade and adopt the geocentric perspective (see Figure 1.1). Worldwide competition has been intensifying, and in time companies that are not internationally inclined will be adversely affected. Rather than being reactive or defensive, a wise marketer must shed a rigid mentality and embrace a more progressive and flexible view of the world market. Potential problems can thereby be transformed into challenges and opportunities.

Sources: "The Stars of Europe: Value Creators," *Business Week*, June 11, 2001, 78; "Nestlé: An Elephant Dances," *Business Week E.BIZ*, December 11, 2000, EB 44; "Nestlé Adopts Regional Strategy," *Bangkok Post*, February 26, 1999; "Nestlé Starting to Slim Down at Last", *Business Week*, October 27, 2003, 56–7; and "The International 500," *Forbes*, July 22, 2002, 124.

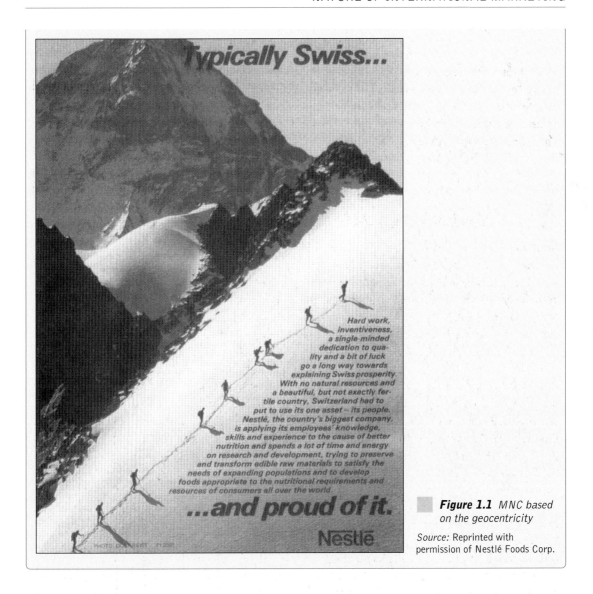

Figure 1.1 *MNC based on the geocentricity*

Source: Reprinted with permission of Nestlé Foods Corp.

PROCESS OF INTERNATIONAL MARKETING

A study of international marketing should begin with an understanding of what marketing is and how it operates in an international context. A definition adopted by the AMA (American Marketing Association) is used as a basis for the definition of international marketing given here: **international marketing** is the multinational process of planning and executing the conception, pricing, promotion, and distribution of ideas, goods, and services to create exchanges that satisfy individual and organizational objectives. Only the word *multinational* has been added. That word implies that marketing activities are undertaken in several countries and that such activities should somehow be coordinated across nations.

This definition is not completely free of limitations. By placing individual objectives at one end of the definition and organizational objectives at the other, the definition stresses a relationship between

3

a consumer and an organization. In effect, it fails to do justice to the significance of **business-to-business marketing**, which involves a transaction between two organizations. In the world of international marketing, governments, quasi-government agencies, and profit-seeking and non-profit entities are frequently buyers. Companies such as Boeing and Bechtel, for example, have nothing to do with consumer products. Likewise, Russia's export agency, Rosoboronexport, has adopted a Western-style marketing approach to sell arms for the country's 1700 defense plants. Its cheery sales representatives and giant TV screens show Russian jets and helicopters in action. In addition, Rosoboronexport offers competitive prices and will modify the products to suit its customers.[1]

Nonetheless, the definition does offer several advantages by carefully describing the essential characteristics of international marketing. First, what is to be exchanged is not restricted to tangible products (goods) but may include concepts and services as well. When the United Nations promotes such concepts as birth control and breast-feeding, this should be viewed as international marketing.

Second, the definition removes the implication that international marketing applies only to market or business transactions. International non-profit marketing, which has received only scant attention, should not be overlooked. Governments are very active in marketing in order to attract foreign investment. Religion is also a big business and has been marketed internationally for centuries, though most people prefer not to view it that way. Even the Vatican is now using modern marketing. The Holy See has launched a mass-licensing program that put images from the Vatican Library's art collection, architecture, and manuscripts on T-shirts, glassware, and candles. The Vatican Radio, wanting to market the Pope's voice in the USA and Europe, has hired a music distributor to market compact disks and cassettes of Pope John II reciting the rosary.[2]

Third, the definition recognizes that it is improper for a firm to create a product first and then look for a place to sell it. Rather than seeking consumers for a firm's existing product, it is often more logical to determine consumer needs before creating a product. For overseas markets, the process may call for a modified product. In some cases, following this approach may result in foreign needs being satisfied in a new way (i.e., a brand new product is created specifically for overseas markets).

Fourth, the definition acknowledges that "place" (distribution) is only part of the marketing mix and that the distance between markets makes it neither more nor less important than the other parts of the mix. It is thus improper for any firms to regard their international function as simply to export (i.e., move) available products from one country to another.

Finally, the "multinational process" implies that the international marketing process is not a mere repetition of using identical strategies abroad. The four Ps of marketing (product, place, promotion, and price) must be integrated and coordinated across countries in order to bring about the most effective marketing mix. In some cases, the mix may have to be adjusted for a particular market for better impact. Coca-Cola's German and Turkish divisions, for example, have experimented with berry-flavored Fanta and a pear-flavored drink respectively. In other cases, a multinational marketer may find it more desirable to use a certain degree of standardization if the existing market differences are somewhat artificial and can be overcome. As in the case of General Electric Co.'s GE Medical Systems, it went too far in localizing its medical imaging products to compete with local competitors. Its managers designed and marketed similar products for different markets. Overcustomizing such big-ticket products is an expensive and wasteful duplication of effort.[3]

INTERNATIONAL DIMENSIONS OF MARKETING

One way to understand the concept of international marketing is to examine how international marketing differs from similar concepts. **Domestic marketing** is concerned with the marketing practices within a researcher's or marketer's home coun[try]. From the perspective of domestic marketing, m[ar]keting methods used outside the home market [are] **foreign marketing**. A study becomes **compara[tive] marketing** when its purpose is to cont[rast] t[he]

[Handwritten note: Two or more sets of environmental factors overlap, indicating that some similarities are shared by the countries involved.]

[Handwritten note: Domestic marketing involves one set of uncontrollables derived from the domestic market. International marketing is much more complex because a marketer faces two or more sets of uncontrollable variables originating from various countries.]

purposes, it is merely a distinction without a difference. As a matter of fact, multinational firms themselves do not make any distinction between the two terms. It is difficult to believe that International Business Machines will become more global if it changes its corporate name to Multinational Business Machines. Likewise, there is no compelling reason for American Express and British Petroleum to change their names to, say, Global Express and World Petroleum. For purposes of the discussion in this text, international, multinational, and global marketing are used interchangeably.

DOMESTIC MARKETING VS. INTERNATIONAL MARKETING

It would beg the question to say that life and death are similar in nature, except in degree. As pointed out by Lufthansa (see Figure 1.2), it would be just as *incorrect to say that domestic and international marketing are similar in nature but not in scope*, meaning that international marketing is nothing but domestic marketing on a larger scale.

foreign laws, and general economic and geopolitical conditions, including inflation and trade relationships.[4]

As shown in Figure 1.3, the two or more sets of environmental factors overlap, indicating that some similarities are shared by the countries involved. A firm's marketing mix is determined by the uncontrollable factors within each country's environment as well as by the interaction between the sets (see Figure 1.4). For optimum results, a firm's marketing mix may have to be modified to conform to a different environment, though wholesale modification is not often necessary. The degree of overlap of th[e]

[Handwritten note: Firms' marketing mix is determined by the uncontrollable factors within each country's environment as well as interaction between the sets. For optimum results, a firm's marketing mix may have to be modified to conform to a different environment.]

Figure 1.2 *Domestic marketing vs. international marketing*

Source: Courtesy of Lufthansa German Airlines.

THE APPLICABILITY OF MARKETING

Marketing is a *universal* activity that is widely applicable, regardless of the political, social, and economic systems of a country. However, it does not mean that consumers in all parts of the world must or should be satisfied in exactly the same way. Consumers from various countries are significantly different due to varying culture, income, level of economic development, and so on. Therefore,

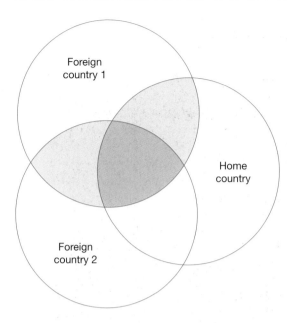

Figure 1.3 *Environmental divergence and convergence*

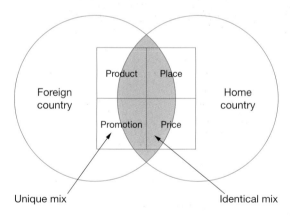

Figure 1.4 *Environmental effect on international marketing mix*

consumers may use the same product without having the same need or motive, and in turn may use different products to satisfy the same need. For example, different kinds of foods are used in different countries to satisfy the same hunger need. Further, Americans and Europeans may use gas or electric heat to keep warm, whereas people in India may meet the same need by burning cow dung.

Too often, marketing mix is confused with marketing principles. Sound marketing principles are universal. One basic principle states that marketers should adopt the marketing concept (i.e., using the integrated marketing approach to satisfy both customers' and corporate goals). Regardless of their nationalities, marketers everywhere should be customer-oriented. However, this universal principle in no way implies a uniform marketing mix for all markets. To be customer-oriented does not mean that the same marketing strategy should be repeated in a different environment.

MULTINATIONAL CORPORATIONS (MNCs)

Pros and cons

Multinational corporations (MNCs) are major actors in the world of international business. The mention of MNCs usually elicits mixed reactions. On the one hand, MNCs are associated with exploitation and ruthlessness (see Marketing Ethics 1.1 and It's the Law 1.1). They are often criticized for moving resources in and out of a country, as they strive for profit without much regard for the country's social welfare. In addition, they erode a nation's sovereignty. One study found that globalization undermined domestic airline competition policy.[5]

Is globalization detrimental to environment? This question is based on a premise that globalization encourages location of polluting industries in countries with low environmental regulations. Based on survey data from companies in China, globalization has positive environmental effects because of self-regulation pressures on firms in low-regulation countries. "Multinational ownership, multinational customers, and exports to developed countries increase self-regulation of environmental performance."[6] According to another study, the size of a domestic market and other factors are much more important than pollution costs. The attractiveness of China is due more to its market size than its relatively lax pollution-control laws. From the 1970s

MARKETING ETHICS 1.1   STARBUCKS: FAIR TRADER OR PREDATOR?

Starbo, a moniker of an old mining camp in Seattle, later became Starbucks, after the first mate in Moby Dick. The founders of Starbucks Coffee felt that the name evoked seafaring romance of early coffee traders and thus chose the mermaid logo. The idea for the modern Starbucks format was copied from a Milan coffee bar. The number of Starbucks coffee shops has zoomed from seventeen in Seattle less than two decades ago to almost 6000 in twenty-eight countries.

Starbucks Coffee's strategy is to cluster stores so as to increase total revenue and market share. Clustering fosters efficiency in terms of delivery and management, and leads to domination of a local market. The strategy is not without controversy. Critics are unhappy with the company's brutal business tactics that have driven many small coffee shops out of business. One tactic is its "predatory real estate" that involves its willingness to pay above-market rate rents in order to keep out competitors.

Starbucks has portrayed itself as a responsible global citizen. It has participated in various programs that aim to increase farmers' wages and improve the local environment. Yet in 2002, it bought only 150,000 pounds of fair-trade coffee from COOCAFE (Consortium of Coffee Cooperatives of Guanacaste and Montes de Oro in Costa Rica). It is the only specialty coffee company that refuses to certify 5 percent of its coffee as "fair trade." In the meantime, with the price of coffee beans at an extremely depressed level, growers are suffering.

Sources: Mark Pendergrast, *Uncommon Grounds: The History of Coffee and How It Transformed Our World*, Basic Books, 2000; and "For Coffee Growers, Not Even a Whiff of Profits," *Business Week*, September 9, 2002, 101ff.

IT'S THE LAW 1.1   FLAGS OF CONVENIENCE

In order to cut operating costs, the tanker industry goes to any country that has few regulatory controls. As a result, ships are often registered in such offshore nations as Liberia and Panama. These "flags of convenience" enable shipowners to sidestep national rules that mandate the use of expensive domestic crews as well as limit their liabilities. As in the case of the World Prodigy tanker, it was made in Greece, registered in Liberia, insured by a Bermuda-based group managed from London, and managed by a Greek shipping magnate.

Carnival Corp., the world's largest cruise line, has advantages over its competitors. The company is incorporated in Panama and has registered many ships in Liberia. As a result, Carnival can escape duties on liquor, often its biggest shipboard money maker. In contrast, the US-flagged American Hawaii pays at least 25 percent more than foreign-flagged vessels. In addition, Carnival is able to skip paying US corporate income tax on most operations. Over a stretch of three years, it paid just $19 million in income taxes on its $2 billion in operating income.

It costs cruise lines hundreds of thousands of dollars a year per ship to dispose of their waste. Naturally, it is tempting for them to simply and illegally dump it instead. Several cruise lines have been fined for dumping oil and refuse. A Royal Caribbean cruise ship, for example, was alleged to have dumped oil in 1994 and 1998. While Royal Caribbean has its headquarters in Miami, it is a Liberian corporation. It claims that, because its ships fly foreign flags, it is immune from criminal prosecution.

Source: "Few Icebergs on the Horizon," *Business Week*, June 14, 1999, 80, 83.

through the early 1990s, the average amount spent by US manufacturers to comply with pollution-control laws accounted for about 1 percent of their total costs, and this cost of pollution control is not high enough to justify international relocation.[7]

On a positive note, MNCs have power and prestige. Also in defense of MNCs, more and more of them have been trying to be responsible members of society. In addition, MNCs create social benefit by facilitating economic balance. Given the fact that natural resources and factors of production are unevenly distributed around the globe, MNCs can act as an effective and efficient mechanism to use these precious resources.

Multinationality and market performance

At one time, it was thought that the relationship between a firm's degree of multinationality and its market performance was a linear and positive one. While studies have found a relationship, the linkage is not straightforward.

One recent study found a curvilinear relationship instead. Increasing levels of multinationality provide significant performance benefits up to a certain optimum level. Once that optimum level is achieved, any further increase of multinationality results in decelerating benefits and accelerating costs. In other words, multinationality has both positive and negative impacts on performance. The positive impacts originate in MNCs' ability to leverage scale economies, access new technologies, and arbitrage factor cost differentials across multiple locations. The negative effects later emerge because of higher costs associated with coordination and control, administrative systems to manage culturally distinct markets, and diverse human resources.[8]

Other factors further complicate the relationship. One cross-sectional analysis of twelve industries over a seven-year period found that the "impact of multinationality on both financial and operational performance is moderated by a firm's R&D and marketing capabilities."[9]

Characteristics of MNCs

MNC is not a one-dimensional concept. There is no single criterion that proves satisfactory at all times in identifying an MNC. Varying definitions are not necessarily convergent. As a result, whether or not a company is classified as an MNC depends in part on what set of criteria is used.

Definition by size

The term *MNC* implies bigness. But bigness also has a number of dimensions. Such factors as market value, sales, profits, assets, and number of employees, when used to identify the largest multinatior will yield varying results (see Table 1.1). As an (ple, although General Motors is No. 118 in ter market value, it is No. 3 in terms of sales.[10] V *Business Week* magazine focuses on market v. *Forbes* magazine ranks the world's largest public companies by using a composite ranking of sales, profits, assets, and market value (see Table 1.2).[11] In the case of the World Investment Report of the United Nations Conference on Trade and Development (UNCTAD), it ranks transnational corporations (TNCs) by their foreign assets (see Table 1.3).[12]

Table 1.1 Global leaders based on market value, sales, and profits

Rank	Market value	Sales	Profits
1	General Electric	Wal-Mart Stores	Citigroup
2	Microsoft	ExxonMobil	General Electric
3	ExxonMobil	General Motors	Altria Group
4	Pfizer	Royal Dutch/Shell	Exxon/Mobil
5	Wal-Mart Stores	BP	Royal Dutch/Shell

Source: Adapted from "Top Global Companies," *Business Week*, July 14, 2003, 60.

Table 1.2 *Global leaders based on a composite ranking*

Rank	Company	Employees (thousands)
1	Citigroup	253.8
2	General Electric	311.5
3	American Intl Group	76.9
4	ExxonMobil	98.8
5	Bank of America	142.7
6	BP	109.2
7	HSBC Group	176.7
8	Fannie Mae	4.3
9	Royal Dutch/Shell	90.0
10	ING Group	112.0

Source: Adapted from "The International 500," *Forbes*, July 22, 2002, 124.

Table 1.3 *The world's top nonfinancial TNCs, ranked by foreign assets (millions of US dollars)*

Rank	Company	Foreign assets	Total assets
1	Vodafone	221,238	222,326
2	General Electric	159,188	437,006
3	ExxonMobil	101,728	149,000
4	Vivendi Universal	93,260	141,935
5	General Motors	75,150	303,100
6	Royal Dutch/Shell	74,807	122,498
7	BP	57,451	75,173
8	Toyota Motor	55,974	154,091
9	Telefonica	55,968	87,084
10	Fiat	52,803	95,755

Source: Adapted from *World Investment Report 2002: Transnational Corporations and Export Competitiveness*, Division on Investment, Technology and Enterprise Development (DITE), UNCTAD, 2002, 86.

Many multinational corporations are indeed large. According to UNCTAD, there are some 65,000 transnational corporations (TNCs) worldwide with more than 250,000 foreign affiliates. Some TNCs are even bigger than a number of countries (see Exhibit 1.1). TNCs control one-third of the world's private sector productive assets.

Ownership of foreign assets is highly concentrated since half of the total is owned by just 1 percent of TNCs. Interestingly, multinationals' overseas investment has progressed to the point where sales generated by them outside their country of origin even exceeded the world trade volume (total world exports).

Is corporate size an accurate indicator of international orientation? According to conventional thought, firm size should positively influence export intensity. The empirical findings have been mixed. One recent study of the Italian manufacturing industry has falsified the proposition concerning the positive relationship between firm size and export intensity.[13] Another study of 14,072 Canadian manufacturers found a positive but only modest relationship between firm size and export propensity. Apparently, although smaller firms have fewer resources, they are still able to engage in international activities.[14]

It is not unusual for corporate size to be used as a primary requirement for judging whether or not a company is multinational. However, based on this criterion, some 300,000 small and medium-sized German companies do not qualify, even though these firms (called the *Mittelstand*, or midranking) contribute mightily to Germany's export success. These medium-sized firms account for two-thirds of the country's gross national product and four-fifths of all workers. It should be noted that IBM did not become multinational because it was large but rather that it became large as a result of going international. Therefore, corporate size should not be used as the sole criterion for multinationalism.

Definition by structure

According to Aharoni, an MNC has at least three significant dimensions: structural, performance, and behavioral.[15] Structural requirements for definition as an MNC include the number of countries in which the firm does business and the citizenship of corporate owners and top managers. Pfizer, stating that it is a truly global company, does business in more than 150 countries.

EXHIBIT 1.1   ARE SOME TNCs BIGGER THAN COUNTRIES?

There is no doubt that TNCs have been growing in size at rates exceeding those of many economies. The sales of the 500 largest firms in the world nearly tripled between 1990 and 2001,[1] while world GDP in current prices increased 1.5 times between these two years. UNCTAD's 100 TNCs also increased their total sales, from $3.2 trillion to almost $4.8 trillion between 1990 and 2000.

However, a comparison of the sales of firms with the GDP of countries is conceptually flawed, since GDP is a value-added measure and sales are not. A comparable yardstick requires that sales be recalculated as value added. For firms, value added can be estimated as the sum of salaries and benefits, depreciation and amortization, and pre-tax income. Based on this measure, the world's largest TNC was ExxonMobil, with an estimated $63 billion in value added in 2000; it ranked 45th in a combined list of countries and non-financial companies. The size of this company equals the size of the economies of Chile or Pakistan in terms of value added. In the top 100 of a combined country–company list for 2000, there were twenty-nine TNCs; half of the largest value-added entities ranked between 51 and 100 were individual firms.

Source: Adapted from *World Investment Report 2002: Transnational Corporations and Export Competitiveness,* Division on Investment, Technology and Enterprise Development (DITE), UNCTAD, 2002, 90.

Rank	Name of TNC/ economy	Value added[1] (billions of dollars)	Rank	Name of TNC/ economy	Value added[1] (billions of dollars)	Rank	Name of TNC/ economy	Value added[1] (billions of dollars)
1	USA	9810	18	Russian Federation	251	35	Israel	110
2	Japan	4765	19	Switzerland	239	36	Portugal	106
3	Germany	1866	20	Sweden	229	37	Iran	105
4	United Kingdom	1427	21	Belgium	229	38	Egypt	99
5	France	1294	22	Turkey	200	39	Ireland	95
6	China	1080	23	Austria	189	40	Singapore	92
7	Italy	1074	24	Saudi Arabia	173	41	Malaysia	90
8	Canada	701	25	Denmark	163	42	Colombia	81
9	Brazil	595	26	Hong Kong	163	43	Philippines	75
10	Mexico	575	27	Norway	162	44	Chile	71
11	Spain	561	28	Poland	158	45	ExxonMobil	63[2]
12	Republic of Korea	457	29	Indonesia	153	46	Pakistan	62
13	India	457	30	South Africa	126	47	General Motors	56[2]
14	Australia	388	31	Thailand	122	48	Peru	53
15	Netherlands	370	32	Finland	121	49	Algeria	53
16	Taiwan	309	33	Venezuela	120	50	New Zealand	51
17	Argentina	285	34	Greece	113			

Notes

1 GDP for countries and value added for TNCs. Value added is defined as the sum of salaries, pre-tax profits and depreciation and amortization.

2 Value added is estimated by applying the 30 percent share of value added in the total sales, 2000, of sixty-six manufacturers for which the data were available.

Citicorp satisfies the requirement for multinationalism through the citizenship of members of its top management. The company has done as much as other major American MNCs to diversify its management. In Asia, a native of Pakistan is in charge of the firm's $800 million finance business for all of Asia apart from Japan. His colleague, an Indian national, heads the consumer business. They are two of the eight non-Americans in the elite group of fifteen executive vice-presidents.[16]

Definition by performance

Definition by performance depends on such characteristics as foreign earnings, sales, and assets. These performance characteristics indicate the extent of the commitment of corporate resources to foreign operations and the amount of rewards from that commitment. The greater the commitment and reward, the greater the degree of internationalization. Japanese and British firms have routinely shown willingness to commit their corporate resources to overseas assets.

Kraft, North America's largest food company, has long dominated US grocery-store shelves with such powerful brands as Philadelphia Cream Cheese, Oreo cookies, Tang, Jell-O, Kool-Aid, Life Savers, Planters peanuts, and Lunchables prepackaged meals for kids. Remarkably, it has sixty-one brands with more than $100 million in sales. Virtually all US grocery stores need some of Kraft's products. Internationally, it is a different matter. In Australia, Kraft Macaroni & Cheese and Oscar Mayer hot dogs are not readily available. While Kraft derives 27 percent of its total revenues from overseas, the figure pales when compared with H.J. Heinz's 44 percent, McDonald's 50+ percent, and Coca-Cola Co.'s 80+ percent. Furthermore, Kraft trails Nestlé and Unilever in foreign markets, with only 9 percent of its sales coming from developing countries.[17]

Human resources or overseas employees are customarily considered as part of the performance requirements rather than as part of the structural requirements, though the desirability of separating lower level employees from top management is questionable. A preferable analysis would be to treat the total extent of the employment of personnel in other countries as another indicator of the structure of the company. In any case, the willingness of a company to use overseas personnel satisfies a significant criterion for multinationalism. Avon, for example, employs 370,000 Japanese women to sell its products house to house across Japan. Siemens, well known worldwide for its consumer and industrial products, has some 300,000 employees in 124 countries.

Definition by behavior

Behavior is somewhat more abstract as a measure of multinationalism than either structure or performance, though it is no less important. This requirement concerns the behavioral characteristics of top management. Thus, a company becomes more multinational as its management thinks more internationally. Such thinking, known as geocentricity, must be distinguished from two other attitudes or orientations, known as ethnocentricity and polycentricity.

Ethnocentricity

Ethnocentricity is a strong orientation toward the home country. Markets and consumers abroad are viewed as unfamiliar and even inferior in taste, sophistication, and opportunity. The usual practice is to use the home base for the production of standardized products for export in order to gain some marginal business. Centralization of decision making is thus a necessity. Caterpillar Inc.'s chairman recalled that, while making sales calls in Africa in his younger days, pricing decisions were often forced upon him from headquarters even though those decisions did not fit the local market.[18]

Polycentricity

Polycentricity, the opposite of ethnocentricity, is a strong orientation to the host country. The attitude places emphasis on differences between markets that are caused by variations within, such as in income, culture, laws, and politics. The assumption is that each market is unique and consequently difficult for outsiders to understand. Thus, managers from the host country should be employed and allowed to have a great deal of discretion in market decisions. A significant degree of decentralization is thus common across the overseas divisions.

A drawback of polycentricity is that it often results in duplication of effort among overseas subsidiaries. Similarities among countries might well permit the development of efficient and uniform strategies.

Geocentricity

Geocentricity is a compromise between the two extremes of ethnocentricity and polycentricity. It could be argued that this attitude is the most important of the three. Geocentricity is an orientation that considers the whole world rather than any particular country as the target market. A geocentric company might be thought of as *denationalized* or *supranational*. As such, "international" or "foreign"

departments or markets do not exist because the company does not designate anything international or foreign about a market. Corporate resources are allocated without regard to national frontiers, and there is no hesitation in making direct investment abroad when warranted.

There is a high likelihood that a geocentric company does not identify itself with a particular country. Therefore, it is often difficult to determine the firm's home country except through the location of its headquarters and its corporate registration. According to Ohmae, business is "nationalityless," and companies should attempt to lose their national identity. As such, a corporation should not mind moving its headquarters to a more hospitable environment.[19] The chairman of Japanese retail giant Yaohan International Group, for example, moved the firm's headquarters as well as his family and personal assets to Hong Kong to take advantage of Hong Kong's low taxes and hub location in Asia. To reward his faith in China, the Chinese government permitted Yaohan to build shopping malls in China.[20]

Geocentric firms take the view that, even though countries may differ, differences can be understood

---

CULTURAL DIMENSION 1.1   HOW TO BE A MULTINATIONAL PERSON

Ten commandments for tourists (as found in a hotel).

1 Thou shalt not expect to find things as thou hast at home, for thou hast left home to find things different.
2 Thou shalt not take anything too seriously, for a carefree mind is the start of a good holiday.
3 Thou shalt not let the other travelers get on thy nerves, for thou hast paid good money to enjoy thyself.
4 Remember to take half as many clothes as thou thinkest and twice the money.
5 Know at all times where thy passport is, for a person without a passport is a person without a country.

6 Remember that if we had been expected to stay in one place we would have been created with roots.
7 Thou shalt not worry, for he that worrieth hath no pleasure, and few things are that fatal.
8 When in a strange land, be prepared to do somewhat as its people do.
9 Thou shalt not judge the people of a country by a person who hath given thee trouble.
10 Remember thou art a guest in other lands and he that treats his host with respect shall be honored.

and managed. In coordinating and controlling the global marketing effort, the company adapts its marketing program to meet local needs within the broader framework of its total strategy. It is important to coordinate the activities of local subsidiaries and those of the headquarters. One study found important divergence between home and away in various aspects of the marketing process. This divergence may result in poor relationships, dysfunctional conflict, and ineffectiveness.[21]

The geocentric approach combines aspects of centralization and decentralization in a synthesis that allows some degree of flexibility. The firm may designate one country subsidiary as its research and development center while appointing another subsidiary in another country to specialize in manufacturing certain products. Although the corporation provides overall guidance so as to achieve maximum efficiency of its global system, the various aspects of the local operations may or may not be centralized as long as they meet local market needs. Geocentric

firms compete with each other on a worldwide basis rather than at a local level.

There is evidence that geocentricity and companies' international practices are related. One study found that managers' worldmindedness was a significant determinant of international trade propensity.[22] Another study employed the GEOCENTRIC scale to measure international human resources managers' mind-set concerning the impact of nationality on the selection and careers of managers (see Exhibit 1.2). The index of a geocentric mind-set was found to be significantly related to the percentage of sales and employees abroad as well as the number of countries with manufacturing operations.[23]

A study of the EPRG (ethnocentrism, polycentrism, regiocentrism, and geocentrism) framework found that firms exhibiting an ethnocentric orientation emphasize the home market and export to psychologically close markets. In addition, these firms believe that marketing adaptation is not necessary.

EXHIBIT 1.2   ARE YOU INTERNATIONALLY INCLINED?

Researchers have used a number of criteria to identify firms and managers that are international in outlook. Such indicators as foreign sales and foreign employees are relatively easy to measure. However, attitudes are more abstract, and it is more difficult to measure a person's attitudes toward overseas consumers and markets.

The GEOCENTRIC scale was designed to measure geocentricity. The scale consists of five questionnaire items. These five statements are constructed as the Likert scale which requires a respondent to indicate the extent of agreement or disagreement with each statement on a 5-point scale. The five statements are:

1   A manager who began his or her career in any country has an equal chance to become CEO of my company.
2   In the next decade, I expect to see a nonUS CEO in my firm.

3   In the next decade, I expect to see one or more nonUS nationals serving as a senior corporate officer on a routine basis.
4   In my company, nationality is unimportant in selecting individuals for managerial positions.
5   My company believes that it is important that the majority of top corporate officers remain American.

A person's index of a geocentric mind-set is a simple sum of these five index items with the order of the last reversed. Higher values represent a more geocentric mind-set. Firms with higher scores frequently use predeparture training for expatriates and make good use of managers returning from overseas assignments.

Source: Adapted from Stephen J. Kobrin, "Is There a Relationship between a Geocentric Mind-Set and Multinational Strategy?" *Journal of International Business Studies* 25 (No. 3, 1994): 493–511.

In contrast, polycentric, regiocentric, and geocentric firms export to psychologically distant markets. Adaptation increases as psychological distance between home and host markets increases.[24]

THE PROCESS OF INTERNATIONALIZATION

The literature describes a number of stages of internationalization. Many companies may have begun as domestic firms concentrating on their own domestic markets before shifting or expanding the focus to also cover international markets. As they become more international, they are supposed to move from being sporadic exporters to being frequent exporters before finally doing manufacturing abroad. It is thus useful to investigate the stages of internationalization.

One study found evidence to support the hypothesis that there are four identifiable stages in a firm's internationalization. The four stages are: nonexporters, export intenders, sporadic exporters, and regular exporters. The process shows how firms were constrained initially by resource limitations and a lack of export commitment, and how they are able to become more and more internationalized as more resources are allocated to international activity.[25]

Based on his review of a number of the internationalization models which specify the various stages of internationalization, Andersen has proposed his own U-model which has received mixed empirical support.[26] According to this model, there are four stages: (1) no regular export activities, (2) export via independent representatives (agent), (3) establishment of an overseas sales subsidiary, and (4) overseas production/manufacturing. The development is supposed to take place initially within a specific country before being repeated across countries.

More recently, an increasingly global economy has given birth to a new theory which states that some companies are destined to go global from the outset, thus bypassing the stages of internationalization. Several Silicon Valley companies do not see the need to have a business model first for the US market before going overseas. Instead, their mission is global almost from birth. As such, from the beginning, they may employ engineers in India, manufacture in Taiwan, and sell in Europe.[27]

At present, there is no conclusive evidence to show that domestic firms have generally indeed progressed from one stage to another as prescribed on their way to becoming more internationally oriented. Likewise, no empirical evidence has been provided so far to support the competing hypothesis that some firms are "born global" in the sense that their mission is to become MNCs which engage in international business activities from the outset.

BENEFITS OF INTERNATIONAL MARKETING

International marketing daily affects consumers in many ways, though its importance is neither well understood nor appreciated. Government officials and other observers seem always to point to the negative aspects of international business. Many of their charges are more imaginary than real.

Survival and growth

For companies to survive, they need to grow. Because most countries are not as fortunate as the USA in terms of market size, resources, and opportunities, they must trade with others to survive. Since most European nations are relatively small in size, they need foreign markets to achieve economies of scale so as to be competitive with American firms.

International competition may not be a matter of choice when survival is at stake. A study of five medical sector industries found that international expansion was necessary when foreign firms entered a domestic market. However, only firms with previously substantial market share and international experience could expand successfully. Moreover, firms that retrenched after an international expansion disappeared.[28]

Even American marketers cannot ignore the vast potential of international markets. The world

15

market is more than four times larger than the US market. In the case of Amway Corp., a privately held US manufacturer of cosmetics, soaps, and vitamins, Japan represents a larger market than the USA.

Sales and profits

Foreign markets constitute a large share of the total business of many firms that have wisely cultivated markets abroad (see Marketing Strategy 1.1). The case of Coca-Cola clearly emphasizes the importance of overseas markets. International sales account for more than 80 percent of the firm's operating profits. In terms of operating profit margins, they are less than 15 percent at home but twice that amount overseas. For every gallon of soda that Coca-Cola sells, it earns 37 cents in Japan – a marked difference from the mere 7 cents per gallon earned in the USA. The Japanese market contributes about $350 million in operating income to Coca-Cola (vs. $324 million in the US market), making Japan the company's most profitable market. With

consumption of Coca-Cola's soft drinks averaging 296 eight-ounce servings per person per year in the USA, the US market is clearly saturated. Non-US consumption, on the other hand, averages only about forty servings and offers great potential for future growth.

Diversification

Demand for most products is affected by such cyclical factors as recession and such seasonal factors as climate. The unfortunate consequence of these variables is sales fluctuations, which can frequently be substantial enough to cause layoffs of personnel. One way to diversify a company's risk is to consider foreign markets as a solution to variable demand. Such markets even out fluctuations by providing outlets for excess production capacity. Cold weather, for instance, may depress soft drink consumption. Yet not all countries enter the winter season at the same time, and some countries are relatively warm all year round. Bird, USA Inc., a

MARKETING STRATEGY 1.1   WHITE MAGIC

Whirlpool Corp. expects demand for big appliances in the US to remain flat through 2009. Luckily, it projects demand overseas to grow by 17 percent to 293 million units. To be successful overseas, Whirlpool has reorganized its global factory network and has made inroads with local distributors. To cut production costs for all appliances, it devises basic models that use about 70 percent of the same parts. The machines are then modified for local tastes.

One of Whirlpool's TV commercials in India shows a mother lapsing into a daydream: her young daughter, dressed as Snow White, is dancing on a stage in a beauty contest. While her flowing gown is an immaculate white, the other contestants' garments are somewhat gray. The mother awakes to the laughter of her adoring family, and she glances proudly at her Whirlpool White Magic washer. This TV spot is based

on four months of research that enables Whirlpool to learn that Indian home-makers prize hygiene and purity which are associated with white. Since white garments often become discolored after frequent machine washing in local water, Whirlpool has custom-designed machines that are especially good with white fabrics.

In India, Whirlpool offers generous incentives to persuade thousands of retailers to carry its products. It employs local contractors who are conversant in India's eighteen languages. They deliver appliances by truck, bicycle, and oxcart. The company's sales have soared, and Whirlpool is now the country's leading brand for fully automatic washers.

Source: "Smart Globalization," *Business Week*, August 27, 2001, 132ff.

Nebraska manufacturer of go-carts and minicars for promotional purposes, has found that global selling has enabled the company to have year-round production.

A similar situation pertains to the business cycle: Europe's business cycle often lags behind that of the USA. That domestic and foreign sales operate in differing economic cycles works in the favor of General Motors and Ford because overseas operations help smooth out the business cycles of the North American market.

Inflation and price moderation

The benefits of export are readily self-evident. Imports can also be highly beneficial to a country because they constitute reserve capacity for the local economy. Without imports (or with severely restricted imports), there is no incentive for domestic firms to moderate their prices. The lack of imported product alternatives forces consumers to pay more, resulting in inflation and excessive profits for local firms. This development usually acts as a prelude to workers' demand for higher wages, further exacerbating the problem of inflation.

Employment

Trade restrictions, such as the high tariffs caused by the 1930 Smoot-Hawley Bill, which forced the average tariff rates across the board to climb above 60 percent, contributed significantly to the Great Depression and have the potential to cause widespread unemployment again. Unrestricted trade, on the other hand, improves the world's GDP and enhances employment generally for all nations.

Unfortunately, there is no question that globalization is bound to hurt some workers whose employers are not cost competitive. Some employers may also have to move certain jobs overseas so as to reduce costs. As a consequence, some workers will inevitably be unemployed. It is extremely difficult to explain to those who must bear the brunt of unemployment due to trade that there is a net benefit for the country.

Standards of living

Trade affords countries and their citizens higher standards of living than otherwise possible. Without trade, product shortages force people to pay more for less. Products taken for granted, such as coffee and bananas, may become unavailable overnight. Life in most countries would be much more difficult were it not for the many strategic metals that must be imported. Trade also makes it easier for industries to specialize and gain access to raw materials, while at the same time fostering competition and efficiency. A diffusion of innovations across national boundaries is a useful by-product of international trade (see Marketing Strategy 1.2). A lack of such trade would inhibit the flow of innovative ideas.

The World Bank's studies have shown that increased openness to trade is associated with the reduction of poverty in most developing countries. Those developing countries which chose growth through trade grew twice as fast as those nations which chose more restrictive trade regimes. "Open trade has offered developing nations widespread gains in material well being, as well as gains in literacy, education and life expectancy."[29]

Understanding of marketing process

International marketing should not be considered a subset or special case of domestic marketing. When an executive is required to observe marketing in other cultures, the benefit derived is not so much the understanding of a foreign culture. Instead, the real benefit is that the executive actually develops a better understanding of marketing in one's own culture. For example, Coca-Cola Co. has applied the lessons learned in Japan to the US and European markets. The study of international marketing can thus prove to be valuable in providing insights for the understanding of behavioral patterns often taken for granted at home. Ultimately, marketing as a discipline of study is more effectively studied.

MARKETING STRATEGY 1.2   MEDICAL VACATION

In Southeast Asia, it is sometimes difficult to distinguish ultramodern hospitals from luxury hotels. Health care and comfort are no longer incompatible concepts. Bangkok's Bumrungrad Hospital is Thailand's top-of-the-range medical facility that has gone well beyond providing Western-trained doctors and up-to-date medical equipment. The hospital also provides guest chefs, bedside Internet access, carpeted wards, and a helicopter rooftop landing pad. Patients and visitors are greeted by a white-gloved doorman, attentive bellhops, and a concierge who shows guests to their rooms (some with wet bars). An escalator connects the first two floors. If you need something to drink or eat, there are on-premise McDonald's and Starbucks outlets.

Private health care spending in Asia has reached $35 billion. Singapore at one time essentially monopolized the high-end market due to its success in attracting well-to-do patients from all over Asia. Because of Asia's lower medical costs and world-class medical treatment, many people choose to combine their vacations with a medical check-up.

Now Thailand and Malaysia are competing with Singapore to become the region's top health care center. The newcomers are able to offer comparable procedures (e.g., heart bypasses, cosmetic surgery) in comparable comfort at savings of as much as 90 percent. They have also joined forces with airlines and travel agents to offer medical package tours. Singapore's hospital operators are fighting back by operating satellite facilities in lower cost Indonesia and Malaysia.

These upscaled medical facilities are not without controversy since they cater only to wealthy customers. The practice thus favors the rich over the poor. The private hospital industry, on the other hand, argues that it has relieved a burden on the public system by taking care of medical tourists who can afford to pay.

Source: "Asia's Middle-Class Sick Find Comfort at Opulent Hospitals," *San Francisco Chronicle*, February 23, 2002.

CONCLUSION

This chapter has provided an overview of the process and of the basic issues of international marketing. Similar to domestic marketing, international marketing is concerned with the process of creating and executing an effective marketing mix in order to satisfy the objectives of all parties seeking an exchange. International marketing is relevant regardless of whether or not the activities are for profit. It is also of little consequence whether countries have the same level of economic development or political ideology, since marketing is a universal activity that has application in a variety of circumstances.

The benefits of international marketing are considerable. Trade moderates inflation and improves both employment and the standard of living, while providing a better understanding of the marketing process at home and abroad. For many companies, survival or the ability to diversify depends on the growth, sales, and profits from abroad. The more commitment a company makes to overseas markets in terms of personnel, sales, and resources, the more likely it is that it will become a multinational corporation. This is especially true when the management is geocentric rather than ethnocentric or polycentric. Since many view MNCs with envy and suspicion, the role of MNCs in society, their benefits as well as their abuses will continue to be debated.

The marketing principles may be fixed, but a company's marketing mix in the international context is not. Certain marketing practices may or may not be appropriate elsewhere, and the degree of appropriateness cannot be determined without careful investigation of the market in question.

CASE 1.1   SONY: THE SOUND OF ENTERTAINMENT

The name Sony, derived from the Latin word *sonus* for sound and combined with the English word *sonny*, was adapted for Japanese tongues. It is the most recognized brand in the USA, outranking McDonald's and Coke. Sony Corp. has $60 billion in worldwide sales, with 80 percent from overseas and 30 percent alone from the USA (more than sales in Japan). Sony's stock is traded on twenty-three exchanges around the world, and foreigners own 23 percent of the stock.

According to the UNCTAD's *World Investment Report 2002: Transnational Corporations and Export Competitiveness*, in terms of value-added sales, Sony is ranked No. 80. In other words, Sony is larger than such economies as Uruguay, the Dominican Republic, Tunisia, Slovakia, Croatia, Guatemala, and Luxembourg. In addition, in terms of foreign assets, Sony is No. 22. Out of its total assets of $68,129 million, it has $30,214 million in foreign assets. It also derives $42,768 million from foreign sales out of its total sales of $63,664 million.

Some years ago, the company made an early move into local (overseas) manufacturing, and 35 percent of the firm's manufacturing is done overseas. For instance, Sony makes TV sets in Wales and the USA, thus enabling the company to earn revenues and pay its bills in the same currency. Sony has recently ceased its production of video products in Taiwan and has moved the operation to Malaysia and China in order to employ cheaper labor. But Sony will establish a technology center in Taiwan for product design, engineering, and procurement.

Sony has some 181,800 employees worldwide, 109,080 of whom are non-Japanese. In the USA, 150 out of its 7100 employees are Japanese. Virtually alone among Japanese companies, Sony has a policy of giving the top position in its foreign operations to a local national. For example, a European runs Sony's European operations.

Sony was also the first major Japanese firm to have a foreigner as a director. Sony's late co-founder, Akio Morita, even talked about moving the company's headquarters to the USA but concluded that the effort would be too complicated.

Sony Corp. of America, located in New York, was Sony's US umbrella company in charge of the US operations that included Sony Pictures Entertainment (formerly Columbia Pictures) and Sony Music Entertainment (formerly CBS Records). Because the president, an American, failed to stop rampant overspending of Sony Pictures Entertainment, Sony ousted him and took a $2.5 billion write-off. Sony's CEO Nobuyuki Idei has stripped the New York headquarters of all operational responsibility for the US market and turned it into a second headquarters and strategic planning center for the USA. The overall management of Sony's US operations will be left to Tokyo. Many of New York's functions will be delegated to Sony Pictures and Sony Music, both of which will report to Tokyo. Idei said: "I want to make [Sony Corp. of America] a more direct extension of Sony headquarters in Japan. We don't need to manage Sony Pictures and Sony Music from New York." Incidentally, Idei has been described by friends as "un-Japanese" because he speaks his mind and demands candor from others.

Sources: "Sony's New World," *Business Week*, May 27, 1996, 100ff. *Business Week/21st Century Capitalism*, 90. "Sony's Idei Tightens Reins Again on Freewheeling US Operations," *Wall Street Journal*, January 24, 1997; "Sony Video Products Shift to Malaysia, China," *San José Mercury News*, September 23, 2000; *World Investment Report 2002: Transnational Corporations and Export Competitiveness*, Division on Investment, Technology and Enterprise Development (DITE), UNCTAD, 2002, 90; and "The Top Foreign Companies," *Forbes*, July 23, 2002, 124ff.

Points to consider

Do you consider Sony to be an MNC (multinational corporation)? What are the criteria that you use to make this determination? You need to provide factual evidence to show how these criteria are or are not met.

QUESTIONS

1   What are the strengths and limitations of the AMA's definition of marketing as adapted for the purpose of defining international marketing?

2   Distinguish among: (a) domestic marketing, (b) foreign marketing, (c) comparative marketing, (d) international marketing, (e) multinational marketing, (f) global marketing, and (g) world marketing.

3   Are domestic marketing and international marketing different only in scope but not in nature?

4   Explain the following criteria used to identify MNCs: (a) size, (b) structure, (c) performance, and (d) behavior.

5   Distinguish among: (a) ethnocentricity, (b) polycentricity, and (c) geocentricity.

6   What are the benefits of international marketing?

DISCUSSION ASSIGNMENTS AND MINICASES

1   Before becoming IBM's chairman and chief executive officer, Louis V. Gerstner, Jr. was a vice-chairman of American Express. While at American Express, he stated: "The split between international and domestic is very artificial – and at times dangerous." Do you agree with the statement? Offer your rationale.

2   Do you feel that marketing is relevant to and should be used locally as well as internationally by: (a) international agencies (e.g., the United Nations); (b) national, state, and/or city governments; (c) socialist/communist countries; (d) LDCs; and (e) priests, monks, churches, and/or evangelists?

3   Some of the best-known business schools in the USA want to emphasize discipline-based courses and eliminate international courses, based on the rationale that marketing and management principles are applicable everywhere. Is there a need to study international marketing? Discuss the pros and cons of the discipline-based approach as compared to the international approach.

4   Do MNCs provide social and economic benefits? Should they be outlawed?

5   According to Dan Okimoto, a professor of political science at Stanford University, "universities in the 21st century will have to be international universities serving a collective good, not simply a national good." Traditionally, American universities have served their international customers by simply admitting them to study in the USA.

Nowadays, no longer content to let foreign students and managers come to them, several American universities are going to their customers instead. The University of Rochester's Simon Graduate School, in conjunction with Erasmus University in Rotterdam, offers an executive MBA program. Tulane University's Freeman School of Business has a joint program with National Taiwan University. The University of Michigan has set up a program in Hong Kong for Cathay Pacific Airways managers. The University of Chicago's Graduate School of Business has transplanted its executive MBA program to Barcelona.

Discuss the merits and potential problems of American business schools offering their graduate programs in a foreign land.

NOTES

1   "Russian Weapons Marketing Gets Glitzier, with Western-Style Sales Pitches, Bargains," *San José Mercury News,* March 18, 2001.

2   "Gucci, Armani, and John Paul II?" *Business Week,* May 13, 1996, 61; and "John Connelly's Holy Hook-Up," *Business Week,* October 7, 1996, 64, 66.

3   "See the World, Erase Its Border," *Business Week*, August 28, 2000, 113–14.

4   Digital Microwave Corporation 2000 Annual Report, 20–1.

5   Joseph A. Clougherty, "Globalization and the Autonomy of Domestic Competition Policy: An Empirical Test on the World Airline Industry," *Journal of International Business Studies* 32 (third quarter, 2001): 459–78.

6   Petra Christmann and Glen Taylor, "Globalization and the Environment: Determinants of Firm Self-Regulation in China," *Journal of International Business Studies* 32 (third quarter, 2001): 439–58.

7   "Do Polluters Head Overseas?" *Business Week*, June 24, 2002, 26.

8   Lenn Gomes and Kannan Ramaswamy, "An Empirical Examination of the Form of the Relationship between Multinationality and Performance," *Journal of International Business Studies* 30 (first quarter, 1999): 173–88.

9   Masaaki Kotabe, Srini S. Srinivasan, and Preet S. Aulakh, "Multinationality and Firm Performance: The Moderating of R&D and Marketing Capabilities," *Journal of International Business Studies* 33 (first quarter, 2002): 79–97.

10 The Global 1000," *Business Week*, July 15, 2002, 58ff.

11 "The International 500," *Forbes*, July 22, 2002, 124.

12 *World Investment Report 2002: Transnational Corporations and Export Competitiveness*, Division on Investment, Technology and Enterprise Development (DITE), UNCTAD, 2002.

13 Andrea Bonaccorsi, "On the Relationship between Firm Size and Export Intensity," *Journal of International Business Studies* 23 (No. 4, 1992): 605–35.

14 Jonathan L. Calof, "The Relationship between Firm Size and Export Behavior Revisited," *Journal of International Business Studies* 25 (No. 2, 1994): 367–87.

15 Yair Aharoni, "On the Definition of a Multinational Corporation," *Quarterly Review of Economics and Business* (October 1971): 28–35.

16 "A Fleet-Footed Team in Asian Finance," *Business Week/21st Century Capitalism*, 1994, 86.

17 "Can Kraft Be a Big Cheese Abroad?" *Business Week*, June 4, 2001, 63–4.

18 "Caterpillar's Don Fites: Why He Didn't Blink," *Business Week*, August 10, 1992, 56–7.

19 Kenichi Ohmae, *The Borderless World* (London: Collins, 1990).

20 "Kazuo Wada's Answered Prayers," *Business Week*, August 26, 1991, 66–7.

21 Chi-fai Chan and Neil Bruce Holbert, "Marketing Home and Away: Perceptions of Managers in Headquarters and Subsidiaries," *Journal of World Business* 36 (No. 2, 2001): 205–21.

22 Robert W. Boatler, "Manager Worldmindedness and Trade Propensity," *Journal of Global Marketing* 8 (No. 1, 1994): 111–27.

23 Stephen J. Kobrin, "Is There a Relationship between a Geocentric Mind-Set and Multinational Strategy?" *Journal of International Business Studies* 25 (No. 3, 1994): 493–511.

24 Aviv Shoham, Gregory M. Rose, and Gerald S. Albaum, "Export Motives, Psychological Distance, and the EPRG Framework," *Journal of Global Marketing* 8 (No. 3/4, 1995): 9–37.

25 T. R. Rao and G. M. Naidu, "Are the Stages of Internationalization Empirically Supportable?" *Journal of Global Marketing* 6 (No. 1/2, 1992): 147–69.

26 Otto Andersen, "On the Internationalization Process of Firms: A Critical Analysis," *Journal of International Business Studies* 24 (No. 2, 1993): 209–31.

27 "New Rules in Silicon Valley: Go Global from the Outset," *San José Mercury News*, May 10, 1998.

28 Will Mitchell, J. Myles Shaver, and Bernard Yeung, "Performance Following Changes of International Presence in Domestic and Transition Industries," *Journal of International Business Studies* 24 (No. 4, 1993): 647–69.

29 Claudia Wolfe, "Building the Case for Global Trade," *Export America* (May 2001): 4–5.

Chapter 2

Trade theories and economic development

If a foreign country can supply us with a commodity cheaper than we ourselves can make it, better buy it of them with some part of our own industry.

Adam Smith

CHAPTER OUTLINE

- Basis for international trade
  - ☐ Production possibility curve
  - ☐ Principle of absolute advantage
  - ☐ Principle of comparative/relative advantage
- Exchange ratios, trade, and gain
- Factor endowment theory
- The competitive advantage of nations
- A critical evaluation of trade theories
  - ☐ The validity of trade theories
  - ☐ Limitations and suggested refinements
- Economic cooperation
  - ☐ Levels of economic integration
  - ☐ Economic and marketing implications
- Conclusion
- Case 2.1 The United States of America vs. the United States of Europe

PURPOSE OF CHAPTER

The case of Botswana illustrates the necessity of trading. Botswana must import in order to survive, and it must export in order to earn funds to meet its import needs. Botswana's import and export needs are readily apparent; not so obvious is the need for other countries to do the same. There must be a logical explanation for well-endowed countries to continue to trade with other nations.

This chapter explains the rationale for international trade and examines the principles of absolute advantage and relative advantage. These principles describe what and how nations can make gains from each other. The validity of these principles is discussed, as well as concepts that are refinements of these principles. The chapter also includes a discussion of factor endowment and competitive advantage. Finally, it concludes with a discussion of regional integration and its impact on international trade.

MARKETING ILLUSTRATION   BOTSWANA: THE WORLD'S FASTEST-GROWING ECONOMY

In 1966, Botswana had only three-and-a-half miles of paved roads, and three high schools in a country of 550,000 people. Water was quite scarce and precious, leading the nation to name its currency *pula*, meaning rain. At the time, Botswana's per capita income was $80 a year.

Fast forward it to the new millennium. Botswana, one of Africa's few enclaves of prosperity, is now a model for the rest of Africa or even the world. Its per capita income has rocketed to $6600. While the other African currencies are weak, the pula is strong – being backed by one of the world's highest per capita reserves ($6.2 billion).

How did Botswana do it? As a land-locked nation in southern Africa that is two-thirds desert, Botswana is a trader by necessity, but, as the world's fastest growing economy, Botswana is a trader by design. Instead of being tempted by its vast diamond wealth that could easily lead to short-term solutions, the

peaceful and democratic Botswana has adhered to free-market principles. Taxes are kept low. There is no nationalization of any businesses, and property rights are respected.

According to the World Bank's *World Development Indicators* (which reports on the world's economic and social health), the fastest growing economy over the past three decades is not in East Asia but in Africa. Since 1966, Botswana has outperformed all the others. Based on the average annual percentage growth of the GDP per capita, Botswana grew by 9.2 percent. South Korea is the second fastest performer, growing at 7.3 percent. China came in third at 6.7 percent.

Sources: "World's Fastest Growing Economy Recorded in Africa," *Bangkok Post,* April 18, 1998; and "Lessons from the Fastest-Growing Nation: Botswana?" *Business Week,* August 26, 2002, 116ff.

BASIS FOR INTERNATIONAL TRADE

Whenever a buyer and a seller come together, each expects to gain something from the other. The same expectation applies to nations that trade with each other. It is virtually impossible for a country to be

completely self-sufficient without incurring undue costs. Therefore, trade becomes a necessary activity, though, in some cases, trade does not always work to the advantage of the nations involved. Virtually all governments feel political pressure when they experience trade deficits. Too much emphasis is

23

often placed on the negative effects of trade, even though it is questionable whether such perceived disadvantages are real or imaginary. The benefits of trade, in contrast, are not often stressed, nor are they well communicated to workers and consumers.

Why do nations trade? A nation trades because it expects to gain something from its trading partner. One may ask whether trade is like a *zero-sum game*, in the sense that one must lose so that another will gain. The answer is no, because, though one does not mind gaining benefits at someone else's expense, no one wants to engage in a transaction that includes a high risk of loss. For trade to take place, both nations must anticipate gain from it. In other words, trade is a *positive-sum game*. Trade is about "mutual gain."

In order to explain how gain is derived from trade, it is necessary to examine a country's production possibility curve. How absolute and relative advantages affect trade options is based on the trading partners' production possibility curves.

Production possibility curve

Without trade, a nation would have to produce all commodities by itself in order to satisfy all its needs. Figure 2.1 shows a hypothetical example of a country with a decision concerning the production of two products: computers and automobiles. This graph shows the number of units of computer or automobile the country is able to produce. The production possibility curve shows the maximum number of units manufactured when computers and

automobiles are produced in various combinations, since one product may be substituted for the other within the limit of available resources. The country may elect to specialize or put all its resources into making either computers (point A) or automobiles (point B). At point C, product specialization has not been chosen, and thus a specific number of each of the two products will be produced.

Because each country has a unique set of resources, each country possesses its own unique production possibility curve. This curve, when analyzed, provides an explanation of the logic behind international trade. Regardless of whether the opportunity cost is constant or variable, a country must determine the proper mix of any two products and must decide whether it wants to specialize in one of the two. Specialization will likely occur if specialization allows the country to improve its prosperity by trading with another nation. The principles of absolute advantage and relative advantage explain how the production possibility curve enables a country to determine what to export and what to import.

Principle of absolute advantage

Adam Smith may have been the first scholar to investigate formally the rationale behind foreign trade. In his book *Wealth of Nations*, Smith used the principle of absolute advantage as the justification for international trade.[1] According to this principle, a country should export a commodity that can be produced at a lower cost than can other nations. Conversely, it should import a commodity that can only be produced at a higher cost than can other nations.

Consider, for example, a situation in which two nations are each producing two products. Table 2.1 provides hypothetical production figures for the USA and Japan based on two products: the computer and the automobile. Case 1 shows that, given certain resources and labor, the USA can produce twenty computers or ten automobiles or some combination of both. In contrast, Japan is able to produce only half as many computers (i.e., Japan

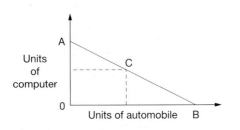

Figure 2.1 *Production possibility curve: constant opportunity cost*

Table 2.1 *Possible physical output*

	Product	USA	Japan
Case 1	Computer	20	10
	Automobile	10	20
Case 2	Computer	20	10
	Automobile	30	20
Case 3	Computer	20	10
	Automobile	40	20

produces ten for every twenty computers the USA produces). This disparity may be the result of better skills by American workers in making this product. Therefore, the USA has an absolute advantage in computers. But the situation is reversed for automobiles: the USA makes only ten cars for every twenty units manufactured in Japan. In this instance, Japan has an absolute advantage.

Based on Table 2.1, it should be apparent why trade should take place between the two countries. The USA has an absolute advantage for computers but an absolute disadvantage for automobiles. For Japan, the absolute advantage exists for automobiles and an absolute disadvantage for computers. If each country specializes in the product for which it has an absolute advantage, each can use its resources more effectively while improving consumer welfare at the same time. Since the USA would use fewer resources in making computers, it should produce this product for its own consumption as well as for export to Japan. Based on this same rationale, the USA should import automobiles from Japan rather than manufacture them itself. For Japan, of course, automobiles would be exported and computers imported.

An analogy may help demonstrate the value of the principle of absolute advantage. A doctor is absolutely better than a mechanic in performing surgery, whereas the mechanic is absolutely superior in repairing cars. It would be impractical for the doctor to practice medicine as well as repair the car when repairs are needed. Just as impractical would be the reverse situation, namely for the mechanic to attempt the practice of surgery. Thus, for practicality, each person should concentrate on and specialize in the craft which that person has mastered. Similarly, it would not be practical for consumers to attempt to produce all the things they desire to consume. One should practice what one does well and leave the manufacture of other commodities to people who produce them well.

Principle of comparative/relative advantage

One problem with the principle of absolute advantage is that it fails to explain whether trade will take place if one nation has absolute advantage for all products under consideration. Case 2 of Table 2.1 shows this situation. Note that the only difference between Case 1 and Case 2 is that the USA in Case 2 is capable of making thirty automobiles instead of the ten in Case 1. In the second instance, the USA has absolute advantage for both products, resulting in absolute disadvantage for Japan for both. The efficiency of the USA enables it to produce more of both products at lower cost.

At first glance, it may appear that the USA has nothing to gain from trading with Japan. But nineteenth-century British economist David Ricardo, perhaps the first economist to fully appreciate relative costs as a basis for trade, argues that absolute production costs are irrelevant.[2] More meaningful are relative production costs, which determine what trade should take place and what items to export or import. According to Ricardo's principle of relative (or comparative) advantage, one country may be better than another country in producing many products but should produce only what it produces best. Essentially, it should concentrate on either a product with the greatest comparative advantage or a product with the least comparative disadvantage. Conversely, it should import either a product for which it has the greatest comparative disadvantage or one for which it has the least comparative advantage.

Case 2 shows how the relative advantage varies from product to product. The extent of relative advantage may be found by determining the ratio of computers to automobiles. The advantage ratio for computers is 2:1 (i.e., 20:10) in favor of the USA. Also in favor of the USA, but to a lesser extent, is the ratio for automobiles, 1.5:1 (i.e., 30:20). These two ratios indicate that the USA possesses a 100 percent advantage over Japan for computers but only a 50 percent advantage for automobiles. Consequently, the USA has a greater relative advantage for the computer product. Therefore, the USA should specialize in producing the computer product. For Japan, having the least comparative disadvantage in automobiles indicates that it should make and export automobiles to the USA.

Consider again the analogy of the doctor and the mechanic. The doctor may take up automobile repair as a hobby. It is even possible, though not probable, that the doctor may eventually be able to repair an automobile faster and better than the mechanic. In such an instance, the doctor would have an absolute advantage in both the practice of medicine and automobile repair, whereas the mechanic would have an absolute disadvantage for both activities. Yet this situation would not mean that the doctor would be better off repairing automobiles as well as performing surgery, because of the relative advantages involved. When compared to the mechanic, the doctor may be far superior in surgery but only slightly better in automobile repair. If the doctor's greatest advantage is in surgery, then the doctor should concentrate on that specialty. And when the doctor has automobile problems, the mechanic should make the repairs because the doctor has only a slight relative advantage in that skill. By leaving repairs to the mechanic, the doctor is using time more productively while maximizing income.

It should be pointed out that comparative advantage is not a *static* concept. John Maynard Keynes, an influential English economist, opposed India's industrialization efforts in 1911 based on his assumption of India's static comparative advantage in agriculture. However, as far back as 1791, Alexander Hamilton had already endorsed the doctrine of **dynamic comparative advantage** as a basis of international trade.[3] This doctrine explains why

Taiwan and India's Bangalore have now become high-technology centers that have attracted investments from the world's top technology companies. It also explains why or how the United Kingdom, forging more steel than the rest of the world combined in 1870, lost the lead to the USA. Andrew Carnegie's mills among others were able to produce twice as much steel as Great Britain three decades later.[4]

EXCHANGE RATIOS, TRADE, AND GAIN

Although an analysis of relative advantage can indicate what a country should export and import, that analysis cannot explain exactly how a country will gain from trading with a partner. In order to determine the extent of trading gain, an examination of the **domestic exchange ratio** is required. Based on Case 2 of Table 2.1, Japan's domestic exchange ratio between the two products in question is 1:2 (i.e., ten computers for every twenty automobiles). In other words, Japan must give up two automobiles to make one computer. But by exporting automobiles to the USA, Japan has to give up only 1.5 automobiles in order to get one computer. Thus, trading essentially enables Japan to get more computers than feasible without trading.

The US domestic exchange ratio is 1:1.5 (i.e., twenty computers for every thirty automobiles). The incentive for the USA to trade with Japan occurs in the form of a gain from specializing in computer manufacturing and exchanging computers for automobiles from Japan. The extent of the gain is determined by comparing the domestic exchange ratios in the two countries. In the USA, one computer brings 1.5 automobiles in exchange, but this same computer will result in two automobiles in Japan. Trading thus is the most profitable way for the USA to employ its resources.

Theoretically, trade should equalize the previously unequal domestic exchange ratios and bring about a new ratio, known as the **world market exchange ratio**, or **terms of trade**. This ratio, which will replace the two different domestic exchange ratios, will lie between the limits established by the pre-trade domestic exchange ratios.

Such benefits derived from trade do not imply that trade must always take place and that all nations will always gain from trade. We will carry the hypothetical example a step further. In Case 3 of Table 2.1, the USA now makes forty automobiles (instead of ten as in Case 1 and thirty as in Case 2). Not only does the USA have absolute advantage for both products, but it also has the same domestic exchange ratio as that of Japan. This situation is graphically expressed by two parallel production possibility curves (Figure 2.2).

Under these circumstances, trade probably will not occur for two principal reasons. First, since the USA is 100 percent better than Japan for each product, the relative advantage for the USA is identical for both products. Second, since both countries have the identical domestic exchange ratio, there is no incentive or gain from trading for either party. Whether in the USA or in Japan, one unit of computer will fetch two automobiles. When such other costs as paperwork and transportation are taken into account, it becomes too expensive to export a product from one country to another. Thus international trade is a function of the varying domestic exchange ratios, and these ratios cause variations in comparative costs or prices.

FACTOR ENDOWMENT THEORY

The principles of absolute and relative advantage provide a primary basis for trade to occur, but the usefulness of these principles is limited by their assumptions. One basic assumption is that the advantage, whether absolute or relative, is determined solely by labor in terms of time and cost. Labor then determines comparative production costs and subsequent product prices for the same commodity.

If labor is indeed the only factor of production or even a major determinant of product content, countries with high labor cost should be in serious trouble. An interesting fact is that Japan and Germany, in spite of their very high labor costs, have remained competitive and have performed well in trade. It thus suggests that absolute labor cost is only

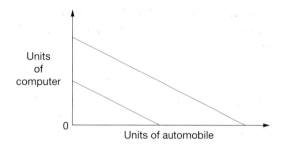

Figure 2.2 *Absolute advantage without relative advantage (identical domestic exchange ratios)*

one of several competitive inputs that determine product value. Tables 2.2 and 2.3 show incomes, working hours, and vacation days across major cities.

It is misleading to analyze labor costs without also considering the quality of that labor. A country may have high labor cost on an absolute basis; yet this cost can be relatively low if productivity is high. Countries with low wages tend to have low productivity. Any subsequent productivity gains usually result in higher wages and currency appreciation.

Furthermore, the price of a product is not necessarily determined by the amount of labor it embodies, regardless of whether or not the efficiency of labor is an issue. Since product price is not determined by labor efficiency alone, other factors of production must be taken into consideration, including land and capital (i.e., equipment). Together, all of these production factors contribute significantly to the creation of value within a particular product.

One reason for the importance of identifying other factors of production is that different commodities require different factor inputs and that no country is well endowed in all production factors. The varying proportion of these factors embodied in various goods has a great deal of impact on what a country should produce. Corn, for instance, is best produced where there is an abundance of land (relative to labor and capital), even though corn can be grown in most places in the world. Oil refining, in contrast, requires relatively more capital and

Table 2.2 *Wage levels around the globe*

City	Gross, Zurich = 100	Net, Zurich = 100	City	Gross, Zurich = 100	Net, Zurich = 100
Zurich	100.0	100.0	Singapore	26.8	28.3
Copenhagen	98.9	74.8	Dubai	26.4	35.2
Basel	97.7	95.8	Lisbon	23.6	25.1
Oslo	94.9	87.0	Manama	22.8	29.4
Geneva	91.1	88.5	Ljubljana	21.2	17.6
New York	84.7	78.6	Johannesburg	19.1	20.0
Lugano	84.3	85.1	Istanbul	17.9	16.7
Chicago	82.5	81.0	Budapest	16.6	15.6
Los Angeles	72.2	72.9	Kuala Lumpur	14.5	16.3
Frankfurt	70.0	59.9	Warsaw	13.0	11.4
Luxembourg	69.4	75.4	Shanghai	12.8	12.5
Tokyo	68.3	70.5	Santiago de Chile	12.7	14.4
Brussels	67.9	56.0	Riga	12.6	12.2
London	65.6	63.9	Tallinn	12.4	11.9
Amsterdam	64.7	57.0	Prague	11.8	12.4
Stockholm	64.7	56.5	Vilnius	11.2	10.1
Berlin	63.9	54.5	Moscow	11.1	13.4
Dublin	63.5	66.1	Sao Paulo	10.4	11.9
Miami	62.4	63.1	Lima	9.9	11.3
Helsinki	58.2	56.6	Bratislava	9.7	9.8
Vienna	55.8	52.3	Caracas	9.2	11.0
Paris	53.4	52.2	Mexico City	9.2	10.7
Toronto	52.6	48.8	Rio de Janeiro	8.4	9.2
Montreal	50.1	48.0	Bogotá	8.3	10.0
Milan	44.5	40.3	Buenos Aires	7.9	8.7
Sydney	40.2	40.7	Bucarest	7.2	11.9
Barcelona	38.0	41.1	Bangkok	6.9	8.6
Rome	37.1	33.4	Jakarta	6.5	7.8
Madrid	35.3	39.2	Manila	5.4	6.0
Athens	34.6	37.3	Sofia	5.3	5.6
Auckland	34.5	35.3	Kiev	5.0	5.8
Tel Aviv	32.8	33.2	Lagos	5.0	6.5
Taipei	32.3	35.5	Nairobi	4.2	4.8
Hong Kong	31.1	36.4	Karachi	3.5	4.1
Seoul	30.6	30.7	Mumbai	3.1	3.6

Source: Prices and Earnings (Zurich: UBS AG, 2003), 7.

Table 2.3 *Working hours and vacation days around the globe*

City	Working hours per year	Vacation days per year	City	Working hours per year	Vacation days per year
Hong Kong	2398	8	Zurich	1872	23
Mumbai	2347	25	Basel	1868	23
Taipei	2327	13	Tokyo	1864	16
Karachi	2302	27	Riga	1862	20
Manila	2301	14	Chicago	1858	15
Mexico City	2281	14	Miami	1856	20
Seoul	2270	20	New York	1843	10
Dubai	2233	26	Vilnius	1833	26
Santiago de Chile	2195	15	Ljubljana	1830	22
Bangkok	2184	10	Montreal	1829	19
Jakarta	2175	11	Tallinn	1826	21
Nairobi	2165	25	Sofia	1824	21
Istanbul	2154	16	Rome	1810	23
Lima	2152	30	Lisbon	1804	22
Kuala Lumpur	2152	17	Rio de Janeiro	1802	30
Singapore	2056	14	London	1787	21
Buenos Aires	2044	17	Moscow	1784	24
Manama	2034	22	Madrid	1782	25
Los Angeles	2022	11	Dublin	1779	22
Auckland	2022	21	Stockholm	1775	25
Budapest	2012	23	Luxembourg	1768	25
Bucharest	1992	20	Sydney	1757	21
Caracas	1989	16	Athens	1744	30
Bogotá	1987	15	Barcelona	1743	30
Tel Aviv	1977	11	Amsterdam	1741	29
Kiev	1958	22	Lagos	1723	31
Shanghai	1958	13	Brussels	1722	22
Prague	1946	22	Milan	1718	23
Sao Paulo	1936	30	Helsinki	1714	28
Lugano	1921	22	Oslo	1703	25
Johannesburg	1910	18	Vienna	1696	26
Toronto	1909	14	Frankfurt	1682	30
Warsaw	1901	26	Berlin	1666	28
Geneva	1895	23	Copenhagen	1658	28
Bratislava	1881	19	Paris	1561	26

Source: Prices and Earnings (Zurich: UBS AG, 2003), 23.

relatively less labor and land because of expensive equipment and specialized personnel. In clothing production the most important input factor is that the economy is labor-intensive.

The varying factor inputs and proportions for different commodities, together with the uneven distribution of such factors of production in different regions of the world, are the basis of the **Heckscher–Ohlin theory of factor endowment**.[5] This theory holds that the inequality of relative prices is a function of regional factor endowments and that comparative advantage is determined by the relative abundance of such endowments. According to Ohlin, there is a mutual interdependence among production factors, factor movements, income, prices, and trade. A change in one affects the rest. Prices of factors and subsequent product prices in each region depend on supply and demand, which in turn are affected by the desires

of consumers, income levels, quantity of various factors, and physical conditions of production.

Since countries have different factor endowments, a country would have a relative advantage in a commodity that embodies in some degree that country's comparatively abundant factors. A country should thus export that commodity which is relatively plentiful (i.e., in comparison to other commodities) within the relatively abundant factor (i.e., in comparison to other countries). This exported item may then be exchanged for goods that would use large quantities of the country's scarce factors if domestically produced. Figure 2.3 lists the Netherland's well-endowed factors, for example. Table 2.4 shows countries with capital scarcity.[6]

Therefore, a country that is relatively abundant in labor but relatively scarce in capital is likely to have a comparative advantage in the production of labor-intensive goods and to have deficiencies in the

Table 2.4 *Capital scarcity. Capital endowments and output per capita are much lower in the Central and Eastern European countries than in Western Europe, implying large potential capital inflows into the region.*

	GDP per worker[1]	Relative marginal product of capital[2]	Potential inflows[3]
Bulgaria	22.9	19.1	753
Czech Republic	53.6	3.5	275
Estonia	31.1	10.3	543
Hungary	55.7	3.2	259
Latvia	20.9	22.9	825
Lithuania	28.5	12.3	596
Poland	38.6	6.7	425
Romania	26.9	13.8	634
Slovak Republic	42.2	5.6	381
Slovenia	72.8	1.9	147
Median	34.9	8.5	484
Minimum	20.9	1.9	147
Maximum	72.8	22.9	825

Notes

1 In percent of German GDP per worker (purchasing-power-parity basis).

2 Cobb-Douglas production function.

3 In percent of initial (Pre-flow) GDP.

Source: Leslie Lipschitz, Timothy Lane, and Alex Mourmouras, "The Tosovksy Dilemma," *Finance & Development,* September 2002, 32.

WordPerfect Grows in Europe Through Dutch Headquarters And Local Customization

In 1978, Alan C. Ashton, a computer science professor at Brigham Young University in Provo, Utah, got together with the director of its marching band, Bruce W. Bastian, to produce software that created the band's marching patterns. Out of their next collaborations grew the world's largest private software company, WordPerfect Corporation of Orem, Utah.

WordPerfect began working in 1984 with a Dutch software distributor, which, in 1985, spun off a distributorship dedicated to WordPerfect products. In 1988, WordPerfect acquired the spin-off and renamed it WordPerfect Europe. WordPerfect Europe moved with WordPerfect Nederland into a new 38,500-square-foot facility near Rotterdam in October 1990 with some 90 employees. According to Mr. Ashton, Holland continues to play a role in the company's European success:

"Bruce and I were impressed by the management skills and the quickness with which the Dutch people developed the technical expertise to sell WordPerfect. Dutch universities are graduating people with the know-how to help us grow our business, not only in the Benelux but also throughout Europe.

"Our Dutch operation became successful because we invested in creating Dutch translations of most of our software products and manuals and included a localized

*Alan C. Ashton, President
WordPerfect Corporation*

Spell-checker, Hyphenation routine and Thesaurus for the WordPerfect product itself. We adhered to this strategy as we expanded. Complete packages have been localized into 12 languages besides U.S. English, with partial packages available in another six, and Russian, Czech and Greek in the works.

"About 20% of WordPerfect's global revenues now come from European customers.

"The Rotterdam office handles technical support and some product development for system configurations that are unique to Europe, such as various printer hardware and UNIX ports. It offers marketing, financial and general management support as needed to our offices in 11 European countries and distributors in another six.

"Through SoftCopy Europe, which was formed in 1988 about a mile from our headquarters in Rotterdam, WordPerfect and other software suppliers have their

master program disks reproduced and packaged with manuals in shrink-wrapped boxes, for shipment directly to customers.

"From our initial telephone call to the Dutch distributor who is now the head of our European operations, our experiences in Holland have been first rate. We always have felt that the Dutch want our business and will do what is necessary to ensure that we, too, are successful."

HIT THE GROUND RUNNING

*For more information,
contact the Netherlands Foreign
Investment Agency in:*
New York
Tel: 212-246-1434   Fax: 212-246-9769
San Mateo
Tel: 415-349-8848   Fax: 415-349-8201
Los Angeles
Tel: 310-477-8288   Fax: 310-312-0771
Ottawa
Tel: 613-237-5030   Fax: 613-237-6471

Netherlands Foreign Investment Agency

This material is published by Ogilvy Public Relations Group, which is registered as an agent of the Government of the Netherlands. It is filed with the Department of Justice, where the required registration statement is available for public inspection. Registration does not indicate approval of the contents by the United States Government.

Figure 2.3 *WordPerfect and the Netherlands' relatively well-endowed factors*
Source: Courtesy of the Netherlands Investment Agency and Ogilvy Adams & Rinehart.

production of capital-intensive goods. This concept explains why China, a formidable competitor in textile products, has to depend on US and European firms for oil exploration within China itself.

Each nation possesses factors of production that may be grouped into these broad categories: human resources, physical resources, knowledge resources, capital resources, and infrastructure. Interestingly or surprisingly, a nation's abundance of a particular production factor may sometimes undermine

instead of enhance the country's competitive advantage.[7]

The quality of human resources is a function of human development. The United Nations Development Program has prepared the Human Development Index (HDI) to measure well-being.[8] The HDI, ranging from zero (low human development) to one (high human development), is an arithmetic average of a country's achievements in three basic dimensions: longevity (measured by life expectancy at birth); educational attainment (measured by combination of adult literacy rate and enrollment ratio in primary, secondary, and tertiary education); and living standards (measured by GDP per capita in US dollars at purchasing power parity). Both the HDI and per capita income are highly correlated with the other widely used measures of poverty. Table 2.5 shows a list of countries based on the HDI.

THE COMPETITIVE ADVANTAGE OF NATIONS

Michael Porter's book, *The Competitive Advantage of Nations*, has received a great deal of interest all over the world.[9] Based on his analysis of over a hundred case studies of industries in ten leading developed nations, Porter has identified four major determi-

Table 2.5 *Human Development Index (HDI), selected countries*

≤ 0.50	0.51–0.70	0.71–0.80	> 0.80
Africa	**Africa**	**Asia**	**Europe/Industrial**
Sudan (0.48)	South Africa (0.70)	Thailand (0.74)	Canada (0.93)
Mauritania (0.45)	Botswana (0.59)	Philippines (0.74)	USA (0.93)
Nigeria (0.44)	Gabon (0.59)	China (0.71)	Australia (0.93)
Congo, Dem. Rep. of	Ghana (0.56)		Japan (0.92)
the (0.43)	Zimbabwe (0.56)	**Transition economies**	United Kingdom (0.92)
Zambia (0.42)	Cameroon (0.53)	Bulgaria (0.77)	France (0.92)
Cote d'Ivoire (0.42)	Kenya (0.51)	Russia (0.77)	Germany (0.91)
Senegal (0.42)	Congo, Rep. of (0.51)	Romania (0.77)	Italy (0.90)
Tanzania (0.41)		Georgia (0.76)	Spain (0.90)
Uganda (0.41)	**Asia**	Ukraine (0.74)	
Angola (0.40)	Vietnam (0.67)	Azerbaijan (0.72)	**Asia**
Malawi (0.38)	Indonesia (0.67)	Albania (0.71)	Singapore (0.88)
Mozambique (0.34)	India (0.56)		Hong Kong SAR (0.87)
Ethiopia (0.31)	Pakistan (0.52)	**Middle East**	Korea, Rep. of (0.85)
Niger (0.29)		Saudi Arabia (0.75)	
Sierra Leone (0.25)	**Transition economies**	Jordan (0.72)	**Transition economies**
	Moldova (0.70)	Iran, Islamic Rep. of	Czech Republic (0.84)
	Uzbekistan (0.69)	(0.71)	Hungary (0.82)
Asia	Tajikistan (0.66)		Poland (0.81)
Lao People's Dem.		**Western Hemisphere**	
Rep. (0.48)	**Middle East**	Mexico (0.78)	**Middle East**
Nepal (0.47)	Syrian Arab Republic	Colombia (0.76)	Israel (0.88)
Bangladesh (0.46)	(0.66)	Brazil (0.75)	Kuwait (0.84)
	Egypt (0.62)	Peru (0.74)	
Middle East	Iraq (0.58)		**Western Hemisphere**
Yemen (0.45)			Argentina (0.84)
	Western Hemisphere		Chile (0.83)
Western Hemisphere	Bolivia (0.64)		Uruguay (0.82)
Haiti (0.44)	Nicaragua (0.63)		
	Guatemala (0.62)		

Source: Paul Cashin, Paolo Mauro, and Ratna Sahay, "Macroeconomic Policies and Poverty Reduction: Some Cross-Country Evidence," *Finance & Development*, June 2001, 46–9.

nants of international competitiveness: (1) factor conditions, (2) demand conditions, (3) related and supporting industries, and (4) firm strategy, structure, and rivalry. These four determinants interact and form the "diamond" which provides the context in which a nation's firms are born and compete.

A nation is competitive when it has specialized assets and skills necessary for competitive advantage in an industry. Firms gain competitive advantage in industries when their home base offers better ongoing information into product and process needs. They gain competitive advantage when owners, managers, and employees support intense commitment and sustained investment. In the end, nations succeed in particular industries because their dynamic home environment stimulates firms to upgrade and widen their advantages over time. Therefore, the effect of one determinant is determined by the state of the others: the advantages in one determinant can enhance the advantages in others.

Porter's theory also includes two additional variables: chance and government. Chance events are developments outside the control of firms, and they include pure inventions, breakthroughs in basic technologies, wars, external political developments, and major shifts in market demand. Government at all levels, on the other hand, can improve or detract from a country's national advantage. Regulations and investment policies can affect domestic rivalry and home demand conditions. The government variable explains why Bermuda and the Cayman Islands, while not being well endowed in terms of factors of production, capture 31.5 percent and 12 percent respectively of the world's captive insurance operations.[10]

The "diamond" promotes the "clustering" of a nation's competitive industries. The country's successful industries are usually linked through vertical (buyer/supplier) or horizontal (common customers, technology) relationships. This cluster of industries is mutually supporting, and the derived benefits flow forward, backward, and horizontally. As in the case of Sweden, it is successful not only in pulp and paper but also in wood-handling machin-

ery, sulphur boilers, conveyor systems, pulp-making machinery, control instruments, paper-making machinery, and paper-drying machinery. Sweden is also internationally competitive in chemicals that are used in pulp and paper making.

Porter's theory seems logical and is supported by empirical evidence. Yet one may wonder whether the broad-based generalizations are warranted. For example, it is doubtful that the theory can explain why Sweden, a relatively small country, is the third largest exporter of music. Likewise, in the case of American pastimes, one has to wonder why foreign-born Latinos are so good at playing baseball to the point that they account for 25 percent of the major league rosters, not counting thousands more from the Caribbean as well as Central and South America who play in the minors.

In fairness, Porter does offer a number of explanations or qualifications. A country's national competitive advantage in a particular industry may be eroded when conditions in the national diamond no longer support investment and innovation to match the industry's evolving structure. Some important reasons for the loss of advantage are: deterioration of factor conditions, local needs not compatible with global demand, loss of home buyers' sophistication, technological change, firms' adjustment inflexibility, and reduction in domestic rivalry. In this regard, Porter has clearly stated that his theory is dynamic. Yet by advocating clustering, the theory also looks static in the sense that it implies that newcomers (nations) will have difficulties in gaining competitive advantage in a new area.

Figure 2.4 shows the world competitiveness scoreboard for nations whose populations exceed 20 million people. Figure 2.5 provides rankings for smaller countries.

A CRITICAL EVALUATION OF TRADE THEORIES

The validity of trade theories

Several studies have investigated the validity of the classical trade theories. The evidence collected by

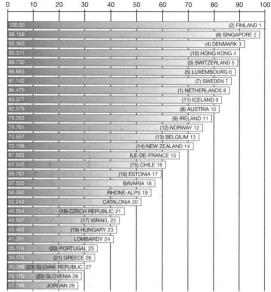

Figure 2.4 *The world competitiveness scoreboard (larger nations), 2002 rankings are in brackets*

Source: *IMD World Competitiveness Yearbook 2003*, 4.

Figure 2.5 *The world competitiveness scoreboard (smaller nations), 2002 rankings are in brackets*

Source: *IMD World Competitiveness Yearbook 2003*, 4.

MacDougall shortly after World War II showed that comparative cost was useful in explaining trade patterns.[11] Other studies using different data and time periods have yielded results similar to MacDougall's. Thus there is support for the claim that relative labor productivities determine trade patterns.

These positive results were subsequently questioned. The studies conducted by Leontief revealed that the USA actually exports labor-intensive goods and imports capital-intensive products.[12] These paradoxical findings are now called the **Leontief Paradox**. Thus, the findings are ambiguous, indicating that, in its simplest form, the Heckscher–Ohlin theory is not supported by the evidence.

In theory, the more different two countries are, the more they stand to gain by trading with each other. There is no reason why a country should want to trade with another that is a mirror image of itself. However, a look at world trade casts some doubt on the validity of classical trade theories. Developed

countries trade more among themselves than with developing countries. There is a tendency for corporations in developed countries to prefer to form direct-investment ties in the other more stable, developed countries while avoiding heavy investment in the fast-growing developing world.

The trade pattern shown is surprising theoretically, because advanced economies have similar climate and factor proportions and thus should not trade with one another since there are no comparative advantages. Apparently, other variables in addition to factor endowment play a significant role in determining trade volume and practices because considerable trade does occur between developed nations.

Limitations and suggested refinements

Trade theories provide logical explanations about why nations trade with one another, but such theories are limited by their underlying assumptions.

Most of the world's trade rules are based on a traditional model that assumes that (1) trade is bilateral, (2) trade involves products originating primarily in the exporting country, (3) the exporting country has a comparative advantage, and (4) competition focuses primarily on the importing country's market. However, today's realities are quite different. First, trade is a multilateral process. Second, trade is often based on products assembled from components that are produced in various countries. Third, it is not easy to determine a country's comparative advantage, as evidenced by the countries that often export and import the same product. Finally, competition usually extends beyond the importing country to include the exporting country and third countries.[13]

In fairness, virtually all theories require assumptions in order to provide a focus for investigation while holding extraneous variables constant. But controlling the effect of extraneous variables acts to limit a theory's practicality and generalization.

One limitation of classical trade theories is that the *factors of production* are assumed to remain constant for each country because of the *assumed immobility* of such resources between countries. This assumption is especially true in the case of land, since physical transfer and ownership of land can only be accomplished by war or purchase (e.g., the US seizure of California from Mexico and the US purchase of Alaska from Russia). At present, however, such means to gain land are less and less likely. As a matter of fact, many countries have laws that prohibit foreigners from owning real estate. Thus, Japan and many other countries remain land-poor. On the other hand, outsourcing and foreign direct investment are a means to gain or use foreign land. Thus, in this regard, one can argue that land is mobile — at least indirectly.

A significant difference exists in the degree of mobility between land and capital. In spite of the restrictions on the movement of capital imposed by most governments, it is possible for a country to attract foreign capital for investment or for a country to borrow money from foreign banks or international development agencies. Not surprisingly, US banks, as financial institutions in a capital-rich country, provide huge loans to Latin American countries. Yet at the same time, a favorable US business climate makes it possible for the USA to attract capital from abroad to help finance its enormous federal deficits. Therefore, capital is far from being immobile.

The extent of money laundering clearly illustrates the high degree of capital mobility (see It's the Law 2.1 and Marketing Strategy 2.1). Even in the case of legal transactions, the so-called hot capital can move instantly in search of a better return. Malaysia has imposed capital controls so as to limit capital flights. It has adopted an exit tax, and investors are taxed according to how quick they withdraw the money. The tax gradually drops to zero for those who leave money in Malaysia for more than a year. The exchange controls continue to be enforced, and the ringgit cannot be traded outside the country. There is a limit on the amount of money one can take out of the country. In any case, an IMF study found that, once financial integration crosses a certain threshold, the positive effects of international capital flows can outweigh the negative effects.[14]

Labor as a factor is relatively mobile because people will migrate — legally or not — in search of a better life (see Marketing Ethics 2.1). It is true that immigration laws in most countries severely limit the freedom of movement of labor between countries. In China, people (i.e., labor) are not even able to select residence in a city of their choice. Still, labor can and does move across borders. Western European nations allow their citizens to pass across borders rather freely. The USA has a farm program that allows Mexican workers to work in the USA temporarily. For Asian nations, most are so well endowed with cheap and abundant labor that Thailand sends laborers to work abroad and the Philippines has a significant number of its citizens work as maids in Hong Kong. China, likewise, would like to export its labor because it is the most well-endowed nation in the world in terms of this resource. In the mid-nineteenth century, many Chinese peasants were brought to the USA for railroad building.

35

IT'S THE LAW 2.1   MONEY LAUNDERING

Like other businesspeople, criminals and terrorists need financing. As such, money laundering is their lifeblood. According to the IMF, poorly supervised financial institutions channel $590 billion in illicit cash a year.

Money laundering is a process to transform proceeds of crime into a usable form and disguise their illegal origins. The illegal profits may be derived from drug or arms trafficking, political corruption, prostitution, and so on. To clean or launder them, criminals move the proceeds through a variety of transactions and financial vehicles before investing them in financial and related assets.

A recent case of money laundering was revealed when three financial institutions reported similar suspicious transactions. It turned out that drug traffickers were using go-betweens who would deliver the cash proceeds of crime to professionals in travel agencies and import/export businesses. The professionals would place the funds in their bank accounts and, for a fee, transfer them on the basis of fake invoices to bank accounts abroad. An estimated $30 million was laundered in this way. However, the coordinated analysis of suspicious transaction reports led to prosecutions in two countries. This case displays many of the common features of money laundering: cash is introduced into the banking system by people far removed from the predicate criminal activity; layering is

achieved by splitting the funds among many small, seemingly innocuous agents (known as "smurfs"); creating a misleading paper trail; and getting funds abroad as soon as possible.

Money laundering is global. If one country's regulations are tightened, criminals will simply shift their laundering activities to a more hospitable environment. The IMF calls for more effective information sharing among authorities. Governments are urged "to create mechanisms to enable collection and sharing, including cross-border sharing of relevant financial information with appropriate supervisory and law enforcement activities."

The USA, in response to terrorist acts, has passed the 2001 USA PATRIOT Act. The US Treasury Department has required banks, credit card companies, and financial institutions to adopt comprehensive programs to combat money laundering. These firms may have to verify the identity of customers. Car dealers and travel agencies may be required to do the same.

Sources: Eduardo Aninat, Daniel Hardy, and R. Barry Johnston, "Combating Money Laundering and the Financing of Terrorism," *Finance & Development*, September 2002, 44–7; "Manila Pushes to Adopt Money-Laundering Law," *Asian Wall Street Journal*, June 26, 2001; "Car, Travel Trades Sought in Fight," *San José Mercury News*, February 27, 2003; "Money Laundering and Terrorist Financing," *IMF Survey*, November 26, 2001, 359.

While immigration laws often restrict labor movement across countries, business laws tend to welcome capital movement to employ labor in a foreign country. When wages in South Korea escalated, Goldstar Co. minimized the labor problem by importing goods from its overseas facilities back into South Korea. It may be said that, in the production of tradable goods, unskilled labor markets in the developed countries have been effectively joined with international markets. As in the case of apparel assembly and footwear which do not lend themselves as yet to technology-intensive methods, a large share of output has already been transferred

to poor countries. Even in Thailand where labor was once plentiful and cheap but where labor cost has moved up, some Thai apparel firms are transferring parts of their production operations to Cambodia and Vietnam. Likewise, Taiwanese shoe companies are establishing new operations on the mainland.

Because workers cannot easily emigrate to another country which has better wages and benefits, wages have not been equalized across countries. Conceivably, computer workstations and communications technology could lessen this problem by allowing a portion of the workforce to work for any company in any part of the world. As mentioned by

MARKETING STRATEGY 2.1   HOW TO MOVE MONEY

It is anticipated that some $177 billion in funds will be transferred globally by 2006. In the case of Mexico, the central bank reported that the amount that Mexicans in the USA sent home ($6.3 billion) exceeded the amounts brought in by tourism ($4.9 billion) and foreign direct investment ($5.2 billion).

In the old days, immigrants used a courier or family member to send money home. Now banks and wire transfer companies fill the void – for a hefty fee. The fees are usually 10 to 15 percent of the amounts sent home. There is a reason why banks account for only 9 percent of the money sent home and why wire transfer companies take 83 percent. Illegal aliens in the USA do not use banks because they need to show US documents. Some are afraid that opening bank accounts may lead to detention or deportation. Interestingly, the nations with the highest number of money-transfer recipients often have the lowest number of people with bank accounts and debit cards.

On the other hand, when workers cash their checks at check-cashing and cash-transfer companies, they lose as much as 3 percent of a check's value. Western Union and MoneyGram dominate international money-transfer business due in part to their live agent relationships. Western Union has 120,000 agent locations, whereas MoneyGram has 50,000. Western Union and MoneyGram handle 40 percent of money transfers to Mexico, and they charge $25 for such a transaction.

Some banks have become innovative and competitive. Citigroup's Grupo Financiero Banamex unit has launched binational accounts for Mexicans working in the USA, where they can deposit into their accounts a specific amount that their relatives in Mexico can withdraw using a Banamex ATM card. These binational savings, checking, or debit accounts will be cheaper than wire transfers or other remittance services. In the case of Bank of America's SafeSend, it allows Mexicans to send $500 home for a $10 fee. SafeSend recipients receive an ATM card that is used to withdraw money for free from an ATM in Mexico.

Sources: "Remittances to Mexico Top Tourism, Other Investment," *San José Mercury News*, September 2, 2003; "Bank Offers Binational Accounts," *San José Mercury News*, April 20, 2002; "More Bankers Are Saying 'Hola,'" *Business Week*, May 13, 2002, 12; "ATMs Make a Play for Money Transfers," *Credit Card Management* (November 2002): 45–6; "Repatriating Money Carries High Fees, Risks," *San José Mercury News*, November 23, 2002.

Andrew Grove, Intel Corp.'s chief executive officer, "capital and work – your work and your counterpart's work – can go anywhere on earth and do a job. . . . If the world operates as one big market, every employee will compete with every person anywhere in the world who is capable of doing the same job."[15] Theoretically, if developments continue along these lines, a worldwide labor market is possible.

In the 1970s and 1980s, workers in the Western world learned a painful lesson: manufacturing could be moved virtually anywhere. History may repeat itself, since it is becoming easier for firms to shift knowledge-based labor as well. This development can be attributed to the worldwide shift to market economies, improved education, and decades of overseas training by multinationals. As a result, a global workforce is emerging, and it is capable of doing the kind of work once reserved for white-collar workers in the West. Advances in telecommunications are making these workers more accessible than ever. In electronics, Taipei, Edinburgh, Singapore, and Malaysia, although far away from the end-user and technological breakthroughs, have emerged as global product-development centers. Therefore, conventional notions of comparative advantage are rapidly changing.

Production factors are now considered more mobile than previously assumed. However, because of government efforts to restrict the mobility of factors of production, production costs and product prices are never completely equalized across countries. Yet the amount of mobility that does exist serves to narrow the price/cost differentials. In

MARKETING ETHICS 2.1   HUMAN TRAFFICKING: THE WORST KIND OF FACTOR MOBILITY

Criminals make money in the worst way – even at the expense of exploiting their fellow human beings. Women and children are particularly vulnerable. In some societies, parents sell their children. In Asia and Eastern Europe, women have been abducted and forced into prostitution. At the Mexican–American border, Mexican police still have not solved the murders of many women who worked in the area or who tried to go across the border into the USA.

In Taiwan, most of its nearly 300,000 foreign contract laborers are from Thailand and the Philippines. Licensed job brokers in Taiwan charge each worker as much as $6000, about the minimum wage for a year's work. A worker on a three-year contract needs two years to pay this fee, leaving only one year for the actual pay.

In the case of Thailand, it is interesting to note that laborers pay brokers to try to secure jobs in Singapore, Taiwan, and wealthy Arab nations. At the same time, labor costs in Thailand have gone up, and many employers have now turned to illegal Burmese aliens instead. While some 200,000 women and children from neighboring countries have been smuggled into Thailand for the sex trade, Thai prostitutes have been sent by gangsters to other Asian and European countries.

The US Trafficking Act ranks countries in terms of their efforts to stamp out human trafficking. Thailand is a Tier 2 country, meaning that it has not met the minimum standards in fighting human trafficking. If it is demoted to Tier 3, Thailand could face economic measures taken by the USA.

Sources: "Taiwan's Invisible Workforce," *San José Mercury News*, September 6, 2000; "US Says Thais Doing Too Little to Stamp Out Human Trafficking," *Bangkok Post*, March 17, 2003.

---

theory, as a country exports its abundant factor, that factor becomes more scarce at home and its price rises. In contrast, as a country imports a scarce factor, it increases the abundance of that factor and its price declines. Therefore, a nation is usually interested in attracting what it lacks, and this practice will affect the distribution of production factors.

Since a country's factors of production can change owing to factor mobility, it is reasonable to expect a shift in the kinds of goods a country imports and exports. Japan, once a capital-poor country, has grown to become a major lender/supplier of money for international trade. Its trade pattern seems to reflect this change.

When considering the factors of production, another item that is very significant involves the level of *quality of the production factors*. It is important to understand that the quality of each factor should not be assumed to be homogeneous worldwide. Some countries have relatively better-trained personnel, better equipment, better-quality land, and better climate.

Although a country should normally export products that use its abundant factors as the product's major input, a country can *substitute* one production factor for another to a certain extent. Cut-up chicken fryers are a good example. Japan imports chicken fryers because a scarcity of land forces it to use valuable land for products of relatively greater economic opportunity. Both the USA and Thailand sell cut-up chicken fryers to Japan. The two countries' production strategies, however, differ markedly. The USA, due to its high labor costs, depends more on automation (i.e., capital) to keep production costs down. Thailand, on the other hand, has plentiful and inexpensive labor and thus produces its fryers through a labor-intensive process. Therefore, the proportion of factor inputs for a particular product is not necessarily fixed, and the identical product may be produced with alternative methods or factors.

Like Joseph Schumpeter before them, some economists argue that innovation (knowledge and its application to real business problems) counts for more than capital and labor, the traditional factors of production. Entrepreneurs, industrial research, and knowledge are what matters.

The discussion so far has dealt with an emphasis of trade theories on the supply side, but *demand* is just as critical, and demand reversal (when it occurs) may serve to explain why the empirical evidence is mixed. Tastes should not be assumed to be the same among various countries. A country may have a scarcity of certain products, and yet its citizens may have no desire for those products. Frequently, less developed countries' products may not be of sufficient quality to satisfy the tastes of industrial nations' consumers. Yugo, for example, tried in vain to convince American consumers that its automobiles, despite their very low prices, were not bad value or of poor quality. Even Renault, in spite of being from a developed country (France), could not win over American consumers.

In some market situations, it is possible for product quality to be too high. Companies in developed countries, for example, sometimes manufacture products with too many refinements, which make the products too costly for consumers elsewhere. German machinery, for instance, has a worldwide reputation for quality. Nonetheless, many less developed countries opt for less reliable machinery products from Taiwan because Taiwan's products are less costly. Such circumstances explain why nations with similar levels of economic development tend to trade with one another, since they have similar tastes and incomes.

Perhaps the most serious shortcoming of classical trade theories is that they ignore the *marketing* aspect of trade. These theories are concerned primarily with commodities rather than with manufactured goods or value-added products. It is assumed that all suppliers have identical products with similar physical attributes and quality. This habit of assuming *product homogeneity* is not likely to occur among those familiar with marketing.

More often than not, products are endowed with psychological attributes. Brand-name products are often promoted as having additional value based on psychological nuance. Tobacco products of Marlboro and Winston sell well worldwide because of the images of those brands. In addition, firms in two countries can produce virtually identical products in physical terms, but one product has different symbolic meaning than the other. Less developed countries are just as capable as the USA or France in making good cosmetic products, but many consumers are willing to pay significantly more for the prestige of using brands such as Estée Lauder and Dior. Trade analysis, therefore, is not complete without taking into consideration the reasons for *product differentiation*.

A further shortcoming of classical trade theories is that the trade patterns as described in the theories are in reality frequently affected by *trade restrictions*. The direction of the flow of trade, according to some critics of free trade, is no longer determined by a country's natural comparative advantage. Rather, a country can create a relative advantage by relying on outsourcing and other trade barriers, such as tariffs and quotas. Protectionism can thus alter the trade patterns as described by trade theories.

The *new trade theory* states that trade is based on increasing returns to scale, historical accidents, and government policies. Japan's *targeted industry strategy*, for example, does not adhere to free-market principles. Therefore, a moderate degree of protection may promote domestic output and welfare. However, as pointed out by Jagdish Bhagwati, it is not easy to differentiate fair trade based on comparative advantage from what may be considered unfair trade. Are trade practices based on work habits, on infrastructure, and on differential saving behavior to be considered unfair? If so, all trade could possible be considered unfair.[16]

ECONOMIC COOPERATION

Given inherent constraints in any system, conditions for the best policy rarely exist. A policy maker must then turn to the second-best policy. This practice applies to international trade as well. Worldwide free trade is ideal, but cannot be attained. The **theory of second best** suggests that the optimum policy is to have economic cooperation on a smaller scale.[17] In an attempt to reduce trade barriers and improve trade, many countries within the same geographic area often join together to establish various forms of economic cooperation. Major regional groups are shown in Exhibit 2.1. As shown in Figure 2.6, some countries are members of multiple groups.

Levels of economic integration

Trade theorists have identified five levels of economic cooperation. They are: free trade area, customs union, common market, economic and monetary union, and political union. Table 2.6 shows a concise comparison of these cooperation levels.

Free trade area

In a free trade area, the countries involved eliminate duties among themselves, while maintaining separately their own tariffs against outsiders. Free trade areas include the NAFTA (North American Free Trade Agreement), the EFTA (European Free Trade Association), and the now defunct LAFTA (Latin-American Free Trade Association). The purpose of a free trade area is to facilitate trade among member nations. The problem with this kind of arrangement is the lack of coordination of tariffs against the non-members, enabling nonmembers to direct their exported products to enter the free trade area at the point of lowest external tariffs.

The first free trade agreement signed by the USA was with Israel in 1985, and the US–Israel Free Trade Area Agreement eliminates all customs duties and most nontariff barriers between the two countries. More recently, the USA has entered into free

Figure 2.6 Regional trading arrangements in Eastern and Southern Africa

Notes
COMESA: Common Market for Eastern and Southern Africa
EAC: East African Community
RIFF: Regional Integration Facilitation Forum
SADC: Southern African Development Community
SACU: Southern African Customs Union

Source: Robert Sharer, "An Agenda for Trade, Investment, and Regional Integration," Finance & Development, December 2001, 16.

Table 2.6 Levels of regional cooperation

Characteristics of cooperation	Free trade area	Customs union	Common market	Economic and monetary union	Political union
Elimination of internal duties	Yes	Yes	Yes	Yes	Probably
Establishment of common barriers	No	Yes	Yes	Yes	Probably
Removal of restrictions on factors of production	No	No	Yes	Yes	Probably
Harmonization of national economic policies	No	No	No	Yes	Probably
Harmonization of national political policies	No	No	No	No	Yes

EXHIBIT 2.1   REGIONAL GROUPINGS AND THEIR NATIONS

African Financial Community: CAEMC and WAEMU members.

AFTA (ASEAN Free Trade Area): ASEAN members.

Andean Group (the Cartagena Agreement): Bolivia, Colombia, Ecuador, Peru, and Venezuela.

ANZCERTA (Australia–New Zealand Closer Economic Relations Trade Agreement): Australia and New Zealand.

APEC (Asia Pacific Economic Cooperation): Australia, Brunei, Canada, Chile, China, Hong Kong, Indonesia, Japan, Korea, Malaysia, Mexico, New Zealand, Papua New Guinea, the Philippines, Singapore, Chinese Taipei (Taiwan), Thailand, and the USA.

Arab/Middle East Arab Common Market: Iraq, Jordan, Sudan, Syria, United Arab Republic, and Yemen.

ASEAN (Association of Southeast Asian Nations): Brunei, Indonesia, Malaysia, the Philippines, Singapore, Thailand, and Vietnam.

Benelux Customs Union: Belgium, the Netherlands, and Luxembourg.

CAEMC (Central African Economic and Monetary Community): Cameroon, the Central African Republic, Chad, the Republic of Congo, Equatorial Guinea, and Gabon.

CARICOM (Caribbean Common Market): Antigua and Barbuda, Bahamas, Barbados, Belize, Dominica, Grenada, Guyana, Jamaica, Montserrat, Saint Christopher-Nevis, Saint Lucia, Saint Vincent and the Grenadines, and Trinidad and Tobago.

Central American Community: Costa Rica, El Salvador, Guatemala, Honduras, Nicaragua, and Panama.

CFA Franc Zone: the Comoros, members of the WAEMU and the CAEMC.

CIS (Commonwealth of Independent States): Armenia, Azerbaijan, Belarus, Georgia, Kazakhstan, Kirgizstan, Moldova, Russia, Tajikistan, Turkmenistan, Ukraine, and Uzbekistan.

East Africa Customs Union: Ethiopia, Kenya, Zimbabwe, Sudan, Tanzania, and Uganda.

ECOWAS (Economic Community of West African States): Benin, Cape Verde, Dahomey, Gambia, Ghana, Guinea, Guinea-Bissau, Ivory Coast, Liberia, Mali, Mauritania, Niger, Nigeria, Senegal, Sierra Leone, Togo, and Upper Volta.

EEA (European Economic Area): Iceland, Norway, and EU members.

EFTA (European Free Trade Association): Austria, Finland, Iceland, Liechtenstein, Norway, Sweden, and Switzerland.

EU (European Union): Austria, Belgium, Denmark, Finland, France, Germany, Greece, Ireland, Italy, Luxembourg, the Netherlands, Portugal, Spain, Sweden, and the UK (plus ten new members).

GCC (Cooperation Council of the Arab States of the Gulf): Bahrain, Kuwait, Oman, Qatar, Saudi Arabia, and the United Arab Emirates.

Group of Three: Colombia, Mexico, and Venezuela.

LAIA (Latin American Integration Association): Argentina, Bolivia, Brazil, Chile, Colombia, Ecuador, Mexico, Paraguay, Peru, Uruguay, and Venezuela.

Mahgreb Economic Community: Algeria, Libya, Tunisia, and Morocco.

Mercosur (Southern Common Market): Argentina, Brazil, Paraguay, and Uruguay.

NAFTA (North American Free Trade Agreement): Canada, Mexico, and the USA.

OECD (Organization for Economic Cooperation and Development): Australia, Canada, Iceland, Japan, New Zealand, Norway, Switzerland, Turkey, the USA, and EU members.

RCD (Regional Cooperation for Development): Iran, Pakistan, and Turkey.

SICA: El Salvador, Guatemala, Honduras, and Nicaragua.

WAEMU: (West African Economic and Monetary Union): Benin, Burkina Faso, Ivory Coast, Guinea-Bissau, Mali, Niger, Senegal, and Togo.

trade agreements with Singapore and Chile, while Mexico has done the same with the EU. Singapore has also concluded free trade deals with Australia and Japan. It should be apparent that countries forming a free trade area do not need to share joint boundaries.

Customs union

A customs union is an extension of the free trade area in the sense that member countries must also agree on a common schedule of identical tariff rates. In effect, the objective of the customs union is to harmonize trade regulations and to establish common barriers against outsiders. Uniform tariffs and a common commercial policy against non-members are necessary to prevent them from taking advantage of the situation by shipping goods initially to a member country that has the lowest joint boundaries. The world's oldest customs union is the Benelux Customs Union. A more recent example is the one formed between Turkey and the European Union; this took effect in 1996.

Common market

A common market is a higher and more complex level of economic integration than either a free trade area or a customs union. In a common market, countries remove all customs and other restrictions on the movement of the factors of production (such as services, raw materials, labor, and capital) among the members of the common market. As a result, business laws and labor laws are standardized to ensure undistorted competition. For an outsider, the point of entry is no longer dictated by member countries' tariff rates since those rates are uniform across countries within the common market. The point of entry is now determined by the members' nontariff barriers. The outsider's strategy should be to enter a member country that has the least non-tariff restrictions, because goods can be shipped freely once inside the common market.

In 1993, the EU and the EFTA formed the world's largest and most lucrative common market

– the European Economic Area. The European Economic Area eliminates nontariff barriers between the EFTA and EU countries to create a free flow of goods, services, capital, and people in a market of more than 400 million people.

Economic and monetary union

Cooperation among countries increases even more with an economic and monetary union (EMU). Some authorities prefer to distinguish a monetary union from an economic union. In essence, monetary union means one money (i.e., a single currency). The Delors Committee, chaired by Jacques Delors, who is President of the European Commission, has issued a report entitled *Economic and Monetary Union in the European Community* that defines monetary union as having three basic characteristics: total and irreversible convertibility of currencies; complete freedom of capital movements in fully integrated financial markets; and irrevocably fixed exchange rates with no fluctuation margins between member currencies, leading ultimately to a single currency. The economic advantages of a single currency include the elimination of currency risk and lower transaction costs. One European Commission study found that European businesses were spending $12.8 billion (0.4 percent of the EU's GDP) a year on currency conversions.

The European Commission's *One Market, One Money* report defines an economic union as a single market for goods, services, capital, and labor, complemented by common policies and coordination in several economic and structural areas.[18] An economic union provides a number of benefits. In terms of efficiency and economic growth, the transaction costs associated with converting one currency into another are eliminated, and the elimination of foreign exchange risk should improve trade and capital mobility. In addition, stronger competition policies should promote efficiency gains. In terms of inflation, the implementation of an economic union is a demonstration of a credible commitment to stable prices.

According to the Delors Committee, the basic elements of an economic union include the following: a single market within which persons, goods, services, and capital could move freely; a joint competition policy to strengthen market mechanisms; common competition, structural, and regional policies; and sufficient coordination of macroeconomic policies, including binding rules on budgetary policies regarding the size and financing of national budget deficits.

A good example of an economic and monetary union is the unification of East Germany and West Germany. The terms of the monetary union called for an average currency conversion rate of M 1.8 to DM 1 and a conversion of East German wages at parity into deutschmarks. The 1 July 1990 German Economic and Monetary Union has resulted in one Germany. In addition to sharing a common, freely convertible currency (the deutschmark), the legal environment, commercial code, and taxation requirements in the German Democratic Republic (East Germany) are now the same as those of the Federal Republic of Germany (West Germany).

Following a transition period, several European currencies were replaced by a new currency called the euro (see Cultural Dimension 2.1). At the beginning of 2002, twelve EU countries (not counting Denmark, Sweden, and the United Kingdom) introduced euro coins and notes. In 2003, following in the footsteps of Denmark three years earlier, the Swedes voted overwhelmingly to reject membership in the European single currency.

The EU member states have ceded substantial sovereignty to the EU. As an example, Denmark was required by the EU to comply with common packaging rules and remove its twenty-year-old ban on beers and soft drinks in metal cans.[19]

CULTURAL DIMENSION 2.1   THE EURO

On January 1, 1999, the European Union adopted the euro as its common currency. As the participating nations adopted the euro, there was a transition cost in terms of the temporary loss of output and the possible increase in unemployment due to the required adjustment to the price stability and fiscal criteria laid out in the Maastricht Treaty. Banks in particular had to bear the cost of $10 billion to $13 billion (about 2 percent of annual operating costs over a changeover period), with software alterations accounting for half of the cost. By 2002, the substitution of euro notes and coins was complete.

Euro is the official name of the European Union's currency. Before the name was finally chosen, some European leaders did the last-minute lobbying for their favored names. French President Jacques Chirac wanted to call the currency the Ecu since the name has historical significance for France. Britain's Prime Minister John Major, on the other hand, preferred names such as the crown, florin, or shilling – all of which have roots in England.

In the end, the European leaders decided against using the name *euro* as a prefix (e.g., euro-mark, euro-pound). Euro was probably chosen because the name was the least offensive.

Robert Kalina was given a task of designing a set of eurobank notes. According to the rules, the designs could not be related to a specific country. So he used bridges and windows to span seven historical periods: Classical, Renaissance, Baroque, Rococo, the age of iron and glass, and modern twentieth-century architecture. One can see through or walk through windows and doors; opening them symbolizes the future. Bridges offer a connecting element: communication. These elements were designed to appeal to 300 million people in twelve countries. However, euro coins have national designs on one side and a universal design on the other.

Sources: "Euro Is Official Name of European Currency," *San José Mercury News*, December 16, 1995; "Now the Hard Part: Imposing a Common Currency," *Wall Street Journal*, July 28, 1995; "Note Design Aims for Broad Appeal," *Bangkok Post*, December 27, 2001.

The EU is unique in the sense that it is the first time that advanced economies have agreed to cooperate economically at such a grand scale. Naturally, with the fall of the Berlin wall in 1989, countries emerging from communism coveted EU memberships, while the EU leaders were stalling them. But the Yugoslav wars made the EU aware of the need to enlarge Europe's security zone. After all, if stability were not exported from the West, instability might be imported instead from the East.[20] So the EU is expanding. Ten new members have been admitted for accession in 2004. The ten new members are: Cyprus, the Czech Republic, Estonia, Hungary, Latvia, Lithuania, Malta, Poland, Slovakia, and Slovenia. Turkey, Bulgaria, and Romania have candidate status. While Bulgaria and Romania are on course for accession in 2007, Turkey was told to wait at least two more years before starting talks on joining.[21]

Political union

A political union is the ultimate type of regional cooperation because it involves the integration of both economic and political policies. With France and Germany leading the way, the EU has been moving toward social, political, and economic integration. The EU's goal is to form a political union similar to the fifty states of the USA. The EU's debate over political union involves issues such as having common defense and foreign policies, strengthening the role of the EU Parliament, and adopting an EU-wide social policy. In late 1991, the member countries of the EU have given the EU authority to act in defense, in foreign, and in social policies.

It is doubtful that pure forms of economic integration and political union can ever become reality. Even if they did, they would not last long because different countries eventually have different goals and inflation rates. More important is that no country would be willing to surrender its sovereignty for economic reasons. The EU, despite great strides, has been plagued by infighting among member states with conflicting national interests.

Although the Treaty of Rome calls for a free internal market and permits market forces to equalize national economic differences, Germany, France, and the Netherlands — which have expensive social welfare programs — argue that the *social dimension* must be taken into account in order to prevent *social dumping*. In other words, they seek to prevent a movement of business and jobs away from areas with high wages and strong labor organizations to areas with low wages, less organized labor forces, and weak social welfare policies. As a result, the EC Commission adopted the Social Charter in 1989 to establish workers' basic rights and to equalize EU social regulations (e.g., a minimum wage, labor participation in management decisions, and paid holidays for education purposes). Member countries accused of social dumping must subject their products to sanctions. European socialists believe that the Social Charter is necessary to prevent countries with the lowest social benefits from gaining a comparative advantage.

Countries with lower labor costs (e.g., Portugal, Spain, and Greece), however, view the Social Charter as something that forces capital-poor countries to adopt the expensive social welfare policies, in effect increasing the cost of labor and unemployment. To them, the Social Charter is nothing more than protectionism in the guise of harmonization. Such expensive policies are also a major concern to European industry. As may be expected, several initiatives are the subject of heated debate.

The European Union is a good case study of how to form economic and political cooperation at a high level. The EU will be the first group of industrial nations to deal with: (1) how to redefine national sovereignty in light of new economic alliances; (2) how to combine various national priorities with a single decision-making process; and (3) how to deregulate separate economies to induce competition among national monopolies.[22]

Economic and marketing implications

Marketers must pay attention to the effects of regional economic integration or cooperation because the competitive environment may change drastically over time. As in the case of the EU, although EU member countries still maintain their national identities, national borders are no longer trade barriers. Marketers must treat the EU as a single market rather than as numerous separate and fragmented markets. They need to rethink their marketing, finance, distribution, and production strategies. Foreign businesses need to make an effort to become familiar with new regulations so as to take full advantage in the changing market. For example, even though standard harmonization may exclude some US firms from the EU markets, the USA should work to influence the process in order to turn the potential barrier into an advantage.

Whereas countries that are not members of the EU view the EU's ambitious goals with some concern, outsider firms can still cope successfully with the Single Internal Market program. Instead of viewing the EU's developments as obstacles, marketers should regard them as both challenges and opportunities. Not unlike coping with a single country's protectionist measures (except on a larger scale), the key to competing effectively in the EU is for an external firm to become an insider. Figure 2.7 shows how the United Kingdom can serve as a strategic location for this purpose.

General Electric Co. has formed joint ventures in major appliances and electrical equipment with Britain's largest electronics firm, has acquired France's largest medical equipment maker, and has planned to build a plastics factory in Spain. Coca-Cola has terminated some licensing agreements and has consolidated its European bottling operations to cut costs and prices. Using acquisitions to build up its European position, Sara Lee Corp. purchased a Dutch coffee and tea company and took control of Paris-based Dim, Europe's largest maker of pantyhose. In addition, Sara Lee has experimented with the "Euro-branding" strategy by printing several languages on a single package and distributing it to several countries.

Initially, new trade policies generally tend to favor local business firms. For example, IBM encountered problems in Europe, where the EU

members wanted to protect their own computer industry. Alternatively, outsider firms may be able to take advantage of the situation to overcome the barriers erected by a particular member of a regional economic cooperation. Facing France's troublesome entry procedure, Japan could first ship its products into Germany before moving them more freely into France.

Because of the favorable economic environment in a cooperative region, additional firms desire entry and the competitive atmosphere intensifies. Firms inside the region are likely to be more competitive owing to the expansion of local markets, resulting in better economies of scale. External firms (those outside the area) are faced with overcoming trade barriers, perhaps through the establishment of local production facilities. For example, Ireland tried to attract foreign investment by mentioning in its advertisements that it is a member of the EU. Nike, a US firm, was able to avoid the EU tariffs by opening a plant in Ireland.

Over time, a region will grow faster than before owing to the stimulation caused by trade creation effects, favorable policies, and more competition, but economic cooperation can create problems as well as opportunities within international markets. The expanded market offers more profit potential, but it may create an impression of collusion when subsidiaries or licensees are granted exclusive rights in certain member countries. The long-term result may be an area-wide antitrust among new firms or nonmember countries wishing to trade within the economically integrated region.

Economic cooperation may either improve or impede international trade, depending on how the result of the cooperation is viewed. Economic integration encourages trade liberalization internally, while it promotes trade protection externally. The tendency is for a member of an economic group to shift from the most efficient supplier in the world to the lowest-cost supplier within that particular economic region. As in the case of NAFTA, the results have been generally positive. Promoting trade between the USA and Mexico has been highly successful. While the US Labor Department has

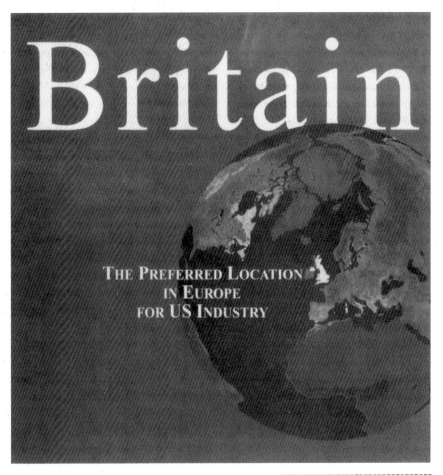

Figure 2.7 *The United Kingdom and its strategic location*

certified that some 316,000 US jobs have been lost or threatened due to trade with Mexico and Canada, the number is far lower than predicted. On balance, NAFTA has increased jobs and reduced inflation without affecting wages.[23]

CONCLUSION

For countries to want to trade with one another, they must be better off with trade than without it. The principles of absolute and comparative advantage explain how trade enables trading nations to increase their welfare through specialization. Trade allows a country to concentrate on the production of products with the best potential for its own consumption as well as for exports, resulting in a more efficient and effective use of its resources.

Absolute production costs are not as relevant as relative costs in determining whether trade should take place and what products to export or import. Basically, a country should specialize in manufacturing a product in which it has the greatest comparative advantage. If no comparative advantage exists, there will be no trade, since there is no difference in relative production costs between the two countries (i.e., a situation of equal relative advantage).

Comparative advantage is not determined solely by labor but rather by the required factors of production necessary to produce the product in question. This advantage is often determined by an abundance of a particular production factor in the country. Thus it is advantageous for a country to export a product that requires its abundant factor as a major production input.

Trade theories, in spite of their usefulness, simply explain what nations should do rather than describe what nations actually do. The desired trade pattern based on those theories related to comparative advantage and factor endowment often deviates significantly from the actual trade practice. It is thus necessary to modify the theories to account for the divergence caused by extraneous variables. Industrial nations' high-income levels, for instance, may foster a preference for high-quality products that less developed countries may be unable to supply. Furthermore, trade restrictions, a norm rather than an exception, heavily influence the extent and direction of trade, and any investigation is not complete without taking tariffs, quotas, and other trade barriers into consideration.

Perhaps the most serious problem with classical trade theories is their failure to incorporate marketing activities into the analysis. It is inappropriate to assume that consumers' tastes are homogeneous across national markets and that such tastes can be largely satisfied by commodities that are also homogeneous. Marketing activities such as distribution and promotion add more value to a product, and the success of the product is often determined by the planning and execution of such activities.

CASE 2.1   THE UNITED STATES OF AMERICA VS. THE UNITED STATES OF EUROPE

The European Union

The European Union (EU), once known as the European Common Market, is a prime example of a very high level of economic cooperation. Formed by the 1957 Treaty of Rome, the EU has grown from six to fifteen members. Sweden, Austria, and Finland joined the EU in 1995. The EU's institutions that function as the three traditional branches of democratic government are the European Parliament (as the legislative branch), the Court of Justice (as a judiciary), and the Council of Ministers of the European Communities (as the executive branch). The Council appoints members of the Commission of the European Communities, which initiates legislative proposals (regulations or directives) for the Council.

The passage in 1985 of the Single European Act (SEA), an amendment to the Treaties of Rome, was largely responsible for the development of the Single Internal Market. Taking effect in 1987, this legal instrument makes it possible for the Council of Ministers to adopt an Internal Market directive or regulation on the strength of a qualified majority (forty-four of sixty-seven votes). Council votes are assigned by a weighted average. The Council of Ministers thus no longer has to reach unanimous agreement for a directive to be passed. However, unanimity is still required for fiscal matters (e.g., taxation), decisions on the free movement of persons, and directives or regulations on the rights and interests of employed persons.

The EU member states have ceded substantial sovereignty to the EU. As an example, the EU's highest court ruled in 2001 that France was breaking an EU law by maintaining a ban on British beef, since the European Commission had already eased a worldwide embargo on British beef exports that was imposed over fears about mad cow disease (BSE).

Because an EMU envisages total fiscal and monetary integration, nations that agree to join the union must work out an economic arrangement in which trade between member countries directly benefits each of the countries' economic objectives. The features of an EMU require a common monetary policy formulated by a single institution; highly coordinated economic policies; and adequate, consistent constraints on members' public sector deficits and their financing.

It should be readily apparent that the formation of an EMU is a complex and exceedingly difficult task because this level of cooperation requires the harmonization of national economic policies – especially in the monetary and fiscal areas. A member country must give up the prospect of currency devaluation as a short-term instrument for solving economic problems. For an EMU to function effectively, member countries should have similar economic conditions. In the case of the EU, economic disparities are highly evident and will probably increase when the EU admits some Eastern European countries as new members.

Under the EU members' EMU agreements, the EU has created a central bank and adopted a single currency. According to the terms of the Maastricht Treaty, the EU nations wishing to join the monetary union must meet the following five economic criteria: annual inflation, public sector budget deficit, public sector debt, long-term interest rates, and exchange rate. In 1999, fixed conversion rates were adopted for the participating nations' currencies, and the European Central Bank (ECB) started to execute a common monetary policy. Following a transition period, the currencies were replaced by a new currency called the euro. At the beginning of 2002, twelve EU countries (not counting Denmark, Sweden, and the United Kingdom) introduced euro coins and notes.

The EU is unique in the sense that it is the first time advanced economies have agreed to cooperate economically on such a grand scale. Naturally, with the fall of the Berlin wall in 1989, countries emerging from communism coveted EU membership. To promote stability in the region, the EU is expanding. Ten new members have been admitted for accession in 2004. The ten new members are: Cyprus, the Czech Republic, Estonia, Hungary, Latvia, Lithuania, Malta, Poland, Slovakia, and Slovenia. Turkey, Bulgaria, and Romania have candidate status. While Bulgaria and Romania are on course for accession in 2007, Turkey was told to wait at least two more years before starting talks on joining.

NAFTA

The North American Free Trade Agreement (NAFTA) is a free trade agreement. Taking effect in January 1994, NAFTA comprises Canada, Mexico, and the USA. NAFTA, in terms of population, is larger than the European Union but slightly smaller than the European Economic Area. In addition, NAFTA's combined output is about 20 percent larger than that of the European Union.

NAFTA progressively eliminates almost all US–Mexico tariffs over a ten-year period and also phases out Mexico–Canada tariffs at the same time. Such barriers to trade as import licensing requirements and customs user fees are eliminated. NAFTA establishes the principle of national treatment to ensure that NAFTA countries will treat NAFTA-origin products in the same manner as similar domestic products. Service providers of the member nations will receive equal treatment. To protect foreign investors in the free trade area, NAFTA has established five principles: (1) nondiscriminatory treatment, (2) freedom from performance requirements, (3) free transference of funds related to an investment, (4) expropriation only in conformity with international law, and (5) the right to seek international arbitration for a violation of the Agreement's protections.

Canada's locus of economic activity has always been along the US border, which stretches for some four thousand miles. It is not too surprising that the natural axis of trade has always been from north to south rather than east to west. Canada is the largest single market for US exports as well as the largest manufactures market of the USA.

The USA is Mexico's most important trading partner, absorbing about two-thirds of total Mexican exports worldwide. On the other hand, Mexico is the third largest US trading partner, ranking after Canada and Japan. Approximately 70 percent of all of Mexico's imports come from the USA, and 15 cents of every additional dollar of Mexican GDP is spent on American goods and services. To modernize its infrastructure and plant facilities, Mexico is purchasing most of the durable goods and industrial materials from the USA. Not surprisingly, Mexico is the fastest growing major US export market. Mexico is, by far, the largest US trading partner in Latin America, accounting for about half of US exports to and imports from the region.

President Vicente Fox of Mexico has advocated a progressive move toward a North American common market that will allow free movement of labor among the three NAFTA members. Neither Canada nor the USA has shown much enthusiasm for the proposal. Instead, the USA is more interested in expanding the free trade area and thus maintaining the same level of economic cooperation.

As the EU expands, the USA itself is trying to persuade the other American countries to join the free trade area. The Free Trade Area of the Americas (FTAA), when completed, will be the world's largest free trade area stretching from the southern tip of Argentina northward to Alaska. In December 1994, at the first Summit of the Americas, the USA and thirty-four other democratically elected leaders in the Western Hemisphere took the first step by committing to establishing the FTAA by 2005. The idea of the FTAA is to allow import tariffs to fall to zero over a decade or more. Nontariff barriers will be gradually eliminated, and trade in services will be liberalized. When formed, the FTAA will be the largest free-trade area in the world.

Points to consider

1 Discuss the obstacles and opportunities presented by the EU market. How should Japanese and American firms adjust their marketing strategies to meet the challenges?
2 Discuss the benefits and difficulties involved as the EU absorbs several new members.
3 Assess the likelihood that the EU will be able to establish a political union.
4 Why is it that organized labor in the USA opposes NAFTA and further expansion when it never objected to the US–Canada Free Trade Agreement which preceded NAFTA?
5 Should the USA advance NAFTA to the next stage to become, say, a common market? Or instead of vertical advancement, should the USA push for horizontal advancement by creating the FTAA?

QUESTIONS

1 Is trade a zero-sum game or a positive-sum game?
2 Explain (a) the principle of absolute advantage and (b) the principle of relative advantage.
3 Should there be trade if (a) a country has an absolute advantage for *all* products over its trading partner, and (b) if the domestic exchange ratio of one country is identical to that of another country?
4 What is the theory of factor endowment?
5 Explain the Leontief Paradox.
6 Discuss the validity and limitations of trade theories.

7   Distinguish among (a) free trade area, (b) customs union, (c) common market, (d) economic and monetary union, and (e) political union.

8   Does economic cooperation improve or impede trade?

DISCUSSION ASSIGNMENTS AND MINICASES

1   Name products or industries in which the USA has a comparative advantage as well as those in which it has a comparative disadvantage.

2   Why is it beneficial for the well-endowed, resource-rich USA to trade with other nations?

3   For a country with high labor costs, how can it improve its export competitiveness?

4   Explain how the advanced economies should cope with the shift in comparative advantage.

5   There was a proliferation of regional trading arrangements in the 1990s. The European Union and the North American Free Trade Agreement in particular have commanded a great deal of world attention. There are numerous reasons for the formation of a regional trading arrangement. Some of the reasons are economic in nature, while others are political. As a policy maker for a medium-sized and developing country, list and explain the reasons that may motivate you to consider forming or joining a regional trade group.

NOTES

1   Adam Smith, *Wealth of Nations* (1776; reprint, Homewood, IL: Irwin, 1963).

2   David Ricardo, *The Principles of Political Economy and Taxation* (1817; reprint, Baltimore: Penguin, 1971).

3   "A Fresh Look at Keynes," *Finance & Development* (December 2001): 60–3.

4   Richard S. Tedlow, *Giants of Enterprise: Seven Business Innovators and the Empires They Built* (New York, NY: HarperBusiness, 2003).

5   Eli Heckscher, "The Effects of Foreign Trade on the Distribution of Income," in *Readings in the Theory of International Trade*, ed. Howard S. Ellis and Lloyd A. Matzler (Homewood, IL: Irwin, 1949); and Bertil Ohlin, *Interregional and International Trade* (Cambridge, MA: Harvard University Press, 1933).

6   Leslie Lipschitz, Timothy Lane, and Alex Mourmouras, "The Tosovksy Dilemma," *Finance & Development*, September 2002, 30–3.

7   Michael E. Porter, *The Competitive Advantage of Nations* (New York, NY: Free Press, 1990).

8   Paul Cashin, Paolo Mauro, and Ratna Sahay, "Macroeconomic Policies and Poverty Reduction: Some Cross-Country Evidence," *Finance & Development* (June 2001): 46–9.

9   Porter, *Competitive Advantage*.

10 *Offshore Finance U.S.A.* (September/October 2001): 66.

11 G. D. A. MacDougall, "British and American Exports: A Study Suggested by the Theory of Comparative Costs," *Economic Journal* (December 1951); Robert Stern, "British and American Productivity and Comparative Costs in International Trade," *Oxford Economic Papers* (October 1962); Bela Balassa, "An Empirical Demonstration of Classical Comparative Cost Theory," *Review of Economics and Statistics* (August 1963).

12 Wassily W. Leontief, "Domestic Production and Foreign Trade: The American Capital Position Re-examined," *Proceedings of the American Philosophical Society* (September 1953); Wassily W. Leontief, "Factor Proportions and the Structure of American Trade: Further Theoretical and Empirical Analysis," *Review of Economics and Statistics* 38 (November 1956): 386–407.

13 "Trade Specialist Calls Current Rules Outdated," *IMF Survey*, July 15, 1991, 209, 216.

14 "Opening Up to Capital Flows? Be Prepared Before Plunging in," *IMF Survey*, May 19, 2003, 137.

15 "'Let Chaos Reign,' Grove Urges Execs," *San José Mercury News*, September 27, 1995.

16 "Economists Discuss Transition to Market-Oriented Economies," *IMF Survey*, February 4, 1991, 34–7.

17 J. E. Meade, *Trade and Welfare* (New York, NY: Oxford University Press, 1955); R. G. Lipsey and K. Lancaster, "The General Theory of Second Best," *Review of Economic Studies* 24 (1956): 11–32.

18 "Report Highlights Benefits of Economic and Monetary Union in Europe," *IMF Survey*, November 26, 1990, 363–5.

19 "Denmark to Lift Ban on Drinks in Cans," *San José Mercury News*, January 15, 2002.

20 "Common Past Fuels Drive to Agree Biggest EU Expansion," *Financial Times*, December 10, 2002.

21 "European Central Bank Plans Reforms to Cope with EU Enlargement," *IMF Survey*, February 3, 2003, 31–2.

22 C. Michael Aho, "'Fortress Europe': Will the EU Isolate Itself from North America and Asia?" *Columbia Journal of World Business* 29 (fall 1994): 33–9.

23 "NAFTA's Scoreboard: So Far, So Good," *Business Week*, July 9, 2001, 54–5.

Chapter 3

Trade distortions and marketing barriers

Trade is not about warfare but about mutual gains from voluntary exchange.

Alan S. Blinder

CHAPTER OUTLINE

PURPOSE OF CHAPTER

Free trade makes a great deal of sense theoretically because it increases efficiency and economic welfare for all involved nations and their citizens. South Korea's trade barriers, however, do not represent an isolated case. In practice, free trade is woefully ignored by virtually all countries. Despite the advantages, nations are inclined to discourage free trade.

The *National Trade Estimate Report on Foreign Trade Barriers (NTE)*, issued by the US Trade Representative, defines **trade barriers** as "government laws, regulations, policies, or practices that either protect domestic producers from foreign competition or artificially stimulate exports of particular domestic products." Restrictive business practices and government regulations designed to protect public health and national security are not considered as trade barriers. The report classifies the trade barriers into ten categories: (1) import policies (e.g., tariffs, quotas, licensing, and customs barriers); (2) standards, testing, labeling, and certification; (3) government procurement; (4) export subsidies; (5) lack of intellectual property protection; (6) services barriers (e.g., restrictions on the use of foreign data processing); (7) investment barriers; (8) anticompetitive practices with trade effects tolerated by foreign governments; (9) trade restrictions affecting electronic commerce (e.g., discriminatory taxation), and (10) other barriers that encompass more than one category (e.g., bribery and corruption).[1]

This chapter catalogs the types and impact of trade and marketing barriers. It examines trade restrictions and the rationale, if any, behind them. By understanding these barriers, marketers should be in a better position to cope with them. It would be impossible to list all marketing barriers because they are simply too numerous. Furthermore, governments are forever creating new import restrictions or adjusting the ones currently in use. For purposes of study, marketing barriers may be divided into two basic categories: tariffs and nontariff barriers. Figure 3.1 on p. 54 provides details of this division. Each category and its subcategories will be discussed in this chapter.

MARKETING ILLUSTRATION   THE BEST THINGS IN LIFE ARE (NOT) FREE

South Korea is the world's sixth largest manufacturer of automobiles, and it exports some 650,000 cars annually. The country is also the world's fastest growing car market. Hyundai Motors and its subsidiary Kia have 75 percent market share. In 1999, Koreans bought almost one million new cars. Yet car imports were so highly restricted that only 2401 imported cars were sold, amounting to about 0.3 percent of the country's domestic car sales (the lowest market penetration in the world). While GM sold sixty-eight cars there, Volkswagen managed to sell two.

Foreign carmakers have long complained about South Korea's highly protected market. Imported cars are subject to the 8 percent tariffs as well as the 15 percent acquisition tax on luxury cars. The government also restricts the number of automobile showrooms and the exhibition space allowed to foreign-owned importers and dealers. Other problems faced by foreign carmakers include restrictions on credit facilities and the tightly regulated advertising market. Since most advertising time on TV and radio is controlled by broadcasting authorities through contracts that may continue indefinitely, large Korean advertisers are able to lock up virtually all prime-time TV spots or sponsored programs. In addition, Korean buyers of high-priced foreign cars can expect special attention from tax officials.

Consumer durables (e.g., refrigerators) are prohibitively expensive because of tariffs and taxes. Even dried peas are classified as luxury goods. Foreign sausages do not necessarily fare any better. Korean inspectors seized a shipment of American-made sausages and held it for months. According to the inspectors, the sausages were incorrectly classified for years by customs officials as a product with a ninety-day expiration period. The sausages are supposed to have only a thirty-day expiration period. Ironically, that is about the length of time it takes for a shipment to reach Korea and undergo the lengthy customs process.

Korea's foreign citrus-licensing system has kept out all but the lowest grade oranges from abroad. When the first shipment of oranges arrived from California, it was held in the hot sun for three weeks while awaiting clearance. After finally admitting the containers, the government then proceeded to reject the oranges as substandard. California's almond growers similarly have to endure customs rules that keep shipments on Korean docks for weeks.

Sources: "From Sausages to Autos, US Products Still Face Trade Hurdles in South Korea," *Wall Street Journal,* May 31, 1994; "South Korea, After US Pressure, Offers Plan to Ease Access for Foreign Cars," *Wall Street Journal,* June 24, 1994; "S. Korean Market Hard to Crack," *San José Mercury News,* October 15, 1995; "Now Detroit's Heavy Artillery Is Trained on Seoul," *Business Week,* September 25, 1995, 78; "Korea, Here We Come," *Business Week,* February 14, 2000, 8; "Foreign Automakers Set Sights on S. Korea," *San José Mercury News,* September 16, 2000.

Figure 3.1
Marketing barriers

Source: Adapted from Sak Onkvisit and John J. Shaw, "Marketing Barriers in International Trade," *Business Horizons* 31 (May to June 1988): 64–72.

PROTECTION OF LOCAL INDUSTRIES

While countries generally do not mind exporting, they simply do not like imports. According to a survey of more than 28,000 people in twenty-three countries, even well-educated workers in poorer countries are against free trade. In addition, workers in the industries that face foreign competition tend to be against free trade. On the other hand, well-educated people in well-educated countries are more likely to favor trade.[2]

Why do nations impede free trade when the inhibition is irrational? One reason why governments interfere with free marketing is to protect local industries, often at the expense of local consumers as well as consumers worldwide. Regulations are created to keep out or hamper the entry of foreign-made products. Arguments for the protection of local industries usually take one of the following forms: (1) keeping money at home, (2) reducing unemployment, (3) equalizing cost and price, (4) enhancing national security, and (5) protecting infant industry.

Keeping money at home

Trade unions and protectionists often argue that international trade will lead to an outflow of money, making foreigners richer and local people poorer. This argument is based on the fallacy of regarding money as the sole indicator of wealth. Other assets, even products, may also be indicators of wealth. For instance, it does not make sense to say that a man is poor just because he does not have much cash on hand when he owns many valuable assets such as land and jewelry. In addition, this protectionist argument assumes that foreigners receive money without having to give something of value in return. Whether local consumers buy locally made or foreign products, they will have to have money to pay for such products. In either case, they receive something of value for their money.

Reducing unemployment

It is standard practice for trade unions and politicians to attack imports and international trade in the name of job protection. Figure 3.2 presents this argument as made by the United Steel workers of America. The argument is based on the assumption that import reduction will create more demand for local products and subsequently create more jobs. Most economists see this kind of thinking as one-sided, though not completely without merits. At the least, import reduction makes foreigners earn fewer dollars with which they can buy US exports. As a result, foreign demand for American products declines. In addition, foreign firms may refuse to invest in the USA. They are inclined to invest only when import demand is great enough to justify building and using local facilities.

Another problem with protectionism is that it may lead to inflation. Instead of using protective relief to gain or regain market share and for competitive investment, local manufacturers often cannot resist the temptation to increase their prices for quick profits.

With higher prices at home, consumers become poorer and buy less, and the economy suffers. To make matters worse, other countries will often retaliate by refusing to import products. On a related subject, note that the establishment of foreign operations is not necessarily harmful to employment at home. In fact, jobs are often created rather than lost.

Equalizing cost and price

Some protectionists attempt to justify their actions by invoking economic theory. They argue that foreign goods have lower prices because of lower production costs. Therefore, trade barriers are needed to make prices of imported products less competitive and local items more competitive. This argument is not persuasive to most analysts for several reasons. First, to determine the cause of price differentials is unusually difficult. Is it caused by labor, raw materials, efficiency, or subsidy? Furthermore, costs and objectives vary greatly among countries, making it impossible to determine exactly what costs need to be equalized.

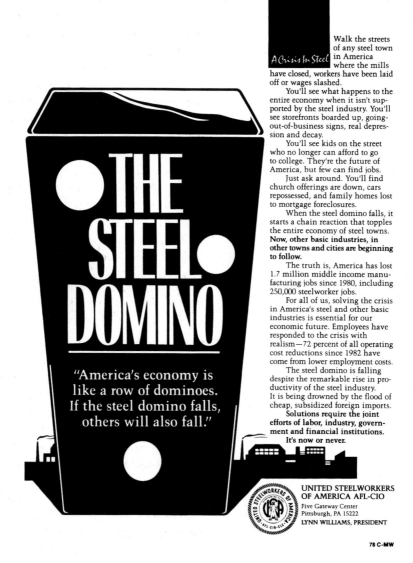

Walk the streets of any steel town in America where the mills have closed, workers have been laid off or wages slashed.

You'll see what happens to the entire economy when it isn't supported by the steel industry. You'll see storefronts boarded up, going-out-of-business signs, real depression and decay.

You'll see kids on the street who no longer can afford to go to college. They're the future of America, but few can find jobs.

Just ask around. You'll find church offerings are down, cars repossessed, and family homes lost to mortgage foreclosures.

When the steel domino falls, it starts a chain reaction that topples the entire economy of steel towns. **Now, other basic industries, in other towns and cities are beginning to follow.**

The truth is, America has lost 1.7 million middle income manufacturing jobs since 1980, including 250,000 steelworker jobs.

For all of us, solving the crisis in America's steel and other basic industries is essential for our economic future. Employees have responded to the crisis with realism—72 percent of all operating cost reductions since 1982 have come from lower employment costs.

The steel domino is falling despite the remarkable rise in productivity of the steel industry. It is being drowned by the flood of cheap, subsidized foreign imports. **Solutions require the joint efforts of labor, industry, government and financial institutions. It's now or never.**

UNITED STEELWORKERS OF AMERICA AFL-CIO
Five Gateway Center
Pittsburgh, PA 15222
LYNN WILLIAMS, PRESIDENT

78 C-MW

Figure 3.2 *Protectionism – Labor's view*

Source: Reprinted with permission of the United Steel Workers of America.

Second, even if the causes of price differentials can be isolated and determined, it is hard to understand why price and cost have to be artificially equalized in the first place. Trade between nations takes place due to price differentials; otherwise, there is no incentive to trade at all.

Although the estimates of the cost of protection vary, they all point to the same conclusion: the costs

to consumers are enormous. While the US International Trade Commission ruled that imports hurt American steel-makers, the Consuming Industries Trade Action Coalition (CITAC) contended that quotas on steel imports could cost American manufacturers nine jobs for every job saved in the steel industry.[3] According to CITAC, tariffs on imported steel would cost consumers between $2 billion and

$4 billion and between 36,000 and 75,000 jobs (or eight times the number of steel industry jobs saved). The steel industry conducted its own study which showed that American steel, due to overcapacity, could easily replace imports, thus adding less than $2 to the cost of each automobile.[4] In any case, the WTO also ruled in 2003 that steel tariffs imposed by the USA were illegal.

If cost/price equalization is a desired end, then international trade may be the only instrument that can achieve it. For example, if wages are too high in one country, that country will attract labor from a lower-wage country. That process will increase the labor supply in the high-wage country, driving the wages down. On the other hand, the labor supply in the lower-wage nation will decrease, driving up wages. Thus, equalization is achieved.

Enhancing national security

Protectionists often use the patriotic theme. They usually claim that a nation should be self-sufficient and even willing to pay for inefficiency in order to enhance national security (see Figure 3.3). That point of view has some justification – to a certain extent.

Opponents of protectionism dismiss appeals to national security. A nation can never be completely self-sufficient because raw materials are not found in the same proportion in all areas of the world. The USA itself would be vulnerable if the supply of certain minerals were cut off. Moreover, national security is achieved at the cost of higher product prices, and money could be used for something more productive to the national interest. In addition, in the case of such scarce resources as oil, if the USA were to try to be self-sufficient, it would quickly use up its own limited resources. The country may be better off exploiting or depleting the resources of others. North Korea's brand of self-sufficiency, coupled with its defense budget, has virtually driven the nation to starvation.

Protecting infant industry

The necessity to protect an infant industry is perhaps the most credible argument for protectionist measures. Some industries need to be protected until they become viable. South Korea serves as a good example. It has performed well by selectively protecting infant industries for export purposes.

In practice, it is not an easy task to protect industries. First, the government must identify deserving industries. Second, appropriate incentives must be created to encourage productivity. Finally, the government has to make sure that the resultant protection is only temporary. There is a question of how long an "infant" needs to grow up to be an "adult." A spoiled child often remains spoiled. A person taught to be helpless often wants to remain helpless or does not know how to stop being helpless. In a practical sense, there is no incentive for an infant industry to abandon protection and eliminate inefficiency.

GOVERNMENT: A CONTRIBUTION TO PROTECTIONISM

Government can be considered to be the root of all evil – at least as far as international trade is concerned. A government's mere existence, even without tariffs or any attempt to interfere with international marketing, can distort trade both inside and outside of its area. At the international level, different governments have different policies and objectives, resulting in different rates for income and sales taxes.

Taxation is not the only cause of tax and income differences. Some governments allow cartels to operate. A cartel is an international business agreement to fix prices and divide markets, in addition to other kinds of cooperation. Such an arrangement is illegal in the USA, but it is permissible and even encouraged in many countries. Australia and New Zealand, for example, allow livestock firms to cooperate with each other in exporting beef to the USA.

Economic cooperation among governments yields economic benefits and problems by significantly affecting internal and external trade patterns. The CAP (Common Agricultural Policy) of the European Union is a good example. The CAP, with more than twenty price systems, was adopted to satisfy France's demand to protect its farmers as a

ITS ONLY A MATTER OF TIME.

We now import more than 40 percent of all the oil we use. And that percentage is growing. Our excessive dependence on foreign oil could blow up in our faces at any moment if our supply were somehow disrupted.

But the more we use nuclear energy, instead of imported oil, to generate our electricity, the less we have to depend on uncertain foreign oil supplies.

America's 112 nuclear electric plants already have cut foreign oil dependence by 4 billion barrels since the oil embargo of 1973, saving us $115 billion in foreign oil payments.

But 112 nuclear plants will not be enough to meet our rapidly growing demand for electricity. We need more plants.

Importing so much oil is a danger we must not ignore. We need to rely more on energy sources we can count on, like nuclear energy.

For a free booklet on nuclear energy, write to the U.S. Council for Energy Awareness, P.O. Box 66080, Dept. BB01, Washington, D.C. 20035.

U.S. COUNCIL FOR ENERGY AWARENESS

Nuclear energy means more energy independence.

© 1990 USCEA

As seen in February 1990 issues of U.S. News & World Report, The New York Times, The Economist, Barrons, and Congressional Quarterly; March 1990 issues of TIME, Sports Illustrated, Newsweek, Business Week, The Washington Post, Forbes, and National Journal; April 1990 issues of Reader's Digest, National Geographic, Ladies' Home Journal, Good Housekeeping, Smithsonian, The Wall Street Journal, Scientific American, Natural History, The Atlantic, American Heritage, Governing, and State Legislatures; and May 1990 issues of The Leadership Network.

Figure 3.3 *National security*

Source: Courtesy of the US Council for Energy Awareness.

condition for joining the European Community. The practice requires the EU to impose variable-levy tariffs on many imported farm products in order to raise prices to European levels so that EU farmers will not be undersold at home regardless of world prices. Furthermore, authorities agree to buy surplus produce to maintain high target prices. The practice encourages farmers to overproduce products, which are later often sold abroad at lower prices. Based on the results of a number of studies, because of the CAP, the EU has experienced an average loss of GDP of about 1 percent as well as a large redistribution of income to farmers from consumers and taxpayers.

Many believe that the USA is the most liberal nation in promoting free trade. This notion is debatable. The USA achieves its protection goals through a variety of means. It has quotas on sugar, processed dairy products (e.g., cheese), and clothespins. Interestingly, in terms of combined ad valorem tariff equivalents (import tariffs as a percentage of the value or price of imported products), US protection is highest on products exported by the least developed countries. Japan is the same with regard to agricultural products. In contrast, the Canadian and EU protectionist measures hurt the low- and middle-income exporters the most.[5]

In conclusion, governments everywhere seem to be the main culprits in distorting trade and welfare arrangements in order to gain some economic and political advantage or benefit. These governments use a combination of tariff and nontariff methods. A discussion of the various kinds of tariff and nontariff barriers and their marketing implications follows.

MARKETING BARRIERS: TARIFFS

Tariff, derived from a French word meaning rate, price, or list of charges, is a customs duty or a tax on products that move across borders. Tariffs may be classified in several ways. The classification scheme used here is based on direction, purpose, length, rate, and distribution point. These classifications are not necessarily mutually exclusive.

Direction: import and export tariffs

Tariffs are often imposed on the basis of the direction of product movement; that is, on imports or exports, with the latter being the less common one. When export tariffs are levied, they usually apply to an exporting country's scarce resources or raw materials (rather than finished manufactured products).

Purpose: protective and revenue tariffs

Tariffs may be classified as protective tariffs and revenue tariffs. This distinction is based on purpose.

The purpose of a protective tariff is to protect home industry, agriculture, and labor against foreign competitors by trying to keep foreign goods out of the country.

The purpose of a revenue tariff, in contrast, is to generate tax revenues for the government. Compared to a protective tariff, a revenue tariff is relatively low. As in the case of the EU, it applies tariffs of up to 236 percent on meat and 180 percent on cereals, while its tariffs on raw materials and electronics rarely exceed 5 percent.[6]

Length: tariff surcharge versus countervailing duty

Protective tariffs may be further classified according to length of time. A tariff surcharge is a temporary action, whereas a countervailing duty is a permanent surcharge. When Harley-Davidson claimed that it needed time to adjust to Japanese imports, President Reagan felt that it was in the national interest to provide import relief. To protect the local industry, a tariff surcharge was used. In this particular case, the tariff achieved its purpose, and the company roared back. In 2002, it shipped 263,653 units, totaled $4.1 billion in sales, earned $580 million in profit, and captured 46 percent of the North American heavyweight motorcycle market.[7] More than 100,000 people rode their Harley-Davidson motorcycles to Wisconsin in 2003 to celebrate the company's 100-year anniversary.

Countervailing duties are imposed on certain imports when products are subsidized by foreign governments. These duties are thus assessed to offset a special advantage or discount allowed by an exporter's government. Usually, a government provides an export subsidy by rebating certain taxes if goods are exported.

Rates: specific, ad valorem, and combined

How are tax rates applied? To understand the computation, three kinds of tax rates must be distinguished: specific, ad valorem, and combined.

Specific duties

Specific duties are a fixed or specified amount of money per unit of weight, gauge, or other measure of quantity. Based on a standard physical unit of a product, they are specific rates of so many dollars or cents for a given unit of measure (e.g., 350 euros/ton on sugar imports into the EU). Product costs or prices are irrelevant in this case. Because the duties are constant for low- and high-priced products of the same kind, this method is discriminatory and effective for protection against cheap products due to their lower unit value; that is, there is a reverse relationship between product value and duty percentage. As product price goes up, a duty when expressed as a percentage of this price will fall. On the other hand, for a cheap product whose value is low, the duty percentage will rise accordingly.

Ad valorem duties

Ad valorem duties are duties "according to value." They are stated as a fixed percentage of the invoice value and applied at a percentage to the dutiable value of the imported goods. This is the opposite of specific duties since the percentage is fixed but the total duty is not. Based on this method, there is a direct relationship between the total duties collected and the prices of products; that is, the absolute amount of total duties collected will increase or decrease with the prices of imported products. The strength of this method is that it provides continuous and relative protection against all price levels of a particular product. Such protection becomes even more crucial when inflation increases prices of imports. If specific duties were used, their effects lessen with time because inflation reduces the proportionate effect. Another advantage is that ad valorem duties provide an easy comparison of rates across countries and across products.

Combined rates

Combined rates (or compound duty) are a combination of the specific and ad valorem duties on a single product. They are duties based on both the specific rate and the ad valorem rate that are applied to an imported product. For example, the tariff may be 10 cents per pound plus 5 percent ad valorem. Under this system, both rates are used together, though in some countries only the rate producing more revenue may apply.

One important fact is that the average tariff rates affect the poor the most. After all, working-class consumers spend a large share of their income on the necessities of daily life, and many such necessities are imported. Affluent consumers, in comparison, are not bothered as much by tariffs because these necessities represent only a fraction of what they earn.

Distribution point: distribution and consumption taxes

Some taxes are collected at a particular point of distribution or when purchases and consumption occur. These indirect taxes, frequently adjusted at the border, are of four kinds: single-stage, value-added, cascade, and excise.

Single-stage taxes

Single-stage sales tax is a tax collected at only one point in the manufacturing and distribution chain. This tax is perhaps most common in the USA, where retailers and wholesalers make purchases without paying any taxes by simply showing a sales tax permit. The single-stage sales tax is not collected until products are purchased by final consumers.

Value-added tax

A value-added tax (VAT) is a multi-stage, noncumulative tax on consumption. It is a national sales tax levied at each stage of the production and distribution system, though only on the value added at that stage. Its important feature is that it credits taxes paid by companies on their material inputs against taxes they must collect on their own sales. In other words, each time a product changes hands, even between middlemen, a tax must be paid, but the tax collected at a certain stage is based on the added value and not on the total value of the product at that point. Sellers in the chain collect the VAT from a buyer, deduct the amount of VAT they have already paid on their purchase of the product, and remit the balance to the government. European Union customs officers collect the VAT upon importation of goods based on the CIF (cost, insurance, and freight) value plus the duty charged on the product.

Even though VAT was first proposed in France in 1920, it was not until 1948 that the first recognizable VAT appeared in France. At that time, this tax was largely unknown outside the theoretical discussions. At present, more than 120 countries rely on it to raise $18 trillion or about a quarter of the world's tax revenue, affecting four billion people or 70 percent of the world's population (see Table 3.1).[8]

VAT is supposed to be nondiscriminatory because it applies both to products sold on the domestic market and to imported goods. The importance of the value-added tax is due to the fact that GATT allows a producing country to rebate the value-added tax when products are exported. Foreign firms trying to obtain a refund from European governments have found the refund process anything but easy.

Since the tax applies to imports at the border but because it is fully rebated on exports, VAT may improve a country's trade balance. The evidence, however, offers a mixed picture.

To strengthen VAT collections, a country should employ a single VAT rate, thus reducing administrative complexity. Value-added taxes should have few exceptions, and any exceptions should apply only to educational, medical, and social services. In addition, only exports should be zero-rated (i.e., VAT exempt).[9]

Cascade taxes

Cascade taxes are collected at each point in the manufacturing and distribution chain and are levied on the total value of a product, including taxes borne by the product at earlier stages (i.e., tax on tax). Of the tax systems examined, this appears to be the most severe of all. For over thirty years, a now-defunct cascade system of taxation in Italy (the IGE) hurt the development of large-scale wholesale business there. Since the IGE was imposed each time the goods changed hands, Italian manufacturers minimized transfers of goods by selling products directly to retailers. The IGE was replaced by a value-added tax in 1973, and it was hoped by foreign manufacturers that the revival of wholesale organizations might facilitate imports of foreign consumer goods. Table 3.2 shows how the tax varies among the three systems.

Table 3.1 *The lure of VAT. After its widespread introduction into Europe and Latin America, VAT has been adopted by a number of developing economies over the past twenty-five years.*

	Sub-Saharan Africa (43)	Asia and Pacific (24)	EU (plus Norway and Switzerland) (17)	Central Europe and BRO[1] (26)	North Africa and Middle East (21)	Americas (26)	Small islands (27)
2001 (April)	27	18	17	25	6	22	8
1989	4	6	15	1	4	16	1
1979	1	1	12	0	1	12	0
1969	1	0	5	0	0	2	0

Note
The figures in parentheses are the total number of countries in each region as of September 1998.
1 Baltic States, Russia, and other countries of the former Soviet Union

Source: Liam Ebrill *et al.*, *The Modern VAT*, IMF, 2001, and Liam Ebrill *et al.*, "The Allure of the Value-Added Tax," *Finance & Development* (June 2002): 44–7.

Table 3.2 *A comparison of distribution taxes*

Point in chain (seller)	Price charged	Payer of tax	Single-stage sales tax	Value-added tax	Cascade tax
Farmer	$4	Manufacturer	None	On $4	On $4
Manufacturer	$5	Wholesaler	None	On $(5–4)	On $5 + previous tax
Wholesaler	$7	Retailer	None	On $(7–5)	On $7 + previous taxes
Retailer	$10	Consumer	On $10	On $(10–7)	On $10 + previous taxes

Excise tax

An excise tax is a one-time charge levied on the sales of specified products. Alcoholic beverages and cigarettes are good examples. It is also common to levy excise taxes on motor vehicles, petroleum, and consumer durables. Excise taxes account for about 19 percent of all tax revenues.[10]

These four kinds of indirect taxes are often adjusted at the border. Border taxes can be used to raise prices of imports or lower prices of exports. Prices of imports are raised by charging imported goods with (in addition to customs duties) a tax usually borne by domestic products. For exported products, their export prices become more competitive (i.e., lower) when such products are relieved of the same tax that they are subject to when produced, sold, and consumed domestically.

MARKETING BARRIERS: NONTARIFF BARRIERS

Tariffs, though generally undesirable, are at least straightforward and obvious. Nontariff barriers, in comparison, are more elusive or nontransparent. Tariffs have declined in importance, reaching the lowest level ever of about 4 percent on average after fifty years and eight global rounds of trade negotiation (see Table 3.3).[11] In the meantime, nontariff barriers have become more prominent. Often disguised, the impact of nontariff barriers can be just as devastating, if not more so, as the impact of tariffs. Figure 3.4 describes how one US firm, Allen-Edmonds Shoe Corporation, intended to overcome frustrating Japanese import barriers.

There are several hundred types of nontariff barriers. According to the US Trade Representative, countries use a variety of barriers that include non-scientific sanitary standards, customs procedures, and government monopolies. Japan's telecommunications, agriculture, and pharmaceuticals sectors have "structural rigidity, excessive regulation, and market access barriers." China, on the other hand, has import standards and sanitary requirements that act as import barriers. China must act to improve the protection of intellectual property rights.[12]

Nontariff barriers may be grouped into five major categories. Each category contains a number of different nontariff barriers.

Government participation in trade

The degree of government involvement in trade varies from passive to active. The types of participation include administrative guidance, state trading, and subsidies.

Administrative guidance

Many governments routinely provide trade consultation to private companies. Japan has been doing this on a regular basis to help implement its industrial policies. This systematic cooperation between government and business is labeled "Japan, Inc." To get private firms to conform to the Japanese government's guidance, the government uses a carrot-and-stick approach by exerting the influence through regulations, recommendations, encouragement, discouragement, or prohibition. Japan's government agencies' administrative councils are

Table 3.3 Trade rounds

Year	Place/name	Subjects covered	Number of countries
1947	Geneva	Tariffs	12
1949	Annecy	Tariffs	13
1951	Torquay	Tariffs	38
1956	Geneva	Tariffs	26
1960–1	Geneva (Dillon round)	Tariffs	26
1964–7	Geneva (Kennedy round)	Tariffs and antidumping measures	62
1973–9	Geneva (Tokyo round)	Tariffs, nontariff measures, "framework" agreements	102
1986–94	Geneva (Uruguay Round)	Tariffs, nontariff measures, rules, services, intellectual property, dispute settlements, textiles, agriculture, creation of WTO	123
2002–4	Doha	All goods and services, tariffs, nontariff measures, antidumping and subsidies, regional trade agreements, intellectual property, environment, dispute settlement, Singapore issues	144

Source: Anne McGuirk, "The Doha Development Agenda," *Finance & Development* (September 2002): 6.

influential enough to make importers restrict their purchases to an amount not exceeding a certain percentage of local demand. The Japanese government denies that such a practice exists, claiming that it merely seeks reports on the amounts purchased by each firm.

Government procurement and state trading

State trading is the ultimate in government participation, because the government itself is now the customer or buyer who determines what, when, where, how, and how much to buy. In this practice, the state engages in commercial operations, either directly or indirectly, through the agencies under its control. Such business activities are either in place of or in addition to private firms.

Although government involvement in business is most common with the communist countries, whose governments are responsible for the central planning of the whole economy, the practice is definitely not restricted to those nations. The US government, as the largest buyer in the world, is required by the Buy American Act to give a bidding edge to US suppliers in spite of their higher prices.

The Government Procurement Act requires the signatory nations to guarantee that they will provide suppliers from other signatory countries treatment equal to that which they provide their own suppliers. This guarantee of "*national treatment*" means that a foreign government must choose the goods with the lowest price that best meet the specifications regardless of the supplier's nationality. The Code requires that technical specifications should not be prepared, adopted, or applied with a view to creating obstacles to international trade. The purchasing agency must adopt specifications geared toward performance rather than design and must base the specifications on international standards, national technical regulations, or recognized national standards, when appropriate.

Subsidies

According to GATT, subsidy is a "financial contribution provided directly or indirectly by a government

63

WHEN THE JAPANESE TOLD US IT WAS CUSTOMARY TO LEAVE OUR SHOES AT THE DOOR, THIS IS THE DOOR THEY HAD IN MIND.

Keep your shoes to yourself. That's the clear message the Japanese government has given Allen-Edmonds and other U.S. shoe manufacturers. Tough licensing, even tougher tariffs and various other obstacles are making it nearly impossible to do business in Japan.

There is a market for our shoes there. The people have shown great interest in our classic styles and our superior quality. But the duty makes them terribly expensive. Fact is, U.S. shoes sold in Japan are taxed up to 60% higher than Japanese shoes sold in this country.

Don't misunderstand. We're not looking for help or sympathy. In fact, we're making headway with some good old-fashioned pushiness. Just recently our president literally crashed a Tokyo trade show we had been excluded from – and promptly sold over 300 pairs of shoes.

The point is this. A company – even a small one like our own – can't wait for political solutions to unfair trade barriers. Manufacturers must initiate action in a friendly but firm manner. Whether it's the Japanese market or any other, for now it's the best way we know to get a foot in the door.

ALLEN EDMONDS
The Handcrafted World of Allen-Edmonds.

Allen-Edmonds Shoe Corporation
Port Washington, WI 53074 U.S.A.
(414) 284-3461   Telex 229715
FAX (414) 284-3462

Figure 3.4 *Japanese import barriers*

Source: Reprinted with permission of Allen-Edmonds Shoe Corp.

and which confers a benefit." Subsidies may take many forms – including cash, interest rate, value-added tax, corporate income tax, sales tax, freight, insurance, and infrastructure. Subsidized loans for priority sectors, preferential rediscount rates, and budgetary subsidies are among the various subsidy policies of several Asian countries.

There are several other kinds of subsidies that are not so obvious. Brazil's rebates of the various taxes, coupled with other forms of assistance, may be viewed as subsidies. Tennessee, Ohio, Michigan, and Illinois, in order to attract foreign automakers to locate their plants in those states, provided such services as highway construction, training of workers, and tax breaks, which are simply subsidies in disguise. Table 3.4 shows the money spent on agricultural support.

Sheltered profit is another kind of subsidy. A country may allow a corporation to shelter its profit from abroad. In 1971 the USA allowed companies to form domestic international sales corporations (DISCs) even though they cost the US Treasury Department more than $1 billion a year in revenue. GATT, the multilateral treaty, eventually ruled that a DISC was an illegal export subsidy. A new US law then allowed companies that met more stringent requirements to form foreign sales corporations (FSCs). As in the case of Boeing Co., it was the biggest user of this tool, enabling it to avoid $130 million in US taxes in 1998, about 12 percent of its entire earnings.[13] Ultimately, FSCs were also found to be illegal.

The **Subsidies Code**, technically named the Agreement on Interpretation and Application of Article VI, XVI and XXIII of the General Agreement on Tariffs and Trade, recognizes that government subsidies distort the competitive forces at work in international trade. The rules of the international agreement negotiated during the Tokyo Round of Multilateral Trade Negotiations differentiate between *export subsidies* and *domestic subsidies*. The Code's rules also differentiate between subsidies paid on *primary products* (e.g., manufactures) and those paid on *nonprimary products* and primary minerals. A primary product is any product of farm,

Table 3.4 Agricultural support. Billions of dollars were spent on agricultural support in 2001.

Country	PSE[1] (millions of US dollars)	Percentage PSE[2]
Australia	827	4
Canada	3928	17
Czech Republic	585	17
European Union	93,083	35
Hungary	580	12
Iceland	108	59
Japan	47,242	59
Korea	16,838	64
Mexico	6537	19
New Zealand	52	1
Norway	2173	67
Poland	1447	10
Slovak Republic	151	11
Switzerland	4214	69
Turkey	3978	15
USA	49,001	21
OECD	230,744	31

Notes
1 Producer support estimate (PSE) is an indicator of the annual monetary value of gross transfers from consumers and taxpayers to support agricultural producers.
2 The percentage PSE is the ratio of the PSE to the value of total gross farm receipts.

Source: "Rich Countries Urged to Lead by Example on Trade Access," *IMF Survey*, October 21, 2002, 322.

forest, or fishery in its natural form or that has undergone such processing as is customarily required to prepare it for transportation and marketing in substantial volume in international trade (e.g., frozen and cured meat). The Code prohibits the use of export subsidies on nonprimary products and primary mineral products.

There is considerable debate over what should be considered manufactured products, since such products are not entitled to any subsidies. For instance, according to the USA, the EU's export subsidies for such manufactured products as pasta and wheat flour are banned by the International Subsidies Code. The EU's position is that pasta and wheat flour are not manufactured products.

Agricultural export subsidies have long been a persistent source of conflict. In 2002, Poland, the Czech Republic, Turkey, and Australia respectively spent $56 million, $35 million, $28 million, and $2 million on agricultural export subsidies. The figures for the following countries are: Switzerland ($292 million), Norway ($128 million), and the USA ($80 million). The EU by itself incredibly spent $5985 million. In 2003, the EU trade ministers applauded an agreement to put limits on the EU's forty-year-old practice of paying farmers subsidies based on the amount of their production. However, the EU has not reduced its $30.5 billion a year paid in production-linked subsidies, nor has it made any changes to its export subsidies – the highest in the world. Developing countries complain bitterly that these subsidies are harmful to trade by encouraging European farmers to sell their produce abroad.[14]

Interestingly, affluent countries have been heavily subsidizing their agricultural businesses (see Table 3.5). Their agricultural subsidies total almost $1 a day (about six times the level of aid to developing countries). While 75 percent of people in Sub-Saharan Africa live on less than $2 a day, an average European cow receives about $2.50 a day in subsidy. On average, a Japanese cow does even better, receiving about $7 a day in subsidy.[15] According to the UNCTAD Secretary-General, "six or seven of the top ten agricultural exporters are developed countries, and I don't think they could reach that status without export subsidies."[16]

Customs and entry procedures

Customs and entry procedures may be employed as nontariff barriers. These restrictions involve classification, valuation, documentation, license, inspection, and health and safety regulations. Exhibit 3.1 describes how software products may be classified and valued.[17]

Classification

How a product is classified can be arbitrary and inconsistent and is often based on a customs officer's judgment, at least at the time of entry. Product classification is important because the way in which a product is classified determines its duty status. A company can sometimes take action to affect the classification of its product. Sony argued that its PlayStation 2, equipped with a 128-bit microprocessor, a DVD player, and Internet connection, was a big improvement over its PlayStation original and that it should thus qualify as a computer. However, the British customs office chose to continue to classify PlayStation 2 in the video games category, in effect imposing a duty of 2.2 percent or about $9. Had Sony prevailed in getting the "digital

Table 3.5 Agricultural distortions. Protectionist policies in agriculture are costly to all regions (billion dollars).

	World	OECD	Non-OECD
Income loss			
Agricultural policy of World	128.2	97.8	30.4
OECD	101.4	92.7	8.7
NonOECD	26.8	5.1	21.7
Forgone export revenue			
World	378.0	255.8	122.2
OECD	257.7	234.9	22.8
NonOECD	120.3	20.9	99.4

Source: Hans Peter Lankes, "Market Access for Developing Countries," *Finance & Development* (September 2002): 8–13.

EXHIBIT 3.1 SOFTWARE CLASSIFICATION AND VALUATION

Do all countries classify software for customs purposes in an identical manner? Many countries, including the USA, will classify software products under an identical Harmonized Tariff System (HTS) category. However, software classification poses similar challenges that arise with other products. Since only the first six digits of the HTS code are harmonized globally, a country may designate a more specific classification beyond those six digits. In rare cases, the customs authority in another country may dispute the general classification of a product altogether based on interpretation of its purpose and use. The rapid evolution of information technology (IT) products is making the process of determining classification more difficult for this sector. Advancements in technologies are outpacing updates to the existing HTS. Therefore, it is prudent to check with the customs authority in the recipient country to ensure proper classification of a product.

How is software valuation determined? Countries vary in their methods for the valuation and assessment of software duties on imports. Under Article VII of the 1984 General Agreement on Tariffs and Trade (GATT), it was declared that software valuation may either be inclusive or exclusive of the cost or value for the intellectual property component of the product. However, it was recommended that software valuation be based on the value or cost of the carrier medium (i.e., optical disk) rather than the "intellectual property" embedded on the medium. This decision was based on the premise that the cost or value of the intellectual property is distinguishable from the value of the medium. This requirement is satisfied if the cost or value of either the medium or the intellectual property is identified separately on the commercial invoice. It is important to note that this GATT ruling does not cover software that includes features such as sound, cinematic, or video recordings. Software incorporating these features (e.g., game software) will be subject to a separate valuation policy. For example, India differentiates entertainment software, health care software, and telecom software from standard software.

This decision has granted customs authorities broad latitude in determining software valuation. Therefore, one may expect to encounter different software valuation regimes. The USA maintains the practice of valuing software on the carrier medium. In general, Canada, Western Europe and many Asian countries also adhere to this method of valuation. In the Middle East, the method of valuing software on its full value or cost is frequently applied. Africa and Latin America are regions where no defined trend for software valuation exists.

An additional consideration with software is the assessment of taxes on the product. Unlike tariffs, taxes on imports from the USA (e.g., value-added taxes imposed at the border) are always assessed on the full value of the software, including intellectual property, unless the USA has a special tax treaty with a particular country.

Is customized software treated differently than packaged software? In most cases, the answer is no. Packaged software is defined as software that is generally available to the public by sale from stock at retail selling points or directly from the software developer or supplier. The vast majority of customs agencies do not treat customized software differently from packaged software. To confirm that the software's destination does not treat the two types of software differently, contact the Trade Information Center or the customs authority in the recipient country.

Source: Dava Kunneman and Jim Golsen, "Issues With Software Exploration," *Export America* (August 2001): 16–17.

processing units" (computers) classification, there would be no import tax.[18]

Valuation

Regardless of how products are classified, each product must still be valued. The value affects the amount of tariffs levied. A customs appraiser is the one who determines the value. The process can be highly subjective, and the valuation of a product may be interpreted in different ways, depending on what value is used (e.g., foreign, export, import, or manufacturing costs) and how this value is constructed. In Japan, a commodity tax is applied to the FOB factory price of Japanese cars. Yet American cars are valued on the CIF basis, adding $1000 more to the final retail price of these cars.

Documentation

Documentation can present another problem at entry because many documents and forms are often necessary, and the documents required can be complicated. Japan held up Givenchy's import application because the company left out an apostrophe for its l'Interdit perfume.

Without proper documentation, goods may not be cleared through customs. At the very least, such complicated and lengthy documents serve to slow down product clearance. France, requiring customs documentation to be in French, even held up trucks from other European countries for hours while looking for products' nonFrench instruction manuals which were banned.

License or permit

Not all products can be freely imported; controlled imports require licenses or permits. For example, importations of distilled spirits, wines, malt beverages, arms, ammunition, and explosives into the USA require a license issued by the Bureau of Alcohol, Tobacco, and Firearms. India requires a license for all imported goods. An article is considered prohibited if not accompanied by a license. It

is not always easy to obtain an import license, since many countries will issue one only if goods can be certified as necessary.

Japan simplified its licensing procedure in 1986. Previously, a separate license application had been required for any new cosmetic product, even when only a change in shade was involved. The new requirements categorize cosmetics into seventy-eight groups and list permitted ingredients. A marketer simply notifies the government of any new product using those ingredients.

Inspection

Inspection is an integral part of product clearance. Goods must be examined to determine quality and quantity. This step is closely related to other customs and entry procedures. First, inspection classifies and values products for tariff purposes. Second, inspection reveals whether imported items are consistent with those specified in the accompanying documents and whether such items require any licenses. Third, inspection determines whether products meet health and safety regulations in order to make certain that food products are fit for human consumption or that the products can be operated safely. Fourth, inspection prevents the importation of prohibited articles.

Marketers should be careful in stating the amount and quality of products, as well as in providing an accurate description of products. Any deviation from the statements contained in invoices necessitates further measurements and determination, more delay, and more expenses.

Inspection can be used intentionally to discourage imports. Metal baseball bats from the USA, for instance, are required to carry a stamp of consumer safety, and this must be "ascertained" only after expensive on-dock inspection.

Health and safety regulations

Many products are subject to health and safety regulations, which are necessary to protect the public health and environment. Health and safety regulations are not restricted to agricultural products. The regulations also apply to TV receivers, microwave ovens, X-ray devices, cosmetics, chemical substances, and clothing.

Concern for safety was used by Japan against aluminum softball bats from the USA. The manufacturing process leaves a small hole in the top which is fitted with a rubber stopper. Japan thus bans the bats on the ground that the stopper might fly out and hurt someone. According to US manufacturers, this fear is unfounded.

Product requirements

For goods to enter a country, product requirements set by that country must be met. Requirements may apply to product standards and product specifications as well as to packaging, labeling, and marking.

Product standards

Each country determines its own product standards to protect the health and safety of its consumers. Such standards may also be erected as barriers to prevent or slow down importation of foreign goods. Because of US grade, size, quality, and maturity requirements, many Mexican agricultural commodities are barred from entering the USA. Japanese product standards are even more complex, and they are based on physical characteristics rather than product performance. Such standards make it necessary to repeat the product approval process when a slight product modification occurs (such as color), even though the performance of the product in question remains the same. Furthermore, these standards are frequently changed in Japan in order to exclude imports.

Packaging, labeling, and marking

Packaging, labeling, and marking are considered together because they are closely interrelated. Many products must be packaged in a certain way for safety and other reasons (see It's the Law 3.1).

Canada requires imported canned foods to be packed in specified can sizes, and instructions contained within or on packages must be in English and French. The Canadian Labeling Act also requires all imported clothing to carry labels in both languages.

Product testing

Many products must be tested to determine their safety and suitability before they can be marketed. This is another area in which the USA has some trouble in Japan. Although products may have won approval everywhere else for safety and effectiveness, such products as medical equipment and pharmaceuticals must go through elaborate standard testing that can take a few years – just long enough for Japanese companies to develop competing products. Moreover, the reviews take place behind the Health and Welfare Ministry's closed doors. In 1995, Japan's Ministry of International Trade and Industry started requiring imported software products to be certified by agents of the Japan Accreditation Bureau. The accreditation requirement may reveal how US software is designed while delaying US bids on public contracts.

The EU's global approach to testing and certification for product safety provides manufacturers with one set of procedures for certifying product compliance with EU health, safety, and environmental requirements. The various means by which manufacturers can certify product conformance include manufacturer self-declaration of conformity, third-party testing, quality assurance audit, and/or approval by a body authorized by an EU member state and recognized by the EU Commission. The mark *CE* on the product signifies that all legal requirements concerning product standards have been met. To be legally marketed in the European Union, more than half of American products must bear the CE mark. Unfortunately, certification of product tests and registrations for information technology, medical devices, and certain products can only be carried out in Europe, and the practice is costly and uncompetitive.

IT'S THE LAW 3.1   WHAT IS THE NATIONALITY OF THAT STEAK?

Imported foods account for a large proportion of US consumption. Imported fish and shellfish, for example, account for 68 percent of such foods consumed in the USA. Likewise, as a percentage of total consumption in a particular food category, the imports of apple juice, asparagus, pecans, and grapes respectively command 63 percent, 60 percent, 47 percent, and 45 percent. In the winter, American consumers enjoy Chilean grapes, peaches, and plums, Mexican cantaloupes and cucumbers, and Argentine apples.

A rule of the US Department of Agriculture, taking effect in 2004, requires supermarkets to either label or display the birthplace of beef, pork, lamb, fish, produce, and peanuts. It is not yet clear as to the kinds of foods that require labeling. The Agriculture Department wants to focus on "whole" foods (i.e., items that keep their identity). As such, whole foods include mixed lettuce in a bag and a tray of ground beef, but they exclude ingredients in a processed item (e.g., apples prepared in a pie). Grocers certainly are not happy about it, contending that such a task should be the responsibility of food companies.

In all likelihood, the rule requires a grocer's label on a steak to reveal where the animal was born,

raised, and slaughtered. About 18 percent of beef consumed by Americans started life outside the USA (e.g., in Canada, Mexico, Australia, and New Zealand). A typical steer can change hands several times before arriving at a packing plant. The rule will be a nightmare for meatpackers who will need to spend tens of millions of dollars per plant to prevent animals of different nationalities from mingling.

While consumerism is used as the justification, protectionism may be the real reason behind the label law. The primary author of the legislation happened to be the Senator from South Dakota where ranchers want to discourage Canadian cattle from entering the US market. In addition, produce growers in Florida and California, facing Mexican competition, were able to persuade several members of the US Congress to go along. Interestingly, chicken, the most popular meat in the USA, does not require labeling, probably due to the fact that the USA imports relatively little chicken meat. In addition, although Americans spend 46 percent of their food dollars outside their home, the restaurant industry does not have to contend with the label law.

Source: "Food Fight: US Grocers Battle Origin Labels," *Asian Wall Street Journal*, June 27–29, 2003.

Product specifications

Product specifications, though appearing to be an innocent process, can wreak havoc on imports. Specifications can be written in such a way as to favor local bidders and to keep out foreign suppliers. For example, specifications can be extremely detailed, or they can be written to closely resemble domestic products. Thus they may be used against foreign suppliers who cannot satisfy the specifications without expensive or lengthy modification. Japan's Nippon Telephone & Telegraph Company (NTT) was able to use product specifications as a built-in barrier when it was forced to accept bids from foreign firms. At one time, it did not even

provide any specifications and bidding details in any language apart from Japanese. Its specifications are highly restrictive and written with existing Japanese products in mind. Instead of outlining functional characteristics, NTT specifies physical features right down to the location of ventilation holes, the details of which are almost identical to those of Nippon Electric. For example, NTT requires metal cabinets for modems, whereas most US makers use plastic. Parts must be made by the Japanese to qualify for bidding. In general, NTT goes well beyond specifications for performance. GATT has established procedures for setting product standards using performance standards rather than detailed physical specifications.

Quotas

Quotas are a quantity control on imported goods. Generally, they are specific provisions limiting the amount of foreign products imported in order to protect local firms and to conserve foreign currency. Quotas may be used for export control as well. An export quota is sometimes required by national planning to preserve scarce resources. From a policy standpoint, a quota is not as desirable as a tariff since a quota generates no revenues for a country. There are three kinds of quotas: absolute, tariff, and voluntary.

Absolute quotas

An absolute quota is the most restrictive of all. It limits in absolute terms the amount imported during a quota period. Once filled, further entries are prohibited. Some quotas are global, but others are allocated to specific foreign countries. Japan imposes strict quotas on oranges and beef. To appease the EU, it has lifted quotas on skimmed milk powder and tobacco for Europe. The most extreme of the absolute quota is an embargo, or a zero quota, as shown in the case of the US trade embargoes against Libya and North Korea.

Tariff quotas

A tariff quota permits the entry of a limited quantity of the quota product at a reduced rate of duty. Quantities in excess of the quota may be imported but are subject to a higher duty rate. Through the use of tariff quotas, a combination of tariffs and quotas is applied with the primary purpose of importing what is needed and discouraging excessive quantities through higher tariffs. When the USA increased tariffs on imported motorcycles in order to protect the US motorcycle industry, it exempted from this tax the first 6000 big motorcycles from Japan and the first 4000–5000 units from Europe.

Voluntary quotas

A voluntary quota differs from the other two kinds of quota, which are unilaterally imposed. A voluntary quota is a formal agreement between nations, or between a nation and an industry. This agreement usually specifies the limit of supply by product, country, and volume.

Two kinds of voluntary quota can be legally distinguished: **VER (voluntary export restraint)** and **OMA (orderly marketing agreement)**. Whereas an OMA involves negotiation between two governments to specify export management rules, the monitoring of trade volumes, and consultation rights, a VER is a direct agreement between an importing nation's government and a foreign exporting industry (i.e., a quota with industry participation). Both enable the importing country to circumvent the GATT's rules (Article XIX) that require the country to reciprocate for the quota received and to impose that market safeguard on a most-favored-nation basis. Since this is a gray area, the OMA and VER may be applied in a discriminatory manner to a certain country. In the case of a VER involving private industries, a public disclosure is not necessary.

The largest voluntary quota is the Multi-Fiber Arrangement (MFA) for forty-one export and import countries. This international agreement on textiles allows Western governments to set quotas on imports of low-priced textiles from the Third World. The treaty has been criticized because advanced nations are able to force the agreement on poorer countries (see Marketing Ethics 3.1).

As implied, a country may negotiate to limit voluntarily its export to a particular market. This may sound peculiar because the country appears to be acting against its own self-interest. But a country's unwillingness to accept these unfavorable terms will eventually invite trade retaliation and tougher terms in the form of forced quotas. It is thus voluntary only in the sense that the exporting country tries to avoid alternative trade barriers that are even less desirable. For example, Japan agreed to restrict and reprice some exports within Great Britain. In reality, there is nothing voluntary about a voluntary quota.

MARKETING ETHICS 3.1 UNNATURAL ADVANTAGE

To protect its processing or manufacturing industry, a country uses tariff escalation. While setting low tariffs on imported materials that are used by its industry, the country sets higher tariffs on imported finished products that could compete with the domestic industry's own products. This form of tax discrimination is a problem for countries that try to move up the technology ladder. They are discouraged from expanding their processing industries. Instead, they are forced to rely on commodities whose prices tend to be volatile.

According to the IMF, the Multi-Fiber Agreement may have cost as many as nineteen million jobs for low-skilled workers in developing countries. When the Multi-Fiber Agreement quotas and tariffs are combined, twenty-seven million jobs may have been lost. Each job saved in this fashion in a developed country replaces thirty-five jobs in developing countries. Furthermore, industrial countries that employ these schemes particularly hurt their own low-income citizens who must spend a larger share of their income on necessities.

Source: Hans Peter Lankes, "Market Access for Developing Countries," *Finance & Development,* September 2002, 8–13.

Financial control

Financial regulations can also function to restrict international trade. These restrictive monetary policies are designed to control capital flow so that currencies can be defended or imports controlled. For example, to defend the weak Italian lira, Italy imposed a 7 percent tax on the purchase of foreign currencies. There are several forms that financial restrictions can take.

Exchange control

An exchange control is a technique that limits the amount of the currency that may be taken abroad. The reason exchange controls are usually applied is that the local currency is overvalued, thus causing imports to be paid for in smaller amounts of currency. Purchasers then try to use the relatively cheap foreign exchange to obtain items that are either unavailable or more expensive in the local currency.

Exchange controls also limit the length of time and money an exporter may hold for the goods sold. French exporters, for example, must exchange the foreign currencies for francs within one month. By regulating all types of capital outflow in foreign currencies, the government either makes it difficult to obtain imported products or makes such items available only at higher prices.

Multiple exchange rates

Multiple exchange rates are another form of exchange regulation or barrier. The objectives of multiple exchange rates are twofold: to encourage exports and imports of certain goods, and to discourage exports and imports of others. This means that there is no single rate for all products or industries, but with the application of multiple exchange rates, some products and industries will benefit and some will not. Spain once used low exchange rates for goods designated for export and high rates for those it desired to retain at home. Multiple exchange rates may also apply to imports. The high rates may be used for imports of particular goods with the government's approval, whereas low rates may be used for other imports.

Since multiple exchange rates are used to bring in hard currencies (through exports) as well as to restrict imports, this system is condemned by the International Monetary Fund (IMF). According to the IMF, any unapproved multiple currency practices are a breach of obligations, and the member may become ineligible to use the Fund's resources. In 1985, South Africa, in trying to stem capital outflow, started to require nonresidents to transact capital transactions at a separately freely floating exchange rate (i.e., the financial rand). The financial rand was much more depreciated than the commercial rand exchange rate. In 1995, as political uncertainty declined, South Africa unified the two exchange rates.

Prior import deposits and credit restrictions

Financial barriers may also include specific limitations on import restraints, such as prior import deposits and credit restrictions. Both of these barriers operate by imposing certain financial restriction on importers. A government can require prior import deposits (forced deposits) that make imports difficult by tying up an importer's capital. In effect, the importer is paying interest for money borrowed without being able to use the money or obtain interest earnings on the money from the government. Importers in Brazil and Italy must deposit a large sum of money with their central banks if they intend to buy foreign goods. To help initiate an aircraft industry, the Brazilian government has required an importer of "flyaway" planes to deposit the full price of the imported aircraft for one year with no interest.

Credit restrictions apply only to imports; that is, exporters may be able to obtain loans from the government, usually at very favorable rates, but importers will not be able to receive any credit or financing from the government. Importers must look for loans in the private sector – very likely at significantly higher rates, if such loans are available at all.

Profit remittance restrictions

Another form of exchange barrier is the profit remittance restriction. ASEAN countries share a common philosophy in allowing unrestricted repatriation of profits earned by foreign companies. Singapore, in particular, allows the unrestricted movement of capital, but many countries regulate the remittance of profits earned in local operations and sent to a parent organization located abroad. Brazil uses progressive rates in taxing all profits remitted to a parent company abroad, with such rates rising to 60 percent. Other countries practice a form of profit remittance restriction by simply having long delays in permission for profit expatriation. To overcome these practices, MNCs have looked to legal loopholes. Many employ various tactics such as countertrading, currency swaps, and other parallel schemes. For example, a multinational firm wanting to repatriate a currency may swap it with another firm which needs that currency, or these firms may lend to each other in the currency desired by each party.

Another tactic is to negotiate for a higher value of an investment than the investment's actual worth. By charging its foreign subsidiary higher prices and fees, an MNC is able to increase the equity base from which dividend repatriations are calculated. In addition, compared to profit repatriations, the higher prices and fees are treated as costs or expenses and are thus paid more freely to the parent firm.

PRIVATE BARRIERS

As conventional trade barriers are lowered, governments are shifting their attention to competition policy to address environmental and labor objectives and private barriers. Private barriers are certain business practices or arrangements between or among affiliated firms.

Japan's *keiretsu* is a good example of private barriers. The *keiretsu* system deals with cooperative business groups. Such a group includes manufacturers, suppliers, retailers, and customers. Members of the group seek long-term security through interlocking directorates and through owning shares in each other's companies. Toyota Motor Corp. provided $83 million to help out Tomen Corp., a money-losing trading firm. Both belong to the same *keiretsu*, and it is a tradition for members of the *keiretsu* to subsidize each other.[19] Mitsubishi even arranges for the executives of its affiliated companies to have lunch together so as to discuss business dealings. Naturally, the companies that belong to the same *keiretsu* will grant preferential treatment to the other members. Korea's *chaebol* system also functions in a similar fashion.

Private barriers are not unique to Asia. In Germany, banks are strong and often take a leadership role. In the case of Deutsche Bank, it owns at least 10 percent of some seventy companies, and its bank executives sit on some 400 corporate boards. As such, it is in a position to encourage its clients to do business with each other – rather than with outsiders.

While nontariff barriers are not as transparent as tariffs, private barriers are the worst in terms of transparency (or the lack of it). It is difficult for an outsider to gain business if potential buyers refuse to explain why they do not want to buy from a foreign firm. Certainly, private barriers will be the next significant challenge.

WORLD TRADE ORGANIZATION (WTO)

Virtually all nations seek to pursue their best interests in international trade. The result is that sooner or later international trade and marketing can be disrupted. To prevent or at least alleviate any problems, there is a world organization in Geneva known as the WTO (with **General Agreement on Tariffs and Trade (GATT)** as its predecessor).

Created in January 1948, the objective of GATT is to achieve a broad, multilateral, and free worldwide system of trading. For example, its code requires international bidding on major projects. GATT provides the forum for tariff negotiations and the elimination of trade discrimination.

The four basic principles of GATT are

1   Member countries will *consult* each other concerning trade problems.
2   The agreement provides a framework for *negotiation* and embodies results of negotiations in a legal instrument.
3   Countries should protect domestic industries *only through tariffs*, when needed and if permitted. There should be no other restrictive devices such as quotas prohibiting imports.
4   Trade should be conducted on a *nondiscriminatory* basis.

Reductions of barriers should be mutual and reciprocal because any country's import increases caused by such reductions will be offset by export increases caused by other countries' reduction of restrictions. This concept is the basis of the principle of the **most favored nation (MFN)**, which is the cornerstone of GATT. According to this principle, countries should grant one another treatment as favorable as treatment given to their best trading partners or any other country. For example, reductions accorded France by the USA should be extended to other countries with which the USA exchanges the MFN principle (e.g., to Brazil). Likewise, if a country decides to temporarily protect its local industry because that industry is seriously threatened, then the newly erected barriers must apply to all countries even though the threat to its industry may come from only a single nation. The MFN principle thus moves countries away from bilateral bargaining to multilateral (or simultaneous bilateral) bargaining. Each country must be concerned with the implications that its concessions for one country would mean for other countries. The only exception is that an advanced country should not expect reciprocity from less developed countries. To better reflect actual practice, the MFN principle is now called the **NTR (Normal Trade Relations)** by the USA.

The USA does not accord MFN status to communist countries that restrict emigration, but this requirement may be waived by the President. After China first received MFN status from the USA in 1980, mushroom imports from China jumped from nothing to nearly 50 percent of all US mushroom imports. This increase owed much to the decline of canned mushroom duties, from 45 percent to 10 percent.

Seven successive rounds of multilateral trade negotiations under GATT auspices produced a decline in average tariff on industrial products in industrial countries from more than 40 percent in 1947 to about 5 percent in 1988. The Uruguay round of multilateral trade negotiations, launched in Punta del Este, Uruguay, in September 1986, aimed to liberalize trade further, to strengthen GATT's role, to foster cooperation, and to enhance the interrelationships between trade and other economic policies that affect growth and development. The Uruguay round attempted to deal with new areas such as services, intellectual property rights, and trade-related investment. Developed nations offered to reduce trade protection to their agriculture and textile industries in exchange for less developed countries' greater imports of services and greater respect for intellectual property. However, the different countries' varying interests repeatedly stalled the talks. Agricultural disputes even led to violent protests by farmers in France, Japan, South Korea, and others.

Not surprisingly, Lee Kuan Yew of Singapore once called GATT the General Agreement to Talk and Talk. Fortunately, delegations from more than a hundred countries were able finally to conclude negotiations at the end of 1993 after seven years of talks. The 109 nations signed the 22,000-page agreement in 1994. This most ambitious and comprehensive global commercial agreement in history provides for a phase-out of the Multi-Fiber Arrangement (MFA) over a ten-year period while reforming trade in agricultural goods. The agreement also lowers tariffs by more than one-third ($700 billion), writes new rules of trade for intellectual property and services, and strengthens the dispute settlement process.

Just like the Uruguay round, the 2002 to 2004 Doha round has generated a great deal of controversy and conflict. While the richer economies press the developing countries to open up their markets, the poorer countries have accused the advanced economies of maintaining a very high level of agricultural supports, thus damaging the poor countries' farm-dependent economies. The talks in Cancun in mid-2003 ended up with the delegates from the poorer countries walking out in protest of the advanced economies' insincere efforts to end agriculture subsidies.[20] As a result, the future of the WTO itself could be jeopardized. Hopefully, logic and practicality should ultimately prevail.

Because GATT was set up in 1948 as a temporary body, the Uruguay round agreement wanted to replace GATT with the World Trade Organization (WTO) in 1995. At the beginning, GATT and the WTO coexisted, but GATT ceased to exist after a one-year period. The WTO, being more permanent and legally secure, will have more authority to settle trade disputes, and will serve along with the International Monetary Fund and the World Bank to monitor trade and resolve disputes. The WTO will encompass the current GATT structure as well as the Uruguay round agreements. It will provide a single, coordinated mechanism to ensure full, effective implementation of the trading system, and it will also provide a permanent, comprehensive forum to address the new or evolving issues of the global market.

The WTO's strengthened dispute settlement system should be better able to limit the scope for unilateral and bilateral actions outside the multilateral system. Under GATT's dispute resolution system, the USA and other members could and indeed did veto the decisions of arbitration boards. As a result, nations could refuse to adopt negative decisions. For example, a GATT panel twice found that the European Union's oilseed subsidies impeded the tariff-free access to the EU market that was promised to the USA in a 1962 trade agreement; yet the EU failed to adequately reform subsidies harmful to US oilseed producers.

Under the WTO, a nation's veto of a panel's decision is eliminated. Other important changes under the new dispute settlement mechanism include: (1) fixed time limits for each stage of the dispute settlement process, (2) automatic adoption of dispute settlement reports, (3) automatic authority to retaliate on request if recommendations are not implemented, (4) creation of a new appellate body to review panel interpretations of WTO agreements, and (5) improved procedural transparency and access to information in the dispute settlement process. The new procedures yield a panel ruling within sixteen months of requesting consultations. Unfortunately for the USA, one early finding involved a challenge of Venezuela and Brazil concerning an Environmental Protection Agency (EPA) regulation governing US imports of gasoline. The

WTO panel ruled that the EPA's treatment of imported gasoline was inconsistent with GATT provisions.

The WTO has 148 members. China, wanting the prestige of being a founding member, tried unsuccessfully to complete its negotiations in 1994 on an accelerated basis. China felt that it should not be held to the same terms which apply to industrialized countries. The USA, however, wanted China to fully observe the WTO rules. After years of negotiation with the EU and the USA, China has finally gained membership. Nepal, one of the poorest countries, became the 148th member in 2003.

Supporters of the WTO have long argued that a reduction of trade barriers will boost global trade. However, there is hardly any rigorous empirical investigation of whether the WTO has an impact on trade or trade policy. While one recent study shows that any impact is very little, another IMF study disagrees with that conclusion.[21]

PREFERENTIAL SYSTEMS

Generalized system of preferences (GSP)

Although the benefits derived from the creation of the WTO are rarely disputed, less developed countries do not necessarily embrace GATT because those countries believe that the benefits are not evenly distributed. Tariff reduction generally favors manufactured goods rather than primary goods. Less developed countries rely mainly on exports of primary products, which are then converted by advanced nations into manufactured products for export back to less developed countries. As a result, a less developed country's exports will usually be lower in value than its imports, thus exacerbating the country's poverty status.

In response to less developed countries' needs, the United Nations Conference on Trade and Development (UNCTAD) was created as a permanent organ of the UN General Assembly. Efforts by the UNCTAD led to the establishment of the New International Economic Order (NIEO) program. This program seeks to assist less developed countries through the stabilization of prices of primary products, the expansion of less developed countries' manufacturing capabilities, and the acquisition by less developed countries of advanced technology.

The goal of the UNCTAD is to encourage development in Third World countries and enhance their export positions. This goal led to the establishment of a tariff preference system for less developed countries' manufactured products. In spite of GATT's nondiscrimination principle, advanced nations agreed to grant such preferences to less developed countries' goods. The UNCTAD also played a key role in the emergence of a maritime shipping code, special international programs to help the least developed countries, and international aid targets.

Under the generalized system of preferences (GSP), developed countries are allowed to deviate from GATT's traditional nondiscrimination principle. Most developing countries have preferential access to the markets of industrial countries. There are about fifteen such arrangements in effect. Although the lower tariffs help the exports of many low-income countries, they also divert trade from some other countries that may be just as poor. Furthermore, according to evidence, the GSP schemes may perpetuate anti-export biases by undermining incentives to engage in trade liberalization.[22]

The US preferential system is known as the generalized system of preferences (GSP). The US Congress passed the Trade Act of 1974, authorizing the initiation of the GSP. The purpose of the act is to aid development by providing duty-free entry on 4000 products from more than thirty developing countries. Products manufactured wholly or substantially (at least 35 percent for single country products) in the designated countries are permitted to enter the United Stats duty-free as long as a particular item does not exceed $50.9 million in sales or 50 percent of all US imports of this product. Not all products qualify for such preferential treatment, however, and one should consult the Harmonized Tariff Schedule of the USA to determine whether a product may enter duty-free.

For a country to qualify, a number of economic variables are considered, such as per capita GNP and living standard. Burma and the Central African Republic had their benefits suspended under the US GSP for failing to meet the labor requirements. Venezuela was challenged as a result of a claim by Occidental Petroleum that its assets were expropriated without compensation. The Four Tigers (Hong Kong, Taiwan, Singapore, and South Korea), once receiving almost 60 percent of the benefits under GSP, were permanently graduated from the program at the beginning of 1989 as a result of their high degree of economic development and export competitiveness. Therefore, Black & Decker, which makes electric irons in Singapore, lost more than $3 million a year because of the new duties. Clearly, foreign exporters and American importers can find the GSP system highly advantageous.

Among the 140 countries and territories covered by the US GSP program, Thailand ranks second behind Angola for receiving the highest GSP privileges. Given the fact that GSP is product-specific and that some of Thailand's products (e.g., silver jewelry, microwave ovens, rubber gloves, and indicator panels) have reached their "competitive need" limit, certain benefits will be either reduced or withdrawn. In general, a product that has export sales of $95 million to the USA is not entitled to GSP tariff reductions. In addition, once a country's per capita GNP exceeds $3115, the country will have officially graduated from the US GSP program.[23]

Caribbean basin initiative (CBI)

Another US preferential system is the Caribbean Basin Initiative (CBI). The Caribbean Basin Economic Recovery Act of 1983 provides trade and tax measures to promote economic revitalization and expanded private sector opportunities in designated countries in the Caribbean Basin region. The main provision of the CBI eliminates US duties on almost all products entering from qualified countries in the Caribbean Basin. The law, however, excludes important products (textiles, apparel, footwear, and leather goods) from duty-free status as a safeguard for domestic (US) industry.

The Customs and Trade Act of 1990 makes the CBI permanent and provides additional trade benefits for the Caribbean countries. The Act provides a significant advantage to import from the region. The products will benefit by cost reductions through tariff elimination compared with imports from non-CBI countries. American firms producing products in the Caribbean may profit further from exporting to Europe, Canada, and South America, because many Caribbean Basin countries have preferential access to one or more of these other markets. The Act thus encourages US firms to open more labor-intensive assembly plants that export back to North America.

Other preferential systems

The Andean Trade Preference Act, similar to the CBI, provides trade benefits to Bolivia, Colombia, Ecuador, and Peru. In addition, the USA has passed the African Growth and Opportunity Act (AGOA) to provide reforming African countries with the most liberal access to the US market available to any country with which the USA does not have a free-trade agreement. The act has designated thirty-five countries to receive the benefits of lower import duty on an approved list of products entering the US market.[24]

SOME REMARKS ON PROTECTIONISM

Protectionist policies rarely achieve their objectives. As noted by a deputy US trade representative, "The price you pay for protection is inefficiency." Inward-looking strategies are based on the *positive externalities* assumption. That is, government intervention is appropriate because the development of a certain industry has a positive impact on a broader segment of the economy. Unfortunately, externalities are usually presumed rather than documented.[25]

No nation can dominate all industries. According to research, the protection of domestic economies against international competition is responsible for major economic losses for most sub-Saharan African countries. These countries need to open up their economies, and structural adjustment programs need to be implemented.

Most politicians are shortsighted; they simply desire to keep wealth within the home country. The possibility of retaliation is not fully considered. They want the best of both worlds. Artificial trade barriers reduce the world output of goods and services, and subsequently the world economic welfare; in the end, everyone suffers. The costs of distortions in agricultural trade are large, probably exceeding $120 billion in welfare costs. Countries, developing and industrial, must pay for protectionism. Elimination of barriers to merchandise trade will result in welfare gains of $250 billion to $620 billion.

A country has a choice of opening or closing its borders to trade. If it adopts the open system, it has a much better chance of fostering economic growth and maximizing consumer welfare. By adopting this approach, Hong Kong has been doing well economically. In response to the first oil price shock in the early 1970s, Brazil and Korea increased protection for domestic industry and got poor economic results. After the second oil price shock in the late 1970s, Korea adopted outward-oriented trade policies and has greatly benefited from international integration and the strong growth of world trade. Brazil's less outward-oriented policies (e.g., substantial import restrictions), in comparison, reduced competitive pressures at home, accelerated inflation, and led to stagnation.[26] The trade regimes are also more restrictive in Africa than in the rest of the world.[27]

Nations usually take a short cut and try to have a quick fix for their trade problems. Preoccupation with immediate problems often makes them lose sight of the long-term objectives. Without proper perspective, they can easily end up with more serious problems later.

Trade barriers slow specialization, diversification, investment efficiency, and growth. Government leaders must have political will to resist protectionist measures. Governments must make concerted and determined efforts to publicize the costs of protectionism. Trade policy should include a systematic consideration of such costs.

Openness of an economy is the degree to which foreigners and nationals can transact without government-imposed costs that are not levied on a transaction between two national citizens. One should note that trade openness and financial openness are complementary. This positive relationship applies both to industrial and developing countries.[28] Even in the case of intra-regional growth, as in China, the evidence shows that the more open areas grow faster than their less open counterparts.[29]

The breadth of evidence on openness, growth, and poverty reduction, and the strength of the association between openness and other important determinants of high per capita income, such as the quality of institutions, should give long pause to anyone contemplating the adoption of a novel (or tested and failed) development strategy that does not center on openness to trade.[30]

CONCLUSION

This chapter has discussed various trade barriers that can inhibit international marketing and, in turn, the world economic welfare of all consumers. It is important to understand that these are only some of the many trade barriers – others are not discussed. For example, more and more countries have now turned to "performance requirements" in order to gain trade advantage. Foreign suppliers are required to use local materials or to do exporting on behalf of an importing nation before they are allowed to sell their products there.

Regardless of the inappropriateness or injustice of many of these practices, they are part of international marketing. Although nations have used the WTO to lessen many of these restrictions, others will undoubtedly remain. In fact, most countries in recent years have initiated more protective measures. Since an international marketer has no control over these wide-reaching forces, the best defense is to understand and to be knowledgable about these trade practices. These barriers may be frustrating but they are not necessarily insurmountable. By understanding them, the marketer can learn what to expect and how to cope. One must always remember that additional problems are often accompanied by additional opportunities – for additional profits (see Marketing Strategy 3.1).

CULTURAL DIMENSION 3.1   BACK TO THE FUTURE

So much has been said about globalization as if it is a relatively new phenomenon. Actually, at the end of the nineteenth century, the world was a highly integrated economy – through mobility of capital, goods, and people. Capital moved freely between continents and states. Even in such protectionist countries as the USA and the German Empire, trade was largely unhindered. Nontariff barriers were rare, and quotas were unknown. People moved around, and they did so without passports. There was really no debate about citizenship as peoples of Asia and Europe braved long journeys across the oceans to unknown lands. Countries that welcomed these immigrants experienced substantial economic growth. Those who did not migrate also benefited from the shrinking populations because of large productivity improvements. The migration eased the desperate poverty of Ireland and

Norway. Capital, trade, and migration were linked. Capital flows made it possible to construct the infrastructure (e.g., railways and cities) to welcome new migrants while creating large overseas markets for European engineering and consumer products.

It was the Great Depression that put an end to the world's experiment with globalization. The states created control mechanisms to shield the countries from the threat of the world economy, but the protection proved to be even more dangerous and destructive than the threat. The Great Depression was a consequence of financial vulnerability that stemmed from the very institutions designed to protect nations from the impact of globalization.

Source: Harold James, "Is Liberalization Reversible?" *Finance & Development* (December 1999): 11–14.

MARKETING STRATEGY 3.1   NEW BALANCE: NEW LAW OF COMPARATIVE ADVANTAGE

According to the principle of comparative advantage, an advanced economy with a high labor cost should let labor-abundant countries perform its labor-intensive tasks, thus freeing its investment and workers to switch to industries that require greater skill and capital investment. After all, the advanced country has a comparative advantage in these areas. The principle assumes that the advanced nation's low-skilled jobs shifted abroad would have stayed low-skilled had they stayed at home. However, if the country can improve the skills so as to make the labor more efficient in performing the same activities, there will be a reduction in gains from moving production overseas.

Take the case of New Balance, an American shoemaker. Relatively speaking, shoes are a labor-intensive product. As a result, the US shoe industry that once employed 235,000 Americans in 1972 has lost 90 percent of those jobs thirty years later. The state of

Maine, once making more shoes than any other state, has been hit particularly hard. If American and Chinese workers were equally efficient, it would be theoretically impossible for New Balance to make shoes in the USA where its labor costs (wages and benefits) are $14 an hour. In China, at 80 cents an hour, labor is so abundant that it can be wasted. However, New Balance has come up with efficient production techniques that combine teams and technology. While Asian factories take three hours to make a pair of shoes, New Balance can do it in twenty-two minutes of labor time. Thus the cost disadvantage of making shoes in the USA has been significantly reduced.

Sources: "Low-Skilled Jobs: Do They Have to Move?" *Business Week*, February 26, 2001, 94; "Technology and Teamwork Helping New Balance Stay 'Made in USA,'" *San José Mercury News*, March 2, 2002.

79

CASE 3.1   GLOBAL WAR ON DRUGS OR TUNA?

Sujata Ramnarayan, San José State University

Senator Bob Graham of Florida proposed lowering tariffs on Ecuadorian tuna as part of an effort to revive the Andean Trade Preferences Act. The renewed act would expand and revive decade-old reductions in tariffs on cut flowers, textiles, packaged tuna, and other goods from Ecuador, Peru, Bolivia, Venezuela and Colombia. These reductions were intended to coax the Andean countries out of the drug business. Little did the Senator know that this bill, intended to combat drugs, would become a worldwide battle for and against tuna tariffs.

THE TUNA INDUSTRY AND THE CANNING PROCESS

The canning of tuna began in the USA in 1903 in Southern California. By the 1960s the operations had spread to the Atlantic coast, the Pacific Northwest, and the offshore territories of Puerto Rico and American Samoa due to low wages and their proximity to fishing areas. By the 1980s public concern for the safety of dolphins along with legislative activity intended to protect these friendly mammals led to shifts in sourcing. In addition, increasingly low-cost imports led to the closure of many of these plants. The Eastern Pacific Region now became a favored source of tuna production due to the fact that the tuna do not run along with dolphins in these waters unlike elsewhere. This led to the shrinkage of the industry in the continental USA, Puerto Rico, and Hawaii.

"Loining" Technology

Tuna is the most widely eaten fish in the USA. Most tuna canneries are located near fishing docks so the fish can be easily unloaded off the vessels. They are then subjected to a process of thawing, butchering, and precooking. After the first cooling process the fish are cleaned by removing the skin and separating the white meat for human consumption from the red meat for pet products. Other by-products include fishmeal and liquid fertilizer. The process of cleaning and separation is followed by packing tuna in water or oil with or without salt. In most canning operations, the cleaning, packing, and seaming equipment areas are located in the vicinity.

Loins are the light, meaty, edible part of the fish. The technology to use loins as the raw material in the canning process is fairly new. In addition, loins weigh less than half of a whole fish since they comprise the edible portion of the fish without all the waste. Their use as raw material in the canning process can result in considerable reduction in freight costs. The production of the loins which includes the butchering and cleaning steps is highly labor intensive, accounting for 60 to 80 percent of the cost of labor in the tuna-processing cannery. Thus, a cannery that contracts to use either fresh or frozen loins as the raw material for its canning operations stands to gain a significant amount of savings.

Tuna market players

The tuna industry is dominated by three major brands – StarKist, Bumble Bee, and Chicken of the Sea – all of which together account for 80 percent of the market in the USA. StarKist Seafood is the US leader with 44 percent of the market, more than the next two – Bumble Bee (23 percent) and Chicken of the Sea (17 percent) – combined.

StarKist and Bumble Bee both have sizable Tuna operations in Ecuador, the region's biggest tuna exporter. However, the two companies now find themselves on the opposite sides of the battle. Bumble Bee would like to see the tariffs continue. The company does all its labor intensive work of "loining" at its 2000-worker Ecuadorian plant. It then ships its cooked fillet to its automated plants in California and Puerto Rico, saving the canning until it enters the USA. This way, the company pays a low duty of 1.5 percent on its product.

StarKist has a different business model for its tuna operations in Ecuador and looks forward to the proposed reduction in tariffs. Its tuna-processing facility in Ecuador cleans, cooks, and packages the tuna for transport to the US in pouches. Depending on whether they are packed in water or oil, the tariffs on its tuna range from 15 to 35 percent.

ASEAN members joining the battle

Meanwhile, the ANDEAN Trade Preference Agreement under review has angered members of the Association of South East Asian Nations (ASEAN). ASEAN members face tariffs as high as 35 percent on their tuna exports to the USA. Ecuadorian tuna exports to the US have grown 600 percent in the past year, due mainly to lower transportation costs. Additional reduction in tariffs would give them an even greater advantage over their Asian counterparts.

While StarKist has spoken up in favor of the tariff reduction, Bumble Bee has teamed up with its Asian rival, Chicken of the Sea, a unit of Bangkok-based Thai Union Frozen PLC based in San Diego, to send a letter to American Samoa's representative in Congress. The two companies have warned Congress that this bill would put US business into foreign hands. In addition, Chicken of the Sea threatens to cut its workforce in Samoa by half.

Samoa sits on the world's richest tuna fishing grounds and the US tax code offers lucrative tax credits to US companies with operations in Samoa. More than 80 percent of the island's economy is driven by two huge tuna packing plants one of which is owned by StarKist, the island's largest employer. Samoan workers earn $3.30 an hour compared to Ecuadorian workers who earn 40 cents an hour. StarKist officials maintain that they have no intention of moving out of Samoa even if the Ecuadorian tuna tariffs are removed.

Sources: This case is adapted from: "The American Samoa Economic Report – 2003," the US Department of Labor; "Tuna Tariff Sparks Trade Fight between Grocery Store Rivals," *Wall Street Journal*, April 29, 2002; "Terrorism, Tariffs and . . . Tuna," The Heritage Foundation, June 14, 2002.

Points to consider

1　Discuss the different environmental factors having an impact on the tuna-processing industry.
2　How can international distribution strategy provide a competitive advantage? Which of the three market players has the best distribution strategy?
3　In what ways are international trade treaties having an impact on the tuna canning industry?
4　How would you have approached this issue as a member country of ASEAN?

QUESTIONS

1　Explain the rationale and discuss the weaknesses of each of these arguments for protection of local industries: (a) keeping money at home, (b) reducing unemployment, (c) equalizing cost and price, (d) enhancing national security, and (e) protecting infant industry.
2　Distinguish between these types of tariffs: (a) import and export tariffs, (b) protective and revenue tariffs, (c) surcharge and countervailing duty, and (d) specific and ad valorem duties.
3　Explain how these distribution/consumption taxes differ from one another: single-stage, value-added, cascade, and excise taxes.

4 Explain these various forms of government participation in trade: administrative guidance, subsidies, and state trading.

5 Other than cash, what are the various forms of subsidies?

6 Explain these customs and entry procedures and discuss how each can be used deliberately to restrict imports: (a) product classification, (b) product valuation, (c) documentation, (d) license/permit, (e) inspection, and (f) health and safety regulations.

7 Explain these various types of product requirements and discuss how each can be used deliberately to restrict imports: (a) product standards, (b) packaging, labeling, and marking, (c) product testing, and (d) product specifications.

8 What is the rationale for an export quota?

9 Distinguish these types of import quotas: (a) absolute, (b) tariff, (c) OMA, and (d) VER.

10 Discuss how these financial control methods adversely affect free trade: exchange control, multiple exchange rates, prior import deposits, credit restrictions, and profit remittance restrictions.

11 What is WTO? What is its purpose?

12 What is GSP?

13 What is CBI?

DISCUSSION ASSIGNMENTS AND MINICASES

1 If the simple existence of government can distort trade inside and outside of its area, should governments be abolished in order to eliminate trade distortion?

2 Will tariffs play a more significant role than nontariff barriers during the 2000s in affecting world trade?

3 Discuss how you can overcome the financial control imposed by the host country.

4 Do you agree that the WTO has served a useful purpose and has achieved its goals?

5 Should the advanced economies continue the GSP system?

6 How should MNCs generally cope with trade barriers?

7 A value-added tax (VAT) is a multi-stage, noncumulative tax on consumption, and it is levied at each stage of the production and distribution system. At the retail level, a retailer sends VAT payments to the government only on the value it adds to a particular product (i.e., its markup). The balance of the VAT on that product is remitted to the government by all other registered firms involved in the production of any inputs used in making or distributing that product. Each party's responsibility is in proportion to its share in the total value added embodied in the final product. Because all the firms involved in the production and distribution will be fully reimbursed by means of successive VAT tax credits, consumers are the ones ultimately bearing the entire VAT liability.

   Some US government officials and elected officials have advocated adoption of the European VAT system for revenue and balance of trade reasons. What is their reasoning? Do you agree with their position? Will VAT enhance US trade competitiveness? Will it discourage tax avoidance and evasion?

8 Presumably a statement of fact, foreign subsidies are supposed to be both unfair and harmful to the US economy. Any American politician would be foolish to argue otherwise. Do you agree with the conventional wisdom that foreign subsidies are unfair? Are subsidies harmful to the USA? How should the USA deal with imported products which are subsidized?

9 As in many countries, the cigarette market in Thailand is a regulated and largely monopolistic one. A quasi-government agency was granted an exclusive right to manufacture and market cigarettes. The US Cigarette Export Association complained that Thailand's discriminatory acts and policies created barriers in the sale

of foreign cigarettes. As a result, American firms lost at least $166 million in exports annually. The Association filed a petition under Section 301 of the US trade law, thus instigating the US Trade Representative's investigation. Subsequently, American trade negotiators put a great deal of pressure on the Thai government. Eventually, Thailand was forced to open its cigarette market to imports in 1990. Do you agree with the US government's involvement in pressuring other countries to open their markets to American products in general and American tobacco products in particular?

NOTES

1   *2003 National Trade Estimate Report on Foreign Trade Barriers*, US Trade Representative, 2003.

2   "Nationalism Can Hurt Trade," *Business Week*, October 8, 2001, 28.

3   "Stronger Support for Steel Quotas," *Business Week*, November 5, 2001, 50.

4   "Steel Tariffs: For and Against," *Business Week*, February 25, 2002, 32.

5   Hans Peter Lankes, "Market Access for Developing Countries," *Finance & Development* (September 2002): 8–13.

6   "The Truth about Industrial Country Tariffs," *Finance & Development* (September 2002): 14–15.

7   "Harley Hits 100," *San José Mercury News*, August 31, 2003.

8. Liam Ebrill *et al.*, *The Modern VAT*, IMF, 2001, and Liam Ebrill *et al.*, "The Allure of the Value-Added Tax," *Finance & Development* (June 2002): 44–7.

9. "How Can Central American Countries Improve Their Tax System?" *IMF Survey*, March 17, 2003, 70–1.

10 "Central American Countries."

11 "Tariff Reductions Aren't Enough," *Asian Wall Street Journal*, June 19, 2001.

12 "US Attacks Use of Non-Tariff Barriers," *AFTA Monitor*, May 15, 2002.

13 "Banned by the WTO, Corporate America Is Scrambling," *Business Week*, March 20, 2000, 118.

14 "WTO Trade Talks are Deadlocked over Concessions," *Asian Wall Street Journal*, July 15, 2003.

15 "Rich Countries Urged to Lead by Example on Trade Access," *IMF Survey*, October 21, 2002, 321–3.

16 "UNCTAD Stresses Gap Between Nations," *San José Mercury News*, February 16, 2000.

17 "Ask the TIC: Issues with Software Exploration," *Export America* (August 2001): 16–17.

18 "PlayStation 2 is Headed to the European Market," *San José Mercury News*, November 23, 2000.

19 "Stop Feeding the Losers, Toyota," *Business Week*, January 13, 2003, 48.

20 "Delegates from Poorer Nations Walk Out of World Trade Talks," *New York Times*, September 15, 2003; and "Coming US Vote Figures in Walkout at Trade Talks," *New York Times*, September 16, 2003.

21 "Do We Really Know That the WTO Increases Trade?" *IMF Survey*, August 18, 2003, 243–5; and "On the Contrary: WTO Makes a Difference," *IMF Survey*, February 2, 2004, 22.

22 Lankes, "Market Access."

23 "Thais Urged to Plan for Loss of Tariff Breaks," *Bangkok Post*, April 16, 2002.

24 "Ask the TIC," *Export America*, July 2001, 16–17.

25 "Structural Policies Shift in Developing Countries," *IMF Survey*, February 6, 1995, 45–6.

26 "Brazil and Korea: Good Policies Matter," *IMF Survey*, May 22, 1995, 161–3.

27 Robert Sharer, "An Agenda for Trade, Investment, and Regional Integration," *Finance & Development* (December 2001): 14–17.

28 "Trade and Finance Links Warrant Closer Attention," *IMF Survey*, September 16, 2002, 273–6.

29 Shang-Jin Wei, "Is Globalization Good for the Poor in China?" *Finance & Development* (September 2002): 26–9.

30 Andrew Berg and Anne Krueger, "Lifting All Boats," *Finance & Development* (September 2002): 16–19.

Chapter 4

Political environment

In an authoritarian state, it is only the prisoner of conscience who is genuinely free.

Nobel laureate Aung San Suu Kyi

CHAPTER OUTLINE

- Multiplicity of political environments
- Types of government: political systems
- Types of government: economic systems
- Political risks
- Privatization
- Indicators of political instability
  - ☐ Attitudes of nationals
  - ☐ Policies of the host government
- Analysis of political risk or country risk
- Management of political risk
- Measures to minimize political risk
  - ☐ Stimulation of the local economy
  - ☐ Employment of nationals
  - ☐ Sharing ownership
  - ☐ Being civic minded
  - ☐ Political neutrality
  - ☐ Behind-the-scenes lobby
  - ☐ Observation of political mood and reduction of exposure
  - ☐ Other measures
- Political insurance
  - ☐ Private insurance
  - ☐ Government insurance
  - ☐ MIGA
- Conclusion
- Case 4.1 Hoa Ni Shoe Company

PURPOSE OF CHAPTER

Whether political interests precede or follow economic interests is debatable, but certainly the two are closely interrelated. A country or company may play politics in order to pursue its economic interests, but economic means may also be used to achieve political objectives. As in the case of the steel industry, President Bush imposed the tariffs in 2002, ranging from 8 percent to 30 percent, on foreign-made steel so as to give the domestic industry time to regroup to become more competitive. Even after the WTO's ruling that the tariffs violated global trade laws, Bush's political advisors did not want to remove the tariffs because it could harm his chance of winning re-election in such steel-making states as Pennsylvania, West Virginia, Ohio, Indiana, and Illinois.[1]

Often, politics and economics do not mix well. For a very long time, the USA imposed economic censure against Vietnam. While the economic sanction was achieving the desired goal of adversely affecting international investment and trade with Vietnam, Asian and European companies took advantage of the absence of American firms and entered the market. Vietnam is an attractive market – not only for its market size and natural resources, but also because of other economic reasons. Vietnam welcomes foreign investment in all economic sectors (except defense industries), offers generous tax concessions and duty exemptions, allows 100 percent foreign ownership, imposes no minimum capital requirement, and promises the unrestricted repatriation of capital and profits. In addition, the political climate has greatly improved. The US government finally permitted American companies to enter the Vietnamese market in the mid-1990s.

The economic interests of MNCs can differ widely from the economic interests of the countries in which these firms do business. A lack of convergent interests often exists between a company's home country and its various host countries. In the absence of mutual interests, political pressures can lead to political decisions, resulting in laws and proclamations that affect business. The example of the US steel industry's lobbying efforts provides an introduction to the political and legal dimensions of international business. Such efforts also show that political risks, thought to be largely uncontrollable, can nevertheless be reasonably managed. It is thus important to understand the role of political risk in international marketing and its impact on each of the four Ps of marketing.

This chapter examines the interrelationships among political, legal, and business decisions. The discussion will focus on how the political climate affects the investment climate. Among political topics covered are forms of government, indicators of political instability, and political risks. The chapter ends with the investigation of strategies used to manage political risks.

MARKETING ILLUSTRATION   HOW TO WIN FRIENDS AND INFLUENCE PEOPLE: FRENCH FRIES VS. FREEDOM FRIES

France and Germany strongly opposed the plan of the USA to invade Iraq in 2003. Interestingly, Germany, America's enemy in two world wars, did not upset Americans very much. A Gallup poll found that 71 percent of Americans had a favorable view of Germany. France, on the other hand, provoked a great deal of anger. While 59 percent still viewed France favorably, this was a drop of almost 20 percent. A former US deputy under-secretary of defense hurled this insult: "Going to war without France is like going deer hunting without an accordion – you just leave a lot of useless, noisy baggage behind." The French felt that Americans misunderstood their country's position which was derived from having to fight two world wars on their soil.

Americans' anger resulted in boycotts of French wine and vacations in France. Even french fries and french toast were not immune; several American restaurants switched from french fries to freedom fries. The shares of Sodexho, a French catering company, forfeited 14 percent in one day because of a radio report mentioning that it had lost a $1 billion contract with the US Marines. To combat the backlash, French companies took action to downplay their identity. The Accor Group allowed its ten Sofitel hotels in the USA to put away French flags. The chairman of Danone proclaimed: "Don't forget Danone in the US is an American company. It is even written in American style D-A-N-N-O-N."

American businesses faced the same problems abroad. To protest the war in Iraq, a number of restaurants in Germany took American items off their menus. Consumers in several Middle Eastern countries boycotted American products. Iran has banned media advertising of American goods. While risks are relatively high for US firms doing business in the Middle East, the risks are heightened when a US brand is a cultural icon. McDonald's and its Golden Arches at 30,000 outlets worldwide is certainly one of the most recognized American symbols. The

company and its American competitors have made it clear that most overseas outlets are owned and operated by local franchisees who buy most products locally. Unfortunately, local consumers often fail to make this distinction.

Even after the war, while softening their tones, the leaders did not change their positions. In his speech to the United Nations General Assembly in September 2003, President George W. Bush wanted to "move forward" but was unapologetic for going to war without a UN endorsement. His speech was preceded by that of UN Secretary Kofi Annan who criticized "the lawless use of force." French President Jacques Chirac followed both and stated that, without Security Council approval, the war has undermined the multilateral system. "In an open world, no one can live in isolation, no one can act alone in the name of all, and no one can accept the anarchy of a society without rules."

Sources: "Hotel Sofitel Puts Its French Flag Away," *San José Mercury News,* March 4, 2003; "French Companies Try to Appear Less French," *San José Mercury News,* March 18, 2003; "US Backlash Against France Targets Wine, Renames Fries," *San José Mercury News,* February 23, 2003; "US Companies Bracing for Hostility Overseas," *San José Mercury News,* March 5, 2003; "US Products Boycotted," *San José Mercury News,* March 26, 2003; "Bush Gets Chilly UN Reception," *San José Mercury News,* September 24, 2003.

MULTIPLICITY OF POLITICAL ENVIRONMENTS

The political environment that MNCs face is a complex one because they must cope with the politics of more than one nation. That complexity forces MNCs to consider the three different types of political environment: foreign, domestic, and international (see Cultural Dimension 4.1). As in the case of the US steel industry, it has received a variety of subsidy and government protection for more than thirty years. George W. Bush continued the assistance by imposing quotas for three years, and politics may have played a role. The action should help Republican candidates in the steel-

producing states. Bush was criticized for shunning free trade for the "pleasure of political opportunism."[2] The measures were like new taxes that would cost consumers of steel products $8 billion.

Although political and economic motives are two distinct components, they are often closely intertwined. A country may use economic sanctions to make a political statement. Likewise, a political action may be taken so as to enhance the country's economic prospects. It is also hardly uncommon for governments as well as companies to ignore politics for the purpose of economic interests. Even while the economic sanctions were in place, the USA was actually importing a large amount of oil from Iraq. While Taiwan and China are supposedly enemies

CULTURAL DIMENSION 4.1   GENETICALLY MODIFIED ORGANISMS

Genes are the materials that contain the blueprint for living beings' make-up. Genetic engineering or bio-engineering is a process that deliberately but not naturally transfers genes from one species to another. Seeds may thus have new traits obtained from gene-splicing. More than 25 percent of corn and roughly 70 percent of soy and cotton grown in the USA are genetically engineered. In general, some 25 to 45 percent of the major crops of the USA use the process.

As a major user and exporter of genetically modified products, the USA feels that the process is safe. However, genetic engineering is highly controversial in Europe and Asia. As an example, a consumer poll conducted by Greenpeace Southeast Asia shows that 95 percent of respondents in Thailand prefer manufacturers to have labels that identify products with genetically modified ingredients. Such concerns have led to an effort to create the world's first global treaty to regulate trade in such modified products. This international cooperation has proposed the Biosafety Protocol that requires exporters of genetically modified organisms to obtain an importing country's prior approval. The idea is to allow countries to minimize ecological risks that may stem from an introduction of genetically altered plants, animals, and microorganisms into the environment.

Even though the Protocol has the support of about 120 countries, six major agricultural exporters (the USA, Canada, Australia, Chile, Argentina, and Uruguay) have rejected it. Monsanto's business activities have complicated the matter further. The company has used genetic engineering to combat farm diseases and improve crop yields. However, its business model emphasizes exclusive uses and patent rights that appear to benefit Monsanto more than farmers.

Nestlé has likewise become a lightning rod. Greenpeace alleges that Nestlé uses genetically modified ingredients only in its products that are sold in developing countries. Nestlé has insisted that it has implemented the same safety and quality standards worldwide. On the other hand, national regulations, availability of raw materials, and consumer attitudes dictate whether the company uses genetically modified ingredients. Nestlé has criticized Greenpeace for rejecting the opinion of international scientific bodies that genetically modified crops are as safe as their conventional counterparts.

Sources: "FDA Looks at Altered Crops," *San José Mercury News*, May 4, 2000; "US Helps Foil Treaty on Genetically Modified Crops," *San José Mercury News*, February 25, 1999; "Some Food for Thought on Bioengineering," *San José Mercury News*, January 13, 2002; and "Nestlé Hits Back at Greenpeace," *Bangkok Post*, May 17, 2002.

that do not want to do business with one another, the truth of the matter is that there are some 50,000 Taiwanese-owned factories in China.[3]

Developing countries often view foreign firms and foreign capital investment with distrust and even resentment, owing primarily to a concern over potential foreign exploitation of local natural resources. **Dependency theory** may partially explain why Latin American countries are reluctant to welcome foreign-based multinational firms. According to this theory, the ongoing economic, political, and social transformations have made it necessary for Latin America to rely on the capitalistic system. Consequently, advanced countries are able to extract surplus value from their less developed counterparts, thus leaving them underdeveloped while perpetuating the existence of class conflicts and oppressive governments.[4]

Developed countries themselves are also concerned about foreign investment. Many Americans have expressed their concern that the increasing foreign ownership of American assets poses a threat to their country's national security, both politically and economically. It should be pointed out that inflows of foreign capital add to the domestic capital stock. This activity contributes to the American standard of living and enhances the country's ability to service its international indebtedness. As a result, the benefits of foreign investment far outweigh the costs.

In some cases, opposition to imported goods and foreign investment is based on moral principle. For example, the citizens of many nations pressured companies in their countries not to invest in South Africa because of that country's policy of apartheid. In the mid-1980s the pressure became so great that the South African government ran advertisements in the USA in an attempt to minimize damage, as shown in Figure 4.1. Ironically, American firms that heeded the anti-apartheid movement's call to divest have found it difficult to re-enter the market and capture back market share.

Regardless of whether the politics are foreign, domestic, or international, the company should

Figure 4.1 *Dealing with political pressure*

Source: Reprinted with permission of the South African Consulate General.

keep in mind that political climate does not remain stationary. The political relationship between the USA and a long-time adversary, China, is a prime example. After decades as bitter enemies, both countries became very interested in improving their political and economic ties so as to dilute the power of the Soviet Union.

Although most companies have little control over affecting changes in international politics, they must be prepared to respond to new developments. Companies can derive positive economic benefits when the relationship between two countries improves or when the host government adopts a new investment policy. As in the case of India, the country was a highly regulated, closed economy which discouraged foreign investment. It was not until 1991 that a new government began a reform program which could transform India into one of the world's most dynamic economies.

On the other hand, serious problems can develop when political conditions deteriorate. A favorable investment climate can disappear almost overnight. In one case, the USA withdrew Chile's duty-free trade status because of Chile's failure to take "steps to afford internationally recognized worker rights." Chile thus joined Romania, Nicaragua, and Paraguay in being suspended from the GSP (generalized system of preferences).

TYPES OF GOVERNMENT: POLITICAL SYSTEMS

A system of the form governments can take can be useful in appraising the political climate. One way to classify governments is to consider them as either parliamentary (open) or absolutist (closed). Table 4.1 shows the political features of oil-exporting nations.

Parliamentary governments consult with citizens from time to time for the purpose of learning about opinions and preferences. Government policies are thus intended to reflect the desire of the majority segment of a society. Most industrialized nations and all democratic nations may be classified as parliamentary.

At the other end of the spectrum are absolutist governments, which include monarchies and dictatorships. In an **absolutist** system, the ruling regime dictates government policy without considering citizens' needs or opinions. Frequently, absolutist countries are newly formed nations or those undergoing some kind of political transition. Absolute monarchies are now relatively rare. The United Kingdom is a good example of a constitutional hereditary monarchy; despite the monarch, the government is classified as parliamentary.

Many countries' political systems do not fall neatly into one of these two categories. Some monarchies and dictatorships (e.g., Saudi Arabia and North Korea) have parliamentary elections. The former Soviet Union had elections and mandatory voting but was not classified as parliamentary because the ruling party never allowed an alternative on the ballot. Countries such as the Philippines under Marcos and Nicaragua under Somoza held elections, but the results were suspect due to government involvement in voting fraud.

Another way to classify governments is by the number of political parties. This classification results in four types of governments: two-party, multi-party, single-party, and dominated one-party. In a **two-party** system, there are typically two strong parties that take turns controlling the government, although other parties are allowed. The USA and the United Kingdom are prime examples. The two parties generally have different philosophies, resulting in a change in government policy when one party succeeds the other. In the USA, the Republican Party is often viewed as representing business interests, whereas the Democratic Party is often viewed as representing labor interests, as well as the poor and disaffected.

In a **multi-party** system, there are several political parties, none of which is strong enough to gain control of the government. Even though some parties may be large, their elected representatives fall short of a majority. A government must then be formed through coalitions between the various parties, each of which wants to protect its own interests. The longevity of the coalition depends

Table 4.1 Oil exporter's political systems. Classifying oil exporters.[1] The type of political system affects how oil revenue is spent.

Political features	Institutional implications	Economic implications
Mature democracy		
Stable party system	Long policy horizon	Saving likely
Range of social consensus	Policy stability, transparency	Expenditure smoothing, stabilization
Strong, competent, insulated bureaucracy	High competitiveness, low transaction costs	Rents transferred to public through government-provided social services and insurance or direct transfers
Competent, professional judicial system	Strong private/traded sector, prostabilization interests vis-à-vis prospending interests	
Highly educated electorate		
Factional democracy		
Government and parties often unstable relative to interest groups	Short policy horizon	Saving very difficult
Political support gained through clientelistic ties and provision of patronage	Policy instability, nontransparency, high transaction costs	Procyclical expenditure; instability
Wide social disparities, lack of consensus	Strong state role in production	Rents transferred to different interests and to public through subsidies, policy distortions, public employment
Politicized bureaucracy and judicial system	Strong interests attached directly to state expenditures; politically weak private non-oil sector and prostabilization interests	
Paternalistic autocracy		
Stable government; legitimacy originally from traditional role, maintained through rent distribution	Long horizon	Procyclical expenditure, mixed success with stabilization
Strong cultural elements of consensus, clientelistic, and nationalistic patterns	Policy stability, nontransparency	Risk of unsustainable long-term spending trajectory leading to political crisis
Bureaucracy provides both services and public employment	Low competitiveness, high transaction costs	Little economic diversification
	Strong state role in production	
	Strong interests attached directly to state expenditures	
	Weak private sector	
Reformist autocracy		
Stable government, legitimized by development	Long horizon	Expenditure smoothing, stabilization
Social range of consensus toward development	Policy stability, nontransparency	State investment complementary to competitive private sector
Constituency in non-oil traded sectors	Drive for competitiveness, low transaction costs	Active exchange rate management to limit Dutch disease
Insulated technocracy	Strong constituency for stabilization and fiscal restraint	
Predatory autocracy		
Unstable government, legitimized by military force	Short horizon	No saving
Lack of consensus-building mechanisms	Policy instability, nontransparency	Highly procyclical expenditure
Bureaucracy exists as mechanism of rent capture and distribution; corrupt judicial system	Low competitiveness, high transaction costs	Very high government consumption, rent absorption by elites through petty corruption and patronage, capital flight
Little or no civic counterweight	Spending interests strong vis-à-vis private sector or prostabilization interests	

Note

1 These classifications are not exhaustive, and some countries have a blend of features from different categories. The aim is not to create a rigid classification of oil countries but to help provide insights into the policy options available to governments. For example, fiscal federalism is one factor cutting across the categories, see, for example, D. Lal, 1995, "Why Growth Rates Differ. The Political Economy of Social Capability in 21 Developing Countries," in *Social Capability and Long-Term Economic Growth*, edited by Bon Ho Koo and Dwight H. Perkins (New York, NY: St. Martin's Press).

Source: Benn Eifert, Alan Gelb, and Nils Borje Tallroth, "Managing Oil Wealth," *Finance & Development* (March 2003): 42.

largely on the cooperation of party partners. Usually, the coalition is challenged continuously by various opposing parties. A change in a few votes may be sufficient to bring the coalition government down. If the government does not survive a vote of no confidence (i.e., it does not have the support of the majority of the representatives), the government is disbanded and a new election is called. Countries operating under this system include Germany, France, and Israel. In the 1991 elections in Poland, twenty-nine parties (including the Polish Beer Lovers' Party) won seats, and no party got more than 13 percent of the vote.

In a **single-party** system, there may be several parties, but one party is so dominant that there is little opportunity for others to elect representatives to govern the country. Egypt has operated under single-party rule for several decades. This form of government is often used by countries in the early stages of the development of a true parliamentary system. Because the ruling party holds support from the vast majority, the system is not necessarily a poor one, especially when it can provide the stability and continuity necessary for rapid growth. But when serious economic problems persist, citizens' dissatisfaction and frustration may create an explosive situation. For example, Mexico has been ruled since its revolution by the Institutional Revolutionary Party (PRI), but economic problems caused dissatisfaction with the PRI in the 1980s. The National Action Party (PAN), Mexico's main opposition party, began gaining strength, possibly foreshadowing a transition away from a single-party system. As a matter of fact, Vicente Fox indeed took Mexico's presidency away from the PRI.

In a **dominated one-party** system, the dominant party does not allow any opposition, resulting in no alternative for the people. In contrast, a single-party system does allow some opposition party. The former Soviet Union, Cuba, Libya, and China are good examples of dominated one-party systems. Such a system may easily transform itself into a dictatorship. The party, to maintain its power, is prepared to use force or any necessary means to eliminate the introduction and growth of other

parties. Such countries as Burma, Cambodia, and Afghanistan have tried to reject outside influences, and it is no accident that they were or are among the most repressive regimes. Understandably, repression or suppression may be their only way of maintaining their ideology.[5]

In addition, countries' electoral systems may be either majoritarianism or proportionality. In the case of **majoritarianism**, a country is ruled by a simple numerical majority in an organized group. **Proportionality** occurs when the number of parliamentary seats is based on vote share. Research shows that spending on social security and welfare is lower under majoritarian systems. In contrast, "certain political factors, such as an electoral system that emphasizes proportionality or a fragmented parliament or government, lead simultaneously to higher transfers, bigger government, and a revenue system that emphasizes labor taxes over consumption taxes."[6]

Freedom House publishes *Freedom in the World*, a survey which reports on freedom around the globe. The publication is an annual comparative assessment of the state of political rights and civil liberties in 192 countries and seventeen related and disputed territories. In 2002, eighty-nine countries were "free" and fifty-six are "partly free." The "not free" category claimed forty-seven countries.[7] Freedom House's *Freedom of the Press 2003: A Global Survey of Media Independence* reveals that press freedom deteriorated in 2002.[8]

One should not be hasty in making generalizations about the ideal form of government in terms of political stability. It may be tempting to believe that stability is a function of economic development. South Africa and Italy, two developed countries, have been beset with internal and external problems. The political atmosphere from time to time is marred by a weak economy, recurring labor unrest, and internal dissension. In contrast, it may be argued that Vietnam, despite being a developing economy, is politically more stable. This stability is due in part to Vietnam's relatively closed economy.

It may be just as tempting to conclude that a democratic political system is a prerequisite for political stability. India, the world's largest democracy, possesses a solid political infrastructure and political institutions that have withstood many crises over time. The democratic system is strongly established in India, and it is almost inconceivable that the Indians would choose any other. Yet India's political stability is hampered by regional, ethnic, language, religious, and economic problems. Unlike such other democratic nations as Australia, where such problems have largely been resolved, India's difficulties remain. These geographic, ideological, and ethnic problems inhibit the government's ability to respond to one sector's demands without alienating others.

Democracy does not guarantee peace. When hateful religious fundamentalists won elections in Algeria, Indonesia, Nigeria, and Pakistan, violence followed. Yugoslavia's citizens appeared to endorse Slobodan Milosevic's policy of ethnic cleansing. Adolf Hitler's rise to power was a result of a free vote. On the other hand, some authoritarian rulers may be more progressive than their followers. While Suharto was in power, his authoritarian style, rightly or wrongly, brought ethnic peace and strong economic growth. Free elections have given power to anti-American Muslim extremists, Christians are being killed, and growth has declined. It is debatable whether elections in Egypt, Jordan, Pakistan, and Saudi Arabia will make the countries better off if fundamentalists come to power.[9]

Dictatorial systems, monarchies, and oligarchies may be able to provide great stability for a country, especially one with a relatively closed society, which exists in many communist countries and Arab nations. If a country's ruler and military are strong, any instability that may occur can be kept under control. The problem, however, is that such systems frequently exist in a divided society where dissident groups are waiting for an opportunity to challenge the regime. When a ruler dies suddenly, the risk of widespread disruption and revolution can be quite high.

Democracy itself is not a perfect system. Japan's recession has been caused in part by its divided, ineffective government. India continues to cope

with the chaos due to a coalition of a dozen fractured parties that runs the government. While representative democracy is generally a good thing, it can create an explosive situation when democracy is combined with capitalism to create "market-dominant minorities." The ethnic Chinese, for example, constitute 1 percent of the Philippines population but control 60 percent of the country's wealth, while two-thirds of the ethnic Filipinos struggle on less than $2 a day. The oppressed majority may violently strike back at the easily identified ethnic minority group (e.g., the ethnic Chinese in the Philippines and Indonesia, the Lebanese in West Africa, the Asian Indians in East Africa, the Jews in Russia, and the whites in Zimbabwe, the indigenous Ibo tribe in Nigeria, and the Tutsi tribe in Rwanda).[10]

Policy makers naturally want to know whether there is a direct relationship between democracy and economic progress. Latin America and Eastern Europe have moved in the democratic direction, and democracies have done relatively well in economic reform. Econometric results also point in the same direction.[11]

TYPES OF GOVERNMENT: ECONOMIC SYSTEMS

Economic systems provide another basis for classification of governments. These systems serve to explain whether businesses are privately owned or government owned, or whether there is a combination of private and government ownership. Basically, three systems may be identified: communism, socialism, and capitalism. Based on the degree of government control of business activity, the various economic systems can be placed along a continuum, with communism at one end and capitalism at another. A movement toward communism is accompanied by an increase in government interference and more control of factors of production. A movement toward capitalism is accompanied by an increase in private ownership.

Communist theory holds that all resources should be owned and shared by all the people (i.e., not by profit-seeking enterprises) for the benefit of the society. In practice, it is the government that controls all productive assets and industries and, as a result, the government determines jobs, production, price, education, and just about anything else. The emphasis is on human welfare. Because profit making is not the government's main motive, there is a lack of incentive for workers and managers to improve productivity.

The term **centrally planned economies** is often used to refer to the former Soviet Union, Eastern European countries, China, Vietnam, and North Korea. These economies tend to have the following characteristics: a communist philosophy, an active government role in economic planning, a nonmarket economy, a weak economy, high foreign debt, and rigid and bureaucratic political/economic systems. A contrast between North Korea and South Korea is quite striking. While North Korea's economy has contracted, South Korea's economy has been booming. South Korea's GDP of $931 billion dwarfs North Korea's GDP of $22 billion. North Korea's exports of $842 million are no match for South Korea's exports of $162.6 billion. It should be noted that North Korea is much better endowed than its southern counterpart in terms of natural resources.

Despite communist countries' preoccupation with control of industries, it would be erroneous to conclude that all communist governments are exactly alike. Although the former Soviet Union and China adhered to the same basic ideology, there was a marked difference between the two largest communist nations. China has been experimenting with a new type of communism by allowing its citizens to work for themselves and to keep any profit in the process. Yet one must remember that "free markets" can exist in China only with the state's permission, and the operations of such markets are still overseen by government officials.

The degree of government control that occurs under **socialism** is somewhat less than under communism. A socialist government owns and operates the basic, major industries but leaves small businesses to private ownership. Socialism is a matter of degree, and not all socialist countries are the same. A socialist country such as Poland leans toward communism, as evidenced by its rigid control over prices, and distribution. France's socialist system, in comparison, is much closer to capitalism than it is to communism.

At one time, Sweden was a role model of what socialism could be, but a middle road between communism and capitalism may now produce stalled economic growth.[12] Sweden's economic decline is due in part to a rapid expansion in regulations and to the rising share of national income spent by central and local governments. During the 1970s and 1980s, Sweden introduced very generous retirement and health benefits, lengthy paid leave for parents, liberal rules for sick workers on taking days off, and many other types of transfer payments. Not surprisingly, on an average day, almost one in four employees is absent from work because of reported illness, parental responsibilities, study leave, and other reasons that allow a worker to stay at home. On a yearly basis, the average Swedish worker is off sick for almost a month of the year while receiving full salary. Moreover, differences in pay by education level, job experience, and other measures of worker productivity have largely disappeared. In the long run, there is no incentive to work hard when one can get paid for staying at home, when education and better jobs do not offer much higher wages, and when taxes offset any increase in pay.

At the opposite end of the continuum from communism is capitalism. The philosophy of **capitalism** provides for a *free-market system* that allows business competition and freedom of choice for both consumers and companies. It is a *market-oriented* system in which individuals, motivated by private gain, are allowed to produce goods or services for public consumption under competitive conditions. Product price is determined by demand and supply. This system serves the needs of society by encouraging decentralized decision making, risk taking, and innovation. The results include product variety, product quality, efficiency, and relatively lower prices. Table 4.2 and Fig. 4.2 ranks the world's free economies.

Table 4.2 *Index of economic freedom rankings*

Rank		2003 Scores	Trade	Fiscal burden of govern- ment	Govern- ment inter- vention	Mone- tary policy	Foreign invest- ment	Banking and finance	Wage/ prices	Property rights	Regula- tion	Black market
1	Hong Kong	1.45	1	2	3	1	1	1	2	1	1	1.5
2	Singapore	1.50	1	2	3	1	1	2	2	1	1	1
3	Luxembourg	1.70	2	4	2	1	1	1	2	1	2	1
3	New Zealand	1.70	2	4	2	1	1	1	2	1	2	1
5	Ireland	1.75	2	3	2	2	1	1	2	1	2	1.5
6	Denmark	1.80	2	4.5	3.5	1	2	1	1	1	1	1
6	Estonia	1.80	1	3.5	2	2	1	1	1	2	2	2.5
6	USA	1.80	2	3.5	2	1	2	1	2	1	2	1.5
9	Australia	1.85	2	3.5	2	2	2	1	2	1	2	1
9	United Kingdom	1.85	2	4	2	1	2	1	2	1	2	1.5
11	Finland	1.90	2	4	2	1	2	2	2	1	2	1
11	Iceland	1.90	2	3	2	2	2	3	1	1	2	1
11	Netherlands	1.90	2	4	2	2	1	1	2	1	3	1
11	Sweden	1.90	2	4.5	2.5	1	1	1	2	1	3	1
15	Switzerland	1.95	2	3.5	3	1	2	1	2	1	3	1
16	Bahrain	2.00	3	2	3	1	2	1	3	1	2	2
16	Chile	2.00	2	2.5	2	2	2	2	2	1	3	1.5
18	Canada	2.05	2	4	2.5	1	3	2	2	1	2	1
19	Austria	2.10	2	4.5	2	1	2	2	2	1	3	1.5
19	Belguim	2.10	2	5	2	1	1	2	2	1	3	2
19	Germany	2.10	2	4.5	2	1	1	3	2	1	3	1.5
22	Bahamas	2.15	5	1.5	2	1	3	2	3	1	1	2
22	Cyprus	2.15	2	3.5	3	1	3	2	2	1	2	2
24	Barbados	2.20	3	4	2	1	3	2	2	1	2	2
24	United Arab Emirates	2.20	2	2	3	1	3	3	2	2	3	1
26	El Salvador	2.25	2	2	2	2	2	2	2	3	2	3.5
27	Norway	2.30	2	4	3	1	3	3	2	1	3	1
27	Taiwan	2.30	2	3	2.5	1	3	2	2	2	3	2.5
29	Italy	2.35	2	5	2	1	2	2	2	2	3	2.5
29	Lithuania	2.35	2	3.5	2	1	2	2	2	3	3	3
29	Spain	2.35	2	4	2.5	2	2	2	2	2	3	2
32	Portugal	2.40	2	4	2	2	2	3	2	2	3	2
33	Israel	2.45	2	5	3	1	2	3	2	2	3	1.5
33	Latvia	2.45	2	4	2	1	2	2	2	3	3	3.5
35	Botswana	2.50	2	3.5	4	3	2	2	2	2	2	2.5
35	Cambodia	2.50	2	2	1	1	3	2	3	4	4	3
35	Czech Rep., The	2.50	3	4.5	2	2	2	1	2	2	3	3.5
35	Japan	2.50	2	4	3	1	3	3	2	2	3	2
35	Uruguay	2.50	3	3.5	2.5	2	2	2	2	2	3	3
40	France	2.55	2	4.5	3	1	3	3	2	2	3	2

Table 4.2 continued

Rank		2003 Scores	Trade	Fiscal burden of government	Government intervention	Monetary policy	Foreign investment	Banking and finance	Wage/ prices	Property rights	Regulation	Black market
40	Kuwait	2.55	2	2.5	3	1	4	3	3	2	3	2
40	Thailand	2.55	4	2.5	1.5	1	3	3	2	2	3	3.5
43	Trinidad and Tobago	2.60	4	3.5	3	2	2	2	2	2	3	2.5
44	Armenia	2.65	1	2.5	3	2	2	2	3	3	4	4
44	Bolivia	2.65	3	3	2	1	1	2	2	4	4	4.5
44	Costa Rica	2.65	2	3	2.5	3	2	3	2	3	3	3
44	Hungary	2.65	3	4	2	3	2	2	3	2	3	2.5
44	Madagascar	2.65	2	2.5	1	3	3	3	2	3	3	4
44	Panama	2.65	3	4	3	1	2	1	2	4	3	3.5
44	Qatar	2.65	3	2.5	3	1	3	3	2	3	4	2
44	South Africa	2.65	3	4.5	2	2	2	2	2	3	3	3
52	Korea, South	2.70	3	3	4	2	2	3	2	2	3	3
52	Malta	2.70	3	4	3	1	3	3	3	1	2	4
52	Namibia	2.70	3	4	3.5	3	2	2	2	2	3	2.5
55	Belize	2.75	4	3.5	2	1	3	3	2	3	3	3
56	Greece	2.80	2	4	2	2	3	3	3	3	3	3
56	Guatemala	2.80	3	2	1	3	3	2	2	4	4	4
56	Jamaica	2.80	4	4	3	3	1	2	2	3	3	3
56	Mexico	2.80	2	3.5	3	3	3	2	2	3	3	3.5
56	Oman	2.80	3	3	4	1	3	3	3	3	3	2
56	Peru	2.80	4	25	3	1	2	2	2	4	4	3.5
62	Jordan	2.85	5	3.5	4	1	2	2	2	3	3	3
62	Philippines, The	2.85	2	2.5	2	2	3	3	3	3	4	4
62	Slovenia	2.85	4	4	2	3	3	3	2	3	2	2.5
62	Uganda	2.85	3	3	2	1	3	3	2	3	4	4.5
66	Poland	2.90	3	4.5	2	3	3	2	3	2	3	3.5
66	Slovak Rep., The	2.90	3	4.5	2	3	2	2	3	3	3	3.5
68	Argentina	2.95	4	3	2	1	3	4	2	4	3	3.5
68	Morocco	2.95	5	4	2.5	1	2	3	2	4	3	3
68	Saudi Arabia	2.95	4	2.5	4	1	3	4	2	3	3	3
68	Tunisia	2.95	5	4	3	1	3	3	2	3	3	2.5
72	Brazil	3.00	4	2.5	3	3	3	3	2	3	3	3.5
72	Colombia	3.00	4	3.5	3	3	2	2	2	4	3	3.5
72	Malaysia	3.00	3	3	3	1	4	4	3	3	3	3
72	Mali	3.00	3	3	3	2	3	3	2	3	3	5
72	Mauritius	3.00	5	3	3	2	3	2	4	2	3	3
72	Mongolia	3.00	2	4.5	2.5	3	3	3	2	3	4	3
72	Nicaragua	3.00	2	3	3	3	2	2	3	4	4	4
72	Swaziland	3.00	2	4	2	3	3	3	3	3	3	4
80	Central African Rep.	3.05	5	2.5	3	1	2	3	3	3	4	4

Table 4.2 *continued*

Rank		2003 Scores	Trade	Fiscal burden of government	Government intervention	Monetary policy	Foreign investment	Banking and finance	Wage/ prices	Property rights	Regulation	Black market
80	Honduras	3.05	3	2.5	3	3	3	3	2	3	4	4
80	Ivory Coast	3.05	4	3.5	1	2	3	2	3	4	4	4
80	Senegal	3.05	4	2.5	3	1	3	3	3	3	4	4
80	Sri Lanka	3.05	3	3.5	3	3	3	3	3	3	3	3
85	Dominican Rep., The	3.10	5	1.5	1	3	3	3	3	4	4	3.5
85	Guinea	3.10	5	3	1	3	3	2	2	4	4	4
85	Kenya	3.10	4	3.5	3	1	3	3	2	3	4	4.5
85	Mauritania	3.10	4	4	2	2	2	2	3	4	4	4
89	Cape Verde	3.15	4	4.5	4	1	3	3	3	3	2	4
89	Croatia	3.15	3	4	2	2	3	3	3	4	4	3.5
89	Gabon	3.15	5	4.5	2	1	3	3	3	3	4	3
92	Guyana	3.20	4	4	3	2	3	3	2	3	4	4
92	Moldova	3.20	2	3.5	3	4	3	3	3	3	4	3.5
94	Algeria	3.25	5	3.5	3	2	2	4	3	4	3	3
94	Burkina Faso	3.25	4	3.5	3	2	2	3	3	4	4	4
94	Lebanon	3.25	5	3.5	3	1	3	2	2	4	4	5
94	Macedonia	3.25	5	2.5	3	2	3	2	2	4	4	5
94	Mozambique	3.25	4	3.5	3	3	2	2	3	4	4	4
99	Djibouti	3.30	4	4	4	1	3	3	2	4	4	4
99	Gambia, The	3.30	4	3	3	2	3	3	3	3	4	5
99	Indonesia	3.30	3	2.5	3	3	3	4	2	4	4	4.5
99	Pakistan	3.30	5	3	3	2	3	3	3	4	3	4
99	Paraguay	3.30	3	2	3	3	3	3	3	4	4	5
104	Albania	3.35	5	3.5	3	2	2	3	2	4	4	5
104	Azerbaijan	3.35	3	3	3	1	4	4	3	4	4	4.5
104	Benin	3.35	4	3.5	3	2	3	3	3	4	4	4
104	Bulgaria	3.35	4	4	2	5	3	3	2	3	4	3.5
104	Cameroon	3.35	5	3	3	1	3	3	3	4	4	4.5
104	Egypt	3.35	4	5	3	1	3	4	3	3	4	3.5
104	Kyrgyz, Rep., The	3.35	4	2.5	2	4	3	3	3	4	4	4
104	Lesotho	3.35	3	4.5	3	3	3	3	3	3	4	4
104	Tanzania	3.35	5	2.5	2	3	3	3	3	4	4	4
113	Chad	3.40	5	4	2	3	3	2	2	4	4	5
113	Fiji	3.40	5	4	3	2	4	2	3	4	3	4
113	Georgia	3.40	4	2	2	4	3	3	3	4	4	5
113	Ghana	3.40	4	3	3	2	3	3	3	4	4	5
113	Niger	3.40	4	3	3	2	3	3	3	4	4	5
118	Ecuador	3.45	4	2.5	2	5	3	3	3	4	4	4
119	Bangladesh	3.50	5	2	3	1	3	4	3	4	5	5
119	Ethiopia	3.50	5	3.5	3	1	4	4	3	4	4	3.5
119	India	3.50	5	4	3	2	3	4	3	3	4	4

Table 4.2 *continued*

Rank		2003 Scores	Trade	Fiscal burden of government	Government intervention	Monetary policy	Foreign investment	Banking and finance	Wage/ prices	Property rights	Regulation	Black market
119	Kazakhstan	3.50	4	3	2	3	4	4	3	4	4	4
119	Nepal	3.50	5	2	2	2	4	4	3	4	4	5
119	Turkey	3.50	3	4.5	3	5	3	3	3	3	4	3.5
119	Venezuela	3.5	4	3	2	4	3	3	4	4	4	4
119	Zambia	3.50	4	4	2	5	3	3	3	3	4	4
127	China	3.55	5	3	4	1	4	4	3	4	4	3.5
128	Equatorial Guinea	3.60	5	2	2	3	3	4	4	4	4	5
128	Haiti	3.60	3	2	2	4	4	3	3	5	5	5
128	Togo	3.60	3	3	3	2	4	4	3	4	5	5
131	Malawi	3.65	4	4	3	5	3	4	3	3	4	3.5
131	Rwanda	3.65	5	2.5	3	2	4	3	3	4	5	5
131	Ukraine	3.65	3	4.5	3	4	4	3	3	4	4	4
131	Yemen	3.65	3	4.5	3	3	3	4	3	4	4	5
135	Congo, Republic of	3.70	5	4	3	1	4	4	3	4	4	5
135	Russia	3.70	4	3.5	2.5	5	3	4	3	4	4	4
135	Vietnam	3.70	5	3	3	1	4	4	3	5	5	4
138	Romania	3.75	4	4.5	3	5	3	3	3	4	4	4
139	Bosnia	3.80	2	4	5	2	4	3	3	5	5	5
140	Nigeria	3.85	5	3.5	3	4	3	4	3	4	4	5
140	Sierra Leone	3.85	5	3.5	2	3	4	4	2	5	5	5
142	Guinea Bissau	3.90	4	4	2	3	3	5	3	5	5	5
143	Suriname	3.95	4	4.5	4	5	3	4	3	3	4	5
143	Syria	3.95	4	4.5	4	1	4	5	4	4	4	5
143	Tajikistan	3.95	3	2.5	3	5	4	5	4	4	4	5
146	Iran	4.15	3	2.5	4	4	4	5	4	5	5	5
146	Turkmenistan	4.15	5	2.5	4	4	4	5	4	4	4	5
148	Burma	4.20	5	2	3	4	5	4	4	5	5	5
149	Uzbekistan	4.25	5	3.5	3	5	4	5	4	4	5	4
149	Yugoslavia	4.25	4	3.5	4	5	5	4	3	4	5	5
151	Belarus	4.30	4	4	3	5	4	4	5	4	5	5
151	Libya	4.30	5	3	4	1	5	5	5	5	5	5
153	Laos	4.40	5	3	3	5	4	5	4	5	5	5
153	Zimbabwe	4.40	5	4	3	5	5	5	4	5	4	4
155	Cuba	4.45	3	4.5	4	5	4	5	5	5	4	5
156	Korea, North	5.00	5	5	5	5	5	5	5	5	5	5

Due to economic and/or political instability, scoring was suspended this year for the following countries:

Angola	n/a
Burundi	n/a
Congo, Dem. Rep. Of	n/a
Iraq	n/a
Sudan	n/a

Source: 2003 Index of Economic Freedom, The Heritage Foundation/Wall Street Journal

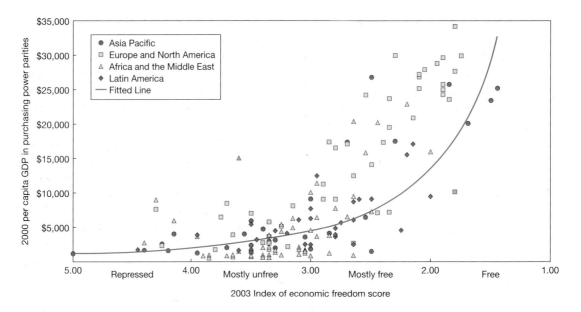

Figure 4.2 *Economic freedom and income*

Note Per capita GDP figures were not available for the following countries: Armenia, The Bahamas, Bahrain, Bosnia, Democratic Republic of Congo, Cuba, Djibouti, Iraq, North Korea, Kuwait, Lebanon, Libya, Malta, Oman, Qatar, Suriname, Taiwan, Tajikistan, United Arab Emirates, Yugoslavia. Per capita GDP figures are in current international dollars and are from 1999.

Source: The World Bank, *2001 Development Indicators on CD-ROM.*

As with the other two economic systems, there are degrees of capitalism. Japan, when compared to the USA, is relatively less capitalistic. Although practically all Japanese businesses are privately owned, industries are supervised very closely by the state. Japan has the MITI and other government agencies that vigorously advise companies what to produce, buy, sell, and so on. Japan's aim is to allocate scarce resources in such a way as to efficiently produce those products that have the best potential for the country overall. Japan's central bank also intervenes by buying shares of the listed companies from banks so as to manipulate the stock market.

In searching for the common characteristics of successful corporations, Chandler examined the 200 largest companies in the USA, Britain, and Germany from the 1880s through the 1940s and found that capitalism took a different form in each country.[13] It was "*managerial capitalism*" in the USA, where managers with little ownership ran companies and competed fiercely for markets and products. In Britain, "*personal capitalism*" took place as owners managed their companies. In Germany, it was "*cooperative capitalism*"; professional managers were in charge, and companies were urged to share markets and profits among themselves. This kind of Rhineland capitalism attempts to forge social consensus through behind-the-scenes deal making among big business, trade unions, and politicians. But global competition is now threatening this type of cooperation.

There are some other variants of capitalism. Quebec has state-assisted capitalism as the government runs the health system, all colleges and universities, liquor stores, and even a parking monopoly in downtown Montreal. While Quebecers seem to endorse the idea that the government is looking after their economic interests, they do not realize that there are hidden costs in terms of higher taxes, higher prices, and lost economic output.

In the case of China, Russia, Cambodia, and Vietnam, their economic system may be called "frontier capitalism". These communist or socialist countries are essentially at a new frontier as they experiment with capitalism. Government agencies themselves may even be involved in production for profit. While they are moving away from communism, their capitalistic infrastructure is not yet quite in place. It is thus difficult for anyone, including the government, to tell with certainty whether the property rights of local and foreign investors will be respected. Business laws simply fail to keep up with economic changes.

At a new frontier are China's economic and legal systems. The Chinese legal system was discarded after the 1949 communist revolution that sent attorneys and law professors to farm collectives. At present, China's rule of law is quite rudimentary. The country has only 150,000 lawyers, while the USA has eight times that number to serve the US population that is only a quarter of the Chinese population. Private business contracts are routinely enforced by bureaucrats who rely on government directives rather than on written case laws. E-commerce sales and contracts are not legally binding, and regulations are largely unpublished.[14]

Similarly, Russia is representative of transition economies. It is difficult to verify and enforce contracts there. Private property rights are neither secure nor credible. Given the lack of efficient methods for resolving commercial disputes, market entry costs increase substantially. Even when one wins in court, it is difficult to collect debts because of a notoriously weak enforcement system. Not surprisingly, most businesspeople, instead of taking their cases to the overburdened courts, prefer to try to resolve any disputes among themselves.

No nation operates under pure communism or pure capitalism, and most countries find it necessary to make some compromise between the two extremes. Even Eastern Bloc countries provided incentives for their managers, and China allows farmers to sell directly to consumers in local markets. Western European countries encourage free enterprise but intervene to provide support and subsidies for steel and farm products. The USA is also not a perfect model of capitalism. It has support prices for many dairy and farm products and has imposed price controls from time to time. Furthermore, the US economy is greatly affected by the Federal Reserve Board's control of the money supply and interest rates. Laissez-faire, the purest form of capitalism, is rare. In any case, there are no nations that allow businesses to be completely controlled by either the private or public sector.

Perhaps the only place that bears a close resemblance to an ideal free-trade market is Hong Kong. It does not even have a central bank, and the legal tender notes are issued by private commercial banks. In 2003, the Washington-based Heritage Foundation gave Hong Kong a rating of 1.45 on a scale of 1 to 5, making it first in terms of freedom from government intervention. The Heritage Foundation's index uses ten criteria (e.g., government policies toward trade, taxation, foreign investment, and money supply) to determine how much a government interferes in economic freedom.[15] The Washington-based Cato Institute also gave first place to Hong Kong. Cato's index, based on an economic freedom scale ranging from 1 to 10, relies on economic variables (e.g., inflation stability, tax rates, government spending) and social indicators (e.g., legal fairness and freedom to open a foreign bank account).

It would be presumptuous to say that capitalism, a system that encourages competition and efficiency, is the ideal system for all countries. It is true that Russia and Poland, for example, once set prices artificially low and thus had a great deal of difficulty in solving a supply dilemma. As a result, citizens were forced to stand in long lines for a small ration to meet their needs. But capitalism may be inappropriate for such countries as China because the system would allow wealth to be concentrated in the hands of a few people and subsequently leave the majority poor and hungry. Market action does not always serve the nation's best interests, particularly in areas of social need. Efficiency may be derived at the expense of jobs for the people, and the profit motive may intensify the inflation problem.

99

In Eastern Europe and to a lesser but significant extent in Latin America, widespread government interference and reliance on inefficient public enterprises have obstructed the normal operation of markets. After decades of state control and ownership, the worldwide movement toward market alliance and political freedom has forced both regions to replace their command systems with thriving private enterprises, which should allow producers to efficiently make the goods that consumers want.

The 1990s witnessed dramatic economic transformations. The former Soviet Union and Eastern European countries abandoned central planning. There was an initial outcry as output declined sharply, but by late 1990s recovery had taken place, albeit unevenly across countries. As in the case of the CIS, real output fell by 50 percent and did not recover until 1999. However, by 2000, Central and Southeastern Europe and the Baltics (CSB) had more than restored their original output levels.[16] Transition economies have shown a varying degree of economic performance. Those that have performed best are the ones which were most committed to the reform at the start and they have carried out reforms rapidly and consistently.[17]

POLITICAL RISKS

There are a number of political risks with which marketers must contend. Hazards based on a host government's actions include confiscation, expropriation, nationalization, domestication, and creeping expropriation. Such actions are more likely to be levied against foreign investments, though local firms' properties are not totally immune. Charles de Gaulle nationalized France's three largest banks in 1945, and more nationalization occurred in 1982 under the French socialists. Coca-Cola Co. managed to re-enter India in 1993, after being thrown out of the country fifteen years earlier by India's socialist government.

Confiscation is the process of a government's taking ownership of a property without compensation. An example of confiscation is the Chinese government's seizure of American property after the Chinese communists took power in 1949. A more recent example involves Occidental Petroleum whose assets were confiscated without compensation by Venezuela.

Expropriation differs somewhat from confiscation in that there is some compensation, though not necessarily just compensation. More often than not, a company whose property is being expropriated agrees to sell its operations – not by choice but rather due to some explicit or implied coercion.

After property has been confiscated or expropriated, it can be either nationalized or domesticated. **Nationalization** involves government ownership, and it is the government that operates the business being taken over. Burma's foreign trade, for example, is completely nationalized. Generally, this action affects a whole industry rather than only a single company. When Mexico attempted to control its debt problem, then-President Jose Lopez Portillo nationalized the country's banking system. In another case of nationalization, Libya's Colonel Gadhafi's vision of Islamic socialism led him to nationalize all private business in 1981. Unlike communists in Hungary and Poland, Czech communists nationalized 100 percent of their economy. Chile nationalized its large copper mines in 1971. By 1980, it had readmitted foreign investment and even provided incentives for foreign investment in the mining sector.[18]

In the case of **domestication**, foreign companies relinquish control and ownership, either completely or partially, to the nationals. The result is that private entities are allowed to operate the confiscated or expropriated property. The French government, after finding out that the state was not sufficiently proficient to run the banking business, developed a plan to sell thirty-six French banks.

Domestication may sometimes be a voluntary act that takes place in the absence of confiscation or nationalization. Usually, the causes of this action are either poor economic performance or social pressures. When situations worsened in South Africa and political pressures mounted at home, Pepsi sold its South African bottling operation to local investors, and Coca-Cola signaled that it would give control to a local company. General Motors followed suit by selling its operations to local South African management in 1986. Shortly thereafter, Barclays Bank made similar moves.

Another classification system of political risks is the one used by Root.[19] Based on this classification, four sets of political risks may be identified: general instability risk, ownership/control risk, operation risk, and transfer risk.

General instability risk is related to the uncertainty about the future viability of a host country's political system. The Iranian revolution that overthrew the Shah is an example of this kind of risk. In contrast, **ownership/control risk** is related to the possibility that a host government might take action (e.g., expropriation) to restrict an investor's ownership and control of a subsidiary in that host country.

Operation risk proceeds from the uncertainty that a host government might constrain the investor's business operations in all areas, including production, marketing, and finance. Finally, **transfer risk** applies to any future acts by a host government that might constrain the ability of a subsidiary to transfer payments, capital, or profit out of the host country back to the parent firm.

The 1970s was the peak period for expropriation activities. The number of expropriation acts peaked at eighty-three (involving twenty-eight countries) in 1975, representing 14.4 percent of all such acts (575) which took place between 1960 and 1992. It is encouraging to note that the trend may have reversed. Based on the 1980 to 1992 data, expropriation is unlikely in the future.[20] As a matter of fact, developing countries now appear to even want to protect foreign investors from it.

Governments' rationale for nationalization varies widely and includes national interests, vote getting, prevention of foreigners' exploitation, and an easy, cheap, and quick way of acquiring wealth. The risk of expropriation will likely be less in the future for several reasons. Many governments have experienced very poor records in running the businesses nationalized and have found that their optimistic projections have not materialized. Furthermore, many nations have realized that such actions have created difficulties in attracting new technology and foreign investment as well as in borrowing from foreign banks. There is also the possibility of open retaliation by other governments.

Although the threat of direct confiscation or expropriation has become remote, a new kind of threat has appeared. MNCs have generally been concerned with coups, revolutions, and confiscation, but they now have to pay attention to so-called creeping expropriation. The Overseas Private Investment Corporation (OPIC) defines creeping expropriation as "a set of actions whose cumulative effect is to deprive investors of their fundamental rights in the investment."[21] Laws that affect corporate ownership, control, profit, and reinvestment (e.g., currency inconvertibility or cancellation of import license) can be easily enacted. Because countries can change the rules in the middle of the game, companies must adopt adequate safeguards. Various defensive and protective measures will be discussed below.

A more recent but increasingly significant risk is creeping expropriation. As in the case of Conoco, it reached a joint venture agreement in 1992 and set up Polar Lights in Russia.[22] At that point in time in the early days of post-communist Russia, potential rewards for a pioneering oil company appeared to exceed risks, but in recent years, Russian government officials have issued demands from time to time to renegotiate the terms of the agreement. The government has claimed that its officials who negotiated the original deal did so illegally. A great deal of confusion and disagreement came from Russia's evolving laws dealing with underground resources. Since Russia is a good example of frontier capitalism, such ambiguities have to be expected.

BP, likewise, invested $500 million in Sidanco.[23] BP was upset when TNK bought Chernogorneft, a prized Siberian oilfield from Sidanco in a 1999 bankruptcy auction. Claiming that the purchase was illegal, BP threatened to leave. An understanding was reached in 2001 to return the oilfield to Sidanco. Subsequently, BP completed the biggest

101

foreign direct investment in post-communist Russia – a $7.7 billion deal giving BP a 50 percent share in the newly formed TNK-BP. Given the fact that Russia is the world's biggest crude oil producer, the country offers a great deal of potential. However, this potential in the country with frontier capitalism is also accompanied by a significant risk.

PRIVATIZATION

Both multinational and local firms should notice a trend toward privatization and its competitive implications. Government-owned enterprises are often characterized by overstaffing, poor financial performance, dependence on subsidies, centralized and politicized organizations, and lack of competition.[24] Among the objectives of privatization are: promotion of competition and efficiency, reduction of debt and subsidies, return of flight capital, and broadening domestic equity ownership.

Countries which are likely to pursue privatization tend to have the following characteristics: high budget deficits, high foreign debt, and high dependence on such international agencies as the World Bank and the International Monetary Fund. In Latin America and Asia, countries pursuing privatization are those which have overused state enterprises and those with the private sector growing faster than average, making them more ready to assume tasks once assigned to state enterprises. In Africa, however, privatization may have been imposed by external agencies, even though these countries are not necessarily ready for this task.[25]

Governments have learned a number of lessons from privatization. Policy makers need to understand that privatization is a political process and that support from the highest political level is necessary. A successful program requires economic reform, and the privatization strategy should be tailored to a country's circumstances. In addition, the privatization process should be transparent.

Should centrally planned economies adopt the *big bang* approach or *gradualism* in reforming their economies? Evidence from the ex-communist countries appears to indicate that it is better to quickly switch to capitalism so that market forces can do their work.[26] In the case of Eastern Europe, all transition economies took the big bang approach by rapidly liberalizing the goods and foreign exchange markets, resulting initially in a steep fall in output. On the other hand, China and Vietnam chose the gradualist approach and have fared better. However, both countries, unlike their Eastern European counterparts, did not begin the reform process in the wake of revolutionary political changes and a collapse of central governing systems which forced the Eastern European economies to move quickly to free prices while imposing current account convertibility. Therefore, the choice of strategy is dependent on the economy's political circumstances and economic structure. In any case, no working model exists of a "functioning market economy with a massive state enterprise sector."[27]

One study examined the impact of governance structures on privatized firms in terms of export intensity. Based on a longitudinal multi-industry set of data involving private firms in Russia, Ukraine, and Belarus, it found that export intensity was mediated by strategies involving product development, acquisitions, and links with foreign partners. The relationship between managerial control and foreign partners changed from positive to negative over time, and it is thus crucial to take a dynamic perspective in transition economies.[28]

INDICATORS OF POLITICAL INSTABILITY

To assess a potential marketing environment, a company should identify and evaluate the relevant indicators of political difficulty. Potential sources of political complication include social unrest, the attitudes of nationals, and the policies of the host government.

The breakup of the Soviet Union should not come as a surprise. Human nature involves monostasy (the urge to stand alone) as well as systasy (the urge to stand together), and the two concepts provide alternative ways of using resources to meet a society's needs.[29] Monostasy encourages competition, but systasy emphasizes cooperation. As explained by Alderson, "a cooperative society tends to be a closed society. Closure is essential if the group is in some sense to act as one." Not surprisingly, China, although wanting to modernize its economy, does not fully embrace an open economy, which is likely to encourage dissension among the various groups. For the sake of its own survival, a cooperative society may have to obstruct the dissemination of new ideas and neutralize an external group that poses a threat. China has apparently learned a lesson from the Soviet Union's experience.

A liberated political climate can easily lead to a call of the long-suppressed national minority groups for cultural and territorial independence. The groups' past conflicts, unsettled but subdued during the communist period, are likely to escalate. Three kinds of conflict may result.[30] First, a domestic dispute may escalate into violence that is confined within the boundaries of the country in question. The civil war that started in 1991 between Serbs and Croats in Yugoslavia is a good example. Another example is the centuries-old ethnic animosity between Christians in Armenia and Muslims ir neighboring Azerbaijan, which led some 60(Armenian nationalists to clash with Soviet soldie during earthquake rescue efforts in Armen Second, an internal dispute may draw interes parties outside the country in question into conflict. For example, problems in Yugosla Macedonia may force Bulgaria and Greece to i vene. Finally, the third form of conflict, res either from the first two kinds of conflict or an international dispute, may lead to a dire frontation between two countries. Romar Hungary, which have deep-rooted gri against each other, could become involve form of conflict.

Attitudes of nationals

An assessment of the political climate i plete without an investigation of the atti citizens and government of the host

nationals' attitude toward foreign enterprises and citizens can be quite inhospitable. Nationals are often concerned with foreigners' intentions in regard to exploitation and colonialism, and these concerns are often linked to concerns over foreign governments' actions that may be seen as improper. Such attitudes may arise out of local socialist or nationalist philosophies, which may be in conflict with the policy of the company's home-country government. Any such inherent hostility is certain to present major problems because of its relative permanence. Governments may come and go, but citizens' hostility may remain. This kind of problem may explain why twelve US firms decides to leave El Salvador in the 1980s. Their departure meant the loss of some 20 percent of US capital investment in that country.

Policies of the host government

Unlike citizens' inherent hostility, a government's attitude toward foreigners is often relatively short-lived. The mood can alter either over time or with a change in leadership, and it can alter for either ~ worse. The impact of a change in mood
~cially in the short run.
~· ·+ busi-

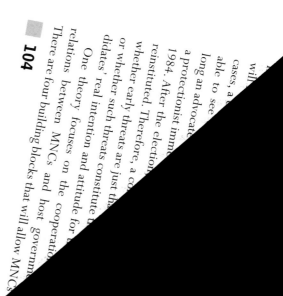

104

There are four building blocks that will allow MNCs
relations between MNCs and host governm
One theory focuses on the cooperatio
didates' real intention and attitude for
or whether such threats constitute t
whether early threats are just th
reinstituted. Therefore, a co
1984. After the election
a protectionist imme
long an advocate
able to see
cases, a
will

MARKETING ETHICS 4.1   A NECESSARY EVIL

The military junta of Myanmar (Burma) is viewed with disdain and disgust in most parts of the world – except by the governments of India and Thailand. While India is the world's largest democracy, it does not mind doing business with the Myanmar dictatorship. To India, it is a matter of necessity. India recognizes that its two threats, China and Pakistan, supply defense equipment to Myanmar. As a result, it feels compelled to engage Myanmar's military regime in a friendly way. India has been quiet about the military junta's policies toward Aung San Suu Kyi and has assisted Myanmar in building crucial border roads.

In spite of worldwide pressure and condemnation, Thailand has refused to join the world community in demanding the Burmese rulers to end their violent oppression of their own people. Thailand's prime minister, Thaksin Shinawatra, even stated that he would side with Myanmar. His deputy prime minister unabashedly proclaimed: "China and Thailand are Burma's good allies." This position is surprising, given the Rangoon government's hostile attitudes toward Thailand. Could it be that the prime minister, who also happens to be a business tycoon, is supporting the Burmese dictators for personal (i.e., business) reasons? As commented by the *Bangkok Post*, "In the future, when the military dictatorship collapses, as they all do, Thailand will be singled out as a junta-friendly reason for the delay in democracy. This will affect the treatment of Thailand and Thais by the next Rangoon government."

Sources: "India's Relations with Burma a Necessary Evil," *Times of India*, October 19, 2000; "Editorial: On the Wrong Side of the Burma Issue," *Bangkok Post*, September 9, 2003.

activities and tactics can very easily create an unwelcome atmosphere for foreign firms. When French politicians cited the fact that one French worker became unemployed for every five to ten Japanese cars imported, the government held up imported cars when the election was a few weeks away. The industry minister used every conceivable excuse to avoid signing the required certificates.

The use of unfriendly rhetoric before an election may be nothing but a smokescreen, and the "bark" not necessarily be followed by a "bite." In such company need not take drastic action if it is through the election. Ronald Reagan, of free trade, became something of diately before his re-election in a policy of free trade was mpany must determine t and nothing more e political can-the future. n-based ent.

to improve their cooperative relationships with governments: (1) resource commitment, (2) personal relations, (3) political accommodation, and (4) organizational credibility. A study of 131 MNCs in China confirms the importance of these blocks.[31]

One model proposes that organizations may employ three political strategies: information, financial incentive, and constituency building. While an MNC may have a particular global strategy when dealing with governments, its subsidiaries may still have to employ specific activities in host-country contexts. As such, a subsidiary's response must be consistent with a host country's characteristics as well as with the imperatives of the headquarters. The more integrated a subsidiary is with its affiliates in a strategic sense, the greater it is integrated with the other subsidiaries in a political sense.[32]

ANALYSIS OF POLITICAL RISK OR COUNTRY RISK

Although political scientists, economists, businesspeople, and business scholars have some ideas about what political risk is, they seem to have difficulties agreeing both on its definition and on methods to predict danger. Perhaps due to this lack of agreement on the definition, many different methods have been employed to measure, analyze, and predict political risks.

Political risk is an uncertainty that stems from the exercise of power by governments and non-governmental actors. Typical hazards include political instability, politicized government policy, political violence, expropriation, creeping expropriation, contract frustration, and currency inconvertibility.

Some assessment methods are country specific in the sense that a risk report is based on a particular country's unique political and economic circumstances. As such, there is lack of a consistent framework that would allow comparison across countries. Since an MNC must decide to allocate resources based on potential opportunities and risk associated with each country, a common methodology is essential.

Even when a systematic attempt is made for cross-national comparisons, the methods used vary greatly. Some are nothing more than checklists consisting of a large number of relevant issues that are applicable to each country. Other systems rely on questionnaires sent to experts or local citizens in order to gauge the political mood. Such scoring systems, which permit numerical ratings of countries, have gained acceptance. Some institutions have turned to econometrics for this purpose. Marine Midland Bank, for example, uses econometrics to rate various countries in terms of economic risk. The method, however, is not perfect.

To many small- and medium-sized firms, doing their own country-risk analyses is out of the question because of the cost, expertise, and resources required. However, there are some alternatives that can provide a useful assessment of political risk. One is to interview people who have some knowledge or experience with the countries of interest, including businesspeople, bankers, and government officials. Molex Inc., a manufacturer of high-technology electrical products, has been able to protect itself by listening to international bankers, lawyers,

and accounting firms. Another method is to rely on the advice of firms specializing in this area. Controlled Risks, a Washington area firm, advises about 400 US companies on the danger of doing business in seventy countries. For fees that can total $9000 a year, the firm offers information and provides training for executives on how to protect themselves, cope with kidnapping and extortion, and guide their employees in political crises.

Many banks can help their clients to assess business risks overseas. Bank of America, for example, provides international economic analyses and forecasts to customers through World Information Services (WIS). Subscribers of WIS receive Country Outlooks, Country Data Forecasts, and Country Risk Monitor. Bank of America uses a ranking system based on a common set of economic and financial criteria to evaluate eighty countries for business risk. In addition to current rankings, a ten-year historical track of each country is also shown. Country Risk Monitor allows risk comparisons of countries with benchmark risk indicators for major country groupings. Updates are regularly provided.

According to one study, in evaluating country creditworthiness, banks use both political instability and economic variables, with larger weight assigned to economic variables.[33] In other words, perceived country creditworthiness is a function of a country's economic performances which reflect longer term political stability. The credit ratings are also affected by the two proxies for political instability: armed conflicts and the frequency of changes in the regime.

Another alternative is to subscribe to reports prepared for this purpose. One valuable report is the **country credit rating** prepared by *Institutional Investor* magazine. Based on a survey of approximately 100 leading international banks concerning a country's creditworthiness and the chance of payment default, rankings are assigned to 100 countries every six months. Greater weight is given to the responses of those banks that have the largest global exposure and which possess the most sophisticated systems of risk analysis. Yet the loan problems encountered by the Bank of America and

Citicorp make it clear that the risk-analysis systems used by some of the world's largest banks are anything but foolproof.

Another relatively simple method is based on **LIBOR (London Interbank rate)**. LIBOR, relatively risk-free, is the interest rate charged for loans between banks. Nonbank borrowers, of course, have to pay a premium over LIBOR, with the premium (i.e., the spread between the loan rate and LIBOR) indicating the extent of risk involved. A borrower from a country with a high risk of default must expect a high premium. The premium is thus a good indicator of risk because it reflects a lender's assessment of the country in terms of debt levels and payment records. Since all loans are not comparable, adjustment must be made for volume and maturity. *Euromoney* magazine has devised a formula to allow for this adjustment, and its formula to compute a country's spread index is the following:

[(volume X spread) / *Euromoney* index] / (volume X maturity)

By simply examining the spread index of a particular country and comparing it with those of other countries, an investor can arrive at the conclusion of a degree of risk associated with the country of interest.

Although *Euromoney*'s and *Institutional Investor*'s country risk ratings are derived in different ways, the two measures are highly correlated and strongly agree on the creditworthiness of the assessed countries. Both magazines' ratings can be replicated to a significant degree with a few economic variables. "In particular, both the level of per capita income and propensity to invest affect positively the rating of a country. In addition, high-ranking countries are less indebted than low-ranking countries."[34]

One study examined the projections of *The Economist*, Political Risk Services (PRS), and BERI (Business Environment Risk Intelligence) against losses incurred in the 1987 to 1992 period. The PRS predictors, when decomposed, appeared to be the most reliable. On the other hand, BERI's projections were superior to *The Economist*'s.[35]

One study examined eleven widely used measures of country risk across seventeen countries over nineteen years. According to the results, "commercial risk measures are very poor at predicting actual realized risks." Yet managers still continue to rely on ratings agencies. One reason is that the purchasing cost of this type of information is miniscule when compared to the amount of FDI to be committed.[36]

As assessment methods of political risks have become more sophisticated, there has been a shift from the earlier conceptual and qualitative approaches to those that are quantitative and derivative of applied research. There is a need, however, to integrate these two major kinds of approaches.

MANAGEMENT OF POLITICAL RISK

To manage political risk, an MNC can pursue a strategy of either avoidance or insurance. **Avoidance** means screening out politically uncertain countries. In this, measurement and analysis of political risk can be useful. **Insurance**, in contrast, is a strategy to shift the risk to other parties. This strategy will be covered in detail below.

There are other strategies that MNCs can use to safeguard their foreign investments. They may want to come to an understanding with a foreign government as to their rights and responsibilities. They can increase and maintain their bargaining power when their technical, operational, and managerial complexity requirements are not within reach of a host country's abilities.

In addition, there are several managerial strategies which are relevant. A firm may try to gain "control" of the situation through political activities, market power, exchange of threats, vertical integration, and horizontal mergers and acquisitions. Or it may try to gain "cooperation" through long-term contractual agreements, alliances, interlocking directorates, interfirm personnel flows, and so on. Furthermore, it may pursue product and/or geographic diversification to gain "flexibility." Operational flexibility can also be achieved through flexible input sourcing and multinational production.[37]

IT'S THE LAW 4.1 "DOS AND DON'TS" FOR EXPORTING TO NORTH KOREA

North Korea is one of the world's most centralized economies. Agricultural production is collectivized, state-owned industry produces nearly all manufactured goods, and the heavy and military industries have traditionally been favored at the expense of consumer goods. North Korea's major industries include military and machinery production, chemical production, mining (coal, iron ore, magnesite, graphite, copper, zinc, lead and precious metals), metallurgy, textiles, and food processing.

Dos

- Be sure that the ultimate purchaser and end-user of the items is not associated with North Korean missile technology exports. This is especially important when a license is not required (e.g., export of an EAR99 item).
- Be aware of the instability of the North Korean financial sector. There is little, if any, fungible capital in the consumer economy since everything is provided by state enterprises. Initially, cash deals with prepayment may be the best way to structure your exports to the North Korean government until you gain confidence that you can be paid by more conventional (e.g., electronic, letters of credit) methods.
- US exporters are encouraged to establish direct contact with the North Korean government, either in Pyongyang itself, through the North Korean mission to the United Nations or the North Korean embassy in Beijing, to ascertain DPRK laws and regulations for doing business in North Korea.

Familiarize yourself with North Korean import guidelines.

- Be sure to make whatever agreements you reach with prospective customers in North Korea contingent on your receiving an appropriate US Department of Commerce export license for the particular export transaction, if goods require a license.

Don'ts

- Don't assume that North Korea is like a Western environment for business and investment.
- Don't expect there to be any real infrastructure for your proposed production or assembly venture in North Korea, or assume that basic industrial resources such as water, electricity, roads, or airports will be available.
- Don't mix controlled and noncontrolled goods in shipments to North Korea.
- Be wary of doing noncash deals, at least until you are comfortable with the payment performance of your North Korean customer.
- Don't expect your customer to obtain the necessary import, export or tariff permits for doing business in North Korea, unless this is required. You are better off approaching North Korean government officials directly with your request.
- Don't ship anything on the Commerce Control List. There is a presumption of denial for all controlled goods to North Korea.

Source: William Golike and Chris Chesterfield, "Export Restrictions on North Korea," *Export America*, 13.

The rapid changes in Eastern Europe present both challenges and opportunities. In the former days of centralization, a trade minister in the capital could speak for the entire nation, but with decentralized decision making, an MNC has to go to the many republics for information and approval. When doing business there, companies need to be creative in terms of long-term thinking and financing.

MEASURES TO MINIMIZE POLITICAL RISK

Political risk, though impossible to eliminate, can at the very least be minimized. There are several measures that MNCs can implement in order to discourage a host country from taking control of MNC assets.

Stimulation of the local economy

One defensive investment strategy calls for a company to link its business activities with the host country's national economic interests. Brazil expelled Mellon Bank because of the banks' refusal to cooperate in renegotiating the country's massive foreign debt.

A local economy can be stimulated in a number of different ways. One strategy may involve the company purchasing local products and raw materials for its production and operations. By assisting local firms, it can develop local allies who can provide valuable political contacts. A modification of this strategy would be to use subcontractors. For example, some military tank manufacturers tried to secure tank contracts from the Netherlands by agreeing to subcontract part of the work on the new tanks to Dutch companies.

In 1985, all the Toyota vehicles sold in America were imported. This practice is no longer in place. Toyota now produces more than half a million vehicles each year in Kentucky and California. The company has invested more than $5 billion in American operations, not counting another $6.2 billion through its Toyota, Lexus, and Toyota Industrial Equipment dealers. It works with more than 400 US suppliers to forge economic ties, and its purchases of American parts and materials have risen to more than $5 billion annually. Toyota boasts that nearly every dollar earned by its US operations since US manufacturing began has been reinvested in American payrolls, purchases, plants, and other facilities. The company's American factories and dealerships employ 123,000 Americans, more than Coca-Cola, Microsoft, and Oracle combined. Toyota's top executives in the USA are increasingly American. The success is easy to see: Toyota is now selling more vehicles in the USA than in Japan, and almost two-thirds of the company's operating profit is derived from the US market.[38]

Sometimes local sourcing is compulsory. Governments may require products to contain locally manufactured components because local content improves the economy in two ways: (1) it stimulates demand for domestic components, and (2) it saves the necessity of a foreign exchange transaction. Further investment in local production facilities by the company will please the government that much more. At one time IBM was the only foreign company allowed to sell switchboards in France because the firm's PBXs were made there.

Finally, the company should attempt to assist the host country by being export oriented. Both United Brands and Castle and Cooke were able to survive the Sandinista revolution in Nicaragua by implementing this strategy. Their export dollars became vital to the Nicaraguan government, thus shielding their Latin American operations from expropriation. AT&T was able to enter the French telephone switch market by agreeing to assist CGE, a French nationalized switch maker, in selling smaller digital switches in the USA.

Employment of nationals

Frequently, foreigners make the simple but costly mistake of assuming that citizens of less developed countries are poor by choice. It serves no useful purpose for a company to assume that local people are lazy, unintelligent, unmotivated, or uneducated. Such an attitude may become a self-fulfilling prophecy. Thus the hiring of local workers should go beyond the filling of labor positions. United Brands' policy, for example, is to hire only locals as managers.

Firms should also carefully weigh the impact of automation in a cheap-labor, high-unemployment area. Automation does not go down well in India, where job creation, not job elimination, is national policy. Technology is neither always welcomed nor always socially desirable. An inability to automate production completely does not necessarily constitute a negative for MNCs. MNCs may gain more in less developed countries by using "intermediate technology" instead of the most advanced equipment. Intermediate technology, accompanied by additional labor, is less expensive, and it promotes goodwill by increasing employment.

Sharing ownership

Instead of keeping complete ownership for itself, a company should try to share ownership with others, especially with local companies. One method is to convert from a private to a public company or from a foreign to a local company. Dragon Airline, claiming it is a real Chinese company, charged that Cathay Pacific Airways' Hong Kong landing rights should be curtailed because Cathay Pacific was more British than Chinese. The threat forced Cathy Pacific to sell a new public issue to allow Chinese investors to have minority interests in the company. The move was made to convince Hong Kong and China that the company had Chinese roots.

One of the most common techniques for shared ownership is to simply form a joint venture. Any loss of control as a result can, in most cases, be more than compensated for by the derived benefits. United Brands' policy in South America is not to initiate any business unless local joint-venture partners can be found to help spread the risk.

In some overseas business ventures, it is not always necessary to have local firms as partners. Sometimes, having co-owners from other nations can work almost as well. Having multiple nationality for international business projects not only reduces exposure; it also makes it difficult for the host government to take over the business venture without offending a number of nations all at once. The political situation in South Africa was one of the reasons Ford chose to merge its automobile operations there with Anglo American. The merger reduced Ford's exposure to a 40 percent minority position.

Voluntary domestication, in most cases, is not a desirable course of action because it is usually a forced decision. The company should therefore plan for domestication in advance instead of waiting until it is required, because by that time the company has lost much of its leverage and bargaining power. This strategy is also likely to be perceived as a gesture of goodwill, an accomplishment in addition to the desired reduction of exposure. A wise strategy may be for the company to retain the marketing or technical side of the business while allowing heavy local ownership in the physical assets and capital-intensive portions of the investment.

Being civic minded

MNCs whose home country is the USA often encounter the "ugly American" label abroad, and this image should be avoided. It is not sufficient that the company simply does business in a foreign country; it should also be a good corporate citizen there. To shed this undesirable perception, multinationals should combine investment projects with civic projects.

Corporations rarely undertake civic projects out of total generosity, but such projects make economic sense in the long run. It is highly desirable to provide basic assistance because many civic entities exist in areas with minimal or nonexistent municipal infrastructures that would normally provide these facilities. A good idea is to assist in building schools, hospitals, roads, and water systems because such projects benefit the host country as well as the company, especially in terms of the valuable goodwill generated in the long run. Toyota has invested in local communities. A portion of its US profits is allocated each year to support community programs. Over a period of three years, it has contributed $38 million to such philanthropic organizations as United Negro College Fund, Teach for America, and Special Olympics. In addition, the company spent more than $1.5 million to help the victims of the Midwest floods, East Coast hurricanes, and the fires and earthquakes in California.

There are many examples of global philanthropy. It is wise to remember that in many less developed countries, a small sum of money can go a long way.

Political neutrality

For the best long-term interests of the company, it is not wise to become involved in political disputes among local groups or between countries. A company should state clearly but discreetly that it is not in the political business and that its primary concerns are economic in nature. Brazilian firms employ this strategy and keep a low profile in matters related to Central American revolutions and Cuban troops in foreign countries. Brazilian arms are thus attractive to the Third World because those arms are free of ideological ties. In such a case, a purchasing country does not feel obligated to become politically aligned with a seller, as when buying from the USA or China.

Behind-the-scenes lobby

Much like the variables affecting business, political risks can be reasonably managed. Companies as well as special interest groups have varying interests, and each party will want to make its own opinion known. When the US mushroom industry asked for a quota against imports from China, Pizza Hut came to China's rescue by claiming that most domestic and other foreign suppliers could not meet its specifications. Pizza Hut has a great deal at stake because it is one of China's largest customers as well as a user of half of some nine million pounds of mushrooms for pizzas – not to mention the desire of PepsiCo, its parent, to open a factory in southern China. Subsequently, the petition of the US mushroom industry was denied.

When practical, firms should attempt to influence political decisions. Mobil Corporation, for example, ran newspaper advertisements emphasizing the importance of the USA–China relations (see Figure 4.3).

Even though a firm's operation is affected by the political environment, the direction of the influence does not have to flow in one direction only. Lobbying activities can be undertaken, and it is wise to lobby quietly behind the scenes in order not to cause unnecessary political clamor. For importers, they must let their government know why imports are crucial to them and their consumers.

Companies may not only have to lobby in their own country, but they may also have to lobby in the host country. Companies may want to do the lobbying themselves, or they may let their government do it on their behalf. Their government can

be requested to apply pressure against foreign governments.

Observation of political mood and reduction of exposure

Marketers should be sensitive to changes in political mood. A contingency plan should be in place. When the political climate turns hostile, measures are necessary to reduce exposure. Some major banks and MNCs took measures to reduce their exposure in France in response to a fear that a Socialist–Communist coalition might gain control of the legislature in the elections of 1978. Their concern was understandable, since most of these companies were on the Left's nationalization list. Their defensive strategy included the outflow of capital, the transfer of patents and other assets to foreign subsidiaries, and the sale of equity holdings to foreigners and French nationals living abroad. Once concluded, such activities made it difficult for the socialist government to nationalize the companies' properties. Prudence required that these transactions be kept quiet so as to avoid reprisals.

Other measures

There are a few other steps that MNCs can undertake to minimize political risk. One strategy could involve keeping a low profile. Because it is difficult to please all the people all the time, it may be desirable for a company to be relatively inconspicuous. For example, in the 1980s, Texas Instruments removed identifying logos and signs in El Salvador.

Another tactic could involve trying to adopt a local personality. A practice approach may require that the company blend in with the environment. There is not much to be gained by a company being ethnocentric and trying to Americanize, Europeanize, or Japanize the host country's citizens. A veteran of international business would very likely realize that it is far better to be flexible and adaptable. Such a firm would know that it should behave like a chameleon, adapting itself to fit the environment. The main reason that McDonald's uses local

China trade:
self-interest and statesmanship

This month, the Congress will again consider the critical American interests related to China and international trade. The House of Representatives will soon vote whether to extend normal trade relations with China for another year. We urge the House to do what it and the rest of the U.S. government have done for many years: support ongoing trade with China, encourage engagement with that country and its people, and underscore America's commitment to open international trade and investment.

Last year, Congress passed and President Clinton signed legislation establishing **permanent** normal trade relations with China. However, permanent normalization was contingent upon China joining the World Trade Organization (WTO). Negotiation of the many bilateral and multilateral agreements necessary to do this has been prolonged, forcing the normal trade status to be renewed annually until China joins the WTO.

President Bush has wisely chosen to continue normal trade. Recently, U.S. Trade Representative Robert Zoellick announced that the U.S. and China have reached consensus on bilateral trade arrangements. This will help pave the way for China's WTO membership, possibly this year.

Because China and the United States have a number of disagreements in important areas unrelated to trade, some in the House would like to "send a message" to China by passing a resolution withdrawing normal trade relations. It is our view that this would be unwise.

The importance of U.S.-China relations transcends dollars and cents

The importance of U.S.-Chinese economic relations transcends dollars and cents. A healthy economic relationship helps establish a solid platform for cooperation and dialogue on many other matters. It presents an arena in which understanding can grow, and a vehicle through which beneficial change can take place.

Normal trade relations are important in promoting economic reform in China. The economic links are vital to Chinese citizens who depend to a great extent on overseas trade for their livelihood and their hopes for the future. And the economic relationship between American and Chinese firms has been a key element in opening China to greater reliance on market-based approaches and greater familiarity with advanced business practices.

Economic relations have been one of the most successful areas of cooperation and growth involving our two countries. China is America's second-largest trading partner, with total trade exceeding $120 billion. U.S. exports to China grew 36 percent in the first quarter of this year, helping cushion the U.S. economic slowdown. U.S. investments in China now approach $30 billion. These economic links strengthen our economy and bring benefits to virtually every American consumer through lower prices.

Accordingly, we urge the House to reject the call for a suspension of normal trade relations with China. Both statesmanship and self-interest argue for continued support of this vital intergovernmental and economic relationship.

ExxonMobil™

Figure 4.3 *Politics and economics*

Source: Mobil Corp.

corporate staff is to make it look like a local company. This is also the goal of Hawley Group. That company is thought to be American in the USA, British in the United Kingdom, and Australian in Australia.

Multinational firms, due to their presence in a large number of countries, must be mindful of terrorist threats. According to the World Markets Research Center, the top ten countries deemed to be the most likely targets of a terrorist attack are: (1) Colombia, (2) Israel, (3) Pakistan, (4) the USA, (5) the Philippines, (6) Afghanistan, (7) Indonesia, (8) Iraq, (9) India, and (10) the United Kingdom.[39]

A survey of US-based MNCs found that less than 50 percent had formal programs to deal with a terrorist attack.[40] Most of the MNCs with anti-terrorist programs focus on security equipment rather than on training executives and their families. Some of the activities included in anti-terrorist training are: defensive driving, self-defense, kidnapping avoidance, behavior after/during kidnapping,

negotiating skills, weapon handling, collecting information from local sources on terrorists, and protection of assets.

Finally, various defensive precautions can be implemented. Automobile drivers should be trained in how to react to a kidnapping attempt, and managers themselves should be instructed in how to deal with the unexpected and taught especially to avoid driving routine routes. Very basic precautions might be undertaken. For example, in El Salvador, Texas Instruments erected protective walls for its facilities and employed extra guards. It is better to be safe than sorry (see Marketing Strategy 4.1).

POLITICAL INSURANCE

In addition to the strategies of risk avoidance and risk reduction, MNCs can employ the strategy of risk shifting. Insurance coverage may be obtained from a number of sources.

MARKETING STRATEGY 4.1 BETTER SAFE THAN SORRY

Chubb, IG and Lloyd's of London are among a small group of insurers which have long offered policies to cover ransom demands for kidnappers. The coverage has been expanded to include legal and psychiatric fees, and compensation for loss of trade secrets and product tampering. Some policies may cover costs incurred when evacuating a politically unstable country. Executives may receive training on how to avoid being kidnapped.

Premiums may run from $1000 to $100,000 a year – depending on the coverage. The premium also varies according to the countries which executives visit most often. As an example, the premium is higher if it involves Latin America, and lower in the case of Europe and Japan. Individuals may buy the insurance if their employers do not provide such a coverage. There is extra cost to cover accidental death and dismemberment. Since it is illegal to purchase

ransom insurance in Germany and Colombia, executives visiting these countries need to buy the coverage elsewhere.

The US government sent $50 billion to state and local governments for homeland security, and private contractors will benefit from it. Security companies guard against employee theft, train bodyguards in evasive driving techniques, teach executives to minimize dangers (e.g., no name and title on a limousine window), and arrange ransom payoffs. They currently offer emergency response (e.g., evacuation and repatriation of overseas personnel), business continuity (e.g., backing up the data system and anti-hacker defenses), vulnerability assessment (e.g., identifying weak points in anti-terror defense), and background checks (identifying problem workers and subcontractors).

Source: "Your Jitters Are Their Lifeblood," *Business Week,* April 14, 2003, 41.

Private insurance

Through ignorance, a large number of companies end up as self-insurers. A better plan would be to follow Club Med's example by shifting political risk to a third party through the purchase of political insurance.

Some insurance companies even insure sales and profits. British Aerospace, for example, has a $70 million policy that guarantees $3.7 billion in revenue from aircraft leasing until the end of 2013. Honeywell has a blanket policy to insure its foreign exchange exposure and other risks, and may expand to include interest rate hedges, weather, and commodity prices.

Currency inconvertibility is often the most common type of political risk claim. A coverage of this type does not protect against currency devaluation. On the other hand, political violence (e.g., civil disturbances and wars) has been increasing. In addition, political disruption can stem from such multilateral bodies as the United Nations, and the disruption includes sanctions and embargoes. Once a company plans to cover commercial risk, it may as well include political risk. After all, the extra premium is not that great.[41]

Although property expropriation seems to be the most common reason for obtaining political insurance, the policy should include coverage for kidnapping, terrorism, and creeping expropriation. Information about most companies' coverage is rather scarce, since it is both imprudent and impermissible for companies to reveal that they are carrying kidnap insurance. Revelation of such coverage would only serve to encourage such activity. While AIG and other insurers have been offering corporate and individual kidnapping-and-ransom insurance policies for quite some time, Chubb now offers a free kidnapping-and-ransom upgrade for homeowners' insurance.[42]

Government insurance

MNCs do not have to rely solely on private insurers. There are nonprofit, public agencies that can provide essentially the same kind of coverage.

For US firms, the two primary ones are OPIC and FCIA.

Overseas Private Investment Corporation (OPIC) is a US government agency that assists economic development through investment insurance and credit financing programs. It is a business-oriented agency whose purpose is to support US private investments. Chartered by Congress in 1981, OPIC is a financially self-sustaining, independent corporation that receives no public funds. Its contracts, however, are fully backed by the US government, a sole owner of the corporation.

OPIC provides several forms of assistance, with political risk insurance as its primary business. It has three type of insurance protection to cover the risks of: (1) currency inconvertibility, (2) expropriation (including creeping expropriation), and (3) loss or damage caused by war, revolution, or insurrection. A typical insurance contract runs for up to twenty years at a combined annual premium of 1.5 percent for all three coverages. Considering that private insurers issue a three-year policy, OPIC's coverage is a positive feature. OPIC's assistance was instrumental in Motorola Inc.'s decision to enter the Nicaraguan market to install, operate, and maintain a cellular telephone service.

The USA has the Ex-Im Export Credit Insurance Program to help American exporters and their export activities by protecting them against risks of nonpayment for political or commercial reasons. Political risks of default, often beyond a buyer's control, are caused by government action, and examples of such risks are political violence or war, government intervention, or cancellation of a firm's license. In contrast, a commercial risk stems from the buyer's inability to fulfill one's payment obligations. This US program thus offers policies that cover single or multiple export sales and leases. Short-term policies cover 100 percent of principal for political risk and 90 to 95 percent for commercial risk, plus a specified amount of interest. Capital goods may be insured for up to five years under a medium-term policy.

Foreign Credit Insurance Association (FCIA) is an association of some fifty leading US companies in the marine and casualty insurance field. Created in 1961, FCIA makes it possible for US firms to become internationally competitive by insuring US exports of both goods and services against commercial and political risks.

MIGA

MIGA (Multilateral Investment Guarantee Agency) was established in 1988 to help its more than 100 member states create an attractive investment climate. Its mission is to promote private investment in developing countries through insuring investment against noncommercial (i.e., political) risk. MIGA works as a co-insurer with, or a reinsurer of, other insurers. It offers four types of coverage: currency transfer, expropriation, war and civil disturbances, and breach of contract. Premiums depend on the type of project, type of coverage, and project-specific conditions. Annual premiums for each coverage are in the range of 0.50 to 1.25 percent of the amount insured. MIGA's rates are slightly higher than those of other national insurers.

In sum, when it comes to political risk, companies tend to be reactive. As a result, they often have to devise an expensive strategy to deal with damage control. It is much more desirable to be proactive by developing a comprehensive and systematic view of the factors that drive risks.[43] There are three basic sets. First, there are external drivers such as political instability (e.g., coups and riots) and poor public policy (e.g., hyperinflation and currency crises). Second, interaction drivers are based on relationships between a company and external actors. Finally, internal drivers include the company's quality of its political risk management processes. In general, the company is not in a position to influence external drivers (e.g., making a host country more politically or economically stable). It should therefore focus on assessing risks and managing their impacts. As an example, since kidnapping is a significant risk, one should assess the likelihood of its occurrence. In statistical terms, it is more likely for a person to become a road traffic accident victim than a kidnap victim. On the other hand, being kidnapped and held for ransom is arguably the most traumatic experience for anyone. As such, firms should train their employees to take precautions and may want to offer them kidnapping and ransom insurance.

CONCLUSION

The international marketer's political environment is complex and difficult due to the interaction among domestic, foreign, and international politics. If a product is imported or produced overseas, political groups and labor organizations accuse the marketer of taking jobs from people in the home country. On the other hand, foreign governments are not always receptive to overseas capital and investment because of suspicions about the marketer's motives and commitment. When both the host country and the home country have different political and national interests, their conflicting policies can complicate the problem further.

This chapter has covered the political dimension of international trade. Due to the diversity of political and economic systems, governments develop varying philosophies. In some circumstances, their political motives overshadow their economic logic. The result is often that political risks – such as expropriation, nationalization, and restrictions – are created against exports and/or imports and are probably inevitable.

Marketing decisions are thus affected by political considerations. When investing in a foreign country, companies must be sensitive to that country's political concerns. Because of the dynamic nature of politics in general, companies should prepare a contingency plan to cope with changes that occur in the political environment. To minimize political risk, companies should attempt to accommodate the host country's national interests by stimulating the economy, employing nationals, sharing business ownership with local firms, and being civic oriented. On the other hand, to protect their own economic interests, companies should maintain political neutrality, lobby quietly for their goals, and shift risks to a third party through the purchase of political insurance. Finally, a company should institute a monitoring system that allows it to systematically and routinely evaluate the political situation.

Some companies view politics as an obstacle to their effort to enter foreign markets and as a barrier to the efficient use of resources. For other companies, political problems, instead of being perceived as entry barriers, are seen as challenges and opportunities. According to firms with the more optimistic view, political situations are merely environmental conditions that can be overcome and managed. Political risks, through skillful adaptation and control, can thus be reduced or neutralized.

CASE 4.1 HOA NI SHOE COMPANY

Lan T. Huong, National Economics University and Gary Oddou, California State University, San Marcos

Hoa Ni Shoe Company (HNSC) was established in 1968 as a prefabrication plant to produce exported leather goods and has for the last three years been listed as a Hanoi Joint Stock Company (though it is not yet listed on the Vietnam Stock Exchange). The employees in the company own 49 percent of the company and the state owns the rest. Before "doi moi" (the economic renovation) Hoa Ni Shoe's main partners were in the East European/Euro-Asian bloc countries of the former Union Soviet Socialist Republic, Czechoslovakia, and East Germany (German Democratic Republic). Prior to "doi moi" and the opening up of Eastern Europe, business was very difficult. HNSC had to seek partners under restricted conditions and somewhat closed markets.

Since the collapse of the East European bloc and the introduction of the more open market policy in Vietnam, businesses in general and with HNSC in particular have been positively affected. For example, in 1992 HNSC began exporting to Italy and Thailand, and in 1996 it found an additional South Korean partner. In more recent years, HNSC has also developed a reputation for on-time deliveries and high product quality. These two elements have been key in retaining its customers and developing new partnerships.

THE COMPANY'S PRODUCTION

Hoa Ni Shoe manufactures products based on its foreign partners' design preferences. Foreign partners are also responsible for supplying the raw materials to HNSC and for helping it distribute and sell its products to international markets. Its products include gloves, shoes, briefcases, and men's wallets.

The domestic market of HNSC is a very small part of its operations, totaling only 2 percent of its total production. However, it has begun to realize that it needs to focus more on the domestic market. For the domestic market, it had produced only for its showrooms in Hanoi and for a small number of local contract customers. Although the quality of the company's product is high, the number of people who are aware of it is very small. It is difficult to find HNSC's products in large shops in Hanoi compared to its competitors' products. In general, its product style has not been as suitable for Vietnamese consumers' taste because their main markets have been outside Vietnam.

The products for the Vietnamese market include women's shoes, women's sandals, small key bags, men's wallets, and briefcases. The shoes and sandals are inexpensive in comparison with other companies' products. Although HNSC has a large product line, the principal strategic products are leather shoes and sandals. In 1998 HNSC produced 600,000 women's shoes, 500,000 gloves, and 600,000 different bags. In addition, the company's turnover was 51.5 billion dong. In the past few years these numbers have grown, but largely because of foreign consumption due to agreements through LEFASO, HNSC's primary regulator.

HNSC is equipped with modern production technology and a modern assembly-line process for producing genuine and artificial leather gloves, safety gloves, leather bags, leather briefcases, and women's shoes. All the sewing machines used in the production of these items are used for products exported to Eastern Europe. Although the sewing machines are part of the older technology in HNSC, equipping production with modern sewing machines is not HNSC's first priority right now.

For production, HNSC's partnering firms are responsible for supplying materials, distributing and selling HNSC's products. The partners will help HNSC with technology and training for the more complex products. However, partners usually contract with HNSC to produce products that are suitable for its machines, facilities, and the skill level of HNSC's production labor.

HNSC is increasing its efforts to enter into cooperative or other join-venture arrangements with multi-sector companies in both local and foreign countries. Currently, however, HNSC has no marketing department. The role and importance of marketing is not understood clearly, and HNSC still has no real marketing strategy for the local consumer market. As a result, it has only just started to attend a few local exhibition or trade shows, but has not had a visible presence at the important Consumption Goods exhibition. Conversely, other shoe companies such as Legamex, Thang Long Shoe Company, Thuong Dinh Shoe Company, and Vina Shoe Company participate in almost all the local exhibitions. As an example of HNSC's lack of domestic focus, when it was possible to celebrate HNSC's thirtieth anniversary, the company did nothing to publicize this event or to promote its name and products to the domestic market. HNSC said that it did not want to "raise a ballyhoo about the company," and that current customers are already clearly aware of Hoa Ni Shoe; therefore promotional activities were neither necessary nor effective.

The way HNSC acquires its domestic customers is through one of three ways: (1) its relationship with LEFASO (Leather and Footwear Association), (2) by direct contact with HNSC from customers approaching HNSC, or (3) contact with other companies through the international trade shows where HNSC exhibits.

LEFASO

LEFASO has three main purposes: it represents the leather and footwear industry within Vietnam, it supports individual companies in their efforts to become competitive, and it also represents the entire Vietnamese leather and footwear industry to similar international and national associations in other countries.

The year 1998 was a turning point for HNSC. At that time, it completed its fully subscribed issue, with all of the stock offering purchased only by employees of HNSC. Although this represented a certain measure of success for HNSC, it also signaled challenging times for the company. Two major directions became clear. First, because domestic markets are estimated as high potential markets, HNSC would like to develop the domestic market and design styles suited to the Vietnamese consumers' taste. To do that, Hoa Ni Shoe has to overcome many obstacles. Currently, the domestic market is full of inexpensive Chinese leather products affordable by most Vietnamese. In addition, many kinds of Italian and French shoes are becoming popular in Vietnam. However, despite this market penetration by foreign companies, HNSC has competitive potential. Vietnamese consumers' confidence in domestic firms' ability to produce high-quality shoes and other products has increased in recent years. This is manifested by the increased sales of such products produced by domestic companies. The second direction HNSC also needs to take is action to obtain more control over foreign markets in order to decrease dependence and improve ever smaller profit margins. Doing this would also increase employees' confidence in HNSC and their trust in management that HNSC is looking out for their interests.

Besides producing leather shoes, leather briefcases and so forth for the domestic market, HNSC wants to become a supplier of material and equipment used in the leather and shoe industry. HNSC plans to increases its overall domestic market share by about 3 to 10 percent for its total product line. Developing the domestic market will improve HNSC's production effectiveness and efficiency from increased production volume and increased savings from using scrap materials.

Currently the domestic market is dominated by several large, well-known and experienced firms: Vina Shoes Company, Legamex, and Hanoi Leather Shoes Company. Unlike HNSC, these competitors produce mainly for domestic consumption. In addition, their products are generally highly esteemed by consumers. Their distribution channels are well established and widespread. As a result, their products are represented in most of the large local markets, such as Hanoi, Ho Chi Minh City, Hue, and so on. These firms are also members of LEFASO.

The Director of HNSC is contemplating how he should go about moving in these two directions, the timing of each and where to concentrate the most effort. He is also wondering how independently he will be able to act without the formal approval of LEFASO for major and less than major decisions. As the markets become more dynamic and more competitive, being able to act quickly and take advantage of opportunities will become a competitive edge. Yet LEFASO, as the major regulator in the Vietnamese leather and footwear products industry, can have a significant effect on member behavior. What should he do?

Obstacles facing LEFASO and Ha Noi Shoes Co.

Most of the leather product companies in Vietnam that export mainly do so with very small profit margins. HNSC is no exception. Foreign partners have integrated themselves into the basic functioning of these leather and footware production firms in Vietnam. They supply materials for the Vietnamese leather and footwear manufacturers and also purchase their products. In general, the shoe industry in Vietnam has been equipped with modern technology from Germany, Italy, and Japan as part of the partnering agreement to produce for them.

The leather industry is also equipped with modern facilities and machinery from France and Italy with similar arrangements. The foreign partners aid in the style and design of the leather goods produced to sell in foreign markets. They also act as distributors and marketers for the Vietnamese leather and footwear industry. The consequence of this foreign dependence is that it is difficult for Vietnamese companies to negotiate with foreign partners in order to get lower supply prices or to increase the price of the finished product being sold to the foreign partners. This leads to imposed prices by the distributors and reduces the productivity of most Vietnamese state-owned firms from 80 percent to 30 percent. The productivity of Hiep Ha Shoe Company (HHSC) — one of the largest companies — was reduced to 19 percent, or 50 percent in special cases, as foreign firms became more integrated into the supply chain affecting HHSC. The total yield of the shoe industry in Ho Chi Minh City has decreased by 12 percent. According to Leaprodexim, the former owner of HNSC, in the first nine months of 1998 there was a decrease of 9.72 percent in the total export of Leaprodexim's units.

The units in Leaprodexim do not want to continue to do business if they only process products for foreign partners who control much of their operation and profits. They no longer want to be dependent on foreign partners.

Points to consider

1   How should the two directions HNSC has identified as its major needs be approached? Should both be pursued equally?
2   What will be the main sources of resistance?
3   What is the role of marketing in the pursuit of the two objectives?
4   Overall, what would be your strategic plan to help HNSC accomplish its goals?

QUESTIONS

1 Explain the multiplicity of political environments.

2 Distinguish between parliamentary (open) and absolutist (closed) governments.

3 Distinguish among these types of governments: two-party, multi-party, single-party, and dominated one-party.

4 Distinguish among these economic systems: communism, socialism, and capitalism.

5 Is country stability a function of (a) economic development, (b) democracy, (c) capitalism?

6 Explain: confiscation, expropriation, nationalization, and domestication.

7 What is creeping expropriation? What is its economic impact on foreign investors?

8 What are the potential sources and indicators of political instability?

9 How can a company do country-risk analysis for investment purposes?

10 Explain these methods of political-risk management: avoidance, insurance, negotiating the environment, and structuring investment.

11 What measures can be undertaken to minimize political risk?

12 What is OPIC and how can it assist US investors abroad?

13 What is FCIA and how can it assist US investors abroad?

14 What is MIGA and how can it assist international marketers?

DISCUSSION ASSIGNMENTS AND MINICASES

1 According to Harvey E. Heinbach, a vice-president of Merrill Lynch, "You're better off making any car in Japan than in the US. But the political realities don't allow that." Discuss this comment from both economic and political perspectives and as related to the USA and Japan.

2 Why is a host country (including the USA) not always receptive to foreign firms' investment in local production facilities?

3 Once viewing each other with great distrust, the USA and China have dramatically improved their economic and political ties. What are the reasons for this development?

4 How likely is it for a country to adopt a system of either 100 percent capitalism or 100 percent communism?

5 Is capitalism the best system – economically as well as socially – for all countries?

6 Indonesia is a country of approximately 200 million citizens. This is a land where Islam, Christianity, and Hinduism coexist. It is a land where there is a huge income gap between the wealthy ethnic Chinese and the remaining 190 million Indonesians. It is also the land which had been ruled for decades with an iron hand by President Suharto who was then in his seventies. Suharto, while calling for more political openness, had ruled like a military strongman. His 1994 crackdown included closures of publications, beatings of demonstrators, and arrests of labor activists. The country, at the time appeared to be relatively stable.

How should Indonesia's type of government be classified: two-party, multi-party, single-party, or dominated one-party? In addition, assess Indonesia in terms of market potential and risks.

NOTES

1 "Panel Supports Tariffs on Steel," *San José Mercury News*, September 22, 2003.

2 George F. Will, "Steel Industry Extracts Billions from Bush," *San José Mercury News*, March 8, 2002.

3 "China," *Business Week*, October 29, 2001, 48–52.

4   Richard Tansey and Michael R. Hyman, "Dependency Theory and the Effects of Advertising by Foreign-Based Multinational Corporations in Latin America," *Journal of Advertising* 23 (March 1994): 27–42.

5   John Kay, "A Poor View of Poverty," *Financial Times*, July 25, 2001.

6   "Politics and Budgets," *IMF Survey*, February 17, 2003, 42–3.

7   *Freedom in the World 2002: Freedom Gains Despite Global Threats*, Freedom House.

8   *Freedom of the Press 2003: A Global Survey of Media Independence* (Freedom House), www.freedom-house.org/pfs2003/pfs2003.pdf.

9   Fareed Zakaria, *The Future of Freedom: Illiberal Democracy at Home and Abroad* (New York, NY: Norton, 2003).

10 Amy Chua, *World on Fire: How Exporting Free Market Democracy Breeds Ethnic Hatred and Global Instability* (New York, NY: Doubleday, 2002).

11 "Fischer Reviews His Eventful Seven-Year Tenure," *IMF Survey*, September 3, 2001, 278.

12 Gary S. Becker, "As Role Models Go, Sweden Is Suspect," *Business Week*, July 9, 1990, 14.

13 Alfred D. Chandler, Jr., *Scale and Scope: The Dynamics of Industrial Capitalism* (Cambridge, MA: Belknap Press, 1990).

14 "Will China Follow WTO Rules?" *Business Week*, June 5, 2000, 42–3.

15 *2003 Index of Economic Freedom*, The Heritage Foundation/*Wall Street Journal*.

16 Pradeep K. Mitra and Marcelo Selowsky, "Lessons from a Decade of Transition in Eastern Europe and the Former Soviet Union," *Finance & Development* (June 2002): 48–51.

17 Stanley Fischer and Ratna Sahay, "Taking Stock," *Finance & Development* (September 2000): 2–6.

18 "Copper Mining in Chile," *IMF Survey*, June 7, 1999, 191.

19 Franklin R. Root, *Foreign Market Entry Strategies* (New York, NY: AMACOM, 1982), 146.

20 Michael S. Minor, "The Demise of Expropriation as an Instrument of LDC Policy, 1980–1992," *Journal of International Business Studies* 25 (No. 1, 1994): 177–88.

21 *Overseas Private Investment Corporation* (Washington, DC: OPIC), 2.

22 "US Oil Giants Are Slow to Invest in Russia," *San José Mercury News*, January 13, 2003.

23 "BP to Own Half of New Russian Energy Company," *San José Mercury News*, August 30, 2003.

24 Ira W. Lieberman, "Privatization: The Theme of the 1990s: An Overview," *Columbia Journal of World Business* 28 (spring 1993): 8–17.

25 Ravi Ramamurti, "Why Are Developing Countries Privatizing?" *Journal of International Business Studies* 23 (No. 2, 1992): 225–49.

26 Gary S. Becker, "Rule No. 1 in Switching to Capitalism: Move Fast," *Business Week*, May 29, 1995, 18.

27 "Reforming Centrally Planned Economies: What Have We Learned?" *IMF Survey*, August 9, 1993, 241, 247–51.

28 Igor Filatotchev *et al.*, "Effects of Post-Privatization Governance and Strategies on Export Intensity in the Former Soviet Union," *Journal of International Business Studies* 32 (fourth quarter, 2001): 853–71.

29 Wroe Alderson, *Dynamic Marketing Behavior* (Homewood, IL: Richard D. Irwin, 1965); Sak Onkvisit and John J. Shaw, "Myopic Management: The Hollow Strength of American Competitiveness," *Business Horizons* 34 (January to February 1991): 13–19.

30 Janusz Bugajski, "Eastern Europe in the Post-Communist Era," *Columbia Journal of World Business* 26 (spring 1991): 5–9.

31 Yadong Luo, "Toward a Cooperative View of MNC–Host Government Relations: Building Blocks and Performance Implications," *Journal of International Business Studies* 32 (third quarter, 2001): 401–19.

32 Timothy P. Blumentritt and Douglas Nigh, "The Integration of Subsidiary Political Activities in Multinational Corporations," *Journal of International Business Studies* 33 (first quarter, 2002): 57–77.

33 Suk Hun Lee, "Relative Importance of Political Instability and Economic Variables on Perceived Country Creditworthiness," *Journal of International Business Studies* 24 (No. 4, 1993): 801–12.

34 Jean-Claude Cossett and Jean Roy, "The Determinants of Country Risk Ratings," *Journal of International Business Studies* 22 (No. 1, 1991): 135–42.

35 Llewellyn D. Howell and Brad Chaddick, "Models of Political Risk for Foreign Investment and Trade: An Assessment of Three Approaches," *Columbia Journal of World Business* 29 (fall 1994): 70–91.

36 Jennifer M. Oetzel, Richard A. Bettis, and Marc Zenner, "Country Risk Measures: How Risky Are They?" *Journal of World Business* 36 (No. 2, 2001): 128–45.

37 Kent D. Miller, "A Framework for Integrated Risk Management in International Business," *Journal of International Business Studies* 23 (No. 2, 1992): 321.

38 "The Americanization of Toyota," *Business Week*, April 15, 2002, 52–4.

39 "Report: US Ranks 4th in World for Terror Risk," *San José Mercury News*, August 17, 2003.

40 Michael G. Harvey, "A Survey of Corporate Programs for Managing Terrorist Threats," *Journal of International Business Studies* 24 (No. 3, 1993): 465–78.

41 Kit Ladwig, "Political Risk Coverage – Is It Worth It?" *Collections and Credit Risk*, February 2001, 43–5.

42 "Insurance Imitates Art," *Business Week*, January 22, 2001, 16.

43 Marvin Zonis and Sam Wilkin, "Driving Defensively through a Minefield of Political Risk," *Mastering Risk, Financial Times*, May 30, 2000.

Chapter 5

Legal environment

The merchant will manage commerce the better, the more they are left to manage for themselves.

Thomas Jefferson, 1800

CHAPTER OUTLINE

PURPOSE OF CHAPTER

The cases in the marketing illustration below provide examples of the complexity of the legal environment. As may be expected, regulations can sometimes be ambiguous. Because regulations do not allow marketers to plead ignorance, they must themselves somehow try to take control of the situation. They must attempt to conform to the legal requirements for each of the product categories they are selling.

    The purpose of this chapter is to discuss the impact of the legal environment on business decisions and to explain how the legal and political dimensions are interdependent. The chapter examines how countries' varying laws and interpretations affect imports, exports, and the marketing mix. In addition to a look at the major legal systems, issues discussed include jurisdiction, extraterritoriality, and bribery. A section is also devoted to discussion of the various legal forms of business organizations.

MARKETING ILLUSTRATION   THE LONG ARM OF THE LAW

The European Court of Justice ruled that eight member nations of the European Union (Denmark, Sweden, Finland, Belgium, Luxembourg, Austria, Britain, and Germany) acted illegally when they signed bilateral air deals with the USA that offered advantages to their national flag carriers. The ruling of the EU high court thus appeared to allow the European Commission to replace national governments in negotiating air-traffic agreements with the other nations.

    To some shoppers, it is a badge of honor to be able to "shop till you drop." It is not easy to "drop" in Germany, where the 1956 law is supposed to protect workers from shopkeepers unduly focusing on money making. Stores are required to close at 8 p.m. during the week and at 4 p.m. on Saturdays. Sunday opening is improbable. The country's powerful trade unions strongly oppose longer shopping hours. They argue that longer hours are unhealthy for retail workers who will be kept away from their families. Besides,

Germans can shop during normal hours since they enjoy more time off than citizens of other countries. In addition, longer hours probably do not add jobs since shoppers would still be spending the same amount of money.

    Until recently, most retailers' associations did not support longer hours due to the extra costs and greater competition. Now they argue instead that longer opening hours would create jobs; also harried customers would be more civil for not having to rush through crowded aisles before closing time. In 2003, the parliament passed a law that allows more time for weekend shopping.

Sources: "EU Court Declares 'Open Skies' Illegal," *San José Mercury News,* November 6, 2002; "German Officials Push Looser Store Hours," *San José Mercury News,* September 15, 2000; "Shop Till You Drop? Not in Berlin," *San José Mercury News,* March 6, 1999; "More Time Approved for Weekend Shopping," *San José Mercury News,* March 14, 2003.

MULTICIPLICITY OF LEGAL ENVIRONMENTS

Much like the political environment discussed in Chapter 4, there are a multiplicity of legal environments: domestic, foreign, and international. At their worst, laws can prohibit the marketing of a product

altogether. To most businesspeople, laws act as an inconvenience. Club Med's policy of rotating its international staff every six months, for example, is hampered by the US immigration law, which makes the process of rotation both time-consuming and costly.

CULTURAL DIMENSION 5.1   SKINNING A COW: THE LANGUAGE OF RELIGION

About 8 percent of Indians are Hindu, and Hindus revere cows. Cows are sacred due to economic and religious reasons. There was a time when an entire village relied on a single cow's milk. As a result, McDonald's refrains from selling beef in India, and foreigners have been told not to give leather gifts. Yet India is also a major producer and consumer of leather (not just from goat, sheep, and buffalo), and the country actually slaughters fourteen million cattle a year – the world's fifth highest. Due to government tax breaks, leather is one of India's biggest exports.

Both business and religious needs can be accommodated. Cows are usually sent to West Bengal and Kerala because cow slaughter is legal in these two communist-influenced states. Muslims do not mind working in slaughterhouses and butcher shops – as long as they do not have to skin an animal that dies naturally. In that case, low-caste Hindus will do the job because the Hindu religion allows the hide of a "fallen" cow to be taken. Higher caste Hindus, on the other hand, operate leather shoe factories. Distance and middlemen make it possible for Indian leather magnates to remove themselves from slaughtered cows and raw cow skins.

Source: "How Many Ways Can You Skin a Cow? In Hindu India, Plenty," *Asian Wall Street Journal*, July 17, 2001.

IT'S THE LAW 5.1   EASY RIDERS

To help the US motorcycle industry, the US government has requested Japan to implement several reforms. In response, Japan instituted motorcycle operator license reforms that improved training and removed restrictive testing requirements, leading to a large increase in the number of qualified riders and a 30 percent increase in sales of US motorcycles. In 2000, Japan agreed to raise the motorcycle highway speed limit to equal the automobile speed limit, allowing motorcycles to move legally at the same speed as other traffic and thus enhancing safety.

Japan, however, continues to prohibit motorcycle tandem riding (carrying a passenger) on expressways. No other country in the world has this kind of ban. Safety research data have shown that expressways are by far the safest roads for motorcycles.

In the case of Taiwan, there is a ban on motorcycles over 150cc. While the ban applies to both domestic and imported products, it has a disproportionate effect on the US motorcycle industry since all American motorcycles are larger than the permitted size. In addition, Taiwan's environmental laws do not take account of the unique pollution signature of these large motorcycles.

Source: "US Consumer Goods," *Export America*, August 2001, 18–23.

There are many products that cannot be legally imported into most countries. Examples include counterfeit money, illicit drugs, pornographic materials, and espionage equipment. It is usually also illegal to import live animals and fresh fruit unless accompanied by the required certificates. Furthermore, many products have to be modified to conform to local laws before these products are allowed across the border. The modification may be quite technical from an engineering standpoint or only cosmetic, as in the case of certain packaging changes.

A company's production strategy can also be affected by the legal environment. The USA bans the importation of the so-called Saturday night specials – cheap, short-barreled pistols – because they are often used in violent crime. Curiously, the gun control legislation does not prohibit the sale of such

123

inexpensive weapons; only the import of such weapons is banned. As a result, Beretta, an Italian gun maker, is able to overcome the import ban by setting up a manufacturing operation in the state of Maryland.

There is no international law per se that prescribes acceptable and legal behavior of international business enterprises. There are only national laws — often in conflict with one another, especially when national politics is involved (see Marketing Ethics 5.1). This complexity creates a special problem for those companies that do business in various countries, where different laws may demand contra-

dictory actions. For example, Wal-Mart Canada, to comply with the demand of the US government, removed 10,000 pairs of Cuban-made pyjamas. Canada was not pleased and ordered the Canadian branch of Wal-Mart to put the pyjamas back on the shelves.[1]

LEGAL SYSTEMS

To understand and appreciate the varying legal philosophies among countries, it is useful to distinguish between the two major legal systems: common law and statute law.

MARKETING ETHICS 5.1   IMMORAL TRADE

In the USA, most cattle ranchers use hormones to speed up beef production. In fact, 63 percent of all cattle and 90 percent of cattle fattened on feedlots are nurtured with hormone to hasten growth. The hormone implants are placed under the skin behind an animal's ear. Unlike American consumers, Europeans simply do not trust the use of hormones for this purpose. For years, the EU has banned hormone-treated beef. The US Trade Representative states that the EU's position on biotechnology is "immoral" as it deprives poor African countries of badly needed food. To the EU, the US claim is nothing but self-serving.

Under international trade agreement, countries can impose trade restrictions based on health concerns only if such concerns are supported by scientific evidence. A panel of the WTO has outlawed the EU's ban on hormone-treated beef because the ban has no scientific evidence that hormones endanger human health. In spite of the WTO's ruling, the EU continues to ban beef produced with growth hormones. A member of the WTO does not have to abide by the WTO's ruling if it either negotiates compensation with an aggrieved party or otherwise absorbs the WTO's trade sanctions. The USA then prepared a list of European goods worth $900 million that could be subjected to 100 percent tariffs. The WTO subsequently allowed the USA to impose punitive tariffs of

$117 million a year, the amount equal to the loss of US beef exports.

The USA and the EU have negotiated how to label the hormone-treated beef so as to inform European consumers who may be concerned about this kind of beef. The USA has offered to label its beef exports as being produced in the USA, but the EU has refused to go along with this because of its high degree of sensitivity to the issue involving altered or adulterated foods.

The dispute has also extended to other farm products. The EU has a long-standing ban on genetically modified food. In the USA, corn and soybeans have been genetically designed to tolerate Monsanto's Roundup herbicide, and they are widely grown. Some biotech crops are resistant to common field pests and have improved yields. The United states, contending that such food is safe, accuses the EU of violating international trade agreements.

The USA and the EU later toned down their rhetoric; both realized that their two-way trade worth $770 billion was at stake.

Sources: "US and EU Trade Shots in Beef War," *International Herald Tribune*, June 4, 1999; "Europe Keep Ban on Beef with Hormones," *San José Mercury News*, May 25, 2000; "US, EU Tone Down Rhetoric in Trade Fight," *San José Mercury News*, March 4, 2003.

There are some twenty-five common law or British law countries. A common law system is a legal system that relies heavily on precedents and conventions. Judges' decisions are guided not so much by statutes as by previous court decisions and interpretations of what certain laws are or should be. As a result, these countries' laws are tradition oriented. Countries with such a system include the USA, Great Britain, Canada, India, and other British colonies.

Countries employing a statute law system, also known as code or civil law, include most continental European countries and Japan. Most countries — over seventy — are guided by a statute law legal system. As the name implies, the main rules of the law are embodied in legislative codes. Every circumstance is clearly spelled out to indicate what is legal and what is not. There is also a strict and literal interpretation of the law under this system.

In practice, the two systems overlap, and the distinction between them is not clear-cut. Although US judges rely greatly on other judges' previous rulings and interpretations, they still refer to many laws that are contained in the statutes or codes. For statute law countries, many laws are developed by courts and are never reduced to statutes. Therefore, the only major distinction between the systems is the freedom of the judge in interpreting laws. In a common law country, a judge's ability to interpret laws in a personal way gives that judge a great deal of power to apply the law as it fits the situation. In contrast, a judge in a civil law country has a lesser role in using personal judgment to create or interpret laws because that judge must strictly follow the "letter of the law."

There are four sources of European Community law: treaties, regulations, directives, and European Court of Justice case law. Member states are bound by European law, and their adopted measures must conform with it. The European Court of Justice ensures that Community law is observed in the interpretation and application of treaties. Treaties are "primary" Community law. Regulations and directives, as "secondary" Community law, expand the treaties and make them more specific. Directives are measures taken by the Community to harmonize the laws of the member states. Directives are binding. Member states' national courts and tribunals must apply Community law alongside provisions of their own national law.[2]

JURISDICTION AND EXTRATERRITORIALITY

There is no international law per se that deals with business activities of companies in the international arena. There are only national laws that vary from one country to another. The EU area, for example, has high minimum wages, generous unemployment benefits, and employment protection measures. Dismissal restrictions include notice and severance pay requirements, and they can affect labor productivity. Among the advanced economies, Portugal is most restrictive in employment protection, and it has particularly stringent dismissal restrictions.[3]

In preparing a contract, a seller or buyer should stipulate a particular legal system that is to take precedence in resolving any contract dispute. The court to be used for legal remedy should also be specified. The company must keep in mind that to earn a legal victory in its home court is one thing, but to enforce a judgment against a foreign party is something else altogether. Enforcement is difficult unless that foreign party has the desire to continue to do business in the country where the judgment is obtained. Given the disparity of national laws, an international marketer will need to seek assistance from either a local lawyer or an international law firm (see Figure 5.1).

It is often necessary to file a lawsuit in the defendant's home country. To make certain that the foreign court will have jurisdiction to hear the case, the contract should contain a clause that allows the company to bring a lawsuit in either the home country or the host country. According to Article 17 of the Brussels Convention on Jurisdiction and the Enforcement of Judgments, the place where the matter in controversy is located is the exclusive forum for disputes regarding real property, status of a corporate entity, public

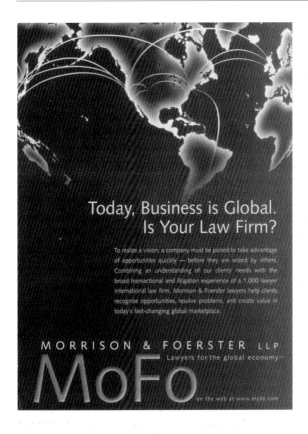

Figure 5.1 *International law firm*

records, trademark, copyright and patent, and enforcement of judgments.[4]

Whenever possible and practical, companies should consider commercial arbitration in place of judicial trials. Arbitration proceedings provide such advantages as an impartial hearing, a quick result, and a decision made by experts. Both IBM and Fujitsu seemed satisfied with the ruling of their two arbitrators in settling a copyright dispute. Intel, in contrast, did not want arbitration and was frustrated by the pace of its copyright lawsuit against NEC.

Three important multilateral agreements on international arbitration address the enforcement of agreements to arbitrate and judicial assistance in the execution of arbitral awards. **The New York Convention** has received broad worldwide acceptance and is now in force in eighty-two countries. The Inter-American Convention, closely paralleling the framework of the New York Convention, states that parties which have agreed to arbitrate may be

compelled to do so, and that arbitral awards shall be recognized and enforced in the same manner as final judicial decisions. **The ICSID Convention** (The Convention on the Settlement of Investment Disputes between States and Nationals of Other States) has established the International Center for the Settlement of Investment Disputes (ICSID) in Washington, D.C. to facilitate the arbitration of disputes between foreign investors and host governments. As of 1994, ICSID has 139 members.

Many Latin American countries adhere to the **Calvo Doctrine** (after the Argentine jurist Carlos Calvo), which is generally hostile to international arbitration. Under the Calvo Doctrine, disputes between foreign investors and a host government must be submitted to the domestic courts of the host government instead of to an independent third party. The general inclination of Latin American countries against ratification or accession to the New York Convention or adoption of ICSID demonstrates the historical aversion those countries have had to arbitration as a substitute for judicial resolution of disputes.[5]

One aspect of the law that does not have universal acceptance involves **extraterritorial application** of the law. A nation wishing to protect its own interests often applies its laws to activities outside its own territory. Spanish laws allow crimes such as genocide to be tried in Spain even though such crimes were not committed there. In 2003, a Spanish judge asked the government to seek the extradition of forty Argentines, including two former leaders of the military junta. Judges in France, Sweden, and Italy also sought the extradition of several former military officers.

Not as clear-cut and much more controversial are the activities of an MNC's foreign subsidiaries and affiliates. In the case of US firms' foreign subsidiaries on foreign soil, it is questionable whether these subsidiaries must comply with the US government's decrees. In response to the US government's prohibition of US firms from doing business with Libya, American firms have complied with the order but do not forbid their foreign subsidiaries from doing business as usual with Libya, as long as American personnel were not stationed there.

According to an Equal Opportunity Commission (EEOC) lawyer, "employers can't go around discriminating, discharging, and harassing people simply because they're overseas." Ali Bouresland, a Lebanese-born naturalized US citizen, claimed that his supervisor at the Arabian American Oil Co. harassed him, denied him time off for Muslim holidays, and fired him because of his race, religion, and national origin. But the Supreme Court stated that a provision of the 1964 Civil Rights Act barring employment bias based on race, sex, religion, and national origin does not apply to US citizens working abroad for American firms. The ruling stressed a principle of American law that limits federal legislation to US territory. As a rule, American courts will not apply laws beyond their border (i.e., extraterritorially) unless Congress expresses a different intent. John Pfeiffer, a high-ranking executive for Wrigley Corp. in the USA,

was protected under US law from discrimination based on his age. After his transfer to a high position in Wrigley's German office, Pfeiffer turned 65 and was immediately fired on the basis of his age. Because of the transfer, he had no recourse.

When a nation attempts to apply its laws extraterritorially, it may upset its trading or political partners. The USA has been placed in this awkward position a number of times in the past. The USA angered Canada when the US government tried to prevent US firms' Canadian subsidiaries from selling products to Cuba. The USA created another uproar in Europe when it prohibited European subsidiaries of American firms from participating in a Soviet pipeline project. In spite of the past mistakes, the USA has once again greatly upset its allies by passing the so-called Helms-Burton law in 1996. The law attempts to tighten economic sanctions against Cuba by penalizing foreign companies investing in Cuba. Mexico, Canada, and the European Union have voiced their strong objection to the extraterritorial measures of the US law which interfere with the foreign policies of the other countries. Reacting to their plans to enact retaliatory laws, the USA has assured these trading partners that the controversial law will not be enforced.

Jurisdiction is crucial for a number of reasons. Plaintiffs want to file lawsuits in countries that give them judicial advantages and maximum compensation. Defendants want to minimize any damage amounts that can be collected. In general, a company prefers a lawsuit in its own home country, but in some cases it is more advantageous to shift the legal action to somewhere else. For example, a lawyer representing fifty-eight Mexicans argued that the accident cases against Bridgestone/Firestone and Ford Motor should be heard in Nashville where the headquarters of Bridgestone/Firestone is located. Furthermore, regarding Firestone and Ford hiding the information that Ford Explorers equipped with Firestone tires were more prone to crash, these allegations took place in the USA. The defendants, on the other hand, argued that the accidents occurred in Mexico and that it would be impractical to take witnesses and plaintiffs to the

USA, not to mention the need to have translators to help English-speaking jurors understand the Spanish-language testimony. The defendants did not mention, however, that plaintiffs could not seek punitive damages in Mexico.[6]

There seems to be a trend toward extraterritoriality. Belgium's law of universal jurisdiction allows its legal system to exert criminal authority over war crimes, genocide, and crimes against humanity that took place anywhere in the world, and it does not matter whether Belgium has any connection with the matter.[7] In other words, the law gives Belgian courts "universal jurisdiction" and allows them to try any person accused of having committed war crimes and genocide anywhere in the world. Cases have been brought against such heads of states as George W. Bush, Tony Blair, and Ariel Sharon. Because of the controversy, Belgium repealed this war crimes law in 2003.

Nations have negotiated a treaty to establish an International Criminal Court. This permanent Court in The Hague is empowered to try individuals accused of genocide, war crimes, and crimes against humanity. The Court should bring order to such ad-hoc tribunals as the ones in Rwanda and Yugoslavia underwritten by the USA. For fifty years, the USA has supported the idea, but when the time came to ratify it, the Bush administration refused. Likewise, those countries targeted for investigations refused to sign, and they include India (for Kashmir), China (for Tibet), Russia (for Chechnya), Iraq, Libya, and Israel. Since sixty-six nations have ratified the treaty, the Court came into existence on July 1, 2002. However, the non-ratifiers are out of reach, unless their crimes occurred in a ratifier's country.[8]

MNCs, by operating in a number of countries, are particularly vulnerable to countries and courts that want to exert their jurisdiction. For instance, the Alien Tort Claims Act was passed in 1789 by the fledgling USA to assure Europe that it would not harbor pirates or assassins. The law allows foreigners to sue in US courts for violations of the "law of nations." Nobody would have thought that the law could be used in 1976 by a Paraguayan doctor who asked the US court to try a former Paraguayan police official for the murder of the doctor's son. A federal appeals court ruled in 1980 that this law permitted foreigners to bring a lawsuit in a US court over acts committed overseas. Now it is Unocal's turn. Burmese citizens asserted that Unocal relied on the Burmese Army to force villagers to clear jungle for this Californian energy giant's natural gas pipeline. Those peasants who resisted were tortured or killed. Unocal denied any knowledge of these acts. It also argued that it had no control over the Burmese military and that it did not actively participate in the alleged human rights violations (unlike the Nazis and their active collaborators at the Nuremberg Trials). According to the Ninth Circuit US Court of Appeals, Unocal could be liable if it "provided practical assistance or encouragement to the Burmese military or if it simply knew that the crimes were taking place." The justices continue to be divided on whether the international or US common law should be used to assess a private corporation's liability of this type.[9] Conceivably, MNCs can be held liable for foreign government's human rights abuses.

Given the fact that cyberspace and e-commerce are inherently international, any attempts to regulate and tax their activities on the Internet through the existing territorial jurisdiction will be problematic. Any successful governance regime will need to involve international public–private sector cooperation. The cooperation may combine self-regulation with government oversight and enforcement.[10]

LEGAL FORM OF ORGANIZATION

Firms doing business in Great Britain have three primary choices for the legal form of organization: British branch, limited company, or partnership. If a limited company is the choice, more decision is needed. A limited company may be either a *public limited company* (PLC), which can raise capital by selling securities to the public, or a *private company* (ltd.), which is not allowed to offer shares or debentures to the public. In general, a public company must meet a number of requirements in terms of registration and capital structure, subscription for shares, and profits and assets available for distribution.

In the USA, a business is able to select from among these forms: sole proprietorship, partnership, and corporation. For firms involved in international trade, the most common choice is the corporation due to the limited liability associated with the corporate form, its relatively permanent structure, and its ability to raise money by selling securities. Most large US firms have a *Corp.* or *Inc.* nomenclature as part of their trade names.

The nomenclature indicating incorporation is different in other countries. For most British Commonwealth countries, corporate names include ltd. or ltd. co. to indicate that the liability of the company is "limited." Equivalencies in civil law countries include the following: in France, S.A. (*société anonyme* or *sociedad anónima*) for a "formal" corporation/stock company and SARL (*société a responsabilité limitée* or *sociedad de responsabilidad limitada*) for an "informal" corporation/limited liability company; in Germany and Switzerland, *A.G.* (*aktiengesellschaft*) for a stock company and *GmbH* (*Gesellschaft mit beschrankter Haftung*) for a limited liability company; in Japan, *K.K.* (*kabushiki kaisha*) for a stock company; in Sweden, *A.B.*; and in the Netherlands, *N.V.* To eliminate confusion and to ensure some uniformity, European countries are now encouraging the use of *PLC* instead of other nomenclature to indicate that a company is incorporated.

BRANCH VS. SUBSIDIARY

One legal decision that an MNC must make is whether to use branches or subsidiaries to carry out its plans and to manage its operations in a foreign country. A branch is the company's extension or outpost at another location. Although physically detached, it is not legally separated from its parent. A subsidiary, in contrast, is both physically and legally independent. It is considered a separate legal entity in spite of its ownership by another corporation.

A subsidiary may either be wholly owned (i.e., 100 percent owned) or partially owned. GE receives some $1 billion in revenues from its wholly owned and partially owned subsidiaries in Europe. The usual practice of Pillsbury, Coca-Cola, and IBM is to have wholly owned subsidiaries. Although a parent company has total control when its subsidiary is wholly owned, it is difficult to generalize about the superiority of one approach over the other.

As a rule, multinationals prefer subsidiaries to branches. Fiat has 432 subsidiaries and minority interests within 130 companies in sixty countries. The question that must be asked is why Fiat, like other MNCs, would go through the trouble and expense of forming hundreds of foreign companies elsewhere. When compared to the use of branches, the use of subsidiaries adds complexity to the corporate structure. They are also expensive, requiring substantial sales volumes to justify their expense.

There are several reasons why a subsidiary is the preferred structure. One reason has to do with *recruitment of management*. Titles mean a great deal in virtually all parts of the world. A top administrator of an overseas operation wants a prestigious title of president, chief executive, or managing director rather than being merely a "branch manager."

Another reason for forming a subsidiary may involve gaining *quick access* to a particular market by acquiring an existing company within the market and making it a subsidiary. The Swiss-based Ciba-Geigy Corporation acquired Airwick, a US firm, with two goals in mind: gaining access to the US consumer market and acquiring a well-known brand.

Furthermore, subsidiaries are preferred because of the *flexibility* created, which may allow the parent company to take advantage of legal loopholes or the opportunity to circumvent certain government requirements. Since 1987, the USA has banned imports of Iranian crude oil. In reality, some $3.5 to $4 billion of Iranian oil have found their way into the USA annually. Exxon bought 250,000 to 300,000 barrels daily from Iran for refineries in Europe and Asia. American oil companies were able to circumvent the ban by using their overseas subsidiaries to buy and sell Iranian crude.

There is an inherent conflict among corporate interests, government policy, and consumer welfare. A company must decide whether it should comply fully with the intention or spirit of the law designed to enhance foreign policy or whether it should look after the interests of consumers or its stockholders. Such a legal loophole probably does not exist if a company's operations abroad are structured as branches rather than subsidiaries. Laws could be changed to close loopholes by requiring foreign subsidiaries and foreign-owned operations to adhere to the same rules. However, the effectiveness of such attempts is questionable, and there is the issue concerning the extraterritorial application of the law.

Another advantage in favor of maintaining subsidiaries is the *tax benefit*. When formed in a foreign country, a subsidiary is considered as a local company, enabling it to receive tax benefits granted to other national companies. Moreover, a subsidiary provides the parent company with some flexibility in terms of when the parent has to pay tax on the income generated by its subsidiary. With a foreign branch, the income is immediately taxable through the parent firm, regardless of whether there is the remittance for the profit. Given this situation, there is no opportunity for the parent to defer any profit or loss.

The *limited liability* advantage may be one of the most important reasons why a subsidiary is formed. With this organizational structure, the parent firm's liability is limited to its investment in the foreign subsidiary; that is, its maximum loss can be no greater than the assets invested in its subsidiary. In addition, the formation of a separate company provides some protection against hostile acts. During World War II, for example, Philips formed North American Philips (NAP) as a separate entity by placing its US operations in a trust in order to protect the company from takeover attempts by the Nazis. The problem in this case was that NAP eventually grew to be too independent and would not even buy the parent's video cassette recorders for

sale in the US market. Philips finally dissolved the trust in 1986, reclaiming the 58 percent interest in NAP in order to have "one face to the world, one central policy."

MNCs generally believe that they are protected against their subsidiaries' actions and liabilities due to the separate incorporation of parent firms and subsidiaries, making them separate legal entities. This precept has come under severe test in a lawsuit filed by India against Union Carbide over an industrial disaster at Bhopal, India. A gas leak at a Union Carbide plant on 3 December 1984 killed 3800 people and injured 200,000 more. In addition to the lawsuit against Union Carbide, victims' lawyers, alleging plant design defects as a contributing factor, sued Humphreys & Glasgow Consultants Pvt. Ltd., Union Carbide's prime contractor. This Bombay-based firm is affiliated with Humphreys & Glasgow Ltd., a London engineering firm, which in turn is owned by Enserch Corp., a Dallas diversified energy company.

The main legal issue in the Bhopal case is whether the parent company is also responsible for the damage caused by its subsidiary. The issue in most cases could probably be decided easily if the parent company owns 100 percent of its subsidiary's voting stock. With full control over a wholly owned subsidiary, there is little question about whether the parent and its foreign subsidiary are indeed independent and separate. In the Union Carbide case, the issue was complicated by the fact that Union Carbide India Ltd. is not a wholly owned subsidiary. Although theoretically and legally autonomous in terms of decision making and responsibility, the subsidiary does not function independently in practice, since its authority is granted by the parent. This is exactly the issue that was legally raised in India in regard to who was responsible for the disaster.

India's contention was that MNCs that are engaged in hazardous activities should not be insulated from their subsidiaries' actions. The liability issue hinged largely on the extent of Union Carbide's involvement in managing its Indian subsidiary. According to India, the two should not be considered legally separate because of their close links. Evidence included the Indian subsidiary's inability to spend large sums of money without authorization from the Connecticut headquarters. Union Carbide's defense was that, although it had the power to veto large outlays as a majority share-holder, the day-to-day operations were run locally. A settlement between India and Union Carbide was finally reached, but many legal issues as well as lawsuits are yet to be resolved.

Warren M. Anderson, the company's chairman, rushed to Bhopal to personally take moral respon-sibility. He was arrested as soon as he stepped off the airplane. The US government intervened, and he was released on bail after six hours. Union Carbide believed it had settled the matter in 1989 when it paid $470 million to the Indian government to settle a civil suit. Many Bhopal residents were unhappy with the settlement, and much of the money has still to reach the victims. Claimants received about $600 for injuries and about $3000 in case of death. Subsequently, the Indian Supreme Court, probably bowing to public pressure, reinstated criminal charges of "culpable homicide" against Anderson. Victims' groups have used the Alien Torts Claims Act to sue American companies in the USA for actions taking place overseas. The lawsuit, charging that Union Carbide violated international law and human rights, states: "the defendants are liable for fraud and civil contempt for their total failure to comply with the lawful orders of the courts of both the USA and India."[11]

LITIGATION VS. ARBITRATION

Litigation, no matter where it takes place, is never an easy thing. In certain countries, it can be much more complicated. Courts in India have twenty-five million cases pending, and it will take more than 300 years to get through this backlog.[12]

In the USA, a lawyer can be found at virtually every corner. Actually, the USA has about 900,000 lawyers, and there is one lawyer for every 400 Americans. According to former Vice-President Dan Quayle, Americans spend more than $80 billion a year on direct litigation costs and higher insurance premiums. Indirect costs which include the expense of avoiding legal liability add another $300 billion a year.

In Japan, there are about 18,000 lawyers, amounting to one lawyer per 7000 Japanese. Japan's legal approach is different. To be a lawyer one must pass the national bar exam, among the world's toughest. Only one attempt per year is allowed. For decades, only the top 500 people passed the bar exam each year. As a non-litigious, consensus-based society, Japan limits the number of attorneys passing the bar exam to only 1 or 2 percent of applicants. On average, a person makes five attempts before successfully passing the bar exam. Not surprisingly, fewer than 1000 new lawyers, judges, and prosecu-tors are certified annually.[13]

Also in Japan, plaintiffs must pay their lawyers an up-front fee of up to 8 percent of damages sought. The system prohibits contingency fees, class actions, and other fee-sharing devices that encour-age filing a lawsuit. Judges, not juries, set damage awards. Even when a victim is killed, awards rarely exceed $150,000. Also in Japan, there is no "dis-covery," thus denying plaintiffs access before trial to an opponent's evidence. In addition, the Japanese culture discourages confrontation and does not view those who sue positively. While the American system encourages excessive and frivolous lawsuits, the Japanese system does not fully protect the rights of the victims. Incidentally, when Hitachi Ltd. was sued by IBM for industrial spying in 1982, Hitachi was shocked to find that its first bill alone from its US law firm exceeded its total payments for legal services in Japan since the founding of the company in 1920.

To save time, expenses, and relationships, it may be wise to look at litigation as the last resort. To resolve a dispute in China, a company has three options: negotiation, arbitration, and litigation (see Marketing Strategy 5.1). Negotiation is usually best because it is quick and inexpensive while preserv-ing a working relationship with one's partner. In fact, most business contracts in China require companies to employ negotiation before pursuing other dispute settlement mechanisms. Chinese

131

MARKETING STRATEGY 5.1 DISPUTE RESOLUTION

There are several ways to deal with a trade dispute with a foreign buyer. One of them is mediation (also known as conciliation). This is a process in which both parties to a dispute appoint a neutral third party to assist them in resolving their disputes. Unlike a judge or an arbitrator, the mediator does not have the power to compel the parties to accept a recommended solution. The goal of mediation is a voluntary negotiated settlement.

One common method of dispute resolution is arbitration. Arbitration is a primary form of alternative dispute resolution. The parties agree to submit their disputes to an arbitrator or a panel of arbitrators. Arbitrators have binding authority to render awards that are enforceable in the courts of most countries. Arbitration is often less costly, less litigious, and less time-consuming, and offers more privacy to the parties than litigation.

The parties agree to arbitration in the event of a dispute in the contracting stage by including an arbitration clause in their contract. Depending on what the parties have agreed to, either the parties will choose their own arbitrators and procedures (ad-hoc arbitration) or submit their dispute to an arbitral institution. There are many different arbitral institutions to which parties may turn in the event of a dispute.

Source: Jim Robb, "Legal Resources and Options for the Exporter," *Export America*, January 2001.

---

government officials may be requested to negotiate a solution. Time limit for this process should be specified. Arbitration is the second best method. Contracts allowing arbitration should specify a choice of arbitration body as well as a choice of law. Because of China's accession to the United Nations Convention on the Recognition and Enforcement of Foreign Arbitral Awards (the New York Convention), arbitral awards rendered in other signatory countries are recognized and enforceable in China, and vice versa.[14]

BRIBERY

At first glance, bribery is both unethical and illegal. A closer look, however, reveals that bribery is not really that straightforward an issue. There are many questions about what bribery is, how it is used, and why it is used. The ethical and legal problems associated with bribery can also be quite complex.

Legal dimension

According to the **Foreign Corrupt Practices Act (FCPA) of 1977**, bribery is "the use of interstate commerce to offer, pay, promise to pay, or authorize giving anything of value to influence an act or decision by a foreign government, politician, or political party to assist in obtaining, retaining, or directing business to any person." A bribe is also known as a "payoff," "grease money," "lubricant," "little envelope," *mordida*, or "bite" (Mexico), and "under-the-table payment," as well as by other terms. A bribe may take the form of cash, gifts, jobs, and free trips. Figure 5.2 describes a bribe as a transaction.

Instances of firms paying bribes are numerous. The US government learned in 1995 of almost ninety cases of foreign firms paying bribes to undercut American firms' efforts to win international contracts worth $45 billion. Germany's Siemens, France's Alcatel Alsthom, and Airbus Industrie are

Figure 5.2 *The anatomy of a bribe*

Source: Sak Onkvisit and John J. Shaw, "International Corporate Bribery: Some Legal, Cultural, Economic, Ethical, Philosophical, and Marketing Considerations," *Journal of Global Marketing* 4 (No. 2, 1991): 6.

among the major practitioners. Germany found 1500 cases of public officials on the take between 1987 and 1995 in Frankfurt, adding 20 to 30 percent to the cost of a building contract. Lockheed Corp. admitted paying $38 million in bribes, kickbacks, and other questionable payments to foreign officials to facilitate aircraft sales between 1970 and 1975. The FCPA was passed as a result of the company's bribery scandal. Also in 1995, Lockheed was forced to admit that it paid $1 million to a member of the Egyptian Parliament so that she would help the company sell three C-130 Hercules transport planes to Egypt. Subsequently, the company paid a record $24.8 million in penalties and for violating the FCPA, and a former vice-president was sentenced to eighteen months in prison.

There are several reasons why a bribe is solicited, offered, and accepted. Low salaries of public officials is one reason; simple greed is another. The loyalties and commitments public servants have to their political parties, families, and friends can cause them to ask for favors that will benefit those groups. The proliferation of bureaucratic regulations seems to be another cause. Complex regulations create the opportunity for bribery because by paying a bribe a company can cut through bureaucratic red tape quickly. Brazil's governmental system is so complicated that it even has the Debureaucratization Ministry. Some of the reasons why businesspeople are often willing and even eager to offer a bribe are:

- To speed up the required work or processing
- To secure a contract
- To avoid the cancellation of the contract
- To prevent competitors from getting the contract.

Bribery is not always an absolute; rather it may be a matter of degree. What may seem like a bribe to one person may not be to another – especially to the one who accepts the payment. This problem of interpretation can perhaps be better understood by considering the tipping system that is so prevalent in the Western world. When viewed in this light, there is a fine line between a bribe and a gratuity.

The tip is given "to ensure promptness" – the same purposes for which a bribe is tendered. Those who provide services expect a tip, and this is true even when the service given may be routine and of poor quality.

The determination of whether or not something is a bribe is complicated further by particular types of payments. When a businessperson gives a public employee a few dollars for extra services so that a delay can be avoided, is this payment a tip or a bribe? The same question in a broader sphere may be asked about compensation and commissions for middlemen. Lockheed paid large sums of money for the services of Prince Bernhardt of the Netherlands and Prime Minister Tanaka of Japan. Under normal circumstances, payments to middlemen pose no problem whatsoever. In the Lockheed case, however, the two middlemen happened to be well-known personalities – a prince and a prime minister – who were in the position of being able to secure favorable treatment for the company. The US Securities and Exchange Commission (SEC) takes the position that payments made to low- and middle-level officials for tasks performed routinely by such officials are not illegal but that payments to high-level government officials for special favors are unlawful.

Another kind of questionable payment involves political contributions. When Gulf Oil was forced to contribute $4 million toward the re-election of Korea's President Park, this was viewed by the Koreans as a political contribution and by US officials as extortion. It is rather ironic that US senators and congressmen would be upset by Gulf's compliance with the Koreans' request when such politicians routinely solicit corporate contributions for their own re-election in the USA. Many attempts to reform political donations in the USA have been slow and difficult.

There has also been debate about gifts. Traditionally, US firms provide Christmas gifts for their customers, employees, and those who have assisted the firm. In foreign countries, gifts may be given for other occasions, such as a New Year holiday or birthday. These gifts are often considered by Westerners as bribes when in reality they serve the same purpose as Christmas gifts.

To answer clearly the question of whether a bribe is illegal and unethical is difficult for two reasons – legal and cultural. Legally speaking, bribery is not an either/or proposition. There are several kinds of payments that fall on the borderline of legality and illegality. To provide clarification, Sections 5001 to 5003 of the 1988 Trade Act amended the FCPA in many respects. The primary change concerns payments to third parties by a US firm "knowing or having reason to know" that the third party would use the payment for prohibited purposes. Under the new law, the US firm must have actual knowledge of or willful blindness to the prohibited use of the payment.

The Act also clarifies the types of payments that are permissible. For example, under the FCPA as originally enacted, although payments to low-level officials who exercise only "ministerial" or "clerical" functions were exempt, the provision provided little guidance to exporters in determining whether a given foreign official exercised discretionary authority. The fact that the Middle East and Africa have part-time officials complicates the matter even more. The Trade Act provides guidance by specifying the types of payment that are permissible rather than which individuals may receive them. A payment for a routine governmental action (e.g., processing papers, stamping visas, and scheduling inspections) may be made without subjecting the exporter to the worry of whether this type of payment may lead to criminal liability. In spite of the clarification, the law still contains several gray areas.

In addition, the interpretation of legality depends on the particular laws of a particular country. What is illegal in one country is not necessarily so elsewhere. In the former Soviet Union, a simple gift – such as clothing for a public official – was considered a bribe. Unlike US laws, the laws of France, Japan, Germany, and Great Britain do not deal specifically with foreign bribery. Canada takes the position that Canadian firms should comply with the host country's law.

Most countries do not provide for legal sanctions for the bribery of foreign officials by their companies or nationals to obtain or retain business. The USA feels that it is important to have equitable competitive conditions. As such, there should be internationally recognized standards of behavior to which marketers may refer so as to be able to refuse to engage in illicit practices. While OECD members have agreed with the US government that international cooperation is needed to discourage companies and public officials from resorting to bribery, it took several years before the twenty-six OECD countries agreed in 1996 to prevent bribes (often listed as fees) from being tax deductible.

The USA has been pushing the OECD members to take a concerted action in criminalizing the bribery of foreign officials in international business transactions. It took more than twenty years for the majority of the leading industrial countries to ratify the OECD Anti-Bribery Convention.

Ethical dimension

Ethical considerations about bribery are even more ambiguous than legal definitions. Generally, ethics precede law. What is illegal is almost always considered unethical, whereas what is unethical may not be illegal. Whether or not bribery is unethical depends on the standards used. Morality exists only in the context of a particular culture. As such, many foreign officials view the holier-than-thou attitude of the USA as being naive and hypocritical. To South Koreans, bribes are part of life. Korean business executives feel obligated to pay each cabinet minister "rice-cake expenses" as holiday gifts.

What is unethical in one culture is not necessarily so in another. Bribery may thus be acceptable in some countries. In many less developed countries, the practice of providing bribes is so common that not to do so may be interpreted as an insult or a lack of respect. The Japanese view payments to foreign officials to secure business deals as normal practice.

There is also another side to ethics. If a company tries to be ethical by refusing to make questionable payments, it may risk having its cargo left on the dock or in a customs warehouse where its goods can easily be damaged or stolen. Moreover, to refuse giving a bribe may result in the loss of a contract, thus harming stockholders and employees. Generally, it is a good idea for a company to maintain its integrity. However, this may be difficult if the company's efforts are adversely affected by competitors that routinely offer bribes and thus take advantage of the company's ethical conduct.

Despite the lack of agreement about what a bribe is and whether bribes are always undesirable, companies must nevertheless cope with the practice. A good rule of thumb may be to be discreet and not to pursue a bribe too aggressively. It may be prudent to wait for the other party either to bring up the issue or to provide a hint. Perhaps occasions for giving should be considered, and holidays can often provide an appropriate excuse. In fact, the absence of a gift at major holidays can be quite conspicuous. In some cultures a gift is acceptable upon being introduced or on meeting someone for the first time. In other cultures an occasion for gift giving is upon the consummation of a deal or when departing. If a US firm decides not to comply with a request for a bribe, it should cite the Foreign Corrupt Practices Act as a legitimate excuse. In any case, no matter how distasteful bribery may appear to be, marketers must realize that it is part of the international "game" that many businesspeople play.

International marketers need to develop strategies to deal with bribery problems (see Figure 5.3, and Exhibits 5.1 and 5.2). Good strategies should include having corporate codes of ethics, sensitization of ethics in managers through training and education, and conducting ethics audits.[15] Regarding the usage and contents of corporate codes of ethics, US firms are more likely than their European counterparts to have adopted codes of ethics. In Europe, adoption of such codes is a relatively new phenomenon, and many of these codes have made their way into Europe via subsidiaries of US firms.

One study found a variation of perceptions of ethical issues by country and type of firm. Therefore, all corporate ethics policies should not look alike since a code of ethics developed in a country in which a firm's headquarters is located may not match the perceptions of ethical issues of the firm's employees in another country. However, country differences do not necessarily preclude a formulation of universal ethical principles.[16] In any case, it is encouraging that companies seem to take ethical behavior more seriously than before.

Marketing professionals' divergence in ethical behavior and attitudes may be attributed to differences in perceptions regarding the importance of ethics and social responsibility. Such perceptions are due to country differences (cultural, economic, and legal/political environments), organizational ethical climate, and demographic variables (gender and age). On the one hand, American, Australian, and Malaysian marketers exhibited different levels of idealism and relativism. On the other hand, irrespective of country, corporate ethical values were positively related to marketers' idealism and negatively related to their relativism. In addition, relativism increased with age, and women were more idealistic than men.[17]

As stated by Peter Eigen, Chairman of Transparency International, "corruption takes many forms and is a universal cancer." As the world's leading anti-corruption organization, Transparency publishes its Corruption Perceptions Index (CPI) and Bribe Payers Index (BPI) annually (see Tables 5.1 and 5.2). Figure 5.4 shows countries' relative positions in terms of corruption control.

One possible solution is for a government to scale down its role in the economy so as to reduce the opportunities for officials to engage in corruption. Such a campaign may have to be a multiple-step process. The focus of a country's anti-corruption efforts should begin with consciousness raising, shift to making the government less susceptible, and then address the problems of a corrupt system.[18]

Corrosive corruption

All around the world, in every language, corruption has a name. Baksheesh. Soborno. Dash. Bribe. And everywhere it occurs, it is corrosive.

Corruption can take many forms, and the effects can accumulate. Where government officials seek special favors or bribes, the costs can discourage honest companies and deter needed investments. Scarce public resources are squandered on nonessential, shoddily built, or too-costly projects, while needed investments go begging. Corrupt officials may thwart the growth of more honest and democratic institutions. Public cynicism, contempt and disillusionment can become widespread.

Companies that participate in corrupted dealings also do themselves no favors. Although a business deal here or there may be obtained, the cost includes creating a culture of dishonesty within the company. If cheating or bribery or fixing the books are tolerated for certain purposes, a company can never again be sure that these dealings are not tolerated for others. The whole organization can come to believe that dishonesty is an accepted approach. That's one reason ExxonMobil maintains strong and clear policies to guard against such dishonesty.

The United States has long been in the forefront of a laudable effort to reduce corruption, and its Foreign Corrupt Practices Act has contributed positively to discouraging extortion and bribery around the world. In 1999, the OECD Convention on Combating Bribery of Foreign Public Officials went into effect. Almost all of the OECD countries have now ratified the convention and enacted enabling legislation.

> **Companies that participate in corrupted dealings do themselves no favors**

This convention holds great promise for reducing corruption, as long as the signatory nations live up to their enforcement obligations.

And some private-sector groups, such as the International Association of Oil & Gas Producers, are helping to meet the OECD standards.

The Organization of American States has also obtained ratification of an Inter-American Convention Against Corruption by most of its member countries. The U.S. ratified the Convention on September 29 of last year.

Also encouraging are steps by international financial institutions such as the World Bank, the International Monetary Fund and the Asian Development Bank to focus more on reducing corruption in the developing world. Innovative arrangements such as the revenue management plan for oil revenues established by the government of Chad and the World Bank are path-breaking advances.

Central to the anti-corruption drive has been the work of the nongovernmental organization Transparency International. Its advisory group of important business and government leaders has included Olusegun Obasanjo, president of Nigeria, who has been at the forefront of efforts to reduce official corruption and private-sector bribery.

There is good reason to be optimistic about the growing efforts to combat the most widespread and damaging effects of corruption. But optimism must be tempered by realism and strengthened by determination, because reducing the impact of corruption will remain a long and difficult struggle.

ExxonMobil™

Figure 5.3 *Corruption and business*

Source: Mobil Corp.

EXHIBIT 5.1 THE COCA-COLA COMPANY: THE CODE OF BUSINESS CONDUCT

Some highlights of the Code

- Employees must follow the law wherever they are around the world.
- Employees must avoid conflicts of interest. Be aware of appearances.
- Financial records – both for internal activities and external transactions – must be timely and accurate.
- Company assets – including computers, materials and work time – must not be used for personal benefit.
- Customers and suppliers must be dealt with fairly and at arm's length.
- Employees must never attempt to bribe or improperly influence a government official.
- Employees must safeguard the company's non-public information.
- Violations of the Code include asking other employees to violate the Code, not reporting a Code violation or failing to cooperate in a Code investigation.
- Violating the Code will result in discipline. Discipline will vary depending on the circumstances and may include, alone or in combination, a letter of reprimand, demotion, loss of merit increase, bonus or stock options, suspension or even termination.
- Under the Code, certain actions require written approval by your Principal Manager. The Principal Manager is your Division President, Group President, Corporate function head, or the General Manager of your operating unit.
- For those who are themselves Principal Managers, written approvals must come from the General Counsel and Chief Financial Officer. Written approvals for executive officers and directors must come from the Board of Directors or its designated committee.
- If you have questions about any situation, ask. Always ask.

This Code should help guide your conduct. But the Code cannot address every circumstance and isn't meant to; this is not a catalogue of workplace rules. You should be aware that the company has policies in such areas as fair competition, securities trading, workplace conduct and environmental protection. Employees should consult the policies of The Coca-Cola Company in specific areas as they apply.

Your responsibilities

- It is your responsibility to read and understand the Code of Business Conduct. You must comply with the Code in both letter and spirit. Ignorance of the Code will not excuse you from its requirements.
- Follow the law wherever you are and in all circumstances.
- Never engage in behavior that harms the reputation of the company. If you wouldn't want to tell your parents or your children about your action – or wouldn't want to read about it in a newspaper – don't do it.
- Some situations may seem ambiguous. Exercise caution when you hear yourself or someone else say, "Everybody does it," "Maybe just this once," "No one will ever know" or "It won't matter in the end." These are signs to stop, think through the situation and seek guidance. Most importantly, don't ignore your instincts. Ultimately, you are responsible for your actions.
- You have several options for seeking guidance. You may discuss concerns with your manager, responsible employees in the Finance or Legal Divisions or, in the case of potential criminal issues, with Strategic Security.

EXHIBIT 5.2 THE COCA-COLA COMPANY: THE CODE OF BUSINESS CONDUCT – WORKING WITH GOVERNMENTS

Overview

Conducting business with governments is not the same as conducting business with private parties. These transactions often are covered by special legal rules. You should consult with company legal counsel to be certain that you are aware of any such rules and you must have approval of local legal counsel before providing anything of value to a government official.

The company prohibits the payment of bribes to government officials. "Government officials" are employees of any government anywhere in the world, even low-ranking employees or employees of government-controlled entities. The term "government officials" also includes political parties and candidates for political office. It is your obligation to understand whether someone you deal with is a government official. When in doubt, consult legal counsel.

In some countries it may be customary at times to pay government employees for performing their required duties. These facilitating payments, as they are known, are small sums paid to facilitate or expedite routine, non-discretionary government actions, such as obtaining phone service or an ordinary license. In contrast, a bribe, which is never permissible, is giving or offering to give anything of value to a government official to influence a discretionary decision.

Understanding the difference between a bribe and a facilitating payment is critically important. Consult with your division legal counsel before acting.

Our company and its subsidiaries must comply with all applicable trade restrictions and boycotts imposed by the US government. (A boycott is a restriction on a company's ability to ship goods into a specific country or do business there.) Moreover, our company and its subsidiaries also must abide by US anti-boycott laws that prohibit companies from participating in any international boycott not sanctioned by the US government. If questions arise, contact legal counsel.

General principles

- The ban on bribes applies to third parties acting on behalf of the company, including all contractors and consultants. Employees must not engage a contractor or consultant if the employee has reason to believe that the contractor or consultant may attempt to bribe a government official.

- The company may hire government officials or employees to perform services that have a legitimate business purpose, with the prior approval of the Principal Manager. For example, an off-duty police officer might provide security. Government officials should never be hired to perform services that conflict with their official duties.

- All facilitating payments must be approved in advance by division legal counsel and recorded appropriately.

- Employees must comply with all US boycott and anti-boycott restrictions.

- The company may operate and fund through its employees one or more political action committees.

- Political contributions by the company must be in accordance with local law. They must be approved by both your Principal Manager and the General Counsel and they must be properly recorded.

- Employees will not be reimbursed for political contributions. Your job will not be affected by your choices in personal political contributions.

The Code in real life

The action: A finance manager paid $20 to an employee of a government-owned telephone company to ensure a telephone line was installed at a company office on time. Even for that small amount, she sought approval from Division Legal Counsel and recorded the transaction as a "facilitating payment."

The decision: That was smart. If the payment had been large, say $600, that might be an indication that this was not a routine governmental action and might constitute a bribe. In every case, employees must seek approval for facilitating payments, and must record these actions appropriately.

The action: An account executive was traveling in a country experiencing civil unrest. A soldier stopped him at a bridge and demanded payment.

The decision: When personal safety is at risk, the employee should, of course, make the payment. Still,

the fee must be reported to the Division Legal Counsel and recorded appropriately.

The action: A general manager entertained a government official in charge of issuing special permits to allow route trucks in a restricted area. During the meeting, the general manager gave a television and DVD player to the official as "a token of respect for the esteemed minister."

The decision: That was a bribe. It was a violation of both the Code and the law.

INTELLECTUAL PROPERTY

Intellectual property (IP), as defined by the World Intellectual Property Organization (WIPO), is "creations of the mind: inventions, literary and artistic works, and symbols, names, images, and designs used in commerce." Individuals and firms have the freedom to own and control the rights to intellectual property (i.e., inventions and creative works). The terms *patent*, *trademark*, *copyright*, and *trade secret* are often used interchangeably. In fact, there are four basic forms of intellectual property, and they hold different meanings. A study found a low correlation of the copyright and trademark variables with Rapp and Rozek's patent variable. This is an indication of the theoretical importance of treating intellectual property law components separately. One component cannot be used as a proxy for the other because countries do not assign equal importance and attention to them.[19]

Categories of intellectual property

A **trademark** is a symbol, word, or object used to identify a product made or marketed by a particular firm. It becomes a registered trademark when the mark is accepted for registration by the Trademark Office.

A **copyright**, which is the responsibility of the Copyright Office, offers protection against unauthorized copying by others to an author or artist for

his or her literary, musical, dramatic, and artistic works. A copyright protects the form of expression rather than the subject matter. A copyright has now been extended to computer software as well. According to the US Supreme Court, databases such as telephone books are not covered by copyright law.

In 1790, the US Congress limited copyrights to fourteen years, renewable for fourteen further years if the author was living. Since then, copyrights have been extended eleven times and are now good for seventy years beyond the life of an author and ninety-five years for copyrights owned by corporations. The latest law is the Sonny Bono Copyright Term Extension Act which was proposed by the Walt Disney Company, thus dubbed the Mickey Mouse Protection Act.[20] Ironically, Walt Disney himself benefited greatly from the value of public domain. By updating an out-of-copyright character, he created Mickey Mouse. The latest extension maintains copyright protection for the early portrayals of Mickey Mouse, George Gerschwin's *Rhapsody in Blue*, Robert Frost's poems, and such films as *Gone With the Wind*, *Casablanca*, and *The Wizard of Oz*.[21]

In European Union countries, copyright protection lasts for fifty years. As a result, recordings made in the early to mid-1950s by such artists as Elvis Presley, Maria Callas, and Ella Fitzgerald have entered public domain. A European company can

139

Table 5.1 *Corruption Perceptions Index*

Rank	Country	CPI 2002 score	Rank	Country	CPI 2002 score
1	Finland	9.7		Mauritius	4.5
2	Denmark	9.5		South Korea	4.5
	New Zealand	9.5	44	Greece	4.2
4	Iceland	9.4	45	Brazil	4.0
5	Singapore	9.3		Bulgaria	4.0
	Sweden	9.3		Jamaica	4.0
7	Canada	9.0		Peru	4.0
	Luxembourg	9.0		Poland	4.0
	Netherlands	9.0	50	Ghana	3.9
10	United Kingdom	8.7	51	Croatia	3.8
11	Australia	8.6	52	Czech Republic	3.7
12	Norway	8.5		Latvia	3.7
	Switzerland	8.5		Morocco	3.7
14	Hong Kong	8.2		Slovak Republic	3.7
15	Austria	7.8		Sri Lanka	3.7
16	USA	7.7	57	Colombia	3.6
17	Chile	7.5		Mexico	3.6
18	Germany	7.3	59	China	3.5
	Israel	7.3		Dominican Rep.	3.5
20	Belgium	7.1		Ethiopia	3.5
	Japan	7.1	62	Egypt	3.4
	Spain	7.1		El Salvador	3.4
23	Ireland	6.9	64	Thailand	3.2
24	Botswana	6.4		Turkey	3.2
25	France	6.3	66	Senegal	3.1
	Portugal	6.3	67	Panama	3.0
27	Slovenia	6.0	68	Malawi	2.9
28	Namibia	5.7		Uzbekistan	2.9
29	Estonia	5.6	70	Argentina	2.8
	Taiwan	5.6	71	Cote d'Ivoire	2.7
31	Italy	5.2		Honduras	2.7
32	Uruguay	5.1		India	2.7
33	Hungary	4.9		Russia	2.7
	Malaysia	4.9		Tanzania	2.7
	Trinidad & Tobago	4.9		Zimbabwe	2.7
36	Belarus	4.8	77	Pakistan	2.6
	Lithuania	4.8		Philippines	2.6
	South Africa	4.8		Romania	2.6
	Tunisia	4.8		Zambia	2.6
40	Costa Rica	4.5	81	Albania	2.5
	Jordan	4.5		Guatemala	2.5

Table 5.1 *continued*

Rank	Country	CPI 2002 score	Rank	Country	CPI 2002 score
	Nicaragua	2.5	93	Moldova	2.1
	Venezuela	2.5		Uganda	2.1
85	Georgia	2.4	95	Azerbaijan	2.0
	Ukraine	2.4	96	Indonesia	1.9
	Vietnam	2.4		Kenya	1.9
88	Kazakhstan	2.3	98	Angola	1.7
89	Bolivia	2.2		Madagascar	1.7
	Cameroon	2.2		Paraguay	1.7
	Ecuador	2.2	101	Nigeria	1.6
	Haiti	2.2	102	Bangladesh	1.2

Source: Transparency International

Table 5.2 *Bribe Payers Index*

Rank	Country	Score	Rank	Country	Score
1	Australia	8.5	12	France	5.5
2	Sweden	8.4	13	USA	5.3
	Switzerland	8.4		Japan	5.3
4	Austria	8.2	15	Malaysia	4.3
5	Canada	8.1		Hong Kong	4.3
6	Netherlands	7.8	17	Italy	4.1
	Belgium	7.8	18	South Korea	3.9
8	United Kingdom	6.9	19	Taiwan	3.8
9	Singapore	6.3	20	People's Republic of China	3.5
	Germany	6.3	21	Russia	3.2
11	Spain	5.8		*Domestic companies*	1.9

Source: Transparency International

thus release albums that were once owned exclusively by particular labels.[22]

The USA has finally joined the eighty-nation **Berne Convention for the Protection of Literary and Artistic Works**, allowing greater protection against foreign pirating of US copyrighted works in twenty-five additional countries. In order to conform to the Berne Copyright Convention, changes in the copyright law in the USA were necessary. Under the new amendment, affixing a copyright notice is optional. For works created after January 1, 1989, mere publication and use are enough to obtain copyright protection.

Even though the copyright notice is no longer required, it is still a good idea to place a ©, the author's name, and date of publication on the original work. A clear notice entitles the author to obtain more effective remedies against infringers.

A **patent** protects an invention of a scientific or technical nature. It is a statutory grant from the government (the Patent Office) to an inventor in

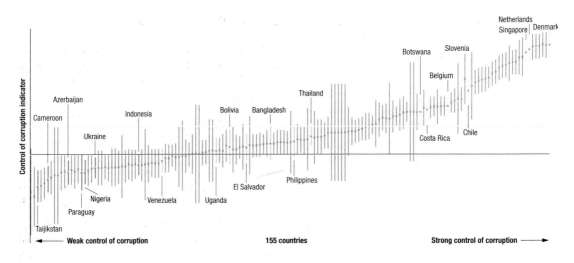

Figure 5.4 *Control of corruption*

Note
This chart shows estimates of control of corruption for 155 countries during 1997–8, with selected countries indicated for illustrative purposes. The vertical bars show the likely range of the governance indicators, and the midpoints of these bars show the most likely value, for each country. The length of these ranges varies with the amount of information available for each country and according to the extent to which different sources' perceptions of corruption coincide. Countries with dark blue (light blue) vertical bars are those for which the governance indicator is statistically significantly in the bottom (top) third of all countries. Countries with mid blue vertical bars fall into neither of the two previous groups. Countries' relative positions are subject to significant margins of error and reflect the perceptions of a variety of public and private sector organizations worldwide. Countries' relative positions in no way reflect the official views of the World Bank or the International Monetary Fund.

Source: Daniel Kaufmann, Aart Kraay, and Pablo Zoido-Lobaton, "Governance Matters: From Measurement to Action," *Finance & Development*, June 2000, 11.

exchange for public disclosure giving the patent holder exclusive right to the functional and design inventions patented and excluding others from using those inventions for a certain period of time (twenty years for a functional patent and fourteen years for a design patent). The purpose of ownership rights is to spur inventiveness. Popular drugs that have recently lost their patent protection include Merck's Zantac (heartburn drug), and Schering-Plough's Claritin (allergy drug),

Some have criticized the US Patent Office for a proliferation of patents – an average of more than 3000 patents a week.[23] The definition of invention has gone beyond substantial and concrete things such as mechanical devices, manufacturing processes, and chemical processes to include genetically engineered animal and human genes and proteins – things that were considered to be mere "discoveries" at one time. Now thought and abstraction can be patented. Software and algorithms used to be unpatentable, but software is now the fastest growing patent category. The trivial devices that have won patent protection include a technique for measuring a breast with a tape to determine a bra size and a technique for executing a tennis stroke while wearing a kneepad.[24]

The top patent holder is IBM.[25] For ten years in a row, IBM generated the most US patents. In 2002, by receiving 3288 patents, it was the only company to be awarded more than 3000 US patents in a single year. The past decade brought IBM 22,357 patents and allowed the company to beat Canon, the next closest rival, by 7000 patents. During the same period, Motorola was the only other American company that managed to land in the top ten. The top ten was dominated by mostly Japanese electronics giants – Canon, NEC, Hitachi, Toshiba, and Sony.

The term **trade secret** refers to know-how (e.g., manufacturing methods, formulas, plans, and so on) that is kept secret within a particular business. This know-how, generally unknown in the industry, may offer the firm a competitive advantage. KFC was alarmed to learn that a handwritten note was found in the basement of a home once owned by Colonel Harland Sanders and that the note might contain his secret KFC recipe. It immediately filed a lawsuit to keep the contents of the note secret but dropped it later after determining that the recipe found did not resemble the Colonel's original recipe of eleven herbs and spices. Colonel Sanders first came up with his famous fried chicken recipe in the late 1930s for his roadside eatery, Sanders Court and Café. Only a few people know the recipe, and they have all signed strict confidentiality agreements.[26]

Infringement occurs when there is commercial use (i.e., copying or imitating) without the owner's consent, with the intent of confusing or deceiving the public. For example, Texas Instruments charged that eight Japanese firms made memory chips based on its patents after the expiration of license agreements, and the US company was able to force the Japanese firms to pay nearly $300 million in royalties. Texas Instruments also obtained an International Trade Commission ruling to seize Samsung's DRAM (dynamic random access memory) chips, which infringed upon Texas Instruments's semiconductor patents. Samsung then joined the eight Japanese companies in agreeing to pay royalties.

In a recent case, Intel filed a lawsuit against Via Technologies, a Taiwanese chip maker. Intel alleged that Via's chip set violated its patents. The legal dispute subsequently led to eleven cases in five countries involving twenty-seven patents. In the end, the two companies settled all litigation related to microprocessors and chip sets. Under the agreement, Via won a three-year license to make Intel-compatible microprocessors and a four-year license to make Pentium 4 chip sets. In addition, both would cross-license each other on patents for ten years.[27]

Legal rights and requirements

Although patent, trademark, and copyright are distinctly different, they all have something to do with the protection of an owner's property. All require applications to be filed – not at the same office, however. Although this section deals with patents more specifically, the same basic ideas apply as well to trademarks and copyrights.

When a firm develops an innovation, a patent should be obtained. The purpose of a patent is to enable the company to exploit its invention commercially while preventing others from interfering. Not all new ideas are patentable. A patent is granted only if the item under consideration is able to satisfy certain criteria. In general, the item must be new, unobvious, and useful, and must also involve an inventive step.

The problem of getting a patent granted is often difficult in many communist countries and LDCs because patent laws do not exist or are ignored. China did not enact its first patent law until 1984. Such countries may refuse to recognize certain patents granted elsewhere, or they may refuse to approve foreign firms' patent applications in their own countries. Items not covered by patents in China include computer software, animals, plants, food beverages, and atomic-energy-related inventions. Also not fully protected are those items related to national defense, the economy, and public health. China does not give patents for chemicals and pharmaceuticals, reasoning that countries at similar stages of economic development have not granted such patents. However, as a new member of the WTO, China is required to observe intellectual property rights.

Patent laws vary widely, and one should not jump to conclusions that patent problems are restricted only to communist or developing countries. Industrial nations may also exclude items from protection. Canada is the only industrialized nation requiring compulsory licensing of drugs. SmithKline had success with Tagamet, a drug for treating ulcers, but Canada issued Novopharm a license for a generic version only four years after Tagamet first appeared on the US market. As a result, SmithKline sued the Canadian government for violation of patent rights.

An inventor should understand that the patent obtained in one country does not extend protection beyond that nation's territorial limits. For further protection, it is necessary for the inventor to file application in other import markets. A few international agreements help simplify this cumbersome process. One such agreement is the **Patent Cooperation Treaty** (**PCT**). The PCT is a multilateral treaty that makes it possible to file an international application simultaneously in up to 115 countries. It thus eliminates the need for separate applications.[28]

Another international agreement is provided by the **Paris Union (Paris Convention)** or the International Convention for the Protection of Industrial Property of 1883. The Paris Union claims about eighty countries as its members. The most important provision is the "**priority right**," which means that the registering of a patent in one member country gives the inventor one year from the filing date to do the same in other countries before losing the protection. In addition, the convention establishes other rules, principles, and rights. The "**national treatment**" rule prevents discrimination by requiring member countries to treat foreign applicants and their own nationals in the same manner. The principle of "**independence of patents**" provides further protection because the revocation or expiration in the country of original filing has no effect on its validity in other countries.

Centralized protection of trademarks is easier to accomplish than centralized protection of patents. One treaty for the purpose of international registration is the **Madrid Agreement for the International Registration of Marks**. Twenty-two countries, mostly in Europe, are signatories, though the USA is not one of them. The Madrid Agreement provides an automatic extension of protection to all member countries when a company pays a single fee of about $300 for the period of protection of twenty years. After a trademark owner has registered a mark in a member country, the **International Bureau of the World Intellectual Property Organiza-**

tion (**WIPO**) in Geneva will then issue and deposit an international registration with the trademark offices in member countries for examination in accordance with their own laws.

The **Trademark Registration Treaty** (**TRT**) simplifies the application process further by not requiring a prior home registration, as in the case of the Madrid Arrangement. If member countries designated in the application do not refuse registration under their national laws in fifteen months, the mark is treated as being registered there.

There are other treaty arrangements. For example, the **European Patent Convention** (**EPC**) establishes a regional patent system for Western Europe. A person can thus file a single international application for a European Patent at the European Patent Office, which administers patent applications. For Latin America, there is the **Inter-American Convention on Inventions, Patents, Designs, and Industrial Models**.

The cost of preparing and registering patents can be quite high. There are costs other than the initial filing fees as well. Periodic maintenance fees (i.e., annual taxes) must be paid during the life of the patent to keep it active. Other requirements must often be met for both the initial patent and its renewal. The required evidence in support of the application usually includes the use and continuous use of the patent.

Because of the high costs associated with patent application and maintenance, the costs must be weighed against the benefits. As a rule of thumb, patent applications and registration are very important and are necessary in the most important markets (i.e., the USA, the EU, and Japan). For other industrialized countries, the potential benefits should justify the costs. In Eastern Europe and Taiwan, it may not be economically worthwhile to file for patents because patent enforcement there is so weak as to be practically nonexistent. Gucci and Rolex fought long and largely unsuccessful battles in those markets.

In spite of the cost, the marketer must realize that, without a valid patent, it can be more costly to do business in the long run. A manufacturer that takes legal action against patent violators is often faced with the burden of proof of ownership. The failure to obtain a patent encourages active infringement, and increases the subsequent legal costs and difficulty of proving a case. The legal costs incurred in a single court can easily exceed the registration costs in several countries.

In the process of filing for patent protection, it is a good idea to make a distinction between common law countries and statute law countries. A common law country determines patent ownership by **priority in use**. In comparison, the ownership in a statue law country is determined by **priority in registration**; that is, the first-to-file is granted a patent even if an innovation was actually created or used earlier by someone else. Europe, Japan, China, and most countries have the first-to-file patent system, and they make patent applications public eighteen months after filing. The USA, as a common law country, relies on the first-to-invent system. The US system's first-to-invent standard is different because it awards patents to the original inventor even though someone else may have got to the patent office first. Based on the US system, the person who had the idea first receives a patent, and patent applications are kept secret – sometimes for years – until a patent is granted. It is true that the European and Japanese systems, by publishing patent information early, encourage imitators, but at the same time, this practice alerts other inventors early enough to avoid redundant research.

The USA was not consistent in treating American and foreign inventors. Although the USA insisted on giving ownership to the first-to-invent, that rule did not protect overseas inventors. US patent law made it clear that research efforts taking place outside the USA could not be used to prove when an invention was conceived. Thus an American inventor would still get ownership if he or she started working on a certain concept before a foreigner's application for a US patent – even though the foreigner actually discovered that idea earlier overseas. After decades of favoritism, the US Patent & Trademark Office, as mandated by GATT, began giving equal treatment to overseas inventors in 1996.

The Japanese patent practices appear to discriminate against foreign applicants who have to wait longer than their Japanese counterparts for a patent to be granted. In contrast, the US, German, and British practices may discriminate against foreign applicants with lower patent grant ratios than for domestic applicants. The USA and Japan seem to have different philosophies concerning patents. In the USA, patents are one's property. In Japan, patents are regarded as public good, and that is why such practices as compulsory licensing and early publication are encouraged.[29]

The USA has complained about other countries' systems, while those countries have urged the USA to become more efficient and consistent with the rest of the world by adopting the system of awarding a patent to the first inventor who applies on an invention. The rationale of the USA is that it attempts to provide a balance between innovation and competition. However, the current practice can and does result in redundant research since other inventors have no knowledge whether someone has filed a patent application on the same idea.

Companies have to put up with the US system because, without US patents, they may be excluded from the world's largest market. Most big companies favor the international first-to-file system due to certainty. One benefit is in terms of the reduction of the threat of "submarine patents" or those applications for major innovations which the Patent Office has kept secret for decades because of indecision about patent approval. When such patents are granted to obscure inventors who claim to have an idea first, they can torpedo other firms which do not know that a patent on the same idea is pending. As in the case of the microprocessor patent, it took the Patent Office twenty years to award a patent to Gilbert P. Hyatt in 1990. As a result, North American Philips Corp. and others had to scramble to obtain a license. Critics feel that some inventors have manipulated the process by continually filing revisions to the original patent applications so as to extend such applications for years or decades. These inventors then suddenly claim patent rights to a widely used technology and demand that companies which use the technology pay them a license fee.

Because of the outcry, in 1994 the USA agreed to bring its patent system in line with those of Japan and Europe. Patent applications will be published eighteen months after filing. At the same time, based on a GATT provision, the seventeen-year patent life after granting was changed to a twenty-year term from the filing date. This change should partially solve the problems of submarine patents.

The WTO has reached a unanimous agreement to alter international trade rules so as to give poor nations greater access to inexpensive life-saving medicine. Poor countries will be able to import generic versions of expensive patented medicines by buying them from countries such as India and Brazil without violating trade laws protecting patent rights. African countries and their supporters in nonprofit health groups have argued that moral and political arguments outweigh commercial considerations in the face of epidemics such as AIDS, malaria and tuberculosis. This agreement could save millions of lives.[30]

COUNTERFEITING

Counterfeiting is the practice of unauthorized and illegal copying of a product. In essence, it involves an infringement on a patent or trademark or both. According to the US Lanham Act, a counterfeit trademark is a "spurious trademark which is identical with, or substantially indistinguishable from, a registered trademark." A true counterfeit product uses the name and design of the original so as to look exactly like the original. On the other hand, some counterfeiters partially duplicate the original's design and/or trademark in order to mislead or confuse buyers. Section 42 of the US Trademark Act prohibits imports of counterfeit goods into the USA.

The extent of counterfeiting is great. Two out of every five recordings sold worldwide are illegal copies. In the case of pirated software as a percentage of the total market, the figures are as follows: Ukraine (89 percent), Russia (88 percent), Bulgaria (78 percent), and Romania (77 percent).[31]

Counterfeiting is a serious business problem. In addition to the direct monetary loss, companies face indirect losses as well. Counterfeit goods injure the reputation of companies whose brand names are placed on low-quality products. In Ecuador, it is easy to see why people earning a minimum wage of $138 a month will have difficulty affording a $15 CD. Consequently, the pirates sold thirteen million CDs in 2002, far eclipsing the 644,274 disks sold legally. To make matters worse, the pirates have entered the export business.[32]

Products affected by counterfeiting cover a wide range. At one end of the spectrum are prestigious and highly advertised consumer products, such as Hennessy brandy, Dior and Pierre Cardin fashion, Samsonite luggage, Levi's jeans, and Cartier and Rolex watches. At the other end of the spectrum are industrial products, such as Pfizer animal feed supplement, medical vaccines, heart pacemakers, and helicopter parts. Counterfeits include such fashion products as Gucci and Louis Vuitton handbags, as well as such mundane products as Fram oil filters and Caterpillar tractor parts. Although fakes are more likely to be premium-priced consumer products, low-unit-value products have not escaped the attention of counterfeiters. Even Coke is not always the "real" thing, as it is very easy for counterfeiters in LDCs to put something else that looks and tastes like Coke into genuine Coke bottles. Fakes can come from anywhere, including industrialized countries. Italy may even be a bigger counterfeit offender than some Asian countries.

Controlling the counterfeit trade is difficult in part because counterfeiting is a low-risk, high-profit venture. It is difficult and time-consuming to obtain a search warrant. Low prosecution rates and minimal penalties in terms of jail terms and fines do not offer a good deterrent. Walt Disney and Microsoft, in winning two trademark-infringement cases in China, were awarded only $91 and $2600 respectively. Moreover, there are many small-time counterfeiters who could just pack up and go to a new location to escape police.

Just as critical, if not more so, is the attitude of law enforcement agencies and consumers. Many consumers understand neither the seriousness of the violation nor the need to respect trademark rights. Law enforcement agencies often believe that the crime does not warrant special effort. The problem is severe in Taiwan, because so many local manufacturers pay no attention to copyrights and patents. The strong export potential for bogus merchandise makes the government there look the other way. In Mexico, one counterfeiter openly operated several "Cartier" stores in American-owned hotels. After many years in Mexican courts and at least forty-nine legal decisions against the retailer, Cartier was still unable to gain the cooperation of Mexican officials to close down the counterfeiter.

The US Trade Representative (USTR) annually submits to Congress a National Trade Estimate Report (NTE) on significant foreign barriers to trade. After submission of the report, the USTR is required to review US trade expansion priorities and identify priority foreign country practices in the Super 301 Report. The **Super 301 Report** identifies foreign practices, if eliminated, that would have the most significant potential to increase US exports. The **Special 301 Report**, on the other hand, identifies annually those countries that deny adequate and effective protection of intellectual property rights (IPR) or that deny fair and equitable market access to Americans which rely on intellectual property protection.[33] Many trade partners of the USA have complained bitterly about the Super 301 and Special 301 reports because of their retaliatory implications. But as far the USA is concerned, this US law has brought results.

Because of China's failure to protect US intellectual property, the USA imposed 100 percent tariffs in 1995 on $108 billion of imports of Chinese products, representing the largest retaliation ever taken by the US government. Soon after that, China signed the Intellectual Property Rights (IPR) Enforcement Agreement and took action to curb piracy. However, although pirated products are no longer sold openly over the counter, the hidden transactions are still common. In addition, while China has done something about illegal retailing, it has not done much about illegal manufacturing. In fact, production of illegal compact disks has greatly increased. The factories making counterfeit products are able to operate quite freely due to their political connections.

It is not sufficient for a company to fight counterfeiting only in its home country. The battle must be carried to the counterfeiters' own country and to other major markets. Apple has filed suits against imitators in Taiwan, Hong Kong, and New Zealand. The overall idea is to prevent bogus goods from entering the industrialized nations that make up the major markets. To make the tactic more effective, it is necessary to go after the distributors and importers in addition to the manufacturers of counterfeit goods. Cartier, for example, has filed 120 lawsuits against retailers in almost every major city. Because it is difficult and time-consuming to shut down foreign counterfeiters in their home countries, major middlemen must be targeted so that they become aware of the risks in handling fakes.

The cooperation a company receives from foreign governments in reducing the amount of counterfeiting varies greatly. Hong Kong has customarily done a credible job of enforcing court judgments against counterfeiters. Taiwan, in contrast, has been reluctant and unpredictable in going after counterfeiters. It has ignored most criticism because its economy depends significantly on the export of bogus goods. In a case such as this, the injured firm should request that its own government intervene by applying pressure on a country that harbors counterfeiters. The US Tariff and Trade Act, passed in 1984, is intended to deal with this problem on an international basis. It allows the USA to deny tariff preferences and duty-free imports to LDCs that do not make a satisfactory attempt to control a counterfeit problem originating in their countries.

Finally, the company must invest in and establish its own monitoring system. Its best defense is to strike back rather than rely solely on government enforcement. One computer firm in Taiwan allows consumers to bring in fakes that it then exchanges for the purchase of genuine computers at a discount. Chanel spends more than $1 million a year on security. It goes after counterfeiters by using a computer to keep track of protected names in various countries, the names of suspected counterfeiters, and the near names, such as Channel, Chabel, or Replica No. 5. Another innovative tactic has been employed by Cartier. It opened its own store directly across the street from the store selling fakes, forcing the retailer of the bogus merchandise to stop selling forgeries in return for a sole local distributorship in Mexico.

When the cost of surveillance is high, it may be more desirable to form an association for the purpose of gathering information and evidence. Apple, Lotus, Ashton-Tate, Microsoft, Autodesk, and Word Perfect formed the Business Software Association as an investigative team. The team was successful in providing information to authorities for the arrest of pirates. This strategy reduces costs while increasing cooperation and effectiveness.

Although counterfeiting is a serious problem, it seems strange that it may still benefit a trademark owner or a patent holder in some way. In the case of software piracy, it provides the shadow diffusion of a software parallel to the legal diffusion in the marketplace, thus increasing the user base in the process. This shadow software diffusion may influence potential software users to adopt the software, and some of them may become new software buyers. Therefore, stopping the shadow diffusion may also impede legal penetration. Marketers need to consider whether software protection strategies may be more harmful to them than piracy.[34]

Business Software Alliance's recent study shows that countries reducing piracy have experienced faster economic growth.[35] Its explanation is that reduction in piracy spurs sales, leading to more jobs and tax revenues. For example, Egypt reduced its piracy rate by 30 percent and saw its software sector grow by 160 percent. Critics of the study, however, countered that it could not be determined whether a country's economic growth was a result of piracy reduction.

CONCLUSION

This chapter has examined the various legal issues related to the conduct of international business activities. Because of the variety of legal systems and the different interpretations and enforcement mechanisms, the discussion must, of necessity, be somewhat general. Based on the same rationale, it is impossible for the top management and legal staff at corporate headquarters to completely master the knowledge of foreign law on their own.

To appreciate the problem and subtlety of foreign law, it is clearly necessary to consult local attorneys to find out how a company's operation may be constrained by particular laws. To deal with problems related to bribery, incorporation, counterfeiting, and infringement, the services of local attorneys are essential. Just as essential is the cooperation of the governments of both the host and home countries.

The legal environment is complex and dynamic, with different countries claiming jurisdiction (or a lack of jurisdiction) over business operations. The interaction among domestic, foreign, and international legal environments creates new obstacles as well as new opportunities. A host country may use an MNC's subsidiary in its country as a method of influencing the MNC and subsequently its home country's policies. Likewise, the home country may instruct the parent company to dictate its foreign subsidiary's activities. It is thus not uncommon to find a situation in which the firm is being pressured in opposing directions by two governments. However, the MNC can use its global network to counter such a threat by shifting or threatening to shift the affected operations to other countries, thus lessening the governments' influence on its behavior. It is this countervailing power that allows the company a great deal of freedom in adjusting its marketing mix strategies.

It is important to keep in mind that legal contracts and agreements can only be as good as the parties who create them and the countries that enforce them. Therefore, a contract cannot be used as a substitute for trust and understanding between parties or careful screening of business partners.

CASE 5.1   INTERNATIONAL AUTO SAFETY AND PATENTS

Peter Spang Goodrich, Providence College

Mercedes-Benz has long been an international industry leader in automobile safety. In 1951, Mercedes-Benz engineer Béla Barényi patented the occupant safety cell. In 1953, the crumple zone premiered with the Mercedes-Benz 180. In 1957, Mercedes installed seat belts, originally used in airplanes.[a] In 1959, the Mercedes 220 had both the rigid passenger cage and integrated crumple zone for cars. The 1981 Mercedes S-Class world premiered the airbag.[b]

Mercedes no doubt had enormous marketing advantages from this corporate image and goodwill; yet Mercedes displayed a high ethical consciousness in its inventiveness. In the early 1950s, Mercedes was the leading team on the Formula 1 auto racing circuit. Mercedes removed its team from participation from racing for over twenty years after a horrific sportscar accident at Le Mans, in which one of its cars careened into the audience killing numerous spectators.

On 23 January 1951, Daimler-Benz AG applied for patent number DBP 854.157, using the unadorned description of "Motor vehicles especially for the transportation of people". Behind this was concealed no less than the invention of the crumple zone. A patent which in the following decades revolutionised the entire automotive industry and became the decisive factor in "passive safety". In more recent times, it has even been applied in railway locomotive and car design.

The ingenious mastermind of the idea was Béla Barényi for whom the maxim of the time – "a safe car must not yield but be stable" – was completely inappropriate. He was the first to discover that in a collision, kinetic energy must be absorbed through deformation in order for the occupants to be protected. He logically split the car body into three "boxes": a soft front section, a rigid passenger cell and a soft rear section. The patent was granted on 28 August 1952.[c]

Patent law allows a company to retain full control over its inventions for seventeen years. Yet Mercedes chose not to enforce its patent rights on the crumple zone so that its competitors could also adopt the technology. As a result, tens of thousands of lives were saved globally.

Points to consider

1   Did Daimler-Benz relinquish its fiduciary responsibilities to its shareholders by failing to maximize profits from its safety innovations?

2   Did Daimler-Benz enhance its marketing strength by its failure to enforce the crumple zone patent rights?

3   What is the difference between Mercedes-Benz's crumple-zone patent protection actions in the 1950s and the current pharmaceutical industry's pricing policies on AIDS drugs to Africa? What would you recommend?

4   Are there certain "intellectual property rights" (patents and copyright) which are so vital to the health and safety of consumers that they should not be allowed to be patented or copyrighted?

Notes

a   In the horrific Mercedes Paris crash which nearly demolished the car and killed Princess Diana, her friend, and the driver, the bodyguard, the only passenger wearing a seat belt, survived.

b   http://www.whnet.com/4x4/crashes.html (accessed May 21, 2003).

c "Patent No. DBP 854.157, Life-saver of thousands." Friday, July 19, 2002. http://forums.benzworld.org/news/news.asp?id=33 (accessed May 21, 2003).

CASE 5.2 BRIBERY: A MATTER OF NATIONAL PERSPECTIVE

Jeffrey A. Fadiman, San José State University

US executives may feel unsure, for example, of how to cope with foreign payoffs, especially when requests for "gifts" take on a form that most Americans consider bribes. Although payoffs obviously exist in the United States, they are detested in our culture. In consequence, this type of solicitation may suggest to even the most overseas-oriented executives that US business values are morally superior to those used abroad.

This conviction, if sensed by foreign colleagues, can shatter the most carefully planned commercial venture. My own initial experience with Third World forms of bribery may serve as an example. It occurred in East Africa during the 1970s and began with this request: "Oh, and, Bwana, I would like [a sum of currency was specified] as Zawadi, my gift. And, as we are now friends, for Chai, my tea, an eight band radio, to bring to my home when you visit."

Both *Chai* (tea) and *Zawadi* (gift) can be Swahili terms for "bribe." These particular suggestions were delivered in tones of respect. They came almost as an afterthought, at the conclusion of negotiations in which details of a projected business venture had been settled one by one. I had looked forward to buying my counterpart a final drink, to symbolically complete the deal in American fashion. Instead, after every commercial aspect had been settled, he expected money.

The amount he suggested seemed huge at the time, but it was his specific request for a radio that angered me. Somehow, it added insult to my injury. Outwardly, I simply kept smiling. Inside, my stomach boiled. I was being asked for a bribe, a request my own culture would condemn. I didn't do it and didn't expect it of others. Beyond that, like most Americans, I expect all monetary discussion to precede the signing of contracts. In this instance, although negotiations were complete, I had been asked to pay once more? Once? How often? What were the rules? Where would it stop? My reaction took only moments to formulate. "I'm American," I declared. "I don't pay bribes." Then, I walked away.

That walk was not the longest in my life. It was, however, one of the least commercially productive. For in deciding to conduct international business by American rules, I terminated more than a commercial venture. I also closed a gate that opened into a foreign culture. Beyond it lay the opportunity to do business in a wholly local fashion, as well as an interpersonal relationship that could have anchored my commercial prospects in that region for years to come.

Points to consider

1 Do you agree with the author's rejection of the request for "gifts"?
2 If you were in a similar situation, how would you handle the situation while considering your own business needs?

QUESTIONS

1 Describe the multiplicity of legal environments.
2 Distinguish between common law and statute law systems.

3 Cite examples of products that cannot be imported into the USA.

4 Explain how the legal environment can have an impact on an MNC's marketing mix.

5 What is the extraterritorial application of law?

6 Why do MNCs prefer to use corporate subsidiaries in foreign markets?

7 Distinguish among patent, trademark, copyright, and infringement.

8 Distinguish between priority in use and priority in registration.

DISCUSSION ASSIGNMENTS AND MINICASES

1 Why is it so difficult for an MNC to deal with bribery?

2 What can trademark owners do to minimize counterfeiting?

3 As an owner of a software product, what form of legal protection will you try to obtain: patent, copyright, or trademark?

NOTES

1 "German Court Rules Against Wal-Mart," *San José Mercury News*, November 13, 2002.

2 Sarah L. Croft and Beatrice Harichaux de Tourdonnet, "France and England: The European Product Liability Directive in Practice," *For the Defense* (February 2000): 8–13.

3 "Offsetting the Costs of Employment Protection?" *IMF Survey*, June 30, 2003, 197–8.

4 Vincenzo Sinisi and Thomas M. Federman, "Commercial Aspects of Italian Law," *Business America*, October 5, 1992, 12–14.

5 Stephen D. McCreary, "International Arbitration in Latin America," *Business America*, February 11, 1991, 17–18.

6 "Mexican Nationals Want Tire Suits Heard in US," *San José Mercury News*, August 24, 2001.

7 "Universal Injustice," *San José Mercury News*, May 16, 2002.

8 "Editorial: World Crime Court Deserves Better Than Denunciation," *San José Mercury News*, May 16, 2002.

9 "Making a Federal Case Out of Overseas Abuses," *Business Week*, November 25, 2002, 78; "Citing Nazis, Lawyers Say Unocal Should Be Tried," *Bangkok Post*, June 19, 2003.

10 Stephen J. Kobrin, "Territoriality and the Governance of Cyberspace," *Journal of International Business Studies* 32 (fourth quarter, 2001): 687–704.

11 "One CEO's Nightmare, Bhopal Ghosts (Still) Haunt Union Carbide," *FORTUNE*, April 3, 2000, 46. "Union Carbide's Former Chief Refusing to Face Bhopal Suit," *San José Mercury News*, March 5, 2000.

12 "Lawlessness and Economics," *IMF Survey*, May 19, 2003, 145–7.

13 "Non-Litigious Japan Faces Critical Shortage of Lawyers," *San José Mercury News*, September 11, 2000; "More Business in Japan?" *Collections and Credit Risk*, May 2000, 10; "Don't Kill All the Lawyers – Send Them to Japan, *Business Week*, June 14, 1999, 66.

14 "Dispute Avoidance and Dispute Resolution in China," *Export America* (June 2001): 14.

15 Sak Onkvisit and John J. Shaw, "International Corporate Bribery: Some Legal, Cultural, Economic, Ethical-Philosophical, and Marketing Consideration," *Journal of Global Marketing* 4 (No. 2, 1991): 5–20.

16 Bodo B. Schlegelmilch and Diana C. Robertson, "The Influence of Country and Industry on Ethical Perceptions of Senior Executives in the US and Europe," *Journal of International Business Studies* 26 (No. 4, 1995): 859–81.

17 Anusorn Singhapakdi *et al.*, "How Important Are Ethics and Social Responsibility? – A Multinational Study of Marketing Professions," *European Journal of Marketing* 35 (No. 1, 2001): 133–53; Kiran Karande, C.P. Rao, and Anusorn Singhapakdi, "Moral Philosophies of Marketing Managers: A Comparison of American, Australian, and Malaysian Cultures," *European Journal of Marketing* 36 (No. 7, 2002): 768–91.

18 Robert Klitgaard, "Subverting Corruption," *Finance & Development* (June 2000): 2–5.

19 Robert L. Ostergard, Jr., "The Measurement of Intellectual Property Rights Protection," *Journal of International Business Studies* 31 (second quarter, 2000): 349–60.

20 "Mickey Mouse Goes to War," *San José Mercury News*, October 4, 2002.

21 "Supreme Court Extends Copyright Protections," *San José Mercury News*, January 16, 2003; "Ruling a Ripoff of Consumers," *San José Mercury News*, January 16, 2003.

22 "Copyrights Expiring in Europe," *San José Mercury News*, January 3, 2003.

23 "Huge Backlog at Patent Office," *San José Mercury News*, April 18, 2003.

24 "Patently Absurd," *The New York Times Magazine*, March 12, 2000, 44–9.

25 "IBM Tops Patents Again," *San José Mercury News*, January 13, 2003.

26 "Sanders' Note Is No Threat to Its Secret Recipe, KFC Says," *San José Mercury News*, January 30, 2001.

27 "Intel Settles Chip-Set Battles," *San José Mercury News*, April 8, 2003.

28 Dean Matlack, "Protecting Intellectual Property Rights Abroad: Resources for US Exporters," *Export America*, June 2002; "The Advantages of Using the Patent Cooperation Treaty," *Export America*, January 2002.

29 Masaaki Kotabe, "A Comparative Study of US and Japanese Patent Systems," *Journal of International Business Studies* 23 (No. 1, 1992): 147–68.

30 "Poor Nations Win More Access to Drugs," *San José Mercury News*, August 31, 2003.

31 "Study Shows Costs of Software Piracy," *Asian Wall Street Journal*, June 26, 2001.

32 "Pirated-Music Sales Flourish in Ecuador," *San José Mercury News*, February 27, 2003.

33 Katherine Wiehagen, "Section 301 Reports," *Export America* (May 2000): 12.

34 Moshe Givon, Vijay Mahajan, and Eitan Muller, "Software Piracy: Estimation of Lost Sales and the Impact on Software Diffusion," *Journal of Marketing* 59 (January 1995): 29–37.

35 "New Study Reveals Significant Decline in World Software Piracy Since 1994," Press release, June 3, 2003.

Chapter 6

Culture

People are tyrannized by their culture.

Edward T. Hall, anthropologist

CHAPTER OUTLINE

- Culture and its characteristics
- Influence of culture on consumption
- Influence of culture on thinking processes
- Influence of culture on communication processes
- Cultural universals
- Cultural similarities: an illusion
- Communication through verbal language
    - ☐ Language acquisition
    - ☐ Translation
    - ☐ The world's best language
    - ☐ Marketing and languages
- Communication through nonverbal language
    - ☐ Language of time
    - ☐ Language of space
    - ☐ Language of agreement
    - ☐ Language of friendship
    - ☐ Language of negotiation
    - ☐ Language of religion
    - ☐ Language of superstition
    - ☐ Language of color
    - ☐ Language of gifts
- Subculture
- Conclusion
- Case 6.1 Cross-cultural marketing: a classroom simulation

PURPOSE OF CHAPTER

A worldwide business success requires a respect for local customs. International marketers need to recognize and appreciate varying cultures. Culture plays a significant role in influencing consumer perception, which in turn influences preference and purchase. A good marketing plan can easily go awry when it clashes with tradition. A marketing mix can be effective only as long as it is relevant to a given culture. One should expect that a product may have to be modified, that a new distribution may have to be found, or that a new promotional strategy may have to be considered.

What is more surprising than the blunders which can occur are the underlying causes for these mistakes. The most fundamental problem appears to be the indifferent attitude of many American firms toward international markets. The firms often enter foreign markets with a complete disregard for the customs and traditions there – something they would never do at home. In marked contrast, many Japanese firms have been highly successful in the USA and elsewhere because of their keen awareness and understanding of the local culture.

In order to develop an appreciation for the role of culture in society as well as the marketing implications of culture, this chapter will explore the following: (1) what culture is, (2) what its characteristics are, and (3) how culture affects consumer behavior. The varying methods of developing cross-cultural communication, verbally and otherwise, are discussed. To lend an understanding of how cultures vary, the chapter will compare a number of cultures. Finally, because population homogeneity within a country is an exception rather than a rule, it is necessary to examine the relevance and bases of subcultural groups.

MARKETING ILLUSTRATION   INNOCENT ABROAD

When marketing products overseas, businesses should be sensitive to local conditions. The countries of the Middle East and North Africa are not a monolith, and there are significant differences among them. Suggestive advertisements may be deemed offensive in Islamic countries, given their more traditional standards of dress and behavior, particularly for women. Advertisements featuring alcohol or pork products are also likely to be poorly received. Arabic and Hebrew script should be used with care to avoid situations like that which befell a company that printed an Arabic phrase on bath towels, not realizing that the phrase had religious connotations.

Regarding greetings and hospitality, handshakes are a typical greeting in the Middle East and are used not only during the first introduction, but may be used each time two people meet, even numerous times in a single day. The common practice in Saudi Arabia is to shake hands at first meeting and again upon leaving.

Typically, people throughout the Middle East maintain closer physical proximity while talking, and conversations often involve more physical contact than is common in the USA. Backing off to increase personal space may feel natural to an American, but will likely be seen as impolite or rude by an Arab or Israeli partner. However, when speaking with a person of the opposite sex, a respectful distance is best. Also, avoid sitting or crossing your legs in such a way that the bottom of your foot faces anyone. This is considered rude.

When a guest in an Arab person's home, avoid making gifts of food or drink. Such gifts imply that the host is inadequate. Gifts of liquor should definitely be avoided in Islamic countries as alcohol is prohibited by the Muslim faith. In Israel, gifts of food or drink are acceptable, but one should ensure that the items are kosher, particularly in the case of Orthodox Jews.

Source: Abridged from Maria Mussler, "Doing Business in the Middle East," *Export America* (December 2002).

CULTURE AND ITS CHARACTERISTICS

Culture, an inclusive term, may be conceptualized in many different ways. Not surprisingly, the concept is often accompanied by numerous definitions. In any case, a good basic definition of the concept is that culture is a set of traditional beliefs and values that are transmitted and shared in a given society. Culture is also the total way of life and thinking patterns that are passed from generation to generation. Culture means many things to many people because the concept encompasses norms, values, customs, art, and mores.

Culture is **prescriptive**. It prescribes the kinds of behavior considered acceptable in a society. As a result, culture provides guidance for decision making. For example, principles enjoining compromise are more salient in East Asian cultures than in North American culture. As confirmed by one study, Hong Kong decision makers are more likely than their American counterparts to compromise.[1]

The prescriptive characteristic of culture simplifies a consumer's decision-making process by limiting product choices to those which are socially acceptable. This same characteristic creates problems for those products not in tune with the consumer's cultural beliefs. Smoking, for instance, was once socially acceptable behavior, but recently it has become more and more undesirable – both socially and medically.

Culture is **socially shared**. Culture, out of necessity, must be based on social interaction and creation. It cannot exist by itself. It must be shared by members of a society, thus acting to reinforce culture's prescriptive nature. For example, at one time Chinese parents shared the preference of wanting their girl children to have small feet. Large feet, viewed as characteristic of peasants and low-class people, were scorned. As a result, parents from the upper class bound a daughter's feet tightly so that her feet would not grow large. It did not matter to the parents that the daughter would grow up having difficulty walking about with distortedly small feet.

Culture **facilitates communication**. One useful function provided by culture is to facilitate communication. Culture usually imposes common habits of thought and feeling among people. Thus, within a given group, culture makes it easier for people to communicate with one another. Yet culture may also impede communication across groups due to a lack of shared common cultural values. This is one reason why a standardized advertisement may have difficulty communicating its message to consumers in foreign countries.

Culture is **learned**. Culture is not inherited genetically – it must be learned and acquired. **Socialization** or **enculturation** occurs when a person absorbs or learns the culture in which he or she is raised. In contrast, if a person learns the culture of a society other than the one in which he or she was raised, the process of **acculturation** occurs. The ability to learn culture makes it possible for people to absorb new cultural trends. Asian countries have complained, sometimes bitterly, about how their cultures are being contaminated by rock music and Western sexual and social permissiveness – foreign elements they consider undesirable and harmful. South Korea has been unsuccessful in banning rock music, as was the former Soviet Union.

Culture is **subjective**. People in different cultures often have different ideas about the same object. What is acceptable in one culture may not necessarily be so in another. In this regard, culture is both unique and arbitrary. As a result, the same phenomenon appearing in different cultures may be interpreted in very different ways. It is customary in many cultures for a bridegroom's family to offer a dowry to a bride's family, either for the bride's future security or to compensate her family for raising her. In India, an entirely different set of cultural rules applies. A woman there is viewed as a burden to both her own family and her husband-to-be. When she marries, her family must offer a dowry to the bridegroom. Some men have been so unhappy with what they perceive as an inadequate dowry that they have set their new wives on fire. Those husbands and in-laws who were angry over small dowry payments killed almost 7000 women in 2001. Although India outlawed dowry payments in 1961, the practice is still being observed by many Hindus who may make both pre- and post-marriage demands. Today, dowries are disguised by families as gifts to newlyweds. Interestingly, according to a survey conducted four decades earlier, almost two-thirds of Indian communities reported that local custom required a groom to pay his bride's family.[2]

Culture is **enduring**. Because culture is shared and passed down from generation to generation, it is relatively stable and somewhat permanent. Old habits are hard to break, and a people tends to maintain its own heritage in spite of a continuously changing world. This explains why India and China, despite severe overcrowding, have a great deal of difficulty with birth control. The Chinese view a large family as a blessing and assume that children will take care of parents when they grow old. They also have a great desire to have sons in order to preserve their family name. The modern Chinese government's mandate of one child per family has resulted in numerous deaths of firstborn daughters. The suspicion is that parents murder their daughters in order to circumvent the quota – they want to be able to have another child, hoping for a son.

Culture is **cumulative**. Culture is based on hundreds or even thousands of years of accumulated circumstances. Each generation adds something of its own to the culture before passing the heritage on to the next generation. Therefore, culture tends to become broader based over time, because new ideas are incorporated and become a part of the culture. Of course, during the process, some old ideas are also discarded.

Culture is **dynamic**. Culture is passed on from generation to generation, but one should not assume that culture is static and immune to change. Far from being the case, culture is constantly changing – it adapts itself to new situations and new sources of knowledge. The dynamic aspect of culture can make some products obsolete and can usher in new buying habits. Japanese tastes, for example, have been changing from a diet of fish and rice to an accommodation of meat and dairy products. In the case of Singapore, it was illegal for concert goers to dance or stand up during performances. The government at first merely tolerated dancing in the audience if it was not violent or offensive. In 2003, the government has finally declared that bar-top dancing is legal, allowing patrons to dance on countertops. The new stance is due to Singapore's desire to transform compliant people into innovators and entrepreneurs in the name of global competitiveness. As endorsed by Prime Minister Goh Chok Tong, "If we want our people to make more decisions for themselves, . . . we must allow some risk-taking and a little excitement."[3]

INFLUENCE OF CULTURE ON CONSUMPTION

Consumption patterns, lifestyles, and the priority of needs are all dictated by culture. Culture prescribes the manner in which people satisfy their desires. Hindus and some Chinese do not consume beef at all, believing that it is improper to eat cattle that work on farms, thus helping to provide foods such as rice and vegetables. In Japan, the per capita annual consumption of beef has increased to 11 pounds, still a very small amount when compared to the more than 100 pounds consumed per capita in the USA and Argentina.

The eating habits of many peoples seem exotic to Westerners. The Chinese eat such things as fish stomachs and bird's nest soup (made from bird's saliva). The Japanese eat uncooked seafood, and Iraqis eat dried, salted locusts as snacks with drinks. Although such eating habits may seem repulsive to Westerners, consumption habits of the West are just as strange to foreigners. The French eat snails, Americans and Europeans use honey (bee expectorate or bee spit) and blue cheese or Roquefort salad dressing, which is made with a strong cheese with bluish mold. No society has a monopoly on unusual eating habits when comparisons are made among various societies.

Not only does culture influence what is to be consumed, but it also affects what should not be purchased. Jews require kosher ("pure") food. Kosher rules about food preparation prohibit pork or shellfish, and there is no mixing of milk and meat products. Coca-Cola was declared kosher in 1935.

Likewise, Muslims do not eat pork, and foods cannot be processed with alcohol and non-halal animal products (e.g., lard). Muslims do not purchase chickens unless they are halal. They also do not smoke or use alcoholic beverages, a rule shared by some strict Protestants. Although these restrictions exist in Islamic countries, the situation is not entirely without market possibilities. The marketing challenge is to create a product that fits the needs of a particular culture. Moussy, a nonalcoholic beer from Switzerland, is a product that was seen as being able to overcome the religious restriction of consuming alcoholic beverages. By conforming to the religious beliefs of Islam that ban alcohol, Moussy has become so successful in Saudi Arabia that half of its worldwide sales are accounted for in that country. Other international brewers have also finally reached the lucrative Middle-East market by promoting malt beverages that resemble beer — without alcohol.[4]

INFLUENCE OF CULTURE ON THINKING PROCESSES

In addition to consumption habits, thinking processes are also affected by culture. When traveling overseas, it is virtually impossible for a person to observe foreign cultures without making reference, perhaps unconsciously, back to personal cultural values. This phenomenon is known as the **self-reference criterion (SRC)**. Because of the effect of the SRC, the individual tends to be bound by his or her own cultural assumptions. It is thus important for the traveler to recognize how perception of overseas events can be distorted by the effects of the SRC.

Animals provide a good illustration of the impact of the SRC on the thinking processes. Americans and Europeans commonly treat dogs as family members, addressing the animals affectionately and even letting dogs sleep on family members' beds. Arabs, however, view dogs as filthy animals. Some in the Far East go so far as to cook and eat dogs — a consumption habit viewed as revolting and

compared to cannibalism by Americans. Hindus, in contrast, revere cows and do not understand how Westerners can eat beef.

In order to investigate a phenomenon in another country, a researcher or marketing manager must attempt to eliminate the SRC effect. The presence of the SRC, if not controlled, can invalidate the results of a research study. Lee suggests a multi-step approach to remove the undue influence of the SRC.[5] First, the problem should be defined in terms of the culture of the researcher's home country. Second, the same problem is defined again, except that it is defined in terms of the cultural norms of the host country. Third, a comparison is made of the two cultural composites. Any difference noted between the composites indicates an existence of the SRC, necessitating another look at the problem with the SRC removed.

The value of this approach is that it forces the manager/researcher to make objective evaluations about assumptions. This, in turn, compels the marketing manager to examine the applicability of initial assumptions in terms of another culture. By being aware of its influence, a manager can isolate the SRC, making it possible to redefine a problem from a more neutral viewpoint. An awareness of this undue influence should sensitize a person to think in terms of the host country's culture. The end result should be that the manager thinks in international terms and not in terms of his or her native culture.

An awareness of the influence of the SRC is valuable because such awareness can help a manager to prevent a transfer of personal cultural norms on a wholesale basis to an overseas market. This awareness should make a manager more customer oriented, and the marketing strategy developed will more likely reflect true market needs. The marketing of fire insurance can be used to explain this rationale. For American consumers, the purchase of fire insurance is a sensible and practical acquisition, but it is difficult to encourage Brazilian consumers to purchase insurance because of superstition. In Brazil, many consumers hold the belief that, by purchasing fire insurance, they may somehow encourage a fire to occur. Therefore, they do not want to think about such an occurrence and avoid the discussion and purchase of fire insurance.

INFLUENCE OF CULTURE ON COMMUNICATION PROCESSES

A country may be classified as either a high-context culture or a low-context culture.[6] The context of a culture is either high or low in terms of in-depth background information. This classification provides an understanding of various cultural orientations and explains how communication is conveyed and perceived. North America and Northern Europe (e.g., Germany, Switzerland, and Scandinavian countries) are examples of **low-context cultures**. In these types of society, messages are explicit and clear in the sense that actual words are used to convey the main part of information in communication. The words and their meanings, being independent entities, can be separated from the context in which they occur. What is important, then, is what is said, not how it is said and not the environment within which it is said.

Japan, France, Spain, Italy, Asia, Africa, and the Middle Eastern Arab nations, in contrast, are **high-context cultures**. In such cultures, the communication may be indirect, and the expressive manner in which the message is delivered becomes crucial. Because the verbal part (i.e., words) does not carry all the information, much of it is contained in the nonverbal part of the message to be communicated. The context of communication is high because it includes a great deal of additional information, such as the message sender's values, position, background, and associations in the society. As such, the message cannot be understood without its context. One's individual environment (i.e., physical setting and social circumstances) determines what one says and how one is interpreted by others. This type of communication emphasizes one's character and words as determinants of one's integrity, making it possible for businesspeople to come to an agreement without detailed legal paperwork.

It is also possible that a subcontext may exist in a broader but different context of a culture. The USA, for example, is a low-context culture that consists of several subcultures operating within the framework of a much higher context. Therefore, communication strategy requires a proper adjustment if it is to be effective.

One common method used by US advertisers is to present an advertisement as an **illustrated lecture**. In this low-context method, a product is discussed in the absence of its natural setting. Such a message is not easily understood in high-context cultures due to the omission of essential contextual and nonverbal details.

According to Hall, cultures also vary in the manner by which information processing occurs.[7] Some cultures handle information in a direct, linear fashion and are thus **monochronic** in nature. Schedules, punctuality, and a sense that time forms a purposeful straight line are indicators of such cultures. Being monochronic, however, is a matter of degree. Although the Germans, Swiss, and Americans are all monochronic cultures, the Americans are generally more monochronic than most other societies, and their fast tempo and demand for instant responses are often viewed as pushy and impatient.

Other cultures are relatively **polychronic** in the sense that people work on several fronts simultaneously instead of pursuing a single task. Both Japanese and Hispanic cultures are good examples of a polychronic culture. The Japanese are often misunderstood and accused by Westerners of not volunteering detailed information. The truth of the matter is that the Japanese do not want to be too direct since, by saying things directly, they may be perceived as being insensitive and offensive. The Japanese are also not comfortable in getting right down to substantive business without first becoming familiar with the other business party. For them, it is premature to discuss business matters seriously without first establishing a personal relationship. Furthermore, American businesspeople consider the failure of the Japanese to make eye contact as a sign of rudeness, whereas the Japanese do not want to look each other in the eye because eye contact is an act of confrontation and aggression.

The cultural context and the manner in which the processing of information occurs may be combined to develop a more precise description of how communication takes place in a particular country. Germany, for example, is a monochronic and low-context culture. France, in comparison, is a polychronic and high-context culture. A lowcontext German may insult his high-context French counterpart by giving too much information about what is already known. Or a low-context German may become upset if he feels that he does not get enough details from the high-context Frenchman.

CULTURAL UNIVERSALS

The failure to consider cultural universals results in a tendency to overemphasize cultural differences. Human beings, regardless of race or religion, all have similar basic needs, and it is reasonable to expect that certain cultural traits transcend national boundaries. For example, people everywhere have a love for music and a need for fun. Some of the cultural universals identified by Murdock are athletic sports, bodily adornment, the calendar, cooking, courtship, dancing, dream interpretation, education, food taboos, inheritance rules, joking, kin groups, status differentiation, and superstition.[8]

Because of the universality of basic desires, some products can be marketed overseas with little modification. The need to have fun, for instance, makes it natural for people everywhere to accept video games. Likewise, culture is not a barrier to computer software dealing with engineering and scientific applications that manipulate schematic drawings and numbers rather than words.

Note that shared values do not necessarily mean shared or identical behavior. The manner of expressing culturally universal traits still varies across countries. Music is a cultural universal, but that does not mean that the same kind of music is acceptable everywhere. Because musical tastes are not internationally uniform, the type of music used must be varied to appeal to a particular country. Likewise, all peoples admire the beautiful, but cultural definitions of beauty vary greatly. In fact, beauty is not a unidimensional concept, and modern-day cultural definitions of beauty are multidimensional. There are different categories of beauty: classic, feminine, sensual, exotic, cute, girl-next-door, sex kitten, and trendy.[9]

The ideal beauty can be both universal and divergent. Many Asian and Hispanic women reshape their minority faces to look more white. Some feel that minorities seeking cosmetic procedures, by getting rid of "ethnic markers," represent the worst kind of ethnic imperialism.[10] In Vietnam, as in other Asian countries, women associate whiteness with beauty. As a result, in the name of beauty, millions of Vietnamese women resort to using gloves, masks, and other things to cover up just about every inch of flesh to block out the sun. Vietnamese men, however, do not have this kind of obsession.[11]

In Niger and many places in Africa, fat is the beauty ideal for women. Amazingly, women take steroids to gain bulk or pills to increase their appetites. Some ingest feed or vitamins for animals. Fattening pills and animal feed are some of the best sellers. Married women do not want to be thin because people may have the idea that they are not being taken care of or that they have been abandoned by their husbands. While the African concept of beauty is the reverse of that in the West, the motivation is the same: seeking men's approval.[12]

Some cultural values remain unchanged over time. For products appealing to basic generic values, certain successful products need not be changed, in spite of the changing environment. Such is the case with *Reader's Digest*'s extraordinary success for more than three-quarters of a century. In the face of violent shifts in lifestyles and cultural tastes around the world, *Reader's Digest* magazine, founded in 1922, has maintained a bland, low-brow editorial formula. It continues to tell people that laughter is the best medicine, that difficulties can be overcome, and that the world is a good, though not perfect, place. The magazine provides people with spirit-lifting stories. These cultural traits are also quite universal, as evidenced by the fact that some 100 million people read the magazine's forty-eight editions in nineteen languages. Its success should remind the marketer that, while cultural values may be constantly shifting, there are basic or generic values that are universal and constant. For some products, that market will always be there as a viable alternative in a fast-changing world.

CULTURAL SIMILARITIES: AN ILLUSION

Cultural universals, when they exist, should not be interpreted as meaning that the two cultures are very similar. Too often, cultural similarities at first glance may be just an illusion. A marketer must thus guard against taking any market for granted. For many Americans, Canada is merely a northward extension of the USA, a notion resented by most Canadians, who resist cultural absorption by the USA.

The perceived cultural difference, real or imagined, explains not only why some American products have been unsuccessful in Canada but also why some Canadian products have failed in the US market. Repeated campaigns to sell the electric tea kettle, an indispensable part of Canadian home life, in the US market have been unsuccessful. Likewise, Vegemite is the closest thing to Australia's national food, with 90 percent of Australian homes having it. Yet this black yeast spread has never been able to find its way into the American consumer's diet.

COMMUNICATION THROUGH VERBAL LANGUAGE

Language is a significant part of culture, and communication is impossible without it. A language may be spoken, written, or nonverbal. There are more than 6000 spoken languages. While Australia has 268 languages, Papua New Guinea has 832 languages. Eight countries claim more than half of all languages, and they are (in order): Papua New Guinea, Indonesia, Nigeria, India, Mexico, Cameroon, Australia, and Brazil.[13] Table 6.1 shows the world's most popular languages.

Some languages are just like endangered species. It is conceivable that more than half of the world's spoken languages could disappear over this century,

Table 6.1 The world's top languages

Rank	Language name	Primary country
1	Chinese, Mandarin	China
2	Spanish	Spain
3	English	United Kingdom
4	Bengali	Bangladesh
5	Hindi	India
6	Portuguese	Portugal
7	Russian	Russia
8	Japanese	Japan
9	German	Germany
10	Chinese, Wu	China
11	Javanese	Indonesia
12	Korean	Korea
13	French	France
14	Vietnamese	Vietnam
15	Telugu	India
16	Chinese, Yue	China
17	Marathi	India
18	Tamil	India
19	Turkish	Turkey
20	Urdu	Pakistan

Source: Adapted from *Ethnologue,* 13th edn, ed. Barbara Grimes (Summer Institute of Linguistics, Inc., 1996).

at the rate of one language death every two weeks.[14] These losses are on top of the thousands of languages that have already disappeared. The Manx language (from the Isle of Man in the Irish Sea) was lost in 1974 when the last speaker died. In 1992, the death of a Turkish farmer was the end of the Ubykh language, which claimed a record of eighty-one consonants. It is difficult to preserve these dying languages when they are spoken by fewer than 2500 people. According to the United Nations Educational, Scientific, and Cultural Organization, a language needs at least 100,000 speakers to pass it from one generation to the next.

Language acquisition

There are a number of theories that explain how people acquire languages. According to the "use it or lose it" hypothesis, people were born with an inherent ability to learn a language. However, this natural ability will diminish with age. Hence, a person must use this ability early. After a certain age, the ability will be lost forever, and one can no longer acquire a language in a natural and effortless way.

Language acquisition may have a biological component. A team of geneticists and linguists has discovered a gene that underlies speech and language. This discovery supports the view that language is acquired and generated by the brain's specific neural circuitry. This gene appears to switch on other genes in developing the brain of a fetus. Some scientists argue that the gene may not be so specific to language. Therefore, the discovery still has not settled a long-standing debate whether the brain handles language through dedicated or general mechanisms.[15]

Several studies have confirmed a widely held belief that the US population in general has very low foreign language fluency. Not surprisingly, many American managers believe that it is not necessary for them to learn another language. They prefer to believe that English is the universal language of business communication. Although this assumption is partially true, it can cause difficulty in carrying out business in parts of the world where English is not spoken.

Many US firms complain that the Japanese market is closed to them, but Japanese officials and businessmen see the situation in another way. They feel that US firms are at fault because US managers do not try hard enough to understand the Japanese market. Japanese managers make a conscientious effort to learn the English language, but very few European and Americans reciprocate. Western managers have difficulty in communicating with Japanese suppliers, distributors, and customers. In addition, such managers cannot lobby effectively for their causes in Japan.

Not all individuals can master a foreign language. There are, however, a few indicators that can predict a person's ability to succeed at learning a language. It is quite easy for a very young person to learn a new language because the ear is still able to pick up the nuances of the spoken word. For older people, some have better linguistic aptitude and are thus better able to acquire another language. Those who are cosmopolitan also do better due to their exposure to foreigners. On the other hand, those who are rigid in their thinking usually encounter learning difficulties in languages. Being too analytical or logical is not a positive attribute. For example, it is not useful to wonder why the German language puts its verb at the end of a sentence or why some letters in certain French words are silent.

If a person wants to learn a foreign language, he or she must attempt to become internationalized in the sense of thinking multilingually or thinking like a foreigner in that foreign language. In other words, one should be able to think in the foreign language without going through a translation process first. As such, the person should be flexible and spontaneous.

Translation

A marketer must be careful even when the same language is used in two or more markets, such as Great Britain and the USA. Although the two countries have a great deal in common, there are many differences important to a marketer. As noted by Oscar Wilde, "The English have really everything in common with the Americans except of course language."

There are significant differences between American English and British English. Different words are used to indicate the same thing, as shown in Table 6.2. For the American *apartment* and *elevator*, the British use *flat* and *lift* respectively. People use *subways* in New York, but they use the *underground* in London.

Citizens of the two countries may sometimes use the same word or phrase when they mean different things. A *billion* is a thousand million to the Americans but a million million to the Britons. When the Americans *table a motion*, the item is set aside without further discussion, while the British take this expression to mean that the item should be placed on the agenda for immediate discussion. A movie that *went like a bomb* was a success to the

Table 6.2 *American English vs. British English*

American	English	American	English
aisle	gangway	mezzanine	dress circle
baby carriage	pram	molasses	black treacle
bacon	gammon	monkey wrench	spanner
baggage room	left luggage office	moving van	removal van
balcony	gallery	mutual fund	unit trust
band-aid	elastoplast	newspaper stand	news agent
bobby pin	kirby grip	one-way ticket	single ticket
bookie	turf accountant	orchestra seats	stalls
checkers	draughts	person-to-person call	personal call
chicory	endive	phone booth	telephone kiosk
coffee with or	black or white	pier	quay
without cream	coffee	popsicle	iced lolly
dessert	sweet	radio	wireless
diaper	nappy	raincoat	mackintosh
druggist	chemist	raisin	sultana
eggplant	aubergine	round-trip ticket	return ticket
electric cord	flex	Scotch tape	sellotape
elevator	lift	second floor	first floor
endive	chicory	sidewalk	pavement
flashlight	torch	soft rolls	baps
French fried potatoes	chips	subway	underground
grade crossing	level crossing	superhighway	motorway
installment buying	hire purchase	suspenders	garters
kerosene	paraffin	thumb tack	drawing pin
lady fingers	boudoir biscuits	tic-tac-toe	naughts and crosses
lawyer	solicitor	toilet	W.C. or cloakroom
lease (rent)	let	trolley car	tram
leash	lead	truck	lorry
line	queue	two weeks	fortnight
liquor store	wine merchant	underwear	smalls
long distance call	trunk call	vacation	holiday
lost and found	lost property	vanilla pudding	blancmange
mail box	post box	yellow turnips	swedes

Briton but a failure to the American. An American vacuums the carpet, but the Briton *hoovers* it instead.

Even when the same word with the same meaning is used, the spelling may vary. For example, *color* and *theater* are used in the USA, whereas *colour* and *theatre* are used in Great Britain. The pronunciation can also be different, especially with the letter Z, which is pronounced as *zee* in the USA but *zed* in the United Kingdom. An American brand name such as E-Z is puzzling in England.

Language differences often necessitate marketing strategy modification. Singer provides its salespeople with instruction books printed in more than fifty languages. Some of these books consist entirely of pictures. In many cases, more than a basic translation of the manual is needed. Computer marketers, for example, have to change software and hardware processes for use in a foreign language. One reason that Japanese computer makers still have difficulty breaking into the US market is because of the problems encountered in exporting software written in Japanese. Accounting and financial programs must be completely rewritten because accounting rules and financial reporting systems vary greatly from country to country.

Less obvious than the variations in accounting and financial rules are the writing and reading rules in different countries. Americans take it for granted that, when they read and write, they should begin from left to right, one row at a time, before going to the next lower row. The Chinese system requires the reader to go from top to bottom, one column at a time rather than row by row. The Chinese also read from right to left (i.e., they start with the column nearest to the right of the page before moving to the next column on the left). These differences usually require a product to be adjusted to some extent. Computer makers have also found that they must change their system for Arab countries, so that the computer can produce a printout reading from right to left.

When a marketing campaign is exported, careful translation is needed. It is crucial to keep in mind that the thought, not the words, must be translated. Examples of careless translation abound. The San José Public Library's huge multilingual welcome banner costs $20,000 and contains twenty-seven languages. *Tuloy Po Kayo* means "welcome" in Tagalog, but what appeared on the banner was *Tuley Po Kayo*, which sounded like "circumcised."

Because differences in languages go beyond differences in words, it is ineffective to have a word-for-word translation. Although they may help a person understand foreign words, dictionaries cannot include subtle differences in syntax, grammar, pitch, and pronunciation. As a result, advertising copy may have to be interpreted rather than translated. As explained by a managing director of a London-based agency,

Translators are usually academic linguists, and know nothing about the art of persuasion or the conventions of marketing; and consumers have an uncanny ability to spot when a piece of copy was never really meant for them in the first place. Translation . . . simply never sounds like free writing. It always rings slightly false, it has a faint odor of foreignness about it, which is anathema to successful selling and brand-building.[16]

Another practice that perplexes non-Americans is the system of dating used in the USA. Americans are taught to begin the date with the month, followed by the day and year. For much of the world, it is more logical to start with the smallest unit (i.e., the day). Therefore, a date written as February 3, 2007 by an American seems illogical to foreigners, who find more sense in 3 February 2007.

The confusion increases significantly when the written date consists solely of numerals. Consider 2/3/2007. Americans read that date as February 3, 2007, whereas others read that date as the second day of the third month (i.e., March) in the year 2007. One can easily imagine the difficulty that may result through a misunderstanding between an American firm and its foreign consumer about delivery and payment dates.

When communicating with customers, it cannot be emphasized strongly enough that there is no place for slang, idioms, and unfamiliar phrases in business correspondence or negotiation. There are many other words or phrases that when translated literally can be misunderstood or insulting. It is wise to avoid such American phrases as "call it a day," "big shot," "lay your cards on the table," and "bottom line."

Safe rules of thumb in international communication are:

- When in doubt, overpunctuate.
- Keep ideas separate, making only one point at a time.
- Confirm discussion in writing.
- Write down all figures using the style of the person you are talking to.

163

- Adjust your English to the level of your foreign counterpart.
- Use visual aids whenever possible.
- Avoid technical, sports, and business jargon.

To put it another way, "Speak to the rest of the world as if you were answering a slightly deaf, very rich auntie who just asked you how much to leave you in her will."[17]

The world's best language

Each native speaker is naturally going to feel that one's own native language is superior. Actually, virtually all languages are not logical. Grammar, spelling, and pronunciation rules are anything but easy. There are exceptions to the rules and even exceptions to the exceptions.

Some may argue that Chinese should be the world's No. 1 language based on the sheer number of speakers. In China, Putonghua ("common speech") or Mandarin, the national language, is used throughout the country. Although the written language in China is uniform, there are actually hundreds of local dialects. Others may additionally counter by saying that Spanish is spoken in more countries. England and France are going to claim that their many former colonies use their languages.

There is no question that English is the world's language of business, diplomacy, and aviation. At Vivendi in France, all board and executive meetings are conducted in English, and all documents are in English. English is also the official language of Totalfina Elf, France's second-largest company. Within Western Europe, English is spoken by 77 percent of college students, 69 percent of managers, and 67 percent of those between 15 and 24 years old.[18]

There are roughly 322 million native English speakers and another billion people who can speak it reasonably well. Some have argued that the popularity of the English language is due to its merit. When compared to the French and German languages, English has a huge vocabulary and a simple grammar, and is open to change to accommodate foreign words and grammatical shifts, not to mention new words or slang (e.g., get crunk, shock jock). But critics can easily point out all those irregular verbs that do not seem to follow any rhyme or reason, not to mention the fact that some irregular verbs have become regularized. To have a command of these verbs and strange pronunciations and spellings, drilling – not reasoning – is the only way to go.

MARKETING STRATEGY 6.1   HOW TO SPEAK ENGLISH PROPERLY

English is the world's must studied language. It is a global language of business, finance, and technology. In countries where English is not a native language, those who can speak English invariably command higher salaries than those who cannot. However, it is important to recognize that non-native English speakers have a smaller vocabulary and that they may take certain words or phrases literally – rather than figuratively. Certainly, they will have difficulties with culture-bound expressions.

To use the English language properly and effectively when interacting with non-native speakers, the following rules should be followed.

- Avoid idioms (e.g., pushing the envelope)
- Avoid jargons (e.g., bottom line) and acronyms (e.g., OECD)
- Avoid complex sentences. Sentences are difficult to follow when they have dependent, coordinate, subordinate, and relative clauses.
- When delivering a message, speak slowly and pause. Do not run words and sentences together. Pause before beginning a new thought, sentence, or point.

Source: Patricia L. Kurtz, "But They Said Everyone Spoke English," Special Advertising Section, *Business Week*, December 17, 2001.

Unlike the English language, which is relatively straightforward, many languages are quite subtle. The Italian language allows several different ways of addressing someone that show a speaker's position and feelings. Likewise, the Japanese language has literary and conversational styles, male and female styles, young and old styles, and various degrees of politeness. In this regard, some may argue that the English language is too black and white and that it does not have words to delineate all subtle meanings.

If there is one language that can lay claim to being truly universal, it is esperanto. This is the UNESCO-resolutioned planned language. The strengths of esperanto are its neutral and universal features. The grammar is extremely regular and easy to learn. The language possesses power, flexibility, and beauty, and promotes as well as protects linguistic cultural diversity. As an international language, esperanto provides a low-cost high-quality trans-Babel communication medium, and it is possible in a short period of time to be fluent in this dialect-free international auxiliary language (see Exhibit 6.1).

Marketing and languages

An observation made by Berlo explains in accurate terms the importance and influence of language. Because languages affect thought, "systems that employ different codes may well employ different methods of thought. A German's language is different from an American's language. It may follow that his methods of thinking are also different."[19]

Marketers should attempt to understand how consumers process linguistic information. The visual nature of the writing system in East Asia, for example, makes East Asians pay more attention to visual information processing as well as to the writing of a name.[20] Empirically, there is evidence to support the position that structural differences between Chinese and English affect mental representations which then affect consumer memory of verbal information.[21] While mental representations of verbal information in Chinese are coded primarily in a visual manner, verbal information in English is coded primarily in a phonological manner. Therefore, Chinese consumers tend to recall information when the visual rather than the phonological memory trace is accessed. English native speakers, on the other hand, are more likely to recall information when the phonological rather than the visual trace is accessed. As far as a brand name is concerned, it is meaningful to structure communications for Chinese consumers by using visually distinct brand-name writings or calligraphy and logo designs that enforce the writing. In contrast, it is more effective to reach English native speakers by using jingles and onomatopoeic name creations to exploit the sound qualities of a brand name.

About a quarter of the world's population read logographs. A prime example is the Chinese logographs that have also been adapted to Japanese kanji and Korean Hancha, thus maintaining the same meanings but not the same pronunciation. While logographs represent meaning, most modern languages use alphabetic scripts consisting of symbols that represent sound. These sound-based scripts include Latin and Arabic. It is thus useful to determine whether cognitive processing of words would vary based on whether such words are written in logographic or alphabetic scripts. Conceivably, processing of words written in alphabetic scripts relies more heavily on storage of the short-term memory's phonological loop. In comparison, processing of words written in logographic scripts may rely more on the storage of visual short-term memory. According to one study, auditory contextual interference was higher for alphabetic words than for logographic words, while visual distracters produced the opposite results. Therefore, advertisements containing alphabetic words should minimize the use of distracting auditory information, but in the case of advertisements containing logographic words, they should minimize use of distracting graphics or complex visual displays.[22]

Many managers and consumers are bilingual. Given the popularity of the English language in world business, it is reasonable to believe that English is the second language of most of these individuals. One marketing question has to do with

EXHIBIT 6.1   QUICK GRAMMAR OF ESPERANTO

Spelling

Every word in Esperanto is pronounced just as it is spelt, with each letter corresponding to a single sound. There are no silent letters. The stress is always on the penultimate a/e/i/o/u, for example, rapide (quickly) is spoken rah-PEA-deh.

- c = ts
- ^c (circumflex over c) = ch, tsh
- g = g (hard as in get)
- ^g (circumflex over g) = g (soft as in ginger), dzh
- h = h (never silent)
- ^h (circumflex over h) (rare) = ch in Scottish loch
- i = ee
- j = y
  - □   aj = eye
  - □   ej = ay in hay
  - □   oj = oy
  - □   uj = u + short I
- ^j (circumflex over j) = s in pleasure, zh
- s = ss (never like z)
- ^s (circumflex over s) = sh
- u = oo
- ù (breve over u) (rare) = w
  - □   aù = ow in now or how
  - □   eù (rare) = e + short u
- x = extending letter. X is not one of the 28 letters of the Esperanto alphabet, but some people do use it to indicate a circumflex or breve on the preceding letter (cx = ^c, gx = ^g, hx = ^h, jx = ^j, sx = ^s, ux = ù). This is only a temporary measure used on the Net: the true Esperanto letters will be used when Unicode WWW browsers become widespread.

Verbs

There are no irregular verbs. All verbs (even esti = to be, havi = to have, iri = to go, and fair = to do/make) take the same simple declination: add -is -as -os -us -u or -I to the root (est- hav- ir- far-). This is illustrated in the following examples.

- -is for past: Li vidis kaj ^si aùdis = He saw and she heard
- -as for present: Mi sidas, sed ili staras = I sit/am sitting, but they stand/are standing
- -os for future: Mi ferios julie = I will go on holiday in July
- -us for conditional: Se me estus rica, (tiam) mi a^cetus helikopteron = If I were rich, (then) I would buy a helicopter
- u for imperative: Envenu! = Come in!
- -i for infinitive: Mi volas na^gi en la maro = I want to swim in the sea

Nouns

There are no word genders in Esperanto, and "the" is always "la". There is no word for "a", so Domo = A house = House. Plurals are always formed by adding -j.

- -o for singular nouns: Viro kun hundo = A man with a dog
- oj (pronounced -oy) for plural nouns: Homoj en la lando de espero = People in the land of hope

  Pronouns are short words ending in an I (li = he, ^se = she, ^gi = it). Objects are without exception formed by adding -n: La kato rigardas lin/^sin/^gin = the cat watches him/her/it.

Adjectives and adverbs

- -a for singular adjectives: Unu verda stelo = One green star
- -aj (pronounced -eye) for plural adjectives: Du feli^caj amantoj = Two happy lovers
- -e for adverbs: Ni kuros rapide = We will run quickly
- -ant => -ing: La ku^santa viro = The lying man (Ku^si = to lie, mensogi = to tell a lie)
- -it => -ed: La fermita pordo = The closed door (fermi = to close)

Asking questions

- ^Cu = Is it true that. This word is used to make simple yes/no questions: ^Cu mi rajtas eniri? = Can (may) I enter?
- **Kial** (pronounced KEE-al) = Why. Kial vi volas transiri? = Why do you want to cross (over)?
- **Kiam** (pronounced KEE-am) = When. Kiam vi devas foriri? = When must you leave?
- **Kie** (pronounced KEE-eh) = Where. Kie oni povas eniri? = Where can you (one) enter?

- **Kio** (pronounced KEE-oh) = What. Kion vi diris? = What did you say? (-n because kio is used as the object here)
- **Kiu** (pronounced KEE-oh) = Who. Kiu donos la bluajn al mia amiko? = Who will give the blue ones to my friend? (No -n because kiu is used as the subject here)

Source: Courtesy of Travlang.com.

the language to be used to communicate with bilingual consumers. One study focusing on how bilingual individuals process advertising messages examines the assumption that advertisements in the consumers' first language gave better results than those advertisements in their second language. The results indicate that second-language messages do not have to result in inferior memory. When the advertisement's picture and text are highly congruent, memory for second-language advertisements, compared to memory for first-language advertisements, was raised to a similar level. At the same time, these second-language advertisements can also maintain product evaluations at a relatively high level.[23]

COMMUNICATION THROUGH NONVERBAL LANGUAGE

People do not always communicate solely through the spoken or written word. Knowingly or not, people routinely communicate with one another in a nonverbal manner (see Exhibit 6.2 and Figure 6.1). Body language includes movement, appearance, dress, facial expressions, gestures, posture, use of silence, use of touch, timing, distance between speakers and listeners, physical surroundings, tone, and rhythm of speech. Some body language "phrases" (e.g., a smile) are universal, but other phrases vary in meaning across cultural lines. Whereas the Japanese view prolonged eye contact as

IT'S THE LAW 6.1
LLANFAIRPWLLGWYNGYLLGOGERYCHWYRNDROBWLLLANTYSILIOGOGOGOCH

Of all the traditional English languages, Welsh faces a tough challenge to survive. Since 1536, Wales, as a constituent part of the United Kingdom, is governed from London. Wales' three million people are overwhelmed by the English majority (forty-nine million). Being unable to comprehend or pronounce names such as Llanystumdwy or Pwllheli, the English outlawed the local language until 1920. Ancient city names were anglicized, and Caerdydd became Cardiff. Such language restrictions led to a protest, and a group of local patriots did so in 1870 by giving their

village a name that no Englishperson could pronounce – Llanfairpwllgwyngyllgogerychwyrndrobwlllantysiliog ogogoch.

The push for Welsh-language instruction began in 1990, and it is now required for all students up to the age of 16. The instruction is the central element in the revival of the language. The strategy is to promote a bilingual Wales so that the two languages can coexist.

Source: "Proud Effort to Revive Tongue Meets Success,"

EXHIBIT 6.2 JAPANESE CULTURE AND BUSINESS PRACTICES

Impressions of each other

Americans talk too much, the Japanese are too polite. Americans are too time-conscious, the Japanese are too slow at making decisions.

These are just some of the perceived and real cultural differences between these two countries that can affect business decisions, according to Hiroki Kato, who spoke at the Pacific Rim Futures Conference on cultural differences. Kato, vice-president of Asian development at the Chicago Mercantile Exchange, listed top complaints Japanese and Americans have of each other from John C. Condon's book, *With Respect to the Japanese: A Guide for Americans.*

Americans believe the Japanese are so polite that no one knows what they're thinking. The Japanese are so ambiguous, it's hard to know where they stand. They are conformists. They are always expressing thanks and appreciation and are always apologizing – sometimes for nothing. They put too much weight on certain actions and are too slow at making decisions. They are very ethnocentric, yet imitative, and they are overly impresses by status. The Japanese are too formal.

What do the Japanese think about Americans?

Besides talking too much, they constantly interrupt other people – even finish sentences. Americans don't listen enough and seem to think if they don't divulge something, no one will know it. Americans are too direct in asking questions, giving opinions and poking fun. They fail to express thanks sufficiently. They are reluctant to admit faults and limitations. American managers give more attention to individuals than to the entire group, which is very embarrassing to the Japanese. Americans do not appreciate the importance of certain formalities in Japan – even to the point of joking about them. Americans are too much in a hurry.

One point was clear in both cultural sessions: Know the proper business etiquette when doing a business. It could make or break the deal.

Source: Ginger Szala, "Are Joint Ventures Worth the Effort?" *Futures* (December 1991): 6. Reprinted from *Futures* Magazine, 219 Parkade, P.O. Box 6, Cedar Falls, Iowa 50613.

---

rude, Americans instead feel that avoidance of eye contact is impolite. In Latino cultures it is also rude to sustain eye contact. In addition, nonverbal cues may vary with a person's gender and social or economic class. Sitting at a table at an angle signals cooperation and active listening. Sitting straight across from one another, on the other hand, may be perceived as being confrontational. Yet sitting side by side makes conversation awkward.

Beckoning someone with a wave of the hand with palm up is fine in America, but very rude in Japan. Foreigners in Indonesia should also think about local nonverbal communication.

Indonesians are polite people. . . . A business guest will often be served something to drink and should not reach for his drink until the host gestures to do so. It is polite to at least sample the drink or any food offered. Indonesians are

not known for their punctuality, so offence should not be taken if events do not start on time or if your guest arrives late. Indonesians avoid the use of the left hand when offering food and other objects, as it is regarded as the unclean hand. It is also considered rude to point with a finger.[24]

Figures 6.2 and 6.3 describe the impact of Asian cultures and how to do business in Japan, Korea, and Singapore.

In a popular and often-quoted article, "The Silent Language in Overseas Business," Edward T. Hall explains that there is a need to appreciate cultural differences in matters concerning the language of time, space, objects, friendship patterns, and agreements. For the purpose of illustration, these languages are discussed here, modified but derived from work done by Hall and by Arning.[25]

You always come back to the basics. JIM BEAM

Figure 6.1 Nonverbal communication and enduring culture

Source: Courtesy of Jim Beam Brands Co.

Language of time

Time has different meanings in different countries. An American and an Asian do not mean the same thing when they say, "Why don't you come over sometime?" In the USA, the statement takes a formal tone, implying that advance notice should be given if the visit is to take place. For an Asian, the meaning is exactly what is said – drop in any time without an appointment, regardless of how early or late it may be in the day. If a person has friends who are moochers, they might conveniently drop by at mealtime so that they will be invited to partake in the food being served.

In Saudi Arabia, a Western-style calendar or daily appointment book is unsuitable as a gift because the 1 January is already halfway into the Islamic year. In Jordan, an Islamic country, the official weekend is on Friday, and the new week begins on Saturday. Therefore, Fridays in Jordan and most of the Middle East are like Sundays in the West. As a result, the outside world can do business with Jordan and other Muslim countries only on Mondays, Tuesdays, Wednesdays, and half of Thursdays (when most businesses close down early).

In the USA, there is a direct relationship between time and the importance of a matter. When a matter is important, it requires immediate attention and action. In some countries, a reverse relationship exists. A matter of importance requires more time to ponder, and to declare a deadline is to exert undue pressure.

Perceptions of time are culture bound, and three different perceptions may be identified: linear-separable, circular-traditional, and procedural-traditional.[26] In the case of **linear-separable time**, common in most European and North American cultures, time is linear in the sense that it has a past, present, and future. Therefore, time is valuable – time spent in the past will make some contribution to the future. In the case of **circular-traditional time**, life is supposed to follow a cycle, and the future thus cannot be altered. As a result, the future is seen as the past repeated, and there is no need to plan because time is not valuable. Finally, in the case of **procedural-traditional time**, the activity or procedure is more relevant than the amount of time spent on it. Time and money are separate, and earnings are determined by task rather than by time. When one activity ends, the next one may begin.

Based on cultural and market-related data collected from the USA, Mexico, Great Britain, France, Germany, Spain, Taiwan, and Korea, advertising strategies appear to be affected by whether or not a culture is linear with regard to perception of time (see Table 6.3 and Figure 6.4). Advertising cultures with a nonlinear perception of time appear to provide scattered and symbolic information without explicit conclusion, and to take the form of a drama-lecture. In contrast, linear cultures tend to use reasoned arguments, visual information, and a credible source that addresses viewers directly.[27]

169

Anyone who does business in Japan knows that aggression often leads to disaster.

The slightest hint of aggression can kill a business deal. Be sure to make your point but don't push it. Many Japanese find it difficult to say no—instead, they may say your request would be hard to fulfill. If you do not get a definite answer, just let the subject drop. Your wisdom should speak for itself.

Bathe in mud.

Or sand. Or sulfur. Or just plain water. You will find all kinds of hot-spring spas and baths throughout Japan. First wash yourself with a bathside basin, leaving no traces of soap, then slip gently into the bath. It's very hot at first, but once you get used to it, there's nothing more relaxing after a hard day's work.

Help!

No problem is too big or small for the Tokyo English Lifeline. They'll answer questions on everything from culture to medical emergencies. Telephone 03/264-4347.

Tipping tips.

There's no such thing as tipping in Japan. More expensive restaurants and hotels add a 10%-15% service charge to your bill, but don't tip cab drivers, waitresses, or bellhops. And do not count your change— it'll be considered a sign of distrust.

Northwest notes.

We now offer exclusive nonstop service from Los Angeles to Osaka and the only daily nonstops from Chicago to Tokyo. And, in addition to providing more service to Japan from the U.S. than any other carrier, we offer something no other airline can: the knowledge that comes from over 40 years of helping people do business in Asia. For international reservations, call your travel agent or Northwest at 1-800-447-4747. To find out more about doing business in Asia, call 1-800-553-2215, ext. 77.

© 1989 Northwest Airlines, Inc.

NORTHWEST AIRLINES
Asia Series

Figure 6.2 *Doing business in Japan*

Source: Courtesy of Northwest Airlines.

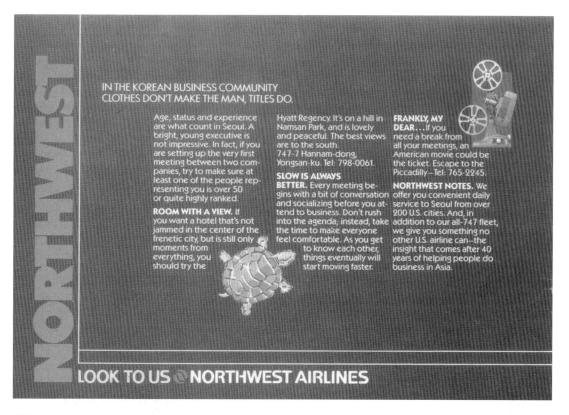

IN THE KOREAN BUSINESS COMMUNITY
CLOTHES DON'T MAKE THE MAN, TITLES DO.

Age, status and experience are what count in Seoul. A bright, young executive is not impressive. In fact, if you are setting up the very first meeting between two companies, try to make sure at least one of the people representing you is over 50 or quite highly ranked.

ROOM WITH A VIEW. If you want a hotel that's not jammed in the center of the frenetic city, but is still only moments from everything, you should try the

Hyatt Regency. It's on a hill in Namsan Park, and is lovely and peaceful. The best views are to the south. 747-7 Hannam-dong, Yongsan-ku. Tel: 798-0061.

SLOW IS ALWAYS BETTER. Every meeting begins with a bit of conversation and socializing before you attend to business. Don't rush into the agenda; instead, take the time to make everyone feel comfortable. As you get to know each other, things eventually will start moving faster.

FRANKLY, MY DEAR... If you need a break from all your meetings, an American movie could be the ticket. Escape to the Piccadilly—Tel: 765-2245.

NORTHWEST NOTES. We offer you convenient daily service to Seoul from over 200 U.S. cities. And, in addition to our all-747 fleet, we give you something no other U.S. airline can—the insight that comes after 40 years of helping people do business in Asia.

NORTHWEST

LOOK TO US ● NORTHWEST AIRLINES

Figure 6.3 *Doing business in Korea*
Source: Courtesy of Northwest Airlines.

Americans tend to value time highly – both work time and leisure time – because "time is money." They often feel that things need to be settled and completed as soon as possible and that they have no time to waste or spare. American impatience is not a virtue in dealing with foreign firms. In general, American negotiators tend to skip the nontask activities and go directly to the agreement stage. Russians, in contrast, have formal classroom training in bargaining and chess. They are patient and careful before making a move, often taking extra time just to gain an advantage in the process of negotiation.

Time takes a more "leisurely walk" in many non-Western societies, where people have ample time and see no need why any situation should be urgent. Whereas Latin American people are usually late,

Swedish people are very prompt. Actually, lack of punctuality may even imply importance and status in some places. But any generalization about punctuality is risky. Asians, for instance, tend not to be punctual, but the Chinese observe strict punctuality for social occasions and appointments. In general, there is a lack of punctuality in Asia and Africa, and it is not uncommon for people to be half an hour or an hour late for an appointment. Usually, no excuse is offered to those who are kept waiting. If an excuse is needed, it may sound something like this: "If I would have hurried through the traffic, I may have been involved in an accident that would have delayed me even more."

Societies hold various views on urgency and punctuality. Time may be important to non-Westerners in different ways. Astrologers and

Table 6.3 Cultural measures by country

Countries*		Cultural dimensions			
		Individualism	Uncertainty avoidance	Power distance	Perception of time
Asia/Pacific	Taiwan	17	69	58	Polychronic
	Korea	18	85	60	Polychronic
	Japan	46	92	54	Polychronic
	Hong Kong	25	29	68	Polychronic
	Australia	90	51	36	Monochronic
	New Zealand	79	49	22	Monochronic
	India	48	40	77	Polychronic
Europe	Norway	69	50	31	Monochronic
	Sweden	71	29	31	Monochronic
	Denmark	74	23	18	Monochronic
	UK	89	35	35	Monochronic
	Netherlands	80	53	38	Monochronic
	Germany	67	65	35	Monochronic
	Belguim	75	94	65	Monochronic
	France	71	86	68	Monochronic
	Austria	55	70	11	Monochronic
	Italy	76	75	50	Monochronic
	Spain	51	86	57	Polychronic
North America	Canada	80	48	39	Monochronic
	USA	91	46	40	Monochronic
	Mexico	30	82	81	Polychronic
South America	Argentina	46	86	49	Polychronic
	Brazil	38	76	69	Polychronic

Note

*Boldface type indicates sample countries.

Source: Fred Zandpour *et al.,* "Global Reach and Local Touch: Achieving Cultural Fitness in TV Advertising," *Journal of Advertising Research* 34 (September/October 1994): 42.

monks are frequently consulted in order to determine the proper time for personal and business matters. The beginning of a construction project, the ceremonial opening of a new building or business, and the right time to marry or to sign a contract are all affected by timing. In India, one should not travel in a time period determined to be unsafe or unlucky. This creates a dilemma for those who are traveling on a plane whose departure time is deemed to be inappropriate. The traveler can, however, circumvent the inappropriate departure time by being flexible. To accommodate both the modern world of travel and the traditional belief concerning the inappropriate departure time of his plane, a traveler may choose to view his departure from home, not from the airport, as the actual time of beginning the travel. If the departure time from home is also inappropriate, the traveler may leave home an hour earlier and drive around for an hour or two before going to the airport.

	Creative strategy				Informativeness			Style	
	Unrelated information	Reasoned argument	Psychological appeals	Symbolic association	Total	Visual	Sound	Drama	Drama-lecture
Asia/Pacific									
Taiwan		░	▓	▓		▓			░
Korea			▓	▓					
Japan	░					▓	▓	▓	
Hong Kong	▓		▓		░				
Australia			░				▓	▓	▓
New Zealand			░				░		
India	▓	░	░				░	░	░
Europe									
Norway							▓		▓
Sweden									▓
Denmark		░			░		▓		
UK									
Netherlands					▓		▓		▓
Germany	░			░				░	░
Belgium		▓		▓		▓	▓	▓	
France		▓						▓	░
Austria	░	░					░		
Italy		▓					▓		
Spain		░	▓		░	░			
North America									
Canada				░				▓	▓
US	░	▓		▓			▓		
Mexico	▓	▓							░
South America									
Argentina	▓			▓			░	░	░
Brazil	▓			▓			░	░	

*Boldface type indicates sample countries

▓ = most likely

░ = least likely

Figure 6.4 *Creative approach, informativeness, and style of TV commercials*

Source: Fred Zandpour et al., "Global Reach and Local Touch: Achieving Cultural Fitness in TV Advertising," *Journal of Advertising Research* 34 (September/October 1994): 49.

Language of space

Space has its own special meaning. Its importance is most evident when people converse with one another. When the other party is nearby, such as in the same room, communication is easily facilitated. Difficulty of communicating increases sharply when the distance between the receiver and sender of a message is great (e.g., when one party is across the street, on another floor, or in another room). In such cases, people have to speak loudly or shout in order to be heard, and the other party may still not hear every word, if any words at all.

Space also has implications for personal selling. Latin Americans are comfortable with ony a few inches of distance between them and repeated embracing. Asians, on the other hand, prefer substantial conversational distance and no physical contact. For Americans, a comfortable distance is something in between these two extremes. An American can give the impression of crowding to an Asian and of running away to a Latin American.

Space is also relative: what is perceived as crowded in the USA may be perceived as spacious somewhere else. A small room with low ceilings, by

US standards, is not small to the Japanese. In US department stores, executive suites are on the top floor and the budget store is in the basement. In Japan, top executives have offices on the ground floor, and the top floor is reserved for bargain-priced merchandise.

Language of agreement

The USA is a very legalistic society. Americans are both specific and explicit in terms of agreement, making legal contracts common and indispensable. Not surprisingly, lawyers become partners in virtually all business deals. When Japan wanted clarification concerning AT&T's products, the company reacted in a typically American fashion by sending a lawyer instead of a manager. Per capita, the USA has more lawyers than any other country in the world. American lawyers earn a good income and are accorded social status not found elsewhere.

According to an old saying in Thailand, "it is better to eat a dog's feces than to engage in a lawsuit." Such thinking explains why the Chinese abhor litigation and why they prefer to withdraw from a deal rather than be involved in potential legal disputes. In many cultures, written contracts are not as binding as one's word. According to people in these societies, if a person cannot be trusted as a friend, then it is futile to expect that person to live up to obligations — written or otherwise.

Even when an agreement is reached, that agreement may not necessarily be ironclad since it can be modified by changing circumstances. In South Korea, a businessperson considers a contract to be a loosely structured consensus statement that allows flexibility and adjustment. In some societies, agreements merely signify intention and have little relation to capacity to perform.

Culture dictates how a disagreement is expressed and resolved. North Americans generally prefer a straightforward approach. Elsewhere, one must be careful in a disagreement never to cause someone else to lose face. Asians, in particular, are sensitive to affronts and can become violent when "loss of face" results. Public humiliation or criticism must thus be avoided in Asia, where politeness is valued over blunt truth.

In Mexico, direct statements of criticism are considered rude, and thus Mexicans practice circumlocution, making it difficult to determine the true meaning. In Latin America, disagreements may be viewed as personal attacks against the individual. Subordinates are expected either to support their managers openly or to keep silent. Similarly, in Japan, silence is perceived as a positive concurrence, and open exchanges and debates are considered inappropriate. Only the top decision maker may comment freely. Japanese stockholders are not allowed to question management critically; companies may hire "guards" to dissuade those who are too curious from asking more questions.

US firms prefer to base decisions on objective criteria, or at least they make that claim. The system makes allowances for those who strongly criticize decisions, but such a process would be unacceptable in countries where it is inappropriate to question an executive's personal judgment. Managers often find themselves in a dilemma, as one cannot consult with others on matters about which one is presumed to be the expert.

As might be expected, the different forms of disagreement may confuse American managers. When potential customers keep quiet, nod their heads, or state that they will think about it, American managers may believe that a deal is developing. But foreign buyers may stay quiet even when the product in question is clearly unsuitable for their needs, because they do not want to offend the American by saying something critical.

Language of friendship

Americans have the unique characteristic of being friendly, even at first meeting. Americans seem to have no difficulty in developing friendship in a very short time, and this trait is carried over into business relationships. American businesspeople are impatient to develop the deep personal ties that are crucial overseas. In many countries, friendship is not taken lightly — it involves real obligations such as

MARKETING ETHICS 6.1   APPRECIATION VS. ACCESS

In Japan, every act of generosity, no matter how small, must be paid back. But the practice also allows people to use it as a disguise to buy access. A renter gives reikin (key money) amounting to two or three months' rent to a landlord as a token of humble appreciation for agreeing to provide an apartment for rental. A few thousand dollars of shiyarei (thankyou money) must be given to entice popular doctors, lawyers, and teachers to take care of you or your family. It is also customary to pay several thousand dollars as thankyou money to a primary school when one's child passes the school's entrance exam, and Catholic schools are not shy about taking this kind of money. Renting a place or getting good medical treatment requires a person to fork out the expected money to a service provider. Money thus defines access or favorable treatment. In these instances, is money an expression of thanks for a special favor, or is it merely a form of institutionalized extortion?

Source: "In Tokyo, You Need a Gift for Giving," *Business Week Online,* June 20, 2001.

---

providing financial and personal help when friends are down and out. It is thus not uncommon that an American businessperson is expected to help his foreign partner to find a school in the USA for the partner's son or daughter. Friendship is not developed as fast in these other countries, but when it is developed it tends to be deeper and longer lasting.

Quite often, it is necessary for potential business partners to become friends first before business is transacted. General Motors Corp. has learned that, in China, the Chinese dine together first before talking business, unlike the US approach of talking business before having a meal together if things go well. Likewise, business is a personal matter in Turkey where friendship should be developed first before determining whether a business relationship is feasible. This is different from the practice in the USA where businesspeople want to do business first before thinking about being friends later.

The manner of addressing a friend can differ depending on the person being addressed, whether a colleague, a business acquaintance, or a customer. The quick friendship characteristic of the USA prompts Americans to use first names in social as well as business encounters soon after a first meeting. This informal approach, claimed to be used to make foreigners feel comfortable, actually makes

Americans themselves comfortable at the expense of foreigners.

The American practice of using first names can be very offensive in other countries, where formality and respect are strongly established traditions. Foreigners find it distasteful for American children to address their parents by their first names. The French as well as most Northern Europeans find the practice offensive. Germans are also formal, and addressing each other by first names is reserved for relatives and close friends. Germans answer the telephone by announcing their last name only. First names, often considered a secret, are revealed only to good friends. In China, it must be understood that the name mentioned first is actually the family name, and thus it would be a mistake to assume that Chinese social customs permit addressing someone by their first or given name.

Addressing someone by their first name is not common outside of the Western hemisphere, unless the first name is accompanied by the proper pronoun or adjective (e.g., Mr. or Mrs.). This formal first-name approach is customary in Asia, Latin America, and the Arab world, whereas the formal last-name approach should be used in Europe. It is thus very important for a businessperson to remember to address foreign counterparts with formal pronouns unless or until being asked to do something else.

175

Language of negotiation

Negotiation styles vary greatly. Hispanic business-people are surprised by Anglos' resistance to bargaining. In the USA, a lack of eye contact is usually viewed as an indication that something is not quite right, but the cultural style of communication negotiation in Japan requires a great deal less eye contact between speakers. Furthermore, in Japan, periods of silence are common during interactions, and a response of silence should not come as a surprise. Americans should learn to be more comfortable with this negotiating tactic, instead of reacting by quickly offering either more concessions or new arguments.

Americans' straightforward style may prove a handicap in business negotiations. Chinese negotiations are generally tough-minded, well prepared, and under no significant time constraints. They are prepared to use various tactics to secure the best deal. While proclaiming ignorance of foreign technology and foreign business practices, these negotiators may actually be willing to play off one competitor against another. In China, foreigners should expect repetitious and time-consuming negotiations. Concessions from the Chinese may not come until Western negotiators, after many days of unproductive negotiations, are ready to give up and head for the airport. Only then will they be called back for further negotiations.

One study found that Chinese executives were more likely than Canadian executives to avoid conflicts. This is understandable because collectivism and group harmony are emphasized in traditional Confucianism and in contemporary socialism. When Chinese managers had to deal with conflicts, however, they were more likely to use negative resolution strategies (i.e., discontinuing or withdrawing negotiation).[28] Another study involved simulated intracultural, one-on-one, buyer–seller negotiations. The findings indicated that Soviet negotiators achieved higher individual profits when employing a competitive approach but that American participants achieved higher profits when employing a more cooperative approach in negotiations.[29]

Language of religion

In search of spiritual guidance, people turn to religion. The major religions are familiar to everyone. In some parts of the world, animism (the belief in the existence of such things as souls, spirits, demons, magic, and witchcraft) may be considered to be a form of religion. Regardless of the religion involved, it is safe to say, specific religious protocols are observed by the faithful (e.g., having evil spirits exorcised).

Religion affects people in many ways because it prescribes proper behavior, including work habits. The Protestant work ethic encourages Christians to glorify God by working hard and being thrifty. Thus many Europeans and Americans believe that work is a moral virtue and disapprove of the idle. Likewise, Islam exalts work, and idleness is seen as a sign of a person's lack of faith in the religion. As such, anyone who is able to work is not allowed to become voluntarily idle. Some religions, however, seem to guide people in the opposite direction. In Hinduism and Buddhism, the emphasis is on the elimination of desires because desires cause worrying. Not striving brings peace, and a person at peace does not suffer.

Marketers must pay attention to religious activities. Buddhists observe the days associated with the birth and death of Buddha and, to a lesser extent, those days of full moon, half moon, and no moon. The entire month of Ramadan is a religious holiday for Muslims, who fast from dawn to dusk each day during that month. Therefore, workers must use part of normal sleeping time for eating. Work productivity can be greatly affected. Furthermore, Muslims pray five times a day, and they stop all work to do so.

There is no doubt that international marketing is affected by religious beliefs. Saudi Arabian publications will not accept any advertisement that has a picture of a woman in it. Sleeveless dresses are considered offensive to Islamic rules, and all advertisements that include pictures of such dresses are banned in Malaysia. Also, religious requirements may prohibit consumption of certain items. Religious taboos include pork and alcohol for

Muslims, beef for Hindus, and pork and shellfish for Jews, and once included meat on Friday for Roman Catholics.

Language of superstition

In the modern world, it is easy to dismiss superstition as nonsense. Yet superstitious beliefs play a crucial role in explaining personal as well as business behavior in all parts of the world. In Asia, fortune telling, palm reading, dream analysis and interpretation, phases of the moon, birthdate, and handwriting analysis, communication with ghosts, and many other beliefs are part of everyday life. Physical appearance is often used to judge a person's character. Long ears, for example, supposedly belong to those who have good fortune.

Some Westerners may be amused to see foreigners taking superstition so seriously. They may not place much credence in animal sacrifices or other ceremonial means used to get rid of evil spirits, but they should realize that their own beliefs and superstitions are just as silly when viewed by foreigners. Americans knock on wood, cross their fingers, and feel uneasy when a black cat crosses their path. They do not want to walk under ladders and may be extra careful on Friday the thirteenth.

It must be remembered that people everywhere are human beings with emotions and idiosyncrasies. They cannot be expected to always behave in a rational and objective manner. In a number of countries (e.g., Colombia), it is not uncommon for priests or monks to bless cars with holy water. While the practice may not have scientific value, it does give owners and drivers peace of mind. Instead of belittling or making fun of superstition, one is prudent to show respect for local customs and beliefs. A show of respect will go a long way in gaining friendship and cooperation from local people.

Language of color

Flowers and colors have their own language and meaning. Preferences for particular colors are determined by culture. Because of custom and taboo,

some colors are viewed negatively. A color deemed positive and acceptable in one culture may be inappropriate in another. According to FTD and Interflora Inc. which send flowers by wire to some 140 countries, the color red is used to cast spells in Mexico, and a white bouquet is necessary to lift the spell. In Spain, red roses are associated more with lust than with love. In France, a dozen as well as thirteen yellow roses are inappropriate: yellow suggests infidelity, and cut flowers by the dozen or any other even number are unlucky. Both the color yellow and the number thirteen are also inappropriate in Latin America where yellow is associated with death rather than with infidelity. In Italy, roses serve as tokens of affection when they are sent in odd numbers to women. In Japan, on the other hand, men are on the receiving end of Valentine's Day. Since a sixteen-petal chrysanthemum is used in the imperial family crest, any other use is disrespectful. Swiss women do not want flowers with strong scents. To Swedish women, a cactus signals the end of a romance.[30]

Other than flowers, colors by themselves have special meaning. Yellow is associated with disease in Africa. White is an appropriate color for a wedding gown in the USA, yet white is used alternately with black for mourning in India, Hong Kong, and Japan. Americans see red when they are angry, but red is a lucky color for the Chinese. It is customary for the Chinese to put money in red envelopes as gifts for employees and children on special occasions, especially on the Chinese New Year's Day.

Using the Luscher color test, a group of researchers asked Chinese, Korean, Japanese, and American respondents about which color they associated with certain words (e.g., expensive, happy, love, and dependable), countries (e.g., Italy, France), institutions (e.g., restaurants, theaters), and product packages (e.g., soft drink label, box of headache remedy). Some colors appear to show cross-cultural consistency. Such colors as purple and gray, however, hold opposite meanings in different cultures.[31]

Marketing managers should be careful when using certain colors since their products because using the wrong color can make or break a deal. A manufacturer of medical systems lost a large order for CAT (computerized axial tomography) scanners in one Middle Eastern country due to the whiteness of the equipment. Parker's white pens did not fare well in China, where white is the color of mourning. Its green pens suffered the same fate in India, where green is associated with bad luck.

Language of gifts

Cultural attitudes concerning the presentation of gifts vary greatly across the globe. Because of varying perceptions of gifts and their appropriateness, good intentions can turn into surprises and even embarrassment when particular gifts violate cultural beliefs. Apparel is not commonly given in the USA, where it is considered too personal a gift, nor in Russia, where it is considered a bribe. In France, Russia, Germany, Taiwan, and Thailand, giving a knife as a present is inappropriate because it may "cut" or "wound" a friendship. Although improper to be given, cutlery can be sold – for a small sum of money as token payment.

Handkerchiefs should never be given in Thailand, Italy, Venezuela, and Brazil because such a gift is akin to wishing a tragedy upon the recipient, implying that something distressing will happen in the near future which will necessitate the use of a handkerchief to wipe away the tears. Prudence requires one not to give potted plants to the sick in Japan because the illness may become more severe by taking deeper root. It is also wise to avoid giving four of anything or any item with four in the name to the Chinese and Japanese because the word sounds like *si* in these languages and means death. Likewise, clocks are a poor choice of gift in China and Taiwan, because the word for a clock sounds like the word for "terminate" or for a pre-funeral visit to the dying.

Many Americans think of gift giving as a waste of time, yet they embrace Christmas gift buying and giving in spite of the excessive commercial overtones. In many parts of the world, a gift is a symbol of thoughtfulness or consideration, and one does not visit another person's home empty-handed. In Japan, the practice is extended to Japanese officials' overseas trips. This old tradition requires the prime minister to carry a gift (miyage) to the country being visited. The gift may take the form of trade policy concessions.

Gift giving is, to a certain extent, an art. Presents are given in Europe only after a personal relationship has developed, but they are given in Japan when people first meet as well as when they part. In Japan, every act of generosity, no matter how small, must be paid back. In addition, form is more important than content. As a result, wrapping (tsutsumi) has been an art in Japan for over ten centuries. Special rules apply to wrapping particular items, and the occasion dictates materials and style. An American businessperson should keep in mind that a gift is often most conspicuous by its absence. Therefore, a cardinal rule in international gift giving is that, when in doubt, one should study closely the customs of the society.

It is useful to distinguish among the parties that receive gifts: good friends, just friends, hi/bye friends, and romantic other. These parties can be arranged on the gift continuum scale (from most to least intimate) of social friendships. There are three models of social exchange that explain gift giving. The first model is mainly economic, and it uses the utilitarian motives of equivalence and equality. The second model relies on the concept of generalized reciprocity and stresses the symbolic value of a gift in strengthening relationships. Such relationships do not seek equivalence and equality, and the relationships permit one-way flows of goods over an extended period of time. The third model is "pure gift." Financial or equivalence considerations are not important. Gift giving is motivated by one's deep desire to please the other person. A Hong Kong study confirms the existence of the gift continuum, which may be used to determine and guide gift exchanges.[32]

SUBCULTURE

Because of differing cultures, worldwide consumer homogeneity does not exist. Neither does it exist in

CULTURAL DIMENSION 6.1   A DIFFERENT KIND OF CUSTOMS BARRIER

- In the People's Republic of China, don't write notes using red ink. This suggests that the writer will die soon. Avoid using the number four at all costs because this, too, signifies death.

- In Thailand, it is considered offensive to show the sole of the shoe or foot to another. Therefore, it is necessary to take care when crossing your legs.

- In Saudi Arabia, the law prohibits the wearing of neck jewelry by men, and Westerners have been arrested for neglecting to observe this rule.

- In Argentina, do not be offended if your business associate arrives thirty to forty minutes late to a meeting.

- In Costa Rica, if you are invited for dinner to a home, bring flowers, chocolates, whisky, or wine. Do not bring calla lilies; they are associated with funerals.

- In Germany, first names are reserved for family members and close friends. Moreover, in German business culture, it is not uncommon for colleagues who have worked together for years not to know of each other's first names.

Source: Margaret Kammeyer, "The Other Customs Barrier," *Export America* (April 2001): 32.

---

the USA. Differences in consumer groups are everywhere. There are white, black, Jewish, Catholic, farmer, truckdriver, young, old, Eastern, and Western consumers, among other numerous groups. Communication problems between speakers of different languages are apparent to all, but people who presumably speak the same language may also encounter serious communication problems. Subgroups within societies use specialized vocabularies. Anyone listening to truckdrivers' conversation on a CB radio could easily verify this point.

In order to understand these diverse groups of consumers, particular cultures must be examined. As the focus is on a subgroup within a society, the more appropriate area for investigation is not culture itself but rather subculture, namely culture on a smaller and more specific level.

A subculture is a distinct and identifiable cultural group that has values in common with the overall society but also has certain characteristics that are unique to itself. Thus, subcultures are groups of people within a larger society. Although the various subcultures share some basic traits of the wider culture, they also preserve their own customs and lifestyles, making them significantly different from other groups within the larger culture of which they are a part. Indonesia, for instance, has more than 300 ethnic groups, with lifestyles and cultures that seem thousands of years apart.

There are many different ways to classify subcultures. Although race or ethnic origin is one obvious way, it is not the only one. Other demographic and social variables can be just as suitable for establishing subcultures within a nation.

The degree of intra-country homogeneity varies from one country to another. In the case of Japan, the society as a whole is remarkably homogeneous. Although some regional and racial diversities as well as differences among income classes are to be found, the differentials are not pronounced. There are several reasons why Japan is a relatively homogeneous country. It is a small country in terms of area, making its population geographically concentrated. National pride and management philosophy also help to forge a high degree of unity. As a result, people work together harmoniously to achieve common goals. The need to work hard together was fostered initially by the need to repair the economy after World War II, and the lessons learned from this experience have not been forgotten.

Canada, in contrast, is a large country in terms of geography. Its population, though much smaller than that of Japan, is much more geographically dispersed, and regional differences exist among the provinces, each having its own unique characteristics. Furthermore, ethnic differences are clearly visible to anyone who travels across Canada.

One study of the relationship between ethnicity and lifestyle found significant differences among English, French, Italian, and Greek Canadians even when sociodemographic variables were controlled. Greek Canadians, for example, are more brand loyal but dislike credit. Each ethnic group, due to its size, may require a differentiated marketing strategy.[33]

Canada's social environment makes it possible for ethnic groups to be active members of Canadian society while having the freedom to pursue their own native customs. The environment thus accommodates what is known as ethnic pluralism. Canadians not only tolerate but even encourage diversity in ethnic customs.

Ethnically speaking, two prominent subcultures emerge: English speaking and French speaking. Studies have repeatedly shown that the French-speaking and English-speaking households differ from each other significantly in terms of demographics, subculture, and consumption habits. French Canadians' consumer behavior is a cross between that of North Americans and that of the continental French, being both similar to and different from those of these two groups. Compared to the French, Quebecers are more direct, less dramatic, and less formal. Compared to other English Canadians, Quebecers move far less often and thus have far less need to make long-distance phone calls to relatives and friends. Although Bell Canada was successful in English Canada with an advertisement that tied together environmental concerns with long-distance service, the advertisement did not work well in Quebec where people are less likely to join a car pool or sort domestic garbage for recycling. As a result, Bell Canada adapted the message to reflect Quebecers' lifestyles by showing a businessman calling home to speak to his daughter.[34]

In the USA, the population increase among blacks, Hispanics, and Asians has been explosive. According to the 2000 US census, these three groups account for 79 million out of 281 million Americans and $1 trillion in annual spending power.

The number of Latinos in the USA is growing at more than twice the rate of blacks, and the Latino population (at 37 million in 2003) is the country's largest minority group. Latinos, making up about 30 percent of California's population, account for a majority of births (about 50 percent) in the state.[35] Demographically, Hispanic households are larger than white households, with 30.6 percent of Hispanic households having five or more people. In addition, they have their own distinctive consumption habits. They are less likely to use credit, and soccer is an integral part of their lives. Latino holidays and cultural events are marketing opportunities. Other than holidays and holy days, religious passageways (christenings, communions, and anniversaries) are important events. Likewise, Quinceanera (a girl's 15th birthday) requires make-up, high heels, nylons, gowns, cards, and so on. Interestingly, the Hispanic population has grown to the point that Procter & Gamble even aired a Spanish-language commercial for its Crest Whitening Plus Scope toothpaste during the Grammy Awards. Titled Goodbye Kiss, the commercial's tagline was in English – "White teeth and fresh breath . . . in any language."[36]

Given the fact that each subcultural group is a part of the larger culture while possessing its own unique cultural, demographic, and consumption characteristics, the issue of market heterogeneity must be recognized. Because individuals' values vary across subcultures, business outcomes may vary as well. As in the case of Brazil's four regional subcultures, subculture affects both motivational domains and business performance.[37] Another study investigated the decision-making patterns of blacks, Hispanics, and whites in the USA when purchasing leisure clothes (value-expressive product) and small electronics (utilitarian product). These groups differed in their informational influences (media and reference group) as well as in their perceptions of store attribute importance, and the patterns also differed between the two product types. Advertisers should thus adjust their advertising messages according to the ethnic groups and product types.[38]

One marketing question is the language that should be used so as to effectively appeal to a particular subculture. According to one study, Spanish-language advertising positively affected Hispanic consumers in the USA by signaling solidarity with the Hispanic community. However, exclusive use of Spanish in advertising also had a negative effect since it appeared to arouse Hispanic insecurities about language use.[39] Therefore, language choice requires more research.

"Ethnic self-awareness" is a temporary state during which a person is more sensitive to information related to one's ethnicity. It occurs when the person engages in a process of self-categorization and uses ethnic criteria as a basis for this categorization. This awareness can be aroused by individual difference variables, situational factors, and other contextual or stimulus primes in environment (e.g., visual or verbal cues that draw attention to ethnicity). When aroused, this awareness can moderate consumer responses to an advertising message. A study of 109 Asian and Caucasian participants found that ethnic prime increased the participants' likelihood to spontaneously mention their ethnicity in self-descriptions. This then led to a more favorable response to the same ethnicity spokesperson and the advertisement that targeted their ethnicity. In other words, the use of ethnic actors alone is not meaningful unless consumers can be aroused first to evoke ethnic self-awareness.[40]

Subculture may provide an effective basis for market segmentation. American firms attempt to attract various subcultural groups in many different ways. Carnival Cruise Lines has an entire cruise ship (Fiesta Marina) just for the Hispanic market. McDonald's has created a Mac Report series of Spanish infomercials. J.C. Penney has outfitted 170 stores to carry merchandise for Hispanic and African-American consumers. AT&T, MCI, and Sprint have advertised their long-distance phone services in a variety of Asian dialects.

While Sears Roebuck and Co. advertises in a generic form of Spanish, it also recognizes regional differences. It adopts a Mexican flavor in the Southwest of the USA and a Caribbean theme in the East. Along the same line, marketers need to appreciate linguistic variations. "Delincuente" means delinquent in Puerto Rico but may mean criminal in Mexico. "Cancelar," depending on a person's origin, may mean either to cancel or to pay off an account. Beans are "frijoles" in Cuba but "habicheulas" in Puerto Rico.[41]

It is not exactly unusual for a company to use a cosmetic line to target an ethnic group. Maybelline's Shades of You and Revlon's Polished Ambers were both aimed at African-American and Latin consumers. Both were unsuccessful and have folded these shades into their conventional lines. Avon hopes to do better. As the world's largest direct seller, Avon has always extended its products beyond the US market. The company's catalog appears in twelve languages and 143 countries. Avon is Latin America's top seller. To attract Hispanic women in the USA, Avon has introduced *Avon Eres Tu* ("It's You"), a bilingual catalog. Instead of simply translating its current catalog, *Eres Tu* also includes new products and beauty tips that do well in Latin American markets. Unlike Maybelline's and Revlon's past efforts, Avon's products are tailored more specifically to Latinas, and the catalog features only Latina models. Because Hispanics vary from being very light to very dark, *Avon Eres Tu* provides shades that perfectly match Latina skin tones.[42]

CONCLUSION

Culture prescribes acceptable beliefs, traditions, customs, and values that are then socially shared. Culture is subjective, enduring yet dynamic, and cumulative. It affects people's behavior in diverse ways through logic, communication, and consumption. Although some cultural traits are universal, many others are unique and vary from country to country. And in spite of national norms, cultural differences as a rule even exist within each country.

While there may be a tendency to misunderstand different cultures and subcultures, this temptation should be resisted. Being the force that it is, the culture of one country should not be judged as superior to the culture of another country. Each culture has its own particular values and social practices, and the international marketer will be much further ahead if he or she tries to walk in the other person's shoes in order to understand more clearly that person's concerns and ideas.

Because marketing takes place within a given culture, a firm's marketing plan assumes meaning or is appropriate only when it is relevant to that culture. A US company should understand that foreign consumers are not obligated to take on American values – nor may those consumers desire to do so. In addition, it is more important to know what a person thinks than what that person's language is. Because of the great differences in language and culture around the world, American firms need to adjust their approach to solving marketing problems in different countries. In a foreign cultural environment, the marketing plan that has worked well at home may no longer be effective. As a result, the firm's marketing mix may have to undergo significant adaptation and adjustment. Effective marketing in this environment will thus mandate that the company be culturally responsive.

CASE 6.1   CROSS-CULTURAL MARKETING: A CLASSROOM SIMULATION

James B Stull, San José State University

This simulation is designed for a fifteen-week, two seventy-five minute periods per week consumer behavior course, with approximately forty students per section; adaptations for course length and size are encouraged. Before commencing with the simulation, naturally an explanation to the students is necessary to show how the simulation meets the objectives of the course.

- ■ *Week 1*   Assign students to research groups, one group for each cultural component (language, attitudes, religion, social organization, education, technology, politics and law); five students per group. Provide groups with bibliographies if available. Have the groups focus on the major considerations within each component.
- ■ *Weeks 1–5*   Pace student research groups through their research procedures, keeping them aware that they will be presenting their findings to the class during weeks six through nine. Provide sufficient in-class time for brainstorming, problem-solving and question-feedback sessions. These first five weeks may also be spent covering or highlighting portions of textbook not highlighted by simulation.
- ■ *Weeks 6–9*   Groups present their findings; for current simulation, one cultural component is presented each class period for eight successive meetings. Students should be encouraged to participate and take notes because the information will be used during the third module of the simulation.
- ■ *Weeks 10–15*   During week 10, form new groups; assign one member from each *research* group to each new group so that each new group has eight members, one specialist from each previous group. Each new group will function as a business organization representing a separate, unique culture. Distribute handout similar to Table 6.4.

Procedure

1   *Each culture should gain its own identity early.* Have each culture consult its specialists to develop a clear understanding of its own identity regarding each component. Focus on developing specific verbal and non-verbal language norms which will be observed during negotiations with other cultures. This may take a few class days.

Table 6.4 Cultural variables

Variables	Culture				
	BWANA	FELIZ	LEUNG	KORAN	DHARMA
Language	Swahili	Spanish	Cantonese	Arabic	Hindi
Religion (major)	Animistic	Catholicism	Buddhism	Muslim	Hindu
Education	Informal	Secondary (urban only)	Formal Tech/trade	*Koran*	Formal/developing
Technology	Low/ developing	Moderate/ developing	Low–moderate developing	Low	Agricultural/low/ developing
Politics	Republic	Republic/ unstable	Communist/ nationalist	Muslim	Socialist–British colony
Legal system	Indigenous	Civil	Common/communist	Muslim	Common
Attitudes	(to find)[1]				
Social organization	(to find)[2]				

Notes

1 Attitudes: find out general attitudes toward time, space, work, achievement, wealth and material gain, change, etc.
2 Social organization: find out general role relationships in terms of families, friendships, reference groups, social classes, unions, etc.

2 Have cultures study other cultures to gain familiarity with each cultural component.

3 Instruct cultures that their overall goal is to market a product (or product line), service or idea to each other culture, and that their success depends upon how well they know their own culture and how it compares with other cultures.

4 Have cultures develop a product, service or idea which they feel is compatible with their own culture and which they feel they can market successfully to each other culture. This does not have to be an invention, merely an innovation for the new market.

5 Have cultures develop a marketing strategy for each other target culture, being sensitive to the idiosyncrasies of each.

6 Have cultures negotiate with each other, persisting until a contract has been settled or until a perceived stalemate has been reached.

7 Discuss the simulation, focusing on affective and cognitive realizations and cultural sensitivity developed.

Each step may take a few class periods, especially those involving cultural self-identity and assessment of other cultures. Depending upon the population of the course, various levels of marketing and advertising activity may be reached by participants.

Discussion

During this simulation, students are exposed to conditions utilizing a variety of communication skills: brainstorming, encoding, decoding, role playing, decision making, problem solving, library research, cultural sensitivity and more.

Further research is currently underway to determine learning, cross-cultural sensitivity development, and student attitudes towards and perceptions of benefits of the simulation. Additional research is being conducted to apply this simulation to Latin American markets.

This simulation also strengthens interpersonal awareness on a *micro* level. If *macro* – cross-cultural – differences are stressed, it may be safe to assume that participants will recognize that any behavioral differences, even where major cultural differences do not apply, are due to the infinite variety of experiences of each member of any society.

Adaptions of this exercise are feasible to meet the needs of industrial and government training programs.

Source: James B. Stull, San José State University. Copyright 1980. Reprinted with permission.

QUESTIONS

1   What are the characteristics of culture?
2   Explain the impact of culture on consumption.
3   What is the SRC (self-reference criterion)?
4   Distinguish between high-context and low-context cultures.
5   Distinguish between monochronic and polychronic cultures.
6   Explain how the meanings of time, space, agreement/disagreement, and friendship can vary from one culture to another. Also discuss their business implications.

DISCUSSION ASSIGNMENTS AND MINICASES

1   Which of the following seems to better characterize the world: cultural commonality or cultural diversity?
2   Because English is the world language of business, is it necessary for US managers to learn a foreign language?
3   Do you agree that the USA is a "melting-pot"?
4   As Hispanic consumers in the USA are also American consumers, is it necessary for marketers to adjust their marketing mix for this market segment?
5   Explain how culture affects the ways people use eating utensils (e.g., fork, spoon, knife, chopsticks).
6   Explain why people in several countries are upset when they see: (a) an advertisement showing an American crossing his legs or putting his legs on a table; and (b) Americans wearing shoes in their homes.
7   According to Edward T. Hall, a renowned anthropologist, Americans are more comfortable with Germans than with the Japanese because Germans generally make eye contact to indicate attention to a speaker. However, the Americans feel that the Germans do not smile often enough. How do the Germans and Japanese regard the Americans' frequent smiles and eye contact?
8   According to William Wells of the DDB Needham Worldwide advertising agency, American TV commercials are usually shown either as an illustrated lecture or as a drama in which a product is a prop (or a mixture of both techniques). Why is the lecture approach (a low-context technique) inappropriate for high-context cultures? Why is the drama approach (a high-context technique) appropriate for Japan? Note that Japanese commercials go to great lengths to present cues that are not product-related before devoting only a few seconds to the product itself at the end. To American advertisers, this advertising approach is ambiguous and puzzling.
9   What are the stereotypes of the following groups: Arabs, Asians, Africans, and Latin Americans? Why is it undesirable to use stereotyping as a basis to understand foreigners? Also identify the positive traits and values of the groups mentioned above.
10   What are some of the unique characteristics of the US culture? What are some of the unique business characteristics of the Japanese culture?

NOTES

1 Donnel A. Briley, Michael W. Morris, and Itamar Simonson, "Reasons as Carriers of Culture: Dynamic versus Dispositional Models of Cultural Influence on Decision Making," *Journal of Consumer Research* 27 (September 2000): 157–78.

2 "India Honors Bride Who Fought Dowry," *San José Mercury News*, May 17, 2003.

3 "Singapore Lets Its Hair Down," *International Herald Tribune*, July 15, 2003.

4 "Malts Hot in Mideast," *San José Mercury News*, February 13, 2003.

5 James A. Lee, "Cultural Analysis in Overseas Operations," *Harvard Business Review* 44 (March to April 1966): 106, 111.

6 Edward T. Hall, *Beyond Culture* (Garden City, NY: Anchor Press/Doubleday, 1976).

7 Hall, *Beyond Culture*.

8 George P. Murdock, "The Common Denominator of Cultures," in *The Science of Man in the World Crisis*, ed. Ralph Linden (New York, NY: Columbia University Press, 1945), 123–42.

9 Basil G. Englis, Michael R. Solomon, and Richard D. Ashmore, "Beauty Before the Eyes of Beholders: The Cultural Encoding of Beauty Types in Magazine Advertising and Music Television," *Journal of Advertising* 23 (June 1994): 49–64.

10 "Plastic Surgery for Minorities," *San José Mercury News*, August 24, 2002.

11 "Vietnamese Women Make an Anti-Sun Fashion Statement," *San José Mercury News*, November 18, 2002.

12 "Fat Is ideal Body Shape in West Africa," *San José Mercury News*, February 17, 2001.

13 "Lost Languages," *San José Mercury News*, August 26, 2001.

14 "Lost Languages."

15 "Gene That Generates Language Found, English Scientists Say," *San José Mercury News*, October 4, 2001.

16 Simon Anholt, "The Problem of International Work: Why Copy Can't Be Translated," *DM News*, January 23, 1995, 13.

17 *The Tower of Business Babel: A Guide for the Correct Use of the English Language in International Trade* (Janesville, WI: Parker Pen Co., 1983).

18 Justin Fox, "The Triumph of English," *FORTUNE*, September 18, 2000, 209ff.

19 David R. Berlo, *The Process of Communication* (New York, NY: Holt, Rinehart, & Winston, 1960), 164.

20 Bernd H. Schmitt, "Language and Visual Imagery: Issues of Corporate Identity in East Asia," *Columbia Journal of World Business* 30 (winter 1995): 28–36.

21 Bernd H. Schmitt, Yigang Pan, and Nader T. Tavassoli, "Language and Consumer Memory: The Impact of Linguistic Differences Between Chinese and English," *Journal of Consumer Research* 21 (December 1994): 419–31.

22 Nader T. Tavassoli and Jin K. Han, "Scripted Thought: Processing Korean Hancha and Hangul in a Multimedia Context," *Journal of Consumer Research* 28 (December 2001): 482–93.

23 David Luna and Laura A. Peracchio, "Moderators of Language Effects in Advertising to Bilinguals: A Psycholinguistic Approach," *Journal of Consumer Research* 28 (September 2001): 284–95.

24 *Investment in Indonesia* (Kantor Akuntan Sudjendro and Peat Marwick, 1985), 15–16.

25 Edward T. Hall, "The Silent Language in Overseas Business," *Harvard Business Review* 38 (May to June 1960): 87–96; H. K. Arning, "Business Customs from Malaya to Murmansk," *Management Review* 53 (October 1964): 5–14.

26 Robert J. Graham, "The Role of Perception of Time in Consumer Research," *Journal of Consumer Research* 7 (March 1981): 335–42.

27   Fred Zanpour *et al.*, "Global Reach and Local Touch: Achieving Cultural Fitness and TV Advertising," *Journal of Advertising Research* 34 (September/October 1994): 35–63.

28   David K. Tse, June Francis, and Jan Walls, "Cultural Differences in Conducting Intra- and Inter-Cultural Negotiations: A Sino-Canadian Comparison," *Journal of International Business Studies* 25 (No. 3, 1994): 537–55.

29   John L. Graham, Leonid I. Evenko, and Mahesh N. Rajan, "An Empirical Comparison of Soviet and American Business Negotiations," *Journal of International Business Studies* 23 (No. 3, 1992): 387–418.

30   Karol Stonger, "If You're Saying It with Flowers, Make Sure the Message Is Clear," *San José Mercury News*, February 8, 1990.

31   Laurence Jacobs *et al.*, "Cross-Cultural Colour Comparisons: Global Marketers Beware!" *International Marketing Review* 8 (No. 3, 1991): 21–30.

32   Annamma Joy, "Gift Giving in Hong Kong and the Continuum of Social Ties," *Journal of Consumer Research* 28 (September 2001): 239–56.

33   Michael Hui *et al.*, "Equivalence of Lifestyle Dimensions across Four Major Subcultures in Canada," *Journal of International Consumer Marketing* 5 (No. 3, 1993): 15–35.

34   Julie Snyder, "Promoting Consumer Goods and Services in Quebec, Canada's Distinct, French-Speaking Market," *Business America*, November 1, 1993, 22–3.

35   "More Than Half of State's Newborns Are Latinos," *San José Mercury News*, February 6, 2003.

36   "Crest's Prime-Time Ad Targets Hispanics," *San José Mercury News*, February 22, 2003.

37   Tomasz Lenartowicz and Kendall Roth, "Does Subculture within a Country Matter? A Cross-Cultural Study of Motivational Domains and Business Performance in Brazil," *Journal of International Business Studies* 32 (second quarter, 2001): 305–25.

38   Youn-Kyung Kim and Jikyeong Kang, "The Effects of Ethnicity and Product on Purchase Decision Making," *Journal of Advertising Research* (March to April 2001): 39–48.

39   Scott Koslow, Prem N. Shamdasani, and Ellen E. Touchstone, "Exploring Language Effects in Ethnic Advertising: A Sociolinguistic Perspective," *Journal of Consumer Research* 20 (March 1994): 575–85.

40   Mark R. Forehand and Rohit Deshpande, "What We See Makes Us Who We Are: Priming Ethnic Self-Awareness and Advertising Response," *Journal of Marketing Research* 38 (August 2001): 336–48.

41   "In Pursuit of El Dorado," *Credit Card Management* (October 2000): 61–8.

42   "Avon Courts Latinas with New Look," *San José Mercury News*, October 4, 2002.

Chapter 7

Consumer behavior in the international context

Psychological and social dimensions

Oh what power . . . to see ourselves as others see us!

Robert Burns

CHAPTER OUTLINE

- Perspectives on consumer behavior
- Motivation
- Learning
- Personality
  - ☐ Personality traits
  - ☐ Hofstede's national cultures
  - ☐ Clustering: commonality and diversity
- Psychographics
- Perception
  - ☐ Formation of perception
  - ☐ Country of origin and perceived product quality
- Attitude
- Social class
- Group
- Family
- Opinion leadership
- Diffusion process of innovations
- Conclusion
- Case 7.1 Beneath Hijab: marketing to the veiled women of Iran

PURPOSE OF CHAPTER

Consumers' perceptions are highly subjective, and consumers can be quite unpredictable. The complex nature of consumers makes the study and understanding of consumer behavior imperative. Sweden and Colombia have both attempted to affect consumer perceptions. The Juan Valdez campaign of the Federation of Colombian Coffee Growers has been successful in creating a desirable image for its product and using it to communicate with consumers. Volvo, likewise, has successfully nurtured an image of safety.

Because the influence of culture has already been discussed in depth in Chapter 6, this chapter covers other relevant concepts. The focus is on the major approaches used to study consumer behavior. The basic purpose of this chapter is to acknowledge the role that determinants other than culture play in influencing consumer behavior. The chapter thus examines the psychological and social dimensions, and these include motivation, learning, personality, psychographics, perception, attitude, social class, group, family, opinion leadership, and the diffusion process of innovations.

MARKETING ILLUSTRATION   IT'S NOT A SMALL WORLD AFTER ALL

To compete with Brazil and Mexico, the Federation of Colombian Coffee Growers needed an image (see Figure 7.1). Based on its composite Colombian coffee man, it wanted a Latin name that was both pronounceable and easy to remember for Americans. Thus Juan was chosen as the first name because it is easy and rhymes with one (coffee beans are picked one by one). Since Rodriguez is too complicated a name for Americans, Valdez was picked as the last name. A nationwide search was arranged for a Colombian actor who would fit the American conception of the Latin male. The screening led to Carlos Sanchez, a relatively impoverished, university-educated silk-screen artist and sometime actor. The Federation's marketing campaign has been very effective.

Sweden, a country of nine million people, has long, harsh, and dark winters to go with its moose-ridden roads; yet it has one of the world's lowest traffic fatality rates. This should not be surprising because safety is part of Sweden's heritage. Volvo and Saab are well known for automotive-safety innovations. Volvo, in particular, is world famous for its automotive safety rather than style (see Figure 7.2). The emphasis on safety guides the car makers to exceed the legal crash-test requirements. Both have studied real-world accidents that have resulted in such innovations as the Saab active head restraint. Saab has even placed

Some people can't wait for their next coffee break.

Figure 7.1 *Colombian coffee and product image*

Source: Courtesy of the National Federation of Coffee Growers of Colombia.

the ignition key in a center console so as to prevent a driver from suffering knee injuries in head-on collisions. The safety expertise was a significant reason for Ford to buy Volvo in 1999 and GM to wholly buy Saab in 2000.

Sources: "The Real Juan Valdez," *San José Mercury News*, March 27, 1989; "Coffee Growers to Open US Stores," *San José Mercury News*, November 29, 2003; and "Why Swedish Means Safe," *San José Mercury News*, April 11, 2003.

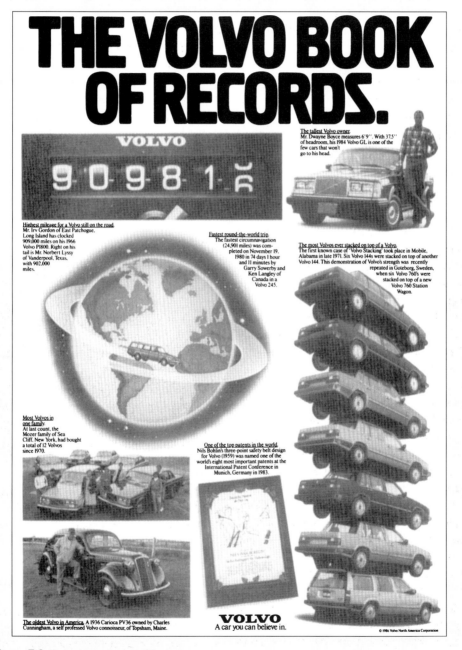

Figure 7.2 *Volvo's product positioning*

Source: Reprinted with permission of Volvo North America Corp.

PERSPECTIVES ON CONSUMER BEHAVIOR

Consumer behavior may be defined as a study of human behavior within the consumer role and includes all the steps in the decision-making process. The study must go beyond the explicit act of purchase to include an examination of less observable processes, as well as a discussion of why, where, and how a particular purchase occurs.

Domestically, marketing scholars have employed a variety of techniques and concepts, including the cultural approach, to study consumer behavior. Yet consumer study on an international basis has employed the cultural approach almost exclusively without much regard for other psychological and social concepts. This is a very curious approach since it is the norm for virtually all consumer behavior textbooks to treat culture as only one of the many theoretical concepts which can affect purchase and the other behavioral dimensions.

It is a questionable practice to rely on culture as the sole determinant of behavior or as the only concept that largely, if not entirely, explains behavior. Culture undoubtedly affects the psychological and social processes and thus affects consumer behavior. However, too much emphasis is placed on a single concept (i.e., culture). Consumer behavior research must include international dimensions.

Differences in behavioral dimensions among national groups "should not be attributed to differences in culture unless components of culture have been specified."[1] For group mean differences to be meaningful, there should be some explanation as to why these differences should exist. Furthermore, there may be a need to develop an international consumer behavior model so that studies of consumer behavior in various countries can be more systematic and better coordinated.[2]

The major behavioral sciences relevant to consumer study are psychology, sociology, and cultural anthropology. **Psychology**, with the *individual* as its central unit of analysis, is the study of individual and interpersonal behavior. Behavior is governed by a person's cognitions, such as values, attitudes, experiences, needs, and other psychological phenomena. Purchase, then, becomes a function of the psychological view of products, and the consumer buys a product not only for consumption but also because of a perception of how a product can be used to communicate with other people. Some psychological concepts relevant to the study of consumer behavior are motivation, learning, personality, perception, and attitude.

Sociology is the study of groups and human interactions. The unit of analysis is not the individual but rather the *group*. The group, consisting of a set of individuals who interact over time, is important because it can exert a significant influence on a person's preferences and consumption behavior. In many instances, it may be useful for a marketer to view consumers as a group. For example, a family, not an individual, often makes a purchase decision that affects all members of the family group. Important sociological concepts are reference group and family.

Cultural anthropology is the study of human culture. Thus, the analytic perspective may be quite large. Culture involves an aggregate, social category level (i.e., a large group), and the social categories are significant in the sense that they influence consumers' cognitive and personality development. The concepts from this discipline usually included in the analysis of consumer behavior are culture, subculture, and social class.

MOTIVATION

Motivation is fundamental in initiating consumer behavior. Motivation may be viewed as a drive that is directed by a motive formed in relation to a particular goal. Once the motive–drive relationship is developed, the consumer initiates some forms of motivated behavior to satisfy a previously recognized need.

Consumer motives are determined largely by buying habits, though motives can vary, and it is important to recognize the various types of motives. Motives may be classified as rational and nonrational. Examples of **rational motives** are price, durability, and economy in operation. **Nonrational appeals**, in comparison, include prestige, comfort, and pleasure. Figure 7.3 is an automobile advertisement that combines both emotional and logical motives.

The problem with the conventional classification (i.e., rational vs. emotional) is that a consumer may not recognize emotional motives and may have a tendency to rationalize personal behavior by assigning only rational and socially acceptable motives. In addition, the process of classification is not always straightforward. Convenience, for instance, can be both rational and nonrational at the same time.

In the end, the success of a product is greatly affected by whether its target customers are properly motivated. Whether a motive is rational or irrational is not particularly important. What is important is to identify specific motives relevant for marketing purposes. A critical task is to select, carefully and properly, a relevant motive for the purpose of product promotion. In addition, the relevance of a particular motive may vary across

21 LOGICAL REASONS TO BUY A SAAB.

In each of us, there is a tough, cold, logical side that wants to have hard facts, data and empirical evidence before it will assent to anything.

So when your impulsive, emotional side saw the exciting photograph on the facing page and yelled "Hey, look at this!," your logical side immediately asked to see some solid and relevant information about the Saab.

Here, then, are some of the more significant hard facts about Saabs, facts that make a strong logical argument in favor of owning a Saab:

1) Front-wheel drive. Once, Saab was one of the few cars in the U.S. that offered this. Since then, most other carmakers have discovered the superior handling and safety of front-wheel drive and have followed Saab's lead.

2) Turbocharging. More power without more engine displacement. Saab's third generation of turbocharging, incorporating an intercooler and Saab's Automatic Performance Control system, is still a generation or two ahead of any competition.

3) Four-valve technology. Doubling the number of valves per cylinder improves engine efficiency enormously. Yet another group of manufacturers is beginning to line up behind Saab.

4) Advanced ergonomics. That's just a way of saying that all instruments, controls and functional elements are designed so that they will be easy and natural to use. A legacy of Saab's aerospace heritage. Saab is the only car manufacturer which

also builds supersonic military jets.

5) Special steel underpanel. The Saab's smooth underside improves its aerodynamics and helps shed water to prevent rust.

6) Balance. 60% of the car's weight is borne by the front wheels, to maintain a consistent slight understeer and superior traction.

7) Rustproofing. A 16-step process that's designed to protect the car from the wetness and saltiness of Sweden's long winters.

8) Climate control. Your Saab is going to be comfortable inside, whatever is happening outside. Air conditioning is standard on all models, and effective insulation helps to control the temperature as well as the noise level inside.

9) High capacity electrical system. For reliable starts in subarctic cold.

10) Advanced Sound System. When you're in the Saab, the AM/FM cassette system sounds wonderful. When you get out, it can come with you, to provide the most theft deterrent possible.

11) One of the world's safest steering wheels. Heavily padded and designed to collapse in a controlled manner in case of heavy impact.

12) Safety cage construction. Last year, the U.S. Highway Loss Data Institute ranked the safety of cars based on actual damage and injury claims. Saab 900's were safer than any other midsize sedans.

13) Fold-down rear seats. This

makes Saab the only performance sedan in the world that can provide up to 56 cubic feet of cargo space.

14) Large, 15-inch wheels. They permit good high-speed control with a very comfortable ride. They also permit larger disc brakes all around.

15) Price. It's modest, particularly when you see it against comparable Audi, BMW, Mercedes or Volvo models.

16) Side-cornering lights. These show you what you're getting into when you signal for a turn at night.

17) Front seats. Firmly supportive, orthopedically shaped and adjustable in practically every dimension you can imagine. They're even heated.

18) Saab dealers. They're all over the country, waiting to help you with specially trained mechanics and comprehensive stocks of Saab parts, and. . .

19) Saab accessories. These may be a bit too much fun for your logical side. They let you customize your Saab with factory-approved performance wheels, floor mats, fog lights and so on. And on. And on.

20) Saab's aircraft heritage. The first Saab automobile was designed by aircraft engineers who established a company tradition of carefully rethinking problems rather than just adopting the conventional solution.

21) The Saab driving experience. Best expressed on the facing page.

The most intelligent cars ever built.

Figure 7.3 *Buying motives*

Source: Reprinted with permission of Saab-Scania of America, Inc.

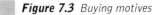

countries. For example, one study of youths in Hong Kong, Singapore, Canada, and Hawaii compared their beliefs in money, business ethics, *quanxi*, and machiavellian personality. Surprisingly, Canadians believe that money can work wonders — even more so than their Hong Kong and Singapore counterparts.[3]

LEARNING

Like all habits, food and drink habits are learned. Before World War II, the British were accustomed to drinking tea, not coffee. Then along came the American troops, who brought the American taste for coffee — at first a relatively light, almost blond coffee. Before long, Britons had learned to drink coffee too. In another example, a large lunch with wine presents no problem to a Swiss, but the same will put an American to sleep. On the other hand, American-style cocktails may prove to be too much for Europeans, who are accustomed to milder drinks. Marketers must take these habits into consideration.

Motives, cultural norms, and consumption habits are all learned. Therefore, a marketer should understand the learning process. Learning is a change in behavior that occurs over time relative to a given set of external stimulus conditions. Baskin-Robbins, as the first fast-food franchise in Vietnam, has to teach the Vietnamese about the concept of fast food. When the ice cream parlor first opened, most Vietnamese customers walked in and sat down, expecting to be waited on. When they were asked to go to the counter, some felt insulted and left. In addition the Vietnamese are accustomed to linger at café tables and are thus not used to having to pay immediately. Naturally, a number of them got angry and felt that Baskin-Robbins did not trust them by asking them to pay for the ice cream immediately. Interestingly, one learned behavior is that the rum raisin flavor, not that popular in the plain vanilla US market, is quite popular among the Vietnamese as well as many other Asians.

A marketer can play a significant role in facilitating the learning process by using a variety of rewards to encourage learning. Infant formula, as

IT'S THE LAW 7.1   FOOD AND RELIGION

Indonesia is the world's largest Islamic country. Halal, an Arabic word for "allowed," is a label for foods that comply with Islamic laws.

MSG (monosodium glutamate) is a taste enhancer that is used by many millions of Asians every single day. Ajinomoto Co., a Japanese food giant, is a dominant brand. Over the years, it has had to combat many rumors that cast doubts on the quality or safety of its MSG product. The company's Indonesian subsidiary, PT Ajinomoto, had one big problem in Indonesia in 2001. The Ulema's Council, a religious body determining whether food products comply with Islamic law, alleged that the Ajinomoto seasoning contained enzymes grown on pork fat. The police even detained eight directors (including three Japanese) for questioning.

Ajinomoto announced that, while its subsidiary used an enzyme from pork to make four products, the enzyme itself was not in the final products. The controversy forced the company to remove hundreds of tons of its products from the market. Indonesia's president, in defense of the Ajinomoto, stated that the council erred in its findings. President Abdurrahman Wahid also mentioned that political forces had unjustly blamed Ajinomoto so as to incite Muslim unrest. After the president's announcement, police released the company's Japanese vice-president from custody.

Sources: "Indonesia Releases Ajinomoto Official," *Asian Wall Street Journal*, January 11, 2001; "Wahid Blasts Ban of Food Product," *Asian Wall Street Journal*, January 10, 2001.

an example, is useful in many non-Western countries for well-to-do women who do not want to bother with breast-feeding. Poor women seek the reward of using this status symbol and of having fatter babies – a benefit implied by this product. Furthermore, young mothers like the prestige of using American or European products.

PERSONALITY

Personality study has long been a subject of interest to marketers due to the assumption that product purchases are an extension of a consumer's personality. Figure 7.4 makes a reference to a person's personality as a factor in choosing a car. Personality, derived from a Latin word meaning "personal" or "relating to person," is the individual characteristics that make a person unique as well as consistent in adjustments to a changing environment. Personality is an integrated system that holds attitude, motivation, and perception together. To study a personality is to study the person as a whole – not only the separate, individual elements that make up a person.

Personality traits

Personality traits are relatively stable qualities, but they do vary in degree from person to person. Because personality study applies to a person rather than to a group, it is difficult to make generalizations about personality traits among people of a particular country. Nevertheless, it is useful to consider the concept of **national character**, which states that "people of each nation have a distinctive, enduring pattern of behavior and/or personality characteristics."[4] The English, for example, are highly impulse-restrained and unassertive.

Despite the difficulty, particular personality traits seem dominant in certain countries. Koreans see themselves as being driven by two complementary passions that are uniquely theirs: *han* (bitterness) and *jong* (devoted love). The interplay of the two explains Korea's ability to be at once intensely productive and violent, to both drive and stall a society, and to be capable simultaneously of love and hate.[5]

While both South Korea and Japan display a mixture of ancient and modern Asian cultures, they also differ in a number of ways. In spite of South Korea's Confucian culture and the bowing, deference, traditions, and formality, the Koreans are also passionate, emotional, intense, energetic, emotional, fun-loving, and impatient. In fact, one of the phrases that is heard most often in South Korea is "balli, balli" (hurry, hurry). Compared to Tokyo, Seoul is more chaotic.[6]

One study used the Myers-Briggs Type Inventory to contrast Canadian and Japanese MBA students and found differences in cognitive style.[7] On the judging–perceiving dimension, the Canadians sought fast decisions and rushed to closure on data collection, while such actions may frustrate the Japanese who showed a preference for larger amounts of information. On the thinking–feeling dimension, the Japanese, as expected, preferred forming personal relationships before business was transacted.

One personality trait that has gained recent attention is consumer ethnocentrism.[8] Adapted from the general concept of ethnocentrism, consumer ethnocentrism explains that, due to patriotic and nationalistic sentiments as well as a personal level of prejudice against imports, some consumers feel that it is inappropriate or even immoral to buy imported products. Highly ethnocentric consumers thus tend to buy domestic products. Table 7.1 shows the CETSCALE which is used to measure consumer ethnocentrism.

The national markets also possess some other personality characteristics which may affect marketing strategies. Scotland set up Project Galore to develop a strategy to promote the commercial power of Scottishness. Based on the reactions received in Scotland and other parts of the world, tenacity is a true Scottish characteristic. Integrity is another core value, since Scotland and the world believe that Scotland has this attribute to a greater extent than most, if not all, other countries. Spirit is another virtue that defines Scotland. However, although the Scots (as well as the English) believe that they have inventiveness, the rest of the world does not seem to subscribe to the same notion, since

TEST DRIVE A SAAB. IT WILL TELL YOU A LOT ABOUT YOURSELF.

Thirty minutes in the driver's seat of a Saab 900 can be more revealing than a session on a psychiatrist's couch.

Will you look at Saab's front-wheel drive as a way to get through winter and the foul weather of the other seasons? You're ruled by your intellect.

Or will you look at front-wheel drive as the means to give a sedan the road-hugging, toe-curling, cornering ability of a sports car? You're ruled by your emotions.

But maybe you see front-wheel drive as both. You're ruled neither by your intellect nor your emotions. You are ruling them.

The ego and the id.

The id, the repository of your instinctual impulses, will want to know, on a test drive, how good a Saab is at, well, burning rubber. Don't repress that feeling.

All the practical considerations for buying a Saab (economy, the reasonableness of its price, the active and passive safety features, the durability in a world where disposability is a perverse virtue) are just as real and just as practical after testing its acceleration as they were before.

Sure, a car's reason for being is to get from Point A to Point B. But a Saab's reason for being is to do that as responsibly as possible without ignoring the romance in the possibilities of Points Q, R, S, T, not to mention X, Y, and Z.

An interpretation of your dreams.

Is the Saab 900 the car of your dreams? Who knows?

We do know it's the car of our engineers' and designers' dreams. There are, you know, seemingly disparate elements on a Saab.

Rack-and-pinion steering, disc brakes on all four wheels, front-wheel drive, 53 (!) cubic feet of cargo space, aerodynamic body, incredible fuel efficiency* considering its performance.

On a Saab, though, they add up to a whole greater than its parts. Saabs somehow feel better to Saab owners than other cars they've owned.

For the first time, they got the performance car they wanted with the responsible car they needed.

They found out the joy of not following the crowd, but of starting a crowd of their own.

Truth is, a 30-minute test drive may not be able to tell you all this. But we'll bet that three years owning one will.

SAAB 900
The most intelligent car ever built.

Saab 16-valve Turbo 5-speed: 19 EPA estimated city mpg, 25 estimated highway mpg. Use estimated mpg for comparison only. Mileage varies with speed, trip length and weather. Saabs range in price from $11,850 for the 900 3-door, 5-speed to $18,620 for the 900 4-door, 5-speed, 16-valve Turbo. Manufacturer's suggested retail prices. Not including taxes, license, freight dealer charges or options.

Figure 7.4 *Personality and car ownership*

Source: Reprinted with permission of Saab-Scania of America, Inc.

Table 7.1 CETSCALE. 17-item CETSCALE[1]

Item		Reliability[2]
1	American people should always buy American-made products instead of imports.	0.65
2	Only those products that are unavailable in the USA should be imported.	0.63
3	Buy American-made products. Keep America working.	0.51
4	American products, first, last, and foremost.	0.65
5	Purchasing foreign-made products is unAmerican.	0.64
6	It is not right to purchase foreign products, because it puts Americans out of jobs.	0.72
7	A real American should always buy American-made products.	0.70
8	We should purchase products manufactured in America instead of letting other countries get rich off us.	0.67
9	It is always best to purchase American products.	0.59
10	There should be very little trading or purchasing of goods from other countries unless out of necessity.	0.53
11	Americans should not buy foreign products, because this hurts American business and causes unemployment.	0.67
12	Curbs should be put on all imports.	0.52
13	It may cost me in the long-run but I prefer to support American products.	0.55
14	Foreigners should not be allowed to put their products on our markets.	0.52
15	Foreign products should be taxed heavily to reduce their entry into the USA.	0.58
16	We should buy from foreign countries only those products that we cannot obtain within our own country.	0.60
17	American consumers who purchase products made in other countries are responsible for putting their fellow Americans out of work.	0.65

Notes
1 Response format is 7-point Likert-type scale (strongly agree = 7, strongly disagree = 1). Range of scores is from 17 to 119.
2 Calculated from confirmatory factor analysis of data from four-areas study.

Source: Terence A. Shimp and Subhash Sharma, "Consumer Ethnocentrism: Construction and Validation of the CETSCALE," *Journal of Marketing Research* 24 (August 1987): 282.

they do not have enough knowledge of Scotland's inventiveness.[9]

While the European Union is unifying markets, it will take time to construct a unified set of European marketing theories. There is still a wide divergence in terms of economic development levels, languages, religions, and legal systems. Generalizations are both difficult and dangerous. Marketers must still consider a country's history, national character, and cognitive styles.[10]

Hofstede's national cultures

Hofstede has strongly indicated that ethnocentric management theories (i.e., based on a particular country's value system) are untenable. Based on his study of work-related values in fifty countries, national cultures have four largely independent dimensions: (1) individualism vs. collectivism, (2) large or small power distance, (3) strong or weak uncertainty avoidance, and (4) masculinity vs. femininity. Power distance describes how a society treats unequal people. "Collectivist countries always show large power distance, but individualist countries do not always show small power distance." Regarding uncertainty avoidance, some countries have weak uncertainty avoidance in the sense that they accept uncertainty and they are thus able to take risks easily. In contrast, strong uncertainty avoidance societies create institutions to offer security and avoid risk. With regard to masculinity/femininity, the classification is derived from whether a society has well-defined roles for men and women. A masculine society clearly expects men to be assertive and dominant and women to assume more service-oriented and caring roles. This society clearly differentiates between what men should do and what women are supposed to do.[11]

Based on Hofstede's research, countries that are low in power distance, masculinity, and uncertainty avoidance include Australia, Canada, Denmark, the United Kingdom, the Netherlands, Norway, New Zealand, Sweden, and the USA. In comparison, those cultures that are low in individualism but high in power distance, masculinity, and uncertainty avoidance include Greece, Mexico, Pakistan, Peru, the Philippines, Taiwan, Thailand, Venezuela, and Japan.[12]

As explained by Hofstede, management is an American invention. However, the practices of management in many parts of the world can deviate greatly from management as practiced in the USA. American management theories emphasize market processes, managers, and individualism – things that assume less significance elsewhere. In Japan, the emphasis is on workers – not managers. In fact, management as practiced in the USA does not bear much resemblance to management practiced in Japan.[13]

A literature review of the five dimensions of national culture (individualism, power distance, masculinity, uncertainty avoidance, and Confucian dynamic) led Nakata and Sivakumar to propose that these dimensions affect new product development – both positively and negatively.[14]

One study of ten countries and sixty regions found that cultural power distance, cultural individualism, and regional socioeconomics affect brand image strategies (see Figure 7.5).[15] In low power distance countries, people are not too focused on social roles and group affiliation, and it is thus appropriate to use functional brand images that

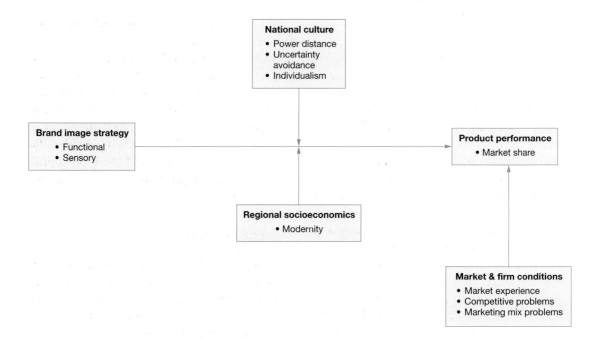

Figure 7.5 *Cultural and socioeconomic factors and brand image strategies*

Source: Martin S. Roth, "The Effects of Culture and Socioeconomics on the Performance of Global Brand Image Strategies," *Journal of Marketing Research* 32 (May 1995): 165.

de-emphasize the social, symbolic, sensory, and experiential benefits of products. However, social and/or sensory needs should probably be stressed in a country with a high degree of power distance. In addition, marketing in high individualism cultures (e.g., European countries) should focus on functional, variety, novelty, and experiential needs, whereas cultures with low individualism (e.g., Asian countries) may find social brand image strategies to be more appealing. Finally, when regional socioeconomics is high, it is appropriate to focus on social and sensory brand images.

The dimensions of national culture have marketing relevance. A study of TV commercials from Japan, Russia, Sweden, and the USA in terms of the masculine–feminine continuum found that feminine countries showed a higher degree of use of relationships for male and female characters. Since not all cultures share the same values, advertising standardization appears to be strategically unwise.[16]

Clustering: commonality and diversity

The impact of Hofstede's fifty-country study requires no debate. It has spawned a great deal of discussion as well as numerous studies. Another rigorous and large-scale study is just as valuable even though it is yet to attract the same kind of attention. Project GLOBE (Global Leadership and Organizational Behavior Effectiveness), based on a collaboration of scholars in all parts of the world, is a study of thousands of middle managers in food processing, finance, and telecommunications industries in sixty-one countries. The study focuses on nine dimensions of national cultures: performance orientation, future orientation, assertiveness, power distance, humane orientation, institutional collectivism, in-group collectivism, uncertainty avoidance, and gender egalitarianism. In the process, six global leadership attributes have been identified.[17]

The project uses discriminant analysis to confirm the ten a priori clusters: South Asia, Anglo, Arab, Germanic Europe, Latin Europe, Eastern Europe, Confucian Asia, Latin America, Sub-Saharan Africa,

and Nordic Europe. The results offer strong support to the existence of these proposed clusters.

Reflecting Latin America's paternalistic orientation, this cluster shows the practices of high power distance, and low performance orientation, uncertainty avoidance, future orientation, and institutional collectivism.[18] The hallmark of the southern Asia cluster is its high power distance and group and family collectivism practices. Charismatic, team oriented, and humane leadership is highly valued.[19] The members of the Anglo cluster are all developed countries, and their orientation is toward individualist performance. A leader is expected to provide charismatic inspiration and a participative style.[20]

The societies found in the Arabic cluster are predominantly Muslim, and they share common literature, architecture, educational background, and religious characteristics. They are highly group oriented, hierarchical, and masculine while being low on future orientation.[21] The cluster of Germanic Europe is a model of cooperation between labor and capital. Co-determination leads to participative leadership.[22]

The Eastern European cluster, reflecting both tradition and transition, stresses high power distance and high family and group collectivism.[23] The Latin Europe cluster scores close to mid-range on all but one dimensions of societal practices on a 7-point measurement scale. The only exception is in terms of a high average of over 5 on power distance. The societies in this cluster attempt to balance the need for competitiveness with their traditional preference for a paternalistic and interventionist government.[24]

PSYCHOGRAPHICS

Because of the disappointing results in using personality to predict purchase behavior, marketers have turned to other meaningful purchase variables that might be used in conjunction with personality characteristics. This area of purchase behavior study is known as psychographics, also known as lifestyle or AIO (activities, interests, and opinions) study. Psychographics is a quantitative analysis of consumers' lifestyles and activities with the purpose of relating these variables to buying behavior. The analysis encompasses both the strength of the qualitative nature of Sigmund Freud's psychoanalytic theory and the statistical and methodological sophistication of trait and factor theories. As a result, questions are well organized, and responses are subject to numerical representation and multivariate analysis.

Questions normally included in psychographic studies are those related to demographics, personality traits, and activities such as media habits, retail patronage, and general interests. People can be classified by their lifestyles and then be contrasted in terms of their consumption habits. For example, respondents from England and Denmark do not view Denmark's furnishing interiors in the same way. The two cultures have different ideas of appropriate product syntax or how furnishing items could and should be combined.[25]

It is generally believed that Japan is so homogeneous that the market should not be segmented and that there will either be a mass response or little response. Actually, psychographics can yield useful information. As an example, the VALS (Values and Lifestyles) instrument was tailored to the Japanese market. Ten Japanese segments have been identified: integrators who are well educated and modern (4 percent), sustainers who are resistant to change (15 percent), self-innovators who are young and self-directed (7 percent), self-adapters who are shy and look to self-innovators (11 percent), *ryoshiki* — "social intelligence" — innovators who are career-oriented and middle-aged (6 percent), *ryoshiki* adapters who are shy and look to *ryoshiki* innovators (10 percent), tradition innovators who are middle-aged and active in the community (6 percent), tradition adapters who are young and affluent (10 percent), high pragmatic who are withdrawn and suspicious (14 percent), and low pragmatic who are attitudinally negative and oriented to inexpensive products (17 percent).[26]

Marketers, in addition to identifying lifestyle variations within a country, may also identify lifestyle groups on a worldwide basis. According to Backer Spielvogel Bates Worldwide, there are five distinct groups of consumers worldwide: (1) strivers (26 percent) – relatively young people who work very hard and seek convenience and instant gratification, (2) achievers (22 percent) – affluent opinion and style leaders who pick brands that make statements about status and quality, (3) pressured (13 percent) – predominantly women who contend with economic and family pressures and have little room for pleasure or enjoyment, (4) adopters (18 percent) – older consumers who live comfortably in a changing world by respecting new ideas without losing sight of time-honored values, and (5) traditionals (16 percent) – those who embody the oldest values of their countries and cultures and resist change while preferring familiar products. However, 5 percent of the consumers did not fit into any of these categories.[27]

PERCEPTION

To learn, a person must perceive. Perception goes beyond sensation by providing meaning to sensory stimulations. It is the process of interpreting nervous impulses or stimuli received that the brain must organize and give meaning through cognitive interpretations. The Chinese, for instance, perceive Coke to look and taste like medicine.

One's culture greatly affects one's perception and behavior. Americans, for example, generally prefer steak on the "rare" side, in order to retain moisture and flavor. Asians, on the other hand, would not dream of eating steak this way, believing meat in that condition to be unsafe. Furthermore, Americans prefer to cook a big piece of meat, to be cut up or sliced on a serving plate at the dining table when they are ready to eat. The Chinese, however, prefer to cut the meat into small, bite-sized pieces before cooking and thus have no need for a knife at the dining table.

Formation of perception

It is important to keep in mind that perceptions are formed though a highly subjective and selective process. The consumer's cognitive map of the environment is not a photograph of that physical environment. It is instead a partial and personal construction of a situation in which certain cues – selected and given emphasis – are perceived in an individual manner. More precisely, when one forms a perception, one is not a photographer but rather an artist who draws or paints an object in the way one thinks it is or should be. Therefore, no object or product is ever perceived exactly in the way it actually appears.

Because of the selectivity and subjectivity characteristics of perception, people "seeing" the same thing can have vastly different interpretations. In Spain, accepting credit is viewed as an inability to pay – a shameful situation. While American consumers take it for granted that, if not satisfied, they can simply return a product for a full refund, German consumers are unlikely to share this view.

Whether or not a product will be successful depends significantly on how it is perceived. A marketer should provide some cues about a product in order to aid consumers in perceiving the product in the desired manner. Volvo, for example, has done quite well through emphasizing safety features.

Country of origin and perceived product quality

One of the cues often used by consumers in evaluating products is where a product is made. It is not unusual for consumers to categorize countries (e.g., rich, poor, developed, developing) and to use these categories to judge product quality. There is evidence of **country-category effect** in the sense that consumers use stereotyping in typing product classes and brands.

At a more specific level, consumers may use **country of origin** as a guide to product quality. Not only do consumers harbor general images about certain countries, but they also form specific attitudes about products made in those countries. This topic has received a great deal of interest and has been researched in depth.[28] Many empirical studies support the hypothesis that consumers have stereotyped opinions about specific products from particular countries. For example, an investigation of product-country images and ethnocentric behaviors found that Turkish consumers' perceptions of product attributes were influenced by products coming from countries at different levels of socioeconomic and technological development.[29]

When a "made in" designation is not favorably received, a marketer may want to deliberately conceal or not mention the product's origin. Many countries, however, including the USA, require proper origin identification in the form of a tag, label, or other identification means before foreign products can be imported.

The effects of country of origin can be moderated by consumer expertise and the type of attribute information. As shown in one study, when encountering unambiguous attribute information, experts based their evaluations on attribute strength, but novices relied on country of origin. In the case that attribute information was ambiguous, both experts and novices then utilized country of origin stereotypes.[30] Likewise, motivational intensity and direction moderate the effect of information type of country of origin evaluations. When country of origin is salient and when consumers find new information relevant to their judgment, evaluations of the country of origin become more favorable.[31]

There is a relationship between consumer ethnocentrism and consumer attitude toward foreign products (when there is no domestic alternative). According to one study, consumers with high levels of consumer ethnocentrism adopt more favorable attitudes toward products from culturally similar countries when compared to products from culturally dissimilar countries.[32]

Country of origin is a multidimensional construct. As such, its effect is neither simple nor straightforward. Two particular dimensions are **country of assembly** and **country of design**. According to traditional wisdom, a manufacturer in a newly developed country or less developed country should conceal the identity of its manufacturing locations. However, if its product is *designed* in an advanced country, that fact can improve consumers' ratings of the product.[33] Another study focused on televisions and stereos in terms of the country of origin for parts, assembly, and design. Respondents have more favorable attitudes and higher purchase intention when a product assembled in the USA uses American parts rather than Mexican parts.[34]

It should be pointed out that *single-cue* studies created larger country of origin effect sizes than did *multiple-cue* studies.[35] The effect of country of origin is strongest when it is the only cue, but when other explicit multiple cues are included, the effect weakens.[36] In addition, to use country of origin to a marketer's advantage, the marketer should emphasize high levels of positive attributes and low levels of negative attributes without ignoring the negative attributes.[37]

In general, products from less developed countries are less favorably received than those from industrialized countries. Yet even for high-risk products from less developed countries, consumers are still willing to buy them as long as they carry known brand names, indicating the power of a brand name to moderate the negative influence of a country's negative image.[38] When there is congruence between brand origin and country of manufacture (e.g., a Sony TV set made in Japan), country of manufacture has impact on product beliefs and brand attitudes. Incongruence takes place when a branded product is made in a country whose image is not as favorable as that of brand origin (e.g., a Sony TV set made in Mexico). In this case, country of manufacture information adversely affects product evaluations – but only for low equity brands rather than high equity brands. Apparently, a brand can be strong enough to mitigate any negative perceptions derived from country of manufacture information.[39]

In addition, attribute claims become more credible when the products are distributed through a prestigious retailer.[40] Distributors and/or retailers can have an impact on how a brand is perceived. Samsung Electronics Co.'s initial strategy was to use Wal-mart Stores Inc. to distribute its low-end electronic gadgets. The company has now outgrown that strategy as it pushes toward innovative, higher margin products, such as voice-activated mobile phones that are also digital music players and personal digital assistants. For many consumers, this will be the very first time they try such products, and it will also be the first time they are exposed to brand names associated with these product categories. So Samsung has an opportunity to create brand equity and loyalty. As a result, it made a tough decision to abandon Wal-mart in favor of specialty stores (e.g., Best Buy and Circuit City). Samsung's strong commitment to its brand strategy has propelled it to be among the world's top fifty brands. In fact, among all brands, Samsung's rise in brand value was the fastest.[41]

It may be incorrect to treat country of origin as a **halo effect**. A country's image varies across product categories. While consumers may prefer Japanese and German cars, they also prefer crystal from Ireland and leather shoes from Italy. Consumer preference is thus a function of **product–country match**. Consumer willingness to buy a country's particular product increases when the country image is also an important characteristic for that product category. American, Irish, and Mexican consumers are interested in buying a car or watch from Japan, Germany, and the USA because these countries have characteristics which are relevant and important to these products. In contrast, consumers are less willing to buy Mexican and Hungarian cars and watches because Mexico and Hungary receive poor evaluations on relevant product dimensions.[42] Another study of Bangladeshi consumers and their perceptions of products from nine foreign countries found that they overwhelmingly preferred Western-made products. At the same time, their perceptions varied across product classes as well as across the sourcing countries.[43]

The findings of the various studies have several marketing implications. Because consumers are more wary of products from developing countries, especially when there is a high degree of financial risk, the developing countries naturally need to solve this marketing problem. Because consumers continuously merge product information with country image, quality control is necessary. The industry association and the government should establish quality standards and provide such incentives as tax benefits and subsidies to exporters who meet the standards, while penalizing those who do not by imposing export taxes or withholding export licenses. To help consumers generalize product information over the country's products, individual marketers can benefit from favorable country image by highlighting products of superior quality from the same country. For example, Mitsubishi may claim that its TV sets are as good as those manufactured by Sony. Alternatively, to prevent consumers from the country's negative image in product evaluation, marketers should dissociate their products from unsuccessful products manufactured in that country.

An international marketer should pay attention to the relationship between country of origin and the perception of product quality. Country of origin information is more important than price and brand information in affecting product quality assessments.[44] In general, engineering and technical products from Germany, electronics products from Japan, fashion products from France, and tobacco products from the USA are favorably received in most parts of the world. In addition, consumers in less developed countries usually prefer imported or foreign goods, believing that those goods are of higher quality and prestige.

A company must keep in mind that a product's image may change if its production facilities are moved from one country to a new location. Lowenbrau lost its image as a prestigious import beer once American drinkers became aware that the beer was licensed to be made by Miller in the USA.

Because of the constancy or stability of perceptions, a negative perception associated with a particular country tends to persist. The failure of Yugoslavia's Yugo automobiles had to do with the negative perception. However, the problem can be overcome if a firm or country perseveres and is determined to improve its product quality. A case in point is Japan. Its initial effort to penetrate the US market after World War II was greeted with the perception that its products were cheap, imitative, and shoddy. Ironically, many consumers, including those in the USA, came to feel that Japanese products are superior to American goods, offering better value for money. South Korea is currently striving to match Japan in this perception game. In the meantime, its Hyundai automobiles have perception hurdles to overcome (see Marketing Strategy 7.1). One experiment manipulated the level of warranty coverage and a warrantor's reputation. The findings indicate that warranty strategies can overcome consumers' negative perception about the quality of a company's hybrid product.[45]

CULTURAL DIMENSION 7.1 FOLK MEMORY

The USA is Waterford Wedgwood's biggest market, accounting for almost half of the total sales. When Irish families emigrated to North America in the nineteenth century, many took a piece of Waterford crystal along as a memento of their homeland. When the company resumed production in the 1950s after a century of dormancy, it was greatly assisted by this "folk memory" that has been maintained over several generations. Because of its status symbol due to its reputation for quality, Waterford even designed and built the Times Square Millennium Ball to herald the year 2000 in New York. It is thus an irony that Waterford has only recently embraced its Irishness – publicly. On the other hand, Ireland does not offer the best kind of association for a luxury product. At least, at one time, it evoked more of the image of "pigs in the parlor" and backwardness.

Source: "Waterford Shatters Stuffy Image in Bid to Boost Sales," *San José Mercury News*, February 18, 2001.

MARKETING STRATEGY 7.1 A NEW IMAGE

Hyundai Excel invaded the US market in the 1980s and left a long-lasting impression: cheap but mechanically fragile. Now Hyundai, Kia, and Daewoo all insist that their vehicles have improved in quality. To get rid of their shoddy image, they offer warranties that are among the best. Hyundai's warranty is the industry's most comprehensive package: ten-year/100,000-mile power-train protection, five-year/60,000-mile bumper-to-bumper coverage, and five-year/unlimited-mile roadside assistance. Daewoo offers free maintenance for an owner's first three years. The efforts seem to be paying off. Hyundai now sells more cars than Mitsubishi and Mazda, and Kia outsells Acura and Isuzu. Daewoo has more sales than Suzuki and Saab. Kia boasts that its cars offer a great deal of content and value and that they are built incredibly well for the price. The Korean car makers' successes may be attributed to improved quality (or at least, improvement of perceived quality).

Source: "Korean Cachet," *San José Mercury News*, August 25, 2000.

ATTITUDE

Attitude is the learned tendency to respond to an object in a consistently favorable or unfavorable way. Attitude is a complex and multidimensional concept. It consists of three components: cognition, affect, and conation (behavioral intention). Based on this definition, a few properties of attitude can be identified. First, the relationship between an individual and an object is not neutral: the reaction to the object is either favorable or unfavorable. Most people, for example, have favorable attitudes toward such automobiles as Mercedes-Benz, BMW, and Rolls-Royce, viewing them as status symbols. On the other hand, except for American consumers who have long been conditioned to prefer large automobiles, most consumers have strong reservations about large cars because they look unsightly and are difficult to maneuver on the narrow roads found in most parts of the world, and they are also more uneconomic in terms of fuel consumption.

Second, attitudes are relatively enduring and patterned and not temporary or transient. As a person becomes older, attitudes become more established. This becomes a challenge for international marketers who want to introduce change. A new product often involves a change in a long-held attitude. Finally, attitude is not innate – it must be learned. One's attitude about an object is formed by one's experience of the object, either directly or indirectly.

There is a relationship between consumer attitudes and their purchases. For instance, many Singaporeans are outshoppers who go to Malaysia to buy food, beverages, and grocery products due to competitive prices and ample parking space. Compared to their infrequent counterparts, frequent outshoppers perceive fewer secondary costs. In addition, since they engage in outshopping primarily for economic reasons, they do not feel guilty (i.e., a lack of national pride or low consumer ethnocentrism).[46]

Attitude is greatly influenced by culture (see Marketing Ethics 7.1). Attitudes toward women, for example, vary from country to country. In many countries, women are still considered as a man's property, and a woman must seek her husband's approval before entering into a contract or being allowed to apply for a visa or passport. In Saudi Arabia, strict Muslim restrictions make it very uncommon for women to work. In Japan, working women are common but rarely have the opportunity to rise to a managerial position. Therefore, when women are portrayed in advertisements, the portrayal should be consistent with the expected role of women in that particular culture.

MARKETING ETHICS 7.1   FIVE-STAR GRAVEYARD

The Chinese are superstitious. Due to ancient belief, they do not like to mention the word for death (*si*) and will instead use other words to imply the phenomenon (e.g., a person passed away, got old, or was gone). In China, land is valuable, and cremation in major cities is mandatory. Despite the government's encouragement, tree burials, in which evergreens are planted in holes containing a deceased's ashes, has not gained much acceptance.

The government's regulations and prodding have a difficult time overcoming the country's 5000 years of burial traditions. A traditional belief is that eternal peace requires a body to be buried comfortably in the ground. While some children do not take good care of their parents, they will spend lavishly on the parents'

burials and graves. The practice is self-serving. After all, when parents are properly buried, their spirits will protect their children.

In spite of the government's pressure, the pendulum seems to be swinging in another direction. The country's movement in the direction of a market economy has coincided with the use of advertising to promote cemeteries. One graveyard claims to offer "five-star" accommodation. In the case of Beijing Heaven Cemetery, it elevated its profile by sponsoring a contest (Century Longevity Stars), and the nine lucky winners won grave sites.

Source: "In China, Burials Restricted to Make Room for the Living," *San José Mercury News*, February 15, 2000.

Attitude can affect marketing plans in other ways. Some countries have favorable attitudes toward foreigners, wealth, and change, making it relatively easy for MNCs to introduce new products. In fact, attitudes toward marketing itself should be considered. In India, marketing is viewed as unnecessary, annoying, and wasteful. Nestlé's infant formula received enormous adverse publicity because of the negative view in less developed countries about the company's marketing activities in poor countries.

One problem firms have in marketing their products overseas involves the negative attitudes toward situations associated with their products and sometimes toward the products themselves. For example, customers may have favorable attitudes toward German machinery but not toward the purchase of such machinery because of the high cost, service, or availability of parts.

It is important for a marketer to distinguish between private and public attitudes, because an expressed public attitude can differ widely from a private attitude, especially when the private attitude contradicts the society's cultural norms.

SOCIAL CLASS

Social class implies inequality. Even in the USA, where all are supposed to be equal, some people seem to be much more equal than others. Social class exists because it provides for and ensures the smooth operation of a society. For a society to exist, many functions must be performed – some of which are not very pleasant. In this regard, members of society are not that different from bees in a hive – different types of bees exist for different purposes (e.g., working bees, queen bees, soldier bees, and so on). In Japan, even though the government long ago abolished the social caste system to allow for the mixing and reshuffling of people at all social levels, the selective access to higher education still impedes certain individuals from becoming career officials within the government.

Many societies see nothing wrong with the existence of a social hierarchy. In fact, many Asian and Middle East countries view status differences positively. Elders and superiors command respect. Connections with socially acceptable persons are often important in securing business.

203

The criteria used to assign people to social classes vary from country to country. In the USA, relevant characteristics generally used in the construction of a social class index for classification purposes are occupation, source of income, house type, and dwelling area. In other countries, occupation and/or amount of income (rather than source of income) are the dominant discriminating variables. In some societies, royalty affiliation is employed as well to distinguish one social class from another.

The US social system differs from those of other countries in several respects. Its greatest representation occurs approximately at the middle (i.e., the lower-middle and upper-lower categories) of the social class scale. Many developing countries have a very large lower class, and the graphic composition of all social classes resembles a pyramid: the upper class is a small minority group at the top and the vast number of lower-class people occupy the large base at the bottom. Furthermore, the US system allows for social class mobility, while systems elsewhere may be much more rigid.

Even when the same distinguishing variable is used in different countries for classification, it may not have the same meaning and does not necessarily yield the same result. If the classification of occupation is considered, in the USA, financial considerations very likely explain why attorneys are accorded the kind of status and prestige rarely found elsewhere. Engineers, on the other hand, are regarded much more highly in societies outside of the USA.

Social class has a great deal of relevance for marketing strategies. It influences store selection, product selection, media selection, advertising appeal selection, and sales promotion selection. Different motives may thus have to be employed for different social classes. Thresher, a British liquor store chain of 990 outlets, used the results of its marketing research to divide its shops into three designations: drinks stores, wine shops, and wine racks. The designations are based on the social status of a neighborhood. The down-market drinks stores are located in working-class areas, and they stock mostly beer. Wine racks, offering a larger selection of wines and champagnes, are found in wealthier locations and have a better educated staff. The middlebrow wine shops are somewhere in between.

GROUP

A group consists of two or more persons who share a set of norms and have certain implicitly or explicitly defined relationships with one another in such a way that their behavior is interdependent. Group norms influence both general behavior and consumption behavior.

Originally formed for defense and survival, a group now serves its members more for needs of social and psychological satisfaction. An individual cannot operate well in isolation because all persons are biologically and socially interdependent. An individual needs to belong to a group to interact with those who can provide identification and help to meet needs in a more efficient manner. The influence of a reference group is derived in part from its capacity to disseminate information.

The relevance and strength of influence of a reference group is not constant across product categories. Its influence is determined in part by the conspicuousness of the product in question. A product can be conspicuous in two ways: by having the qualities of visibility and by standing out. The more the product is visible and stands out, the more conspicuous it becomes. Product conspicuousness allows a reference group to operate in exerting its influence on consumer behavior. For example, Philip Morris's Galaxy brand was perceived at one time as a "diet" cigarette, and for that reason Brazilians became ashamed to be seen with it because social and personal pressures were placed on those who smoked Galaxy.

The relevance of group appeal may be dictated by cultural norms. In contrast to Americans, who are more individually oriented, the Japanese are more committed to group membership and are consensus oriented. Group pressure is very great in Japan. The Fishbein behavioral intentions model was found to reflect cultural differences (i.e., the collectivist culture of Korea and the individualistic culture of the USA). The greater importance of subjective norm in Korea and of attitude toward an act in the USA indicates that social pressures, while having a relatively weak influence on Americans, play a major role in the formation of Koreans' behavioral intentions. Therefore, international marketers operating in Confucian cultures should keep in mind that a product may not be evaluated independently of group conformity and face saving. A marketing mix program should take into account these social factors.[47]

FAMILY

In the USA, the word "family" has a narrow meaning because it encompasses only the husband, wife, and their offspring (if any). This family is known as a nuclear or conjugal family. In other parts of the world, the word has a much broader meaning because it is based on the concept of an extended or consanguine family. A family can be vertically extended when it includes several generations. It can also be horizontally extended when such family members as uncles, aunts, and cousins are included. Thus non-Americans count vertical and horizontal relatives of either the husband or wife or both as part of their family. It is not uncommon for a son to live in his parents' home even after getting married. When his parents become old, it will become his responsibility to take care of his parents, the home, and the business. In such a country, nursing homes are relatively rare, and the placement of elderly or ill parents in homes for the aged is frowned upon.

The Chinese culture emphasizes familial over private self. Attainment of family-oriented goals is a measure of self-realization and self-fulfillment. Boundaries of familial self may include romantic partners and close friends who are "like family." In family and like-family contexts, there is no need for reciprocity.[48]

As a subset and special kind of reference group, the family can be distinguished by its characteristics. First, a family allows its members ample opportunity to interact with one another on a face-to-face basis. In effect, each member operates as both a counselor and an information provider. Second, the family is a consuming unit in the sense that most members share the consumption of many products, especially those that are durables or that affect family budget. Third, individual needs are usually subordinated to family needs. Finally, one member is often assigned the primary duty of buying products for other users, thus acting as a gatekeeper or purchasing agent.

Americans and non-Americans raise their families in very different ways. Americans emphasize individual freedom, and children are taught to be self-sufficient and independent. In Japan and China, the family is the main focal point. Similar to the Hispanics' family orientation, the Japanese feel a strong sense of responsibility and obligation toward their families, and these obligations predominate in family decisions.

Because of the emphasis on family orientation, nepotism is an expected and accepted practice in most parts of the world. The tradition may even be carried on to include business partners. In Japan, close bonds among all members of a manufacturer's distribution channel explain why unprofitable members are not dropped from the system. Pillsbury has to accommodate this different style of doing business in Japan, where the emphasis is on long courtship, trust, sincerity, and Asian "old friends." Joint ventures are akin to a marriage, and a divorce of this kind is strongly frowned upon. The family tradition also explains why Japanese corporate priorities are employees, suppliers, customers, community, government, bankers, and finally shareholders.

A family functions more efficiently when its members specialize in the roles they are most comfortable with or are capable of performing better than other family members. A marketers must determine the kind of decision making that is relevant to the product. Once that fact is known, the marketer can direct promotional effort toward the party making the purchase decision. It is thus useful to consider and to assess the relative influence of each spouse in the decision-making process.

A study of two cultures – the USA and China – found that emphasis on joint, husband-dominated, and wife-dominated decisions varied by stage of the decision process as well as by stage–culture interaction. Compared with the US sample, the Chinese sample exhibited: (1) lower levels of egalitarianism, (2) more husband-dominated decisions, and (3) fewer joint decisions.[49]

Similarly, in the case of Hispanic ethnic identification groups, the effect of ethnic identification on marital roles in decision making was found to interact with the phase of the purchase decision process. In addition, there is a positive relationship between ethnic identification and husband dominance in decision making.[50]

OPINION LEADERSHIP

Within each social group, there are some individuals who are able to exert a significant influence on other members in such a way as to affect their thinking and behavior in a desired direction. These individuals are known as opinion leaders. In the context of consumer behavior, their opinions about products can affect subsequent purchases made by others.

In marketing products overseas, MNCs should attempt to appeal to opinion leaders. In general, these are likely to be people who command respect from others. In Ghana, government health workers gain better cooperation and reception by asking for village witch-doctors' approval before inoculating people or spraying huts to fight malaria. In developing countries, it is a good strategy to market new ideas to teachers, monks, or priests first, because their opinions influence the acceptance of these ideas by others.

When it is doubtful who the opinion leaders are, marketers should try to identify those with influence and affluence. BMW, for example, sells its cars at a discount to diplomats, believing that its target consumers will take notice of the kind of cars driven by those in power. In foreign countries, business periodicals and English-language newspapers are usually an effective means of reaching government and business leaders who are potential opinion leaders.

DIFFUSION PROCESS OF INNOVATIONS

The diffusion process of innovations is an acceptance over time of a product or idea by consumers, linked to a given social structure and a given system of values or culture. Innovators possess certain characteristics that distinguish them from noninnovators. Innovators are frequently opinion leaders, and it is thus desirable to identify and contact innovators.

The diffusion process varies from culture to culture. The conservative business etiquette in South Korea is reflected in Korean firms' organizational structure as well as in their managerial approach, which emphasizes harmony and structure over innovation and experimentation. Diffusion of the Internet differs between the USA and Japan. Japan, as a collectivist culture, values high uncertainty avoidance and has large power distance. As such, Japan has a slower adoption process.[51]

One study investigated consumer innovativeness in a cross-cultural context by examining data collected from 2283 consumers in eleven EU countries. According to the findings, innovation orientation differs both among consumers and among countries, reflecting the fact that national cultural variables can explain systematic differences in innovativeness between countries. In collectivistic countries, a marketing message should emphasize social acceptance and a product's local origin. In contrast, Australia, New Zealand, the United Kingdom, the USA, and Canada have national cultures that are characterized by low uncertainty avoidance, high individualism, and high masculinity. As such, they are receptive to product innovations.[52]

Culture not only affects the diffusion process in general, but it also exerts a great deal of influence on the adoption of a product in particular. A product that is suitable in one culture may be totally inappropriate elsewhere. The Italian and Asian preference for fresh meat and vegetables has hampered the acceptance of frozen foods. In Italy and Southeast Asia, markets open and close early, and shoppers who wish to select the best items must get to market very early in the morning. By the early afternoon the market is ready to be closed, with only a few inferior items left.

As explained by the international product life-cycle concept, a new product is not adopted at the same time or at the same rate in various countries. It is thus necessary to ask whether innovators should be classified on a national (local) or international (worldwide) basis. If innovators are defined as the first 10 percent of adopters, how should a consumer be classified if he is not in the first 10 percent internationally but well within the first 10 percent of purchasers within his home country? The answer is that the diffusion rate should be based on segmentation criteria for each target market. Special consideration must be given to certain ethnic groups, age levels, social classes, geographic areas, and so on. Therefore, innovators should be classified as the first 10 percent of a particular target market, regardless of the percentages of adoption in other countries or on a worldwide scale.

It should be pointed out that innovators are small in number and that their influence is not always positive in that they may reject a new product. Although innovators are important, the evidence suggests that "the basic strategy should be aimed at imitators in the market in order to stimulate demand for the new product. Furthermore, the product should be tailored carefully to the needs and wants of that segment.[53]

CONCLUSION

Consumer behavior, as a discipline of study, has been researched extensively in the USA at both the macro and micro levels. Surprisingly, it has not been so rigorously and diligently investigated in the international context. All too frequently, studies that compare consumers in various countries attribute differences in consumer characteristics and behavior to cultural differences. This convenient approach (i.e., culture) is inadequate by itself and does not enhance the understanding of consumption behavior overseas.

Instead of explicitly or implicitly attempting to use culture to explain most variations in consumption, researchers should redirect their attention toward smaller units of analysis. This requires a study of psychological concepts as well as social concepts which are not based solely on cultural determinants.

At the psychological level, relevant concepts such as motivation, learning, personality, psychographics, perception, and attitude should be closely examined. Because consumer needs vary across countries, as does the degree of importance attached to a particular need, it is unrealistic to expect consumers everywhere to be motivated in the same way. The varying motives that occur are due in part to individual personality traits and lifestyles. The learning and perception of a product and the attitude toward it will also affect consumers' motivations in acquiring the product.

At the social level, it is redundant to state that consumer behavior is affected by the cultural environment. It is more important to list specifically the cultural norms in a country and to understand why those norms vary from country to country. It is thus important to appreciate how these norms are shaped by reference groups, social class, family, opinion leadership, and the diffusion process of innovation. Consumer preference depends in part on how well a product fits into the cultural circumstances and on whether the product will have the approval of a consumer's reference group, social class, and family.

In conclusion, marketers and researchers should guard against using culture as a catch-all term and should not use it on a wholesale basis to explain overseas behavior. It is necessary to go beyond noticing cultural differences and instead to attempt to understand the underlying causes of cultural variations. This goal requires researchers to be more specific and rigorous in their investigation by extending the application of relevant psychological and social concepts to the international scene. It is time to move away from a vague and generic explanation of consumption behavior to a more precise and better-focused avenue of research.

CASE 7.1   BENEATH HIJAB: MARKETING TO THE VEILED WOMEN OF IRAN

Jeffrey A. Fadiman, San José State University

Hijab means modest dress, and that is how Muslim women cover themselves. To Muslim women wearing *hijab*, one of the most annoying questions asked by Western women is, "Why?"

In defense of the practice, *Mahjubah: The Magazine for Moslem Women* (an English-language journal published in Iran for foreign distribution) ran an article examining *hijab* from the perspective of Muslim women. According to the article, men and women are physically and psychologically different. Muslim women are equal to men but not the same as men. Each sex has its own rights and place in society. Women wear *hijab* not because they are weak but because of the high status given to them by Allah and because of their desire to adhere to Islamic morality. As such, *hijab* means more than an outer garment; the heart must be modest as well.

Muslim women, on the other hand, often wonder why Western women wear skimpy, skin-tight dresses that are impractical and uncomfortable. Why must Western women be slaves to appearance, forever listening to the media about how to be glamorous? Why must they have to look beautiful for strangers to ogle them in public places? Why do Western feminist groups want to turn women into men? Muslim women wonder whether such questioning of gender roles is a sign of strength or actually a sign of weakness.

Points to consider

Assume that Iran's new leaders now welcome US businesses, requiring only that the members of each firm respect the religious, ethical, and moral beliefs of the nations. Consider that before the Ayatollah Khomeini's revolution, Iran's women showed enormous and increasing interest in a wide range of US goods, often wearing them "beneath the *hijab*," in deference to the opinions of Iranian men. Then came Khomeini, labeling the United States "the Great Satan." As a consequence, Western goods became equated with religious evil. Now the market has opened once more, after a drought of years.

How can you reawaken that demand? How can you stimulate the demand for Western goods (or services) among Iranian women without generating anxiety on the part of Iran's (all male) religious and secular authorities?

Your responses to this question should take the form of an essay, suggesting a number of specific measures that might be taken. The essay should include your responses to the following:

1   *Product selection.* What type of product (goods or service) could you, as the marketing director of a small US firm, attempt to test market to the female population of Iran? Describe in detail. Justify your choice of product.

2   *Market segment.* Which segment of the market should you target as an initial clientele? Describe in detail, including sex, age, social class, residential pattern (rural, suburban, urban), and so on. Justify your choice of segment.

3   *Product modification.* In what ways should the product (or service) be modified to stimulate demand by women, particularly those who continue to wear the black *chadur*, thereby conforming to *hijab* either by preference or in deference to male authority? Justify your modifications.

4   *Product image.* In what ways should the product image be modified to conform to Iranian religious, ethical, and moral norms, considering that these are entirely imposed by men? Justify your modifications. In addition, consider media selection, potential distribution outlets, point-of-purchase strategies, and so on.

5   *On-site project head.* Considering both the legacy of hostility that Iranians feel toward America and their long-range fascination with Western goods, what type of individual would you select to launch this first-time

effort within the country? Based on the data available to you at this moment, who among your classmates would appear to be the best selection? Justify your choice.

As you write your essay, you should consider specifics about Iranian distribution outlets. Iran's cities, like many in the Middle East, can be described as three communities in one:

- *Modern core.* Department stores, specialty shops; luxury goods (pre-Khomeini) elitist, Western-oriented clientele; also patronized by the middle class.
- *Traditional core.* Middle-Eastern marketing patrons – open bazaars, with separate sections for specialists (e.g., street of the silversmiths), family go-downs (small general stores), clustered along tiny streets; lower-middle-class, "traditional," and urban worker clientele.
- *Worker zones.* Concentric circles around both cores, each less wealthy than its predecessor, extending outward until they blend into the rural villages, from which the cities draw their food.

QUESTIONS

1 Distinguish among these three disciplines in terms of the unit of analysis: psychology, sociology, and anthropology.
2 Are rational motives more effective than their emotional counterparts in motivating consumers to make a purchase?
3 Are consumers' perceptions of products affected by the information concerning the products' countries of origin?
4 Explain how attitudes toward (a) marketing and (b) women may vary across countries.
5 Do social classes exist in the USA, the so-called land of equality?

DISCUSSION ASSIGNMENTS AND MINICASES

1 Do you feel that consumer differences can be adequately explained by the all-encompassing concept of culture? Is it a waste of time to employ other psychological and social concepts to understand consumer behavior?
2 Are the same buying motives effective worldwide?
3 Because personality is related to an individual person, is it possible for citizens of a country to have unique personality traits? Does a nation have its own national character?
4 Compared to Americans, are Asians and Africans: (1) more group oriented, (b) more family oriented, and (c) more concerned with social status? How might such orientations affect the way you market your product to Asian and African consumers?
5 Do you think it is worthwhile to appeal to opinion leaders and innovators in foreign markets?

NOTES

1 Saeed Samiee and Insik Jeong, "Cross-Cultural Research in Advertising: An Assessment of Methodologies," *Journal of the Academy of Marketing Science* 22 (No. 3, 1994): 205–17.

2   A. Coskun Samli, "Toward a Model of International Consumer Behavior: Key Considerations and Research Avenues," *Journal of International Consumer Marketing* 7 (No. 1, 1994): 63–84.

3   Swee Hoon Ang, "The Power of Money: A Cross-Cultural Analysis of Business-Related Beliefs," *Journal of World Business,* 35 (No. 1, 2000): 43–60.

4   Terry Clark, "International Marketing and National Character: A Review and Proposal for an Integrative Theory," *Journal of Marketing* 54 (October 1990): 66.

5   Michael Shapiro, *The Shadow in the Sun: A Korean Year of Love and Sorrow* (New York, NY: Atlantic Monthly Press, 1990).

6   "Frenetic People in a Hurry," *Financial Times,* May 28, 2002.

7   Neil R. Abramson *et al.*, "A Comparison of Canadian and Japanese Cognitive Styles: Implications for Management Interaction," *Journal of International Business Studies* 24 (No. 3, 1993): 575–87.

8   Terence A. Shimp and Subhash Sharma, "Consumer Ethnocentrism: Construction and Validation of the CETSCALE," *Journal of Marketing Research* 24 (August 1987): 280–9; Subhash Sharma, Terence A. Shimp, and Jeongshin Shin, "Consumer Ethnocentrism: A Test of Antecedents and Moderators," *Journal of the Academy of Marketing Science* 23 (winter 1995): 26–37.

9   Kate Hamilton, "Project Galore: Qualitative Research and Leveraging Scotland's Brand Equity," *Journal of Advertising Research* 40 (January to April 2000): 107–11.

10 Frederic Jallat and Allan J. Kimmel, "Marketing in Culturally Diverse Environments: The Case of Western Europe," *Business Horizons* 45 (July to August 2002): 30–6.

11 Geert Hofstede, "The Cultural Relativity of Organizational Practices and Theories," *Journal of International Business Studies* 14 (fall 1983): 75–89.

12 Geert Hofstede, *Culture's Consequences: International Differences in Work-Related Values* (Beverly Hills, CA: Sage Publications, 1980).

13 Geert Hofstede, "Cultural Constraints in Management Theories," *Academy of Management Executive* 7 (No. 1, 1993): 81–94.

14 Cheryl Nakata and K. Sivakumar, "National Culture and New Product Development: An Integrative Review," *Journal of Marketing* 60 (January 1996): 61–72.

15 Martin S. Roth, "The Effects of Culture and Socioeconomics on the Performance of Global Brand Image Strategies," *Journal of Marketing Research* 32 (May 1995): 163–75.

16 Laura M. Milner and James M. Collins, "Sex-role Portrayals and the Gender of Nations," *Journal of Advertising* 29 (spring 2000): 67–79.

17 Mansour Javidan and Robert J. House, "Leadership and Cultures around the World: Findings from GLOBE," *Journal of World Business* 37 (spring 2002): 1–2; Robert House *et al.*, "Understanding Cultures and Implicit Leadership Theories Across the Globe: An Introduction to Project GLOBE," *Journal of World Business* 37 (spring 2002): 3–10.

18 Vipin Gupta, Paul J. Hanges, and Peter Dorfman, "Cultural Clusters: Methodology and Findings," *Journal of World Business* 37 (spring 2002): 11–15.

19 Vipin Gupta *et al.*, "Southern Asia Cluster: Where the Old Meets the New?" *Journal of World Business* 37 (spring 2002): 16–27.

20 Neal M. Ashkanasy, Edwin Trevor-Roberts, and Louise Earnshaw, "The Anglo Cluster: Legacy of the British Empire," *Journal of World Business* 37 (spring 2002): 28–39.

21 Hayat Kabasakal and Muzaffer Bodur, "Arabic Cluster: A Bridge between East and West," *Journal of World Business* 37 (spring 2002): 40–54.

22 Erna Szabo *et al.*, "The Germanic Europe Cluster: Where Employees Have a Voice," *Journal of World Business* 37 (spring 2002): 55–68.

23 Gyula Bakacsi *et al.*, "Eastern European Cluster: Tradition and Transition," *Journal of World Business* 37 (spring 2002): 69–80.

24 Jorge Correia Jesuino, "Latin Europe Cluster: From South to North," *Journal of World Business* 37 (spring 2002): 81–89.

25 Simon Ulrik Kragh and Malene Djursaa, "Product Syntax and Cross-Cultural Marketing Strategies," *European Journal of Marketing* 35 (No. 11, 2001): 1301–20.

26 Lewis C. Winters, "International Psychographics," *Marketing Research* 4 (September 1992): 48–9.

27 Jon Lafayette, "Backer Predicts Material World," *Advertising Age*, July 29, 1989, 79.

28 For a list of studies focusing on country of origin, see the previous editions of this textbook.

29 Erdener Kaynak and Ali Kara, "Consumer Perceptions of Foreign Products: An Analysis of Product–Country Images and Ethnocentrism," *European Journal of Marketing* 36 (No. 7, 2002): 928–49.

30 Durairaj Maheswaran, "Country of Origin as a Stereotype: Effects of Consumer Expertise and Attribute Strength on Product Evaluations," *Journal of Consumer Research* 21 (September 1994): 354–65.

31 Zeynep Gurhan-Canli and Durairaj Maheswaran, "Determinants of Country-of-Origin Evaluations," *Journal of Consumer Research* 27 (June 2000): 96–108.

32 John J. Watson and Katrina Wright, "Consumer Ethnocentrism and Attitudes toward Domestic and Foreign Products," *European Journal of Marketing* 34 (No. 9, 2000): 1149–66.

33 Paul Chao, "Partitioning Country of Origin Effects: Consumer Evaluations of a Hybrid Product," *Journal of International Business Studies* 24 (No. 2, 1993): 291–306.

34 Paul Chao, "The Moderating Effects of Country of Assembly, Country of Parts, and Country of Design on Hybrid Product Evaluations," *Journal of Advertising* 30 (winter 2001)

35 Robert A. Peterson and Alain J.P. Jolibert, "A Meta-analysis of Country-of-Origin Effects," *Journal of International Business Studies* 26 (No. 4, 1995): 883–900.

36 Jeen-Su Lim, William K. Darley, and John O. Summers, "An Assessment of Country of Origin Effects under Alternative Presentation Formats," *Journal of the Academy of Marketing Science* 22 (No. 3, 1994): 274–82.

37 Ravi Parameswaran and R. Mohan Pisharodi, "Facets of Country of Origin Image: An Empirical Assessment," *Journal of Advertising* 23 (March 1994): 53–6.

38 Victor V. Cordell, "Interaction Effects of Country of Origin with Branding, Price, and Perceived Performance Risk," *Journal of International Consumer Marketing* 5 (No. 2, 1993): 5–20; Victor V. Cordell, "Effects of Consumer Preferences for Foreign Sourced Products," *Journal of International Business Studies* 23 (No. 2, 1992): 251–69.

39 Michael K. Hui and Lianxi Zhou, "Country-of-Manufacture Effects for Known Brands," *European Journal of Marketing* 37 (No. 1, 2003): 133–53.

40 Chol Lee, "Modifying an American Consumer Behavior Model for Consumers in Confucian Culture: The Case of Fishbein Behavioral Intention Model," *Journal of International Consumer Marketing* 3 (No. 1, 1990): 27–50.

41 "The Best Global Brands," *Business Week*, August 6, 2001, 50–7; "The Best Global Brands," *Business Week*, August 5, 2002, 92–99.

42 Martin S. Roth and Jean B. Romeo, "Matching Product Category and Country Image Perceptions: A Framework for Managing Country-of-Origin Effects," *Journal of International Business Studies* 23 (No. 3, 1992): 477–97.

43 Erdener Kaynak, Orsay Kucukemiroglu, and Akmal S. Hyder, "Consumers' Country-of-origin (COO) Perceptions of Imported Products in a Homogeneous Less-Developed Country," *European Journal of Marketing* 34 (No. 9, 2000): 1221–41.

44 Marjorie Wall, John Liefeld, and Louise A. Heslop, "Impact of Country-of-origin Cues on Consumer Judgments in Multi-cue Situations: A Covariance Analysis," *Journal of the Academy of Marketing Science* 19 (spring 1991): 105–13.

45 Soo J. Tan *et al.*, "Warranty and Warrantor Reputations as Signals of Hybrid Product Quality," *European Journal of Marketing* 35 (No. 1, 2001): 110–32.

46 Francis Piron, "International Outshopping and Ethnocentrism," *European Journal of Marketing* 36 (No. 1, 2002): 189–210.

47 Chol Lee and Robert T. Green, "Cross-Cultural Examination of the Fishbein Behavioral Intentions Model," *Journal of International Business Studies* 22 (No. 2, 1991): 289–305.

48 Annamma Joy, "Gift Giving in Hong Kong and the Continuum of Social Ties," *Journal of Consumer Research* 28 (September 2001): 239–56.

49 John B. Ford, Michael S. LaTour, and Tony L. Henthorne, "Perception of Marital Roles in Purchase Decision Processes: A Cross-Cultural Study," *Journal of the Academy of Marketing Science* 23 (spring 1995): 120–31.

50 Cynthia Webster, "Effects of Hispanic Ethnic Identification on Marital Roles in the Purchase Decision Process," *Journal of Consumer Research* 21 (September 1994): 319–31.

51 Carrie La Ferle, Steven M. Edwards, and Yutaka Mizuno, "Internet Diffusion in Japan: Cultural Considerations," *Journal of Advertising Research* (March to April 2002): 65–79.

52 Jan-Benedict E.M. Steenkamp, Frenkel ter Hofstede, and Michel Wedel, "A Cross-national Investigation into the Individual and National Cultural Antecedents of Consumer Innovativeness," *Journal of Marketing* 63 (April 1999): 55–69.

53 Hirokazu Takada and Dipak Jain, "Cross-national Analysis of Diffusion of Consumer Durable Goods in Pacific Rim Countries," *Journal of Marketing* 55 (April 1991): 48–54.

Chapter 8

Marketing research and information system

The faster and further you move information, the more valuable it becomes.

Glen McG. Renfrew, managing director, Reuters Holdings PLC

CHAPTER OUTLINE

PURPOSE OF CHAPTER

Lack of knowledge and unfamiliarity with foreign markets usually heighten the risks for a company wanting to do business in a foreign land. The problem is further complicated by the fact that international marketing research is more difficult and more complex than domestic research. The case of Toyota illustrates the value of marketing information and how such information can make the difference between success and failure. The data allow the firm to make timely adjustments to its marketing mix, and the company's understanding of consumer habits makes it possible for Toyota to better satisfy its customers' needs.

Given the complexity of today's fast-changing world and the unpredictability of consumer demands, the use of marketing research is essential if a company is to reduce the serious risks associated with marketing a product. Thus the purpose of this chapter is to examine the nature and techniques of international marketing research. The chapter investigates such topics as types of data, types of data collection methods, sampling, and measure. The discussion emphasizes the difficulties associated with cross-cultural research and the necessity for adapting marketing research techniques to international markets.

MARKETING ILLUSTRATION   KEEPING TABS ON CUSTOMERS

In addition to consumer interviews, Toyota's product teams attended a cocktail party at a Houston country club and learned that car owners preferred a distinctive grille that made the car more impressive when brought to the door by a valet. The teams also measured how close cars were parked to one another at the ballparks, leading the company to implement sliding doors instead of swing-open doors in its minivans. By observing that adults take their children along when shopping and return to the car with their arms full, Toyota realized the need to have an easy-to-open door mechanism that also opens the trunk.

Toyota and its US subsidiaries often disagree on the design choices for the US market, and the disagreements range from major product-strategy decisions to minor ones such as interior color schemes. In the late 1990s, Toyota's Japanese product planners did not endorse the idea of their American counterparts to build a V8 pickup truck. As a result, the American executives took the Japanese colleagues to a Dallas Cowboys football game. To their surprise, the Japanese saw rows of full-size pickup trucks at the Texas Stadium parking lot. They quickly realized that, to many Americans, a pickup was more than just a commercial vehicle since it was considered to be primary transportation as well. Thus the successful Toyota Tundra was born.

Sources: "Japan's Building Motor City II in S. California," *San José Mercury News,* May 11, 1990; "The Americanization of Toyota," *Business Week,* April 15, 2002, 52–54.

NATURE OF MARKETING RESEARCH

According to the American Marketing Association, **marketing research** involves the "systematic gathering, recording, and analyzing of data about problems relating to the marketing of goods and services." This definition provides a useful description of the nature of marketing research, but it fails to

include preresearch analysis, which is an important aspect of the research process. Before data collection, careful planning is required to specify both the kind of information needed and the purpose of such information. Without preresearch activities, there is a great danger that critical information may not be obtained and that what is obtained may turn out to be irrelevant or unsuitable. The letter in Exhibit 8.1

shows a lack of problem definition, research objectives, and preresearch activities.

The gathering of information can never be a substitute for good managerial judgment. A story told by the founder of Bata (the world's largest shoe company) illustrates this point. Two shoe salesmen from two companies visited the same island and came away with vastly different interpretations of people not wearing shoes there. One was returning home immediately because of a non-existent marketing opportunity. The other salesman, however, was very enthusiastic since all these potential customers were still without shoes. The moral of the story is that marketing research is only one part of the equation, and proper analysis and judgmental decisions are required.

In terms of marketing research expenditures, the USA is a leader. According to ESOMAR (European Society for Opinion and Marketing Research), commercial firms' total worldwide expenditures for marketing, advertising, and opinion research totaled $15.5 billion in 2000. The top twenty-five firms accounted for 61 percent of the total world expenditures.[1]

EXHIBIT 8.1   POORLY FORMULATED RESEARCH

To: International Trade Administration
US Department of Commerce
Washington, D.C.

Dear Sir/Madam:

I am in the process of planning the importation of a foreign product into the USA for wholesale distribution.

I have not yet determined the nature of the product. I am certain, however, that it is neither a food item nor automotive products. I am also undecided about the country of origin, even though I am leaning in the direction of the European or Asian manufacturing firms. These requirements should be able to minimize the research required to locate the research materials which I would like to receive from you.

Thank you for your assistance in providing me with the requested information.

Sincerely,

Potential Importer

CULTURAL DIMENSION 8.1   FEWER DEPENDENTS, MORE INDEPENDENCE

One measure of an economy's consumption capacity is the ratio of the dependents to the employed. There is more money per capita when each employed person has fewer dependents. From the absolute standpoint, China is certainly not a wealthy country; yet, relative to the number of dependents, China looks strong because it has one of the lowest dependency ratios. At 0.78 in 2000, each wage earner in China supports him or herself and 0.78 other. In other words, if a person earns $1000, he and his dependent end up with $561 each. India, however, is a different story. Each wage earner has to support himself plus 2.73 dependents. If an Indian worker earns $1000, the amount has to be divided among 3.73 persons, leaving $268 for each.

Among Asian countries, China, Thailand, and Japan have a ratio of less than one. For Hong Kong, South Korea, Taiwan, and Indonesia, their ratios are between 1 and 1.5. But in the case of the Philippines, Malaysia, and India, their ratios exceed 1.5.

As young dependents enter the work force, they will transform themselves into independents. This trend will take place in India, the Philippines, Thailand, Malaysia, and Indonesia, resulting in an improvement in their ratios.

Source: "Supporting People," *Asian Wall Street Journal,* June 19, 2001.

215

MARKETING INFORMATION SOURCES

Once a researcher has identified the marketing problem and has completed a preresearch analysis, the relevant information must be collected. The two major sources of information are primary data and secondary data.

Primary data may be defined as information that is collected firsthand, generated by original research tailor-made to answer specific, current research questions. The major advantage of primary data is that the information is specific, relevant, and up-to-date. The desirability of primary data is, however, somewhat moderated by the high cost and amount of time associated with the collection of this type of data.

Secondary data, in contrast, may be defined as information that has already been collected for other purposes and is thus readily available. Note that the advantages of primary data are the disadvantages of secondary data, and that the advantages of secondary data become the disadvantages of primary data.

As a rule, no research should be done without a search for secondary information first, and secondary data should be used whenever available and appropriate. To determine the suitability of the secondary data, a researcher should employ relevant criteria to evaluate the purpose, methodology, definitions of the concepts, and time period covered in the study yielding the secondary information. Transition economies, in particular, pose a special challenge in terms of data quality. Extreme caution should be used when interpreting the foreign trade statistics in the Baltics, Russia, and the other countries of the former Soviet Union. With the economic transformation, coupled with an elimination of the large foreign trade organizations that relied on one currency with an administratively established exchange rate, the methodology of collecting and recording data has changed markedly.[2]

The evaluation process becomes much more complicated if secondary data from various countries must be compared in order to analyze the business potential of each country. A problem for marketers is that secondary data on international marketing may not be comparable for several reasons. First, countries may employ different data collection methods. Second, there may be a problem with classification differences. Third, the unit of measurement employed could differ. Finally, definitional differences are another common problem because countries tend to use various definitions in collecting the same kind of information. For example, regarding the "urban" concept, Denmark defines it as a locality of 200 or more inhabitants, while it must be at least 20,000 for Nigeria. In the case of Bermuda and Singapore, the entire countries comprise an urban area.

SECONDARY RESEARCH

There are many different ways to collect secondary data, and there are many information sources for this purpose. Such sources may be grouped under either public or private sources.

Private sources

A very basic method of finding business information is to begin with a public library or a university library. A library with a reasonable collection should contain standard reference guides, commercial and industrial directories, financial reference manuals, and other materials containing pertinent business information.

One useful source of information is the World Trade Centers Association (WTCA) which has more than 300 World Trade centers in eighty-nine countries. Established as a nonprofit organization in 1970, the WTCA promotes international business relationships through a network of members worldwide. These centers offer referrals, contacts, and information for businesses. A local chamber of commerce in a metropolitan area pays a $165,000 licensing fee to join the WTCA.

Another good source of information is a community's chamber of commerce. Being well informed on local business, this organization is capable of providing helpful advice. In addition to a chamber of commerce at the national level (e.g., the US Chamber of Commerce), there are local chambers of commerce, which are often some of the best sources of information on trade and industry in specific localities. Larger organizations may publish classified buyers' guides, manufacturers' guides, or lists of international traders in their areas. Finally, foreign chambers of commerce are in a position to provide a great deal of relevant information about their countries because they act as public relations offices.

Concerning country information, Dun's Marketing Services offers *Exporter's Encyclopaedia*, which provides comprehensive country-by-country information for over 200 markets. Several large accounting firms also publish their own country-by-country books.

Public sources

Public sources of market information are numerous. Foreign governments, their embassies and consulates, and trade promotion agencies either have the information desired or are in a position to guide the marketer to the proper source of information. Germany, for example, has the Society for Information and Documentation, which promotes development of information science and exchanges scientific and technical data with other countries. France's Center for Information and Documentation offers services similar to those provided by US information brokers. Furthermore, regional and international organizations, such as the World Bank, the OECD, and the IMF, routinely collect information on population and a nation's financial circumstances.

The World Bank and its affiliates offer a number of publications. As in the case of its *Global Development Finance*, it allows users to: (1) generate market analysis, forecasts, and comparisons, (2) examine current trends and assess their impact on investment opportunities, (3) develop investment strategies, and (4) analyze the investment risks associated with specific emerging markets. The World Bank has launched the Country Analytic Work Website to enable multilateral agencies to share information. Donor agencies share analysis, good practices and advice, and they develop and implement country strategies. Both the donors and their clients, through the website, can use development resources more efficiently while avoiding duplication.[3]

The Organization for Economic Cooperation and Development (OECD) is the international organization of the industrialized, market economy countries of Western Europe, North America, and Asia. At OECD headquarters in Paris, it regularly gathers statistical information on the foreign trade of its member countries and makes the statistics internationally comparable by converting the information into uniform units. The OECD Secretariat compiles economic data and policy information, formulates forecasts, and provides analytical work to support the work of government representatives.

The IMF has worldwide information-gathering resources. The IMF's research activities rely on the expertise of its more than 1100 economists who conduct a wide range of financial and monetary studies. Based on these studies, the IMF publishes the *Occasional Papers* and *Economic and Financial Surveys* series, both of which are proven references. *Occasional Papers* are studies on economic and financial subjects of importance to the world economy. *World Economic and Financial Surveys* series, in contrast, are special-topic studies, and the core of the series is derived from *World Economic Outlook*. Twice a year, the IMF prepares *World Economic Outlook* which is a comprehensive assessment of each country's economic situation and prospects. Each May, *World Economic Outlook* examines what is happening and what is likely to happen in various countries; each October, it provides updated projections, showing the impact of key developments. In addition, the IMF's *Staff Country Reports* cover a variety of topics on economic developments in individual member countries. Each in-depth report includes an overview, economic and financial data, analysis of trends, factors to consider in forecasting, comparative charts and graphs, and tabular presentations with interpretive comments. Because the IMF's

217

projections affect the decisions of the IMF and its member countries, the IMF's research is based on the latest facts and figures.

The World Trade Organization (WTO) has several resources for global trade statistics. Its website provides selected statistics on trade in merchandise and services at world and regional levels, developments in major product categories, and historical developments in international trade at the aggregate level. Its trilingual (English, French, and Spanish) CD-ROM contains statistical reports.[4]

For US firms, the most logical public source of information is the US government and its agencies. A good starting point would be to contact the International Trade Division of the Department of Commerce. The International Trade Division maintains reference libraries in major cities where one can talk to trade experts and find statistical and trade reports for each country. At its main office in Washington, DC, there are experts assigned to cover a particular country. One US company interested in selling microwave toilets to Nigeria avoided a costly mistake after being advised that what Nigeria really needed was basic sewage systems.

Getting information from the US government has become easier. The federal government now offers a one-stop data site. Its firstgov.com is a one-stop site that has consolidated some 20,000 government sites and twenty-seven million web pages into one. One can learn about statistics, laws, and regulations.[5] The CIA publishes the *World Factbook* that provides countries' basic statistics (e.g., demographic data), and cultural and political/legal information. The *World Factbook* can also be accessed online.

In conclusion, the US government collects large amounts of relevant data that it makes available at reasonable cost. From this large database, several data products and services are produced. Many of these services differ only in terms of how the information is retrieved and packaged for sale. A marketer should thus consult the International Trade Administration before ordering too many services, some of which may turn out to be redundant.

PRIMARY RESEARCH

When secondary data are unavailable, irrelevant, or obsolete, the marketer must turn to primary research. One decision that must be made is whether to compile or buy the information. In other words, the question to be decided is whether outside agencies such as marketing research firms should be used to collect the information needed or whether the firm should use its own personnel for this purpose.

A list of international marketing research firms may be found in the US Department of Commerce's *Trade List: Market Research Organizations Worldwide*, the American Marketing Association's *International Directory of Marketing Research Houses and Services* (Green Book), and *Bradford's Directory of Marketing Research Agencies and Management Consultants in the USA and the World*. Figure 8.1 shows that marketing research firms can help marketers obtain marketing data in Japan.

If outside personnel are to be used, the company should make a distinction among different types of information brokers who differ in terms of the extent to which value is added to the information delivered. Some merely retrieve printed materials ordered by their clients who know what they want. Other brokers add value by locating information sources and may proceed to conduct interviews on behalf of their clients.

If a marketer decides to conduct his or her own research without hiring outside consultants or researchers, there are many alternatives available to collect primary information. First, the marketer should subscribe to the newspapers in the competitor's home country. These newspapers should include the local language papers and dailies with large circulations. Even a newspaper in a small town near the potential market area is useful, because that paper is likely to cover the news concerning a major company or employer in the area. Second, the marketer can learn about a foreign market by personally visiting it or by being a member of a trade mission. By attending trade fairs, the marketer can observe competitors' display booths and have the

Figure 8.1 *Marketing research in Japan*

Source: a Courtesy of A&S MRS Co., Ltd.; b Courtesy of ASI Market Research.

opportunity to talk with potential customers and distributors.

A company should make an attempt to determine the effectiveness of the planned marketing mix. Some type of *experimental study* may be necessary to determine a cause-and-effect relationship. One type of field experimentation is test marketing. The technique may be used to test a planned national marketing program for a new product in a limited geographic area. A good test market should possess the following characteristics: (1) representativeness, (2) self-contained media, and (3) self-contained trading area.

The concern about representativeness involves demographic comparability. The test market should be demographically similar to the country of which it is part and its population should portray the country's typical characteristics. This market should be large enough to provide meaningful data and yet not be so large as to make the costs of the study prohibitive.

The market should be self-contained from a media standpoint in order to avoid media spillage out of the market. If the market is not isolated in terms of media coverage, communication costs are wasted because an audience is being contacted outside of the intended market. Media should also be available at a reasonable cost. A city such as Tokyo is unsuitable for test marketing because of the exorbitant prices charged for TV time – time not at all readily available.

Finally, the test market should be self-contained in terms of trading area. This is necessary in order to avoid trans-shipments into and out of the area. If the city population increases during the daytime because outside people travel into the city for work or if a distributor delivers the product to others nearby cities, it is difficult to achieve accurate readings of sales, because the sales figure is actually overstated. Cities such as Tokyo and New York are definitely not self-contained.

In North America, Winnipeg, the capital of the Canadian province of Manitoba, is considered a premier test market. Its fairly cosmopolitan and conservative population displays the same characteristics as a larger target audience or general market. This city is favorably isolated because the nearest urban centers are Regina, Saskatchewan, and Minneapolis, Minnesota, both of which are approximately 300 miles away. Thus, the market is controllable because its residents are not exposed to conflicting or competing information from outside sources. In terms of media, Winnipeg has its own newspapers and TV stations; their easy access eliminates any problems related to media availability and waste. Winnipeg has been used to test several product concepts before those products were made available in the US market. McDonald's first tested its chicken product in Winnipeg by combining it with french fries. Consumers, however, considered chicken to be a diet food and preferred the product without a bun or fries. Subsequently, McDonald's Chicken and Chips became Chicken McNuggets.

If certain countries are demographically and psychologically similar, a firm can use a city in one country as a test market to research market conditions in another country. As in the case of Hong Kong, empty nesters or people over age 40 whose children have entered the workforce, accounting for 36 percent of all adults, will jump to 54 percent by 2020. This demographic shift makes Hong Kong a useful test market to determine the future of the other affluent Asian markets. Hong Kong is leading the trend, and a product's success here may influence market development elsewhere.[6]

SAMPLING

As with virtually all consumer market studies, it is neither feasible nor practical for a researcher to contact all the members of the population. The general rule is to contact a select group of consumers considered to be representative of the entire population. This practice is known as *sampling*.

There are several kinds of sampling techniques, with probability and nonprobability sampling methods being the two major categories. In probability sampling, it is possible to specify in advance the chance that each element in the population will have of being included in that sample, though not necessarily in equal probability for every element. In nonprobability sampling, it is not possible to determine such probability or to estimate the sampling error.

The problem of poor sampling methods is not always under the control of the researcher. An ideal sampling method, for instance, may not be practical for many reasons when used in the various markets of the world. In the USA, it is possible to use virtually all types of probability and nonprobability sampling methods that closely reflect the population of a target market. The luxury of these options may not be available in other advanced countries. This problem is of a greater magnitude with sampling in developing economies.

Probability sampling methods, though theoretically superior, may be difficult to employ, and the temptation to use nonprobability methods becomes great. There are several reasons for this difficulty. A map of the country may not be available or out of date. Some cities in Saudi Arabia, for example, have no street names, and houses have no numbers. In Hong Kong, a large number of people live on boats. The unavailability of block statistics thus precludes meaningful stratification. Lists of residents may be nonexistent or inaccurate. Poor people may illegally build shacks and pay their neighbors to allow illegal hookups of electricity and water – thus, even utility companies' lists may not be as accurate as they might first appear.

Poor road systems can create another problem because they preclude the use of the dispersed sample. Even when a proper location is identified, it is still difficult to identify the selected sample element. For example, if the element is a homemaker of a particular housing unit, the researcher may be surprised upon arrival that that particular household has more than one home-maker. This can be a common situation in many parts of the world. The prevalence of extended families and joint tenancy makes it very easy for a housing unit to comprise several primary family units. In some countries, a husband may be a polygamist, and all his wives may live together in the same house. In sum, while one should pay attention to sampling

design, one should not be obsessed with it in light of sampling limitations in most parts of the world.

In cross-national studies, sampling procedures become even more complicated. A researcher may desire to use the same sampling method for all countries in order to maintain consistency. Theoretical desirability, however, often gives way to practicality and flexibility. Sampling procedures may have to vary across countries in order to ensure reasonably the comparability of national groups. For durable products, a random sample may work well in the USA and the European Union, but a judgmental sample based on the more upscale segment of the population may be more meaningful in a less developed country, because relatively affluent consumers there are more likely to purchase and use such products. Thus, the relevance of the sampling method depends on whether it will yield a sample that is representative of a country's population and on whether comparable samples may be obtained from the intended groups of different countries. Furthermore, a researcher may have to distinguish samples obtained from rural and urban areas because dual economies exist in many countries, resulting in rural and urban inhabitants being distinctly different.

It is quite rare for a study to simultaneously investigate some forty or fifty countries. A researcher conducting international business research typically focuses on a few countries for comparison. Sivakumar and Nakata have proposed a methodology that aims to choose country combinations so as to strengthen hypothesis testing.[7] Using a series of algorithms, they have rank-ordered the sets of countries by their power in hypothesis testing. Their tables eliminate judgmental or ad-hoc selection so that a sample can be better justified in terms of methodological rigor. Still, in the end, practical considerations must also be given to access to field-sites, availability of research collaboration, and non-culture variables to be studied.

The experience of Honda demonstrates why it is critical to have an appropriate sample. Honda initially pushed to recycle a platform developed in Japan for its American sport-utility vehicle (SUV),

221

while the American team insisted on a genuine American platform. The American subsidiary wanted an "apartment on wheels" SUV to target surfers, mountain bikers, and other youthful outdoor types who could live in a vehicle while on the road. It was critical for this SUV, Acura MDX, to have American features that included a third row of seats. On the other hand, the top Japanese product development executives felt that people who needed a third row would buy a minivan instead. To overcome this resistance, the American team insisted that a top research-and-development Japanese executive visit Denver. There, he went to the homes of the families that drove Ford Expeditions, and he observed how mothers transported their own children and those of the neighbors to soccer games. He also saw firsthand how so many families used a vehicle's third row for their dogs. Had the research been done in Japan, the Japanese executive would have missed the dog-friendly behavior of the American middle class.[8]

BASIC METHODS OF DATA COLLECTION

There are two principal methods for the collection of primary data: (1) observation, and (2) the administration of survey questions. In the case of observation, respondents are visually observed, regardless of whether they realize it or not. When the survey question method is used, respondents are asked certain questions relating to their characteristics or behavior.

Observation

The principal advantage of the observation method is that, on a theoretical basis, it is supposed to be more objective than the use of survey questions. When using observation, a researcher does not have to depend on what respondents say or are willing to say. Another reason why the observation method tends to yield more objective information lies in the fact that there is no influence exerted by an interviewer, regardless of whether such influence would be real or imagined by respondents. The lack of

social interaction eliminates the possibility of influencing the respondent.

Individuals are usually reluctant to discuss personal habits or consumption, and observation avoids this problem. In the Middle East, Latin America, and Asia, interviewers are suspected of being tax investigators in disguise, making it difficult to obtain data about income and purchases. The degree of openness in a society may also vary. Because of the effectiveness of the observation technique, Edward T. Hall, an internationally known anthropologist, has replaced listening and asking with watching.

There are conflicting opinions about the kind of personnel that should be involved in direct observation. Some contend that local observers should be used because of their familiarity and understanding of the local culture, while others believe that familiarity breeds carelessness. Local observers, by being familiar with local events, tend to take those occurrences for granted. Consequently, essential and rich detail may be left out of a report. For example, a local observer may fail to notice that students wear school uniforms if that is a common local practice. The failure to include this piece of information may be quite crucial for an American firm wanting to sell clothing to schoolchildren. If an American observer were used in the same way, it would be unlikely that such information would be missing, since school uniforms are the exception in the USA. Of course, the situation can also be reversed. An American observer may see nothing unusual about students wearing blue jeans to school, but this kind of behavior might be very conspicuous to a non-American observer.

Whereas familiarity may result in some details being left out, lack of familiarity may lead an inexperienced observer to draw the wrong conclusion. An American observer seeing two foreign males holding hands could draw a hasty conclusion that these men must be homosexual. But this conclusion could be based on an ignorance of the local culture. In many countries, there is nothing sexual or unusual about friends of the same sex holding hands. In such countries, what is unusual is for members of the opposite sex to hold hands in public.

The only safe conclusion that can be made about observers is that there is no substitute for careful training. Observers must be explicitly instructed about what they are supposed to notice. Training and practice are necessary if desired details are to be systematically noted and recorded. If bias cannot be completely eliminated through training, it may be necessary to use observers from various backgrounds to cover each other's blind spots.

Clearly, no company can learn about the competition by interviewing competitors. This is one situation where the observation technique can prove useful in gathering information. One common method used to gather data involves such traditional sources as media and business indexes. A marketer can learn about competitors by reading newspaper or magazine stories about those companies. Problems with such sources are that stories appearing in the print media may be too general and that standard business sources are often outdated. Furthermore, print media may not provide information on competitors' plant operations, capacity, sales force, management structure, and distribution.

Questioning

Survey questions can be used more frequently than observation because of speed and cost. With questioning, data can be collected quickly and at a minimum cost because the researcher does not have to waste time waiting for an event to happen to be observed. The survey question method is also quite versatile, because it can be used to explore virtually all types of marketing problems. Survey questions can be employed to acquire information on the past, present, and future. They are even useful to learn about a consumer's internal workings – such as motives and attitudes – that are not immediately observable.

There are three basic ways of administering questions: personal interview, telephone interview, and mail questionnaire. The popularity of each questioning mode varies from country to country. In many developing countries, telephone and mail surveys are impractical for a variety of reasons.

Although personal, door-to-door, in-home interviews are the dominant mode for gathering research data in Great Britain and Switzerland, central location/street interviews are the dominant technique in France. While the telephone interview is quite popular in the USA, face-to-face interviews account for 77 percent of all interviews conducted in Portugal. In the Nordic countries, where the education level is very high, mail interviews are common.[9]

When the **personal interview** is used, an interviewer must know and understand the local language. This imperative can present a problem in a country such as India, where there are fourteen official languages. In addition, a great deal of personal and social interaction occurs in a personal interview, and the appearance of the interviewer must thus be taken into account. If an interviewer is dressed too smartly, farmers and villagers may be intimidated and may claim to use expensive products just to impress the interviewer.

Personal interview style and technique may need to be adjusted from country to country. A researcher will not be able to ask too many questions in Hong Kong. People there are constantly in a hurry, and will not tolerate lengthy interviews.

Telephone interviews pose a special challenge for international researchers. State-run telephone monopolies are usually associated with poor service, and it is therefore difficult and at times impossible to conduct a telephone survey. It is exceedingly difficult for residents in many countries to receive their own telephone lines – something Americans have always taken for granted. Consumers in other countries may have to pay several hundred dollars for the privilege of being put on a waiting list in the hope that new telephone lines and numbers become available. Often, a person will wait several years before eventually receiving a telephone.

Assuming that private telephones are available, there remain several problems associated with a telephone interview. First, some cities do not have telephone books. Second, foreign telephone owners are much more likely than their Western counterparts to be members of the educated and higher-income groups, making them untypical of the larger population. Finally, telephone conversational habits can be vastly different, and an interviewer may experience great difficulty in obtaining information over the telephone. Some people may be reluctant to give any information over the telephone to an unknown person.

The **mail questionnaire** is a popular survey method due to its low cost and high degree of standardization. Despite these advantages, its effectiveness is contingent on the country in which it is used. Unilever, for instance, will not use the mail questionnaire in Italy.

One problem involves the scarcity of good mailing lists. No population is as mobile as the US population, but people in most countries generally do not bother to report their new address, not even for the purpose of forwarding mail. As a result, a government's list based on the census report and household registration is, as a rule, woefully out of date.

Another problem is illiteracy. Without doubt, this is a significant problem in many less developed countries, but the USA is hardly immune to this problem. Lack of familiarity with the mailed survey question method should be given careful consideration, because many people are not used to responding by mail. This may be due in part to the low volume of mail received outside of the USA. Finally, poor postal service, especially in rural areas, is a cause for complaint in most parts of the world.

ESOMAR's website provides tips on nuances to consider when conducting business research overseas. The site offers a guide to opinion polls. There are guidelines on tape and video recording, interviewing children, mystery shopping, and pharmaceutical marketing research.[10]

MEASUREMENT

The best research design and the best sample are useless without proper measurements. A measuring method or instrument that works quite satisfactorily in one culture may fail to achieve the intended purpose in another country. Special care must therefore be taken if the reliability and validity of the measurement are to be ensured. Questions and scales must be assessed in order to make certain that they perform the function properly.

A measuring instrument exhibits **reliability** when it yields the same result repeatedly, assuming no change in the object being measured. As an example, if a person steps on a weighing scale five times and gets five different results, then something is certainly wrong with the scale, since that person's weight does not change appreciably within a short span of time.

The same reliability problem applies to international marketing research. An English-language questionnaire, when used within foreign markets, increases the chances that misinterpretation, misunderstanding, and administration variation will occur. Respondents' inconsistent answers are likely to be an indicator of the possible unreliability of the instrument.

Validity is an indication of whether a measuring instrument is able to measure what it purports to measure (i.e., whether the measure reflects an accurate representation of the object being measured). A thermometer has been universally accepted as being a valid instrument for measuring temperature, but its validity must be seriously questioned if it is used to measure something else, such as the length of a room or the amount of rainfall.

Reliability is a prerequisite for the existence of validity. If an instrument is not reliable, there are no circumstances under which it may be valid. Reliability, although a necessary condition for validity, is not a sufficient condition. Just because an instrument is reliable, the instrument is not automatically valid.

Linguistic and conceptual nonequivalencies in questionnaire instruments that are used in cross-national surveys could conceivably operate to produce differences in the reliability of measurements, thus affecting the validity of conclusions drawn about market similarities or differences. The occurrence of reliability differentials in cross-national samples varies according to the type of variable.

MARKETING ETHICS 8.1   I SPY – FOR MONEY

According to the American Society for Industrial Security (ASIS), in 1997 there were more than 1100 documented incidents of economic espionage and 550 suspected incidents that could not be fully documented. American companies lost $25 billion in 1995 as a result of economic espionage. The loss jumped to $1 trillion in 2000. The highly prized information includes research and development strategies, manufacturing and marketing plans, and customers lists.

The CIA has reported that intelligence services of several countries (including some close US allies) are active in stealing US proprietary economic information, company trade secrets, and critical technologies. Japan, the United Kingdom, South Korea, Taiwan, China, and France have been known to target the USA for industrial spying.

The French, in particular, are notorious for their active industrial espionage. Their tactics include: (1) steering US defense officials and business executives to bugged Air France seats as well as bugged Paris hotel rooms, (2) tapping French phone lines to obtain contract bids and new product designs faxed to France by American companies, (3) placing moles in US computer firms in Paris and Silicon Valley to pass along breakthrough technology, (4) stealing garbage in Houston in search of industrial secrets, (5) posing as nondefense customers to obtain classified US "stealth" technology for France's aerospace industry, and (6) recruiting French people employed by the US Embassy in Paris to spy on visiting American VIPs.

There are other techniques that are probably legal but not necessarily ethical. Industrial spies can attend trade shows and talk to their clients' competitors. One technologist regularly attends scientific conferences. When technical experts present their papers, she is able to learn about a competitor's new product development.

To protect the security of the high-technology industry, the US Congress passed the Economic Espionage Act of 1996. As a result, theft of trade secrets is a federal crime. Foreign economic spies, if caught, face penalties as high as twenty-five years in jail and $10 million dollars in fines. It is not easy to implement the law, however, because criminal intent must be proven.

What can be done to minimize a company's vulnerability? Precautions must be taken when a person possessing valuable information is on the move. That is when proprietary information is most vulnerable. In addition, executives must carefully weigh the costs and benefits of employing foreign nationals. They must also sensitize their employees to possible consequences of leaking information. After all, the ultimate cost is a loss of jobs if the company loses markets.

Sources: "French Techno-spies Bugging US Industries," *San José Mercury News*, October 21, 1992; John J. Fialka, *War by Others Means*, Norton, 1999; "Attention, Business Travelers: You May Be Targeted by Spies," *San José Mercury News*, March 12, 2000; "Foreign Spies in High Tech Hard to Catch," *San José Mercury News*, February 11, 2001.

Conceptual equivalence

Conceptual equivalence is concerned with whether a particular concept of interest is interpreted and understood in the same manner by people in various cultures. Such concepts as hunger and family welfare are universally understood and pose little problem. Other concepts, however, are culturally specific. The concept of dating between the sexes, which is taken for granted by Americans, is incomprehensible to citizens of countries where the arranged marriage is the norm and where a man can see a member of the opposite sex only in the presence of her family or a chaperon. Culture-specific concepts such as these can have implications for marketers. For example, Pizza Hut initially found that it could not conduct marketing research in Thailand because Thai consumers at the time did not know what a pizza was.

Demographics, in spite of being apparent and easily understood, should not be readily embraced in terms of conceptual equivalence without an examination of the varying frames of reference. A demographic variable such as sex is universal, and a question of this nature can be used in a cross-cultural study. Age, on the other hand, is not always considered in the same way – the Chinese include the time during pregnancy in their age. Educational level, likewise, does not have the same meaning everywhere. The meaning of primary school, grade school, secondary school, high school, college, and university varies greatly. A primary school can range from four years to eight years, depending on the country. In some countries, a college may be nothing more than a vocational school. A college education in one country may not at all be equivalent to that in another. It is thus wise in many instances to ask about the number of years of schooling attended by the respondent.

Let us consider the measurement of poverty. The measurement process usually comprises three steps: (1) choosing an indicator of individual economic welfare (which tends to be household expenditure or income over a certain period, adjusted for differences in household size and cost of living), (2) setting a poverty line (which defines the level of welfare deemed necessary for an individual to escape poverty), and (3) identifying an aggregate poverty measure (one which summarizes the information from the first two steps).[11]

The three steps mentioned are anything but easy because the process has a number of contentious issues. There are several conceptual difficulties associated with each step. In the case of the household welfare indicator, the disputes include such issues as: should the indicator be consumption or income, what should each one include, and whether and how should it consider cost-of-living differences? Regarding the poverty line, at what overall level should it be set, and should the level vary in real terms by subgroup or date? Finally, with regard to the aggregate poverty measure, how should it treat inequality among the poor? One has to wonder whether economists are well equipped to answer these questions or whether behavioral scientists (e.g., psychologists) can do a better job by focusing on individuals' perceptions of their well-being.

The measurement issues and debates mentioned above play an important role in the debate over globalization's impact on poverty and inequality. While some point out that the proportion of people living in extreme poverty in the developing world fell sharply in 1990s, others argue that globalization has created greater poverty. Some contend that income equality has been rising in the world, whereas others argue the opposite. Such conflicting claims stem not only from differences in data and methods used but also from the important conceptual distinctions discussed above. The opposing positions of proglobalizers and antiglobalizers represent a question of interpretation.

One kind of conceptual equivalence a researcher should pay close attention to is **functional equivalence**. A particular object may perform varying functions or may satisfy different needs in different countries. A bicycle is a recreation device in some countries and a basic transportation device in others. Antifreeze is used to prevent freezing of engine coolant in cold countries but to prevent overheating in countries with warm climates. A hot milk-based drink is perceived as having restful, relaxing, and sleep-inducing properties in the United Kingdom; Thai consumers, in contrast, view the same drink as stimulating, energy giving, and invigorating. Thais consume hot milk as either a substitute for or a supplement to breakfast. Therefore, a valid comparison requires the use behavior to have been developed in response to similar problems in different cultures. Use differences must be built into the measuring instrument if meaningless results are to be avoided.

Definitional or **classification equivalence** is another type of conceptual equivalence that requires careful treatment. This factor involves the way in which an object is defined or categorized – either perceptually by consumers or officially by law or government agencies. In addition, even demographic characteristics are subject to the problem of definitional or classification equivalence. Age is one such example. Persons in the same age group in different countries are not necessarily at the same stage of life or family life. When a boy becomes a man or a legal adult depends on the definition used by a particular country. The age of legal adulthood may vary anywhere from the very early teens to 21 years. In India, a "boy" of only 13 or 14 years of age can legally marry a girl who is a few years younger. As a result, chronologically identical age groups within two or more countries do not necessarily lead to comparable equivalent groups. It is thus not possible to standardize age groupings and have the same definitional or classification equivalence on an international basis.

Instrument equivalence

In devising and using a measure, a researcher should distinguish between two kinds of measuring instruments: emic and etic. **Emic instruments** are tests constructed to study a phenomenon within one culture only. **Etic instruments**, on the other hand, are those that are "culture universal" or "culture independent." As such, when properly translated, etic measuring instruments may be used in other cultures.

International marketing research often necessitates some measurement adaptation to overcome the problems of reliability and validity. The rest of this section on measurement is devoted to the problems and adjustments of measurement in terms of conceptual equivalence, instrument equivalence, linguistic equivalence (translation), response style, measurement timing, and external validity.

A measuring instrument should be evaluated in terms of its international suitability. Let us consider the CETSCALE instrument which is used to measure consumer ethnocentrism. Consumers who are ethnocentric do not like to purchase foreign products because such purchases are unpatriotic and harm the domestic economy and employment. The instrument was originally validated with samples of American consumers only. Subsequently, the instrument was applied to samples from France, Japan, Germany, and the USA. The CETSCALE was found to be a reliable measure across the four countries.

It also has some degree of validity as evidenced by the consistent pattern of correlations across each country's sample.[12]

An investigation of product-country images, lifestyles, and ethnocentric behaviors of Turkish consumers detected the robustness of the CETSCALE, thus lending further support to the earlier studies which were conducted in Western countries.[13] Another study investigated whether the CETSCALE could be used as a measure of consumer ethnocentrism on an international basis. In order to assess the instrument's reliability and validity in as many countries and different conditions as possible, the study focused on Spanish consumers' ethnocentric tendencies. The findings indicated that the scale measured a unidimensional construct and that the degree of measurement error was quite acceptable.[14]

In consumer research, the most popular rating scales are the Likert scale and the semantic differential scale. When a **Likert scale** is employed, a respondent is asked to respond by indicating agreement (or disagreement) and the relative intensity of such an agreement to each item or question. The degree of agreement (or disagreement) usually ranges from "strongly agree" to "strongly disagree."

The **semantic differential scale** measures the meaning of an object to a respondent who is asked to rate that concept on a series of bipolar rating scales (i.e., the extremes of each scale employ adjectives of opposite meanings).

A researcher must keep in mind that the Likert and semantic differential scales, though proven to be satisfactory in measuring behavior and opinion in the USA, may not be understood or may not elicit the same manner of response in other markets. One study found significant main effects due to country (China, South Korea, Japan, and the USA) and type of scale used (Likert and semantic differential) as well as the interaction effects. The Likert and semantic differential scales appear to have emic (culture-bound) properties and should be treated as culture-specific instruments.[15]

The nature of the measurement scale can affect responses. Asking whether a particular object is a

10 on a scale of 1 to 10 may be meaningful to American respondents but may not be understood by respondents in most other countries where this rating scheme is uncommon. It is imperative that scales be tailor-made and tested carefully in each culture in terms of relevance and appropriateness.

One issue that may pose a problem is whether a scale should be in balance. A balanced scale is one that has the same number of choices for the positive side as well as for the negative side of the scale. Should scales have a positive or negative skew? It is possible that people in certain cultures may tend to rate positively. As such, should a researcher offer a larger number of alternatives among the positive categories to achieve discrimination?

Another issue related to rating scales is the number of choices (possible answers) provided with each question. A 7-point scale, for example, may not yield more information than a 5-point scale in the USA, but the former may prove useful elsewhere. In general, a higher-point scale is needed when a group is relatively homogeneous, since more information is required to distinguish among members of the group.

According to one study, the 3-category scales were more equivalent than the 5-category scales. This finding raises several interesting questions. "Do scales with fewer categories pose fewer equivalence problems? Is it more difficult to systematically bias scales with fewer categories because choices are constrained? If so, it would create a tradeoff between designing items to capture variance more accurately and designing items less susceptible to response bias."[16]

Content validity should be routinely examined. Content validity is critical when a measuring instrument developed for one population is going to be used with another population. A test has content validity when it consists of items or questions judged to be representative of the specified universe of content. A test to measure the spelling ability of fifth-grade students should comprise words which students at that level of education are supposed to have learned. If a test were to contain a relatively large number of sports terms, for example, it would not have content validity because it would be unfair to those not interested in sports. One researcher has constructed a scale to measure *Guanxi*, a behavior that is pervasive in China. Naturally, the items used must reflect the typical activities in Chinese society.[17]

Standardized tests, such as IQ, SAT, and GMAT tests, are somewhat controversial due to content validity or the lack of it. In the USA, such tests are criticized by the poor and various ethnic minorities for being biased because the questions purportedly reflect the experience of white, middle-class Americans. As such, the questions are not representative of the universe of content of interest. The problem is greatly amplified when US colleges require foreign students to take these standardized tests to determine admission eligibility.

Uniformity is usually desirable, but that should be achieved at the expense of content validity. A researcher must keep in mind that some questions are culturally specific, making them difficult for foreigners, no matter how acculturated or smart they may be, to understand. Some of the questions in US are meaningful to Americans but incomprehensible to Britons. A foreign language can complicate matters even more. It would be unreasonable to say that non-English-speaking children are unintelligent just because they cannot answer questions written in English.

A researcher must remember that the content validity of an instrument depends on the purpose of the study as well as on the groups of people under investigation. The universe of content can vary from group to group and from culture to culture. Standardized tests, therefore, may not necessarily work. Identical questions do not guarantee comparable data from different countries, and some variations in questions may be necessary.

Linguistic equivalence

Linguistic differences can easily invalidate the results of a study. There is no question that poor translation works against sound research methodology. Particularly disadvantageous are imprecise literal translations made without regard to the intended purpose or meaning of the study. **Linguistic equivalence** must be ensured when cross-cultural studies are conducted in different languages.

The goal of linguistic equivalence requires the researcher to pay close attention to potential translation problems. According to Sekaran, translators should pay attention to idiomatic vocabulary, grammatical and syntactical differences in languages, and the experiential differences between cultures as expressed in language.[18] Vocabulary equivalence requires a translation that is equivalent to the original language in which the instrument was developed. Idiomatic equivalence becomes a problem when idioms or colloquialisms unique to one language cannot be translated properly into another. Grammatical and syntactical equivalence poses a problem when long passages must be translated. With regard to experiential equivalence, care should be taken that accurate inferences in a given statement are drawn by respondents from various cultures. As in the case of one study exploring strategic alliances in the emerging Latin American countries, the survey instrument was developed in English and was translated into Portuguese and Spanish by native speakers who were business professors. Back translation was later performed on each local language instrument until conceptual and functional equivalence was achieved.[19]

There are several translation techniques that can be used: back translation, parallel-blind translation, committee approach, random probe, and decentering.[20] With *back translation*, the research question is translated by one translator and then translated back into the source language by another translator. Any discrepancy between the first and last research questions indicates translation problems.

In a *parallel-blind translation*, the question is translated by several individuals independently, and their translated statements are then compared. The *committee approach* differs from the *parallel-blind* technique in the sense that the former permits committee members to discuss the research questions with one another during the translation.

A *random probe* involves placing probes at random locations in both the source and translated question during pretesting in order to ensure that the respondents understand questions in the same way. In *decentering*, both the source version and target version are viewed as open to modification. If translation problems are recognized for the source document, then it should be modified to be more easily translatable. Consequently, the source question becomes more lucid and precise. For example, the statement "I am an aerobic instructor" may be changed to "I am a dance-exercise teacher."

Regardless of the method of translation, there will always be concepts that cannot be translated into certain languages or that cannot be asked in a meaningful way in certain cultures. 7Up's "uncola" slogan is an example of such a concept. Some language purists may even contend that linguistic comparability is an unattainable goal. In any case, none of the translation methods can guarantee linguistic equivalence, but the recognition of potential translation difficulties should at least minimize problems.

When Gillette globally launched Venus, a triple-blade razor for women, the product hit twenty-nine countries simultaneously.[21] A global campaign must pay attention to local languages and requirements; so a website was designed to serve as a global template for fifteen regional sites. Since a package might contain as many as three languages, the company set up a translation war room in London filled with designers, translators, and lawyers. Because the promotional phrases of "soft, protective cushions" and "reveal the goddess in you" carried significance nuances, the translators were required to express back the core idea in their native language. In the case of the word "goddess," Gillette chose the lower case so as to avoid a cultural or religious controversy.

Response style

Response styles are "tendencies to respond systematically to questionnaire items on some basis other than what items were specifically designed to measure."[22] Some common response styles are:

acquiescence, extreme responding, use of the middle response category on the rating scales, and socially desirable responding (see Exhibit 8.2). Such response styles, by contaminating respondents' answers to substantive questions, threaten the validity of empirical findings of both domestic and international marketing research. One large, representative sample of consumers from eleven European Union countries showed systematic effects of response styles on the scale scores as a function of two scale characteristics (proportion of reverse-scored items and extent of deviation of scale mean from the midpoint of the response scale). The correlations between the scales could be biased upward or downward depending on correlation between response style components. Furthermore, a secondary analysis of a comprehensive collection of measurement scales found many scales to fail to control adequately for response styles.

People from different cultures have different response styles when dealing with the same questions. Asian people, for example, are generally very polite and may avoid making negative statements about a product. In such a case, a researcher may have to employ an even-number scale (e.g., yes/no) in order to receive an objective response. The even-number scale, however, may create another problem in the sense that it may elicit an opinion that does not truly exist. A researcher may then want to consider whether to use an odd-number scale so that respondents have an option of making a neutral response.

Another issue concerning response style variation is the willingness – or lack of it – on the part of a respondent to take an extreme position, especially when such a position is not a popular one. It may thus be appropriate to adjust for respondents' extreme positions and/or response style by using "normalized" scores rather than raw scores.

More often than not, one must be sensitive to the logic of a language. English-speaking people, for example, use the words *yes* and *no* in a manner that differs from the way non-English-speaking people do. Thus, "yes" is not always "yes," and sometimes "no" may mean "yes" instead. The English and Western languages require the answer to be "yes" when the answer is affirmative. It is "no" when the answer is negative. For other languages, however, "yes" or "no" refers to whether a person's answer affirms or negates the question asked. Consider the question, "Don't you like it?" An American who does not like the item in question would say "no," but a non-Westerner would probably say "yes," indicating agreement with the question. For the non-Westerner, the statement "Yes, I don't like it" is perfectly logical. Therefore, it is a good idea to phrase questions in simple, positive terms. Questions with negatives should be avoided.

It should be noted that an interviewer is part of the measuring instrument. As such, the charac-

---

EXHIBIT 8.2   RESPONSE STYLES

Acquiescence: the tendency to agree with items regardless of content. Also called agreement tendency, yea-saying, or positivity.

Disacquiescence: the tendency to disagree with items regardless of content. Also called disagreement tendency, nay-saying, or negativity.

Extreme response: the tendency to endorse the most extreme response categories regardless of content.

Response range: the tendency to use a narrow or wide range of response categories around the mean response.

Midpoint: the tendency to use the middle scale category regardless of content.

Noncontingent: the tendency to respond to items carelessly, randomly, or nonpurposefully.

Source: Adapted from Hans Baumgartner and Jan-Benedict E.M. Steenkamp, "Response Styles in Marketing Research: A Cross-National Investigation," *Journal of Marketing Research* 38 (May 2001): 145.

teristics of the interviewer may interact with a respondent's response style. As shown in one study, response quality was affected by interaction effects of respondent and interviewer gender and ethnicity.[23] Overall, Anglos and female interviewers were able to generate more responses. Also in support of the general deference theory, both Hispanic and Anglo respondents deferred to an interviewer from a different background when asked about the interviewer's culture but not when queried about noncultural questions.

Measurement timing

A cross-national study can be done simultaneously, sequentially, or independently. A researcher may initially think it advantageous for a study to be conducted simultaneously in the countries of interest. But simultaneous studies in different markets may present problems of data comparability, especially due to seasonal factors. Consider a study of soft drink consumption, which is generally highest in the summer. Winter in Canada occurs when it is summer in Argentina. Simultaneous studies in such a case would yield invalid results.

History is a specific external event that may affect the outcome or respondent behavior within a study. Acting as an extraneous variable, history complicates cross-national studies. For example, an important election (i.e., history) held in one country and not in another may considerably affect the results of a study. Likewise, sales in the USA during the Christmas season are much higher than sales during the rest of the year, whereas sales in China and Hong Kong tend to be higher than normal during the period of the Chinese New Year.

Another complicating factor can be a product's life-cycle stage. The same product may be in different stages of its life cycle in different countries. Because of the phenomenon of an international product's life cycle, less developed countries may lag behind more advanced nations in adopting the product. The sales of the product in two or more countries for the same period may not be comparable, casting doubt on the wisdom of conducting simultaneous studies. Because of this problem, it may be better in some cases to conduct "simultaneous" studies when the countries are in the same product-life-cycle stage. In addition, it may be prudent to conduct sequential studies for a particular stage in the product's life cycle when the product is not introduced at the same time in the countries of interest.

External validity

There are two major types of validity: internal and external. So far this chapter has only discussed internal validity. A study is said to have **internal validity** when it accurately measures the characteristic or behavior of interest.

However, a researcher is prudent to ask whether the findings concerning a particular sample in a particular study will hold true for subjects who did not take part in the study. **External validity** is concerned with the generalization of research results to other populations. Ordinarily, there is a limit on how far research findings can be generalized. Consequently, the findings may not be applicable to other groups or populations, other products, other cities, other countries, or other cultures.

Consider the health concerns about the use of saccharin. Many studies have provided evidence for a link between saccharin and cancer. The scientific evidence has shown that saccharin is a carcinogen (cancer-causing substance) and that it may act as a cancer catalyst in the sense that it assists the carcinogen to work. Internal validity has never been much of an issue because studies have repeatedly proven that saccharin indeed causes cancer, at least in laboratory rats. Critics of this evidence have concentrated on the issue of external validity. According to the critics, producing a disease in rats is not a valid basis for predicting the effect of saccharin on humans. The US Food and Drug Administration (FDA), however, has dismissed this criticism by pointing out that the analysis is not accompanied by any proof that the mechanism causing cancer in rats would be different in humans. As far as the FDA is concerned, the studies in question are both internally and externally valid. Ironically, after several decades, new evidence seems to indicate that saccharin is safe for consumption after all.

The FDA, surprisingly, has reacted conservatively when test results submitted have used foreign subjects. Although the FDA has accepted results using rats (whether American or not) as surrogates for human beings, it had long shown great reluctance in accepting foreigners as being similar to Americans in terms of the impact of drug treatment. New FDA rules now permit a drug company to submit the results of clinical studies done abroad to support claims of safety and efficacy. Such studies are permitted as long as they have been conducted by competent foreign researchers, can be validated, and are applicable to the US population.

External validity is generally not a problem when the matter of concern is physiological in nature. The same cannot be said about psychological matters. Thus, people may have similar demographics but diverse attitudes and behavior. The behavior of one consumer group or the general behavior of people in one country should not simply be extended to another group or people. It may not be reasonable to assume that a study of a marketing problem in one country or the results obtained within one culture will also be applicable to a marketing problem or people in other cultures. Because of differences between cultures, the problem of external validity is amplified when marketers engage in international marketing research.

Since research in the area of satisfaction has focused primarily on American subjects, the degree of generalization of the results must be evaluated. Toward this end, one study tests the basic disconfirmation of expectations model in a very different culture (Taiwan).[24] Based on the matched samples of American and Taiwanese respondents, the results confirm the generalizability of the model in this particular Asian culture. Along the same lines, 100 American and 100 Chinese Singaporean customers were used to study whether the Fishbein behavioral intention model could be used to explain their retail bargaining behavior. While the Chinese have a higher level of bargaining intention as well as a more competitive bargaining style, the two groups' bargaining attitudes and subjective norms do not differ.[25]

Another study evaluates the applicability of the Narver and Slater market orientation scale in the context of service firms in Central Europe's transition economies.[26] The survey measures the levels of market orientation in 205 business-to-business services companies and 141 consumer services companies in Hungary, Poland, and Slovenia. The results are consistent with the prediction found in predominantly Western marketing literature, thus establishing the scale's reliability and validity. Service firms with the higher levels of market orientation are: (1) more often found in turbulent, rapidly changing markets, (2) more likely to pursue longer term market-building goals (vs. short-term efficiency objectives), (3) more likely to pursue differentiated positioning through superior levels of service, and (4) better performers on both financial and market-based criteria.

MARKETING INFORMATION SYSTEM

A marketing information system (MIS) is an integrated network of information designed to provide marketing managers with relevant and useful information at the right time and place for planning, decision making, and control. As such, the MIS helps management identify opportunities, become aware of potential problems, and develop marketing plans. The MIS is an integral part of the broader management information system. For example, Benetton's stores around the world are linked by computer. When an item is sold, its color is noted. The data collected make it possible for Benetton to determine the shade and amount of fabric to be dyed each day, enabling the firm to respond to color trends very quickly.

In spite of computer and other advanced technologies, "dark age" methods of data collection and maintenance are still prevalent. In many parts of the world, a knowledge and application of modern management systems is nonexistent. In many offices, scores of desks are crammed together in the same room. Each employee may have his or her own unique and disorganized system for filing documents and information. New employees inherit these filing and accounting systems and modify them to fit their needs. The unindexed filing system, a long honored custom, makes each employee practically indispensable since no one knows how to find a document that has been filed by someone else. Such problems are not confined only to less developed countries. Advanced nations such as some European countries and Japan are still struggling with the automation of their information systems.

There is often a misconception that an MIS must be automated or computerized. Although many firms' systems are computerized, it is possible for a company to set up and use a manual system that can later be computerized if desired. With modern technology and the availability of affordable computers, it seems quite worthwhile for an international firm to install a computer-based information system. Yet no one should assume that the computer is a panacea for all system problems, especially if flaws are designed into the MIS. A poorly designed system, whether computerized or not, will never perform satisfactorily.

System development

For the MIS to achieve its desired purpose, the system must be carefully designed and developed. Development involves the three steps of system analysis, design, and implementation. **System analysis** involves the investigation of all users' information needs. The relevant parties must be contacted to determine the kinds of information they need, when it is needed, and the suitable format through which the information is made available. Because information is not cost free, it may not be feasible to satisfy all kinds of information needs. The benefit of the information provided must be compared with the cost of obtaining and maintaining it. Only when the benefit is greater than the cost can a particular information need be accommodated.

System design should be the next major consideration. System design transforms the various information requirements into one or more plans that clearly specify the procedures and programs in obtaining, recording, and analyzing marketing data. Alternative or competing plans are developed and compared, and the most suitable one is ultimately selected.

The final step comprises **system implementation**. The chosen system is installed and checked to make certain that it functions as planned. Both those who operate the system and those who use it must be trained, and their comments should be evaluated to ensure the smooth operation of the system. Even after implementation, the system should continue to be monitored and audited. In this way, management can make certain that the system serves the needs of all users properly while preventing unqualified persons from gaining access to the system. Security Pacific Bank, for example, lost $10.3 million when a consultant was able to obtain an electronics fund transfer code and use it to deposit money into his Swiss bank account.

Desirable characteristics

For the MIS to be effective and efficient, it should possess certain characteristics. In general, the system should be user-oriented, systematic, expandable, comprehensive, flexible, integrated, reliable, timely, and controllable. Marketing and environmental information should be routinely received, evaluated, and continuously updated.

As implied above, certain characteristics are universal in the sense that all information systems, whether large or small and whether domestic or global, should possess them. However, unlike a domestic MIS, an international marketing information system (IMIS) needs to satisfy additional criteria in order to ensure that the system can effectively serve a company's international marketing strategy. Some of these criteria are time independence, location independence, cultural and linguistic compatibility, legal compatibility, standardization/uniformity, flexibility, and integration. An IMIS should

233

be time independent by providing around-the-clock services. Being location independent means that the system must be capable of allowing submission and use of data at the various strategic points globally. Cultural knowledge and linguistic capability, whenever possible, should be built into the software and system. Naturally, the implementation of an IMIS must conform to local laws. To assure uniformity, certain kinds of information need to be standardized. Yet some degree of flexibility is required as well since a good information system should be user oriented. Finally, given the number of users, countries, and locations involved, an IMIS must be designed to allow data integration.

According to the CEO of Peoplesoft, there are twelve imperatives for a real-time enterprise: (1) standardization of business processes, (2) pure Internet architecture, (3) minimizing customizations, (4) holding software vendors accountable, (5) accommodating multiple databases, (6) highly scalable applications, (7) multilingual, multicurrency, (8) interoperability between vendors, (9) embedded business analytics, (10) fewer vendors, broader product lines, (11) change management, and (12) CIO.[27] Regardless of size, each company needs to have the capability to operate on a global basis. Therefore it is important that, whenever possible, business processes should be standardized across subsidiaries, geographies, and divisions.

When operating in multiple countries, a company may have a number of databases (or sub-databases). Such databases should be defined by international standards so as to allow efficient access and data comparison. While such factors as language, consumption habits, and retail trade structure may continue to maintain a distinct local character, the uniform methods allow for a quick examination of market situations across the world or a particular region.

A company that has only one website for the world needs to design the site that takes national or cultural differences into account. The needs of local consumers must be accommodated. To improve service, the company must design the registration and order forms to accept foreign addresses and currencies. A US website thus must add a "country" field and set the postal code to accept more than five alphanumeric digits, while not making "state" a mandatory field.[28]

Subsystems

The MIS consists of several systems: internal reporting, marketing research, and marketing intelligence. The internal reporting subsystem is vital to the system because a company handles a great deal of information on a daily basis. The marketing department has sales reports. The consumer service department receives consumers' praises and complaints. The accounting department routinely generates and collects such information as sales orders, shipments, inventory levels, promotional costs, and so on. All of these types of internally generated information should be kept and made available to all concerned and affected parties.

For externally generated information, the MIS should consist of two subsystems. One of these is the marketing research subsystem. The activities of this subsystem have already been discussed extensively. The other subsystem is the marketing intelligence or environmental scanning subsystem. The responsibility of this subsystem is to track environmental changes or trends. This subsystem collects data from salespersons, distributors, syndicated research services, government agencies, and from publications about technology, social and cultural norms, the legal and political climate, economic conditions, and competitors' activities.

The implementation of the MIS must conform to local laws (see It's the Law 8.1). Many countries, concerned with citizens' privacy, have laws that restrict free flow of information. In England, data users are required by the Data Protection Act to register with the Office of Data Protection Registrar; otherwise, heavy fines are levied. Computer users must state how personal information was obtained and how it will be used. Furthermore, British residents have the right to see personal data about themselves. Similarly, Quebec's privacy legislation restricts the activities of direct marketers who

MARKETING STRATEGY 8.1   HOW TO ADDRESS THE ADDRESS PROBLEMS

There are two underlying problems with the quality of international names and addresses. One problem has to do with storing and manipulating such data in traditional domestic customer databases. The other problem focuses on finding the address standardization tools that are capable of handling international data. Fortunately, there are several products and services that are designed to clean up international addresses.

It is important to deal with data at the reformatting stage. In Singapore, customer names are from three different cultures: Chinese, Malay (Islamic), and Western. Chinese names are presented in last–middle–first order, while Islamic names (e.g., Mohammed bin Abdullah) are approximately (but not exactly) last–first order. For Western-style names, they are first–middle–last order. Caribbean addresses need to be understood and parsed as either American style or Spanish style.

To accommodate international data, a typical US record layout will have to be modified. For example, the length of fields must be extended to accept longer names and addresses. The phone and fax numbers field should include a country code and handle more than ten digits. In the case of the address fields, they may have to be lengthened beyond Address1 and Address2 to include Address3 and perhaps even Address4. In addition, the layout needs to support the expanded character and/or Unicode character sets. The rules behind the postal code field must be evaluated to allow

for alphabetical characters and spaces. Additional fields are required to accommodate country name, region name, and geographic code (e.g., Asia, Sales Territory 1, etc.). It is desirable to consider parsing first name, last name, and multiple last names (e.g., Hispanic names). Finally, be sure to accommodate multiple international currencies.

A firm's database should be flexible enough to accommodate each country's preferred style in maintaining names and addresses. Concerning addresses, in France, Germany, and Italy, the postcode usually precedes the town on a single line. In Britain, the postcode should follow the country name. If the country name is omitted, the postcode follows the town or city. In France and the United Kingdom, the house number precedes the street name. In Germany, Italy, and other European countries, it is the opposite.

Regarding address windows, the window should go on the left-hand side in the case of Britain, the Netherlands, and Ireland. But in France, Sweden, Belgium, and Germany, the right-hand side is the norm. Regarding field sizes, flexibility is a necessity. The German language may require up to one-third more characters than the English-language equivalent.

Sources: "Cher or Chere? (And a Few Other Format Issues)," *DM News*, April 11, 1994, 29; "Ode to International Merge/Purge," *Anchorline*, Anchor Computer's Newsletter, Summer 1998; "Long-Range Missives," *Direct*, March 1, 2002, 33–5.

---

target the French-speaking province. The law requires marketers to notify customers that a file is being created on them and to explain why a database record has been set up. Consumers must be given a "reasonable opportunity" to remove their names from mailing lists.

The MIS should be designed to do more than data collection and maintenance. It should go beyond data collection by adding value to the data so that the information will be of most use to users. The

MIS thus requires an analytical component that is responsible for conceptually and statistically analyzing the data. This component may even go a step further by offering conclusions and recommendations based on the analysis of data. In the case of Shiseido Co., a new computer network finally links factories, sales staff, and 16,000 stores, and enables managers to more accurately forecast demand for its beauty products. As a result, the company has reduced inventory by one-third.[29]

IT'S THE LAW 8.1   THE SAFE HARBOR PRINCIPLES

Notice: An organization must inform individuals about the purposes for which it collects and uses information about them, how to contact the organization with any inquiries or complaints, the types of third parties to which it discloses the information, and the choices and means the organization offers individuals for limiting its use and disclosure. This notice must be provided in clear and conspicuous language when individuals are first asked to provide personal information to the organization or as soon thereafter as is practicable, but in any event before the organization uses such information for a purpose other than that for which it was originally collected or processed by the transferring organization or discloses it for the first time to a third party.

Choice: An organization must offer individuals the opportunity to choose (opt out) whether their personal information is (a) to be disclosed to a third party or (b) to be used for a purpose that is incompatible with the purpose(s) for which it was originally collected or subsequently authorized by the individual. Individuals must be provided with clear and conspicuous, readily available, and affordable mechanisms to exercise choice.

Safe harbor sensitive information principle: For sensitive information (i.e. personal information specifying medical or health conditions, racial or ethnic origin, political opinions, religious or philosophical beliefs, trade union membership or information specifying the sex life of the individual), they must be given affirmative or explicit (opt in) choice if the information is to be disclosed to a third party or used for a purpose other than those for which it was originally collected or subsequently authorized by the individual through the exercise of opt in choice. In any case, an organization should treat as sensitive any information received from a third party where the third party treats and identifies it as sensitive.

Onward transfer: To disclose information to a third party, organizations must apply the Notice and Choice Principles. Where an organization wishes to transfer information to a third party that is acting as an agent, it may do so if it first either ascertains that the third party subscribes to the Principles or is subject to the Directive or another adequacy finding or enters into a written agreement with such third party requiring that the third party provide at least the same level of privacy protection as is required by the relevant Principles. If the organization complies with these requirements, it shall not be held responsible (unless the organization agrees otherwise) when a third party to which it transfers such information processes it in a way contrary to any restrictions or representations, unless the organization knew or should have known the third party would process it in such a contrary way and the organization has not taken reasonable steps to prevent or stop such processing.

Security: Organizations creating, maintaining, using or disseminating personal information must take reasonable precautions to protect it from loss, misuse and unauthorized access, disclosure, alteration and destruction.

Data integrity: Consistent with the Principles, personal information must be relevant for the purposes for which it is to be used. An organization may not process personal information in a way that is incompatible with the purposes for which it has been collected or subsequently authorized by the individual. To the extent necessary for those purposes, an organization should take reasonable steps to ensure that data is reliable for its intended use, accurate, complete, and current.

Access: Individuals must have access to personal information about them that an organization holds and be able to correct, amend, or delete that information where it is inaccurate, except where the burden or expense of providing access would be disproportionate to the risks to the individual's privacy in the case in question, or where the rights of persons other than the individual would be violated.

Enforcement: Effective privacy protection must include mechanisms for assuring compliance with the Principles, recourse for individuals to whom the data relate affected by non-compliance with the Principles, and consequences for the organization when the Principles are not followed. At a minimum, such mechanisms must include (a) readily available and affordable independent recourse mechanisms by which each individual's complaints and disputes are investigated and resolved by reference to the Principles and damages awarded where the applicable law or private sector initiatives so provide; (b) follow up procedures for verifying that the attestations and assertions businesses make about their privacy practices are true and that privacy practices have been implemented as presented; and (c) obligations to remedy problems arising out of failure to comply with the Principles by organizations announcing their adherence to them and consequences for such organizations. Sanctions must be sufficiently rigorous to ensure compliance by organizations.

Source: "The Safe Harbor Principles," *Export America,* January 2001, 25.

CONCLUSION

This chapter has discussed the need for information on the one hand and the difficulty of managing information on the other. The primary goal is to provide a basic understanding of the research process and the use of information. Special attention has been given to the information collection process and the use of marketing information. This coverage is far from being exhaustive, and the reader should consult marketing research textbooks for specific details related to particular research topics.

Regardless of where the intended market is, a company must understand the market and its consumers. Japan and Western Europe are successful abroad because of their adoption of the marketing concept. Basically, the marketing concept requires companies to understand consumer needs, and marketing research is a necessary undertaking in making that determination. Although it may be true that foreign market information is frequently lacking or of poor quality, this general problem can be a blessing in disguise, because competitors do not have either adequate or reliable information. A company that does a better job in acquiring information can gain a competitive advantage.

A marketer should initiate research by searching first for any relevant secondary data. There is a great deal of information readily available, and the researcher needs to know how to identify and locate the various sources of secondary information both at home and abroad. Private sources of information are provided by general reference publications, trade journals from trade and business associations, syndicated services, and marketing research agencies. Government sources also have many kinds of information available in various forms for free or at reasonable cost.

When it is necessary to gather primary data, the marketer should not approach its collection from a perspective of the home country. A marketer should be aware of numerous extra constraints that exist overseas, since such constraints can affect virtually all steps of the research process. Because of these constraints, the process of data collection in the international context is anything but simple. One cannot simply replicate the methodology used in one country and apply it in all countries. The marketer should expect to encounter problems unique to a particular country, and some adaptation in research strategies may be necessary. In order to make certain that a study is reliable and internally and externally valid, it is important to have conceptual, instrumental, and linguistic equivalence.

A company should set up an MIS to handle the information efficiently and effectively. The system should integrate all information inputs from the various sources or departments within the company. For a multinational operation, this means the integration and coordination of all the information generated by the overseas operations as well. The system should be capable of being more than a compilation of data. It should routinely make meaningful outputs available in the desired format for its users in a timely fashion. With the advanced development of artificial intelligence, it may be possible in the near future for a computer to perform all necessary functions, including making recommendations for marketing strategies. However, in the final analysis, every marketer must keep in mind that information can never replace judgment. Remember, it is useless to have "data, data everywhere, and not a thought to think."

CASE 8.1   B&R BANK: DEVELOPING A NEW MARKET

Lan T. Huong, National Economics University, and Gary Oddou, California State University, San Marcos

Since October 1990, when the new banking decrees were established, Vietnam's banking system has undergone a restructuring process. While the state bank is responsible for managing the whole system, local commercial banks now have the freedom to carry out currency trading, banking services, and financial services. Foreign banks have come to Vietnam in increasing numbers due to the banking system reforms which Vietnam's government has recently instituted. B&R Bank is one of those banks in Vietnam. B&R Bank supplies retail banking services and is interested in developing credit card service in Vietnam, especially corporate credit card service.

Today, there are three banks issuing individual and corporate credit cards in Vietnam. These are Vietcombank (Vietnam foreign trade bank), Asian Commercial Bank and Firstvina Bank, the latter two being foreign banks. Currently, commercial banks in Vietnam accept five types of credit card including MasterCard, Visa, Amex, JCB and Diners Club.

However, most credit cards are used by foreigners who travel to Vietnam for business or tourism and by some corporations including Vietnamese companies, joint-venture companies, foreign companies and representative offices in Vietnam.

The banking industry in Vietnam

Vietnam's economy is growing and developing relatively quickly after more than a decade of "doi moi" policy ("Doi moi" refers to the economic reforms the Vietnamese government instituted to create more competitive and open markets in Vietnam). Vietnam in general and the banking industry in particular has overcome the financial crisis that hit Asia in the late 1990s.

Vietnam has four large state-owned banks including Vietcombank, VBARD (Vietnam Bank for Agriculture and Rural Development), BIDV (Bank for Investment and Development of Vietnam), and Industrial and Commercial Bank; there are also forty-six joint-stock banks, more than twenty foreign banks with branches in Vietnam; more than forty foreign banks with representative agents in Vietnam; five joint-venture banks with Malaysia, Indonesia, Thailand, South Korea, and Laos, and two financial companies.

It is the transition to a market economy that has affected the development of the banking system in Vietnam. Over the past years, there have been basic changes in local banking activities. Banks have expanded the scope of their operations to cover all economic sectors to meet the needs of businesses for new equipment purchases, modern technology transfers, import and export activities, and for mobilizing capital.

Banking industry in Hanoi

In Hanoi, the banking sector has made outstanding achievements in providing good and high-quality services to attract more customers. The Hanoi banking system includes over twenty branches of state-owned commercial banks, more than thirteen joint-stock banks, ten branches of overseas banks, and four joint-venture banks.

The mechanism of payment in the banking system has been readjusted, step by step, to meet the demands of businesses in the multi-sector economy. All of the banks provide different services, such as opening individual banking and savings accounts; giving short-term, medium-, and long-term loans; and participating in financing leasing programs.

B&R Bank

B&R is a foreign bank and was established in 1835. Its name has changed three times, the last time in 1970 when the name B&R Bank was adopted. B&R Bank is one of the largest corporations and is ranked among the 100 largest banks throughout the world. B&R operates in forty-one countries and maintains correspondent relationships with over 6000 banks in 157 countries.

The business strategy of B&R is to focus on the Middle East, South and East Asia, and the Pacific area. These regions are of greatest potential and economic relevance to B&R because they represent much of the economically developing regions.

General operations: Operations in B&R are centralized. All the main functions have been brought together in one head office. All the investment banking activities are the responsibility of one business unit.

Operations in Vietnam: In 1994, B&R established its branch in Hanoi and opened another branch in Ho Chi Minh City in 1995. B&R is one of few foreign banks having two branches in Vietnam. B&R offers a wide range of banking services in both Hanoi and Ho Chi Minh City.

Most of the foreign banks in Vietnam (except joint-venture banks) are only involved in wholesaling banking services. B&R is one of a few foreign banks providing retail and wholesale banking services. This is a competitive advantage for B&R compared to other foreign banks. In Vietnam, B&R is the first bank providing credit card services and issuing credit cards. Users of the credit card service in Vietnam are mostly foreign customers but there are also individual Vietnamese customers. The Vietnamese customers tend to be internationally experienced businesspeople and some government personnel.

B&R plans to expand its activities in Vietnam and would like to begin issuing corporate credit cards with the eventual hope of entering the consumer credit card business as time proceeds. B&R is currently researching whether it should invest in corporate credit cards in Vietnam, especially in Hanoi and Ho Chi Minh City. Issues it needs to consider include the level of current and future competition in the corporate credit card sector, how issuing corporate credit cards might affect B&R's reputation, the lack of tradition in using credit cards, and so on.

Credit card environment in Vietnam

In Vietnam, the five accepted cards are MasterCard, Visa, American Express (Amex card), Diners Club and JCB. Credit cards are still a new kind of payment instrument. The Vietnamese are accustomed to cash transactions and bank transfers both at the business-to-consumer level and the business-to-business level. The habit of using cash for purchases is a significant obstacle for card issuers. However, because credit cards can facilitate purchases, there is a clear motivation toward providing credit card services to as many business sectors and markets as possible.

Many commercial banks of Vietnam have become agents for international credit card issuers. In addition, three Vietnamese banks and one joint-venture bank (Vietcombank, ACB Bank, Exim Bank and Firstvina Bank) have also begun issuing credit cards. In April 1996, Vietcombank issued its international credit card (VCB-MasterCard) in Hanoi and Ho Chi Minh City for foreign and high-income Vietnamese. Then, VCB Bank received a license to issue another kind of credit card, VCB-Visa. VCB bank has issued about 2000 VCB-Visa cards and 1500

VCB-MasterCard cards. Seventy percent of them represent individual credit card users and the remainder represent the corporate credit card market.

In 1996, Asia Commercial Bank (ACB) also issued ACB-MasterCard cards, targeting businessmen and travelers as its customers.

In general, individual credit cards and corporate credit cards are not yet popular in Vietnam. Credit cards are accepted only in large cities such as Hanoi and Ho Chi Minh City and only in limited "high-class" establishments, such as very high-end department stores (of which there are only a few) and higher end hotels. Besides the advantages of using credit cards, there are some disadvantages, such as more complex banking procedures, and current limitations in accepting credit cards as an alternative to cash purchases. However, credit cards are seen to hold a huge potential in the future, especially for the corporate credit card market.

From interviewing and sending questionnaires to thirteen banks and twenty joint-venture and foreign companies in Vietnam, B&R has gathered some data on supply and demand, and about the current and future prospects of the corporate credit card market (see appendices).

Points to consider

1   Do you think B&R should issue corporate credit cards in Vietnam? Why or why not?
2   What additional type of market research should B&R conduct? What are the sources of information for that research?

Appendix 1 Banks issuing corporate credit cards and banks planning to issue corporate credit card

Type of banks	Number	Issuing credit cards	Plan to issue
State-owned banks	4	1	1
Joint-stock banks	3	1	2
Joint-venture banks	1	0	0
Foreign banks	5	0	1

Appendix 2 Number of companies using corporate credit cards and the national origin of banks issuing the credit cards

Type of companies	Total	Using corporate credit card		Issuing banks	
		Number	%	Banks in other countries	Banks in Vietnam
Joint venture	13	5	38	5	
Foreign	7	2	29	1	1

Appendix 3 Interest level in using corporate credit cards by thirteen companies that still do not use them (Scale: 1–7; 1: not interested in using corporate credit card, 7: very interested in using corporate credit cards in the future)

Type of companies	Number	Interest level				Time frame for using
		6–7	3–5	1–2	No response	
Joint venture	8	25	25	12.5	37.5	
Foreign companies	5	20	60	20		20 percent interested in using corporate credit cards in next two years

QUESTIONS

1   What are the difficulties in using and comparing secondary data from a number of countries?
2   Why is it difficult to employ probability sampling techniques in developing countries?
3   Distinguish among: back translation, parallel-blind translation, committee approach, random probe, and decentering.
4   Distinguish between internal and external validity. What are the implications of external validity for international marketers?
5   What are the desirable characteristics of the MIS and IMIS?

DISCUSSION ASSIGNMENTS AND MINICASES

1   Would Tokyo be a good test market? Why or why not?
2   Do you prefer observation or questioning in collecting overseas data?
3   Cite certain kinds of behavior so common in the USA that they are often taken for granted by Americans – but not by foreign observers.
4   Discuss the reliability and validity problems in conducting a cross-national comparison study with the use of a standardized questionnaire.
5   Dieting and jogging are concepts which Americans can easily relate to. Are they understood by non-Americans?
6   Do demographic variables have universal meanings? Is there a likelihood that they may be interpreted differently in different cultures?
7   After learning of no import barriers to its product, a US processed food manufacturer conducted market research in Japan to determine the degree of interest in cake mixes. The results were encouraging: the Japanese enjoy eating cakes. Concluding that there was no reason why Japanese consumers would not want to buy ready-made cake mixes, the company proceeded to persuade Japanese supermarkets to carry its product. The sales were extremely disappointing. Did the Japanese interviewed mislead the manufacturer? Or did the manufacturer fail to ask enough or the right questions?
8   As a researcher, you have just been asked to do market research in order to make recommendations on how to market coffee in a number of Asian, European, and South American countries. What questions do you need to ask in order to understand the varying buying motives, consumption habits, and uses of this particular product?

NOTES

1   Jack Honomichl, "Global Growth Forges Ahead at a Steady Pace," *Marketing News,* August 19, 2002, H3.
2   "Transition Economies' Progress in Structural Reform Helps Determine Trade Patterns," *IMF Survey,* April 6, 1998, 110–11.
3   "World Bank Launches Website for Country Analytic Information," *IMF Survey,* November 18, 2002, 358.
4   "Ask the TIC," *Export America,* 14–15.
5   "Government Offers One-Stop Data Site," *San José Mercury News,* September 24, 2000.
6   "Asian Demographics: Stages of Life," *Asian Wall Street Journal,* July 24, 2001.

7   K. Sivakumar and Cheryl Nakata, "The Stampede Toward Hofstede's Framework: Avoiding the Sample Design Pit in Cross-Cultural Research," *Journal of International Business Studies* 32 (third quarter 2001): 555–74.

8   "Tailoring Cars to US Tastes," *Asian Wall Street Journal*, January 16, 2001.

9   "US Research Firms Must Put Time, Thought into European Studies," *Marketing News*, September 11, 2000.

10 "European Studies."

11 "Measuring Poverty: Pitfalls, Prescriptions, and Policy Implications," *IMF Survey*, March 17, 2003, 76–7.

12 Richard G. Netemeyer, Srinivas Durvasula, and Donald R. Lichtenstein, "A Cross-National Assessment of the Reliability and Validity of the CETSCALE," *Journal of Marketing Research* 28 (August 1991): 320–7.

13 Erdener Kaynak and Ali Kara, "Consumer Perceptions of Foreign Products: An Analysis of Product-Country Images and Ethnocentrism," *European Journal of Marketing* 36 (No. 7, 2002): 928–49.

14 Teodoro Luque-Martinez, Jose-Angel Ibanez-Zapata, and Salvador del Barrio-Garcia, "Consumer Ethonocentricism Measurement – An Assessment of the Reliability and Validity of the CETSCALE in Spain," *European Journal of Marketing* 34 (No. 11, 2000): 1353–74.

15 Julie H. Yu, Charles F. Keown, and Laurence W. Jacobs, "Attitude Scale Methodology: Cross-Cultural Implications," *Journal of International Consumer Marketing* 6 (No. 2, 1993): 45.

16 Michael R. Mullen, "Diagnosing Measurement Equivalence in Cross-National Research," *Journal of International Business Studies* 26 (No. 3, 1995): 573–96.

17 Swee Hoon Ang, "The Power of Money: A Cross-Cultural Analysis of Business-Related Beliefs," *Journal of World Business,* 35 (No. 1, 2000): 43.

18 Uma Sekaran, "Methodological and Theoretical Issues and Advancements in Cross-Cultural Research," *Journal of International Business Studies* 14 (fall 1983): 61–72.

19 Masaaki Kotabe *et al.*, "Strategic Alliances in Emerging Latin America: A View from Brazilian, Chilean, and Mexican Companies," *Journal of World Business* 35 (No. 2, 2000): 114–32.

20 Charles S. Mayer, "Multinational Marketing Research: The Magnifying Glass of Methodological Problems," *European Research* 6 (March 1978): 77–83.

21 "Rising," *PROMO* (April 2001): 53ff.

22 Hans Baumgartner and Jan-Benedict E.M. Steenkamp, "Response Styles in Marketing Research: A Cross-National Investigation," *Journal of Marketing Research* 38 (May 2001): 143–56.

23 Cynthia Webster, "Hispanic and Anglo Interviewer and Respondent Ethnicity and Gender: The Impact on Survey Response Quality," *Journal of Marketing Research* 33 (February 1996): 62–72.

24 Richard A. Spreng and Jyh-shen Chiou, "A Cross-Cultural Assessment of the Satisfaction Formation Process," *European Journal of Marketing* 36 (No. 7, 2002): 829–39.

25 Don Y. Lee, "Retail Bargaining Behaviour of American and Chinese Customers," *European Journal of Marketing* 34 (No. 1, 2000): 190–206.

26 Graham Hooley *et al.*, "Market Orientation in the Service Sector of the Transition Economies of Central Europe," *European Journal of Marketing* 37 (No. 1, 2003): 86–106.

27 Craig Conway, President and CEO, Peoplesoft, Keynote address, Digital Economy Conference, December 2001.

28 "Worldwide-Friendly Sites Draws Returns," *Marketing News*, September 2, 2002, 24.

29 "Quick Studies," *Business Week*, November 18, 2002, 48–9.

Chapter 9

Foreign market entry strategies

A merchant, it has been said very properly, is not necessarily the citizen of any particular country. It is in great measure indifferent to him from what places he carries on his trade; and a very stifling disgust will make him move his capital, and together with the industry which it supports, from one country to another.

Adam Smith

CHAPTER OUTLINE

PURPOSE OF CHAPTER

Red Bull has demonstrated a practical way to enter foreign markets. Likewise, Heineken has not entered all markets with a one-track mind and a single-entry method. Even a large multinational corporation, with all its power, still has to adapt its operating methods and formulate multiple entry strategies. The dynamic nature of many overseas markets makes it impossible for a single method to work effectively in all markets.

This chapter is devoted to a coverage of the various market entry strategies. Some of these techniques – such as exporting, licensing, and management contracts – are indirect in the sense that they require no investment overseas. Other techniques, however, require varying degrees of foreign direct investment. These foreign direct investment methods range from joint venture to complete overseas manufacturing facilities, with such strategies as assembly operations, turnkey operations, and acquisitions falling somewhere in between. These strategies do not operate in sequence, and any one of them can be appropriate at any time. Further, the use of one strategy in one market does not rule out the use of the other strategies elsewhere. The methods vary in terms of risk accepted and, to a certain extent, the degree of commitment to the foreign market.

Another purpose of this chapter is to discuss the advantages and disadvantages associated with each method of market penetration. Factors that have an impact on the appropriateness of entry methods are covered in order to provide guidelines for the selection of market entry strategies. The chapter ends with an examination of foreign trade zones, which may be used to complement most entry strategies.

MARKETING ILLUSTRATION RAGING BULL

Chaleo Yoovidhya, the founder of T.C. Pharmaceutical Co. in Thailand, developed several decades ago a formula for Krating Daeng, an energy drink. The brand is a huge success in Thailand, predominantly among blue-collar workers (e.g., truckers, laborers).

Then came Dietrich Mateschitz, an Austrian sales-man from a cosmetics company that was represented in Thailand by the Yoovidhya family. The salesman was intrigued by Krating Daeng and obtained a license to make it in Austria. Krating Daeng became Red Bull, a literal translation. Yoovidhya and Mateschitz formed Red Bull GmbH, each taking a 49 percent stake. Yoovidhya's son got the other 2 percent. Red Bull was marketed in Austria in 1987 before charging into Hungary, its first foreign market, in 1992.

Unlike the way it is marketed in its motherland (Thailand), Red Bull is promoted aggressively as a trendy product associated with extreme sports. It has become a global success. With a sales volume of more than one billion cans a year in eighty-three countries, Red Bull commands 70 percent of the world's energy drink market. That is enough to propel Yoovidhya into the ranks of the world's billionaires. According to Forbes magazine, Yoovidhya ranks No. 383 out of 476 billionaires.

Sources: "Red Bull Tycoon Joins Elite Club," *Bangkok Post*, March 1, 2003; and "Red Bull Takes Flight," *PROMO* (February 2004): 18–19.

FOREIGN DIRECT INVESTMENT (FDI)

Economists usually advocate a free flow of capital across national borders because capital can then seek out the highest rate of return. Owners of capital can diversify their investment, while governments will be less able to pursue bad economic policies. In addition, a global integration of capital markets spreads best practices in corporate governance, accounting rules, and legal traditions.

However, some critics point out that free capital flows are driven by speculative and short-term considerations. For some reason, one noticeable feature of FDI flows is that their share in total inflows is higher in countries where the quality of institutions is lower. In other words, a high share of FDI in a country's total capital inflows may reflect its institutions' weakness instead of its strengths. However, empirical evidence indicates that FDI benefits developing host countries.[1]

MARKETING ETHICS 9.1   WHITE-COLLAR GLOBALIZATION

To take advantage of the global economy, companies have been cutting costs by moving jobs to lower-cost areas. The first wave involved an exodus of jobs making shoes, cheap electronics, and toys. Next came simple service work (e.g., processing credit card receipts). Now the high-end sophisticated jobs can also be exported. The jobs that are moving offshore include life sciences, legal, art/design, business operations, computer, architecture, sales, and office support. Investment banks wonder why they should pay an analyst in London when they can employ an analyst in India to do the same kind of job at a much lower salary. Not surprisingly, British banks (e.g., HSBC Securities Inc.) have large back offices in China and India. French companies have call centers in Mauritius. German multinationals have turned to Russia, the Baltics, and Eastern Europe.

The loss of jobs in the USA and Western Europe is often Asia's gain. American Express, Intel, Microsoft, and others like the Philippines because of its low wages, generous tax breaks, and English-language speakers. Accenture has 5000 workers there, while Procter & Gamble has 650.

One big beneficiary is India. Infosys Technologies has 250 engineers to develop IT applications for Bank of America., and its staffers process home loans for Greenpoint Mortgage of California. At Wipro Ltd., its five radiologists work to interpret thirty CT scans a day for Massachusetts General Hospital. At midnight, Wipro Spectramind Ltd. has 2500 college graduates process claims for a major insurance company and provide help-desk support for a big US Internet service provider – for up to 70 percent lower than the cost in the USA. The company also has seven staff members with Ph.D.s in molecular biology who go through scientific research for Western pharmaceutical companies.

While 35,000 mechanical engineers a year graduate from American universities, China is producing twice as many. Bangalore is India's Silicon Valley, and it alone produces 25,000 software and computer science engineers, almost as many as the entire USA. Because the average wage of $12,000 is only about one-fifth of that in the USA, Cisco, SAP, and the others have shifted their research work to India. General Electric, Intel, and Delta Air Lines have 20,000, 3000, and 6000 workers respectively in India. SAP's 500-engineer facility in Bangalore develops new applications for notebook PCs.

Since capital will constantly chase cheaper labor, does it benefit a society when companies race in search of the bottom of international labor prices? While consumers should benefit from this phenomenon, one has to wonder about workers – especially in the high-cost countries.

Sources: "Is Your Job Next?" *Business Week*, February 3, 2003, 50ff.; "The Way, Way Back Office," *Business Week*, February 3, 2003, 60; "Calling Bangalore," *Business Week*, November 25, 2002, 52–3.

One indisputable fact is that developed countries are both the largest recipients and sources of FDI. The phenomenon is dominated by the triad of the European Union, the USA, and Japan, accounting for 71 percent of inward flows and 82 percent of outward flows.[2] Table 9.1 shows the ten FDI recipients as well as the ten largest sources. Table 9.2 shows inflows by region.

Certain countries have managed to attract large amounts of FDI. In the case of Africa, to attract FDI, African countries have relied on their natural resources, locational advantages, and targeted policies. Above all, the countries that are successful in attracting FDI have certain traits: political and macroeconomic stability and structural reforms (see It's the Law 9.1). "Strong, pro-democracy political leadership that has embraced policies to overcome social and political strife and a firm commitment to economic reform are key factors linked with sizable FDI inflows."[3] Therefore, even those countries that lack natural resources or location advantages still can attract foreign investors by adopting sound economic policies within an open political environment. Figure 9.1 shows that Cyprus has been successful in attracting a number of multinational corporations to locate their operations there.

Corruption has a negative impact on FDI. From the ethics standpoint, foreign investors generally avoid corruption because it is morally wrong. From the economic standpoint, investors prefer not to have to manage such costly risks.[4]

Table 9.2 2001 FDI inflows (by region)

Region	Billions of US dollars
World	760
Developed countries	510
Developing countries	225
Africa	10
Latin America and the Caribbean	80
Asia and the Pacific	125
South, East and South-east Asia	120
Central and Eastern Europe	25

Source: Adapted from *IMF Survey*, October 8, 2001, 314.

EXPORTING

Exporting is a strategy in which a company, without any marketing or production organization overseas, exports a product from its home base. Often, the exported product is fundamentally the same as the one marketed in the home market.

The main advantage of an exporting strategy is the ease in implementing the strategy. Risks are minimal because the company simply exports its excess production capacity when it receives orders

Table 9.1 FDI recipients and sources

FDI recipients	Billions of US dollars	FDI sources	Billions of US dollars
USA	281	United Kingdom	250
Germany	176	France	173
United Kingdom	130	USA	139
Belgium/Luxembourg	87	Belgium/Luxembourg	83
Hong Kong	64	Netherlands	73
Canada	63	Hong Kong	63
Netherlands	55	Spain	54
France	44	Germany	49
China	41	Canada	44
Spain	37	Switzerland	40

Source: Adapted from *IMF Survey*, October 8, 2001, 315.

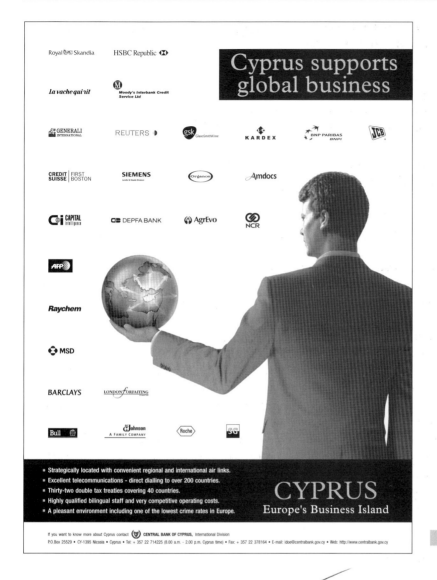

Figure 9.1
Cyprus and FDI

from abroad. As a result, its international marketing effort is casual at best. This is very likely the most common overseas entry approach for small firms. Many companies employ this entry strategy when they first become involved with international business and may continue to use it on a more or less permanent basis. R.R. Donnelley Japan K.K., for example, has issued American Showcase/Japan which is a "catalog of catalogs." This marketing program involves several American catalogers, and allows Japanese consumers to request American catalogs and order merchandise.

The problem with using an exporting strategy is that it is not always an optimal strategy. A desire to keep international activities simple, together with a lack of product modification, make a company's marketing strategy inflexible and unresponsive.

The exporting strategy functions poorly when the company's home country currency is strong. In the 1970s, the Swiss franc was so strong that Swiss companies found it exceedingly difficult to export and sell products in the US market. Swiss companies had to resort to investing abroad in order to reduce the effects of the strong franc. During the first term

IT'S THE LAW 9.1   NOT JUST ANOTHER BANANA REPUBLIC

Costa Rica's traditional exports are coffee and bananas. Unfortunately, these commodities are vulnerable to price swings. To diversify, Costa Rica used its well-educated workforce (the highest literacy rate in Latin America) to attract electronics companies. In the meantime, Intel was planning to build another assembly/test plant. Intel's strategy is to spread such plants around the world to minimize risks of concentrating production in one region as well as to benefit from plentiful, cheap labor and tax incentives in many developing countries. Intel decided to go with Costa Rica – instead of Mexico, Singapore, and Taiwan – because of the country's friendly and stable government and literate workforce. Of course, it helps that Costa Rica offers eight years without taxes, four more years with a 50 percent discount, and bulk rate on electricity.

Both Costa Rica and Intel have greatly benefited from their collaboration. The output from Intel's plant accounts for 37 percent of Costa Rica's exports, more than the exports of coffee and bananas combined. It is also the largest share of a country's exports by a single company anywhere in the world. Costa Rica has room to grow if it can create a local electronics industry. While an Intel plant in Taiwan or Singapore buys 80 percent of its supplies locally, the San José plant in Costa Rica has to import more than 90 percent of its supplies.

Source: "A Silicon Republic," *Newsweek*, August 28, 2000, 42–4.

of the Reagan administration, the US dollar had also gained an extremely strong position. US firms not only found it extremely difficult to export US products but they also had to contend with a flood of inexpensive imports that became even more inexpensive as the dollar became stronger. A currency can remain strong over a stretch of several years, creating prolonged difficulties for the country's exports. Continuing the long-term trend, the Japanese yen surged 20 percent against the US dollar in early 1995 and greatly harmed Japanese exporters.

Austria represents a small but open economy that requires international exchange. Based on a study of the effects of determinants on export performance, the most promising predictors of export performance are firm size, management's motives to internationalize, and use of the differentiation strategy.[5] Another study of small and medium-sized exporters found that decision makers' cosmopolitanism influenced export initiation. These decision makers often learned of foreign opportunities through their existing social ties – rather than formal scanning and market research. The findings were consistent across different industrial settings.[6]

One study measured the export-entrepreneurial orientation construct so as to derive a high versus low export-entrepreneurial taxonomy. While Nigerian firms in the study perceive domestic environmental problems, high export-entrepreneurial firms appear to be better able to adapt and subsequently exhibit a higher tendency to initiate exporting. In addition, high export-entrepreneurial firms are more proactive and innovative in developing exporting while being less averse to exporting risks.[7]

It should be noted that research in international exchange tends to focus on the perspective of exporters. A more complete understanding requires an inclusion of the perspective of importers in the dyad. Based on a study of thirty-six exporter–importer dyads operating in four countries, the best performing dyads exhibited a maintenance of close relationships by people on either side.[8]

LICENSING

When a company finds exporting ineffective but is hesitant to have direct investment abroad, licensing can be a reasonable compromise. Licensing is an agreement that permits a foreign company to use industrial property (i.e., patents, trademarks, and copyrights), technical know-how and skills (e.g., feasibility studies, manuals, technical advice), architectural and engineering designs, or any combination of these in a foreign market. Essentially, a licensor allows a foreign company to manufacture a product for sale in the licensee's country and sometimes in other specified markets.

Examples of licensing abound. Some 50 percent of the drugs sold in Japan are made under license from European and US companies. *Playboy* used to take licensed materials from France's *Lui* for its *Oui* magazine, which was distributed in the US market. *Playboy*'s more common role, however, is that of a licensor, resulting in nine *Playboy* foreign editions. *Penthouse* magazine, likewise, has Japanese and Brazilian versions under license in addition to those in Spain, Australia, and Italy. German-speaking countries account for *Penthouse*'s largest overseas edition.

Licensing is not only restricted to tangible products; a service can be licensed as well. Chicago Mercantile Exchange's attempt to internationalize the futures market led it to obtain licensing rights to the Nikkei stock index. The exchange then sublicensed the Nikkei index to the SIMEX for trade in Singapore in 1986.

In spite of a general belief that foreign direct investment is generally more profitable and thus the preferred scheme, licensing offers several advantages. It allows a company to spread out its research and development and investment costs, while enabling it to receive incremental income with only negligible expenses. In addition, granting a license protects the company's patent and/or trademark against cancellation for nonuse. This protection is especially crucial for a firm that, after investing in production and marketing facilities in a foreign country, decides to leave the market either temporarily or permanently. The situation is especially common in Central and South America, where high inflation and devaluation drastically push up operating costs.

There are other reasons why licensing should be used. Trade barriers may be one such reason. A manufacturer should consider licensing when capital is scarce, when import restrictions discourage direct entry, and when a country is sensitive to foreign ownership. The method is very flexible because it allows a quick and easy way to enter the market. Licensing also works well when transportation cost is high, especially relative to product value. Although Japan banned all direct investment and restricted commercial loans in South Africa, Japan's success there was due to licensing agreements with local distributors.

A company can avoid substantial risks and other difficulties with licensing. Most French designers, for example, use licensing to avoid having to invest in a business. In another example, Disney obtains all of its royalties virtually risk-free from the $500 million Tokyo Disneyland theme park owned by Keisei Electric Railway and Mitsui. The licensing and royalty fees as arranged are very attractive: Disney receives 10 percent of the gate revenue and 5 percent of sales of all food and merchandise. Moreover, Disney, with its policy of using low-paid young adults as park employees, does not have to deal with the Japanese policy of lifetime employment.

An owner of a valuable brand name can benefit greatly from brand licensing. In addition to receiving royalties from sales of merchandise bearing its name or image, the trademark owner receives an intangible benefit of free advertising which reinforces the brand's image. Another benefit is that the brand is extended into new product categories in which the trademark owner has no expertise. Coca-Cola, for example, has licensed its brand name to more than 3000 products which are marketed by 200 licensees in thirty countries.

Nevertheless, licensing has its negative aspects. With reduced risk generally comes reduced profit. In fact, licensing may be the least profitable of all entry strategies.

It is necessary to consider the long-term perspective. By granting a license to a foreign firm, a manufacturer may be nurturing a competitor in the future – someone who is gaining technological and product knowledge. At some point, the licensee may refuse to renew the licensing contract. To complicate the matter further, it is anything but easy to prevent the licensee from using the process learned and acquired while working under license. Texas Instruments had to sue several Japanese manufacturers to force them to continue paying royalties on its patents on memory chips.

Another problem often develops when the licensee performs poorly. To attempt to terminate the contract may be easier said than done. Once licensing is in place, the agreements can also prevent the licensor from entering that market directly. Japanese laws give a licensee virtual control over the licensed product, and such laws present a monumental obstacle for an investor wishing to regain the rights to manufacture and sell the investor's own product.

Inconsistent product quality across countries caused by licensees' lax quality control can injure the reputation of a product on a worldwide basis. This possibility explains why McDonald's goes to extremes in supervising operations, thus ensuring product quality and consistency. McDonald's was successful in court in preventing a franchisee from operating the franchises in France because the franchisee's quality was substandard. Anheuser-Busch, likewise, requires all licensees to meet the company's standards. The licensees must agree to import such ingredients as yeast from the USA.

Even when exact product formulations are followed, licensing can still sometimes damage a product's image – that is, psychologically. Many imported products enjoy a certain degree of prestige or mystique that can disappear rapidly when the product is made locally under license. The Miller brewery became aware of this perception problem when it started brewing Lowenbrau, a German brand, in Texas.

In some cases, a manufacturer has no choice at all about licensing. Many developing countries force patent holders to license their products to other manufacturers or distributors for a royalty fee that may or may not be fair. Canada, owing to consumer activism, is the only industrialized nation requiring compulsory licensing for drugs.

Licensing, in spite of certain limitations, is a sound strategy that can be quite effective under certain circumstances. Licensing terms must be carefully negotiated and explicitly treated (see Figure 9.2). In general, a license contract should include these basic elements: product and territorial coverage, length of contract, quality control, grantback and cross licensing, royalty rate and structure, choice of currency, and choice of law.

When licenses are to be granted to European firms, a firm must consider the antitrust rules of the EU, specifically Article 85 of the Rome Treaty. This article prohibits those licensing terms (with some exemptions) that are likely to adversely affect trade between EU countries. Such arrangements as price fixing, territorial restrictions, and tie-in agreements are void.

A prudent licensor does not "assign" a trademark to a licensee. It is far better to specify the conditions under which the mark can or cannot be used by the licensee. From the licensee's standpoint, the licensor's trademark is valuable in marketing the licensed product only if the product is popular. Otherwise, the licensee would be better served by creating a new trademark to protect the marketing position in the event that the basic license is not renewed.

Licensing should be considered a two-way street because a license also allows the original licensor to gain access to the licensee's technology and product. This is important because the licensee may be able to build on the information supplied by the licensor. Unlike American firms, European licensors are very interested in grantbacks and will even lower the royalty rate in return for product improvements and potentially profitable new products. Thus an intelligent practice is always to stipulate in a contract that license for new patents or products covered by the return grant are to be made available at reasonable royalties.

Finally, the licensor should try not to undermine a product by overlicensing it. For example, Pierre Cardin diluted the value of his name by allowing some 800 products to use the name under license. Subsequently, he created Maxim's as the second

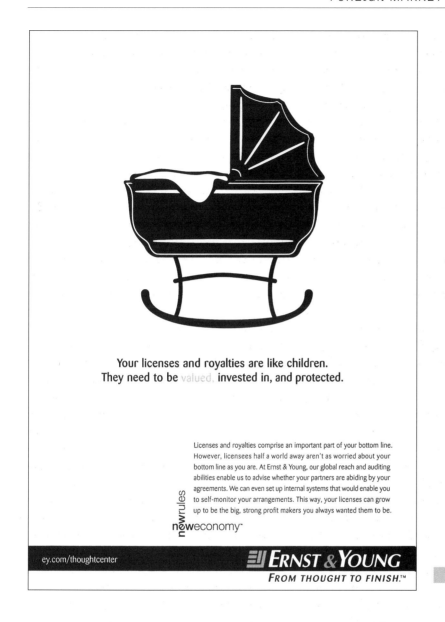

Figure 9.2
Licensing strategy

brand for restaurants, hotels, and food items. Similarly, fashion legend Yves Saint Laurent put his name (YSL) on numerous products ranging from baseball caps to plastic shoes. A luxury brand can lose its cachet when it has too much exposure. Gucci Group paid $1 billion for YSL's ready-to-wear and perfume businesses and quickly moved to restore the brand's image. Production, marketing, and distribution were overhauled. Even though YSL's licensing agreements contributed 65 percent of YSL's rev-enues, Gucci Group decided to walk away from revenues for the sake of the brand's luxury image. In three months, eleven franchised stores were bought back, and a ready-to-wear factory in Tours was sold. Overall, Gucci terminated 152 of 167 licenses to stop the brand's slide in quality and reputation. Some critics felt that Gucci paid too much for YSL by underestimating how far the brand has fallen.[9]

Neither extreme of overlicensing nor under-licensing is desirable. Underlicensing results in

251

potential profit being lost, whereas overlicensing leads to a weakened market through overexposure. Overlicensing can increase income in the short run, but in the long run it may mean killing the goose that laid the golden egg. Some of the risks associated with licensing are suboptimal choice, opportunism, quality, production, payment, contract enforcement, and marketing control. The methods to manage such risks include planning, licensee selection, compensation choices, ongoing relationship, contract specification, and organization of the licensing function.[10]

MANAGEMENT CONTRACT

In some cases, government pressure and restrictions force a foreign company either to sell its domestic operations or to relinquish control. In other cases, the company may prefer not to have any FDI. Under such circumstances, the company may have to formulate another way to generate the revenue given up. One way to generate revenue is to sign a management contract with the government or the new owner in order to manage the business for the new owner. The new owner may lack technical and managerial expertise and may need the former owner to manage the investment until local employees are trained to manage the facility.

Management contracts may be used as a sound strategy for entering a market with a minimum investment and minimum political risks. Club Med, a leader in international resort vacations, is frequently wooed by developing countries with attractive financing options because these countries want tourism. Club Med's strategy involves having either minority ownership or none at all, even though the firm manages all the resorts. Its rationale is that, with management contracts, Club Med is unlikely to be asked to leave a country where it has a resort.

Management contract is a common strategy in the hotel business. Accor SA, a French hotel giant, for example, has purchased a large stake in Zenith Hotels International.[11] Zenith itself manages nine hotels in China and one hotel in Thailand without owning them, and most of its hotels do not carry the Zenith name. Accor's acquisition is an attempt to catch up in China with Bass PLC, the parent of Holiday Inn. It hopes to use Zenith's connections and experience to land more management contracts. Accor's Sofitel brand also has a hotel in China. In the USA, the Motel 6 chain is also operated by Accor.

JOINT VENTURE

The joint venture is another alternative a firm may consider as a way of entering an overseas market. A joint venture is simply a partnership at corporate level, and it may be either domestic or international. For the discussion here, an international joint venture is one in which the partners are from more than one country.

Much like a partnership formed by two or more individuals, a joint venture is an enterprise formed for a specific business purpose by two or more investors sharing ownership and control. Time Warner Entertainment and Taiwan Pan Asia Investment Company, for instance, have formed a joint venture in Taiwan called Tai Hua International Enterprise Co., Ltd. for the purpose of providing products and services to Taiwan's emerging cable TV industry. The US-based McDonald's owns 50 percent of McDonald's Holdings in Japan.

One recent joint venture involves Advanced Micro Devices (AMD) and Fujitsu to replace a previous joint venture (Fujitsu–AMD Semiconductor Ltd.). The previous joint venture allowed the partners to jointly develop flash memory chips. The arrangement was for them to have separate sales forces and geographic territories while competing against each other in selling these jointly developed chips in Europe. Unlike the previous 50–50 joint venture, AMD owns 60 percent of the new company (called FASL LLC), while Fujitsu owns the rest. The three manufacturing plants in Japan, owned by the former joint venture, are folded into the new venture. With the new joint venture, both partners combine all sales, research, engineering, and marketing.[12]

Joint ventures, like licensing, involve certain risks as well as certain advantages over other forms of entry into a foreign market. In most cases, company resources, circumstances, and the reasons for wanting to do business overseas will determine if a joint venture is the most reasonable way to enter the overseas market. According to one study, firms tend to use joint ventures when they enter markets that are characterized by high legal restrictions or high levels of investment risks.[13]

Marketers consider joint ventures to be dynamic because of the possibility of a parent firm's change in mission or power. There are two separate overseas investment processes that describe how joint ventures tend to evolve. The first is the "natural," nonpolitical investment process. In this case, a technology-supplying firm gains a foothold in an unfamiliar market by acquiring a partner that can contribute local knowledge and marketing skills. Technology tends to provide dominance to the technology-supplying firm. As the technology partner becomes more familiar with the market, it buys up more or all equity in the venture or leaves the venture entirely. A contributor of technology, however, is not likely to reduce its share in a joint venture while remaining active in it. The second investment process occurs when the local firm's "political" leverage, through government persuasion, halts or reverses the "natural" economic process. The foreign, technology-supplying partner remains engaged in the venture without strengthening its ownership position, the consequence being a gradual takeover by the local parties.[14]

Partners' commitment to a joint venture is a function of the perceived benefits (satisfaction and economic performance) of the relationship. Conflict, on the other hand, reduces efficiency and thus adversely affects satisfaction.[15]

There are several reasons why joint ventures enjoy certain advantages and should be used. One benefit is that a joint venture substantially reduces the amount of resources (money and personnel) that each partner must contribute.

Frequently, the joint venture strategy is the only way, other than through licensing, that a firm can enter a foreign market. This is especially true when wholly owned activities are prohibited in a country.

Centrally planned economies, in particular, usually limit foreign firms' entry to some sort of cooperative arrangement. China has made it quite clear that only those car makers with long-term commitments will be allowed to assemble foreign models with local partners. Foreign manufacturers must agree to have less than 50 percent control of the joint ventures.

Sometimes *social* rather than legal circumstances require a joint venture to be formed. When Pillsbury planned to market is products in Japan, it considered a number of options, ranging from exporting and licensing to the outright purchase of a Japanese company. Although foreign ownership laws had been relaxed, Pillsbury decided to follow traditional business custom in Japan by seeking a good partner. It thus got together with Snow Brand to form Snow–Brand/Pillsbury.

Joint ventures often have social implications. The familial and tightly knit relationship between suppliers and middlemen is prevalent in many countries. In Japan, this relationship is known as *keiretsu*, which means that family-like business groups are linked by cross-ownership of equity. Such customs and business relationships make it difficult for a new supplier to gain entry. Even in the event that the new supplier is able to secure some orders, those orders may be terminated as soon as a member of the family is able to supply the product in question. A joint venture thus provides an opportunity for the foreign supplier to secure business orders through the back door.

A joint venture can also simultaneously work to satisfy social, economic, and political circumstances since these concerns are highly related. In any kind of international business undertaking political risks always exist, and a joint venture can reduce such risks while it increases market opportunities. In this sense, a joint venture can make a difference between securely entering a foreign market or not entering it at all. Many American firms seek Saudi partners to establish joint ventures so that they can deal effectively with Saudi Arabia's political demands.

Joint ventures are not without their shortcomings and limitations. First, if the partners to the joint venture have not established clear-cut decision-making policy and must consult with each other on all decisions, the *decision-making process* may delay a necessary action when speed is essential.

Problem →

Whenever two individuals or organizations work together, there are bound to be *conflicts* because of cultural problems, divergent goals, disagreements over production and marketing strategies, and weak contributions by one or the other partner. Although the goals may be compatible at the outset, goals and objectives may diverge over time, even when joint ventures are successful. Dow–Badische was set up in the USA with BASF providing the technology to make chemical raw materials and fibers and Dow supplying the marketing expertise. A split eventually occurred despite good profits when BASF wanted to expand the fiber business – Dow felt that the venture was moving away from Dow's mainstream chemical business. BASF ultimately bought out Dow and made the business its wholly owned subsidiary.

Another potential problem is the matter of *control*. By definition, a joint venture must deal with double management. If a partner holds less than 50 percent ownership, that partner must in effect allow the majority partner to make decisions. If the board of directors has a 50–50 split, it is difficult for the board to make a decision quickly or at all. Dow's experience with its Korea Pacific Chemical joint venture illustrates this point. When prices plunged, the joint venture lost $60 million. To stem the loss, Dow wanted to improve efficiency but was opposed by its Korean partner. The government-appointed directors boycotted board meetings and a decision could not be reached. Both sides eventually ended up bringing lawsuits against each other.

There are several factors that may determine whether a company wants to take equity ownership in international joint ventures. These source country factors are exchange rate, cost of borrowing, export capability, and management orientation. Based on a study of 8078 international joint ventures in China, parent firms are more likely to take equity ownership when they are from a source country with a strong currency, low cost of borrowing, strong export capability, and high uncertainty avoidance.[16]

It is interesting to note that, while cultural differences indeed affect international joint venture performance, culture distance stems more from differences in organizational culture than from differences in national cultures. A survey of Indian executives and their partners from other countries confirmed this relationship.[17]

MANUFACTURING

The manufacturing process may be employed as a strategy involving all or some manufacturing in a foreign country. IBM, for example, has sixteen plants in the USA and eighteen more in other countries.

One kind of manufacturing procedure, known as sourcing, involves manufacturing operations in a host country, not so much to sell there but for the purpose of exporting from that company's home country to other countries. This chapter is concerned more with another manufacturing objective: the goal of a manufacturing strategy may be to set up a production base inside a target market country as a means of invading it. There are several variations on this method, ranging from complete manufacturing to contract manufacturing (with a local manufacturer) and partial manufacturing.

From the perspective of the host countries, it is obvious as to why they want to attract foreign capital. Although job creation is the main reason, there are several other benefits for the host country as well. Foreign direct investment, unlike other forms of capital inflows, almost always brings additional resources that are very desirable to developing economies. These resources include technology, management expertise, and access to export markets.

There are several reasons why a company chooses to invest in manufacturing facilities abroad. One reason may involve gaining access either to raw materials or to take advantage of resources for its manufacturing operations. As such, this process is known as *backward vertical integration*. Another reason may be to take advantage of lower labor costs or other abundant factors of production (e.g., labor, energy, and other inputs). Hoover was able to cut its high British manufacturing costs by shifting some of its production to France. The strategy may further reduce another kind of cost – transportation. British publishing firms have begun to print more books abroad because they can save 25 to 40 percent in production and shipping costs. Figure 9.3 shows how Galician Institute for Economic Promotion has attracted more than 10,000 companies to do business in Galicia, Spain.

Manufacturing in a host country can make the company's product more price competitive because the company can avoid or minimize high import taxes, as well as other trade barriers. Honda, with 68 percent of its car sales coming from exports and 43 percent from the US market, has a good reason to be sensitive to trade barriers. In order to avoid future problems of this nature, it set up plants in Ohio.

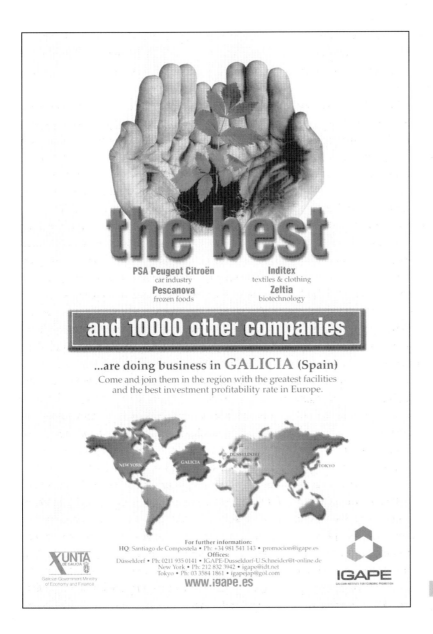

Figure 9.3 *Doing business in Spain*

MARKETING STRATEGY 9.1   DYNAMIC COMPARATIVE ADVANTAGE

Taiwan is one of the Asian tigers. Starting out as an impoverished island, Taiwan has transformed itself into a high-technology center. In 1983, Taiwan was known for making shoes, electric fans, bicycles, umbrellas, and sewing machines. Now, it is a major manufacturer of laptops, monitors, foundry wafers, motherboards, and power supplies.

Taiwan was able to weather the 1997–98 Asian economic crisis because of its role as a manufacturing center for Dell, Compaq, IBM, and others. Taiwan's transformation is continuing, resulting in the hollowing of industry. In 2000, only half of its $40 billion-worth of PCs, peripherals, and semiconductors were made in Taiwan. First International Computer

Inc., like its Taiwanese counterparts, has been moving production to China. While it still does research and development in Taiwan, it also believes that China will soon have enough talent to do it – at one-third of the cost. Conceivably, First International Computer may end up using Taiwan only for its headquarters.

The next stop of transformation: Taiwan policy makers want to use the island's brainpower, entrepreneurial skills, and capital to build an economy of ideas, specifically targeting software and biotechnology.

Sources: "Taiwan Feels Global Shift," *San José Mercury News*, October 7, 2000; "Minds over Matter," *Business Week*, November 27, 2001, 142.

A manufacturer interested in manufacturing abroad should consider a number of significant factors. One study investigated the incentive preferences of MNCs and found absence of restrictions on intercompany payments to be the most important determinant. The other important incentives include: no controls on dividend remittances, import duty concessions, guarantees against expropriation, and tax holidays.[18]

From the marketing standpoint, *product image* deserves attention. Although Winston cigarettes are made in Venezuela with the same tobaccos and formula as the Winston cigarettes in the USA,

Venezuelans still prefer the more expensive US-made Winston. Philip Morris and R.J. Reynolds face this same problem in Russia when setting up manufacturing plants there. Unilever had a similar problem when it began manufacturing locally in Nepal where people prefer Indian-made products (see Cultural Dimension 9.1).

Competition is an important factor, since to a great extent competition determines potential profit. Another factor is resources of various countries, which should be compared to determine each country's comparative advantage. The comparison should also include production considerations,

CULTURAL DIMENSION 9.1   ALL-PURPOSE SOAP

Nepal, with a per capita GDP of $150 to 200, is one of the world's poorest countries. Selling personal care products there can be tricky. In Nepal, consumers use inexpensive laundry soap to wash plates and hair. Lever is the leader in the Nepalese soap market.

Multinational corporations have begun to do more manufacturing of their foreign brands in Nepal. Unfortunately, there is a strong consumer bias against

the made-in-Nepal label. One shopkeeper complains about Lux soaps that are now made in Nepal by Nepal Lever: "We no longer get real Indian soaps." Unilever has thus launched a campaign to change the impression that Nepalese-made goods are inferior.

Source: "Battle for Dominance in the Soap Market Washes over Nepal," *Asian Wall Street Journal*, June 28, 2001.

including production facilities, raw materials, equipment, real estate, water, power, and transport. Human resources, an integral part of the production factor, must be available at reasonable cost.

Manufacturers should pay attention to absolute as well as relative changes in *labor costs* (see Figure 9.4). A particular country is more attractive as a plant's location if the wages there increase more slowly than those in other countries. The increase in labor costs in Germany led GM's Opel to switch its production facilities to Japan and led Rollei to move its production to Singapore. Several Japanese firms have been attracted by the $1 hourly wage rate in Mexico, a rate even lower than the hourly pay in Singapore and South Korea. A manufacturer must keep in mind, however, that labor costs are determined not only by compensation but also by productivity and exchange rates. Mexico's labor costs, already absolutely low, become even lower because of the country's falling exchange rate, but this advantage is offset somewhat because Mexican workers are relatively unskilled and thus produce more defective products.

The *type of product* made is another factor that determines whether foreign manufacturing is an economical and effective venture. A manufacturer must weigh the economies of exporting a standardized product against the flexibility of having a local manufacturing plant that is capable of tailoring the product for local preferences.

Taxation is another important consideration. Countries commonly offer tax advantages, among other incentives, to lure foreign investment. Puerto Rico does well on this score. In addition, there are no exchange problems since the currency is the US dollar.

Just as important as other factors is the *investment climate* for foreign capital. The investment climate is determined by geographic and climatic conditions, market size, and growth potential, as well as by the political atmosphere. As mentioned above, political, economic, and social motives are highly related, and it is hardly surprising that countries, states, and cities compete fiercely to attract foreign investment and manufacturing plants.

Multinational corporations have been investing more and more overseas, with Asia and Latin America as their prime targets. It should be pointed out that the importance of cheap, unskilled labor in attracting manufacturing investment has diminished in recent years and is likely to continue. Because of technology development in products and processes, there is a greater need for human skill in product manufacturing. Therefore, developing countries that can successfully influence plant location decisions will be those that have more highly skilled labor at relatively low wages.[19]

ASSEMBLY OPERATIONS

An assembly operation is a variation on a manufacturing strategy. According to the US Customs Service, "Assembly means the fitting or joining together of fabricated components." The methods used to join or fit together solid components may be welding, soldering, riveting, gluing, laminating, and sewing.

In this strategy, parts or components are produced in various countries in order to gain each country's comparative advantage (see Figure 9.5). Capital-intensive parts may be produced in advanced nations, and labor-intensive assemblies may be produced in a less developed country, where labor is abundant and labor costs low. This strategy is common among manufacturers of consumer electronics. When a product becomes mature and faces intense price competition, it may be necessary to shift all of the labor-intensive operations to less developed countries.

An assembly operation also allows a company to be price-competitive against cheap imports, and this is a defense strategy employed by US apparel makers against such imports. As far as pattern design and fabric cutting are concerned, a US firm can compete by using automated machines, but sewing is another matter altogether, since sewing is labor-intensive and the least automated aspect of making the product. To solve this problem, precut fabrics can be shipped to a low-wage country for sewing before bringing them back for finishing and

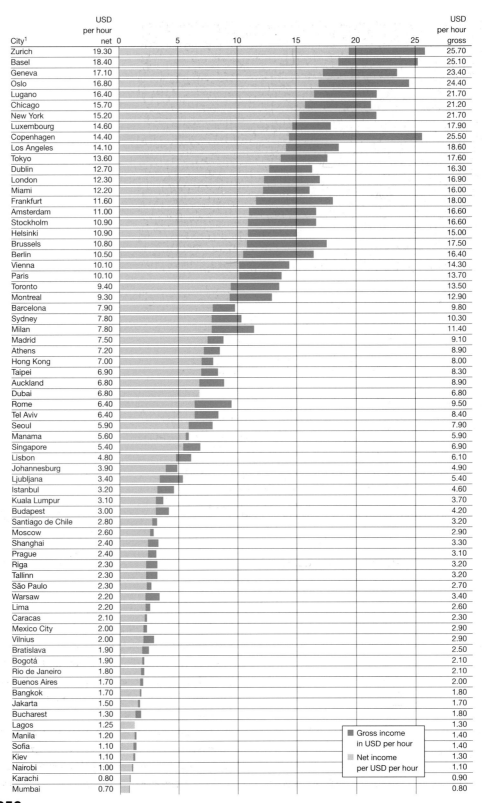

City[1]	USD per hour net	0	5	10	15	20	25	USD per hour gross
Zurich	19.30							25.70
Basel	18.40							25.10
Geneva	17.10							23.40
Oslo	16.80							24.40
Lugano	16.40							21.70
Chicago	15.70							21.20
New York	15.20							21.70
Luxembourg	14.60							17.90
Copenhagen	14.40							25.50
Los Angeles	14.10							18.60
Tokyo	13.60							17.60
Dublin	12.70							16.30
London	12.30							16.90
Miami	12.20							16.00
Frankfurt	11.60							18.00
Amsterdam	11.00							16.60
Stockholm	10.90							16.60
Helsinki	10.90							15.00
Brussels	10.80							17.50
Berlin	10.50							16.40
Vienna	10.10							14.30
Paris	10.10							13.70
Toronto	9.40							13.50
Montreal	9.30							12.90
Barcelona	7.90							9.80
Sydney	7.80							10.30
Milan	7.80							11.40
Madrid	7.50							9.10
Athens	7.20							8.90
Hong Kong	7.00							8.00
Taipei	6.90							8.30
Auckland	6.80							8.90
Dubai	6.80							6.80
Rome	6.40							9.50
Tel Aviv	6.40							8.40
Seoul	5.90							7.90
Manama	5.60							5.90
Singapore	5.40							6.90
Lisbon	4.80							6.10
Johannesburg	3.90							4.90
Ljubljana	3.40							5.40
Istanbul	3.20							4.60
Kuala Lumpur	3.10							3.70
Budapest	3.00							4.20
Santiago de Chile	2.80							3.20
Moscow	2.60							2.90
Shanghai	2.40							3.30
Prague	2.40							3.10
Riga	2.30							3.20
Tallinn	2.30							3.20
São Paulo	2.30							2.70
Warsaw	2.20							3.40
Lima	2.20							2.60
Caracas	2.10							2.30
Mexico City	2.00							2.90
Vilnius	2.00							2.90
Bratislava	1.90							2.50
Bogotá	1.90							2.10
Rio de Janeiro	1.80							2.10
Buenos Aires	1.70							2.00
Bangkok	1.70							1.80
Jakarta	1.50							1.70
Bucharest	1.30							1.80
Lagos	1.25							1.30
Manila	1.20							1.40
Sofia	1.10							1.40
Kiev	1.10							1.30
Nairobi	1.00							1.10
Karachi	0.80							0.90
Mumbai	0.70							0.80

Gross income in USD per hour

Net income per USD per hour

258

Mercedes-Benz excellence means more than just outstanding cars.

As the world automobile industry celebrates the 100th anniversary of the automobile, the Mercedes-Benz three-pointed star has achieved universal recognition as a symbol of undisputed technological advancement and excellence.

This high standard of excellence applies also to Mercedes-Benz trucks throughout America. The three-pointed star gives assurance that Mercedes-Benz trucks provide value:
● Proven product reliability
● A full range of 126-250 HP engines for both tractors and straight trucks to handle the most demanding jobs
● The only guaranteed parts-availability

program in the industry
● 18-months unlimited warranty
● A nationwide dealer network for support
● American craftsmanship: Mercedes-Benz trucks are assembled in a modern, state-of-technology plant in Hampton, Virginia, by workers whose record for quality is the finest anywhere.

The Mercedes-Benz three-pointed star stands for excellence of each and every Mercedes-Benz truck in America. The majority of parts and components for these trucks are sourced from Mercedes-Benz do Brasil, the largest producer of trucks over six tons in the southern hemisphere.

Mercedes-Benz do Brasil S.A.

Figure 9.5 *Assembly operations*

Source: Reprinted with permission of Mercedes Benz do Brasil S.A.

Figure 9.4 *Gross and net hourly pay*

Notes
It was only possible to use official wage data; unofficial customary wage supplements (e.g. cash) could account in some cities, such as Kiev, for more than 50 percent official gross wages.
Methodology: Effective hourly pay in 13 occupations, taking into account working hours, public holidays and vacation days; weighted by occupation.
1. Order based on index levels for net hourly pay.

Source: Prices and Earnings (Zurich: UBS AG, 2003), 22.

packaging. Warnaco and Interco save on aggregate labor costs by cutting fabrics in the USA and shipping them to plants in Costa Rica and Honduras to be sewn. The duties collected on finished products brought back are low.

Assembly operations also allow a company's product to enter many markets without being subject to tariffs and quotas. The extent of freedom and flexibility, however, is limited by local product-

259

content laws. South American countries usually require that 50–95 percent of components used in products be produced domestically. Note that as the percentage of required local content increases, the company's flexibility declines and the price advantage is eroded. This is so because domestic products can be sheltered behind tariff walls, and higher prices must be expected for products with a low percentage of local content.

In general, a host country objects to the establishment of a **screwdriver assembly** that merely assembles imported parts. If a product's local content is less than half of all the components used, the product may be viewed as imported, subjected to tariffs and quota restrictions. The Japanese, even with joint ventures and assembly operations in Europe, keep local content in foreign production facilities to a minimum while maximizing the use of low-cost Japanese components. British Leyland's Triumph Acclaim is one such example. Made in the United Kingdom under license from Honda, Acclaim contained over 55 percent Japanese parts. Italy considered Acclaim as a Japanese, not a European, car. Since the EU's rule of thumb seemed to be at least 45 percent local content, Italy asked the European Commission to decide what percentage of local content a product must have to be considered "made in Europe." An assembly manufacturing operator must therefore carefully evaluate the trade-off between low-cost production and the process of circumventing trade barriers.

TURNKEY OPERATIONS

A turnkey operation is an agreement by the seller to supply a buyer with a facility fully equipped and ready to be operated by the buyer's personnel, who will be trained by the seller. The term is sometimes used in fast-food franchising when a franchisor agrees to select a store site, build the store, equip it, train the franchisee and employees, and sometimes arrange for the financing. In international marketing, the term is usually associated with giant projects that are sold to governments or government-run companies. Large-scale plants requiring technology and large-scale construction processes unavailable in local markets commonly use this strategy. Such large-scale projects include building steel mills; cement, fertilizer, and chemical plants; and those related to such advanced technologies as telecommunications.

Owing to the magnitude of a giant turnkey project, the winner of the contract can expect to reap huge rewards. Thus it is important that the turnkey construction package offered to a buyer is an attractive one. Such a package involves more than just offering the latest technology, since there are many other factors important to less developed countries in deciding on a particular turnkey project. Financing is crucial, and this is one area in which US firms are lacking. European and Japanese firms are much more prepared to secure attractive financing from their governments for buyers. Another factor for consideration involves an agreement to build a local plant. All equipment must be installed and tested to make certain that it functions as intended. Local personnel must be trained to run the operation, and after-sales services should be contracted for and made available for the future maintenance of the plant.

ACQUISITION

When a manufacturer wants to enter a foreign market rapidly and yet retain maximum control, direct investment through acquisition should be considered. The reasons for wanting to acquire a foreign company include product/geographical diversification, acquisition of expertise (technology, marketing, and management), and rapid entry. For example, Renault acquired a controlling interest in American Motors in order to gain the sales organization and distribution network that would otherwise have been very expensive and time-consuming to build from the ground up. After being outbid in 1994 when Forstmann Little & Co. bought Ziff-Davis Publishing, a company well known for its *PC Magazine* and other computer-related publications, Japan's Softbank Corp. was able finally to acquire the publisher a year later, albeit at a much higher price ($2.1 billion). The deal made the Japanese software company the world's largest computer magazine publisher and the largest operator of computer trade shows including Comdex.

Acquisition is viewed in a different light from other kinds of foreign direct investment. A government generally welcomes foreign investment that starts up a new enterprise (called a **greenfield** enterprise), since that investment increases employment and enlarges the tax base. An acquisition, however, fails to do this since it displaces and replaces domestic ownership. Therefore, acquisition is very likely to be perceived as exploitation or a blow to national pride – on this basis, it stands a good chance of being turned down. There was a heated debate before the United Kingdom allowed Sikorsky, a US firm, to acquire Westland, a failing British manufacturer of military helicopters. That episode caused the Thatcher government to halt its negotiation with Ford concerning the acquisition of British Leyland's Austin–Rover passenger-car division. A greenfield project, while embraced by the host country, implies gradual market entry.

A special case of acquisition is the **brownfield** entry mode. This mode happens when an investor's transferred resources dominate those provided by an acquired firm. In addition, this hybrid mode of entry requires the investor to extensively restructure the acquired company so as to assure fit between the two organizations. This is not uncommon in emerging markets, and the extensive restructuring may yield a new operation that resembles a greenfield investment. As such, integration costs can be high. However, brownfield is a worthwhile strategy to consider when neither pure acquisition nor greenfield is feasible.[20]

Due to the sensitive nature of acquisition, there are more legal hurdles to surmount. In Germany, the Federal Cartel Office may prohibit or require divestiture of those mergers and acquisitions that could strengthen or create market domination.

Nestlé, in a space of three months, completed three major deals.[21] First it paid $10.3 billion in cash for Ralston Purina Co., a pet-food powerhouse. Second, it paid over $2.6 billion in stock for a controlling stake in Dreyer's Grand Ice Cream Inc., the largest US maker of ice cream. Another $2.6 billion deal followed for Chef America Inc. Nestlé spent almost a year convincing American regulators to allow it to acquire Dreyer's Grand Ice Cream. The US Federal Trade Commission blocked the proposed deal because the takeover would eliminate brand and price competition for such premium brands as Häagen-Dazs and Godiva. Nestlé, Dreyers, and Unilever control 98 percent of superpremium ice cream sales in the USA.

There does not appear to be any sign that mergers and acquisitions are abating. Anheuser-Busch has negotiated in 2003 to increase its stake in Tsingtao Brewery, China's biggest brewer, from 4.5 percent to 27 percent over seven years at the cost of $182 million. Several of Ford Motor Co.'s premium brands are a result of acquisitions, and they include Volvo (1999), Jaguar (1989), and Aston Martin (1987). A 2000 acquisition was a payment of nearly $3 billion to BMW Group for the British-born Land Rover line of sport-utility vehicles. BMW acquired Rover Group Ltd. in 1995 and lost $1.25 billion on this investment over five years. To cut the loss, BMW sold Rover Group's Rover and MG brands to a British investment group and Land Rover to Ford.

The value of a currency may either reduce or increase the costs of an acquisition. A buyer whose home currency is getting weaker will see its costs go up but will benefit if its currency becomes stronger. As in the case of Hoechst, a German chemical giant, it bid $7.2 billion for the US-based Marion Merrell Dow Inc. and was able to save at least $250 million because the value of the dollar plunged in the meantime.

International mergers and acquisitions are complex, expensive, and risky. The problems are numerous: finding a suitable company, determining a fair price, acquisition debt, merging two management teams, language and cultural differences, employee resentment, geographic distance, and so on. Acquirers thus must exercise due diligence. Sometimes, it may be better to walk away from a deal. The reasons for exiting from a deal include:

high price, no agreement on governance issues, no synergies, poor quality of management, environmental issues, ethical reasons, no strategic fit, detection of significant unrecorded/undisclosed liability, potential problems with antitrust laws, and uncertainty about legal/tax aspects.[22]

Quite often, the future synergies due to vertical integration are elusive. Unicord PLC, a large fish processor located in Thailand, paid $280 million to acquire Bumble Bee Seafood Inc., a San Diego tuna canner. The acquisition was a failure, and the founder of Unicord committed suicide in 1995 as lenders sought payment. Japan's Bridgestone Corp. paid $2.6 billion to acquire money-losing Firestone Tire & Rubber Co. and lost $1 billion in the first five years after the acquisition while enduring a bitter and lengthy strike. Overall, foreign acquirers pay almost twice as much as would domestic buyers. The US market in particular, due to its size, tends to force foreign acquirers to pay a premium price.

According to a study by *Business Week* and Mercer Management Consulting Inc. of 150 deals worth at least $500 million, mergers and acquisitions do not benefit stockholders. When judged by stock performance in relation to Standard & Poor's industry indexes, about half of the 150 deals harmed shareholder wealth, while another one-third hardly contributed anything. Yet, in spite of the high failure rate for cross-border acquisitions, more and more international deals may be expected. A follow-up study showed that transatlantic mergers had a better chance to succeed – far better than the usual success ratio of American domestic or intra-European deals. One contributing factor is that such deals tended to expand geographic reach, reducing the need to cut costs by disruptively merging overlapping operations. In addition, because of the hassles of having to pass the scrutiny of antitrust regulators on both sides of the ocean, companies choose to pursue only the most promising prospects.[23]

STRATEGIC ALLIANCES

As discussed, to gain access to new markets and technologies while achieving economies of scale,

international marketers have a number of organization forms to choose from: licensing, partially owned or wholly owned subsidiaries, joint ventures, and acquisitions. A relatively new organizational form of market entry and competitive cooperation is strategic alliance. This form of corporate cooperation has been receiving a great deal of attention as large multinational firms still find it necessary to find strategic partners to penetrate a market.

There is no clear and precise definition of strategic alliance. There is no one way to form a strategic alliance. Strategic alliances may be the result of mergers, acquisitions, joint ventures, and licensing agreements. Joint ventures are naturally strategic alliances, but not all strategic alliances are joint ventures. Unlike joint ventures which require two or more partners to create a separate entity, a strategic alliance does not necessarily require a new legal entity. As such, it may not require partners to make arrangements to share equity. Instead of being an equity-based investment, a strategic alliance may be more of a contractual arrangement whereby two or more partners agree to cooperate with each other and use each partner's resources and expertise to penetrate a particular market.

America Online is a good example of strategic alliances. In 2000, America Online and Bertelsmann AG formed a global alliance to expand the distribution of Bertelsmann's media content and electronic commerce properties over America Online's interactive brands worldwide. Earlier, a strategic alliance between America Online and Sun Microsystems, Inc. involved a joint development of a comprehensive suite of easy-to-deploy, end-to-end solutions to assist companies and Internet service providers in entering the electronic commerce market and scale their electronic commerce operations. America Online has committed to buy systems and services worth approximately $400 million from Sun. In return, in 2000, America Online received $123 million in licensing, marketing and advertising fees, and about $317 million in minimum revenue commitments.[24]

Airlines are a good example of the international nature of strategic alliances. Almost all major airlines have joined one of the three strategic groups: Star, SkyTeam, and Oneworld. The SkyTeam group consists of Delta, Air France, Aeromexico, Alitalia, Czech Airlines, and Korean Air. Oneworld comprises American, British Airways, Aer Lingus, Cathay Pacific, Finnair, Iberia, LanChile, and Qantas. The Star alliance, the largest group, comprises United, Air Canada, Air New Zealand, ANA, Austrian, British Midland, Lauda, Lufthansa, Mexicana, Scandinavian, Singapore, Thai, Tyrolean, and Varig. While the alliances vary in size and degree of integration, most have code sharing by offering seats on a partner's flights. In addition, passengers earn frequent-flier points on their home carrier when flying with the alliance members. These members also provide reciprocal access to their airport lounges.

Companies enter into alliance relationships for a variety of reasons. Those in the emerging Latin American economies are similar to their counterparts in many other nations in terms of their motivations. In general, through alliances with foreign partners, they seek resource acquisition, competitive posturing, and risk/cost reduction.[25] While companies have paid attention to the hard side of alliance management (e.g., financial issues and other operational issues), the soft side also requires attention. The soft side has to do with the management of relationship capital in an alliance. Relationship capital focuses on the socio-psychological aspects of the alliance, and the two important areas of relationship capital are mutual trust and commitment.[26]

There are at least three types of strategic alliances: shared distribution, licensed manufacturing, and research and development (R&D) alliances.[27] Examples of shared distribution include Chrysler's distribution of Mitsubishi cars in the USA and the shared routes of SAS, KLM, Austrian Air, and Swiss Air. Matshushita's manufacturing of IBM PCs is an example of licensed manufacturing, enabling the partners to fill unused capacity while avoiding an investment in a new plant and equipment. In the case of R&D alliances, one recent example is an alliance between Sony and Philips which competed with another alliance led by Toshiba in developing DVDs.

ANALYSIS OF ENTRY STRATEGIES

To enter a foreign market, a manufacturer has a number of strategic options, each with its own strengths and weaknesses. Many companies employ multiple strategies. IBM has employed strategies ranging from licensing, joint ventures, and strategic alliances on the one hand to local manufacturing and subsidiaries on the other hand. Likewise, McDonald's uses joint ventures in the Far East while licensing its name without putting up equity capital in the Mideast. Walt Disney Co. has a 39 percent stake in Euro Disney while collecting management and royalty fees which amount to $70 million a year.

One would be naive to believe that a single entry strategy is suitable for all products or in all countries. For example, a significant change in the investment climate can make a particular strategy ineffective even though it worked well in the past. There are a number of characteristics that determine the appropriateness of entry strategies, and many variables affect which strategy is chosen. These characteristics include political risks, regulations, type of country, type of product, and other competitive and market characteristics.

The impact of culture on FDI is somewhat ambiguous. One study found no support for the belief that foreign direct investments first took place in foreign markets close to the home country before spreading to more culturally distant markets.[28] Another study involved service multinational firms and found that their foreign investments were negatively related to the cultural distance between the home and host countries.[29] Interestingly, multinational corporations with social knowledge (i.e., ability to understand others' general patterns of behavior) have less need to resort to ownership for control purposes.[30]

Viacom Inc. appears to take culture into account in deciding on entry strategies. In the case of its MTV channel, the company generally does not have partners, but in the case of its Nickelodeon channel, the firm has made an effort to have local partners. It is difficult to tell Europeans that they should have the same cultural underpinnings inherent in American children's programming. Although children may watch programming from other countries, they are more inclined to watch their own programs.

Markets are far from being homogeneous, and the type of country chosen dictates the entry strategy to be used. One way of classifying countries is by the *degree of control exerted on the economy by the government*, with capitalism at one extreme and communism at the other. Other systems are classified somewhere in between depending on the freedom allowed to private citizens in conducting their business activities. In free-enterprise economies, an MNC can choose any entry strategy it deems appropriate. In controlled economies, the options are limited. Until recently, the most frequent trade entry activity in controlled economies was exporting, followed by licensing for Eastern Europe.

Market entry strategies are also influenced by *product type*. A product that must be customized or that requires some services before and after the sale cannot be exported easily to another country. In fact, a service or product whose value is determined largely by an accompanied service cannot be distributed practically outside of the producing country. Any portion of the product that is service-oriented must be created at the place of consumption. As a result, service-intensive products require particular modes of market entry. The options include management contract to sell service to a foreign customer, licensing so that another local company (franchisee) may be trained to provide that service, and local manufacturing by establishing a permanent branch or subsidiary there.

A product that is basically a *commodity* may require local production in order to reduce labor and shipping costs. For a *value-added or differentiated product*, a firm can depend on the exporting mode because of the higher profit margin. Furthermore, local manufacturing may destroy the product's mystique and thus diminish a previously existing market.

A study of foreign direct investment entries in the USA found that 65 percent entered the USA through acquisitions and that joint ventures and greenfields accounted for 9 percent and 26 percent respectively. Foreign acquisitions of American firms

were more likely to fail than foreign greenfield investments. Foreign-controlled firms failed less often than domestically owned firms.[31] There may be a relationship between ownership entry modes and performance. According to one study of 321 Japanese firms entering the North American market, new ventures outperform joint ventures, and joint ventures outperform acquisitions.[32]

There are two schools of thought that explain how multinational corporations select ownership structures for subsidiaries. The first has to do with what the firm wants, and MNCs want structures that minimize the transaction costs of doing business abroad (e.g., whole ownership). Factors affecting what the firm wants include the capabilities of the firm, its strategic needs, and the transaction costs of different ways of transferring capabilities. The second school of thought, related to what the firm can get, explains that what it wants may differ from what it can get (e.g., joint venture). In this case, ownership structures are determined by negotiations, whose outcomes depend on the relative bargaining power of the firm and that of the host government. The statistical analysis supports the bargaining school, in that attractive domestic markets increase the relative power of host governments. However, there is no support for the prediction that firms in marketing- and R&D-intensive industries have more bargaining power than others. MNCs prefer whole ownership when they have a lot of experience in an industry or a country, when intrasystem sales of the subsidiary are high, or when the subsidiary is located in a market-intensive industry. The joint venture is the preferred mode when MNCs rely on local inputs of raw materials and skills.[33]

In practice, American manufacturers prefer joint ventures in the Far East because of legal and cultural barriers. Regarding how American manufacturers want to enter the European Union market, the preferred methods of entry (and the percent of preference) are: joint venture (26 percent), sales representative (21 percent), branch/subsidiary (19 percent), distribution facility (17 percent), increasing exports (9 percent), and expanding existing facilities (8 percent). Their preferred European locations are: Britain (30 percent), Germany (24 percent), France (9 percent), Italy (9 percent), the Netherlands (8 percent), Belgium (8 percent), Ireland (5 percent), Spain (5 percent), and Denmark (3 percent).[34]

A company's entry choice of joint ventures versus wholly owned subsidiaries may be influenced by its competitive capabilities as well as market barriers. In the case of Japanese investors entering the US market, they choose joint ventures when facing high market barriers. However, they prefer to establish wholly owned subsidiaries when they possess competitive capabilities. These ownership decisions are influenced more by marketing variables than by technological factors. One caveat: the results vary across industries (low technology vs. high technology) and products (consumer products vs. industrial products).[35] The costs of organizing a business in transition economies influence entry mode choice. Host country institutions have an impact because underdeveloped institutions drive up costs of establishing wholly owned ventures.[36]

Institutional isomorphism seems to exist as later entrants often use the entry mode patterns established by earlier entrants. In addition, this behavior exists within a firm as companies exhibit consistency in their entry mode choices across time.[37]

In the case of China, a company's timing of entry is associated with non-equity modes, competitors' behavior, and lower levels of country risk. Firms cannot delay their entry when the competitors are moving in. In addition, a firm's entry is accelerated if a non-equity mode of entry is chosen. Favorable risk conditions (locational features), likewise, accelerate entry timing. In addition, corporate size facilitates early entry. A firm of good size is able to muster resources, extend support among the related products sectors, and capitalize on economies of scale. This is consistent with the resource-based arguments that early entrants differ from late entrants in terms of resources and capabilities.[38]

One study focuses on conflicting results which show that cultural distance is associated with wholly owned modes in some studies and with joint ventures in other studies. The evidence shows that, for Western firms investing in Central and Eastern Europe, investment risk moderates the relationship between cultural distance and entry mode selection. Firms entering culturally distant markets that are low in investment risk preferred cooperative modes of entry. However, if such culturally distant markets pose high investment risk, wholly owned modes of entry are preferred.[39] However, although cultural distance is routinely used as an independent variable which supposedly influences performance and entry mode choice, it is conceivable that the relationship may be reversed. A case can be made that cultural distance is a dependent variable because entry mode and performance may affect the perceived distance.[40]

FOREIGN TRADE ZONES (FTZs)

When entering a market, a company should go beyond an investigation of market entry modes. Another question that should be asked is whether a foreign trade zone (FTZ) is involved and needs consideration. The decisions concerning market entry and FTZs are somewhat independent. An FTZ may be used regardless of whether the entry strategy is exporting or local manufacturing.

An FTZ is a secured domestic area in international commerce, considered to be legally outside a country's customs territory. It is an area designated by a government for the duty-free entry of goods. It is also a location where imports may be handled with few regulations, and little or no customs duties and excise taxes are collected. As such, goods enter the area without any duty being payable. The duty would be paid only when goods enter customs territory of the country where an FTZ is located.

Variations among FTZs include freeports, tariff-free trade zones, airport duty-free arcades, export processing zones, and other foreign grade zones. FTZs are usually established in countries for the convenience of foreign traders. The zones may be run by the host government or by private entities. FTZs vary in size from a few acres to several square

265

miles. They may be located at airports, in harbor areas, or within the interior of a country (e.g., Salt Lake City). In addition to the FTZs (general-purpose zones), there are also subzones throughout the USA. Subzones are special-purpose facilities for companies unable to operate effectively at public zone sites.

One popular misconception about FTZs is that they are used basically for warehousing. Although goods may be stored for an unlimited length of time in an FTZ, any gain from doing so is small when compared to the alternative of a bonded warehouse, which allows temporary storage without duty. Actually, the future of FTZs lies in manufacturing (product manipulation), not storing.

FTZs offer several important benefits, both for the country and for companies using them. One benefit is job retention and creation. When better facilities and grants are provided to attract MNCs, FTZs can generate foreign investment and jobs. For example, in Buffalo, New York, FTZ was able to attract a Canadian automobile assembly operation and a Japanese camera importer to establish operations there. China has set up Special Economic Zones (SEZs) for manufacturing, banking, exporting and importing, and foreign investment. These SEZs provide a more liberal environment than that of the rest of the country. SEZs, when compared to the rest of China, are unique in the sense that they enjoy considerable administrative autonomy and they offer numerous economic incentives.[41]

Some countries, due to political reasons, are not able to open up their economies completely. Instead they have set up **export processing zones**, a special type of FTZ, in order to attract foreign capital for manufacturing for export. However, for export processing zones to be effective, exporters should not be isolated from other firms.[42]

There is evidence that manufacturers take free trade zones into account when selecting a site for their foreign operations. Plant location is related positively to size of free trade zones, per capita GNP, exchange rate devaluation, length of income tax holidays, political stability, and manufacturing concentration. On the other hand, the location of export-oriented manufacturing investment is related negatively to wage rate, inflation rate, transportation cost, and profit repatriation restrictions.[43]

The benefits of FTZ use are numerous. Some of these benefits are country-specific in the sense that some countries offer superior facilities for lower costs (e.g., utilities and telecommunications). Other benefits are zone-specific in that certain zones may be better than others within the same country in terms of tax and transportation facilities. Finally, there are zone-related benefits that constitute general advantages in using an FTZ. Some of the zone-related benefits are: lower theft rate, lower insurance costs, delay of tax payment, and reduction of inventory in transit.

FTZs provide a means to facilitate imports. Imported merchandise can be sent into FTZs without formal customs entry and duty payment until some later date. Both foreign and domestic goods may be moved into FTZs and remain there for storage, assembling, manufacturing, packaging, and other processing operations. Goods that were improperly marked or cannot meet standards for clearance can be remarked and salvaged. Moreover, goods can be cleaned, mixed, and used in the manufacturing of other products. One Swiss cosmetics company imports in bulk and employs US labor to repackage its goods for retailing. In fact, importers can even display and exhibit merchandise and take orders in FTZs without securing a bond. For retailers, benefits derived by using FTZs include the sorting, labeling, and storing of imports.

FTZs not only facilitate imports but also facilitate export and re-export, though the gain from this practice is small when compared to the alternatives of duty drawback and temporary import bond. However, domestic goods can be taken into an FTZ and are then returned free of quotas and duty, even when they have been combined with other articles while inside the zone. Sears uses the New Orleans FTZ to inspect foreign cameras it subsequently ships to Latin America. Seiko Time Corporation of America opened a 200,000-square-foot facility in the New Jersey FTZ to store and ship watches to Canada and Latin America. One European medical supply firm that makes kidney dialysis machines uses German raw materials and American labor in a US FTZ for assembly purposes, and then exports 30 percent of the finished product to Scandinavia.

CONCLUSION

If a company wants to avoid foreign direct investment when marketing in foreign markets, it has a number of options. It can export its product from its home base, or it can grant a license permitting another company to manufacture and market its product in a foreign market. Another option is to sign a contract to sell its expertise by managing the business for a foreign owner.

If the firm is interested in making foreign direct investment, it can either start its business from the ground up or acquire another company. The acquisition, however, may receive a less than enthusiastic response from the foreign government. If the company decides to start a new business overseas, it must consider whether a sole venture or joint venture will best suit the objective. Sole ventures provide a company with better control and profit, whereas joint ventures reduce risk and exploit the strengths of a local partner. Regardless of whether a sole venture or joint venture is used, the company must still decide whether local production is going to be complete or partial (i.e., assembly). Finally, foreign sales to governments often take the form of giant turnkey projects that require the company to provide a complete package, including financing, construction, and training.

Once a particular market is chosen, management needs to decide on the market entry strategy. In addition, the company should consider the feasibility of operating all or some of its international business in a free trade zone, since such a zone can complement many of the market penetration options.

Each market entry strategy has its own unique strengths and weaknesses. In most circumstances the strategies are not mutually exclusive. A manufacturer may use multiple strategies in different markets as well as within the same market. No single market penetration is ideal for all markets or all circumstances. The appropriateness of a strategic option depends on corporate objectives, market conditions, and political realities.

CASE 9.1 HOW TO EXPORT HOUSES

Prefabricated houses are not new. Some well-known mail-order retailers started selling such houses in the USA decades ago. Nearly all houses built today contain some prefabricated components such as roof trusses, floor trusses, prehung doors, windows, and so on. The site-built or stick-built housing industry has long realized that using ready-made components for selected parts of a house results in a significant saving of time and money in overall construction.

Factory-built housing has come a long way since its early trailer park days back in the 1950s. Dramatic advances in design and technology have transformed these once small, creaky single-sectioned mobile campers into attractive, spacious, multi-sectional family dwellings. In 1999, US manufacturers exported $72 million in prefabricated homes and housing trailers. Prefabricated housing has been gaining in popularity in the USA and has also been expanding into overseas markets. This is mostly because of lower transportation costs and improvements in styling and engineering technology.

Prefabricated houses are assembled from components that are manufactured in an enclosed central production facility. The assembled structures are either fabricated in the factory into an almost complete module (a modular house) or the components are transported for assembly to the construction site (panelized, precut, or log homes). Housing is a highly varied product.

Modular structures are the most sophisticated complete types of all prefabricated buildings, being 95 percent complete when they leave the factory, with interior and exterior walls, wiring, plumbing, insulation, windows/doors, kitchen/bathroom appliances/fixtures, heating and cooling equipment, water heater and all other mechanical items. The entire set-up process usually takes only a few hours and all remaining work on the building is completed in less than two weeks.

An important type of modular housing is mobile homes. Manufactured housing units (mobile homes) are shipped as single-section units or as single-wide sections of multi-section structures. Most are built for housing purposes but some are made for light commercial uses, such as offices, clinics, or classrooms.

Panelized buildings are the most popular type of prefabricated structure for both domestic and international sales due to ease of transportation via containers. Design flexibility, cost reduction advantages, and improvements in quality control are just some of the advantages of using this system for both housing and light commercial applications. Wall panels, some including doors and windows, are ready for assembly immediately after delivery to the building site. Addition of the roof and completion of the building takes only a few days.

The precut building is the most basic type of manufactured structure requiring the least amount of factory fabrication. All the wooden structural members of a building are precut at the factory with each component numbered or coded to key it to a set of assembly instructions or blueprints.

One advantage of prefabricated housing is quick assembly – only a few days are needed. Another buying incentive is the lower price achieved through mass production. Another advantage of the assembly-line approach is better quality control. The major disadvantage is, of course, the product's image. There is no prestige in living in a prefab house, and the uniform look does not enhance consumer perception. Although mass production has generally negative connotations, it does not appreciably hurt such durables as refrigerators, automobiles, and sound equipment. Yet, for housing, the negative image is quite overwhelming.

In Japan, where land and housing costs are outrageous, prefab houses are a necessity for many. One Japanese firm that has acquired technical know-how in manufacturing prefab houses is Misawa Homes. Ones of its popular designs is House 55. This model has ten capsules, requiring five large containers for transportation. The model's advantage is that rough assembly can be accomplished in only two hours. Another strength is its price – 20 percent lower than conventional prefab houses and 30 percent lower than wood houses. The model was exhibited at trade fairs in Europe and received a great deal of interest. Encouraged, Misawa Homes wanted to export its House 55 houses to Europe and the USA.

Points to consider

1 Do you think that such prefab houses as House 55 can gain consumer acceptance in the USA and Europe?
2 Even supposing the absence of US consumers' negative reactions, are there any factors that pose no problem in Japan and yet would create difficulties in the USA?
3 What should be Misawa's strategy to enter overseas markets with the product?

Source: This case was based in part on Patrick MacAuley and Pat Smeller, "Exporting US Manufactured Housing," *Export America*, December 2000, 19–23.

QUESTIONS

1 Briefly explain these market entry strategies: exporting, licensing, joint venture, manufacturing, assembly operations, management contract, turnkey operations, and acquisition.
2 What is cross-licensing or grantback?
3 What are the factors that should be considered in choosing a country for direct investment?
4 What is an FTZ? What are its benefits?

DISCUSSION ASSIGNMENTS AND MINICASES

1 Since exporting is a relatively risk-free market entry strategy, is there a need for a company to consider other market entry strategies?

2 Can a service be licensed for market entry purposes?

3 In spite of the advantages of foreign trade zones, most companies have failed to use them effectively. What are the reasons? Can anything be done to stimulate the interest?

4 One of the most celebrated joint ventures is NUMMI (New United Motor Manufacturing, Inc.), a joint venture between General Motors and Toyota. It seems surprising that the two largest competitors would even think of joining forces. GM is the number one manufacturer in the USA as well as in the world. Toyota, on the other hand, is number one in Japan and number two worldwide. NUMMI is a fifty–fifty joint venture with the board of directors split equally between the two companies. Initially, the venture was to manufacture the Toyota-designed subcompact, and the name chosen for the car was Nova. The total number of vehicles assembled at NUMMI in 2002 was 369,856: Toyota Tacoma (164,550), Toyota Corolla (137,642), Pontiac Vibe (59,556), Toyota Voltz (8108). What are the benefits each partner may expect to derive from the NUMMI joint venture? Do you foresee any problems?

5 Each year, foreign companies generate some $10 billion in capital and 300,000 new jobs for the US economy. As may be expected, US politicians, states, and local governments have competed aggressively for foreign direct investment. Discuss the business of attracting foreign corporations from the viewpoints of both the companies and the states. What are the matters of concern to companies which they will take into consideration when making their location decisions? What are the incentives which states can offer to lure businesses to locate in a particular state?

NOTES

1 Prakash Loungani and Assaf Razin, "How Beneficial Is Foreign Direct Investment for Developing Countries?" *Finance & Development* (June 2001): 6–9.

2 "Foreign Direct Investment Flows Soar in 2000, But Are Likely to Decline Sharply in This Year," *IMF Survey*, October 8, 2001, 314–15.

3 "FDI in Africa: Why Do Select Countries Do Better?" *IMF Survey*, March 25, 2001, 91–2.

4 Mohsin Habib and Leon Zurawicki, "Corruption and Foreign Direct Investment," *Journal of International Business Studies* 33 (second quarter 2002): 291–307.

5 Artur Baldauf, David W. Cravens, and Udo Wagner, "Examining Determinants of Export Performance in Small Open Economies," *Journal of World Business* 35 (No. 1, 2000): 61–75.

6 Paul Ellis and Anthony Pecotich, "Social Factors Influencing Export Initiation in Small and Medium-Sized Enterprises," *Journal of Marketing Research* 38 (February 2001): 119–30.

7 Kevin I.N. Ibeh and Stephen Young, "Exporting as an Entrepreneurial Act – An Empirical Study of Nigerian Firms," *European Journal of Marketing* 35 (No. 5, 2001): 566–86.

8 Ashley Lye and R.T. Hamilton, "Search and Performance in International Exchange," *European Journal of Marketing* 34 (No. 1, 2000): 176–89.

9 "Saint Laurent's Newest Look," *Business Week*, July 31, 2000, 82, 84; "Making Over YSL Is No Stroll Down the Catwalk," *Business Week*, January 28, 2002, 54.

10 Sandra Mottner and James P. Johnson, "Motivations and Risks in International Licensing: A Review and Implications for Licensing to Transitional and Emerging Economies," *Journal of World Business* 35 (2), 2000, 171–88.

11 "Accor Buys Zenith Stake to Life China Exposure," *Asian Wall Street Journal*, January 4, 2001.

12 "AMD to Form New Venture with Fujitsu," *San José Mercury News*, March 31, 2003; "Fujitsu, AMD Expand Venture," *San José Mercury News*, April 1, 2003.

13 Keith D. Brouthers, "Institutional, Cultural and Transaction Cost Influences on Entry Mode Choice and Performance," *Journal of International Business Studies* 33 (second quarter, 2002): 203–21.

14 Linda Longfellow Blodgett, "Partner Contributions as Predictors of Equity Share in International Joint Ventures," *Journal of International Business Studies* 22 (No. 1, 1991): 63–78.

15 Robert J. Rolfe *et al.*, "Determinants of FDI Incentive Preferences of MNEs," *Journal of International Business Studies* 24 (No. 2, 1993): 335–55.

16 Yigang Pan, "Equity Ownership in International Joint Ventures: The Impact of Source Country Factors," *Journal of International Business Studies* 33 (second quarter, 2002): 375–84.

17 Vijay Pothukuchi *et al.*, "National and Organizational Culture Differences and International Joint Venture Performance," *Journal of International Business Studies* 33 (second quarter, 2002): 243–65.

18 Joel Bergsman and Xiaofang Shen, "Foreign Direct Investment in Developing Countries: Progress and Problems," *Finance & Development* (December 1995): 6–8.

19 Robert R. Miller, "Determinants of US Manufacturing Investment Abroad," *Finance & Development*, March 1993, 16–18.

20 Klaus E. Meyer and Saul Estrin, "Brownfield Entry in Emerging Markets," *Journal of International Business Studies* 32 (third quarter, 2001): 575–84.

21 "Can Nestlé Resist This Morsel?" *Business Week*, September 2, 2002, 60, 62.

22 Philippe Very and David M. Schweiger, "The Acquisition Process as a Learning Process: Evidence from a Study of Critical Problems and Solutions in Domestic and Cross-border Deals," *Journal of World Business* 36 (No. 1, 2001): 11–31.

23 "Mergers: Will They Ever Learn?" *Business Week*, October 30, 1995, 178; and "Is the European Grass Greener?" *Business Week*, January 29, 2001, 28.

24 AOL 2000 Annual Report.

25 Masaaki Kotabe *et al.*, "Strategic Alliances in Emerging Latin America: A View from Brazilian, Chilean, and Mexican Companies," *Journal of World Business* 35 (No. 2, 2000): 114–32.

26 John B. Cullen, Jean L. Johnson, and Tomoaki Sakano, "Success Through Commitment and Trust: The Soft Side of Strategic Alliance Management," *Journal of World Business* 35 (fall 2000): 223–40.

27 Johny K. Johansson, "International Alliances: Why Now?" *Journal of the Academy of Marketing Science* 23 (fall 1995): 301–4.

28 Gabriel R. G. Benito and Geir Gripsrud, "The Expansion of Foreign Direct Investments: Discrete Rational Location Choices or a Cultural Learning Process," *Journal of International Business Studies* 23 (No. 3, 1992): 461.

29 Jiatao Li and Stephen Guisinger, "The Globalization of Service Multinationals in the 'Triad' Regions: Japan, Western Europe and North America," *Journal of International Business Studies* 23 (No. 4, 1992): 675–96.

30 Jung Hoon and Derick Sohn, "Social Knowledge as a Control System: A Proposition and Evidence from the Japanese FDI Behavior," *Journal of International Business Studies* 25 (No. 2, 1994): 295–324.

31 Jiatao Li and Stephen Guisinger, "Comparative Business Failures of Foreign-controlled Firms in the USA," *Journal of International Business Studies* 22 (No. 2, 1991): 209–24.

32 C. Patrick Woodcock, Paul W. Beamish, and Shige Makino, "Ownership-based Entry Mode Strategies and International Performance," *Journal of International Business Studies* 25 (No. 2, 1994): 253–73.

33 Benjamin Gomes-Casseres, "Firm Ownership Preferences and Host Government Restrictions: An Integrated Approach," *Journal of International Business Studies* 20 (No. 1, 1990): 1–22.

34 *US Manufacturing Firms' Attitudes toward 1992*, Economics Department of The Bank of Boston, 1989.

35 Shih-Fen S. Chen and Jean-Francois Hennart, "Japanese Investors' Choice of Joint Ventures Versus Wholly-Owned Subsidiaries in the US: The Role of Market Barriers and Firm Capabilities," *Journal of International Business Studies* 33 (first quarter, 2002): 1–18.

36 Klaus E. Meyer, "Institutions, Transaction Costs, and Entry Mode Choice in Eastern Europe," *Journal of International Business Studies* 32 (second quarter, 2001): 357–67.

37 Jane W. Lu, "Intra- and Inter-organizational Imitative Behavior: Institutional Influences on Japanese Firms' Entry Mode Choice," *Journal of International Business Studies* 1 (first quarter, 2002): 19–37.

38 Vibha Gaba, Yigang Pan, and Gerardo R. Ungson, "Timing of Entry in International Market: An Empirical Study of US Fortune 500 Firms in China," *Journal of International Business Studies* 33 (first quarter, 2002): 39–55.

39 Keith D. Brouthers and Lance Eliot Brouthers, "Explaining the National Cultural Distance Paradox," *Journal of International Business Studies* 32 (first quarter, 2001): 177–89.

40 Oded Shenkar, "Cultural Distance Revisited: Towards a More Rigorous Conceptualization and Measurement of Cultural Differences," *Journal of International Business Studies* 32 (third quarter, 2001): 519–35.

41 Arvind Panagariya, "What Can We Learn from China's Export Strategy?" *Finance & Development* (June 1995), 32–5.

42 Ann Harrison, "The Role of Multinationals in Economic Development: The Benefits of FDI," *Columbia Journal of World Business* 29 (winter 1994): 6–11.

43 Douglas P. Woodward and Robert J. Rolfe, "The Location of Export-Oriented Foreign Direct Investment in the Caribbean Basin," *Journal of International Business Studies* 24 (No. 1, 1993): 121–44.

Chapter 10

Product strategies
Basic decisions and product planning

Because of the level of reliability and confidence consumers have in a certain [brand] name, they would expect more within reason.

Allen Vangelos, vice president, Marketing/Customer Relations,
Castle & Cooke's Fresh Foods Division

CHAPTER OUTLINE

- What is a product?
- New product development
- Market segmentation
- Product adoption
- Theory of international product life cycle (IPLC)
  - Stages and characteristics
  - Validity of the IPLC
  - Marketing strategies
- Product standardization vs. product adaptation
  - Arguments for standardization
  - Arguments for adaptation
- A move toward world product: international or national product?
- Marketing of services
  - Importance of services
  - Types of services
  - The economic and legal environment
  - Marketing mix and adaptation
  - Market entry strategies
- Conclusion
- Case 10.1 McDonaldization

PURPOSE OF CHAPTER

Just because a product is successful in one country, there is no guarantee that it will be successful in other markets. A marketer must always determine local needs and tastes and take them into account (see Cultural Dimension 10.1. p. 274). Some products have universal appeal, and little or no change is necessary when these products are placed in various markets. But for every so-called universal product there are many others, as mentioned above, that have a narrower appeal. For products in this category, modification is necessary in order to achieve acceptance in the marketplace. It is generally easier to modify a product than to modify consumer preference. That is, a marketer should change the product to fit the need of the consumer rather than try to adjust consumers' needs to fit product characteristics. An awareness of application of this marketing concept in an international setting would provide definite advantages to an international merchant. Although the principle has been universally accepted in domestic marketing, it has often been ignored in international marketing.

The purpose of this chapter is to study *product* in an international context. The discussion focuses on the meaning of product and the necessities of market segmentation and product positioning. Other topics include product development and services. There is also a critical look at the controversial issue of product standardization versus product adaptation, as well as the theory of international product life cycle and that theory's marketing applications.

MARKETING ILLUSTRATION EAST IS EAST AND WEST IS WEST

Appealing to 1.1 billion Muslims, LG Electronics has introduced a mobile phone that includes an electronic compass. Muslims pray five times a day facing Mecca. The phone, equipped with location tracking software, is able to point toward Mecca.

Hillary Rodham Clinton's autobiography, *Living History*, is a bestseller in China. It sold more than 200,000 copies in just over one month, making it the most popular foreign political memoir in Chinese history. Although China's imprisonment of Harry Wu, a prominent human rights activist, almost caused Hillary Clinton to cancel her plan to attend a UN women's conference in Beijing in 1995, the officially licensed Chinese edition of the book merely identified Wu as a person who was "prosecuted for espionage and detained awaiting trial." In addition, Clinton's criticisms of Communist Party social controls and human rights politics were either shortened or selectively excerpted. The Chinese publisher admitted that it made changes in the text but that these minor and technical changes did not affect the integrity of the book. When informed of the changes, Clinton expressed outrage.

At one time, the Atlanta headquarters of Coca-Cola dictated advertising, packaging, and product decisions for its overseas operations. Now Coke has embraced localism. It has introduced new flavors specifically for Europe. Its Turkish division offers a pear-flavored drink, while the German division markets a berry-flavored Fanta. Due to legal requirements, the products' ingredients may have to be modified from country to country. The combinations of low-calorie sweetener used in each country varied according to both local consumer tastes and local regulations.

Japanese owners, like other Asians, wash their cars a lot. Hence they become more intimate with areas of the car not seen by others. This is one reason why NUMMI has to remove three burrs — tiny metal bumps — from the tailpipes of its Voltz vehicles during the assembly process. One was inside the tailpipe, while another was outside it. The third was located where the tailpipe was welded to the main exhaust system. When Japanese customers clean their cars, they will want to clean inside the pipe where some exhaust residue has accumulated, so that they achieve a nice shiny finish. American buyers do not notice these burrs in the exhaust pipes that bother their Japanese counterparts.

KFC's name in Chinese is kendeji (kun-duh-jee) or Kentucky. Blending local cuisine with its American-style poultry fare, KFC offers Beijing duck. This new item is Chicken Roll of Old Beijing, rolled in a thin pancake with scallions, cucumber slivers and traditional sauce – typical accompaniments to Beijing-style roast duck. The product contains fried chicken instead of duck meat. Certainly, to maintain global success, KFC cannot afford to cling to American tastes without giving due consideration to diversified cultures and customs of local consumers in other countries.

Sources: "LG Reaches Out to Muslim Callers," *San José Mercury News*, September 9, 2003; "Chinese Censorship Angers Sen. Clinton," *San José Mercury News*, September 24, 2003; "For Coke, Local Is It," *Business Week*, July 3, 2000, 122; "No banned Sweetener in Coke Light or Coca-Cola," *Bangkok Post*, April 19, 2001; "Fremont Plant to Produce Autos for Japan Sale," *San José Mercury News*, May 18, 2002; "KFC's New Secret Recipe in China Draws on Traditional Beijing Duck," *San José Mercury News*, February 15, 2003.

CULTURAL DIMENSION 10.1   JAPAN'S MOST INFLUENTIAL INVENTION: *RAMEN*

Ramen is a Japanese word for *lo mein* (Chinese boiled noodles). Momofuku Ando first introduced his instant chicken ramen in 1958 which had flavoring already infused in the noodles. At the time, at a price of 10 cents a packet, the product cost six times the price of a bowl of fresh *ramen*. Ando persevered and ultimately succeeded, even though it took nearly half a century for the world to come around. China consumes 17.8 billion packets, while the figures for Indonesia, Japan, South Korea, and the USA respectively are: 9.9 billion, 5.35 billion, 3.64 billion, and 3 billion.

Ando's Nissin Food Products has perfected a process to preserve cooked noodles. Fresh *ramen* is steamed, molded into blocks, dried, cooled, and packaged. He improved flavor by packaging powdered soup mix separately from the brick of wavy noodles.

When asked to name Japan's most influential invention of the twentieth century, people ranked *ramen* first, ahead of Sony Walkman, Toyota cars, and Nintendo video games. No longer limited to mild variations, *ramen* now comes in a variety of hot and spicy flavors.

The global noodle king produces more than four billion packs and cups a year and controls 40 percent of the Japanese market and 10 percent of the world market. Nissin operates twenty-five plants in eight countries and uses shrimp from India and cabbage from China. To conquer the world, Nissin has adapted its products to the peculiarities of foreign markets. Shorter noodles are offered to accommodate forks rather than chopsticks.

Sources: "The Universal Appeal of Ramen," *San José Mercury News*, February 26, 2003; "Chicken Ramen Maker Used His Noodle," *San José Mercury News*, February 12, 2001.

WHAT IS A PRODUCT?

A product is often considered in a narrow sense as something tangible that can be described in terms of physical attributes, such as shape, dimension, components, form, color, and so on. This is a misconception that has been extended to international marketing as well, because many people believe that only tangible products can be exported. A student of marketing, however, should realize that this definition of product is misleading since many products are intangible (e.g., services). Actually, intangible products are a significant part of the American export market. For example, American movies are distributed worldwide, as are engineering services and business-consulting services. In the financial market, Japanese and European banks have been internationally active in providing financial assistance, often at handsome profits. Even when tangible products are involved, insurance services and shipping are needed to move the products into their markets.

In many situations, both tangible and intangible products must be combined to create a single, total product. Perhaps the best way to define a product is to describe it as *a bundle of utilities or satisfaction*. Warranty terms, for example, are a part of this bundle, and they may be adjusted as appropriate (i.e., superior versus inferior warranty terms). Purchasers of Mercedes-Benz cars expect to acquire more than just the cars themselves. In hot and humid countries, there is no reason for a heater to be part of the automobile's product bundle. In the USA, it is customary for automatic transmission to be included with other standard automobile equipment.

One marketing implication that may be drawn is that a multinational marketer must look at a product as a total, complete offering. Consider the Beretta shotgun. The shotgun itself is undoubtedly a fine product, quite capable of superbly performing its primary function (i.e., firing shotgun ammunition). But Beretta also has a secondary function in Japan, where the Beretta brand is perceived as a superior status symbol. Not surprisingly, a Beretta can command $8000 for a shotgun, exclusive of the additional amount of a few thousand dollars for engraving. In this case, Beretta's secondary function conceivably overshadows its primary objective. Therefore, a complete product should be viewed as a satisfaction derived from the four Ps of marketing (product, place, promotion, and pricing) – and not simply the physical product characteristics.

Since a product can be bundled, it can also be unbundled. One problem with a bundled product is the increased cost associated with the extra benefits. With the increased cost, a higher price is inevitable. Thus a proper marketing strategy, in some cases, is to unbundle a product instead so as to get rid of the frills and attract price-sensitive consumers. As an example, Serfin is a mid-tiered bank in Mexico, and is owned by Spain's Banco Santander Central Hispano. Serfin has launched Serfin Light, a new credit card that offers no points or air miles. Instead, its key feature is an interest rate of 24 percent rather than 40 percent charged by the main competitors. The word "Light" is appropriate because Mexico is the world's largest consumer per capita of soft drinks, and Diet Coke is sold as Coke Light. The "light" concept has a significant meaning in Mexico. The success of Serfin Light prompted Banorte, the largest bank in northern Mexico, to change its slogan to "better than a light card, a strong card."[1]

NEW PRODUCT DEVELOPMENT

There are six distinct steps in new product development. The *first step* is the *generation of new product ideas*. Such ideas can come from any number of sources (e.g., salesperson, employees, competitors, governments, marketing research firms, customers). As in the case of Japan, already one out of five Japanese is age 65 or older, and the trend has adversely affected baby food. From the peak of $252 million in 1999, sales of baby foods fell to $235 million in 2001. Searching for new sources of revenue, Japanese food companies were intrigued to learn that the same characteristics which make baby food appealing to babies (soft, small morsels, low salt, easy preparation) also attracted old people.

MARKETING ETHICS 10.1   IN THE NAME OF FREE TRADE: DYING FOR PROFITS

It is an undeniable fact that cigarette smoking kills 4.9 million people every year. Once young people start smoking, many will be hooked for life. If cigarettes are a brand new product that is introduced to the market for the very first time, it is doubtful whether any governments would allow this harmful product to be marketed. A case can be made that cigarettes should be classified as an illegal drug.

Health officials all over the world have been prodding their governments to discourage smoking as well as the marketing of cigarettes. After all, health costs are enormous. While the USA has forced tobacco firms to curtail their marketing activities in the US market, it seems to have taken the opposite approach abroad. While the US cigarette market is now a mature or even declining one, such overseas markets as China and Russia are very attractive. The Chinese and Russian markets are big, and people there are not as concerned about the health issues. There is no question that cigarettes are a highly profitable industry and that American tobacco firms have dominated markets worldwide. But should the USA push to open up markets abroad for American cigarettes by using free trade as an excuse? The Bush administration has even tried to interfere with international controls on tobacco by opposing the Framework Convention on Tobacco Control.

Bush tries to have it both ways. He wanted countries to be able to approve the pact while also being able to "take reservations" (i.e., opting out of individual clauses). The rationale or excuse is that the USA needs the flexibility to deal with constitutional issues (e.g., tobacco companies' freedom of speech) and matters that are under state governments' jurisdiction. The problem with this proposal is that it undermines the effectiveness of the treaty.

The World Health Organization has spent three years working out an agreement with 171 countries to control the spread of smoking-related diseases. The treaty bans tobacco advertising, except where such a ban would be in conflict with national laws. The treaty additionally imposes a substantial tax on tobacco products and mandates warning labels on cigarette packages. Strangely, the USA, citing free speech, seems to be more concerned with the welfare of the tobacco industry, which happened to give $6.4 million to the 2002 campaign chests of Republican candidates. Moreover, the Bush administration has rejected a global warming agreement, an international criminal court, and a treaty on women's rights.

Sources: "Deadly Export," *San José Mercury News*, May 21, 2002; "Tobacco Treaty Changes Sought," *San José Mercury News*, April 30, 2003; "US Feeds the World's Tobacco Habit," *San José Mercury News*, May 4, 2003.

Thus food makers have come out with ready-to-eat treats: soft-boiled fish, bite-size shrimp meatballs, chop suey with tofu, and dozens of others. These "Fun Meals" or "Food for Ages 0–100" only hint at the target demographic group without embarrassing older consumers.[2]

The *second step* involves the *screening of ideas*. Ideas must be acknowledged and reviewed to determine their feasibility. To determine suitability, a new product concept may simply be presented to potential users, or an advertisement based on the product may be drawn and shown to focus groups to elicit candid reactions. As a rule, corporations usually have predetermined goals that a new product must meet. Kao Corporation, a major Japanese manufacturer of consumer goods, is guided by the following five principles of product development: (1) a new product should be truly useful to society, not only now but also in the future, (2) it should make use of Kao's own creative technology or skill, (3) it should be superior to the new products of competitors, both from the standpoint of cost and performance, (4) it should be able to stand exhaustive product tests at all stages before it is commercialized, and (5) it should be capable of delivering its own message at every level of distribution.[3]

The *third step* is *business analysis*, which is necessary to estimate product features, cost, demand, and profit. Xerox has small so-called product synthesis teams to test and weed out unsuitable ideas. Several competing teams of designers produce a prototype, and the winning model that meets preset goals then goes to the "product development" team.

The *fourth step* is *product development*, which involves lab and technical tests as well as manufacturing pilot models in small quantities. At this stage, the product is likely to be handmade or produced by existing machinery rather than by any new specialized equipment. Ideally, engineers should receive direct feedback from customers and dealers. Goldstar Co., by letting its engineers out of the laboratories and into the market to see what Korean customers want, got an idea to make a refrigerator that can keep *kimchi* (fermented pickled cabbage or radishes which are Korea's national dish) fresh and odorless for a long time. The refrigerator was an instant hit and enabled Goldstar to regain the top position which it lost to Samsung in South Korea in the late 1980s.[4]

The *fifth step* involves *test marketing* to determine potential marketing problems and the optimal marketing mix. Anheuser Busch pulled Budweiser out of Germany after a six-month Berlin market test in 1981. Its Busch brand was another disappointment in France, where this type of beer did not yet correspond to French tastes.

Finally, assuming that things go well, the company is ready for *full-scale commercialization* by actually going through with full-scale production and marketing.

It should be pointed out that not all of these six steps in new product development will be applicable to all products and countries. Test marketing, for example, may be irrelevant in countries where most major media are more national than local. If the television medium has a nationwide coverage, it is not practical to limit a marketing campaign to one city or province for test marketing purposes.

In any case, so many new products are tested and marketed each year. In Japan, because consumers constantly demand fresh, new products, some 700 to 800 drinks are launched annually. To keep pace, Coca-Cola has built a product development center which allows it to cut launch time for new drinks from ninety days to a month, enabling it to release fifty new beverages a year.

Unfortunately, it is easier for a new product to fail than to succeed. Naturally, so many things can go wrong. Therefore, it is just as crucial for a company to know when to retreat as when to launch a product. Coca-Cola's Ambasa Whitewater, a lactic-based drink, was removed from the market after eighteen months when sales started to decline.

MARKET SEGMENTATION

Market segmentation is a concept to which marketers and academics like to pay a great deal of attention. All conceivable possibilities for segmenting the US market have been thoroughly studied. For example, Visa has designed its consumer credit products and non-credit products for diverse market segments. Some of its products are: Visa Classic, Visa Gold, Visa Platinum, Visa Signature, Visa Infinite, Visa check card, and Visa Buxx.

Yet on the international scale, American marketers are prone to treat market segmentation as an unknown and unfamiliar concept, and they apparently leave their knowledge about market segmentation at home when they go abroad. More often than not, there is hardly any serious or conscious attempt by American businessmen to segment a foreign market. This phenomenon probably derives from an assumption that, by going abroad, geographic segmentation has been implemented. But geographic segmentation, an obvious choice, is often overemphasized and is usually inappropriate. Marketers fail to realize that the purpose of segmentation is to satisfy consumer needs more precisely – not to segment the market just for the sake of the segmentation.

Another mistake marketers make in foreign countries is in attempting to capture the total market at once. The resulting disappointment in market performance demonstrates that two major problems have been overlooked. First, consumers in a foreign country are unlikely to be homogeneous. Usually, marketers must distinguish urban consumers from rural consumers. Even in largely homogeneous Japan, American Express found it necessary to segment Japanese consumers. It introduced the luxury gold yen card for the affluent segment and the green card for the middle-income segment.

Second, a "total market" strategy places the company in head-to-head competition with strong, local competitors. The success of Japanese products in the USA and in many other countries may be explained in part by the explicit and conscientious attempt by the Japanese to segment the market. Japanese firms usually pick their targets carefully, avoiding head-to-head competition with major US manufacturers in mature industries. Starting at the low end of the product spectrum, a Japanese firm establishes a reputation for product excellence, and eventually gets customers to trade up over time. The strategy has worked exceedingly well in the automobile and consumer-electronics industries. Japanese computer makers have used the same marketing strategy in breaking into the US computer market. Japanese firms market commodity products such as personal computers, disc drives, printers, and other peripherals before attempting to trade up with their customers to the larger systems, which have the highest profit margins. This strategy makes a great deal of strategic sense because the marketer does not arouse the US giants early in the game. US toolmakers' strategic mistake was their emphasis on large machines for major users, while leaving room at the low end for entry to foreign competitors with product lines at the $150,000 price level.

The most important reason behind the employment of market segmentation is market *homogeneity/heterogeneity*. Based on the national boundary, homogeneity can be *vertical* (i.e., homogeneous within the same country) or *horizontal* (i.e., homogeneous across countries). Therefore, two countries exhibiting the lack of vertical homogeneity within

their borders may still be homogeneous horizontally when a particular segment of one country is similar to an equivalent segment of another country.

Nevertheless, market segmentation is not always necessary or desirable. This is especially true when either consumer needs within a country are largely homogeneous or a mass market exists.

PRODUCT ADOPTION

In breaking into a foreign market, marketers should consider factors that influence product adoption. As explained by diffusion theory, at least six factors have a bearing on the adoption process: relative advantage, compatibility, trialability/divisibility, observability, complexity, and price. These factors are all perceptual and thus subjective in nature.

For a product to gain acceptance, it must demonstrate its *relative advantage* over existing alternatives. Products emphasizing cleanliness and sanitation may be unimportant in places where people are poor and struggle to get by one day at a time. Wool coats are not needed in a hot country, and products reducing static cling (e.g., Cling Free) are useless in a humid country. A sunscreen film attached to auto windshields to block out sunlight may be a necessity in countries with a tropical climate, but it has no such advantage in cold countries. Dishwashing machines do not market well in countries where manual labor is readily available and inexpensive.

A product must also be *compatible* with local customs and habits. A freezer would not find a ready market in Asia, where people prefer fresh food. In Asia and such European countries as France and Italy, people like to sweep and mop floors daily, and thus there is no market for carpet or vacuum cleaners. Deodorants are deemed inappropriate in places where it is the custom for men to show their masculinity by having body odor. Dryers are unnecessary in countries where people prefer to hang their clothes outside for sunshine freshness. Kellogg's had difficulties selling Pop Tarts in Europe because many homes have no toaster. Unlike American women, European women do not shave their legs, and thus have no need for razors for that purpose. The

Japanese, not liking to have their lifestyles altered by technology, have skillfully applied technology to their traditional lifestyle. The electrical *kotatsu* (foot warmer) is a traditional form of heater in Japan. New *kotatsu* are equipped with a temperature sensor and microcomputer to keep the interior temperature at a comfortable level.

A new product should also be compatible with consumers' other belongings. If a new product requires a replacement of those other items that are still usable, product adoption becomes a costly proposition.

A new product has an advantage if it is capable of being *divided* and *tested* in small trial quantities to determine its suitability and benefits. This is a product's *trialability/divisibility* factor. Disposable diapers and blue jeans lend themselves to trialability rather well, but when a product is large, bulky, and expensive, consumers are much more apprehensive about making a purchase. Thus, washers, dryers, refrigerators, and automobiles are products that do not lend themselves well to trialability/divisibility. This factor explains one reason why foreign consumers do not readily purchase American automobiles, knowing that a mistake could ruin them financially. Many foreign consumers therefore prefer to purchase more familiar products, such as Japanese automobiles, that are less expensive and easier to service and whose parts are easier to replace.

Observation of a product in public tends to encourage social acceptance and reinforcement, resulting in the product's being adopted more rapidly and with less resistance. If a product is used privately, other consumers cannot see it, and there is no prestige generated by its possession. Blue jeans, quartz watches, and automobiles are used publicly and are highly observable products. Japanese men flip their ties so that labels show. Refrigerators, on the other hand, are privately consumed products, though owners of refrigerators in the Middle East and Asia may attempt to enhance observability (and thus prestige) by placing the refrigerator in the living room, where guests can easily see it. In any case, a distinctive and easily recognized logo is very useful.

Complexity of a product or difficulty in understanding a product's qualities tends to slow down its market acceptance. Perhaps this factor explains why ground coffee has had a difficult time in making headway to replace instant coffee in many countries. Likewise, 3M tried unsuccessfully in foreign markets to replace positive-acting printing plates with presensitized negative subtractive printing plates, which are very popular in the USA. It failed to convert foreign printers because the sales and technical service costs of changing printers' beliefs were far too expensive. Computers are also complex but have been gradually gaining more and more acceptance, perhaps in large part because manufacturers have made the machines simpler to operate. Ready-made software can also alleviate the necessity of learning computer languages, a time-consuming process.

The first four variables are related positively to the adoption process. Like complexity, *price* is related negatively to product adoption. Prior to 1982, copiers were too big and expensive. Canon then introduced personal copiers with cartridges that customers could change. Its low price (less than $1000) was so attractive to consumers (but not to competitors) that Canon easily dominated the market.

THEORY OF INTERNATIONAL PRODUCT LIFE CYCLE (IPLC)

The international product life cycle theory, developed and verified by economists to explain trade in a context of comparative advantage, describes the diffusion process of an innovation across national boundaries. The life cycle begins when a developed country, having a new product to satisfy consumer needs, wants to exploit its technological breakthrough by selling abroad. Other advanced nations soon start up their own production facilities, and before long less developed countries do the same. Efficiency/comparative advantage shifts from developed countries to developing nations. Finally, advanced nations, no longer cost-effective, import products from their former customers. The moral

279

of this process could be that an advanced nation becomes a victim of its own creation.

IPLC theory has the potential to be a valuable framework for marketing planning on a multinational basis. In this section, the IPLC is examined from the marketing perspective, and marketing implications for both innovators and initiators are discussed.[5]

Stages and characteristics

There are five distinct stages (Stage 0 through Stage 4) in the IPLC. Table 10.1 shows the major characteristics of the IPLC stages, with the USA as the developer of innovation in question. Figure 10.1 shows three life cycle curves for the same innova-

tion: one for the initiating country (i.e., the USA in this instance), one for other advanced nations, and one for LDCs (less developed countries). For each curve, net export results when the curve is above the horizontal line; if under the horizontal line, net import results for that particular country. As the innovation moves through time, directions of all three curves change. Time is relative, because the time needed for a cycle to be completed varies from one kind of product to another. In addition, the time interval also varies from one stage to the next.

Stage 0 – Local innovation

Stage 0, depicted as time 0 on the left of the vertical importing/exporting axis, represents a regular and highly familiar product life cycle in operation within its original market. Innovations are most likely to occur in highly developed countries because consumers in such countries are affluent and have relatively unlimited wants. From the supply side, firms in advanced nations have both the technological know-how and abundant capital to develop new products.

Many of the products found in the world's markets were originally created in the USA before being introduced and refined in other countries. In most instances, regardless of whether a product or not is intended for later export, an innovation is designed initially with an eye to capture the US market, the largest consumer nation.

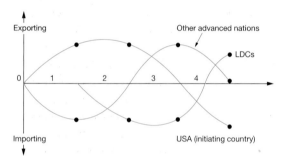

Figure 10.1 IPLC curves

Source: Sak Onkvisit and John J. Shaw, "An Examination of the International Product Life Cycle and Its Application within Marketing," Columbia Journal of World Business 18 (fall 1983): 74.

Table 10.1 IPLC stages and characteristics (for the initiating country)

Stage	Import/export	Target market	Competitors	Production costs
(0) Local innovation	None	USA	Few: Local firms	Initially high
(1) Overseas innovation	Increasing export	USA and advanced nations	Few: local firms	Decline due to economies of scale
(2) Maturity	Stable export	Advanced nations and LDCs	Advanced nations	Stable
(3) Worldwide imitation	Declining export	LDCs	Advanced nations	Increase due to to lower economies of scale
(4) Reversal	Increasing import	USA	Advanced nations and LDCs	Increase due to comparative disadvantage

Source: Sak Onkvisit and John J. Shaw, "An Examination of the International Product Life Cycle and Its Application within Marketing," Columbia Journal of World Business 18 (fall 1983): 74.

Stage 1 – Overseas innovation

As soon as the new product is well developed, its original market well cultivated, and local demands adequately supplied, the innovating firm will look to overseas markets in order to expand its sales and profit. Thus this stage is known as a "pioneering" or "international introduction" stage. The technological gap is first noticed in other advanced nations because of their similar needs and high income levels. Not surprisingly, English-speaking countries such as the United Kingdom, Canada, and Australia account for about half of the sales of US innovations when first introduced to overseas countries with similar cultures, and economic conditions are often perceived by exporters as posing less risk and thus are approached first before proceeding to less familiar territories.

Competition in this stage usually comes from US firms, since firms in other countries may not have much knowledge about the innovation. Production cost tends to be decreasing at this stage because by this time the innovating firm will normally have improved the production process. Supported by overseas sales, aggregate production costs tend to decline further due to increased economies of scale. A low introductory price overseas is usually not necessary because of the technological breakthrough; a low price is not desirable due to the heavy and costly marketing effort needed in order to educate consumers in other countries about the new product. In any case, as the product penetrates the market during this stage, there will be more exports from the USA and, correspondingly, an increase in imports by other developed countries.

Stage 2 – Maturity

Growing demand in advanced nations provides an impetus for firms there to commit themselves to starting local production, often with the help of their governments' protective measures to preserve infant industries. Thus these firms can survive and thrive in spite of relative inefficiency.

Development of competition does not mean that the initiating country's export level will immedi-

ately suffer. The innovating firm's sales and export volumes are kept stable because LDCs are now beginning to generate a need for the product. Introduction of the product in LDCs helps offset any reduction in export sales to advanced countries.

Stage 3 – Worldwide imitation

This stage means tough times for the innovating nation because of its continuous decline in exports. There is no more new demand anywhere to cultivate. The decline will inevitably affect the US innovating firm's economies of scale, and its production costs thus begin to rise again. Consequently, firms in other advanced nations use their lower prices (coupled with product differentiation techniques) to gain more consumer acceptance abroad at the expense of the US firm. As the product becomes more and more widely disseminated, imitation picks up at a faster pace. Toward the end of this stage, US export dwindles almost to nothing, and any US production still remaining is basically for local consumption. The US automobile industry is a good example of this phenomenon. There are about thirty different companies selling cars in the USA, with several on the rise. Of these, only two (General Motors and Ford) are US firms, with the rest being from Western Europe, Japan, South Korea, and others.

Stage 4 – Reversal

Not only must all good things end, but misfortune frequently accompanies the end of a favorable situation. The major functional characteristics of this stage are *product standardization and comparative disadvantage*. This innovating country's comparative advantage has disappeared, and what is left is comparative disadvantage. This disadvantage is brought about because the product is no longer capital-intensive or technology-intensive but instead has become labor-intensive – a strong advantage possessed by LDCs. Thus LDCs – the last imitators – establish sufficient productive facilities to satisfy their own domestic needs as well as to produce for the biggest market in the world, the

USA. US firms are now undersold in their own country. Black-and-white TV sets, for example, are no longer manufactured in the USA because many Asian firms can produce them much less expensively than any US firm. Likewise, the USA hardly produces color TV sets either. Consumers' price sensitivity exacerbates this problem for the initiating country.

Validity of the IPLC

Several products have conformed to the characteristics described by the IPLC. The production of semiconductors started in the USA before diffusing to the United Kingdom, France, Germany, and Japan. Production facilities are now set up in Hong Kong and Taiwan, as well as in other Asian countries. Similarly, at one time, the USA used to be an exporter of typewriters, adding machines, and cash registers. However, with the passage of time, these simple machines (e.g., manual typewriters) are now being imported, while US firms export only the sophisticated, electronic versions of such machines. Other products that have gone through a complete international life cycle are synthetic fibers, petrochemicals, leather goods, rubber products, and paper. The electronics sector, a positive contributor to the trade balance of the USA for a long time, turned negative for the first time ever in 1984 with a massive $6.8 billion deficit. A deficit also occurred at the same time for communications equipment, following the trend set by semiconductors in 1982.

The IPLC is probably more applicable for products related through an emerging technology. These newly emerging products are likely to provide functional utility rather than aesthetic values. Furthermore, these products likely satisfy basic needs that are universally common in most parts of the world. Washers, for example, are much more likely to fit this theory than are dryers. Dishwashing machines are not useful in countries where labor is plentiful and cheap, and the diffusion of this kind of innovation as described in IPLC is not likely to occur.

Marketing strategies

For those advanced economies' industries in the worldwide imitation stage (e.g., automobiles) or the maturity stage (e.g., computers), things are likely to get worse rather than better. The prospect, though bleak, can be favorably influenced. What is crucial is for firms in the advanced economies to understand the implications of the IPLC so that they can adjust marketing strategies accordingly.

Product policy

The IPLC emphasizes the importance of cost advantage. It would be very difficult for firms in advanced economies to match labor costs in low-wage nations since costs are only 0.5 cent in China. Still, the innovating firm must keep its product cost competitive. One way is to cut labor costs through automation and robotics. IBM converted its Lexington (Kentucky) plant into one of the most automated plants in the world. Japanese VCR manufacturers are counting on automation to help them meet the challenge of South Korea.

Another way to reduce production costs is to eliminate unnecessary options, since such options increase inefficiency and complexity. This strategy may be crucial for simple products or for those at the low end of the price scale. In such cases, it is desirable to offer a standardized product with a standard package of features or options included.

To keep costs rising at a minimum, an initiating firm may use local manufacturing in other countries as an entry strategy. The company can not only minimize transportation costs and entry barriers but also indirectly slow down potential local competition starting up manufacturing facilities. Another benefit is that those countries can eventually become a springboard for the company to market its product throughout that geographic region. In fact, sourcing should allow the innovator to hold down labor costs at home and abroad and retain the original market as well.

Manufacturers should examine the traditional vertical structure in which they make all or most components and parts themselves because in many instances outsourcing may prove to be more cost-effective. **Outsourcing** is the practice of buying parts or whole products from other manufacturers while allowing a buyer to maintain its own brand name. For example, Ford Festiva is made by Kia Motors, Mitsubishi Precis by Hyundai, Pontiac Lemans by Daewoo, and GM Sprint by Suzuki.

A modification of outsourcing involves producing various components or having them produced under contract in different countries. That way, a firm takes advantage of the most abundant factor of production in each country before assembling components into final products for worldwide distribution.

Solectron and Flextronics are examples of contract manufacturers that do manufacturing for many well-known brands. Solectron, a contract electronics maker, makes components and finished products for electronics companies, and its customers include Cisco Systems, HP, and Ericsson. A recent deal involves Solectron making optical networking equipment worth as much as $2 billion for Lucent Technologies for three years. Xerox has a five-year contract that transfers about half of Xerox's manufacturing operations to Flextronics and represents more than $1 billion in annual manufacturing costs. Flextronics, based in Singapore, is a $12 billion global electronics manufacturing services company, manufacturing Xerox office equipment and components at a modest premium over book value. These copiers and printers are used worldwide.[6]

Once in the maturity stage, the innovator's comparative advantage is gone, and the firm should switch from producing simple versions to producing sophisticated models or new technologies in order to remove itself from cut-throat competition. Japanese VCR makers used to make 99 percent of the machines sold in the USA and 75 percent of all machines sold worldwide, but they still cannot compete with low-wage Korean newcomers strictly on price, because labor content in VCRs is substantial. To retain their market share, the Japanese rely on new technology, such as 8-mm camcorders.

For a relatively high-tech product, an innovator may find it advantageous to get its product system to become the industry's standard, even if it means lending a helping hand to competitors through the licensing of product knowledge. Otherwise, there is always a danger that competitors will persevere in inventing an incompatible and superior system. A discussion of product adoption above should make it clear that several competing and incompatible systems serve only to confuse potential adopters who must acquire more information and who are uncertain as to which system will survive over the long term.

The worst scenario for an innovating firm is when another system supplants the innovators' product altogether to become the industry's standard. Sony's strategic blunder in guarding its Betamax video system is a good case to study. Matsushita and Victor Co. took the world leadership position away from Sony by being more liberal in licensing its VHS (Video Home System) to their competitors. Philips and Grundig did not introduce their Video 2000 system until VHS was just about to become the industry's standard in Europe and the world. By that time, despite price cutting, it was too late for Video 2000 to attract other manufacturers and consumers. The problem was so bad that Philips' own North American subsidiary refused to buy its parent's system. Ironically, Sony itself had to start making VHS-format machines in 1988. In 2002, Sony ended its bitter experience by discontinuing the Betamax machines.

A more recent case of competing technologies and strategic alliances involves the digital videodisc (DVD) which can also store audio and computer data and software. Toshiba's system competed with the Multimedia Compact Disc system offered by Sony and Philips. In addition, Toshiba aggressively courted movie makers (e.g., Warner Bros., MCA, and MGM/UA) while offering "open" licensing to other electronics companies. As a result, such manufacturing giants as Matsushita, Thomson, and Pioneer chose to ally with Toshiba. In the end, Sony and Philips had to come to a compromise by adopting a single format that was closer to Toshiba's system than theirs.

Matsushita and Sony recently faced off again as both tried to make their products the industry standard so as to control the market of related digital consumer products. The battle involved flash memory cards which are used to record data on digital cameras, music players, and next-generation mobile phones and computers. Matsushita, playing catch-up, has the support of nearly ninety manufacturers worldwide, while Sony has fifty-eight. In addition, Matsushita's DVD audio player is not compatible with Sony's SACD (Super Audio CD), and its first recordable DVD player uses DVD-RAM that is not compatible with the DVD-RW format led by Pioneer and supported by Sony.

Pricing policy

Initially, an innovating firm can afford to behave as a monopolist, charging a premium price for its innovation. But this price must be adjusted downward in the second and third stages of IPLC to discourage potential newcomers and to maintain market share. Anticipating a Korean challenge, Japanese VCR makers cut their prices in the USA by 25 percent and were able to slow down retailers' and consumers' acceptance of Korean brands. IBM, in comparison, was slow in reducing prices for its PC models. The error in judgment was the result of a belief that the IBM PC was too complex for Asian imitators. This proved to be a costly error because the basic PC hardly changed for several years. Before long, the product became nothing but an easily copied, standardized commodity suitable for intensive distribution – the kind that Asian companies thrive on. Commodity pricing now dominates the market. In the end, IBM stopped manufacturing desktop PCs in most parts of the world. Instead, its PCs are now made by Sanmina-SCI, a contract manufacturer.

In the last stage of the IPLC, it is not practical for the innovating firm to maintain low price because of competitors' cost advantage. However, the firm's above-the-market price is feasible only if it is accompanied by top-quality or sophisticated products. A high standard of excellence should partially insulate the firm's product from direct price competition. US car makers failed in this area – high prices are not matched by consumer perception of superior quality.

Promotion policy

Promotion and pricing in the IPLC are closely related. The innovating firm's initial competitive edge is its unique product, which allows it to command a premium price. To maintain this price in the face of subsequent challenges from imitators, uniqueness can be retained only in the form of superior quality, style, or services.

The innovating marketer must plan for a non-price promotional policy at the outset of a product diffusion. Timken is able to compete effectively against the Japanese by offering more services and meeting customers' needs at all times. For instance, it offers technological support by sending engineers to help customers design bearings in gearboxes.

One implication that may be drawn is that a new product should be promoted as a premium product with a high-quality image. By starting out with a high-quality reputation, the innovating company can trade down later with a simpler version of the product while still holding on to the high-priced, most profitable segment of the market. One thing the company must never do is to allow its product to become a commodity item with prices as the only buying motive, since such a product can be easily duplicated by other firms. Aprica has been very successful in creating a status symbol for its stroller by using top artists and designers to create a product for mothers who are more concerned with style than price. The stroller is promoted as "anatomically correct" for babies to avoid hip dislocation, and the company uses the snob appeal and comfort to distinguish its brand from those of Taiwanese and Korean imitators. Therefore, product differentiation, not price, is most important for insulating a company from the crowded, low-profit market segment. A product can be so standardized that it can be easily duplicated, but image is a very different proposition.

A more recent example is a treatment for impotence. Viagra was the first to hit the market, generating an incredible amount of discussion worldwide. It is important for Viagra to create brand awareness and preference. Within a few short years, a number of rivals entered the market with improved products. Bayer and GSK, using vardenafil, markets Levitra which works regardless of the cause of a patient's impotence – depression, heart disease, high blood pressure, diabetes, and so on. Eli Lilly's Cialis claims to work for up to thirty-six hours or seven times as long as Viagra, thus having an advantage in terms of picking the right moment.[7]

Place (distribution) policy

A strong dealer network can provide the US innovating firm with a good defensive strategy. Because of its near-monopoly situation at the beginning, the firm is in a good position to be able to select only the most qualified agents/distributors, and the distribution network should be expanded further as the product becomes more diffused. Caterpillar's network of loyal dealers caused difficulty for Komatsu to line up its own dealers in the USA. In an ironic case, GM's old policy of limiting its dealers from carrying several GM brands inadvertently encouraged those dealers to start carrying imports. A firm must also watch closely for the development of any new alternative channel that may threaten the existing channel.

When it is too late or futile to keep an enemy out, the enemy should be invited in. US firms – manufacturers as well as agents/distributors – can survive by becoming agents for their former competitors. This tactic involves providing a distribution network and marketing expertise at a profit to competitors who in all likelihood would welcome an easier entry into the marketplace. American car makers and their dealers seem to have accepted the reality of the marketplace and have become partners with their Japanese and foreign competitors, as evidenced by General Motors's ventures with Toyota, Suzuki, and Isuzu (to produce Nova,

Sprint, and Spectrum respectively), American Motors' with France's Renault (prior to the subsequent sale to Chrysler), Chrysler's with Mitsubishi and Maserati, and Ford's with Mazda and the Korean Kia Motors.

Once a product is in the final stage of its life cycle, the innovating firm should strive to become a specialist, not a generalist, by concentrating its efforts in carefully selected market segments, where it can distinguish itself from foreign competitors. To achieve distinction, US firms should either add product features or offer more services. For the alert firm, there are early warning signals that may be used to determine whether the time has come to adopt this strategy. One signal is that the product becomes so standardized that it can be manufactured in many LDCs. Another warning signal is a decline in the US exports owing to the loss of narrowing of the US technological lead. By that time, certain forms of market segmentation and product differentiation are highly recommended. As in the case of consumer electronics, such great American brands as Marantz and Scott were once synonymous with good sound and top quality but have since been bought up or driven out of business by Japanese and European manufacturers. American firms continue to dominate the segment of high-end stereo equipment where top systems may cost up to $100,000. American firms are successful because of the precision required and because production runs are short and usually done by hand.

PRODUCT STANDARDIZATION VS. PRODUCT ADAPTATION

Product standardization means that a product designed originally for a local market is exported to other countries with virtually no change, except perhaps for the translation of words and other cosmetic changes. Revlon, for example, used to ship successful products abroad without changes in product formulation, packing (without any translation, in some cases), and advertising. There are advantages and disadvantages to both standardization and individualization.

Arguments for standardization

The strength of standardization in the production and distribution of products and services is its *simplicity* and *cost*. It is an easy process for executives to understand and implement, and it is also cost-effective. If cost is the only factor being considered, then standardization is clearly a logical choice because economies of scale can operate to reduce production costs. Yet minimizing production costs does not necessarily mean that profit increases will follow. Simplicity is not always beneficial, and costs are often confused with profits. Cost reductions do not automatically lead to profit improvements, and in fact the reverse may apply. By trying to control production costs through standardization, the product involved may become unsuitable for alternative markets. The result may be that demand abroad will decline, which leads to profit reduction. In some situations, cost control can be achieved but at the expense of overall profit. It is therefore prudent to remember that cost should not be overemphasized. The main marketing goal is to maximize profit, and production-cost reductions should be considered as a secondary objective. The two objectives are not always convergent.

When appropriate, standardization is a good approach. For example, when a *consistent company or product image* is needed, product uniformity is required. The worldwide success of McDonald's is based on consistent product quality and services. Hamburger meat, buns, and fruit pies must meet strict specifications. This obsession with product quality necessitates the costly export of french fries from Canada to European franchises because the required kind of potato is not grown in Europe. In 1982, a Paris licensee was barred through a court order from using McDonald's trademarks and other trade processes because the licensee's twelve Paris eateries did not meet the required specifications.

Some products by their very nature are not or cannot be easily modified. *Musical recordings and works of art* are examples of products that are difficult to differentiate, as are books and motion pictures. When this is the case, the product must rise and fall according to its own merit. Whether such products will be successful in diverse markets is not easy to predict. Films that do well in the USA may do poorly in Japan. On the other hand, movies that were not box-office hits in the USA have turned out to be money makers in France (e.g., most of Jerry Lewis' films). Yet in the case of Ricky Martin, his worldwide fame has to do in part with his France '98 World Cup theme song ("The Cup of Life") – in Spanish, English, and French.

With regard to high-technology products, both users and manufacturers may find it desirable to reduce confusion and promote compatibility by introducing *industry specifications* that make standardization possible. A condition that may support the production and distribution of standardized products exists when certain products can be associated with particular *cultural universals*; that is, when consumers from different countries share similar need characteristics and therefore want essentially identical products. Watches are used to keep time around the world and thus can be standardized. The diamond is another example. Levi Strauss' attempt to penetrate the European market with lighter-weight jeans failed because European consumers preferred the standard heavy-duty American type.

Another study also found that industrial managers and managers of consumer goods regarded certain marketing-related factors differently, thus implying that product standardization or customization depends in part on the type of product. Furthermore, respondents consistently regarded competitive environment as the most important variable affecting the extent of marketing standardization.[8]

While market conditions tend to support localization, Western companies tend to favor standardization, but there is some logic behind the practice. Most Central and Eastern European countries are too small to pay off for customization. In addition, within a decade, these markets may converge to Western Europe market structures and rules.[9]

Arguments for adaptation

There is nothing wrong with standardized products if consumers prefer those products. In many situations, domestic consumers may desire a particular design of a product produced for the American market. However, when the product design is placed in foreign markets, foreign buyers are forced either to purchase that product from the manufacturer or not purchase anything at all. This manner of conducting business overseas is known as the "big-car" and "left-hand-drive" syndromes. Both describe US firms' reluctance and/or unwillingness to modify their products to suit their customers' needs.

According to the **big-car syndrome**, US marketers assume that products designed for Americans are superior and will be preferred by foreign consumers. US car makers believe (or used to believe) that the American desire for big cars means that only big cars should be exported to overseas markets.

The **left-hand-drive syndrome** is a corollary to the big-car syndrome. Americans drive on the right-hand side of the road, with the steering wheel on the left side of the automobile. But many Asian and European countries have traffic laws requiring drivers to drive on the left side of the road, and cars with steering wheel on the left present a serious safety hazard. Yet exported US cars are the same left-hand-drive models as are sold in the USA for the right-hand traffic patterns (see Figure 10.2). According to the excuse used by US car makers, a small sales volume abroad does not justify converting exported cars to right-hand steering: as GM's president explained, "There's a certain status in having a left-hand steer in Japan." This is one good reason why American automobile sales abroad have been disappointing. A half-hearted effort can only result in a half-hearted performance. American exporters have failed time and time again to realize that when in Rome one should do as the Romans do. Japanese car makers have not shown the same kind of indifference to market needs; Japanese firms have always adapted their automobiles to American driving customs (see Figure 10.3).

Those American firms that have understood the need for product modification have done well even in Japan. Du Pont has customized its manufacturing and marketing for the Japanese market, and its design units work with Japanese customers to design parts to their specifications. Sprite became the best selling clear soft drink in Japan after being reformulated – the lime taste was taken out because Japanese were found to prefer a purer lemon flavor.[10] Yamazaki-Nabisco's Ritz crackers sold in Japan are less salty than the Ritz crackers sold in America; similarly, Chips Ahoy are less sweet than versions sold elsewhere. Responding to the Japanese demand for quality, Ajinomoto-General Foods used a better grade of bean for its Maxim instant coffee.

Firms must choose the time when a product is to be modified to better suit its market. According to the Conference Board, important factors for product modification mentioned by more than 70 percent of firms surveyed are long-term profitability, long-term market potential, product–market fit, short-term profitability, cost of altering or adapting (e.g., retooling), desire for consistency (e.g., maintaining a world image), and short-term market potential. These factors apply to consumer nondurable and durable products as well as to industrial products.

Product adaptation is necessary under several conditions. Some are mandatory, whereas others are optional. In addition, firm characteristics and environmental characteristics have a significant impact on a firm's overall performance and marketing mix strategy.[11]

Mandatory product modification

The mandatory factors affecting product modifications include the following: government's mandatory standards (i.e., country's regulations), electrical current standards, measurement standards, and product standards and systems.

The most important factor that makes modification mandatory is **government regulation**. To gain entry into a foreign market, certain

What's right with this picture?

You want to see very many Accord Coupes that look like this one. There is no question about that. Unless, of course, you happen to work at Honda's factory located in Marysville, Ohio. Or live in Japan.

Carefully, built and assembled at one of the automotive industry's most advanced manufacturing facilities, the

Accord Coupe is made only in America. But that's not the only place it's sold.

Thousands of new Accord Coupes are expected to Japan each and every year. Where they are prized for their engineering, craftsmanship and value. Just as they are here.

But the other reason the Japanese are fond of this car is because it comes

with right-hand drive. Which is fitting since they drive on the opposite side of the road in Japan.

Most you producing both right-hand and left-hand drive cars from the same assembly line takes a lot of extra effort. The fact that Honda is the only U.S. carmaker to do so speaks for itself. It's this kind of innovation and true

commitment to people's needs which makes Honda, well, Honda.

Because even though we sell more Accord Coupes in America, it's just as important to satisfy our customers in other parts of the world.

After all, when you look at the big picture, that's what it's all about.

HONDA

Figure 10.2 *Honda: built-in product adaptation*

Source: Reprinted with permission of American Honda Motor Co., Inc.

Back in 1957 we brought our first two cars to America. And took them home again.

They were the best cars we'd ever made. They'd been bestsellers in Japan. But how would they do in the bigtime — in America?

We didn't know. We couldn't know, until we brought them here.

We brought them in August, 1957. And showed them with great hope. And even greater fear. What would happen if America didn't like them?

As it turned out, America *didn't* like them; our cars, the critics said, were "overpriced, underpowered, and built like tanks."

We had to start all over.

The message was painful and very clear: if we wanted to sell cars in a place like America, we had to start all over. And make a better car.

So we started over. And worked very hard for many frustrating years.

We stretched our technology farther than we had ever stretched it before.

We tried out ideas that had never been tried before.

We made every mistake that we could possibly make.

And one day we did it: we made a better car.

And the rest, as they say, is history.

And now comes the future.

Toyota is now, and has been for years, America's leading auto import.

But soon this import will be made right here.

On May 5 we broke ground for a new Toyota manufacturing plant in Kentucky.

The plant will cost $800,000,000, will employ 3,000, and will produce 200,000 cars a year.

Site of Toyota's new $800,000,000 auto plant in Kentucky.

It's a major investment in the future of the American automobile industry, and in the future of the American economy.

It's also a down payment on our debt.

We owe a lot to America. America gave us a chance when we were small and scared. It gave us the challenge that helped us become who we are.

This is something we will never forget.

TOYOTA

Figure 10.3 *Toyota's product adaptation*

Source: Reprinted with permission of Toyota Motor Corporation.

requirements must be satisfied. Regulations are usually specified and explained when a potential customer requests a price quotation on a product to be imported. Avon shampoos had to be reformulated to remove the formaldehyde preservative, which is a violation of regulations in several Asian countries. Food products are usually heavily regulated. Added vitamins in margarine, forbidden in Italy, are compulsory in the United Kingdom and Holland. In the case of processed cheese, the incorporation of a mold inhibitor may be fully allowed, allowed up to the permissible level, or forbidden altogether.

Frequently, products must be modified to compensate for differences in **electrical current standards**. In many countries there may even be variations in electrical standards within the country. The different electrical standards (phase, frequency, and voltage) abroad can easily harm products designed for use in the USA, and such improper use can be a serious safety hazard for users as well. Stereo receivers and TV sets manufactured for the US 110- to 120-volt mode will be severely damaged if used in markets where the voltages are twice as high. Therefore, products must be adapted to higher voltages. When there is no voltage problem, a product's operating efficiency may be impaired if

the product is operated in the wrong electrical frequency. Alarm clocks, tape-recorders, and turntables designed for the US 60-Hz (60 cycles per minute) system will run more slowly in countries where the frequency is 50 Hz. To solve this problem, marketers may have to substitute a special motor or arrange for a different drive ratio to achieve the desirable operating RPM or service level.

As with electrical standards, **measurement systems** can also vary from country to country. Although the USA has adopted the English (imperial) system of measurement (feet, pounds), most countries employ the metric system, and product quantity should or must be expressed in metric units. Starting in 2010, the EU countries will no longer accept nonmetric products for sale. Many countries even go so far as to prohibit the sale of measuring devices with both metric and English markings. One New England company was ordered to stop selling its laboratory glassware in France because the markings were not exclusively metric (see It's the Law 10.1 and 10.2).

In 1982, in order to save $2 million, the US Congress abolished the US Metric Board as well as a voluntary program for conversion to the metric system. That decision was shortsighted. Metric demands adversely affect US firms' competitiveness

---

IT'S THE LAW 10.1 POUNDS FOR KILOS

The European Union directive, passed in the mid-1980s, gave Great Britain more time to go metric. The time came on January 1, 2000. All shops are now required to operate in metric measurements. In spite of the agreement, the metric requirement has created an uproar. British politicians and consumers are angry. Tesco PLC, Britain's biggest supermarket chain, interviewed 1000 customers and learned that more than half felt that metric measurements were confusing. According to Tony Bennett of the UK Independence Party, "We gave away shillings and pence in 1971, then we had to switch from gallons to liters in 1995. Gradually we've been forced to give

up Fahrenheit for Celsius, and now it's pounds for kilos." A fishmonger, upset by having to measure fish in kilograms, states: "if it's good enough for [British Prime Minister] Tony Blair to have his new baby weighed in pounds and ounces, then it's good enough to sell fish in." Likewise, a butcher declares: "It's disgusting how a person can go into an Englishman's shop and make him into a criminal for selling in pounds and ounces." Of course, the EU officials are not amused either.

Source: "Weighty Matter: Tradition Hangs in the Balance of English Kilo War," *Asian Wall Street Journal*, July 24, 2000.

IT'S THE LAW 10.2   THE METRIC

The metric system is the international standard of measurement and most countries require, or will soon require, metric units for measurements. Many non-metric US products are not readily exportable to certain markets. More importantly, customers in other nations have lifelong experience with the metric system and expect products made according to metric measures. They are neither familiar nor comfortable with US pints, ounces, inches, and pounds.

The International System of Units, universally abbreviated as SI, is the modern metric system of measurement. The General Conference on Weights and Measures (CGPM) established the SI in 1960 and is the international authority that ensures SI dissemination and modification to reflect the latest advances in science and technology. The CGPM is an intergovernmental treaty organization which boasts forty-nine member states, including the USA and all the major industrialized countries, and remains the basis of all international agreements on units of measurement.

Every industrialized nation in the world, except for the USA, prefers the metric system for weights and measures. Thus the USA's trading partners require at least dual labeling (US units and metric units), if not metric-only measurement units on product labels.

Europe

The long-standing European Union (EU) Metric Directive mandated that after January 1, 2000, all products sold in the EU needed to specify and label in metric measurements only. Prior to implementation, the European Commission recommended a ten-year deferral of the metric-only directive, allowing companies to use dual labeling through 2009. After the EU Directive takes effect, member and associated countries will no longer permit dual indications of measurement. US exporters can no longer label or print inches, pounds, or any other non-metric measurement on shipments. This affects labels, packaging, advertising, catalogs, technical manuals, and instructions. Legal units of measurement will now be referred to as SI units (International System), and enforcement mechanisms are already in place.

Asia

In Asia, Korea is changing from the older versions of the metric system to the SI. The revised Korean Metrology Law prescribes strict new guidelines effective from July 1, 2001, mandating that measurements be expressed only in SI units. Both manufacturers and importers are required to adhere to metrification rules, which include technical requirements for weighing and measuring devices. Strict punishment for noncompliance may include fines and a prison term. The Japanese market strongly prefers metric labeling and its Measurement Law requires that all imported products and shipping documents show SI units. The Philippine government prohibits importation of non-metric measuring devices, instrumentation, and apparatus without prior clearance from its Bureau of Product Standards.

Latin America

In Latin America and the Caribbean, metric is increasingly becoming the standard. Chile requires that all labels must contain, in Spanish, size and weight converted to the metric system. Goods not complying with these measurements may be imported, but not sold to consumers until the conversion is made. Costa Rican law requires the exclusive use of the metric system. In Brazil, product labels should have a Portuguese translation and use metric units or show a metric equivalent.

Africa

Countries in Africa have similar metric requirements. Mauritius and Eritrea require metric weights and measures. Cameroon recommends French and English labeling, with all measurements in the metric system. Côte d'Ivoire also prefers French labeling, and requires imported equipment adapted to run according to European electrical and metric standards. South Africa requires metric weights and measures on the bill of lading. All items entering Nigeria must be labeled in metric terms exclusively, and products with dual or multi-markings will be confiscated or refused entry.

Source: David Averne and Jim McCracken, "The Metric System: The International System for Measurement and Commerce," *Export America*, January 2002, 14–15.

because many American firms do not offer metric products. A Middle-Eastern firm, for example, was unable to find an American producer that sold pipe with metric threads for oil machinery. A European firm had to rewire all imported electrical appliances because the US standard wire diameters did not meet national standards. It is difficult to find a US firm that cuts lumber to metric dimensions. Fortunately, the new trade act now requires the US government and industry to use metric units in documentation of exports and imports as prescribed by the International Convention on the Harmonized Commodity Description and Coding System. The Harmonized System is designed to standardize commodity classification for all major trading nations. The International System Units (Systeme International d' Unites (SI)) is the official measurement system of the Harmonized System.

Very few countries still cling to the obsolete nonmetric systems. Among them are the USA, Burma, Brunei, and Liberia. Robert Heller of the Federal Reserve Board of Governors made the following comment:

> Only Yemen and India have as low an export-to-GDP ratio as the USA. Would it come as a surprise to you to know that the US and Yemen share something else in common? They are the only two countries in the world that have not yet gone metric! If an American manufacturer has to retool first in order to sell his wares abroad, his incentive to do so is considerably reduced, and it makes his first step into export markets all that much more expensive.[12]

Some products must be modified because of different **operating systems** adopted by various countries. Television systems provide a good example (see Exhibit 10.1). There are three different TV operating systems used in different parts of the world: the American NTSC (National Television Systems Committee), the French SECAM (Systeme Electronique Pour Couleur Avec Memoire), and the German PAL (Phone Alternating Lines). In 1941, the USA became the first country to set the national standards for TV broadcasting, adopting 525 scanning lines per frame. Most other nations later decided to adopt 625 lines for a sharper image. In most cases, a TV set designed for one broadcast system cannot receive signals broadcast through a different operating system. When differences in product operating systems exist, a company unwilling to change its products must limit the number of countries it can enter, unless proper modification is undertaken for other market requirements.

Optional product modification

The conditions dictating product modification mentioned so far are mandatory in the sense that without adaptation a product either cannot enter a market or is unable to perform its function there. Such mandatory standards make the adaptation decision easy: a marketer must either comply or remain out of the market. Italy's Piaggio withdrew its Vespa scooters from the US market in 1983, choosing not to meet US pollution control standards for its few exports.

A more complex and difficult decision is optional modification, which is based on the international marketer's discretion in taking action (see Marketing Strategy 10.1). Nescafé in Switzerland, for instance, tastes quite different from the same brand sold just a short distance across the French border.

One condition that may make optional modification attractive is related to **physical distribution**, and this involves the facilitation of product transportation at the lowest cost. Since freight charges are assessed on either a weight or volume basis, the carrier may charge on the basis of which ever is more profitable. The marketer may be able to reduce delivery costs if the products are assembled and then shipped. Many countries also have narrow roads, doorways, stairways, or elevators that can cause transit problems when products are large or are shipped assembled. Therefore, a slight product modification may greatly facilitate product movement.

Another determinant for optional adaptation involves **local use conditions**, including **climatic conditions**. The hot/cold, humid/dry

EXHIBIT 10.1   WORLD TELEVISION STANDARDS

NTSC

Antigua	Costa Rica	Jamaica	Puerto Rico
Bahamas	Cuba	Japan	Saipan
Barbados	Dominican	South Korea	Samoa
Belize	Republic	Mexico	Surinam
Bermuda	Ecuador	Netherlands	Taiwan
Bolivia	El Salvador	Antilles	Trinidad
Burma	Greenland	Nicaragua	Tobago
Canada	Guam	Panama	USA
Chile	Guatemala	Peru	Venezuela
Colombia	Honduras	Philippines	Virgin Islands

PAL

Afghanistan	Gibraltar	Netherlands	Swaziland
(Kabul)	Hong Kong	New Guinea	Sweden
Algeria	Iceland	New Zealand	Switzerland
Argentina	India	Nigeria	Tanzania
Australia	Indonesia	Norway	Thailand
Austria	Ireland	Oman	Turkey
Bangladesh	Italy	Paraguay	United Arab
Belguim	Jordan	Portugal	Emirates
Brazil	Kenya	Qatar	United Kingdom
Brunei	North Korea	Saudi Arabia	Uruguay
China	Kuwait	Sierra Leone	Yemen
Cyprus	Liberia	Singapore	Yugoslavia
Denmark	Luxembourg	South Africa	Zambia
Finland	Malaysia	Spain	Zimbabwe
Germany	Malta	Sri Lanka	
Ghana	Monaco	Sudan	

SECAM

Albania	Guadeloupe	Madagascar	Russia
Benin	French	Martinique	Senegal
Bulgaria	Guyana	Mauritius	Syria
Congo	Haiti	Mongolia	Tahiti
Czechoslovakia	Hungary	Morocco	Togo
Djibouti	Iran	New Caledonia	Tunisia
Egypt	Iraq	Niger	Vietnam
France	Ivory Coast	Poland	Zaire
Gabon	Lebanon	Reunion	
Greece	Libya	Romania	

MARKETING STRATEGY 10.1   THE GOAT

GM wants to trumpet its ability to marshal global resources and well-known brands. As an example, Saturn, well known for its reliable compact cars and no-haggle pricing policy, was to rely on GM's Opel unit for its L-series. But the execution of the plan was difficult. European and American engineers had never worked together before. Differences in engineering standards slowed production and harmed quality in the US plant. American engineers found out later that their German counterparts had slightly different specifications for many of the thousands of variables that make a car's parts work together. As a result, plastic parts and body panels did not fit. Opel originally planned to make minor changes in its midsize Vectra for the L-series. However, Saturn insisted on major changes – making the car longer and wider and using Saturn's trademark plastic panels (which are attached differently from the traditional sheet-metal variety). Even a small change was a problem. German engineers could not understand the need to have a cup holder large enough to accommodate giant-sized drinks.

GM's Pontiac division is well known for its GTO muscle cars (also called the Goat or the GreaT One). To leverage its resources, GM pasted its legendary GTO name on an Australian car (Monaro) produced by its Holden subsidiary. The transformation focused on power, exhaust note, and launch feel. In addition to the powertrain alterations, other changes were required to conform to the US crash safety standards to improve the car's durability against corrosion. To live up to its reputation, the GTO generates about 350 horsepower, whereas the Monaro makes about 300.

While some Americans have criticized GM for putting a famous American name on an Australian car, the engineering manager of the GTO made no apology for the Australian accent and defended it as a global vehicle.

Sources: "Australia's Monaro Inspired Pontiac GTO," *San José Mercury News,* July 18, 2003; "G'Day, GTO," *San José Mercury News,* July 18, 2003.

---

conditions may affect product durability or performance. Avon modified its Candid moist lipstick line for a hot, humid climate. Certain changes may be required in gasoline formulations. If the heat is intense, gasoline requires a higher flashpoint to avoid vapor locks and engine stalling. In Brazil, automobiles are designed to run on low-quality gas, to withstand the country's rough dusty roads, and to weather its sizzling temperatures. As a result, these automobiles are attractive to customers in LDCs, especially when the automobiles are also durable and simple to maintain. American automobiles can experience difficulties in these markets, where people tend to overload their cars and trucks and do not perform regular maintenance, not to mention the unavailability of lead-free gasoline.

Another local use condition that can necessitate product change is **space constraint**. Sears' refrigerators were redesigned to be smaller in dimensions without sacrificing the original capacity, so that they could fit into the compact Japanese home. Philips, similarly, had to reduce the size of its coffee maker. In contrast, US mills, for many years, resisted cutting plywood according to Japanese specifications, even though they were told repeatedly that the standard Japanese plywood dimensions were 3 × 6 ft – not the US standard of 4 × 8 ft. In a related case, Japanese-style homes have exposed wood beams, but US forest-products firms traditionally allow 2 × 4 studs to be dirty or slightly warped, since in the USA these studs will almost always be covered over with wallboard. The firms have refused to understand that wood grain and quality are important to the Japanese because an exposed post is part of the furniture. Furniture is not easily exported because it has two inherent problems: size/weight and different ways furniture is designed and used in other cultures. Some foreign manufacturers are still able to be successful in Japan, especially those who are willing to reduce the size of some products and make necessary modifications so as to appeal to Japanese consumers.[13]

Consumer demographics as related to **physical appearance** can also affect how products are used and how suitable those products are. Habitat Mothercare PLC found out that its British products were not consistent with American customs and sizes. Its comforters were not long enough to fit American beds, and its tumblers could not hold enough ice. Philips downsized its shavers to fit the smaller Japanese hand. One US brassière company did well initially in Germany yet failed to win repeat purchases. The problem was that German women have a tendency not to try on merchandise in the store and thus did not find out until later that the product was ill-fitting because of measurement variations between American and German brassières. Furthermore, German customers do not usually return a product for refund or adjustment.

Even a doll may have to be modified to better resemble the physical appearance of local people. The Barbie doll, though available in Japan for decades, became popular only after Mattel allowed Takara (which holds the production and marketing agreement) to reconstruct the product. Out of sixty countries, Japan is the only market where the product is modified. Barbie's Western-style features are modified in several ways: her blue eyes become brown, her vividly blonde hair is darkened, and her bosom size is reduced.

Local use conditions include **users' habits**. Since the Japanese prefer to work with pencils – a big difference from the typed business correspondence common in the USA – copiers require special characteristics that allow the copying of light pencil lines. Microsoft's plant in Ireland was charged with the task of localizing Windows 95 into more than fifty languages. IBM, likewise, localized its OS/2 Warp system. It took four months for IBM to translate it for the Czech Republic. The words on the screen had to be translated first from Czech to English. Later, the program was adapted to the Czech operating system. However, on the first try, the OS/2 could not accept any Windows applications due to the differences in the Czech system. Another month of adjustment was necessary before the Czech version was ready. The Polish, Hungarian, and Russian language versions were also made available.

Finally, other **environmental characteristics** related to use conditions should be examined. Examples are endless. Detergents should be reformulated to fit local water conditions. IBM had to come up with a completely new design so that its machine could include Japanese word-processing capability. Kodak made some changes in its graphic arts products for Japanese professionals, most of whom have no dark-rooms and have to work in different light environments.

Price may often influence a product's success or failure in the marketplace. This factor becomes even more crucial abroad because US products tend to be expensive, but foreign consumers' incomes tend to be at lower levels than Americans' incomes. Frequently, the higher quality of American products cannot overcome the price disadvantage found in foreign markets. To solve this problem, American companies can reduce the contents of the product or remove any nonessential parts or do both. Foreign consumers are generally not convenience-oriented, and an elaborate product can be simplified by removing any "frills" that may drive up the price unnecessarily. This approach is used by General Motors in manufacturing and selling the so-called Basic Transportation Vehicle in less-industrialized nations.

One reason that international marketers often voluntarily modify their products in individual markets is their desire to maximize profit by **limiting product movement across national borders**. The rationale for this desire to discourage gray marketing is that some countries have price controls and other laws that restrict profits and prices. When other nearby countries have no such laws, marketers are encouraged to move products into those nearby countries where a higher price may be charged. A problem can arise in which local firms in countries where product prices are high are bypassed by marketers who buy directly from firms handling such products in countries where prices are low. In many cases, due to antitrust laws, international marketers who wish to maintain certain market prices cannot ban this kind of product movement by threatening to cut off supply from those firms re-exporting products to high-priced countries. Johnson & Johnson, for example, was fined $300,000 by the EU for explicitly preventing British wholesalers and pharmacists from re-exporting Gravindex pregnancy tests to Germany, where the kits cost almost twice as much.

In spite of authorities' efforts to prevent companies from keeping lower-priced goods out of higher-priced countries, marketers may do so anyway as long as they do not get caught. Some manufacturers try to hinder these practices by deliberately varying packaging, package coding, product characteristics, coloring, and even brand names in order to spot violators or to confuse consumers in markets where products have moved across borders.

Perhaps the most arbitrary yet most important reason for product change abroad is because of **historical preference**, or **local customs and culture** (see Marketing Strategy 10.1). Product size, color, speed, grade, and source may have to be redesigned in order to accommodate local preference. Kodak altered its film to cater to a Japanese idea of attractive skin tones. Kraft's Philadelphia Cream Cheese tastes different in the USA, Great Britain, Germany, and Canada. In Asia, Foremost sells chocolate and strawberry milk instead of low-fat and skimmed milk. Asians and Europeans by tradition prefer to shop on a daily basis, and thus they desire smaller refrigerators in order to reduce cost and electrical consumption.

When products clash with a culture, the likely loser is the product, not the culture. Strong religious beliefs make countries of the Middle East insist on halaled chickens. In soup-conscious Brazil, Campbell soups did not take off because home-makers there have strong cultural traditions of a home-maker's role, and serving Campbell soup to their families would be a soup served not of their own making. As a result, these home makers prefer dehydrated products manufactured by Knorr and Maggi, used as a soup starter to which the home-

maker can add her own flavors and ingredients. Campbell soups are usually purchased to be set aside for an emergency, such as if the family arrives home late.

Product changes are not necessarily related to functional attributes such as durability, quality, operation method, maintenance, and other engineering aspects. Frequently, aesthetic or secondary qualities must also be taken into account. There are instances in which minor, cosmetic changes have significantly increased sales. Therefore, functional and aesthetic changes should both be considered in regard to how they affect the total, complete product.

One company that incorporates multiple features of product modification in appealing to local tastes is Pillsbury. In marketing its Totino's line of pizzas in Japan, Pillsbury found it wise to make several mandatory and optional changes in its product.[14] Japanese food standards ban many preservatives and dyes. The ban often necessitates an extensive redesign of a product just to get it into the Japanese market. Totino's pizzas are basically a "belly stuffer" in the USA, a confirmation of many foreigners' perceptions that Americans have pedestrian tastes in food. But the Japanese "eat" with their eyes, too — all foods have an aesthetic dimension. They perceive American foods as being too sweet, too large, and too spicy, making it necessary to alter the ingredients to suit the Japanese palate. Furthermore, the pizza size had to be reduced from the US 12-ounce size to the Japanese 6.5-ounce size to fit into smaller Japanese ovens. In effect, Totino's frozen pizza and packaging were completely redesigned for the Japanese market, and Pillsbury's success confirms that its efforts were worthwhile.

In conclusion, marketers should not waste time resisting product modification. The reluctance to change a product may be the result of an insensitivity to cultural differences in foreign markets. Whatever the reason for this reluctance, there is no question that it is counter-productive in international marketing. Product adaptation should rarely become an important issue to the marketer. A good marketer compares the incremental profits against the incremental costs associated with product adaptation. If the incremental profit is greater than the associated incremental cost, then the product should be adjusted – without question. In making this comparison, marketers should primarily use only future earnings and costs.

A MOVE TOWARD WORLD PRODUCT: INTERNATIONAL OR NATIONAL PRODUCT?

Product standardization and modification may give the impression that a marketer must choose between these two processes and that one approach is better than the other. In many instances, a compromise between the two is more practical and far superior than selecting either procedure exclusively. Black and Decker has stopped customizing products for every country in favor of a select few global products that may be sold everywhere. Such US publishers as Prentice-Hall and Harper have also adopted the "world book" concept, which makes it possible for an English-language world book to have world copyright. Publishers change, if necessary, only the title-page, cover, and/or jacket.

World product and standardized product may sometimes be confused with each other. A **world product** is a product designed for the international market. In comparison, a **standardized product** is a product developed for one national market and then exported with no change to international markets. Zenith and RCA TV sets are standardized products, whereas a German subsidiary of ITT makes a world product by producing a "world chassis" for its TV sets. This world chassis allows assemblage of TV sets for all three color TV systems of the world (i.e., NTSC, SECAM, and PAL) without changing all circuitry on the various modules.

A move by a company toward a world product is a logical and healthy move. If a company has to adapt its product for each market this can be a very expensive proposition, but without the necessary adaptation a product may not sell at all. Committing to the design of a world product can provide the solution to these two major concerns faced by most firms

dealing in the international marketplace. GE, for example, produces a numerical control system suitable in both metric and English measures. In addition, it has designed machines to operate under the wide differences in voltage among the different European countries. GE refrigerators are built in such a way that they can be used regardless of whether the frequency is 50 Hz or 60 Hz. This emerging trend toward world products is also attractive for items with international appeal or for those items purchased by international travelers. Electric shavers made by Norelco and portable stereo radios made by Sony and Crown are produced having a universal-voltage feature.

One might question whether a world product would be more expensive than a national or local product, since the world product may need multipurpose parts. Actually, the world product should result in greater saving for two reasons. First, costly downtime in production is not needed to adjust or convert equipment to produce different national versions. Second, a world product greatly simplifies inventory control because only one universal part, rather than many individual parts, has to be stocked.

A world product may also be able to lower certain production costs by anticipating necessary local adaptation and thus being adaptation-ready. As an example, the Japanese government requires thirty-two changes on most US-built cars, including: replacing headlamps that, because of the left-hand drive, dip in the wrong direction; changing "sharp-edged" door handles; replacing outside rearview mirrors; and filling in the gap between the body and the rear bumper to prevent catching the sleeves of kimono-clad women. Honda is able to sell its US-made cars in Japan at relatively low prices because it produces the car ready for sale in Japan (see Figure 10.2). Since cars manufactured by GM, Ford, and Chrysler are built for the American market, they must undergo expensive alterations to meet Japanese regulations. The American car makers have taken some steps to remedy the problem.

It must be pointed out that a world product has some inherent problems as well. As illustrated by Ford Escort, the car was designed in Europe as

Ford's world car. The company's American executives, however, proceeded to thoroughly redesign it for the US market. Similarly, design choices are often a source of conflict between Toyota's Japanese headquarters and its US subsidiary. Even interior color schemes, while minor, are also in dispute.[15] Therefore, corporate commitment is a necessity. There must be mechanisms to take care of the conflicting views of executives working in the different countries.

The Ford 2000 project, relying on centralization, uses vehicle centers to better use common parts and engineering ideas. However, due to differences in gasoline prices, consumer income, and tastes, the same vehicle does not have the same appeal in many parts of the world. While Americans are crazy about Ford's trucks and sports-utility vehicles, Europeans like smaller, more fuel-efficient passenger cars. While Europeans prefer flashier interiors, their American counterparts want wider seats while toning down the interiors.[16]

As a product of compromise, a world product may have to be bland enough to partially please everyone while not really pleasing anyone; that is, it must satisfy the lowest common denominator of taste in different markets. Ford's Mondeo has done well in Europe, but American consumers have found the back seat of the American versions (Ford Contour and Mercury Mystique) to be too tight. Likewise, GM's 1997 front-drive minivan is just right for the Europeans but a little too small for the Americans. As far as the automobile industry is concerned, a world car has another problem: it has to meet the world's toughest environmental and safety rules, thus increasing costs.

The trend toward an international or world product and away from a national product will continue as MNCs become more aware of the significance of world marketing. The willingness of several companies to consider designing a universal product for the world market is indeed a good indicator that this trend will continue. Consider the case of Vaillant.[17] This German boiler company is Europe's biggest maker of central heating boilers. The boiler market does not accommodate the pan-European plans well. Due to a huge variation in customer tastes and building standards, a company has to offer hundreds of different models. As a result, local suppliers largely dominate individual countries' boiler markets, and the industry's cross-border selling is much less developed than that found in most other industries. As noted by Vaillant's manager, products such as toilet cisterns and refrigerators have far less product divergence across the continent. However, Vaillant's strategy is to focus on a few common components while producing hundreds of different types of boiler. While boilers must still be developed to meet individual countries' specifications, they will share as many common features (e.g., burners and controls) as is logical. Therefore, the costs of customization can be minimized without minimizing customer choice.

International marketers pursuing a global strategy will need to consider how to standardize the existing product offerings and marketing activities while making unique adjustment in a local market. According to one study investigating sixteen supposedly global product attributes across three product categories in France and Malaysia, two attributes (product quality and appearance) are universal and may thus be standardized. The relevance of the other fourteen attributes though is based on international market contingencies.[18]

MARKETING OF SERVICES

Services, broadly defined, encompass all economic activities – other than agriculture, manufacturing, and mining. The service section has a great variety of industries that include: banking and insurance, travel and tourism, entertainment, wholesale and retail trade, legal and other business services, telecommunications, health care, education and training, publishing, transportation, energy, and environmental services, as well as architecture, construction, and engineering services.

The impact of service can also be indirect. As countries become more developed economically, they also become more service oriented. Firms in mature Western markets seem to gain a competitive advantage with a strong service orientation. Likewise, the evidence, while quite limited, shows that a private, more service-oriented Slovenian bank outperformed a large, older, state-supported bank.[19]

Importance of services

Internationally, the "invisible" trade is responsible for one-fifth of the value of world exports. The share of commercial services in world trade has been rising. Due to information technology, communication costs will decline further. As a result, trade in services is very likely to continue to expand rapidly.

In Hong Kong, the services sector has traditionally dominated the economy, accounting for 85 percent of GDP (mostly financial services and trade and tourism).[20]

The USA is the world's leading producer and exporter of services. The service sector is the largest component of the US economy. It accounts for 79 percent of the private sector output and 83 percent of the private non-farm employment (93 million people).[21] The top US services exports are: tourism, transportation (see Figure 10.4), financial, education, and training, business, telecommunications, equipment (installation, maintenance, and

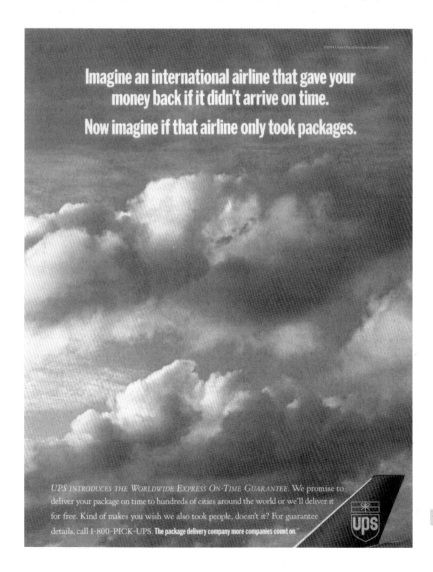

Figure 10.4
Marketing of service: transportation

repair), entertainment, information, and health care. The major markets for American services exports, in order, are: the European Union, Japan, and Canada.

Education and tourism in particular are significant earners for the USA. Some 583,000 foreign students attend US colleges and universities, and one-third or more of science and engineering degrees go to foreigners.[22] Likewise, travel and tourism exports are unique because buyers must travel to the USA to buy and consume the products. The top three reasons why international visitors travel to the USA are: vacation, visiting friends and relatives, and business meetings.

Types of services

There are two major categories of services: consumer and business services. Business services that are exported consist of numerous and varied types, including advertising, construction and engineering, insurance, legal services, data processing, and banking. Among the consulting and technical services are personnel training and supervision, management of facilities, and economic and business research.

Services such as hairdressing are often cited as a classic example of nontradables. However, technological advancement has made it possible for many services to be embodied in goods that are traded internationally (e.g., software on diskettes and films on videotape). Technology has also greatly benefited information-intensive services (e.g., research and development, accounting, legal services) as well as knowledge-based services (e.g., professional and technical services, banking, insurance, education).[23] The Indian software industry has been able to capture about 12 percent of the international market for customized software. Figure 10.5 shows the international nature of management education.

The economic and legal environment

Like merchandise trade, exports of services are influenced by changes in relative economic conditions and exchange rates. As shown by the travel industry, when the dollar was strong in the early 1980s, the increased buying power of the dollar made foreign travel by Americans a bargain, but when the dollar weakened, foreign travelers vacationed in the USA.

The primary competition for American service firms comes from Western Europe, with new challenges being mounted by Latin American and East Asian companies. Countries such as India view service as an infant industry that must be nurtured and protected. Not surprisingly, service exports/ imports are subject to many nontariff trade barriers (e.g., local labor and content of service requirements, ownership restrictions, foreign exchange controls, employment bans, quotas, local standards, and discriminatory taxation policies). International marketers may even face outright bans on investing in certain businesses altogether. For example, foreign life insurers are not allowed to set up shop in South Korea.

The National Committee for International Trade in Education publishes a report on barriers to trade in education services. The report states that American providers face numerous barriers when delivering their services abroad. The barriers highlighted include: national legislation and policy that inhibit foreign education providers from obtaining national licenses; qualifications authorities that have difficulty recognizing foreign educational credentials; telecommunications laws that restrict the use of national satellites and receiving dishes; foreign currency controls that limit direct investment by foreign education providers, place minimum capital investment requirements on foreign-owned firms and assess prohibitively high taxes on all revenue made by foreign entities; limitations on foreign ownership; and disregard for international agreements concerning intellectual property rights.[24]

Although service providers must abide by local laws, they may still want to try to change unfavorable laws or oppose proposed regulations that can adversely affect business activities. Since the move for fixed exchange rates will threaten the existence of the Chicago Mercantile Exchange's currency contracts, the CME established the American Coalition

Figure 10.5
Marketing of service: management education

for Flexible Exchange Rates to present the alternative point of view to that of the advocates of fixed rates.

One good sign is that services are being liberalized. One successful aspect of the Uruguay Round is the adoption of the General Agreement on Trade in Services (GATS). This agreement has extended multilateral rules (e.g., most-favored-nation status, national treatment, removal of quantitative restrictions) to services.

Marketing mix and adaptation

Services have several unique characteristics; they are intangible, person-oriented, and perishable. Yet virtually all marketing concepts and strategies used to market tangible products are relevant to the marketing of services.

Like a product, a company's service should also be defined broadly. American Express, for instance, does not regard itself as being in the credit-card business. Instead, the company is in the communications and information-processing business, and its computer center in Phoenix processes a quarter of a million credit-card transactions each day from all over the world.

Services also require adaptation from time to time for foreign markets. Even movies distributed abroad, more often than not, must be packaged differently. At the very least, movies distributed internationally require subtitles or overdubbing. Most Japanese were perplexed by Disney's policies of serving no alcohol and prohibiting bringing in food from outside the park. Disney, however, has made a few changes. It added a Japanese restaurant to serve older patrons. There was no Nautilus submarine. In addition, to protect against rain and snow, more areas are covered.

Service providers usually have more flexibility in providing services than products because it is more difficult for consumers to ascertain and compare the quality of services among suppliers. Their prices must still be competitive, especially when the services offered are standardized (see Table 10.2).

Market entry strategies

Regarding market entry strategies, a service firm's unique characteristics (e.g., low capital intensity and the inseparability of production and consumption) may have some impact on entry–mode choice. In general, service firms prefer full-control modes, but firms with low asset specificity, in responding to the rising costs of integration or the diminishing ability to integrate, may have to relinquish control and seek shared-control ventures.[25]

In practice, service firms can use virtually all market entry strategies when they are appropriate. In the financial services industry, American firms have entered into partnership and joint venture agreements with European and Japanese firms. Wells Fargo and Nikko Securities have formed a joint venture to operate a global investment management firm. Merrill Lynch and Société Générale have discussed a partnership to develop a French asset-backed securities market.

In the case of Toronto-based Four Seasons Hotels Inc., it was relatively unknown in Asia even though it manages Inn on the Park in Europe and The Pierre and The Ritz-Carlton in North America. To quickly become a dominant high-end hotelier worldwide, Four Seasons paid $122 million for a 25 percent stake in the Hong Kong-based Regent International Hotels Ltd. (which is owned by Japan's EIE International Corp.). As part of the deal, Four Seasons also gains the rights to manage the luxury chain, thus managing forty-three hotels in seventeen countries. This acquisition strategy coupled with the management contract strategy has made it possible for Four Seasons to gain an exposure in Asia that otherwise would have taken years to develop on its own.

CONCLUSION

A product provides a bundle of satisfaction that the consumer derives from the product itself, along with its promotion, distribution, and price. For a product or service to be successful in any market, whether at home or overseas, it must therefore primarily satisfy consumer needs. In order to satisfy these needs more precisely, marketers should employ market segmentation, product positioning, and other marketing techniques. In the past, American marketers have been slow to realize that they must adapt their marketing practices when selling abroad. American marketers have overlooked the particular preferences and needs of customers overseas and have not adapted exported products, brands, and packages to meet these needs. For companies that have committed themselves seriously to their international market needs, performance can be very encouraging. Texas Instruments and Du Pont, for example, have done remarkably well in Japan, a market misunderstood by many, by assigning their best marketing personnel in that market. Du Pont, recognizing the importance of this market, maintains thirteen laboratories in Japan to work closely with customers in order to tailor products to meet customers' needs.

Although product modification for local markets is a necessity in many cases, it does not mean that

Table 10.2 Prices of services

City	USD	Index Zurich= 100	City	USD	Index Zurich= 100
Oslo	558	115.1	Barcelona	270	55.7
London	552	113.9	Lisbon	259	53.5
Tokyo	514	106.0	Taipei	258	53.3
Zurich	485	100.0	Manama	257	53.0
Copenhagen	482	99.5	Singapore	248	51.2
Stockholm	474	97.9	Moscow	244	50.3
Chicago	469	96.7	Istanbul	239	49.4
Helsinki	466	96.2	Warsaw	236	48.6
New York	463	95.5	Tallinn	234	48.2
Basel	457	94.3	Budapest	221	45.6
Geneva	441	91.1	Ljubljana	221	45.6
Hong Kong	436	89.9	Jakarta	211	43.5
Lugano	435	89.7	Bangkok	210	43.4
Paris	428	88.4	Lima	208	42.9
Vienna	376	77.6	Santiago de Chile	207	42.7
Athens	369	76.1	Shanghai	206	42.6
Luxembourg	365	75.2	Riga	199	41.1
Los Angeles	363	74.9	Kuala Lumpur	197	40.6
Frankfurt	355	73.3	Vilnius	191	39.4
Milan	355	73.3	Johannesburg	188	38.8
Amsterdam	353	72.8	Caracas	183	37.8
Dublin	353	72.8	Manila	179	36.9
Miami	348	71.8	Nairobi	169	34.9
Brussels	330	68.1	Lagos	168	34.6
Sydney	327	67,4	Bogotá	165	34.0
Berlin	316	65.3	Prague	164	33.8
Dubai	315	65.0	São Paulo	162	33.4
Rome	310	64.0	Rio de Janeiro	153	31.6
Mexico City	302	62.2	Kiev	150	31.0
Montreal	296	61.0	Sofia	150	31.0
Auckland	290	59,8	Bratislava	148	30.5
Madrid	287	59.2	Buenos Aires	136	28.1
Seoul	287	59.2	Mumbai	114	23.6
Tel Aviv	285	58.8	Bucharest	102	21.0
Toronto	277	57.1	Karachi	97	19.9

Source: Prices and Earnings (Zurich: UBS AG, 203), 20.

all products must be changed. A standardized product designed for one market may fit many other markets as well. But this situation is relatively rare, and the standardized product that is suitable in many markets should be considered as a fortunate random occurrence. A world product, on the other hand, should be created with the world market in mind in order to maximize consumer satisfaction and simplify the production process in the long run. If a world product is not possible due to environmental diversity or other circumstances, a marketing manager should re-examine product characteristics and consumer needs. If there is a possibility that there is a convergence in the characteristics and needs, then it may be possible to standardize the product. When the characteristics and need variables do not converge, then it becomes a matter of changing the product to fit consumer needs, as long as the associated costs are not prohibitive. The time has clearly come for the export marketer to think less nationally and more internationally. It may in fact be as fundamental as determining that, if the product can satisfy a need at a reasonable price, the product will sell in its international market.

CASE 10.1 MCDONALDIZATION

McDonald's Corp. is often used as an example of Americanism (and globalization) owing to its strict quality control and worldwide success. McDonald's has some 30,000 outlets in 121 countries to serve about 46 million customers every day, totaling more than $41 billion in annual sales.

The company has highly detailed specifications and rules that must be strictly followed. In England, its high standard for coffee aroused the ire of a British coffee supplier, and the company built its own plant when it could not get quality hamburger buns. McDonald's provides assistance to Thai farmers for cultivation of Idaho russet potatoes. When suitable supplies are unavailable in Europe, the company does not hesitate to import french fries from Canada and pies from Oklahoma.

As reported by *Advertising Age*, the *Wall Street Journal*, and *Direct Marketing*, the company, however, permits some degree of flexibility and creativity on the part of its franchisees. In Southeast Asia, it serves durian-flavored milk shakes made from a tasty tropical fruit whose aroma is acceptable to Asians but is considered foul by Westerners. Coconut, mango, and tropic mint shakes may be found in Hong Kong.

Menu changes are also necessary in Europe. McDonald's sells near beer, which does not require a liquor license in Switzerland, and chicken on the Continent (to head off Kentucky Fried Chicken). McDonald's on the Champs-Élysées offers a choice of *vin blanc* or *vin rouge*, and the coffee comes in a tiny cup with about half a dozen spoonsful of very strong black coffee. In England, tea is available and will have milk in it unless black tea is ordered.

McDonald's Australian outlets formerly offered mutton pot pie; outlets in the Philippines, where noodle houses are popular, offer McSpaghetti. Likewise, in Mexico, McDonald's offers the McPollo chicken sandwich and jalapeno sauce as a hamburger condiment. Since eating the Midwest-American beef is like eating soft pebbles to the Japanese, McDonald's hamburger in Japan has a different texture and spices. In many countries, consumers consider fast food to be primarily a snack rather than a regular meal.

Furthermore, the company's operating philosophy has to be altered as well. In order to attract foreign partners who are well qualified and well financed, McDonald's grants territorial franchises instead of the usual practice of granting franchises store by store.

In spite of its strong American image and sandwiches, McDonald's has done quite a bit of localization. Consider the following non-US products: Taiwan (rice dishes with curry beef, ginger beef and spicy tomato chicken), India (vegetarian sandwich with eggless tomato mayonnaise), New Zealand (hamburger with a fried egg and slice of pickled beet), Turkey (spicy meat patty with a yogurt and tomato sauce), the Philippines (pasta in a red sauce),

Egypt (deep-fried patties of ground beans and spices), India (aloo tikka), Japan (teriyaki burgers), Amman (flat-bread McArabia), Israel (kosher McNuggets), and France (cheese and ham between two thin slices of toasted bread).

McDonald's Restaurants Taiwan is almost entirely run by Taiwanese. It added rice dishes in late 2002, following the trend in Hong Kong, the Philippines, Indonesia, and Thailand. McDonald's controls 70 percent of Taiwan's fast-food market and hopes that rice dishes will add to the market share by enticing adults to eat with their kids in its outlets. However, the management is mindful of the fact that the success in Taiwan is due to the core business (i.e., the traditional McDonald's business).

McThai Co. Ltd. adds a Thai feeling to McDonald's. About 15 percent of menu items are locally oriented products to suit local tastes. The menu includes khao man somtan (coconut milk rice with spicy papaya salad), and desserts such as sago and coconut pie. In addition, the managing director plans to introduce the concept of *eatingtainment* that combines entertainment and eating. Activities such as karaoke hours and contests have been planned.

In Europe, a local flavor is evident. The McDonald's outlets in England are the first in the world to sell fresh fruit (grapes and sliced apples), fruit juice with "no extra sugar," and a 266-calorie pasta salad with less than 5 percent fat. France is perhaps even more crucial to McDonald's, and the company opens a new outlet every six days. Surprisingly, a typical French customer spends $9 per visit, more than twice as much as the US average of $4. For McDonald's which is a model of efficiency, McDonald's France appears to ignore the model. It refits restaurants with chic interiors and extras (e.g., music videos) to encourage customers to linger over their meals. Instead of streamlining its menus to speed up service, as do its US counterparts, the French outlets add items. A hot ham-and-cheese sandwich (Croque McDO) is especially popular. In terms of architecture, McDonald's France has adapted the restaurant designs to blend with local architecture. Some outlets in the Alps have wood-and-stone interiors reminiscent of a chalet. While the updated styling found in half of the more than 900 French outlets adds 20 percent more to the standard designs, sales at these outlets have also gone up by as much as 20 percent.

Conceivably, the French approach may not work in the USA because fast-food customers simply want quick service and cheap, tasty foods. The McCafé concept from Australia was imported but failed in the USA. Likewise, McDonald's did not do well with pizza.

Points to consider

Some managers of McDonald's, buoyed up by the success in Asia and Moscow, want to "McDonaldize" the world. Discuss the implications of this statement. Should McDonald's try to standardize its product mix? What aspects of McDonald's are universal and thus can be exported to other countries? Should the company introduce into the USA the products that are successful in Europe and Asia?

QUESTIONS

1   By marketing in a foreign country, must a firm automatically employ geographic segmentation or other segmentation bases?

2   Explain (in the international context) how these product attributes affect product adoption: relative advantage, compatibility, trialability/divisibility, observability, complexity, and price.

3   Describe briefly the IPLC theory and its marketing implications.

4   Describe the factors that make it feasible to offer a standardized product.

5   Offer your arguments for product adaptation.

6 Explain the "big-car" syndrome and "left-hand-drive" syndrome.

7 Why do foreign governments erect barriers to US exports of services?

DISCUSSION ASSIGNMENTS AND MINICASES

1 Provide examples of products for each of these IPLC stages: (0) local innovation, (1) overseas innovation, (2) maturity, (3) worldwide imitation, and (4) reversal.

2 Given the implications of the IPLC theory, how should US innovating firms adjust their marketing strategies?

3 Why are US manufacturers unwilling to modify their products for overseas customers?

4 Is it practical to offer a world product? (NB: this term should be differentiated from a standardized product.)

5 Can standard marketing techniques (e.g., market segmentation) be used to market services locally and internationally?

NOTES

1 "Credit Due for Transparency," *Financial Times*, May 28, 2002.

2 "Eat Your Baby Food, Gramps," *Business Week*, March 3, 2003, 14.

3 Masashi Kuga, "Kao's Marketing Strategy and Marketing Intelligence System," *Journal of Advertising Research* 30 (April/May 1990): 20–5.

4 "Goldstar Is Burning Bright," *Business Week*, September 26, 1994, 129.

5 This section is based largely on Sak Onkvisit and John J. Shaw, "An Examination of the International Product Life Cycle and Its Application within Marketing," *Columbia Journal of World Business* 18 (fall 1983): 73–9.

6 "Solectron Gets 3-Year Deal with Lucent," *San José Mercury News*, March 29, 2002; and "Xerox to Transfer Work to Singapore," *San José Mercury News*, October 3, 2001.

7 "Rivals to Viagra Get Ready to Offer Stiff Competition," *Financial Times*, May 28, 2002; and "Firms' New Drug Will Challenge Viagra in Europe," *San José Mercury News*, March 8, 2003.

8 Imad B. Baalbaki and Naresh K. Malhotra, "Standardization versus Customization in International Marketing: An Investigation Using Bridging Conjoint Analysis," *Journal of the Academy of Marketing Science* 23 (summer 1995): 182–94.

9 Arnold Schuh, "Global Standardization as a Success Formula for Marketing in Central Eastern Europe?" *Journal of World Business* 35 (No. 2, 2000): 133–47.

10 Robert C. Christopher, *Second to None: American Companies in Japan* (New York: Crown, 1986).

11 Aron O'Cass and Craig Julian, "Examining Firm and Environmental Influences on Export Marketing Mix Strategy and Export Performance of Australian Exporters," *European Journal of Marketing* 37 (No. 3, 2003): 366–84.

12 "How to Compete," *San José Mercury News*, February 18, 1990.

13 "US Consumer Goods," *Export America* (August 2001): 18–23.

14 "Pillsbury Unlocks Japan by Doing as Japanese Do," *Chicago Tribune*, February 11, 1982.

15 "The Americanization of Toyota," *Business Week*, April 15, 2002, 52–54.

16 "Ford Attempts to Boost Its Sales by Rearranging Global Structure," *San José Mercury News*, October 16, 1999.

17 "Fired Up to Introduce New Ideas," *Financial Times*, December 10, 2002.

18 G. Tomas M. Hult, Bruce D. Keillor, and Roscoe Hightower, "Valued Product Attributes in an Emerging Market: A Comparison between French and Malaysian Consumers," *Journal of World Business* 35 (No. 2, 2000): 206–19.

19 Monty L. Lynn, Richard S. Lytle, and Samo Bobek, "Service Orientation in Transitional Markets: Does It Matter?" *European Journal of Marketing* 34 (No. 3, 2000): 279–98.

20 "Hong Kong SAR Projected to See Significant Effects from China's WTO Accession," *IMF Survey*, June 19, 2000, 207–08.

21 Josephine Ludolph, "Services: Exporting's Hidden Giant," *Export America* (May 2001): 14–16.

22 "How the War on Terror Is Damaging the Brain Pool," *Business Week*, May 19, 2003, 72–73.

23 Carlos A. Primo Braga, "The Impact of the Internationalization of Services on Developing Countries," *Finance & Development* (March 1996): 34–37.

24 Jennifer R. Moll, Susan Gates, and Lesley Quigley, "International Education and Training Services: A Global Market of Opportunity for US Providers," *Export America* (May 2001): 19–21.

25 M. Krishna Erramilli and C. P. Rao, "Service Firms' International Entry-Mode Choice: A Modified Translation-Cost Analysis Approach," *Journal of Marketing* 57 (July 1993): 19–38.

Chapter 11

Product strategies

Branding and packaging decisions

The protection of trademarks is the law's recognition of the psychological function of symbols.
Justice Felix Frankfurter, US Supreme Court

CHAPTER OUTLINE

PURPOSE OF CHAPTER

The purpose of this chapter is to acknowledge the strategic significance of branding and packaging and to examine some of the problems commonly faced by MNCs. Among the subjects discussed are brandless products, private brands, manufacturers' brands, multiple brands, local brands, worldwide brands, brand consolidation, brand protection, and brand characteristics. The strengths and weaknesses of each branding alternative are evaluated. The chapter also examines both mandatory and optional packaging adaptation. The emphasis of the chapter is on the managerial implications of both branding and packaging.

MARKETING ILLUSTRATION THE NAME GAME

Accor manages a network of worldwide hotels. Its Sofitel brand offers 160 prestige hotels in fifty countries. Its Novotel brand has international standards and good value and consists of 370 hotels in fifty-six countries. The Mercure brand, in contrast, has 740 mid-scale hotels in forty-three countries. The Coralia brand focuses on 200 resorts in thirty-five countries. The Ibis hotel chain of over 600 hotels in thirty-four countries offers simplicity, quality, and value for money. In the USA, Accor has recently reminded people that Motel 6 is an Accor hotel.

For decades, the name *Hyundai* was synonymous with South Korea's economic development. Due to its financial troubles, the government-controlled creditor banks have urged Hyundai Group, the nation's largest conglomerate, to spin off affiliates and unload assets. Hyundai Electronics Industries, one of the world's major computer chip makers, is the first major affiliate to distance itself by discarding the name of Hyundai. It has become Hynix Semiconductor.

Nestlé licenses its Kit Kat brand to Hershey for the US market. If Hershey is for sale but bought by someone else other than Nestlé, chances are good that Nestlé will take back the rights to Kit Kat. Since Kit Kat may be worth as much as $1 billion, it is likely that the other potential buyers will not want to pay as much without having the rights to the Kit Kat brand.

Among the top 100 global brands in terms of value, American brands claim eight of the top ten spots while dominating the list with sixty-two brands. The list is based on a detailed analysis of how a product's sales are driven by brand name, weighted for market leadership, stability, and ability to cross national borders, among other factors. Many of these global brands have been around for so long that many consumers are not aware of their origins. In surveys, many believe that Heineken is a German beer and that Nokia is a Japanese firm. They also do not realize that Haagen-Dazs and Estée Lauder were born in the USA. Even when consumers are aware of the origins of the brands, they are inclined to think of these brands as global rather than national. The top ten brands are: Coca-Cola, Microsoft, IBM, GE, Intel, Nokia, Disney, McDonald's, Marlboro, and Mercedes. Among the non-US brands, Samsung Electronics, SAP, L'Oréal, and Toyota have made the biggest gains in value.

Sources: "Kit Kat License Likely to Be Worth $1 Billion," *San José Mercury News*, July 27, 2002; "Brands in an Age of Anti-Americanism," *Business Week*, August 4, 2003, 68–78.

BRANDING DECISIONS

To understand the role of trademark in strategic planning, one must understand what a trademark is from a legal standpoint. According to the US Lanham Trade-Mark Act of 1947, trademark "includes any word, name, symbol, or device or any combination thereof adopted and used by a manufacturer or merchant to identify these goods and distinguish them from those manufactured or sold by others." If a trademark is registered for a service, it is known as a service mark (e.g., Berlitz).

A trademark can be something other than a name. Bibendum, the roly-poly corporate symbol, is Michelin's trademark in France, and it is known as Bi-bi-deng in China. It should be noted that the Michelin Man, a 100-plus-year-old mascot, seems recently to have lost some weight while becoming more muscular. Nipper, the familiar fox terrier sitting next to a phonograph along with the phrase "His Master's Voice," is RCA's official symbol. Other easily recognized logos include Ralph Lauren's polo player and Goodyear's wingfoot. Figure 11.1 shows the logos of General Foods' well-known brands. Figure 11.2, in contrast, shows the trademarks of multinational firms that have direct investment in Cyprus.

A trademark can be more than a name or logo. Harley Davidson tried unsuccessfully to register the sound of its heavy motorcycles as a trademark. H.J. Heinz Company had better luck in registering a color in England. While words and logos account for a vast majority of trademarks registered in England and while it is unusual for a food company to be granted a trademark on a color alone, the Trademarks Registry granted legal protection to Heinz Baked Beans' distinctive use of turquoise. The Trademarks Registry has determined that Heinz Baked Beans' turquoise has "achieved distinctiveness through use." As the number one brand of baked beans in the United Kingdom for generations, the product is an important part of the British culture, and almost everyone recognizes the turquoise can.[1]

Although companies spend millions of dollars developing logos, some are more effective than others. One study asked consumers to judge a company's image by looking at its name alone as well as with its logo. Motorola Inc., for example, received a positive score of 55 percent, meaning that the logo adds a sense of quality and trustworthiness. British Airways and Infiniti, on the other hand, received negative scores of −20 percent and −16 percent respectively. In the latter case, the logos, instead of being helpful, may actually hurt corporate image.[2]

A logo, when inappropriate, ineffective, or dated, should be modified. In the case of Audi, which wanted to further differentiate itself from its parent Volkswagen, replaced its corporate logo in 1995 with a new one featuring the four silver rings with the Audi name written underneath in red.

In many countries, branding may be nothing more than the simple process of putting a manufacturer's name, signature, or picture on a product or its package. Many US firms did precisely this in the old days, as illustrated by King Gillette's own portrait being used as a trademark for his Gillette razor-blades.

The basic purposes of branding are the same everywhere in the world. In general, the functions of a brand are to: (1) create identification and brand awareness, (2) guarantee a certain level of quality, quantity, and satisfaction, and (3) help with promotion. All of these purposes have the same ultimate goal: to induce repeat sales. The Spalding name, for example, has a great deal of marketing clout in Japan. In fact, a group of investors bought the company in 1982 because they felt that Spalding was the best-known name in sports in the free world and that the name was underused.

For American consumers, brands are important. Overseas consumers are just as brand-conscious – if not more so – because of their social aspirations and the social meanings that brand names can offer. Eastern European consumers recognize many Western brand names, including some that are unavailable in their countries. Among the most powerful brand names are Sony, Adidas, Ford, Toyota, Volvo, BMW, and Mercedes. When International

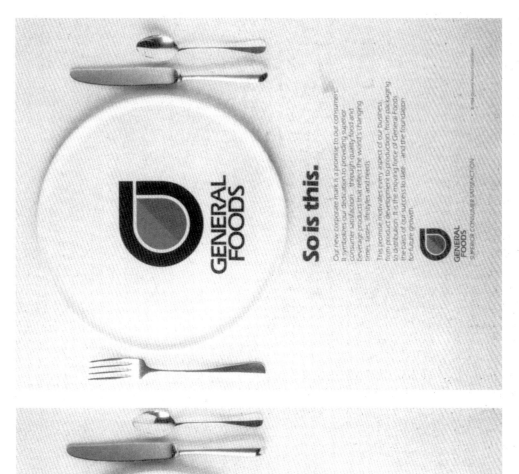

Figure 11.1 *General Food's registered trademarks and logos*

Source: Reprinted with permission of General Foods Corporation.

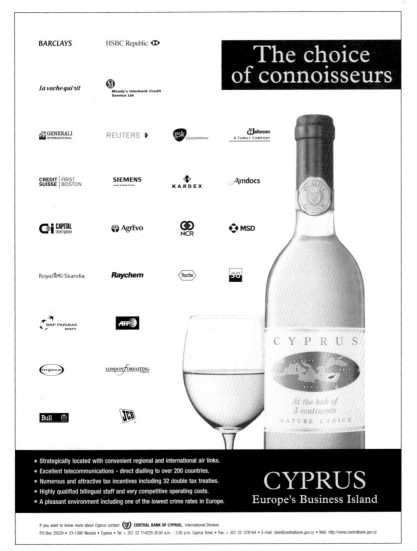

Figure 11.2
Trademarks and foreign direct investment

Source: Courtesy of Central Bank of Cyprus.

Semi-Tech Microelectronics Inc. acquired troubled SSMC Inc., the most important asset was probably the Singer trademark.

When a company is for sale, the remainder of the purchase price after deducting the fair value of the physical assets is called goodwill, "going concern value," or an intangible asset. In the case of service businesses, nearly all of the purchase price that companies generate tends to be goodwill. The brand has brand equity when there is value that is attached to that brand. Perhaps Coca-Cola's most valuable asset is its brand equity which is worth $39 billion.

Taking into consideration the importance of branding as a marketing tool, one would expect that corporate headquarters would normally have a major role in brand planning for overseas markets. As a component of an MNC's marketing mix, branding is the area in which standardization appears to be relatively high. Westinghouse, for example, requires its Westinghouse do Brasil affiliate to use the common logo, resulting in all the MNC's Brazilian companies using the familiar circled W symbol in their promotion programs. Thus brand centralization is a common practice.

One study found that international marketing managers considered some cultural and socioeconomic conditions of foreign countries in making global brand image strategy decisions.[3] If the markets are similar, a firm may be able to use the standardization strategy by extending its brand image theme to the other markets. However, when markets differ in cultural uncertainty avoidance, individualism, and national socioeconomics, managers tend to employ the image customization strategy.

Other than merely using the same brands worldwide, MNCs are also interested in creating a global identity via some degree of standardization of a corporate visual identity system (CVIS) in their multinational operations. As in the case of British companies operating in Malaysia, they have increasingly adopted a standardized CVIS, stimulated in part by global restructuring, merger, or acquisition.[4] Their reasons include aiding the sale of products and services, creating an attractive environment for hiring employees, and increasing the company's stature and presence.

BRANDING LEVELS AND ALTERNATIVES

There are four levels of branding decisions: (1) branding versus no brand, (2) private brand versus manufacturer's brand, (3) single brand versus multiple brands, and (4) local brands versus worldwide brand. Figure 11.3 shows an outline of the decision-making process when branding is considered; Figure 11.4 provides a branding model for decision making; and Exhibit 11.1 lists the advantages of each branding alternative.

Branding vs. no brand

To brand or not to brand, that is the question. Most products are branded, but that does not mean that all products should be. Branding is not a cost-free proposition due to the added costs associated with marking, labeling, packaging, and legal procedures. These costs are especially relevant in the case of commodities (e.g., salt, cement, diamonds, produce, beef, and other agricultural and chemical products). *Commodities* are "unbranded or undifferentiated products which are sold by grade, not by brands." As such, there is no uniqueness, other than grade differential, that may be used to distinguish the offerings of one supplier from those of another. Branding is then probably undesirable because brand promotion is ineffective in a practical sense and adds unnecessary expenses to operations costs. The value of a diamond, for example, is determined by the so-called four Cs – cut, color, clarity, and

Figure 11.3 Branding decisions

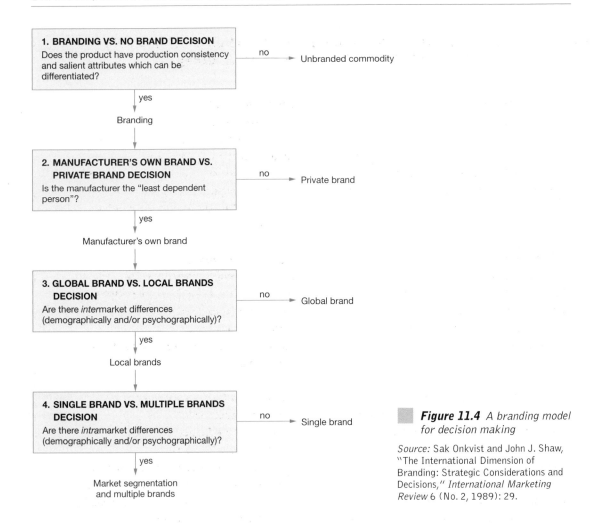

1. BRANDING VS. NO BRAND DECISION
Does the product have production consistency and salient attributes which can be differentiated?

— no → Unbranded commodity

yes ↓

Branding

2. MANUFACTURER'S OWN BRAND VS. PRIVATE BRAND DECISION
Is the manufacturer the "least dependent person"?

— no → Private brand

yes ↓

Manufacturer's own brand

3. GLOBAL BRAND VS. LOCAL BRANDS DECISION
Are there *inter*market differences (demographically and/or psychographically)?

— no → Global brand

yes ↓

Local brands

4. SINGLE BRAND VS. MULTIPLE BRANDS DECISION
Are there *intra*market differences (demographically and/or psychographically)?

— no → Single brand

yes ↓

Market segmentation and multiple brands

Figure 11.4 *A branding model for decision making*

Source: Sak Onkvist and John J. Shaw, "The International Dimension of Branding: Strategic Considerations and Decisions," *International Marketing Review* 6 (No. 2, 1989): 29.

carat weight – and not by brand. This is why DeBeers promotes the primary demand for diamonds in general rather than the selective demand for specific brands of diamonds.

On the positive scale, a brandless product allows flexibility in quality and quantity control, resulting in lower production costs along with lower marketing and legal costs.

The basic problem with a commodity or unbranded product is that its demand is strictly a function of price. The brandless product is thus vulnerable to any price swing or price cutting. Farmers can well attest to this vulnerability because prices of farm products have been greatly affected by competition from overseas producers. Yet there

are ways to remove a company from this kind of cut-throat competition.

Branding, when feasible, transforms a commodity into a product (e.g., Chiquita bananas, Dole pineapples, Sunkist oranges, Morton salt, Holly Farms fryers, and Perdue fryers). A product is a "value-added commodity," and this bundle of added values includes the brand itself as well as other product attributes, regardless of whether such attributes are physical or psychological and whether they are real or imaginary. The 3M company developed brand identity and packaging for its Scotch videotapes for the specific purpose of preventing them from becoming just another commodity item in the worldwide, price-sensitive market.

EXHIBIT 11.1   ADVANTAGES OF EACH BRANDING ALTERNATIVE (FROM MANUFACTURER'S VIEWPOINT)

No Brand

Lower production cost

Lower marketing cost

Lower legal cost

More flexibility in quality and quantity control (i.e., possibility of less rigidity in control)

Good for commodities (undifferentiated items)

Brand

Better identification

Better awareness

Better chance for product differentiation

Better chance for repeat sales

Possible premium pricing (i.e., removal from price competition)

Possibility of making demand more price inelastic

Private Brand

Ease in gaining dealers' acceptance

Possibility of larger market share

No promotional hassles and expenses

Good for small manufacturer with unknown brand and identity

Manufacturer's Brand

Better control of products and features

Better price due to more price inelasticity

Retention of brand loyalty

Better bargaining power

Assurance of not being bypassed by channel members

Multiple Brands (in single market)

Utilization of market segmentation technique

Creation of excitement among employees

Creation of competitive spirits

Avoidance of negative connotation of existing brand

Gain of more retail shelf space

Retention of customers who are not brand loyal

Allowance of trading up or down without hurting existing brand

Single Brand (in single market)

Better marketing impact

Permitting more focused marketing

Brand receiving full attention

Reduction of advertising costs due to better economies of scale and lack of duplication

Elimination of brand confusion among employees, dealers, and consumers

Good for product with good reputation and quality (halo effect)

Local Brands

Legal necessity (e.g., name already used by someone else in local market

Elimination of difficulty in pronunciation

Allowance for more meaningful names (i.e., more local identification)

Elimination of negative connotations

Avoidance of taxation on international brand

Quick market penetration by acquiring local brand

Allowance of variations of quantity and quality across markets

Worldwide Brand

Better marketing impact and focus

Reduction of advertising costs

Elimination of brand confusion

Good for culture-free product

Good for prestigious brand

Easy identification/recognition for international travelers

Good for well-known designer

Branding makes premium pricing possible because of better identification, awareness, promotion, differentiation, consumer confidence, brand loyalty, and repeat sales. According to one Supreme Court decision (No. 649, May 4, 1942, Mishawaka Rubber and Woolen Manufacturing Co. vs. S. S. Kresge, 53 USPQ 323), "The owner of a mark exploits this human propensity by making every effort to impregnate the atmosphere of the market with the drawing power of a congenial symbol. . . . Once established, the trademark owner has something of value."

Although branding provides the manufacturer with some insulation from price competition, a firm must still find out whether it is worthwhile to brand the product. In general, the following prerequisites should be met:

- Quality and quantity consistency, not necessarily the best quality or the greatest quantity.
- The possibility of product differentiation.
- The degree of importance consumers place on the product attribute to be differentiated.

As an example, Nike's unique designs (e.g., the waffle sole) allowed the company to differentiate its brand from others and to become the top-rated brand among serious joggers.

Private brand vs. manufacturer's brand

Branding to promote sales and move products necessitates a further branding decision: whether the manufacturer should use its own brand or a distributor's brand on its product. Distributors in the world of international business include trading companies, importers, and retailers, among others; their brands are called private brands. Many portable TV sets made in Japan for the US market are under private labels. In rare instances, Japanese marketers put their brands on products made by US companies, as evidenced by Matsushita's purchases of major appliances from White and D&M for sale in the USA. The Oleg Cassini trademark is put on the shirts actually made by Daewoo.

Even though it may seem logical for a distributor to carry the manufacturer's well-known brand, many distributors often insist on their own private brands for several reasons. First, a distributor may be able to create a unique product by bundling or unbundling product attributes and then adjusting the price to reflect the proper value.

Carrefour, a French retail giant, sells some 3000 in-house products at prices about 15 percent lower than national brands. J. Sainsbury PLC, a British retailer, has a private brand that is able to win 30 percent of the detergent market, moving it ahead of Unilever's Persil and just behind Procter & Gamble's Ariel which is the market leader. It is believed that private-label products now account for one-third of supermarket sales in the United Kingdom and a quarter in France.

Second, a private brand is a defensive strategy which guarantees that a distributor is not bypassed by its supplier. For example, Ponder and Best, after losing the Rolleiflex and Olympus distributorships, came up with its own brand of photographic products, Vivitar.

Third, distributors can convert fixed production costs into variable costs by buying products made by others. Sperry's products are made by more than 200 manufacturers (e.g., Sperry's personal computer is manufactured by Mitsubishi). With this practice, Sperry is able to save cash and research-and-development expenses. Of course, it is important for a distributor with a private brand to have a reliable supplier.

The fourth and perhaps the most important reason for a distributor's insistence on a private brand is due to brand loyalty, bargaining power, and price. In spite of the lower prices paid by the distributor and ultimately by its customers, the distributor is still able to command a higher gross margin than what a manufacturer's brand usually offers. The lower price may also be attributed to the distributor's refusal to pay for the manufacturer's full costs. A distributor may want to pay for the manufacturer's variable costs but not all of the fixed costs. Or a distributor may want to pay for production costs only but not the manufacturer's promotional expenditures, because a distributor gets no benefit from the goodwill of a manufacturer's advertised brand. If a firm has any problem with the supplier (manufacturer), it has the flexibility of switching to another supplier to make the identical product, thus maintaining brand loyalty and bargaining power without any adverse effect on sales. RCA, for example, switched from Matsushita to Hitachi for its portable units of VCRs.

There are a number of reasons why the strategy of private branding is not necessarily bad for the manufacturer. First, the ease in gaining market entry and dealers' acceptance may allow a larger market share overall while contributing to offset fixed costs. Toronto-based Cott Corp., once an obscure regional bottling company, has emerged as a leading private-label player by being involved with dozens of store-brand sodas. It sells more than one billion servings of soft drinks to Wal-Mart Stores Inc. under the label of Sam's American Choice. Cott bottles Sainsbury Classic Cola for J. Sainsbury PLC which is the top food retailer in Britain. In the USA, Safeway Inc. is one of Cott's largest customers. Safeway feels that it can give consumers value while earning better margins than on national brands.

Second, there are no promotional headaches and expenses associated with private branding, thus making the strategy suitable for a manufacturer with an unknown brand. Suzuki cars are sold in the USA under the GM Sprint brand name. Ricoh's facsimile machines are sold under AT&T's well-known name. Brother has had virtually no name recognition because it has marketed its many products under the private labels of US major retail chains; to secure recognition, it has begun to mount a major campaign.

Third, a manufacturer may judge that the sales of its own product are going to suffer to a greater or lesser degree by various private brands. In that case, the manufacturer may as well be cannibalized by one of those private brands made by the manufacturer.

There are also reasons why private branding is not good for the manufacturer. By using a private brand the manufacturer's product becomes a commodity, at least to the distributor. To remain in business and retain sales to the distributor, the manufacturer must compete on the basis of price, since the distributor can always switch suppliers. Cott Corp., for example, lost its contract to brew its President's Choice beer for Loblaw Cos., Canada's top supermarket, when John Labatt Ltd. paid Loblaw $28 million for the contract.

By not having its own identity, the manufacturer can be easily bypassed. Furthermore, it loses control over how its product should be promoted – this fact may become crucial if the distributor does not do a good job in pushing the product. For example, Mitsubishi, which manufactures Dodge Colt and Plymouth champ for Chrysler, felt that its products did not receive Chrysler's proper attention. As a result, Mitsubishi began to create its own dealer network and brand identity (e.g., Mitsubishi Mirage). Ricoh used to sell copiers in the USA only under such private brands as Savin and Nashua, whose sales lagged. After switching to its own brand name in 1981, Ricoh's sales increased tenfold to take second place in unit sales behind only Canon.

The manufacturers' dilemma is best illustrated by Heinz's experience in the United Kingdom, where consumer recognition for its brand is stronger than in any other country in the world. Whereas Campbell Soup and Nestlé's Crosse & Blackwell make some products under private labels to accommodate giant supermarkets' insistence, Heinz produces products only under its own brand because, as the largest supplier of canned foods there, it has the most to lose. To preserve its long-term market leadership at the expense of short-term earnings, Heinz has held down prices, stepped up new product introductions, launched big capital-spending programs, and increased advertising. Heinz does make private-label merchandise in the USA, where private brands account for 10 percent of its US sales. Its logic is that the slow growth of US private labeling does not pose a serious threat as it does in the United Kingdom.

Clearly, the manufacturer has two basic alternatives: (1) its brand, or (2) a private brand. Its choice depends in part on its bargaining power. If the distributor is prominent and the manufacturer itself is unknown and anxious to penetrate a market, then the latter may have to use the former's brand on the product. But if the manufacturer has superior strength, it can afford to put its own brand on the product and insist that the distributor accept that brand as part of the product.

The hypothesis of the "least dependent person" can be quite applicable in determining the power of the manufacturer and that of its dealer. The stronger party is the one with resources and alternatives, and that party can demand more because it needs the other party less. The weaker party needs the other partner more due to a lack of resources and/or alternatives, and thus the weaker must give in to the "least dependent" party. In most cases, the interests of both parties are interdependent, and neither party may have absolute power. For instance, Kunnan, a maker of a high-quality tennis racket, lost some of its well-known customers when they began doing their own manufacturing. When those companies discovered later that they could not produce so well in terms of cost and quality, they came back to Kunnan for the private-brand manufacturing.

Private branding and manufacturer's branding is not necessarily an either/or proposition: a compromise may often be reached to ensure mutual coexistence. If desired, both options can be employed together. Michelin, for instance, is world renowned for its own brand, and most people do not realize that Michelin also makes tires for Sears and Venture. Sanyo, another major international brand, is relatively unknown in the USA because it has relied heavily on private-label sales to Sears and other big companies. To rectify this identity problem, Sanyo has been pushing its own name simultaneously.

Manufacturers cannot treat private brands as simply generic competitors. After all, retailers that carry the private labels are both customers and competitors at the same time.[5] The popularity of private brands varies from country to country. In England, the key factors that have contributed to the evolution of retail brands within British grocery retailing are changing the basis and use of retail power in the distribution channel, centralization of management activities, and appreciation of

what constitutes retail image. British grocery retailers have successfully managed these factors. As a result, their retail brands are regarded by consumers as being as good as, if not better than, the established manufactured brands.[6]

The discussion so far has focused primarily on the practice of distributors or middlemen having their own private brands manufactured by the other companies. A new trend in the high-technology arena is for manufacturers with top brands to have their products manufactured by someone else. IBM, the company responsible for the worldwide acceptance of personal computers, has stopped making desktop PCs in most parts of the world. It has signed a three-year, $5 billion agreement with Sanmina-SCI, a contract manufacturer, to make the IBM-brand PCs.[7]

High-technology firms have been relying more on contract manufacturers and original design manufacturers (ODMs). Quanta Computer Inc. is a contract manufacturer that does all the manufacturing and logistics.[8] This Taiwan company makes Apple's Titanium G4 PowerBook. It also takes care of just about everything in less than forty-eight hours for HP's notebook unit, from hardware to software and from testing the final product to shipping it to customers. Compaq Computer did not design nor make its iPaq Pocket PC. This handheld PC and its system of interchangeable accessory sleeves are actually the products of HTC, an ODM in Taiwan. Samsung, LG Electronics, and Acer are ODMs that make products for others as well as their own brands. Samsung's Q10 notebook is almost indistinguishable from Dell Latitude X200 and Gateway 200. In the end, customers cannot rely on tangibles to tell these brands apart and must trust such intangibles as warranty and technical support.

The branding and manufacturing strategy mentioned above illustrates the potential benefits and problems of private branding. By putting their brands on the computers made by outside suppliers, the brand owners are able to take care of the gap in their product lines quickly and economically while solving their inventory problems. However, this new strategy will make product differentiation more difficult. Well-informed consumers may not see a good reason to pay extra for these brands.

Single brand vs. multiple brands

When a single brand is marketed by the manufacturer, the brand is assured of receiving full attention for maximum impact. However, a company may choose to market several brands within a single market based on the assumption that the market is heterogeneous and thus must be segmented. Consequently, a specific brand is designed for a specific market segment. In the case of Intel, it spent several hundred million dollars to promote Centrino, a new brand for wireless computing. Figure 11.5 shows Anheuser-Busch's various brands for the US market.

The watch industry provides a good illustration for the practice of using multiple brands in a single market for different market segments. Bulova is a well-known brand, as are the Accutron and Caravelle brands. Citizen, in its attempt to capture the new youth and multiple-watch owners' market, traded down to include a new brand called Vega. Likewise, Hattori Seiko is well known for its Seiko brand, which is sold at the upper-medium price

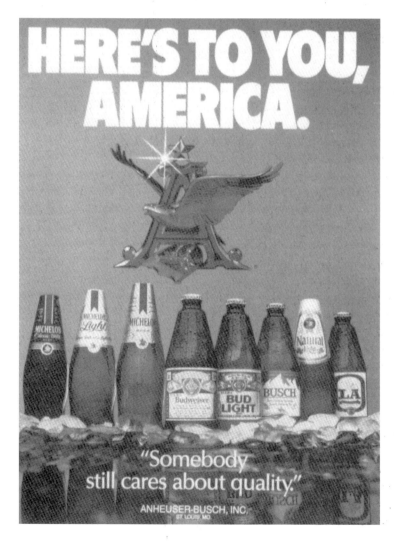

Figure 11.5
Anheuser-Busch's multiple brands for a single market

Source: Reprinted with permission of Anheuser-Busch, Inc.

319

range in better stores; to appeal to a more affluent segment, the firm traded up with the Lassale name. Seiko's strategy is to deliberately divorce the Seiko and Lassale names, once used together in the public mind, with the gold-plated Lassale line and the karat-gold Jean Lassale line. Lassale watches have Seiko movements but are made only in the USA and Western Europe in order to curb parallel trading, and they are distributed only through jewelers and department stores. The company also trades down, with Pulsar, Lorus, and Alba for Asia. Swatch Group Ltd. has more than 50 percent of the Swiss watch industry. Swatch owns a number of well-known brands that include Omega, Longines, Tissot, and Calvin Klein. It recently spent $75 million to acquire the French watchmaker Breguet.[9]

Multiple brands are suitable when a company wants to trade either up or down because both moves have a tendency to hurt the firm's main business. If a company has the reputation for quality, trading down without creating a new brand will hurt the prestige of the existing brand. By the same rationale, if a company is known for its low-priced, mass-produced products, trading up without creating a new brand is hampered by the image of the existing products. Casio is perceived as a manufacturer of low-priced watches and calculators, and the name adversely affects its attempt to trade up to personal computers and electronic musical instruments. To overcome this kind of problem, Honda uses the Acura name for its sporty cars so that Acura's image is not affected by the more pedestrian Honda image.

China has a long way to go before it can become synonymous with quality in the eyes of Western consumers. Not surprisingly, Chinese companies have downplayed the origin of their products. In the case of TCL Corp., a TV and cellular-phone maker, it acquired the bankrupt German TV maker Schneider in 2002. Although the TCL name has done well in Asia, the company believes that it needs a better known brand to succeed in Europe. To this end, Schneider, a century-old brand, should do better.[10]

Local brands vs. worldwide brand

When the manufacturer decides to put its own brand name on the product, the problem does not end there if the manufacturer is an international marketer. The possibility of having to modify the trademark cannot be dismissed. The international marketer must then consider whether to use only one brand name worldwide or different brands for different markets or countries. To market brands worldwide and to market worldwide brands are not the same thing.

A single, worldwide brand is also known as an international, universal, or global brand. A Euro-brand is a slight modification of this approach, since it is a single product for a single market (i.e., the European Union and the other Western European countries), with an emphasis on the search for intermarket similarities rather than differences.

For a brand to be global or worldwide, it must, by definition, have a commonly understood set of characteristics and benefits in all of the markets where it is marketed.[11] Coca-Cola is a global brand in the sense that it has been successful in maintaining similar perceptions across countries and cultures. However, most other brands do not enjoy this kind of consistency, thus making it debatable whether a global brand is a practical solution.

A worldwide brand has several advantages. First, it tends to be associated with status and prestige. Second, it achieves maximum market impact overall while reducing advertising costs because only one brand is pushed. Bata Ltd., a Canadian shoe marketer and retailer in ninety-two countries, found out from its research that consumers generally believed Bata to be a local concern, no matter the country surveyed. The company thus decided to become an official sponsor of World Cup soccer in order to enhance Bata's international stature. For Bata and others, it is easier to achieve worldwide exposure for one brand than it is for multiple local brands. Too many brands create confusion and fragmentation.

Third, a worldwide brand provides a convenient identification, and international travelers can easily recognize the product. There would be no sense in creating multiple brands for such international products as *Time* magazine, American Express credit card, Diner's Club credit card, Shell gasoline, and so on.

Finally, a worldwide brand is an appropriate approach when a product has a good reputation or is known for quality. In such cases, a company would be wise to extend the brand name to other products in the product line. This strategy has been used extensively by GE. In another case, 3M perceived commonalities in a consumer demographics and market development worldwide; in response, it devised a "convergence marketing" strategy to develop global identity for its Scotch brand of electronic recording products, whose design displays prominently the Scotch name and a globelike logo.

Global consumer culture positioning (GCCP) is a positioning tool that suggests one pathway through which a brand may be perceived by consumers as "global." GCCP is a construct that associates a brand with a widely understood and recognized set of symbols which constitute an emerging global consumer culture. A significant number of advertisements employ GCCP (instead of positioning the brand as a member of a local or specific foreign consumer culture).[12]

ACNielsen's Global Mega Brand Franchises report uses a number of criteria to identify mega brands. A megabrand must be available in at least fifteen out of fifty countries that account for 95 percent of the global economic output. It must be marketed under the same name in at least three different product categories in three or more regions. Based on these criteria, the megabrands are dominated by the highly extendable personal care and cosmetics manufacturers and by food and drinks manufacturers. The queen of megabrands is Nivea, a brand owned by the German consumer products group Beiersdorf. This skin-care brand is a huge success, and the brand has been extended to at least nineteen product categories (shampoos, after-shave, wrinkle lotion, and bath foam) in every part of the world. In contrast, Coke as a brand does not have much of this power of extendability.[13]

The use of multiple brands, also known as the local or individual approach, is probably much more common than many people realize. Discover Financial Services, while using the Discover name in the USA, issues a consumer credit card in England under the Morgan Stanley Dean Witter. In the case of Unilever, its fabric softener is sold in ten European countries under seven names. Due to decentralization, the multinational firm allows country managers to choose names, packages, and formulas that will appeal to local tastes. More recently, the company, while keeping local brand names, has been gradually standardizing packaging and product formulas.

There are several reasons for using local brands. First, developing countries resent international brands because the brands' goodwill is created by an advertising budget that is much greater than research-and-development costs, resulting in no benefit derived from research and development for local economies. In addition, local consumers are forced to pay higher prices for advertising and goodwill, benefiting MNCs but hindering the development of local competitive capacity. Such resentment may explain why India's ministries, responding to domestic soft drink producers' pressure, rejected Pepsi's 35 percent Pepsi-owned joint venture. Some governments have considered taxing international brands or limiting the use of such brands, as in the case of South Korea, which has considered placing restrictions on foreign trademarks intended for domestic consumption.

Second, when the manufacturer is unable to ensure uniform product quality across countries, it should consider local brands. Third, when an existing brand is difficult to pronounce, a new brand may be desirable. Sometimes, consumers avoid buying a certain brand when it is difficult to pronounce because they want to avoid the embarrassment of a wrong pronunciation.

Fourth, a local brand is more easily understood and more meaningful for local consumers. By considering foreign tastes and preferences, a company achieves a better marketing impact. Post-it note pads made by 3M are marketed as Yellow Butterflies in France. Grey, an international advertising agency, worked with Playtex to create appropriate names for Playtex's brassières in different languages. The result was Wow in England and Traumbügel (dream wire) in Germany. Translation may also make a brand more meaningful. This approach is sometimes mistaken for a single-brand approach when in fact a new brand is created. Close-Up (toothpaste) was translated as Klai-Chid (literally meaning "very close") in Thailand; the translation retained the meaning and the logo of the brand as well as the package design.

Fifth, a local brand can avoid a negative connotation. Pepsi introduced a non-cola under the Patio name in America but under the Mirinda name elsewhere due to the unpleasant connotation of *patio* in Spanish.

Sixth, some MNCs acquire local brands for quick market penetration in order to save time, not to mention money, which otherwise would be needed to build the recognition for a new, unknown brand in local markets. Renault would have been foolish to abandon the AMC (American Motors) name after a costly acquisition. Thus Renault 9, for example, became AMC Alliance in the USA. Chrysler subsequently bought AMC from Renault, one reason being AMC's coveted Jeep trademark.

Seventh, multiple brands may have to be used, not by design but by necessity, due to legal complications. One problem is the restrictions placed on the usage of certain words. Diet Coke in countries that restrict the use of the word *diet* becomes Coke Light. Antitrust problems can also dictate this strategy. Gillette, after acquiring Braun A.G., a German firm, had to sign a consent decree not to use the name in the US market until 1985. The decree forced Braun to create the Eltron brand, which had little success.

The eighth and perhaps most compelling reason for creating new local brands is because local firms may have already used the names that multinational firms have been using elsewhere. In such a case, to buy the right to use the name from a local business can prove expensive. Unilever markets Sure antiperspirant in the United Kingdom but had to test

market the product under the Trust name in the USA, where Sure is Procter & Gamble's deodorant trademark.

In an interesting case, Anheuser-Busch bought the American rights to the Budweiser name and recipe from the brewer of Budweis in Czechoslovakia; Budejovicky Budvar Narodni Podnik, the Czech brewer, holds the rights in Europe. Operating from the town of Ceske Budejovice, known as Budweis before World War I, this brewer claims exclusive rights to the Budweiser name in the United Kingdom, France, and several European countries. Courts have ruled that both companies have the right to sell in the United Kingdom, but Anheuser-Busch has to use the Busch name in France and the corporate name in other parts of Europe.

Ninth, a local brand may have to be introduced due to price control. This problem is especially acute in countries with inflationary pressures. Price control is also one reason for the growth of the so-called gray marketers, as the phenomenon contributes to price variations among countries for the same product. Thus, instead of buying a locally produced product or one from an authorized distributor/importer, a local retailer can buy exactly the same brand from wholesalers in countries where prices are significantly lower. A manufacturer will have a hard time prohibiting importation of gray market goods, especially in EU countries where products are supposed to be able to move freely. Parallel trading can be minimized by having different national brands rather than only a worldwide brand.

As mentioned above, brand standardization is a common strategy. Companies tend to brand globally but advertise locally. Interestingly, although the McDonald's logo is one of the most recognizable trademarks in the world, McDonald's has changed its advertising logo for Quebec, perhaps the only market in the world which receives this special treatment. The most well-known logo in Quebec is J'M. This is a play on "j'aime" which means "I love" in French.[14]

The strategy of using a worldwide brand is thus not superior (or inferior) to using multiple local brands. Each strategy has its merits and serves its own useful functions. This is where managerial judgment comes in. Unilever, for example, considers consumer responses to a particular brand mix. It uses an international brand for such products as detergents and personal products because common factors among countries outweigh any differences. Food products, however, are another story. Food markets are much more complex due to variations in needs and responses to different products. The southern half of Europe uses mainly oil for cooking rather than margarine, white fats, or butter. The French more than the Dutch consider butter to be an appropriate cooking medium. German home makers, when compared to British home makers, are more interested in health and diet products. Soup is a lightweight precursor to the main dish in Great Britain but can almost be a meal by itself in Germany. Under such circumstances of preferential variations, the potential for local brands is greatly enhanced.

When creating local brand names in the multi-lingual international market, companies have three translation methods to consider: phonetic (i.e., by sound), semantic (i.e., by meaning), and phonosemantic (i.e., by sound plus meaning). The effectiveness of translation depends on the emphasis of the original English name and the translation method used previously for brand names within the same category. When the phonetic naming method is used, brand-name evaluations are more favorable for names that emphasize an English word than for those names that emphasize a Chinese word.[15]

BRAND CONSOLIDATION

Frequently, it is either by accident or lack of coordination that multiple local brands result. Despite the advantages offered by the multiple-brand strategy, it may be desirable to consolidate multiple brands under one brand when the number of labels reaches the point of being cumbersome or confusing. National BankAmericard used to issue cards around the world under twenty-two names before consolidating them all under the Visa umbrella. Unilever markets a vast array of beauty, home-care,

and food products under numerous names. Some of its well-known brands include: ice cream (Breyer's, Good Humor), soap (Dove, Caress, Lever 2000, Lifebuoy), hair care (Suave, ThermaSilk), oral care (Close-Up, Pepsodent, Aim), fragrances (Calvin Klein, Elizabeth Arden, Elizabeth Taylor), and personal care (Vaseline, Q-Tips, Pond's). However, this portfolio of 1600 brands, although well recognized, has proven to be unmanageable. So Unilever has decided to focus mainly on some 400 brands while eliminating up to 75 percent of its products.[16]

Another way of consolidating the brand franchise is simply to drop weak brands. Assuag-SSIH weeded out all but its most prominent watch brands. Its Eterna brand, for example, was never marketed in the USA, and that brand was eventually sold to another company.

Brand consolidation on a global scale is a strategy that has been hotly debated. As in the case of Scott Paper Co., the company felt that the Scott name, just like Coca-Cola, should command respect all over the world.[17] In addition, global branding would allow Scott to use common advertising messages internationally while saving costs. So the company has been phasing out local brand names in its eighty national markets. Even Andrex, a top-selling toilet tissue in England, will suffer the same fate, thus diluting or destroying the goodwill that has been earned.

When a marketer wants to change brands or consolidate them under one brand in order to unify all marketing efforts, the process is complex and extremely costly on an international scale. Although a unified brand across frontiers provides cost savings by eliminating duplication of design and artwork, production, distribution, communications, and other related issues, such a change is fraught with pitfalls and, if not well planned and executed, can cause more problems than it solves. Nestlé uses a gradual, evolutionary process in preparing its European brands for 1992. Its package–design unification involves having the Nestlé name appear along with the local brand. The Nestlé name will be gradually enlarged over a period of four or five years until it replaces the local brand names entirely.

Another kind of problem presents when a brand is well known but the corporate name is not, complicating communication for the company. In this situation, it is probably easier to change the corporate name to fit the better-known brand, a strategy used by Sony, Aprica, Olympus, and Amoco.

Nissan's name change, in comparison, was risky because it followed an opposite route. Nissan's half-hearted entry into the US market led to the use of the Datsun name to avoid embarrassment in case the effort failed. However, the company was also unhappy that the proud corporate name was not as widely recognized as its Datsun brand, which enjoyed an 85 percent recognition rate in the USA (compared to 10 to 15 percent for Nissan). The company decided to institute a worldwide brand by phasing out Datsun and phasing in Nissan. Some critics questioned the move because the change cost Nissan $150 million. Furthermore, years of goodwill gained from the Datsun name would be lost. To minimize this problem, both Nissan and Datsun names appeared together at first. Its initial TV commercials and print advertisements emphasized that Datsun was a product of Nissan.

It is debatable whether the corporate name and the product's brand name should even be the same. When the name is the same, a brand that performs poorly or gains notoriety through bad publicity hurts the corporate image as well, since the images of the corporation and the product are so intertwined. Firestone is a prime example of how a brand could damage the same corporate name due to the accidents caused by its tires. The strategy is even riskier for fashion products because fashion comes and goes. Using the same name, however, is a relatively safe strategy and should work well if a firm has good quality control and the reputation of its nonfashion products has withstood the test of time.

Brand consolidation is never an easy process, especially when well-known brands have to be replaced. Because of BP's acquisition of Amoco, BP Amoco has rebranded Amoco gas stations to erase the Amoco name from all 9000 stations in the USA. The decades-old Amoco torch has been replaced by a new, lower-case BP logo and an eighteen-point green-and-yellow sun. The remodeling of all 19,000 BP stations worldwide is expected to cost up to $4.5 billion over four years. The 1725 recently acquired Arco stations are keeping the Arco name.[18]

Figures 11.6 and 11.7 show how Agere Systems and Wyeth promote their new corporate names. In the case of Unilever, it has to deal with complications related to its effort to replace its Jif brand with the Cif brand (see Marketing Strategy 11.1).

BRAND ORIGIN AND SELECTION

Brand names can come from a variety of sources, such as from a firm's founders (e.g., Francois Michelin, Albert G. Spalding, Pierre Cardin, and Yves St. Laurent), places (e.g., Budweiser), letters and numbers (e.g., IBM), and coined words (e.g., Ikea based on a combination of the initials of the Swedish-born founder, Ingvar Kamprad, with those of the farm, Elmtaryd, and the village, Agunnaryd, where he grew up).

Sometimes, it is easier simply to purchase an existing brand from another company. Hong Kong's Universal International bought Matchbox, a British toy car maker. W. Haking enterprises, another Hong Kong company, acquired the Ansco name from GAF, and most Americans do not realize that the brand of Haking's low-priced cameras is actually a Hong Kong brand. North American Philips (NAP) bought the Schick shaver trade name. Underscoring the value of this name, Remington even filed a complaint alleging that the Schick name enabled NAP to avoid spending $25 million needed to launch a new shaver to supplement the Norelco line.

Brand selection is far from being an exact science, as illustrated by the origins of many successful brands. Gabrielle Chanel liked the scent of the fifth sampled bottle in 1921. Feeling that 5 was a pretty number, she named the perfume Chanel No. 5. Denmark's Lego Group, well known for its interlocking plastic bricks, is the world's fifth-largest toy maker with annual sales of about $1 billion. The founder, Ole Kirk Kristiansen, named

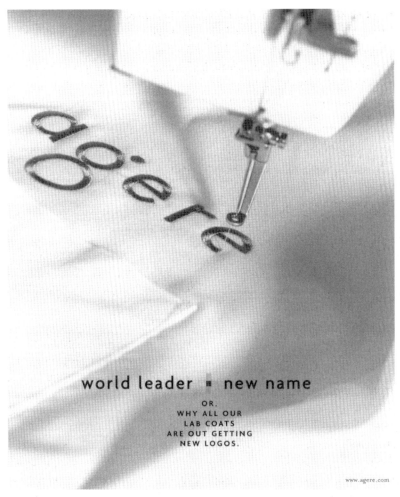

world leader ▪ new name

OR,
WHY ALL OUR
LAB COATS
ARE OUT GETTING
NEW LOGOS.

www.agere.com

Once we were Lucent's Microelectronics Group. Today we're Agere Systems. A company that has put generations of innovations to work. A world leader in optical components and communications chips. An organization with the focus, expertise and global resources to lead the way in communications technology. Agere Systems. Same smart people. New lab coats.

© 2001 Agere Systems Inc. Agere, the Agere Systems logo and How communications happens are trademarks of Agere Systems Inc.

agere systems
How communications happens™

Figure 11.6
Agere Systems and a corporate name change

his company Lego which is a combination of the Danish words leg godt, meaning "play well."

More recently, brand selection has shifted away from being an art and is becoming more of a science. There are several companies that specialize in creating brand and corporate names, and they use computer programs that can run prefixes, suffixes, and other word combinations.

However, it must be pointed out that marketers often do not have the luxury of picking and choos-ing names they like. Nor is it always feasible to conduct marketing research to investigate the appropriateness of a name. In Brazil, Philip Morris chose the Galaxy name without marketing research because it happened to be one of the company's reg-istered names. NUMMI's use of the Nova trademark for cars produced jointly with Toyota and General Motors was due in part to GM's ownership of the Nova brand name.

325

*The future
of medicine has
a new name.*

Wyeth

Announcing the new name of American Home Products Corporation.

As it has grown over its 76-year history, American Home Products has become one of the world's most advanced pharmaceutical companies, with a rich portfolio of innovative medicines.

We've built a research powerhouse unique in its ability to discover and develop novel treatments across three platforms: pharmaceuticals, vaccines and biotechnology. Equally important, we link these efforts to maximize our potential to find solutions to health care problems around the world.

To better reflect our focus and mission, we have selected Wyeth – a name that expresses our pharmaceutical heritage – as our Company's new corporate name. Our symbol on the New York Stock Exchange changes to WYE.

In addition to prescription medicines, Wyeth will continue to bring you leading non-prescription brands as well as innovative products in the field of animal health.

With a proud past and an exciting pipeline to the future, we at Wyeth renew our commitment to a single mission: Leading the way to a healthier world.

WYE
LISTED
NYSE

Pharmaceuticals. Vaccines. Biotechnology. All add up to **Wyeth**®

©2002 Wyeth   www.wyeth.com

Figure 11.7 *Wyeth: a corporate name change*

BRAND CHARACTERISTICS

A good brand name should possess certain characteristics, and such characteristics are thoroughly discussed in most advertising and marketing textbooks. In essence, a brand should be short, distinctive, easy to pronounce, and able to suggest product benefits without negative connotations. In the international arena, these qualities are also relevant.

In selecting a brand name, a marketer should first find out whether a brand name has any negative connotation in the target market. One company in the business of brand-name selection felt that

Probe was an inappropriate name for Ford's car, having an unpleasant gynecological reference. One reason why Japan's Daihatsu Motor Co. Ltd. did not succeed in the USA may have to do with its name. According to research, many American consumers thought that the company was Korean, and it was a negative association.

An international brand name should reflect the desired product image. Toward this end, consumer perception should be taken into account. For instance, worldwide consumers usually perceive French perfumes to be superior, and French-sounding names for this kind of product may prove beneficial.

MARKETING STRATEGY 11.1   JIF VS. CIF

Unilever PLC, the Anglo-Dutch consumer goods giant, has a bulging brand portfolio, and it wants to get rid of 1800 marginal brands so that it can focus on some 400 top brands (e.g., Lipton tea and Calvin Klein fragrances). Its Persil laundry detergent in Britain is called Omo elsewhere. Another interesting case is its household cleanser sold in sixty countries. The company uses either Jif or Cif, depending on ease of pronunciation in a local language. Thus it was launched as Jif in England in 1974, and Malaysia and Australia also got Jif. But in France and thirty-eight other countries, it is Cif. To add to the complexity, the brand was called Vim in Canada, Viss in Germany (for trademark reasons), and Vif in multilingual

Switzerland. Neither Jif nor Cif is sold in the USA where Procter & Gamble markets Jif peanut butter. To simplify its brand names sold in various countries, Unilever has changed the name of Jif to Cif in the UK, even though Jif was the company's best-selling household cleanser there. Interestingly, the two names have traded places before. In 1998, both Jif in Greece and Vif in Switzerland became Cif – without much trouble. The company did not anticipate much problem in England either. The British focus groups were unimpressed by the name change; they neither loved nor hated the new name.

Source: "Unilever Renames Cleanser to Simplify Brand," *Asian Wall Street Journal*, December 28, 2000.

Likewise, good watches are perceived to be made in Switzerland, toiletries in the USA, machinery and beers in Germany, and so on. If appropriate, brands should reflect such images. Russian-sounding names may be used to position a vodka brand positively. Smirnoff originated in the Soviet Union but has been made in the USA for decades – a fact not known by many Americans.

Marketers may want to consider foreign branding which is a strategy of pronouncing or spelling a brand name in a foreign language. Foreign branding, by triggering cultural stereotypes, may influence product perceptions and attitudes. As shown in one experimental study, a brand name's French pronunciation affects the perceived hedonism of the products as well as attitudes toward the brand name and the brand. Even with the presence of direct sensory experience, French branding still changes perceptions of a product.[19]

One way of creating a desired image is to have a brand name that is unique or distinctive. Exxon has this quality. Aprica, a status-symbol stroller, is also unique in several respects. In choosing the name, Kenzo Kassai, the company's owner, wanted something cute like "apple" for his folding stroller. During a trip to Italy, he found *apri* – an appropriate name

for something that opens and closes. As "stroller" in Japanese is translated as "baby car," the *ca* syllable (for "car") is a natural ending. In effect, Aprica is a blend of English, Italian, and Japanese, meaning "open to the sun."

A unique name often renders itself to graphic design possibilities, another desirable feature of a trademark. Exxon was chosen because of its distinctiveness, usefulness in work markets, and graphic design possibilities. After rejecting Hot-Line and Sound-About for not being appealing, Sony selected Walkman because of the distinctive logotype with two legs sticking out from the bottom of the letter *A* in *walk*.

An international product should have an international brand name, and this name should be chosen with the international market in mind. When possible, the name should suggest significant benefits. Although Emery Air Freight ships everything large and small anywhere in the world, its name gave no indication of this advantage. To overcome a secretary's fear of shipping a letter to foreign countries with a carrier specializing in freight, the corporate name was changed to Emery Worldwide. Not wanting the trademark to be closely identified with USA, US Rubber adopted Uniroyal to reflect

327

its diverse businesses around the world. The former French-born chairman of Revlon viewed Amoresse as unsuitable for a fragrance for the international audience; consequently, the name was changed to Jontue.

One way of making a brand name more international is by paying special attention to pronunciation. Many languages do not have all the alphabet characters, and the English language is no exception. The Spanish alphabet does not include the letter w, and the Italian language has no j, k, w, or y. Exhibit 11.2 examines the vowels and consonants that pose pronunciation problems to the Chinese.

Stenographers can easily see why many American words are misunderstood overseas because shorthand notations are based on how a word is pronounced and not on the way it is spelled. In general, any prefix, suffix, or word containing such letters as ph, gh, ch, and sh invites difficulty. Phoenix sewing machines provide a good example – it is inconceivable to many foreign consumers how the brand can be pronounced fe-nix and not pe-nix or fo-nix. It is difficult to understand why the o and not the e is silent in this case. Also, if the o is silent, why should it be in there in the first place? By the same token, people in many countries do not make any distinction, as far as pronunciation is concerned, between the following pairs: v and w; z and s; c and z; and ch and sh. A similar lack of distinction often exists with the trio of j, g, and y. The letter c in English words can be confusing because it can be pronounced like an s, as in the words audience and fragrance, or like a k, as in the words cat and cost. The letter y also poses some problems because it can sound like an a at one time and an i at another. Consider the hair product Brylcream. Foreign consumers may think that the e is silent and that the y should sound like a long i. A simple test could have easily revealed any pronunciation difficulties. Figure 11.8 shows how Hoechst tried to overcome the pronunciation difficulty while producing a promotional message at the same time.

Finally, the legal aspect of branding definitely cannot be overlooked. A name that is similar to other firms' trademarks should be avoided. Toyota's Lexus was sued in 1988 by Lexis, which is Mead

EXHIBIT 11.2 "A BRIEF GUIDE TO A PRONUNCIATION OF ROMANIZED CHINESE"

There are four Romanized Chinese consonants which cause pronunciation problems. Here is a guide to pronouncing them accurately:

- c equals the *ts* of *tsar* or i*ts*; thus "cai" (finance) sounds like "tsai"
- q equals the *ch* of *Ch*ina or *ch*ile; thus *Qin* (a Dynasty) sounds like *chin*
- x equals the *sh* of *sh*ine or *sh*eet; thus xi (west) sounds like *shee*
- zh equals the *j* of *J*im or *j*ig; thus Zhang (a surname) sounds like Jang

Chinese vowels are broader and longer than American vowels, otherwise they are very close in pronunciation, except for the Chinese *e* as in the names Hebei and Henan. The Chinese *e* is somewhat like the *o* of *other*.

Unless otherwise indicated, two Chinese vowels placed next to one another are pronounced as one sound, i.e. as a dipthong. The sister state of Illinois, Liaoning, is a two syllable word – *lyao-ning*.

Chinese surnames come first. The given names are not hyphenated in modern Chinese. Thus Huan Zhirong (the Chinese consul general) should be addressed as Mr. Huang.

Sometimes, Chinese, especially those from Beijing, have a tendency to add an *r* sound at the end of certain words. Don't be confused by it. It is analogous to a Harvard *r*.

Source: US Department of Commerce.

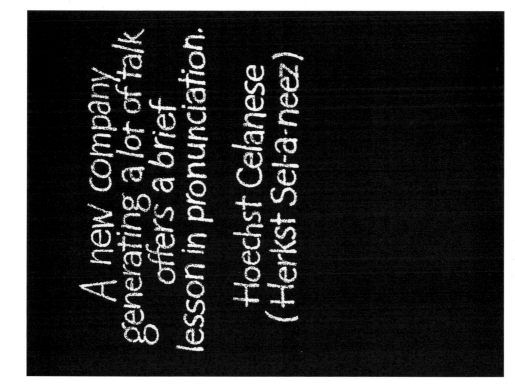

The recent merger of American Hoechst and Celanese has made our new name the subject of more and more conversations.

That's to be expected.

After working together for 25 years, we've joined forces to create one of the most exciting science and market driven chemicals—pharmaceuticals—fibers—advanced materials companies in the U.S.

Last year our combined sales totalled $4.6 billion, and with an annual R&D budget of over $1 billion backing us, we will be in an even better position to develop and market a broader range of products and services.

All of which should be enough to keep people talking about us—even if our name (again, that's pronounced Herkst Sel-a-neez) doesn't fall trippingly off the tongue.

Hoechst Celanese

Hoechst ⬣

Hoechst Celanese Corporation, Route 202-206 North, Somerville, NJ 08876

Figure 11.8 *Overcoming a pronunciation difficulty*

Source: Reprinted with permission of Hoechst Celanese Corporation

Data Central Inc.'s information retrieval service. Lexus was originally prevented from using the name nationally in the USA until it won a decision from an appeals court. Likewise, Altima Systems Inc., a California computer business, wanted to stop Nissan from also using the name before finally reaching a confidential agreement in 1992. Directed Electronics Inc., another California automobile security company, owns the name "Viper" for its line of automobile security alarm systems. A legal challenge followed when Chrysler started using the name for its Dodge car. Both sides reached an out-of-court settlement in 1992, agreeing to coexist.

BRAND PROTECTION

The job of branding cannot be considered done just because a name has been chosen. The brand must also be protected (see Marketing Ethics 11.1 and It's the Law 11.1). The first protective step is to obtain trademark registration (see It's the Law 11.2). Because of the cost involved, it may be neither practical nor desirable to register the name in all countries, especially in places where demand seems weak. It is inexcusable, however, not to do so in major markets. Even Queen Elizabeth II has registered her two private homes (Sandringham in

Norfolk and Balmoral Castle in Scotland) as trademarks so that she can sell her own merchandise under the brand names of Sandringham and Balmoral. The names have been registered with the British Trade Marks Registry and represent the first time the Queen has exploited the names of her houses for commercial purposes.[20]

There are international arrangements that simplify the registration process. The **Paris Convention (International Convention for the Protection of Industrial Property)** is the most significant multilateral agreement on trademark rights because it establishes reciprocity, which allows a foreign trademark owner to obtain the same protection in other convention member countries as in the owner's home country. Although preventing discrimination against non-nationals, the degree of protection varies with individual national laws. In the case of the **Madrid Convention**, nationals of the participating countries can have simultaneous trademark filing among all member countries. The **Trademark Registration Treaty (TRT)** allows a company to file for trademark protection with the International Bureau of the World Intellectual Property Organization (WIPO) without being required, as in the case of the Madrid Agreement, to have a prior home registration.

MARKETING ETHICS 11.1 THE "BUCKS" STOP HERE

Starbucks Corp. is known for its round green logo, and the logo has the words "Starbucks Coffee" in block white letters against a green background. Starbucks filed a temporary injunction against Doutor Coffee, a Japanese competitor, claiming that consumers were confused by a similar logo. Doutor uses an oval-shaped green logo and signage for its Excelsior Café chain, and the logo also uses block white letters that say Excelsior Café Espresso against a green background. While Starbucks has a picture of a goddess (Seiren) in white against a black background, Excelsior Café has a red, white, and green picture of a steaming cup of coffee in the middle of its logo,

against a black background.

HaidaBucks Café is a modest diner in the remote islands off frigid Canadian coasts. The last thing it expected was to receive a letter from Starbucks threatening a lawsuit. Starbucks alleged that the eatery's name posed a challenge to its trademark. While Starbucks found the word "Haida" to be acceptable, it claimed that "Bucks" is a clear association with its trademark. Bucks refers to young men in the culture of First Nations, and one of the diner's owners is a member of Haida First Nation.

Source: "Starbucks Warns Diner Over Name," *San José Mercury News*, April 17, 2003.

IT'S THE LAW 11.1   YOUR APPLE OR MINE?

Apple Corps Ltd. started out as Apple Records in the mid-1960s. The company was formed by the Beatles to distribute their music, and the trademark was registered in nearly all countries where the Beatles' music was sold.

Steve Jobs and Steve Wozniak formed Apple Computer in 1977. The founders chose the Apple name because they wanted their company to be listed ahead of rival Atari Corp. in the telephone book. Apple Computer's logo is a multicolored apple with a bite taken out of it. Apple Records, on the other hand, has a logo which is a shot of the exterior of a green apple and the inside of an apple sliced in half.

Apple Corps asserted its right to the trademark and wanted to collect royalties on Apple Computer's computer sales. The lengthy negotiations led to an agreement in 1981. Apple Computer agreed to pay an undisclosed sum for the right to use the Apple name on apparel, personal computers and related equipment "that didn't synthesize or reproduce music."

The legal problem resurfaced in 1984 when the Macintosh computer was introduced because the Mac had a semiconductor chip that made it possible for the machine to record and synthesize sound. In 1988, Apple Corps claimed that the Macs were musical instruments and demanded royalties from Apple Computer.

Apple Computer counterattacked by filing legal actions in many countries to have Apple Corps' trademark cancelled or declared invalid based on the time that has elapsed since the breakup of the Beatles. Apple Corps, however, was able to obtain an injunction from the British court to stop Apple Computer challenging the validity of Apple Corps' trademark country by country. According to Apple Corps' argument, the 1981 settlement required the computer firm to respect the validity of the Beatles' trademark in other countries and to recognize British law as the ultimate authority on the matter. Apple Corps wanted tens of millions of dollars in royalties, interest, and legal fees. While continuing its legal fight, Apple Computer wrote off $38 million in 1991 as a reserve for a lawsuit against it by Apple Corps. Later, the two companies signed an agreement which specified the rights each would have to use the Apple trademark.

Now that Apple Computer has got into the music business in a big way with its iTunes Music Store and iPod music player, Apple Corps is back to sue for another trademark infringement. Apple Computer issued a written statement: "Unfortunately, Apple and Apple Corps now have differing interpretations of this agreement and will need to ask a court to resolve this dispute."

Sources: "You Say It's Your Trademark," *San José Mercury News*, October 27, 1990; "Apple Against Apple," *San José Mercury News*, February 23, 1989; "Let It Be? Not on Your Life," *Business Week*, August 5, 1991, 31; "The Long and Winding Trademark Dispute," *San José Mercury News*, September 13, 2003.

Other treaties include the **Central American Arrangement and the African Intellectual Property Organization (OAPI)**. The **Arrangement of Nice [France] Concerning the International Classification of Goods and Services to Which Trade Marks Apply** is the most widely used trademark classification system. Adopted by the USA and some sixty countries, the system has thirty-four product and seven service categories.

The USA has two registers. The **Principal Register** provides federal protection, a benefit not provided for by the Supplemental Register. A trademark owner who is unable to place a mark on the Principal Register may be able to do so later when the mark has acquired distinctiveness over the years. The **Supplemental Register** is still useful for US marketers who must obtain registration in the home country before becoming eligible to do the same in host countries.

IT'S THE LAW 11.2   TRADEMARK REGISTRATION

Practically anyone can file for and own a registered trademark for almost every good or service imaginable. A registered trademark provides public notice as to the origin and source of a product or service and establishes a property interest.

Costs

Costs for filing a single class trademark application vary, but usually range from $800 to $2,000 for a smooth filing with few obstacles to publication and registration. To minimize your costs, bear in mind the range of products or services you wish to use the trademark with and a good idea of what you want the trademark to look like. In addition, if there is a design element to your mark, have the image on a transferable medium, such as a disk.

Most important to cutting costs is to have some idea whether you are the only user of the proposed trademark. In fact, the most common but easily avoidable legal obstacle is when someone else has previously filed for, or holds, a registration to the same mark as yours for the same or similar goods or services. To aid your attorney, you can easily conduct what is called a "common law" search by searching the US Patent and Trademark Office (USPTO) online trademark database (www.uspro.gov), surfing the Internet, checking phone books, trade journals and other product listings, such as the *Thomas Register*.

Filing process

The trademark application process begins by filing with the appropriate government authority. The process is called "prosecuting a trademark" and entails communication between the trademark authority and your representatives. Following the filing, the application is reviewed by an examiner. Once the examiner finds that the application has no defects, or all defects have been properly addressed, the application is passed for publication. It is rare for a trademark application to have no defects. If detects are found, the examiner issues an official report or "action to the attorney of record" detailing the defects and statutory deadline for response. In many countries, an examiner is obligated by law to issue at least two actions before making a rejection final. When the corrective actions are not sufficient and the rejection by the examiner is made final, only an appeal will get the mark reviewed again.

However, if all defects are resolved, the application is passed for publication, which may take several months. Depending on the country, the mark is published in the official trademark reporter or a time period allowed for the public to submit comments. If comments concerning your mark are received, they will be considered before the mark can continue. If the mark passes publication unscathed, it will move on to registration.

Once registered, the mark can be safely marked as registered by using the registration symbol or the ® as a superscript to your mark. This demarcation gives notice to the world that you are rightfully using the word, phrase or design as a lawful trademark for the goods or services to which it is attached.

Maintenance of trademark

Continued maintenance of your trademark registration is an important responsibility of trademark ownership. Careful attention should be paid to deadlines for such filings, since the dates differ from jurisdiction to jurisdiction. Many businesses not only maintain the registration of their trademarks in use, but also actively protect their marks from improper use by other entities. These trademark owners do so by hiring law firms or "trademark watch" firms to ensure that no one except authorized users is using their trademarks in conjunction with certain goods and services.

Source: Jaylene M. Sarracino, "Small Business Primer to Filing for Trademarks in a Foreign Country," *Export America*, March 2001, 16–17.

The courts have developed a hierarchy of registration eligibility. Moving from highly protectable to unprotectable, these categories are: fanciful (Kodak), arbitrary (Camel), suggestive (Eveready), descriptive (Ivory), and generic (aspirin). In general, for a trademark to be eligible for registration, it must be "distinctive" or, if not, must be "capable of being distinctive."

A **fanciful mark** is a term coined solely for the purpose of identifying a particular product. An **arbitrary mark** is an ordinary word that is used on a product in a totally nondescriptive way. A **suggestive mark** subtly indicates something about a product, and consumers must thus use their imagination to understand that the mark represents a product's characteristic. A **descriptive mark**, in contrast, immediately conveys, without requiring use of imagination, a product's characteristic, quality or feature. Interestingly, pharmaceutical companies are quite good at creating fanciful marks. Based on the total cost of direct-to-consumer advertising, the top ten are: Nexium, Vioxx, Celebrex, Viagra, Allegra, Advair Diskus, Zocor, Paxil, Zoloft, and Zyrtec.

Although a valid brand name can suggest or imply a product's benefits, it cannot merely describe the fact or the product. A suggestive mark is registrable, but a descriptive name is not legally acceptable unless it has acquired distinctiveness through long-continued exclusive use. Even if the descriptive mark might somehow have been registered, the mark can still be cancelled for lack of distinctiveness. Of course, it is not always easy to distinguish a suggestive mark from a descriptive mark. Weedless, as a lawn-care product, may be either suggestive or descriptive.

A generic term merely identifies the product rather than the maker of that product. As such, it receives no protection and cannot function as a trademark. Labatt, a Canadian brewer, attempted to win US trademark protection for the name "ice beer" by claiming that it invented the manufacturing process. Anheuser-Busch Cos. sued and was awarded $5 million in punitive damages when a St. Louis jury ruled that ice beer was not a trademark.

The policy of the US government is to contest applications for generic trademarks abroad (e.g., Wash-and-Wear, or such foreign variants as Lava y Listo). If allowed to be registered, such trademarks could create significant problems in international trade. A US exporter, for example, will find it impossible to use common product names in advertising abroad without the risk of being sued for trademark infringement, or the exporter may find that the goods are refused entry into a foreign country altogether.

Most countries do not require the display of a trademark in a specific language or the translation of that trademark. However, to be registered, a foreign trademark may have to be written in a local language in such a way as to give the equivalent pronunciation. China requires a trademark to be displayed in Chinese characters. Coca-Cola, depending on a group of Chinese characters used, may have the right sound but the wrong interpretations. The original registered characters (Koo-kah- koo-lah, when translated, mean either "a wax-fattened mare" or "bite the wax tadpole." The company then varied the new characters slightly to read Kah-koo-kah-lah, which translates as "May the happy mouth rejoice."

Unlike patents, trademark registrations can be renewed indefinitely. To keep registrations in force, trademark owners are required to pay an annual tax or maintenance fee in most countries (though not in the USA). The technical requirements must also be observed. Some countries (e.g., Australia) allow the fees to be paid by a foreign trademark owner residing abroad or by the owner's representative/agent in a third country. In other countries (e.g., Brazil), the fees may be paid by only a local or domestically domiciled representative/agent.

Politics may make registration and maintenance of a trademark difficult. Most US companies have lost their trademarks in Vietnam due to invalidation of those trademark registrations which were obtained in South Vietnam before 1975 and which were not re-registered in the Socialist Republic of Vietnam by 1982. While McDonald's registered its trademark in South Africa in 1968, the company did not open a restaurant there due to international economic sanctions. According to South African law, a foreign company could lose its right for not using the trademark for five years. As a result, when McDonald's finally entered the market in 1995, a local court ruled that the company did not have an exclusive right to its various trademarks. In fact, Dax Properties, which opened its own MacDonald's hamburger outlet there selling such things as Little Mac, even tried to bar the real McDonald's from using the name. Under international pressure, South Africa passed a new law in 1995 to conform to international law and to offer protection to world-recognized names.

Registration by itself does not offer automatic or complete protection. Other legal requirements must be met in order to maintain copyright. Use is a universal requirement. In China, publication, advertising, and exhibiting a product with the trademark all constitute use. To establish use in most countries, a manufacturer must sell or make that product in the intended market.

The legal procedure to acquire and maintain a trademark varies from country to country. Whereas some countries recognize registration but not prior use, other countries do exactly the opposite. In most countries, a company can register a mark subject to cancellation if that mark is not used or continued to be used within a reasonable period of time. The failure to register, even with actual prior use, may force the company to forfeit its rights to another person who registers the same mark later but before anybody else. The first user can be held to ransom in this way.

Going back as far as the 1870s, trademark rights in the USA were based on the "no trade, no trademark" premise. Until recently, the US Patent and Trademark Office was practically alone in the world in requiring a potential mark owner to put the trademark into interstate or foreign commercial use first before it could even be registered. The US Trademark Act of 1946 (the Lanham Act) has been updated, and several changes have been made. One change involves intent-to-use trademark applications; the change permits companies to file an application based on projected future use. Now a declaration of a bona fide intent to use the mark in commerce is sufficient. A trademark registration is subsequently issued when the applicant files a statement showing evidence of actual use of the mark in commerce. To demonstrate use of the mark, specimens in the form of containers, labels, tags, or displays associated with the goods must be filed. There is no penalty for reserving names that are never actually used. The second change is the constructive-use provision. For goods or services specified in the Principal Registration, an applicant receives a nationwide priority effect as though the applicant had used the mark throughout the nation as of the filing date. The definition of "use of the mark" has been changed to require that use be in the ordinary course of trade, and token use is prohibited. To reserve a mark, the intent-to-use application becomes the sole avenue. Finally, the term of federal registration has been reduced from twenty to ten years to clear out trademarks no longer used.

Although a single use of mark may be adequate to register the mark, a company must exploit the mark commercially in good faith to prevent its loss.[21] The rationale is to prevent a company from abusing the law to its advantage when the owner has no intention of using the trademark other than to bar potential competitors with genuine interests from using a competitive tool. An example is Snob perfume, a name owned in France by Le Galion, a French company, and in the USA by Jean Patou, an American company. Le Galion was able to challenge Patou's rights successfully because Patou (1) sold only eighty-nine bottles of Snob perfume in twenty-one years, (2) never supported the product with promotion, and (3) made only $100 in gross profit. Thus Patou was suspected of registering the name just to bar a potential competitor from entering the market.

The quickest way to lose a trademark is by not using it. Failure to use a registered trademark for three years terminates all rights in China. In the case of South Korea, nonuse after a period of one year is grounds for cancellation of registrations. In Central and South America, due to inflation, currency devaluations, and political uncertainty, a manufacturer may find it difficult to maintain operations there. However, the company risks losing its trademark if it stops the business activities. It is thus wise to consider some temporary licensing agreements with local firms until the situation improves. By doing so, brand awareness and trademark ownership are sustained. This is exactly what some international firms did while being forced to retreat from South Africa at the height of the anti-apartheid movement.

Another caveat is to make sure that the brand does not become so generic that it is identified with the product itself. A loss of trademark can occur if the name becomes part of the language; that is, when members of the consuming public use the brand name to denote the product or its common function rather than the producer of the product. Yo-Yo (a foreign trademark), Roquefort cheese, and Champagne are proprietary names in France but generic names in the USA. The reverse is true of Ping-Pong, a US-registered trademark that is a generic name in China for table tennis. In Japan, there is no word for vulcanized rubber, and the Goodyear name is used to identify this product. Cyanamid has had to fight to keep Formica from denoting all plastic laminate or laminated wood. Bayer's loss of the Aspirin trademark in the USA was due partly to the anti-German sentiment during World War II and partly to its failure to create a generic word for the product, whose chemical name is acetylsalicylic acid. Bayer would have been on more solid legal ground if it had established a generic term for household use (e.g., headache tablet or pain relief tablet).

To avoid this problem of a brand name becoming a generic name, a firm must never use the brand name in a generic sense (i.e., using it as a verb or adjective to denote the product). Promotional materials should reflect the proper usage, and the public should be informed accordingly. Willy Motors always emphasizes that Jeep is a trademark and uses an advertisement to inform consumers not to use Jeep as an adjective (e.g., jeeplike, jeepy, or jeep-type), a verb (e.g., jeep around or go jeeping), a plural (e.g., jeeps), or a generic without

the capital J. In the Philippines, however, Jeep has become a generic name, and people there use privately owned small buses known as jeepnies for transportation. Jeep is now a registered trademark of DaimlerChrysler.

It is not legally sound to combine trademarks. It may seem unlikely that Honda will have trouble with its Honda Accord and Honda Civic marks, but the fact remains that the second mark (Accord, Civic) is in jeopardy through inference that it is the product's generic name. The public may thus assume that manufacturers other than Honda also make Accord and civic cars.

Tabasco provides a good illustration of the various legal issues that have been discussed. Unlike Worcestershire sauce and soy sauce, Tabasco is a properly registered trademark. It is the name of a river and a state of southern Mexico. One may question how a geographic name could ever have been accepted for registration, since the name is not distinctive. The answer is that the name was capable of being distinctive and did become so because it has been used continuously and exclusively by the manufacturer for a long time. Thus, the name has become associated with this particular company. Furthermore, Tabasco is the official botanical name of the hot red peppers, but those peppers were actually named for the sauce (i.e., product) and not the other way around. Tabasco is aware that consumers might use the brand to denote the product (i.e., hot sauce) rather than the marker of the product. It has thus hired two legal firms to police the world for any misappropriation of the trademark. Its vigorous enforcement enabled it to defeat B.F. Trappey Sons' legal bid for the right to use the word.

To hold the legal rights to a registered trademark is one thing, but to prevent others from illegally using it through counterfeiting is another matter altogether. In fact, counterfeiters, though acknowledging the illegality of the activity, may see nothing morally wrong with the activity. In China, the basic cultural values relevant to counterfeiting are neutral – it is not a violation to copy someone's ideas. Great artists' works, for example, are copied as a sign of respect.

335

To prevent the importation into the USA of counterfeits and, to a lesser extent, gray market goods, a trademark owner whose mark is accepted for the Principal Register can register a mark with the US Customs Service for the purpose of preventing entry of goods from bearing an infringing mark. The Customs Service distinguishes colorable imitation from counterfeit trademark. A **colorable imitation** is a mark so similar as to be confused with a registered mark, whereas a **counterfeit trademark** is basically indistinguishable from a registered trademark. Colorable imitations are treated more leniently in that they can still gain entry as long as the objectionable mark is removed. However, in the case of counterfeits, the Customs Reform and Simplification Act of 1978 allows the seizure as well as forfeiture to the government of any articles bearing a counterfeit trademark.

PACKAGING: FUNCTIONS AND CRITERIA

Much like the brand name, packaging is another integral part of a product. Packaging serves two primary purposes: functional and promotional. First and foremost, a package must be functional in the sense that it is capable of protecting the product at minimum cost.

If a product is not manufactured locally and has to be exported to another country, extra protection is needed to compensate for the time and distance involved. A country's adverse environment should also be taken into account. When moisture is a problem, a company may have to wrap pills in foil or put food in tin boxes or vacuum-sealed cans. However, the type of package chosen must be economical. In Mexico, where most consumers cannot afford to buy detergents in large packages, detergent suppliers found it necessary to use plastic bags for small packages because cardboard would be too expensive for that purpose.

For most packaging applications, marketers should keep in mind that foreign consumers are more concerned with the functional aspect of a package than they are with convenience. As such, there is usually no reason to offer the great variety of package sizes or styles demanded by Americans. Plastic and throw-away bottles are regarded as being wasteful, especially in LDCs, where the labor cost for handling returnables is modest. Non-American consumers prefer a package to have secondary functions. A tin box or a glass bottle can be used after the product content is gone to store something else. Empty glass containers can be sold by consumers to recoup a part of the purchase price.

From the marketing standpoint, the promotional function of packaging is just as crucial as the functional aspect. To satisfy the Japanese preference for beautiful packaging, Avon upgraded its inexpensive plastic packaging to crystalline glass. Similarly, BSR packs its product into two cartons, one for shipping and one for point-of-purchase display, because Japanese buyers want a carton to be in tip-top condition. The successful campaign for Bailey's Irish Cream in the USA included a fancy gold foil box package that promotes this whiskey-based drink's upscale image. In any case, packaging does not have to be dull. Novel shapes and designs may be used to stimulate interest and create excitement.

MANDATORY PACKAGE MODIFICATION

A package change may be either mandatory or at the discretion of the marketer. A mandatory change is usually necessitated by government regulations. Sometimes, it is for safety and other reasons. Sometimes, packaging regulations are designed more for protection against imports than for consumer protection.

Several countries require bilinguality (e.g., French and English in Canada, and French and Flemish in Belgium). This requirement may force the manufacturer to increase package size or shorten messages and product name, since a bilingual package must have twice the space for copy communications. In some cases, modification is dictated by mechanical or technical difficulties, such as the unavailability of certain typographic fonts or good advertising typographers.

In many cases, packaging and labeling are closely related. Packages may be required to describe contents, quantity, manufacturer's name and address, and so on in letters of designated sizes. Any pictorial illustration that is used should not be misleading. In Singapore, certain foods must be labeled to conform to defined standards. When terms are used that imply added vitamins or minerals (e.g., enriched, fortified, vitaminized), packages must show the quantities of vitamins or minerals added per metric unit. In addition, if the product is hazardous in any way, marketers should adopt the United Nations' recommendations for the labeling and packaging of hazardous materials.

Exporters of textile products must conform to countries' varying regulations. Spain has specific and extensive requirements concerning fiber content, labeling, and packaging. In addition to its flammability requirements, Sweden's labeling regulations include size, material, care, and origin. Venezuela requires all packaged goods to be labeled in metric units while specifically prohibiting dual labeling to show both metric and nonmetric units. Germany wants the description of fiber content to be in German, but labeling for Denmark must be in Danish or kindred. In the case of France, care labeling (if used) must meet an International Standardization Organization (ISO) directive.

As discussed in Chapter 10, countries' different measurement systems may necessitate some form of product modification, and necessity applies to packaging as well. Product, toiletries included, cannot be sold in Australia in ounces. The Australian regulations require products to be sold in metric numbers, in increments of 25 mm. In Germany, liquid products must be bottled or packaged in standard metric sizes. Interestingly, the USA, a nonmetric nation, has the same requirement for liquor products.

The European Union's Directive on packaging and packaging waste, taking effect in 1994, harmonizes the national measures on the management of packaging waste among the member states while ensuring that restrictions on packaging do not create trade barriers. Setting targets for both recovery and recycling of waste, the Directive requires the member states to ensure that 50 to 65 percent of all waste is recovered for waste stream and that 25 to 45 percent is recycled.[22]

OPTIONAL PACKAGE MODIFICATION

Optional package modification, although not absolutely necessary, may have to be undertaken for marketing impact or for facilitating marketing activities. Through accidents and history, users in many countries have grown accustomed to particular types of packages. Mayonnaise, cheese, and mustard come in tubes in Europe, but mustard is sold in jars in the USA. Orange bottles are popular in the Netherlands. While non-Dutch beer drinkers all over the world readily recognize a green Heineken bottle, the domestic Heineken beer comes in a brown bottle. Alfred H. Heineken designed the famous green bottle and logo with the red star and the black banner bearing the brand name.

In selecting or modifying a package, a marketer should consider local conditions related to purchasing habits. Products conventionally sold in packs in the USA are not necessarily sold that way elsewhere and may require further bulk breaking. This phenomenon is partly the result of lower income levels overseas and partly the result of a lack of unit pricing, which makes it difficult for buyers to see any savings derived from the purchase of a bigger package. Foreign consumers may desire to buy one bottle of beer or soft drink at a time instead of buying a six-pack or eight-pack. Likewise, one cigarette, not the whole pack, may be bought in a purchase transaction.

For Unilever, the $50 billion Anglo-Dutch consumer goods multinational has mastered the art of selling products in tiny packages costing a few cents each. Its Indian subsidiary, Hindustan Lever Ltd., began selling single-use sachets of Sunsilk shampoo for 2 to 4 cents. These mini-packages now account for half of Hindustan Lever's $2.4 billion in sales in India. Unilever's Rexona brand deodorant sticks sell for 16 cents and up, and are very popular in India, the Philippines, Bolivia, and Peru. A nickel-size Vaseline package and a tube containing enough Close-Up toothpaste for twenty brushings sell for about 8 cents each. In Nigeria, Unilever sells 3-inch-square packets of margarine that don't need refrigeration.[23]

In addition to conditions of use, other cultural factors should be taken into consideration since such factors often determine and influence consumer preference. Although the UHT (ultra-high temperature) process for packaging milk and juices in unrefrigerated cartons has long been popular in Europe and Asia, it took quite a while for American consumers who were accustomed to fresh products to start accepting aseptic packaging.

Symbols and colors of packages may have to be changed to be consistent with cultural norms. If packages are offensive, they must be made more acceptable if the product is to be marketed successfully. For example, the controversial Jovan packages, with their sexual connotations, can prove to be too suggestive in some countries. In Japan, since manufacturers of condoms have female customers in mind, packaging tends to be cute.

Sometimes, it is difficult to tell whether package modification is mandatory or optional. Take the case of Germany's "green dot" packaging laws. Since the early 1990s, Germany has required manufacturers, distributors, and retailers to take back sales packaging (used packaging materials) either directly from the consumer's domicile or from designated local collection points. Those manufacturers who participate in the "green dot" program are exempted from this requirement. The green dot is the symbol which has been adopted by the Duales System Deutschland GmbH (DSD – Dual System of Germany), a corporation established in 1990, with over 400 participating companies (shareholders). The DSD collects a fee from the participating manufacturers for the right to display the green dot symbol on the products. The revenue is used to finance local packaging waste collection and recycling programs. The green dot tells consumers that such packaging may not be returned to the retailer but should be consigned to specially designated collection containers or be taken to the local recycling center. The symbol also indicates that the packaging will be recycled or reused rather than dumped or incinerated. While goods without the green dot are not illegal, they are unlikely to be accepted by the market – retailers, wholesalers, and importers. The

DSD estimates that over ten billion units currently being marketed in Germany carry the green dot.

Most other European Union countries have initiated similar green dot programs. Japan's Packaging Recycling Law requires manufacturers to pay costs associated with collection, sorting, transportation, and recycling of all paper and plastic containers and packaging. Importers are held responsible for paying the recycling costs of imported products.

One helpful sign that should reduce packaging confusion is the European Union's standardization attempt. Changes in the EU's food packaging requirements should allow foreign food manufacturers and packaging agents to follow one unified EU regulation. Although size requirements differ by product, the EU has harmonized the sizes of sealed packages and containers. The uniformity assists consumers in comparing prices for the same quantity, thus abolishing the need for unit pricing. EU packaging regulations also help to promote conservation by decreasing the amount of paper used in packaging.

Because there is no EU-wide general product-labeling directive, manufacturers have to label their products differently for each country, thus increasing expenses. There is also a question about language requirements. The EU suggests that most products should have at least two EU official languages so as to increase the marketability of the products. In terms of what is to be placed on the product label, EU officials recommend the following: (1) the name of the product, (2) a name of the manufacturer or distributor within the marketing country, (3) any care conditions, (4) special storage conditions, (5) country of origin, especially where labels might mislead, (6) metric requirements, and (7) list of chemicals/ingredients included.

CONCLUSION

A product is a bundle of utilities, and the brand and package are part of this bundle. There is nothing unusual about consumers' reliance on brand names as a guide to product quality. As shown by the perfume industry, the mystique of a brand name may be so strong as to overshadow the product's physical attributes. When practiced and well exe- cuted, branding allows a commodity to be trans- formed into a product. In doing so with the aid of product differentiation, brand loyalty is created, and the product can command a premium price.

Branding decisions involve more than merely deciding whether or not a product should be branded. Branding entails other managerial deci- sions. A manufacturer must decide whether to use its own brand or that of its dealer on its product. A marketer must also determine whether to use a single brand for maximum impact or multiple brands to satisfy the different segments and markets more precisely. Regardless of the number of brands used, each brand name must be selected carefully with the international market in mind. Once selected, the brand name must be protected through registration, and other measures should be taken to prevent any infringement on that name.

Like the brand name, which may have to be varied from one country to another, packaging should be changed when needed. Mandatory mod- ification of packaging should not be considered a problem because the marketer has no choice in the matter – if a marketer wants to market a product, the marketer must conform to the country's stated packaging requirements. Unilever, for instance, has to conform to the French requirement of selling cube-shaped, not rectangular, packs of margarine. Its descriptions for mayonnaise and salad dressing also have to vary from country to country.

Optional or discretionary packaging modifica- tion, in contrast, is a more controllable variable within a marketer's marketing mix. Usually, discre- tionary packaging is related more to product pro- motion, and it can take on the same importance as mandatory packaging. Soft-drink containers are a good example of how packaging requirements must be observed. In many countries, bottles are manu- factured in metric sizes because of government requirements, and the containers must be made of glass because consumers abroad regard plastic throw-away bottles as being wasteful. Therefore, both mandatory and optional packaging changes should be considered at the same time.

CASE 11.1 PLANET RALPH: THE GLOBAL MARKETING STRATEGY OF POLO RALPH LAUREN

Deirdre Bird, Providence College, and Helen Caldwell, Providence College

Polo Ralph Lauren (PRL) is a highly successful US company. The thirty-fifth anniversary of the company has been covered in glowing terms across the globe. For example, Ralph Lauren was interviewed for the prestigious British broadsheet, *The Sunday Times*, followed by a lecture at The British Museum in London. *Vogue* magazine profiled Lauren as "The Man Behind the Mega-Brand" while making the cover of both *GQ* (as a Man of the Year) and *Architectural Digest*. *Time* magazine presented Ralph Lauren as "A Bronx Cowboy in Europe," outlining Lauren's rise from Bronx kid Ralph Lifschitz to world-famous designer Ralph Lauren.

Today's world of luxury in fashion

The primary customers for luxury products tend to be women aged between 30 and 50 in the upper income brack- ets, where the household earns over $100,000. In the USA, this categorization accounts for over fifteen million households. In the upper-middle category (with household incomes of $75,000 to $100,000), there are an addi- tional twelve million households. However, in what has come to be termed the "democratization of luxury," people in all income brackets want to participate in the luxury market, even if that means buying nothing more than a $4 chai latte at Starbucks, or a $20 scarf at Gucci. Ralph Lauren recognized this himself when he described the desire for luxury as "aspirational."

Approximately thirty-five companies share 60 percent of the luxury goods market. The six top competitors, one of which is Polo Ralph Lauren, have annual revenues greater than $1 billion; fifteen to twenty companies have revenues between $500 million and $1 billion; and ten have revenues between $100 million and $500 million. These companies tend to have a product focus and thus do not all compete on equal terms in the various luxury categories. For instance, Richemont, a Swiss conglomerate, deals largely in watches, jewelry, and writing instruments, with brands such as Cartier, Piaget, and Mont Blanc. Hermes focuses on leather goods, selling ladies' bags for upwards of $4000. LVMH is the industry leader in luxury goods, followed by Richemont, and Gucci Group. Coming in fourth in the industry is Polo Ralph Lauren.

The Polo Ralph Lauren concept

PRL is a family-controlled company, in that its Chairman and CEO is designer and founder Ralph Lauren. However, the company is quoted publicly on the New York Stock Exchange. The company derives its revenues from three sources: retail, wholesale, and licensing.

The retail segment operates over 236 outlet and full-price stores, including the magnificent flagship stores in Manhattan, London, Paris, Boston, and Brussels. Retail sales contributed almost $1 billion to revenue in 2002.

The wholesale segment consists of two units: Polo Brands and Collection Brands, with each unit selling its own discrete brands to department and specialty stores, and to PRL-owned and licensed retail stores. This segment is responsible for the majority of the corporation's net sales (almost $1.2 billion in fiscal year 2002).

The licensing segment accounts for almost 10 percent of total sales, generating revenue from royalties through licensing alliances, whereby the licensee is granted the right to use the company's trademarks in connection with manufacturing and sale of certain products in specific geographical areas. As a result of a corporate strategy of increasing its global presence, PRL acquired its Italian licensee, Poloco S.A.S., thus allowing for greater integration of its European wholesale operations.

The Polo Ralph Lauren strategy

PRL intends to grow by brand extension and by globalization. In its brand extensions, the company aims to expand by "creating luxury and lifestyle brands that inspire people to live their dreams." The company has developed apparel labels which segment the upper end of the luxury market into Purple Label, Women's Collection and Black Label, and in its home furnishings division it has developed the Ralph Lauren Home collection. At a lower price point, Polo Blue Labels have been developed, and will be distributed exclusively in PRL stores in the USA, and in specialty stores in Europe, Asia, and Australia. In arrangements with its licensees in department stores, the company has developed Lauren for women and Lauren bedding and bath products. The recently acquired Club Monaco concept (formerly a fifteen-category Canadian company) has been rationalized to three categories of men's, women's, and accessories.

This brand extension strategy has required, and will continue to require, a very large advertising budget. The company uses a combination of television and multi-page magazine advertising, intended to illustrate the luxurious aspect of the brands. Advertising expenses in 2002 amounted to almost $80 million, or approximately 4 percent of net sales.

The global strategy

Based on a belief that there are enormous opportunities in Western Europe the company has plans to open new Ralph Lauren stores in Europe through the next several years. Similarly, development is planned in Asia, specifically in Japan, Hong Kong, and Korea, these latter countries being managed by licensed partners.

Currently, the USA accounts for almost 73 percent of company sales. Europe and Japan represent approximately 10 percent each, and Canada, Korea, Australia, and other small markets account for the remaining 7 percent of sales. Thus in the past Lauren has relied heavily on US sales. Much of this has come from department stores.

Points to consider

As Lauren ponders his corporation's future, the questions he needs to address are as follows:

1 Can an American brand built on the quintessential "American dream" succeed globally?
2 Will the PRL form of lifestyle marketing succeed globally?
3 Which brands would present the best global opportunities for PRL?

Sources: "Every Cloud Has a Silver Lining," *The Economist*, March 21, 2002; Rebecca Gardyn, "Oh, The Good Life," *American Demographics*, November 2002; Lauren Goldstein, "Lauren: A Bronx Cowboy in Europe," *Time: Global Business*, September 2002; Claire A. Kent *et al.*, "Making the Sale," *Morgan Stanley Dean Witter*, March 11, 1999; and Polo Ralph Lauren, Annual Corporate Report, 2002.

CASE 11.2   MAJORICA S.A. VS. R.H. MACY

Majorca is a place well known for its pearls. One Spanish firm, Majorica S.A., has used Majorica, an ancient name for Majorca, since 1954 as its trade name as well as a brand name to describe its pearls.

Majorica was alarmed to learn that R.H. Macy, a major US department store chain, was selling Majorca-labeled pearls that were made by Hobe Cie. Ltd., a competitor of Majorica S.A. Contacts with Macy produced no fruitful results in resolving the difficulty. Macy felt that it had a right to use the name in question because Majorca was the name of an island and because the pearls in question were indeed made there.

Subsequently, Majorica filed a lawsuit in a federal court, asking for a judgment to stop Macy using the name. Majorica S.A. cited trademark infringement as the reason for seeking relief. It argued that Macy's action caused confusion among consumers as well as erosion of goodwill.

Points to consider

1 Is Majorica a valid brand name or just a generic trademark? Does the fact that it is the name of a place (i.e., island) affect the registration eligibility and legal protection of Majorica S.A.?
2 Was Macy's action legally defensible? Assuming that you are a federal court judge, do you think that Macy's use of the name could cause consumer confusion? Do you think that Macy's labeling constituted trademark infringement? Can the branding/labeling be somehow modified to prevent consumer confusion?

QUESTIONS

1 What are the requirements that must be met so that a commodity can effectively be transformed into a branded product?
2 Explain the "least dependent person" hypothesis and its branding implications.
3 When is it appropriate to use multiple brands in (a) the same market and (b) several markets/countries?

4 What are the characteristics of a good international brand name?

5 Explain these legal requirements related to branding: (a) registration, (b) registration eligibility, (c) use, (d) renewal, and (e) generic trademark.

6 Distinguish colorable imitation from counterfeit trademark.

7 Cite the factors that may force a company to modify its package for overseas markets. Discuss both mandatory and optional modification.

DISCUSSION ASSIGNMENTS AND MINICASES

1 Should farmers brand their exported commodities (e.g., soybean, corn, beef)?

2 Some retailers (e.g., Sears) and manufacturers (e.g., General Motors) place their trademarks on products actually made by foreign suppliers. Discuss the rationale for these actions by these firms.

3 Discuss how certain English letters, prefixes, suffixes, syllables, or words create pronunciation difficulties for those whose native language is not English.

4 Is Hyundai a good name to use for an international brand? On what do you base your evaluation?

5 Go to the soft drink section of a supermarket. How many different types of soft-drink packages are there (in terms of size, form, and so on)? Should any of them be modified for overseas markets?

NOTES

1 *H.J. Heinz Company 2000* (second quarter), 9.

2 "In Business This Week," *Business Week*, September 27, 1993, 50.

3 Martin S. Roth, "Effects of Global Market Conditions on Brand Image Customization and Brand Preference," *Journal of Advertising* 24 (winter 1995): 55–75.

4 T.C. Melewar, John Saunders, and John M.T. Balmer, "Cause, Effect and Benefits of a Standardised Corporate Visual Identity System of UK Companies Operating in Malaysia," *European Journal of Marketing* 35 (No. 3, 2001): 414–27.

5 Peter C. Verhoef, Edwin J. Nijssen, and Laurens M. Sloot, "Strategic Reactions of National Brand Manufacturers towards Private Labels: An Empirical Study in the Netherlands," *European Journal of Marketing* 36 (No. 11, 2002): 1309–26.

6 Steve Burt, "The Strategic Role of Retail Brands in British Grocery Retailing," *European Journal of Marketing* 34 (No. 8, 2000): 875–90.

7 "In Desktop PCs, IBM Clicks on 'Quit,'" *Business Week*, January 21, 2002, 40.

8 "Quanta's Quantum Leap," *Business Week*, November 5, 2001, 79–81; "Don't Be Fooled by the Name on the Box," *Business Week*, June 17, 2002, 18.

9 "Swatch: Ready for Net Time?" *Business Week*, February 14, 2000, 61.

10 "Breaking into the Name Game," *Business Week*, April 7, 2003, 54.

11 Stuart J. Agres and Tony M. Dubitsky, "Changing Needs for Brands," *Journal of Advertising Research* 36 (January/February 1996): 21–30.

12 Dana L Alden, Jan-Benedict E.M. Steenkamp, and Rajeev Batra, "Brand Positioning Through Advertising in Asia, North America, and Europe: The Role of Global Consumer Culture," *Journal of Marketing* 63 (January 1999): 75–87.

13 "Nivea, Nestlé (AAC) Extend Bounds in Global Mega Brand Survey," *Bangkok Post*, April 3, 2003.

14 Julie Snyder, "Promoting Consumer Goods and Services in Quebec, Canada's Distinct, French-Speaking Market," *Business America*, November 1, 1993.

15 Shi Zhang and Bernd H. Schmitt, "Creating Local Brands in Multilingual International Markets," *Journal of Marketing Research*, 38 (August 2001): 313–25.

16 "Drastic Cuts Are in Store for Unilever," *San José Mercury News*, February 23, 2000.

17 "Scott Rolls Out a Risky Strategy," *Business Week*, May 22, 1995, 48.

18 "For Sale: Amoco Signs, Cheap," *Business Week*, August 14, 2000, 8.

19 France Leclerc, Bernd H. Schmitt, and Laurette Dube, "Foreign Branding and Its Effect on Product Perceptions and Attitudes," *Journal of Marketing Research* 31 (May 1994): 263–70.

20 "UK Queen Registers Trade Marks," *The Nation*, July 8, 2000.

21 Sidney A. Diamond, *Trademark Problems and How to Avoid Them*, rev. edn (Chicago: Crain Books, 1981), 20–2.

22 Jim Golsen, "Packaging and Recycling Requirements," *Export America* (May 2000).

23 "Ideas for a Changing World," *Business Week*, August 26, 2002, 112–14.

Chapter 12

Channels of distribution

In a market system, all aspects of economic activity are interdependent, and the whole cannot function properly if any major element is not in its place.

Michel Camdessus, Managing Director, International Monetary Fund

CHAPTER OUTLINE

PURPOSE OF CHAPTER

All products need competent distribution. Unfortunately, the distribution of blood diamonds is relatively competent. In any case, any products, no matter how good they are, are unlikely to gain market acceptance without being made available at a time and place that are convenient to final users.

The purpose of this chapter is to discuss the various channels of distribution that are responsible for moving products from manufacturers to consumers. Both international and domestic channels are examined. The chapter describes the varieties of intermediaries (i.e., agents, wholesalers, and retailers) involved in moving products between as well as within countries. The tasks and functions of the various intermediaries will be examined. It should be kept in mind that certain types of intermediaries do not exist in some countries and that the pattern of use as well as the importance of each type of intermediary varies widely from country to country.

A manufacturer is required to make several decisions that will affect its channel strategy, including the length, width, and number of distribution channels to be used. The chapter examines the various factors that influence these decisions. For an operation to be a success, a good relationship among channel members is vital. There is no one single distribution method that is always ideal in all markets. Thus this chapter examines channel adaptation.

MARKETING ILLUSTRATION   BLOOD DIAMONDS AND DEBEERS

One needs money to wage war, and diamonds are just as good as money. Diamonds are portable and anonymous. Most of Sierra Leone's diamonds are smuggled into Liberia for sale. It is practically impossible to identify the origins of diamonds. As a result, diamonds are a currency of choice for thugs and rebels in Africa. At one time, diamonds from the African war zones accounted for 10 to 15 percent of the world supply.

In Angola, diamonds helped Unita, an Angolan rebel group, to launch a civil war in the 1990s. Such blood diamonds resulted in half a million Angolans being killed and four million Angolans being displaced. The Revolutionary United Front, a rebel unit that barters diamonds for weapons, is unbelievably brutal. Its soldiers chopped off limbs of innocent people to cause fear. Unita's cruelty led the USA to impose a diamond embargo on the group in 1998. While the United Nations Children's Fund has declared that Angola is the worst place on earth to be a child, it took the United Nations six years before imposing the embargo.

Unita does not act alone. It has many accomplices to help it to use diamonds to finance its ruthless operations. Corrupt governments, pitiless rebels, and porous borders in Angola, Congo, and Sierra Leone have allowed diamonds to become agents of slave labor, dismemberment, murder, mass exodus, and economic collapse. Many diamond dealers in Antwerp do not care to know where the stones are from, and the world's largest diamond bourse in Antwerp has "extremely lax regulations." At the same time, Liberia, Uganda, Rwanda, and Zimbabwe have passed off smuggled diamonds as their own by supplying false but official certificates of origin.

Finally, governments and the diamond industry have reached a global accord that stops trade in diamonds from the conflict zones. For rough diamonds to be exported, they must be certified that they are not from the territory held by the rebels. Any private exporters or importers who break the rules will lose their trading licenses. Countries that break rules will be barred from selling diamonds, and they may face international sanctions.

345

To maintain its control on the supply of diamonds, De Beers bought Unita's diamonds. In its defense, De Beers claimed that it did not deal directly with the rebels and that it stopped all deals after the 1998 embargo. The company's own annual reports nonetheless showed that the cartel's deals had brought large amounts of money to the rebels. As the world is flooded with diamonds, De Beers found it to difficult

to maintain expensive inventory and prices, and its image was also taking a heavy beating. The company managed to solve both problems at the same time by not buying diamonds from Angola any longer, except from a government-controlled mine.

Sources: "Africa's Gems: Warfare's Best Friend," *New York Times,* April 6, 2000; "New Rules Set for Diamond Trading," *San José Mercury News,* November 6, 2002.

CULTURAL DIMENSION 12.1 HOLLYWOOD AND BOLLYWOOD

All superpowers have attempted to spread their cultures. The Roman, Japanese, Soviet, and British empires are no exception. Many Asian and European countries have been complaining rather bitterly about the American media and their spread of "cultural imperialism." Certainly, Hollywood movies and American rock-and-roll music are widely distributed and played. Most Americans probably see nothing wrong with spreading American culture around the globe. What can be wrong with pushing individual freedom while glorifying violence and rebellion?

In reality, foreign companies have invaded the US entertainment industry, and several major Hollywood studios are either owned or run by foreign firms or executives. While France has been particularly vocal in speaking against US cultural imperialism, it is an irony that the French media conglomerate Vivendi acquired Universal Studios (before having to resell it to GE in 2003 due to heavy debts). Sony acquired Columbia Pictures more than a decade ago with an

aim to create content and merchandising opportunities for its audio and video products. Rupert Murdoch, a former Australian, now controls the Fox film studios and TV network.

India produces more movies than Hollywood. Indian movies have a simple formula. The popular films simply rely on a few plots involving love, revenge, and, occasionally, social issues. These movies, often three hours long, are concoctions of melodrama with quite a bit of overacting. They must have big song-and-dance routines, with one scene involving kissing or rolling in the rain. Inevitably, there is a strong, flawless male hero pursuing a coy heroine. Bollywood movies, while colorful, see the world in black and white in the sense that the villains are clearly defined, leaving no doubt as to who are the good or the bad guys.

Sources: "The Real French Connection," *Bangkok Post,* June 23, 2000; "'Cultural Imperialism' Is No Joke," *Business Week,* November 30, 1998; "'Bollywood' Has Eyes on Hollywood," *San José Mercury News,* March 24, 2002.

DIRECT AND INDIRECT SELLING CHANNELS

A manufacturer can sell directly to end users abroad, but this type of channel is generally not suitable or desirable for most consumer goods. In foreign markets, it is far more common for a product to go through several parties before reaching the final consumer. Figures 12.1 and 12.2 show

how two major Japanese companies (Sony and Kikkoman), by acting as middlemen, offer their distribution expertise to help American firms market their products in Japan.

Companies use two principal channels of distribution when marketing abroad: (1) indirect selling, and (2) direct selling. **Indirect selling**, also known as the local or domestic channel, is employed when a manufacturer in the United Kingdom, for example,

SONY PLAZA WANTS MORE

U.S. PRODUCTS TO SELL IN JAPAN

"International trade requires efforts in importing as well as in exporting. There's an excellent market for American products in Japan. Our economy is strong. Japanese customers want diversity and are attracted by American brands. Sony has the sales force and knowledge of the Japanese market to help American firms find ready acceptance among Japanese consumers. This kind of trade will be beneficial both to Japan and to the American firms coming into the market."
——————A. MORITA   SONY Chairman

With this philosophy, Sony Plaza Co., Ltd. was established by Sony Corporation, a Company known for it's own fine exports. Sony Plaza has made famous such names as Fieldcrest, Royal Copenhagen, Paddington Bear, Famous Amos, Goody, etc. in the Japanese market. And you? Sony Plaza wants to import yours.

If you're interested please talk to us. In the U.S. please write to: Ms. Michele Classe, Sony Corp of America, America Export to Japan Div., 9 West 57th Street, New York, N.Y. 10019. In Japan: Mr. Y. Maki, Sony Plaza Co., Ltd., Sony Bldg. 5-3-1 Ginza, Chuo-ku, Tokyo. 104, Japan.

Figure 12.1 Sony's distribution expertise

Source: Reprinted with permission of Sony Corporation of America

markets its product through another British firm that acts as the manufacturer's *sales intermediary* (or middleman). As such, the sales intermediary is just another local or domestic channel for the manufacturer because there are no dealings abroad with a foreign firm. By exporting through an independent local middleman, the manufacturer has no need to set up an international department. The middleman, acting as the manufacturer's external export organization, usually assumes responsibility for moving the product overseas. The intermediary may be a **domestic agent** if it does not take title to the

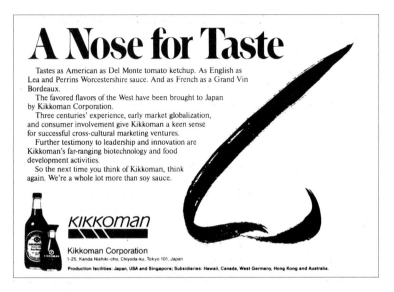

Figure 12.2 Kikkoman's distribution expertise

Source: Courtesy of Kikkoman Corp.

goods, or it may be a **domestic merchant** if it does take title to the goods.

There are several advantages to be gained by employing an indirect domestic channel. For example, the channel is simple and inexpensive. The manufacturer incurs no start-up cost for the channel and is relieved of the responsibility of physically moving the goods overseas. Because the intermediary very likely represents several clients who can help share distribution costs, the costs for moving the goods are further reduced.

An indirect channel does, however, have limitations. The manufacturer has been relieved of any immediate marketing costs but, in effect, has given up control over the marketing of its product to another firm. This situation may adversely affect the product's success in the future. If the chosen intermediary is not aggressive the manufacturer may become vulnerable, especially in cases where competitors are careful about their distribution practices. Moreover, the indirect channel may not necessarily be permanent. Being in the business of handling products for profit, the intermediary can easily discontinue handling a manufacturer's product if there is no profit or if a competitive product offers a better profit potential.

Export intermediaries' performance is a function of their possession of valuable, unique, and hard-to-imitate resources. Such resources reduce their client's transaction and agency costs.[1] A related study, focusing on 20,000 French firms, found that export intermediary firms tend to export products with a high commodity content rather than products with a low commodity content, thus confirming the role of product complexity.[2]

Direct selling is employed when a manufacturer develops an overseas channel. This channel requires that the manufacturer deal directly with a foreign party without going through an intermediary in the home country. The manufacturer must set up the overseas channel to take care of the business activities between the countries. Being responsible for shipping the product to foreign markets itself, the manufacturer exports through its own internal export department or organization.

One advantage gained in using the direct-selling channel is active market exploitation, since the manufacturer is more directly committed to its foreign markets. Another advantage is greater control. The channel improves communication because approval does not have to be given to a middleman before a transaction is completed. Therefore, the channel allows the company's policy to be followed more uniformly.

Direct selling is not without its problems. It is a difficult channel to manage if the manufacturer is unfamiliar with the foreign market. Moreover, the channel is time consuming and expensive. Without a large volume of business, the manufacturer may find it too costly to maintain the channel. Hiram Walker, a Canadian distiller, used to have its own marketing operation in New York City to distribute such brands as Ballantine Scotch, Kahlua, and CC Rye. Poor earnings finally forced the company to phase out its costly US selling organization along with its New York City marketing operation.

In the case of multinational corporations with foreign subsidiaries, cooperation can enhance performance of products across markets. Cooperative marketing operations between the headquarters and its foreign subsidiaries enhance performance of products in subsidiaries' markets. National culture in foreign markets moderates the effect of trust on relational behaviors. As a firm attempts to standardize its marketing programs, subsidiaries' acquiescence becomes increasingly important.[3]

TYPES OF INTERMEDIARIES: DIRECT CHANNEL

There are several types of intermediaries associated with both the direct and indirect channels. Figure 12.3 compares the two channels and lists the various types of domestic and foreign intermediaries.

Foreign distributor

A foreign distributor is a foreign firm that has exclusive rights to carry out distribution for a manufacturer in a foreign country or specific area. For example, when Don Wood returned to Detroit, he still remembered the MG sports car he drove in England during World War II. His letter asking MG's chairman to sell and ship one car to him brought the response that MG's policy was to sell only through authorized distributors, but MG was willing to appoint Wood as its Midwest distributor if he would order two cars instead. Wood agreed to do so and went on to become a successful distributor.

Figure 12.3 *International channels of distribution*

Orders must be channeled through the distributor, even when the distributor chooses to appoint a subagent or subdistributor. The distributor purchases merchandise from the manufacturer at a discount and then resells or distributes the merchandise to retailers and sometimes to final consumers. In this regard, the distributor's function in many countries may be a combination of wholesaler and retailer, but in most cases, the distributor is usually considered as an importer or foreign wholesaler. The length of association between the manufacturer and its foreign distributor is established by a contract that is renewable provided the continued arrangement is satisfactory to both.

In some situations, the foreign distributor is merely a subsidiary of the manufacturer. Seiko USA., for example, is a distributor for its Japanese parent (Hattori Seiko), which manufactures Seiko watches. More frequently, however, a foreign distributor is an independent merchant. Charles of the Ritz Group has been the US distributor for Opium, a very popular perfume made in France. A distributor may sometimes take on the name of the brand distributed even though the distributor is an independent operator and not owned by the manufacturer. Brother International Corp. is an independent US distributor of Brother Industries, Ltd., a Japanese firm. Longines-Wittnauer Watch Co. distributes the Swiss-made Longines watch in the US market. This distributorship is actually a subsidiary of the Westinghouse Electric Corp.

There are a number of benefits in using a foreign distributor. Unlike agents, the distributor is a *merchant* who buys and maintains merchandise in its own name. This arrangement simplifies the credit and payment activities for the manufacturer. To carry out the distribution function, the foreign distributor is often required to warehouse adequate products, parts, and accessories and to make facilities and personnel immediately available to service buyers and users. However, the manufacturer must be careful in selecting a foreign distributor or it may end up with a distributor who is deficient in marketing and servicing the product.

Foreign retailer

If foreign retailers are used, the product in question must be a consumer product rather than an industrial product. There are several means by which a manufacturer may contact foreign retailers and interest them in carrying a product, ranging from a personal visit by the manufacturer's representative to mailings of catalogs, brochures, and other literature to prospective retailers. The use of personal selling or a visit, although expensive due to travel costs and commissions for the manufacturer's representative, provides for a more effective sales presentation as well as for better screening of retailers for the distribution purpose. The use of direct mail, although less expensive, may not sufficiently catch the retailers' attention.

For such big-ticket items as automobiles or for high-volume products, it may be worthwhile for a manufacturer to sell to retailers without going through a foreign distributor. In fact, most large retailers prefer to deal directly with a manufacturer. In Europe, for example, a number of retail food chains are becoming larger and more powerful, and they prefer to be in direct contact with foreign manufacturers in order to obtain price concessions.

State-controlled trading company

For some products, particularly utility and telecommunications equipment, a manufacturer must contact and sell to state-controlled companies. In addition, many countries, especially those in Eastern Europe, have state-controlled trading companies, which are companies that have a complete monopoly in the buying and selling of goods. Hungary has about a hundred state trading organizations for a variety of products, ranging from poultry to telecommunications equipment and for both imported and exported products.

Being government sanctioned and controlled for trading in certain goods, buyers for state-controlled trading companies are very definitely influenced by their governments' trade policies and politics. Most opportunities for manufacturers are limited to raw materials, agricultural machinery, manufacturing equipment, and technical instruments rather than consumer or household goods. Reasons for this limitation include shortage of foreign exchange, an emphasis on self-sufficiency, and the central planning systems of the communist and socialist countries.

End user

Sometimes, a manufacturer is able to sell directly to foreign end users with no intermediary involved in the process. This direct channel is a logical and natural choice for costly industrial products. For most consumer products, the approach is only practical for some products and in some countries. A significant problem with consumer purchases can result from duty and clearance problems. A consumer may place an order without understanding his or her country's import regulations. When the merchandise arrives, the consumer may not be able to claim it. As a result, the product may be seized or returned on a freight-collect basis. Continual occurrence of this problem could become expensive for the manufacturer.

To solicit orders, a manufacturer may use publications to attract consumers. Many US magazines receive overseas distribution, and the advertisements inside are read by foreign consumers. Other US magazines, including *Time*, *Newsweek*, and *Business Week*, facilitate the ordering process since they publish international editions. Of course, an advertiser can also place its advertisements directly with foreign publishers. This is the process many countries follow in order to promote the local tourism industry. The 7-11 outlets in Japan also facilitate the manufacturer–end user channel by allowing consumers to come in to inspect the merchandise shipped to them before making a payment.

TYPES OF INTERMEDIARIES: INDIRECT CHANNEL

For a majority of products, a manufacturer may find it impractical to sell directly to the various foreign parties (i.e., foreign distributors, foreign retailers, state-controlled trading companies, and end users). Other intermediaries, more often than not, have to come between these foreign buyers and the manufacturer. This section examines the roles of those middlemen located in the manufacturer's country.

With an indirect channel, a manufacturer does not have to correspond with foreign parties in foreign countries. Instead, the manufacturer deals with one or more domestic middlemen, who in turn move and/or sell the product to foreign middlemen or final users. Although there are many kinds of local sales intermediaries, all may be grouped under two broad categories: (1) domestic agents, and (2) domestic merchants. The basic difference between the two is ownership (title) rather than just the physical possession of the merchandise. **Domestic agents** never take title to the goods, regardless of whether or not the agents take possession of the goods. **Domestic merchants**, on the other hand, own the merchandise, regardless of whether or not the merchants take possession. An agent represents the manufacturer, whereas a merchant (e.g., a distributor) represents the manufacturer's product. The merchant has no power to contract on behalf of the manufacturer, but the agent can bind the manufacturer in authorized matters to contracts made on the manufacturer's behalf.

Agents can be further classified according to the principal whom they represent. Some agent intermediaries represent the buyer; others represent the interest of the manufacturer. Those who work for the manufacturer include export brokers, manufacturer's export agents or sales representative, export management companies, and cooperative exporters. Agents who look after the interests of the buyer include purchasing (buying) agents/offices and country-controlled buying agents.

Export broker

The function of an export broker is to bring a buyer and a seller together for a fee. The broker may be assigned some or all foreign markets in seeking a potential buyer. It negotiates the best terms for the seller (i.e., manufacturer) but cannot conclude the transaction without the principal's approval of the arrangement. As representative of the manufacturer, the export broker may operate under its own name or that of the manufacturer. For any action performed, the broker receives a fee or commission. An export broker does not take possession or title to the goods. In effect, it has no financial responsibility other than sometimes making an arrangement for credit. An export broker is less frequently involved in the export (shipping) of goods than in the import (receiving) of goods.

The export broker is useful due to its extensive knowledge of the market supply, demand, and foreign customers. This knowledge enables the broker to negotiate the most favorable terms for the principal. The broker is also a valuable associate for highly specialized goods and seasonal products that do not require constant distribution. An export broker may thus be used on a one-time basis by small manufacturers with limited financial resources who are selling in broad markets.

Manufacturer's export agent or sales representative

Because of the title of this intermediary, one might easily mistake an export agent or sales representative for a manufacturer's employee when, in fact, this is an independent businessperson who usually retains his or her own identity by not using the manufacturer's name. Having more freedom than the manufacturer's own salesperson, a sales representative can select when, where, and how to work within the assigned territory. Working methods include presenting product literature and samples to potential buyers. An export agent pays his or her own expenses and may represent manufacturers of related and noncompeting products. The person may operate on either an exclusive or nonexclusive basis.

Like a broker, the manufacturer's export agent works for commission. Unlike the broker, the relationship with the manufacturer is continuous and more permanent. The contract is for a definite period of time, and the contract is renewable by mutual agreement. The manufacturer, however, retains some control because the contract defines the territory, terms of sale, method of compensation, and so on.

The manufacturer's export agent may present some problems to the manufacturer because an agent does not offer all services. Such services as advertising, credit assistance, repair, and installation may be excluded. An export agent may take possession but not title to the goods and thus assumes no risk – the risk of loss remains with the manufacturer. Finally, the manufacturer relinquishes control over marketing activities, and this can hurt a manufacturer whose volume is too small to receive the agent's strong support. The experience of Arthur C. Bell, a British firm, is a case in point. James B. Beam, its previous agent in the USA, neglected Bell because its salespeople had too many other products to handle. Bell switched to Monsieur Henri as its new agent. However, this hardly improved the situation because Henri also preferred to concentrate on larger accounts. As a result, Bell was left out of Christmas catalogs or dropped by many retailers. Bell thus contemplated acquiring a US importer to have stronger control over its own marketing destiny.

Under certain circumstances, it may not be justifiable for a small manufacturer to set up its own sales force and distribution network. Such circumstances include the following:

1   When the manufacturer has a geographically widespread market – the usual case in international marketing.
2   When some overseas markets are too thin.
3   When the manufacturer's product is new and the demand is uncertain.
4   When the manufacturer is inexperienced in international marketing.
5   When the manufacturer wants to simplify business activities.

A manufacturer can avoid fixed costs associated with having its own sales and distribution organization when it employs an agent, since the commission is paid only when sales are made. A manufacturer's export agent has extensive knowledge of specific foreign markets and has more incentive to work than the manufacturer's own salesperson. In addition, the agent carries several product lines, and the result is that the expense of doing business is shared by other manufacturers. This arrangement allows the manufacturer to concentrate time, capital, and expertise on the production of goods rather than on having to deal with the marketing aspect. Of course, if the product is successful, the manufacturer can always set up its own sales force.

Export management company (EMC)

An export management company manages, under contract, the entire export program of a manufacturer. An EMC is also known as a **combination export manager (CEM)** because it may function as an export department for several allied but non-competing manufacturers. In this regard, those export brokers and manufacturer's export agents who represent a combination of clients may also be called EMCs. When compared with export brokers and manufacturer's export agents, the EMC has greater freedom and considerable authority. The EMC provides extensive services, ranging from promotion to shipping arrangement and documentation. Moreover, the EMC handles all, not just a portion, of its principal's products. In short, the EMC is responsible for all of the manufacturer's international activities.

Foreign buyers usually prefer to deal directly with the manufacturer rather than through a third party. Therefore, an EMC usually solicits business in the name of the manufacturer and may even use the manufacturer's letterhead. Identifying itself as the manufacturer's export department or international division, the EMC signs correspondence and documents in the name of the manufacturer. This may be an advantageous arrangement for small and medium-sized firms that lack expertise and adequate human and financial resources to obtain exports. This arrangement may be a good way for a firm to develop foreign markets while creating its own identity abroad. The EMC, on the other hand, faces a dilemma because of a double risk: it can easily be dropped by its clients either for doing a poor job or for making the manufacturer's products too successful.

American EMCs are typically small, and a majority of them have six employees or fewer. It is normal for an EMC to have only one or a few managers or market specialists. An EMC typically requires at least a one-year contract to handle a manufacturer's products. More often, it is a three-year contract. This is understandable because it takes at least six to twelve months to produce significant results.[4]

EMCs are compensated in several ways. Frequently, compensation is in the form of a commission, salary, or retainer plus commission. Depending on the product, the commission may be as high as 20 percent, with the 6 to 10 percent range being the most prevalent. Some EMCs may require a manufacturer to pay a one-time project fee, and such start-up costs may range from a few hundred dollars to tens of thousands of dollars. Meridian Group, a Los Angeles EMC, has stated that it can help handle sales, distribution, credit, shipping, and everything else. Typically, an export manager charges a fee of between 10 and 15 percent of a shipment's wholesale value.[5]

Many EMCs are also traders (i.e., export merchants). As both agents and merchants, they sometimes act as agents and rely on the commission arrangement. When acting as merchants, they engage in the buy-and-resell arrangement. In such cases, they buy merchandise outright and thus take title to the goods. They are compensated by receiving discounts on goods purchased for resale overseas, and such discounts may be greater than what other middlemen receive for the domestic market. They may receive promotion allowances as well. For example, Overseas Operations, Inc., markets builders' hardware, housing accessories, door closures and locks, and computer software and accessories. As an exclusive representative of a number of American manufacturers, the company buys products when orders are received and makes its profit on the markup.

353

There are several reasons why a firm uses an EMC. It has international marketing expertise and distribution contacts overseas. For the many services provided, an EMC's costs are relatively low due to the efficiencies of scale; that is, costs can be spread over the products of several clients. In addition, the EMC provides shipping efficiency because it can consolidate several manufacturers' products in one shipment. The orders are consolidated at the port and shipped on one ocean bill of lading to the same foreign buyer. By consolidating shipments of products from several principals, a company obtains better freight rates. In addition, many EMCs provide financial services. By guaranteeing payments and collecting from overseas buyers, a manufacturer is assured of immediate payment. By providing all of these services, the EMC allows the manufacturer to concentrate on internal efforts and its domestic market.

Using EMCs, like using other types of intermediaries, does have is disadvantages. First, an EMC prefers new clients whose products complement the EMC's existing product lines. The EMC is very likely not interested in unknown products or new technologies that require too much time and effort in opening new markets overseas. A problem for a small manufacturer may be the extent of support it receives. If a firm seeks to do business with a large EMC, the EMC is not likely to give the small client adequate attention. If a small EMC is used, the EMC may be too small to give attention to all the products of its clients. In general, most EMCs do make a serious effort and are willing and able to provide sufficient services for new clients.

Cooperative exporter

A cooperative exporter is a manufacturer with its own export organization that is retained by other manufacturers to sell in some or all foreign markets. Except for the fact that this intermediary is also a manufacturer, the cooperative exporter functions like any other export agents. The usual arrangement is to operate as an export distributor for other suppliers, sometimes acting as a commission representative or broker. Because the cooperative exporter arranges shipping, it takes possession of goods but not title.

The cooperative exporter's motive in representing other manufacturers primarily involves its own financial interest. Having fixed costs for the marketing of its own products, the cooperative exporter desires to share its expenses and expertise with others who want to sell in the same markets abroad. Because of these activities, a cooperative exporter is often referred to as a *mother hen*, a *piggyback exporter*, or an *export vendor*. Examples of cooperative exporters include such well-known companies as GE, Singer, and Bog-Warner. By representing several clients, the cooperative exporter is regarded as a form of EMC.

The relationship between the cooperative exporter and its principal is a long-term one. The arrangement provides an easy, low-risk way for the principal to start marketing overseas, and the relationship should ordinarily continue as long as unrelated or noncompetitive products are involved. A problem may arise if the principal decides to market a new product that competes directly with the cooperative exporter's own product or those of the exporter's other clients.

Purchasing/buying agent

An export agent represents a seller or manufacturer; a purchasing/buying agent represents a foreign buyer. By residing and conducting business in the exporter's country, the purchasing agent is in a favorable position to seek a product that matches the foreign principal's preferences and requirements. Operating on the overseas customer's behalf, the purchasing agent acts in the interest of the buyer by seeking the best possible price. Therefore, the purchasing agent's client pays a fee or commission for the services rendered. The purchasing agent is also known by such names as commission agent, buyer for export, export commission house, and export buying agent. This agent may also become an export-confirming house when confirming payment and paying the seller after receiving invoice and title documents for the client.

The buying agent is valuable for manufacturers because it seeks out those firms and offers them its services. However, since the agent operates on an order basis, the relationship with either seller or buyer is not continuous. This arrangement thus does not offer a steady volume of business for the manufacturer and neither does it offer any reduction in financial risk. In any case, the transaction between the manufacturer and the buying agent (or the agent's customer) may be completed as a domestic transaction in the sense that the agent will take care of all shipping arrangements. Otherwise, the manufacturer will have to make its own arrangements.

Country-controlled buying agent

A variation on the purchasing agent is a country-controlled buying agent. This kind of agent performs exactly the same function as the purchasing/buying agent, the only distinction being that a country-controlled buying agent is actually a foreign government's agency or quasi-governmental firm. The country-controlled buying agent is empowered to locate and purchase goods for its country. This agent may have a permanent office location in countries that are major suppliers, or the country's representative may make formal visits to supplier countries when the purchasing need arises.

Resident buyer

Another variation of the purchasing agent is the resident buyer. As implied by the name, the resident buyer is an independent agent that is usually located near highly centralized production industries. Although functioning much like a regular purchasing agent, the resident buyer is different because it is retained by the principal on a continuous basis to maintain a search for new products that may be suitable. The long-term relationship makes it possible for the resident buyer to be compensated with a retainer and a commission for business transacted.

The resident buyer provides many useful services for a manufacturer. It can offer a favorable opportunity for a supplier to maintain a steady and continuous business relationship as long as the supplier remains competitive in terms of price, service, style, and quality.

For a foreign buyer, the resident buyer offers several useful services, one of which is the purchasing function. The resident buyer uses its judgment to make decisions for its overseas client, which does not have the time to send someone to visit production sites or firms, or which cannot wait to examine samples. Another service provided by the resident buyer is the follow-up function. The resident buyer can make certain that delivery is made as promised. A late delivery can make the purchase meaningless, especially in the case of seasonable or fashion products. If the foreign client decides to visit manufacturing plants or offices, the resident buyer can assist by making hotel reservations, announcing visits to suppliers, arranging vendor appointments, and so on.

Export merchant

The intermediaries covered so far have certain factors in common: they take neither risks nor title, preferring to receive fees for their services. Unlike these middlemen, domestic merchants are independent businesses that are in business to make a profit rather than to receive a fee. There are several types of domestic merchants. Because they all take title, they are distinguished by other features, such as physical possession of goods and services rendered.

One kind of domestic merchant is the export merchant. An export merchant seeks out needs in foreign markets and makes purchases from manufacturers in its own country to fill those needs. Usually the merchant handles staple goods, undifferentiated products, or those in which brands are unimportant. After having the merchandise packed and marked to specification, the export merchant resells the goods in its own name through contacts in foreign markets. In completing all these arrangements, the merchant assumes all risks associated with ownership.

The export merchant's compensation is a function of how product is priced. The markup is affected by the profit motive as well as by market conditions. In any case, the export merchant hopes that the price at which the product is sold will exceed all costs and expenses in order to provide a profit. An export merchant may sometimes seek extra income by importing goods to complement its export activities. The merchant may or may not offer a steady business relationship to his supplier.

Export drop shipper

An export drop shipper, also known as a *desk jobber* or *cable merchant*, is a special kind of export merchant. As all these names imply, the mode of operation requires the drop shipper to request a manufacture to "drop ship" a product directly to the overseas customer. It is neither practical nor desirable for the shipper to physically handle or possess the product. Based on this operational method, the shipper's ownership of the goods may last for only a few hours.

Upon receipt of an order from overseas, the export drop shipper in turn places an order with a manufacturer, directing the manufacturer to deliver the product directly to the foreign buyer. The manufacturer collects payment from the drop shipper, who in turn is paid by the foreign buyer.

Use of a drop shipper is common in the international marketing of bulky products of low unit value (e.g., coal, lumber, construction materials). The high freight volume relative to the low unit value makes it prohibitively expensive to handle such products physically several times. Minimizing physical handling reduces the cost accordingly.

One may question why a manufacturer does not simply deal directly with a foreign buyer, bypassing the drop shipper and saving money in the process – the shipping instructions would reveal the name and address of the foreign buyer. The answer is that the manufacturer can reduce the risk while simplifying the transactional tasks. It is a great deal easier for the manufacturer to call the export drop shipper in the manufacturer's own country instead of trying to sell to and collect from the buyer in a far-away destination.

There are also good reasons why the foreign buyer may not be able to or want to bypass the export drop shipper. The buyer may not have adequate product knowledge or supply knowledge, and the buyer's order may be too small to entice the manufacturer to deal directly. The drop shipper is thus valuable because this kind of merchant is highly specialized in knowing the sources of supply and markets. The drop shipper also has information and advice about the needed product and can arrange all details for obtaining it.

Export distributor

Whereas export merchants and drop shippers purchase from a manufacturer whenever they receive orders from overseas, an export distributor deals with the manufacturer on a continuous basis. This distributor is authorized and granted an exclusive right to represent the manufacturer and to sell in some or all foreign markets. It pays for goods in its domestic transaction with the manufacturer and handles all financial risks in foreign trade.

An export distributor differs from a foreign distributor simply in location. The foreign distributor is located in a particular foreign country and is authorized to distribute and sell the product there. The export distributor, in comparison, is located in the manufacturer's country and is authorized to sell in one or more markets abroad. Consider Mamiya, a Japanese manufacturer. J. Osawa is Mamiya's worldwide distributor (i.e., export distributor). Bell and Howell: Mamiya is in turn J. Osawa's exclusive US distributor (i.e., foreign distributor).

The export distributor operates in its own name or in that of the manufacturer. It handles all shipping details, thus relieving the manufacturer of having to pay attention to overseas activities. In other words, the sale made to the export distributor is just like another domestic transaction for the manufacturer. Because the export distributor, as a rule, represents several manufacturing firms, it is sometimes regarded as a form of EMC.

The export distributor usually sells the manufacturer's product abroad at the manufacturer's list price and receives an agreed percentage of the list price as remuneration; that is, the export distributor is either paid by commission or allowed a discount for its purchase. The manufacturer may bill a foreign buyer directly or may let the distributor bill the buyer to obtain the desired margin.

Trading company

Those that want to sell and those that want to buy often have no knowledge of each other or no knowledge of how to contact each other. Trading companies thus fill this void. In international marketing activities for many countries, this type of intermediary may be the most dominant form in volume of business and in influence. Many trading companies are large and have branches wherever they do business. They operate in developing countries, developed countries, and their own home markets. Half of Taiwan's exports are controlled by trading companies. In Japan, general trading houses are known as *sogo shosha*, and the largest traders include such well-known MNCs as Mitsubishi, Mitsui, and C. Itoh. The nine largest trading firms handle about half of Japan's imports and exports. Even large Japanese domestic companies buy through trading companies.

A trading company performs many functions: the term describes many intermediaries that are neither brokers nor import merchants. A trading company may buy and sell as a merchant. It may handle goods on consignment, or it may act as a commission house for some buyers. By representing several clients, it resembles an EMC, except for the fact that it (1) has more diverse product lines, (2) offers more services, (3) is larger and better financed, (4) takes title (ownership) to merchandise, (5) is not exclusively restricted to engaging in export trade, and (6) goes beyond the role of an intermediary (which provides only export facilitation services) by engaging directly in production, physical distribution channel development, financing, and resource development.

As the name implies, the trading company trades on its own account for profit. By frequently taking title to the goods it handles, its risks of doing business greatly increase. A trading company does not merely represent manufacturers and/or buyers, thus reducing risks, because increased risks are usually accompanied by increased rewards. In the case of WSJ International, which is a trader as well as a representative, profit margins gained on trading are about four times greater than margins on representative sales. It is thus not surprising that trading accounts for half of the company's revenues.

Manufacturers and buyers use trading companies for good reasons. The trading company gathers market information; does market planning, finds buyers; packages and warehouses merchandise; arranges and prepares documents for transportation, insurance, and customs; provides financing for suppliers and/or buyers; accepts business risks; and serves foreign customers after sales. It is, in short, a valuable entity in overcoming cultural and institutional barriers. Nanodata, for example, concluded that it was too expensive to reach unfamiliar and distant market areas. The company hired TKB Technology Trading Corporation, a trading company, to identify good European markets for Nanodata's computer and to develop a distribution channel by choosing agents, distributors, or direct subsidiaries. TKB offered entry without expensive staff buildup until Nanodata was ready to do so on its own.

Like other intermediaries, however, the trading company must always face the possibility of being bypassed by its clients, and it thus must offer something of value to its customers. This holds true even for Mitsubishi, the world's largest trader with more than $164 billion in sales. Without its own production, this company could be squeezed out by Japanese clients that would set up their own marketing departments. Mitsubishi's solution in keeping old customers and getting new ones is to give buyers and sellers an incentive to do business with it. It has formed joint ventures with American and Japanese partners with an aim to acquire ownership influence with both its suppliers and customers. Furthermore, this firm cannot be easily replaced because of its long experience, expertise, and established networks.

Japanese trading companies

Because of the spectacular success of the huge Japanese trading companies, many companies – especially those in the USA – would like to emulate or duplicate them. Japanese trading companies perform a number of marketing functions: market identification and analysis, sales forecasts, buying goods from manufacturers, selling goods to customers, and bearing financial risks (see Figure 12.4).

Japanese trading companies have several distinct characteristics. They are supported by domestic Japanese business. They are partners with groups of banks and other financial intermediaries, allowing them easy, convenient, and almost permanent access to enormous amounts of capital and financing.

Traditionally, Japanese manufacturers prefer to separate manufacturing from marketing, leaving the marketing function to trading firms. A new breed of Japanese manufacturers, however, prefers to have more marketing control and has been shifting away from this pattern of specialization by pursuing forward integration. Responding to this adverse

Marubeni has built some big markets for the U.S.A. in Japan, in close tie with its subsidiary, Marubeni America. And not by chance. Success like this takes more than sales skills: it requires deep insight into the realities that create the Japanese marketplaces, and investment to help shape them. We're the kind of "hands on" trading companies that are geared to meet these challenges squarely.

Consider our record with American high-tech products. Marubeni's had tremendous success marketing sophisticated computers and semiconductor manufacturing equipment from the U.S.A. in Japan. The reason: we've built a complete subsidiary, Marubeni HYTECH, and staffed it with specialists and engineers who know these products inside out. Far beyond sales, our people provide a brand of on-call support

WE EXPORTED

$3.3 Billion

TO JAPAN LAST YEAR FROM AMERICA

and service to customers that's much better than what other importers can do. We even feed back user comments to makers, for product improvement.

Right now, HYTECH is handling sales and support of electronic-industry design systems from such U.S. companies as ECAD, Zycad, Viewlogic and others. Sales of these systems to Japan's IC manufacturers are growing rapidly.

Of course we handle a great many more "Made in U.S.A." goods, too: we export America's agricultural produce and consumer products, we license its services and sell its high-fashion clothing, and we introduce partners for the venture businesses that build the future. Marubeni America Corp. is today, in fact, one of the leaders in increasing U.S. exports, as its $3.3 billion in sales to Japan and $2.2 billion elsewhere attest.

We build world trade in other ways as well. By providing customized financing, investment, leasing, supply of natural resources—even turnkey plant or infrastructure project management.

Take advantage of our skills. Marubeni's 192 offices worldwide are on-line channels of business opportunity, linked by 24-hour satellite telecommunications. Our 13 offices in America are waiting and willing to talk over the business potentials in Japan, or anywhere, any time you'd like.

Always with and for you.

Marubeni

C.P.O. Box 595, Tokyo 100-91, Japan

Marubeni America Corporation Head Office:
42nd Fl., Pan American Bldg., 200 Park Avenue, New York, N.Y. 10166 Tel. 212-599-3700
Los Angeles Tel. 213-972-2700 San Francisco Tel. 415-954-0100 Chicago Tel. 312-222-6211 Houston Tel. 713-654-4000 Seattle Tel. 206-624-5850 Portland Tel. 503-224-3760 Dallas Tel. 214-880-9001 Detroit Tel. 313-353-7060 Boston Tel. 617-273-4940 St. Louis Tel. 314-291-1127 Washington D.C. Tel. 202-331-1161 Nashville Tel. 615-885-2530

Figure 12.4
Japanese trading company

Source: Reprinted with permission of Marubeni America Corporation.

trend, the *sogo shosha* is emphasizing its core competence: information gathering. It has transformed itself into an information-based organization.

Export trading companies

In the USA, the Export Trading Company (ETC) Act was passed in 1982. Title III of the 1982 Act allows domestic competitors to obtain binding antitrust preclearance for specified export activities. By granting prior antitrust immunity, the antitrust threat was removed, creating a favorable environment for the formation of joint export ventures.

The firms that have recently formed ETCs are from various backgrounds. Some are manufacturers with subsidiaries that have ready access to the parents' products. GE Trading Company, for example, has access to GE's 300,000 products. Retailers such as Sears and Kmart have a great deal of bargaining power because of their enormous purchases, and this leverage serves them well in marketing US exports through foreign retail chains. Other organizations forming ETCs are banks, which seem natural for this purpose. Because banks can own up to 100 percent of an ETC's stock, these ETCs are guaranteed to have adequate financial resources. In some cases, banks and other business firms may want to form a joint venture, as in the case of First Chicago and Sears World Trade, Inc.

One problem with ETCs is that the ETC Act is designed to promote only US exports. Thus ETCs' import activities must take a secondary position, undertaken only when they are needed to promote exports. Consequently, ETCs may lack an efficient infrastructure for developing two-way trade. In this regard, ETCs differ greatly from Japanese trading companies, which achieve their efficiencies through domestic, foreign, and third-country trading activities. American ETCs may thus lack a comprehensive international perspective.

CHANNEL DEVELOPMENT

The suitability of a particular channel depends greatly upon the country in which it is used. A par-

ticular type of intermediary that works well in one country may not work well elsewhere or may lose effectiveness over time. This does not necessarily mean that each country requires a unique channel. However, a company may find that a country classification system is useful, a system that can be used to determine how the distribution strategy should be set up from one group of countries to another.

Litvak and Banting suggest the use of a country temperature gradient to classify countries.[6] Their classification system is based on the following environmental characteristics: (1) political stability, (2) market opportunity, (3) economic development and performance, (4) cultural unity, (5) legal barriers/restrictions, (6) physiographic barriers, and (7) geocultural distance. Based on these characteristics, countries may be classified as hot, moderate, or cold. A hot country is one that scores high on the first four characteristics and low on the last three. A cold country is exactly the opposite, and a moderate one is medium on all seven characteristics.

The USA generally falls in line with the characteristics of a hot country. So does Canada, even though its cultural unity is moderate (rather than high) and its physiographic barriers are moderate (rather than low). Germany, likewise, is a hot country in spite of some slight interference in the sense that its legal barriers and geocultural distance are moderate rather than low. Brazil, in contrast, largely conforms to a cold country's characteristics.

It is a judgment call whether so many characteristics are necessary for the purpose of classifying countries. The level of economic development could be used as the sole indicator, but such a classification would be misleading because hot countries are not the same as industrialized countries. However, one must question whether refinement and improvement in the classification process justifies the extra effort necessary to wade through all relevant characteristics, especially since the level of economic development correlates well with these characteristics. For practicality, a short-cut appears to be desirable.

Classification is a means to an end, and the purpose of the country temperature gradient is to determine which intermediary should be used in a given country. The temperature gradient also indicates which kind of intermediary is likely to be functioning in a country. In a cold country, competitive pressures on institutional change are not dynamic. Legal restrictions, for example, can prevent or slow down new distribution innovations. Consider Egypt as an example. Only persons born of Egyptian fathers or Egyptian legal entities can represent foreign principals. Being "comfortably cold," middlemen see few threats to their existence. In China, all tobacco must be sold through the China National Tobacco Co. monopoly.

For a hot country, environmental forces may be so hot that new institutional structures arise. Middlemen who fail to adjust will be bypassed and go out of existence. The survival of a channel member is thus a function of the ability to adapt to changing environmental conditions because the channel member cannot hide behind local regulations for protection. For example, in the United Kingdom, either the principal or the intermediary can terminate an agency relationship provided reasonable notice is given.

The country temperature gradient has implications for all channel members. A foreign manufacturer can exercise maximum control over the evolutionary process in the distribution channel. The firm can rely initially on middlemen/distributors. If sales increase, the manufacturer can bypass the intermediary by setting up a sales branch or subsidiary. This is the trend being followed by foreign liquor suppliers in the US market. These suppliers now very much control their own destiny by being responsible for their own distribution. E. Remy Martin & Co. took its cognac away from Glenmore Distillers and became its own US distributor through its Premier Wine Merchants. Distillers Co., a Scottish firm, acted likewise by buying Somerset Importers from Esmark. Pernod Ricard and Monet-Hennessy adopted the same strategy by buying Austin Nichols and Schieffelin, respectively.

A local manufacturer should be alert to any new channel since the new channel may pose a threat to this existing channel. When possible, the manufacturer must pre-empt the competition from using it.

Xerox was successful and secure with its direct sales force channel – so secure that, when the Japanese competition entered the market, Xerox was totally unprepared. The Japanese invaded the US market quickly and cheaply by using independent office equipment dealers, a channel that had been ignored by Xerox. The Japanese firms had their own direct sales force in large metropolitan areas, but they also supplied their machines to such US firms as IBM, Monroe, and Pitney Bowes, thus exploiting these US firms' extensive sales and distribution networks. Xerox was forced to experiment with such alternative channels as retail stores, direct mail, and part-time representatives.

Wholesalers, especially those involved in high-margin, low-volume operations, are particularly vulnerable to the threat posed by modern institutions. Wholesalers can easily be bypassed if they are successful in promoting their principals' products. Superscope, for example, lost the Sony franchise. On the other hand, if wholesalers do the job poorly, they are also likely to be eliminated or their authority and responsibility reduced. Mitsubishi was so unhappy with Chrysler's performance that the Japanese company developed its own independent dealer network in order to catch up with Toyota and Nissan.

Innovations tend to take place in a hot country before spreading to other hot countries and finally developing countries. Retailing innovations that conform to this description include self-service stores, discount houses, and supermarkets, all of which developed initially in the USA. Hypermarche, on the other hand, is a mass-merchandising method developed in Europe. This retail store is an enormous self-service combination of foods and general merchandise, generally displayed in shipping containers. A single set of checkout counters is used. This innovation has had only limited success when introduced in the USA.

The success of an innovation is affected not only by the country temperature gradient but also by several other factors. A certain minimum level of economic development is required to support any form of outlet beyond simple retailing methods.

General stores, a dying breed in the USA, are still very common in many countries. Firms' aggressive behavior will also be a determinant of the success of a new retailing method. Other cultural, legal, and competitive factors play an important role too. In developing countries, where there is plenty of low-cost labor and where people are accustomed to being waited on, self-service stores, discount houses, and supermarkets are slow in gaining widespread acceptance. In developed countries, by comparison, various factors work in favor of large modern discount stores/supermarkets, including high population density, urbanization, literacy, and labor costs. In addition, the high income level and relatively even income distribution make refrigerators and automobiles affordable and accommodate infrequent shopping trips and large purchases.

CHANNEL ADAPTATION

Because the standardized approach to international marketing strategy may not apply to distribution strategy in foreign markets, it is imperative that international marketers understand the distribution structures and patterns in those markets. Toward this end, comparative marketing analysis should be conducted. Distribution is likely to be highly adapted to the different conditions in Africa, Latin America, and Asia. These regions' government regulations as well as local customs act as a barrier to distribution standardization.

Some channel adaptation is frequently a necessity. Suspicion and privacy can limit the effectiveness of door-to-door selling or other direct selling methods. Avon has had to develop other distribution methods in Japan and Thailand. Discount retailing may not be effective in countries where there are many middlemen handling small volumes of merchandise. A traditional distribution channel may seem inefficient, but it may maximize the use of inexpensive labor, leaving no idle resources.

A manufacturer must keep in mind that, due to adaptation, a particular type of retailer may not operate in exactly the same manner in all countries. Whereas a US supermarket emphasized a low gross margin, its foreign counterpart may have a relatively high gross margin, emphasizing specialty goods and imported goods to a high degree. Furthermore, the foreign counterpart often operates a ready-to-eat food section. Interestingly, American supermarkets, especially those that have been converted into superstores, have begun to do the same.

A particular distribution concept proven useful in one country may have to be further refined in another. Although 7–11 pioneered the convenience food store concept in Japan, the Japanese operation has evolved into being more sophisticated than its original counterpart in the USA. 7–11 Japan offers its customers steaming fish cakes, canned tea, and rice balls, while accepting payment for utility bills and accepting orders from Tiffany's catalog. To provide the most popular and latest products, about two-thirds of a typical store's 3000 items will change in a year.

CHANNEL DECISIONS

As in any domestic market, the international market requires a marketer to make at least three channel decisions: length, width, and number of channels of distribution. **Channel length** is concerned with the number of times a product changes hands among intermediaries before it reaches the final consumer. The channel is considered long when a manufacturer is required to move its product through several middlemen. The channel is considered short when the product has to change hands only one or twice. If the manufacturer elects to sell directly to final consumers, the channel is direct.

Channel width is related to the number of middlemen at a particular point or step in the distribution channel. Channel width is a function of the number of wholesalers and the different kinds that are used, as well as a function of the number and kind of retailers used. As more intermediaries or more types are used at a certain point in the channel, the channel becomes wider and more intensive. If only a few qualified intermediaries are needed to provide proper product support at a particular level or at a specific location, the channel is selective. The product, though perhaps not available everywhere, is still carried by at least a few qualified middlemen within the same area. Finally, the distribution becomes exclusive if only one intermediary of one type is used in that particular area.

The watch industry and its distribution strategies provides a good illustration of an industry with various channel widths. Timex, as a low-priced, mass-market product, is intensively distributed in the sense that any intermediary, no matter what kind, is allowed to carry the brand. Seiko is more selective. Seiko, as an upper-medium-priced brand, is sold through jewelry stores and catalog showrooms and is less likely to be found in discount or drug stores. Patek Philippe, in order to promote an image of elegance and exclusivity, limits its U.S. outlets to 100 meticulously selected fine jewelry stores. Figure 12.5 shows that Patek Philippe chooses a channel that enhances an image.

A PATEK PHILIPPE DOESN'T JUST TELL YOU THE TIME.

It seems to us that there are certain unique qualities that can be found among the men and women who, over the centuries, have chosen to wear Patek Philippe watches.

Intelligence, for one thing. A delight in logic, for another. An appreciation of beauty. And perhaps most important, as great a respect for *internal* integrity as for *external* appearance.

Of course, we have the advantage of knowing the names of many of the great historical and contemporary figures who have been clients of Patek Philippe.

But we believe that even if you were to judge the watch solely on its own merits, without reference to some of its notable owners, you would come to the same conclusions about their characters as we have.

Here are some of the things that might guide your opinions. For esthetics, as well as function, every working part, down to the tiniest screw or the finest wheel, is microscopically rounded off and polished by hand, to a tolerance of no more than one-hundredth of a millimeter–a virtually frictionless state.

Cutting and pivoting the wheels and pinions alone involve 100 different operations, each one done by hand. And the pinions are lapped and polished on both sides.

In the Patek Philippe mechanical watch as well as the Patek Philippe quartz watch, many internal parts are plated with gold, again for function *and* appearance.

Our *horlogers complets*, complete watchmakers, mount the tiniest parts of a Patek Philippe by hand during the eight to nine month span that it takes to create each individual watch.

And once it is totally assembled, it is taken apart for further refinements.

During manufacture, each movement undergoes a total of 600 or more hours of testing, including testing for its response to cold, heat, humidity, and for wear, in five different positions. Actually, almost half the time of our watchmakers is spent on examination and re-examination of parts and final polishing.

Our quartz watch has only one-third fewer mechanical parts than our mechanical watch, and takes eight months to complete. Almost as long as our mechanical watch.

And the tiny 2.5mm Patek Philippe quartz movement comes from our own electronics factory, where we have been honing our skills in this twentieth century science of electronic timekeeping since 1952.

Ultimately, there is as much difference between a Patek Philippe quartz watch and other quartz watches as there is between a Patek Philippe mechanical watch and other mechanical watches.

For 144 years, our single-minded dedication to perfection has been the context for our company's existence–ever since the French watchmaker, Adrien Philippe, joined forces with the exiled Polish nobleman, Count Antoine de Patek–to create the world's finest watches.

Now that you know a little about the details of our meticulous timepieces, what do you think the ownership of a Patek Philippe, mechanical or quartz, might tell you about yourself?

Something very reassuring, perhaps?

The Patek Philippe pictured is self-winding, mechanical, with date. For a new and comprehensive presentation of Patek Philippe timepieces, please send $5–or for a brochure of current styles write–to Patek Philippe, 10 Rockefeller Plaza, Suite 629-B, NY, NY 10020.

PATEK PHILIPPE GENEVE

IT TELLS YOU SOMETHING ABOUT YOURSELF.

Figure 12.5 *Patek Philippe's channel of distribution*

Source: Reprinted with permission of Henri Stern Watch Agency, Inc.

Channel width is relative. Both Seiko and Omega employ selective distribution, though Omega is much more selective. Omega's tighter policy of selective, limited distribution results in the brand being available only in top jewelry, specialty, and department stores. Due to the relative nature of channel width, it is inappropriate to compare width at the retail level with wholesale width. Because there are many more retailers than wholesalers, the issue of channel width applies only to a particular distribution level rather than through distribution levels. The degree of selectivity depends on the relative, not the absolute, number of intermediaries at a particular distribution level. As a product moves closer to end users, the distribution channel tends to become broader. At a point closer to the manufacturer, the channel is not as broad. For example, at the distributor level, Brother International is the exclusive US distributor for Japan's Brother Industries.

Another decision that concerns the manufacturer is the **number of distribution channels** to be used. In some circumstances, the manufacturer may employ many channels to move its product to consumers. For example, it may use a long channel and a direct channel simultaneously. The use of dual distribution is common if the manufacturer has different brands intended for different kinds of consumers. Another reason for using multiple channels may involve the manufacturer setting up its own direct sales force in a foreign market where the manufacturer cannot remove the original channel (e.g., agents) for strategic or legal reasons. Although Seiko, Lassale, and Jean Lassale are all made by the same Japanese firm, dual channels are used for these brands. Seiko and Lassale are sold through distributors in the USA, whereas Jean Lassale is sold by the manufacturer directly to retailers (jewelers).

DETERMINANTS OF CHANNEL TYPES

There is no single across-the-board solution for all manufacturers' channel decisions; yet there are certain guidelines that can assist a manufacturer in making a good decision. Factors that must be taken into account include legal regulations, product image, product characteristics, middlemen's loyalty and conflict, and local customs.

Legal regulations

A country may have specific laws that rule out the use of particular channels or middlemen. France, for example, prohibits the use of door-to-door selling. Saudi Arabia requires every foreign company with work there to have a local sponsor who receives about 5 percent of any contract. Not surprisingly, many Saudis, acting as agents, have become millionaires almost overnight.

The overseas distribution channel often has to be longer than desired. Because of government regulations, a foreign company may find it necessary to go through a local agent/distributor. In China, foreign firms cannot wholly own retail outlets, and they cannot engage in wholesaling activities. In addition, only fourteen foreign retail ventures have direct import authority, forcing those without direct import authority to add another layer of middlemen. Foreign retailers are required to operate through joint ventures, and they can own a maximum of 65 percent of such joint ventures. It is an Asian tradition, however, to circumvent ownership restrictions by having silent partners who have nothing to do with daily operations. Carrefour S.A., for example, essentially wholly owned its three northeastern supermarkets – until the government cracked down on the practice. As a result, Carrefour was forced to transfer 35 percent of the ownership to two domestic trading firms.[7]

Channel width may be affected by the law as well. In general, exclusive representation may be viewed as a restraint of trade, especially if the product has a dominant market position. In Germany, the Federal Cartel Office may intervene with exclusive dealing and distribution requirements. Due to the EU's single market program, geographic barriers between national markets have blurred, making it possible for consumers outside national sales territories to gain greater access to products and services. Therefore, EU antitrust authorities have increased their scrutiny of "national" and exclusive sales agreements. The Treaty of Rome prohibits distribution arrangements that affect trade or restrict competition (i.e., restrictions on territory, non-competition clauses, and grants of exclusivity). In fact, in the case of automobiles, the Commission has determined that exclusive distribution limited trade between the member countries and that manufacturers thus had less incentive to price cars on a competitive basis. It has directed the manufacturers to allow distributors to sell to other dealers and consumers throughout the EU.

Product image

The product image desired by a manufacturer can dictate the manner in which the product is distributed. A product with a low-price image requires intensive distribution. On the other hand, it is not necessary nor even desirable for a prestigious product to have wide distribution. Clinique's products are sold in only sixty-four department stores in Japan. Waterford Glass has always carefully nurtured its posh image by limiting its distribution to top-flight department and specialty stores. At one time, it did not take on any retail accounts for a period of a year. Its effort to create an air of exclusivity has worked so well that Waterford Glass commands a quarter of the US market, easily making it the bestselling fine crystal.

Although intensive distribution may increase sales in the short run, it is potentially harmful to the product's image in the long run. This is a problem faced by Aprica as it moves its strollers beyond department and specialty stores into mass-market outlets such as JCPenney and Sears. Tiffany & Co. lost many upper-class customers when it broadened its clientele base. Cartier, in trying to restore its esteem, has pared its retail distribution network, which had proliferated unwisely, by 50 percent in the USA and 25 percent worldwide.

Product characteristics

The type of product determines how the product should be distributed. For low-priced, high-turnover convenience products, the requirement is for an intensive distribution network. The intensive distribution of ice cream is an example. Walls' (formerly Foremost's) success in Thailand may be attributed in part to its intensive distribution and channel adaptation. Walls has tailored its distribution activities to the local Thai scene by sending its products (ice cream, milk, and other dairy products) into the market in every conceivable manner. Such traditional channels as wholesalers and such new channels as company-owned retail outlets (modern soda fountains) and pushcarts are also used. Pushcarts are supplied by the company and manned by independent retailers (i.e., sidewalk salesman) who keep a 20 percent margin. However, traditional channels employing wholesalers, small stores, restaurants, hotels, and schools still account for a majority of sales.

For high-unit-value, low-turnover specialty goods, a manufacturer can shorten and narrow its distribution channel. Consumers are likely to do some comparison shopping and will more or less actively seek information about all brands under consideration. In such cases, limited product exposure is not an impediment to market success.

One should always remember that products are dynamic, and the specialty goods of today may be nothing more than the shopping or even convenience goods of tomorrow. Consider computers, which were once an expensive specialty product that required a direct and exclusive channel. Since the early 1980s, computers have become more of a shopping good, necessitating a longer and more intensive channel. Now computers, like TV sets, are sold in discount stores.

Middlemen's loyalty and conflict

One ingredient for an effective channel is satisfied channel members. As the channel widens and as the number of channels increases, more direct competition among channel members is inevitable. Some members will perceive major competing members and self-service members as being unfair. Some members will blame the manufacturer for being motivated by greed when setting up a more intensive network. In effect, intensive distribution reduces channel members' cooperation and loyalty as well as increasing channel conflict. Michelin has been accused of undercutting its own dealers in the US market by not only expanding its dealer network by 50 percent but also adding a direct channel to take national accounts away from dealers. Both actions increased price competition and reduced dealers' loyalty. Apple's problems in Japan were due in part to its addition of new channels, even though it already had a major distributor.

One survey measured cooperative decisions involving export managers from the USA and Peru, during a sequence of three simulated interactions with business partners. During the initial stage of the relationship, decisions of Peruvian export managers reflect less trust than do those of their American counterparts. During the second stage, Peruvian exporters respond differently to weak cheating. Results generally are consistent with cultural differences in attitudes toward in-group versus out-group members. However, influence of cultural differences gradually erodes in favor of personal characteristics and relationship-specific history. Therefore, cultural differences between business partners decline in importance as they get to know each other.[8]

Local customs

Local business practices, whether outmoded or not, can interfere with efficiency and productivity and may force a manufacturer to employ a channel of distribution that is longer and wider than desired. Because of Japan's multitiered distribution system, which relies on numerous layers of middlemen, companies often find it necessary to form a joint venture with a Japanese firm, such as Pillsbury with Snow Brand, Xerox with Fuji, and KFC with Mitsubishi. Japan's many-layered distribution system is not entirely unique in that part of the world, since the custom in many Far-Eastern countries is to have multiple intermediary markups on imported goods. Yet the rule of thumb in Hong Kong is that there should be no more than two layers between a US exporter of finished goods and Hong Kong consumers, usually consisting of an importer, agent retailer, or distributor.

Domestic customs can explain why a particular channel is in existence. Yet customs may change or be overcome, especially if consumer tastes change. For example, there are some 82,000 British pubs, 50,000 of which are owned by brewing companies; the problem they face is the trend toward beer consumption at home. The pubs have had to adjust by emulating trendy American bars, selling more wine and food such as hamburgers.

MARKETING STRATEGY 12.1   HOT AND COLD

Prêt à Manger, a British sandwich maker, has expanded into overseas markets. The New York expansion started in 2000 and won wide acclaim. To appeal to Americans, the company offers cookies and bagels while adding cream cheese to its standard smoked salmon sandwich. The operations in Hong Kong pose a bigger challenge. Because people in Hong Kong are not so keen on very strong cheeses, the Hong Kong branches make fewer of them or none at all. To introduce a local flavor, the company has a bigger fish, pork, and seafood offering.

The Chinese usually do not like cold dishes. Even when a dish is served cold, the food has been heated first. That explains why Delifrance and Oliver's have a growing selection of hot food along with their sandwiches. At lunchtime, their customers tend to buy at least one hot item (e.g., a curry puff at Delifrance or pasta at Oliver's). This kind of local preference makes Prêt consider selling soup in Hong Kong.

Source: "U.K. Sandwich Maker Aims for Its Own Slice of Hong Kong Market," *Asian Wall Street Journal,* October 31, 2001.

It is difficult for new firms to enter Russia. The market has a great deal of structural and institutional impediments. The impediments include: horizontal dominance (significant seller and buyer contraction in regional markets), a high degree of vertical integration and exclusive buyer–seller relationships in certain industrial sectors, geographic segmentation, interregional barriers to trade and investment, and policies that make entry difficult for new firms. The anticompetitive market structure, coupled with the existing dominant firms' anticompetitive conduct, does not leave enough structural economic space for new entrants.[9]

Power and coercion

The "least dependent person" hypothesis, mentioned in Chapter 11, states that the one party with resources and alternatives can demand more because it needs the other party less. As such, the least-dependent member of the channel has more power and may be able to force other channel members to accept its plan. This hypothesis explains why it has been difficult for Japanese and Korean semiconductor manufacturers to recruit US distributors to reach customers who are too small to buy directly from computer chip manufacturers. The major US semiconductor manufacturers have long adopted a tacit policy of not allowing their distributors to sell Japanese competitors' products. Avnet Inc., the largest distributor in the USA, had to stop buying chips from Japan's NEC Corp. Samsung Semiconductor was initially happy when Arrow Electronics Inc., the nation's second largest distributor of semiconductors, agreed to sell its products. Arrow abruptly terminated the agreement a few weeks later, citing changing business conditions. What happened was that Intel Corp. and Texas Instruments reduced the amount of business conducted with Arrow. It is thus not surprising that only one of the electronics industry's top ten distributors distributes Japanese or Korean chips.

Conceivably, dealers in a developing country do not retaliate against a manufacturer's use of coercive influence strategies. When dealers are highly dependent on manufacturers, they have higher tolerance than dealers in other channel contexts.

One must be careful in applying Western models overseas because their impact may differ in developing countries. The applicability of those models may vary from country to country as well. How distributors perceive influence can affect control and conflict in the relationship. Consequently, influence, as practiced in Western channels, may not be effective in relationships with Asian or Latin American firms.

One study investigated how resource- and market-based assets influenced power in international relationships. Based on a sample of distributors from Canada, Chile, Great Britain, and the Philippines, a distributor's power is influenced by asset specificity, predictability, and market knowledge gap. Investments in assets specific to the relationship that cannot be easily obtained by an American manufacturer provides an overseas distributor with power over its US manufacturer.[10]

Control

If it has a choice, a manufacturer that wants to have more control over its product distribution may want to both shorten and narrow its distribution channel. The EU integration and competitive pressures may encourage manufacturers to get closer to final customers by setting up sales subsidiaries instead of relying on distributors or agents. Absolut vodka, a product of Vin and Sprit (a company in Sweden), is distributed in the USA by Future Brands. The product is distributed in Europe by Maxxium. To maintain a measure of control, it bought 49 percent of a joint venture with Future Brands, and it became a fourth partner in Maxxium.[11]

In conclusion, there are a number of factors that affect channel decisions. Some of these factors are interrelated. Empirically, it has been shown that overseas distribution channel choice is affected by culture and other product constraints. One study of 269 manufacturers also found that a choice between foreign-based agents and distributors is affected by market diversity, type of transaction-specific asset, and production cost economies. Agents are used only to find customers when manufacturers want to safeguard technology by self-performing most of the export functions.[12]

DISTRIBUTION IN JAPAN

One good way to understand how a foreign distribution system might differ from that of the Western world is to examine Japan's distribution system. Japan's many-layered distribution system appears to be counter-productive. In modern societies where production is revered, Japan's distribution system seems ancient and inefficient. Employing 8.6 million people, the system consists of multiple layers of overstaffed intermediaries – overstaffed in part due to nepotism. The distribution network has more wholesalers and retailers per capita than any of the advanced industrial nations.

At the wholesale level, Japanese wholesalers perform the warehousing and financing functions in great detail. Because retailers are small and inadequately financed, the retailers shift warehousing and financing responsibilities to their suppliers by placing frequent but small orders. Wholesalers are expected to extend lengthy credit and to accept the risk of selling on consignment. Wholesalers are also expected to stock an extensive assortment of goods and to provide rapid delivery. Supplier reliability and wholesaler ability to deliver with a short lead time outweigh any concern about price advantage.

Another distinctive feature of the Japanese wholesaling business is the close and frequent interaction among wholesalers. It is common business practice for wholesalers there to resell products to other wholesalers. Distribution channels in Japan are characterized by multiple layers of wholesalers and many small retailers. Japanese wholesalers have close, personal relationships with other wholesalers, manufacturers, importers, and retailers. Because of these intimate relationships which serve as an informal barrier, foreign firms have difficulties in directly reaching end users or retailers. Even though the population of Japan is about half that of the USA, and Japan is smaller in geographic size

than the state of California, the number of retail outlets in Japan is nearly the same as that in the USA. Overall, the Japanese system of distribution is both complex and inefficient.[13]

The Japanese distribution system exists to serve social as much as economic purposes, and the social or societal goal sometimes overshadows economic logic. Channel members are not altogether different from family members, with all levels and members being tightly interlocked by tradition and emotion. It is a traumatic and sometimes tragic decision if channel members have to be dropped, and such members may be unable to bear the social consequence of losing face.

The familial relationship of firms makes doing business easier, and it is customary for members of the same family unit to prefer sourcing from one another to sourcing on the outside. This tightly knit vendor–customer family relationship is perceived by some foreign firms as a trade barrier, but it is more likely that these foreign manufacturers have failed to understand the system. However, it is not as much a case of the Japanese versus foreign suppliers but rather a case of an insider against an outsider. Any newcomer, Japanese or foreign, will have a difficult time penetrating the family unit's close organizational ties. The key to succeeding within this network is to work long and hard to become part of the family.

Compared to corporate groups in Germany, Spain, France, and Korea, the well-diversified industrial groups of Japan called *keiretsu* are similar but larger. There are six major *keiretsu* in Japan: Mitsui, Mitsubishi, Sumitomo, Fuyo, Sanwa, and Dai-Ichi. The *keiretsu* system has three major characteristics: (1) cross-ownership of equity (which allows the costs of a negative industry-specific shock to be shared by all other member firms from other industries), (2) close ties to the group's "main bank" (which provides the majority of the firm's debt financing), and (3) product market ties with the other firms in the group (which limit competition by discriminating against outside buyers/sellers).[14]

Legal barriers pose a problem for distribution efficiency. Foreign car makers have to contend with the high cost of opening dealerships in Japan. Japanese regulations prohibit local automobile dealers from sharing facilities with importers even though these dealers may sell products that have nothing to do with automobiles. In the USA, Japanese exporters have no difficulty in lining up American dealers to share their outlets.

For almost thirty years, Japan's controversial Large Scale Retail Store Law protected small and medium-sized retailers by restricting a larger store's size, hours, and operating days. Large retailers, those ones most likely to carry imported goods, were thus unable to modernize the distribution system. One has to be careful about what one may wish for, however. Because of the pressure from the USA to open its economy to more efficient international competitors, Japan finally abolished the law in 2000. Unfortunately, Japan has replaced it with the Large Scale Retail Store Location Act that has even more restrictions. Store developers must build enough parking spaces so that, even on the busiest shopping day, no shopper will ever have to wait for a parking space. This requirement is easier said than done. After all, in Japan, land is expensive and lot sizes are narrow, not to mention a burdensome task of land transfer. On top of all these obstacles, it is exceedingly difficult for any developer to do enough to reduce traffic so as to win building approval.[15]

In spite of the apparent rigidity which exists in Japan, it must be pointed out that Japan, as a "hot" country, is ripe for changes. Japanese retailing, once highly weak and fragmented, has been evolving rapidly. Small retail firms have declined in number by 20 percent, and the total number of retail establishments has decreased as well. These developments clearly show a consolidation of the Japanese retail sector.

Due to structural change in Japan, foreign manufacturers may want to experiment with alternative distribution channels. It is possible to circumvent the Japanese distribution system. Instead of cracking Japan's multitiered distribution system, foreign marketers may want to employ certain alternative distribution channels. One channel is to use direct marketing (e.g., telemarketing, mail order, and door-to-door selling). Amway Japan Ltd. has been spectacularly successful by adopting the parent's highly successful direct sales technique. The company rewards Japanese distributors for performance and gives them such titles as Diamond Direct distributors.

Another alternative channel is to establish a retail store. This is what Toys "Я" Us has done. Costco has followed suit. Costco operates more than 390 outlets worldwide to sell merchandise in big packages under a membership system. It will take time for Japanese consumers to get used to this type of distribution. Many Japanese are accustomed to go on foot to shop daily at local stores. In addition, Japanese homes are small and have only limited storage space. In the end, though, the convenience of driving to big stores and stocking up at lower prices may change their attitudes.[16]

SELECTION OF CHANNEL MEMBERS

Because the success of a product depends so much on the efforts of channel members, manufacturers must carefully screen all potential members. Most Hong Kong trading companies handle such a wide range of products that they may have inadequate time to devote to any additional product. To make matters worse, some agents in Hong Kong are known to take on a new product line for the sole purpose of denying it to other agents, knowing full well that they are not capable of being of much assistance to the new client.

Manufacturers and their intermediaries should determine whether their marketing plans are compatible. It is unwise to assume that a common European (or Asian) business mentality exists across European (or Asian) countries.

Since it is difficult for a manufacturer to learn about distant potential dealers, short of a personal and lengthy visit, there is a need to depend on other sources of information. Countries with export promotion programs usually have local offices in their major foreign markets that can provide information on how exporters may contact importers in such markets. Figure 12.6 illustrates how Hong Kong tried to attract US importers.

One good source of information in the USA is the International Trade Administration, which has available trade lists by industry and country. The US Department of Commerce's *Agent/Distributor Service (ADS)* is designed for firms seeking to identify potential foreign agents or distributors interested in a business relationship. It is a customized overseas search for interested and qualified foreign representatives on behalf of a US client. US commercial officers abroad conduct the search and prepare a report identifying up to six foreign prospects that have personally examined the US firm's product literature and have expressed an interest in representing it.

REPRESENTATION AGREEMENT AND TERMINATION

Firms often assume that, in the absence of provisions to the contrary, clauses appointing foreign distributors or agents are nonexclusive. Actually, the opposite is often the case. Indonesia prohibits a

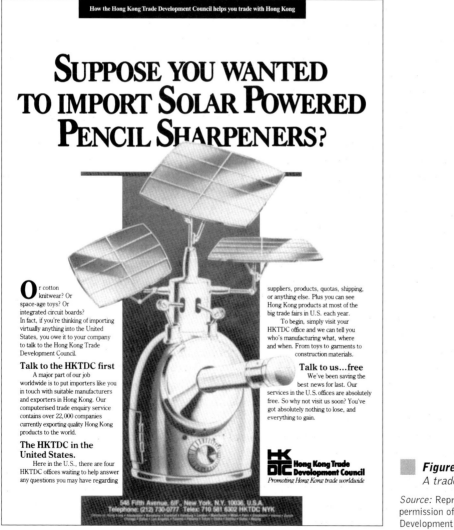

Figure 12.6
A trade inquiry service

Source: Reprinted with permission of Hong Kong Trade Development Council.

supplier from appointing more than one distributor or representative in the same territory. Colombia presumes that a sales agent's appointment is exclusive unless the agreement specifically states that the appointment is a nonexclusive one.

It may not be easy to terminate a representation agreement. Based on the assumption that an agent or distributor often invests considerable effort and money to develop the local market for the principal, many countries have enacted **agency termination laws** to protect the interests of agents and distributors. Such laws have a tendency to penalize unilaterally foreign principals that have terminated the agency relationships. These laws often forbid a manufacturer from terminating its relationships with even incompetent channel members without a lengthy notice in advance or without an expensive settlement. For example, without just cause, Bolivia may not allow a principal's product to enter the country. In Abu Dhabi, an agent with a compensation claim pending can legally prevent the importation of the former principal's products.

Despite some variations, contract termination laws of various countries have several common characteristics. First, these laws are constructed in such a way that they provide the agent with considerable leverage. The principal can terminate or refuse to extend an agency agreement without being penalized economically only upon a showing of just cause. For example, the reasons and situations under which the agreement may be validly terminated in Chile are: (1) expiration of the contract term, (2) agent's resignation, (3) death, (4) bankruptcy or insolvency of either party, (5) legal incompetence of either party, (6) marriage of a woman agent, and (7) termination of the functions of the principal, if the agency was based on the exercise of such functions.

Second, the principal is obliged to compensate the agent when the relationship is terminated without just cause. If a fixed-term contract has run for more than one year, Mexico sets the compensation at the value of six months' remuneration plus twenty days' remuneration for every year of service after the first year. In Austria, the damage payment may amount to between one year's and fifteen years'

average commission. Puerto Rico's required compensation in the event of unjust termination can be excessive, since it includes (1) actual value of expenses incurred by the agent in setting up and running the business, (2) value of the agent's inventories and stock, (3) loss of the agent's profits, and (4) value of the agent's goodwill. The agent may also claim an amount equal to the agent's profit experience for the previous five years or five times the average annual profit.

Third, the compensation and other rights granted to the agent may not be waived in some countries. Sweden, for instance, does not allow the agent to waive the termination notice requirements.

Fourth, the agency contract may not allow the parties to elect another country's law to govern the contract. Bolivia voids choice-of-law clauses since Bolivian law is the sole applicable law.

Fifth, the agent may be considered as an employee of the principal and is thus entitled to the protection of local labor laws concerning dismissal and compensation. The compensation may take the form of a pension.

Sixth, the principal may be required to give notice prior to termination, and the agent may have the right to contest the termination decisions. Sweden stipulates that the notice term be three months when an indefinite-term agreement has been in effect for at least one year. In Switzerland, the law requires a two-month minimum period for termination notice after the first year, and the termination can be effective only at the end of each calendar quarter.

To minimize risk and problems, the principal should carefully structure the representation agreement. In general, certain contract terms must be included. The written contract should identify the parties and their rights and obligations. A time period during which the agreement will be in effect should be stated. When legally permissible, the contract should specify the jurisdiction to handle legal disputes. Arbitration clauses specifying the arbitration body should be included. To avoid ambiguity, it is highly advisable to have an English version that is expressly allowed to prevail.

In Italy, most distribution agreements involve repeated sales of stock to distributors because there is no compensation upon expiration of the contract unless otherwise stipulated. It is more favorable for a manufacturer to avoid an agency relationship which will entitle an agent to certain guarantees. When an agency relationship is established, the manufacturer must make a contribution to an agent's insurance fund (ENASARCO) in order to provide sickness, termination, and pension benefits. Upon termination, the agent receives compensation for the termination itself from the ENASARCO fund. In addition, the agent will also receive compensation for the clientele already provided to the principal, and the compensation is based on the annual value of clientele served by the agent.[17]

MNCs should avoid **evergreen contracts**, which allow agreements to remain in effect or to be automatically renewed until terminated by one of the parties.[18] Such a contract may substantially increase the potential compensation obligations of the exporter under foreign laws on termination of distributors and sales representatives. Exporters should therefore have specific expiration dates in their foreign distributorship and sales representative agreements. Many countries regard the third or fourth renewal of even one- or two-year agreements as evidence of an evergreen contract. When renewing agreements, it is thus a good practice for the exporter to change the language of prior texts sufficiently in order to avoid creating the appearance of an evergreen contract. Another useful method of reducing or avoiding compensation payments is to include "just cause" termination provisions. The agreement should have the legally permissible grounds (just causes) for terminating distributors and sales representatives in the foreign country in question.

BLACK MARKET

Economic activities in search of profit will always take place regardless of what the laws say. Naturally, virtually all countries, regardless of their religious, political, and legal orientations, must contend with the black market. For millennia, smuggling has been a way of life in land-locked Afghanistan. Smuggling is facilitated by the Afghan Trade Transit Agreement (ATTA), signed in 1950, that allows goods to pass from the port of Karachi through Pakistan and over the Afghan border duty-free. Almost all goods bound for Afghanistan make a "U-Turn" and end up back in Pakistan. As an example, a buyer in Afghanistan may import air-conditioners through the Karachi port and move them across the Afghan border 620 miles away. After the trucks unload the appliances on the Afghan side, they go back to Pakistan and wait for the very same appliances to re-enter Pakistan illegally, carried by donkeys, camels, or on tribesmen's backs. Such goods sell for much less in Pakistan than legally imported items. Incidentally, a trucking industry controlled largely by Afghan refugees is used for the transportation of these products. According to the World Bank, this illegal trade amounted to $2.5 billion in 1997.[19]

While the legality of a gray market is uncertain, a black market is most certainly illegal. While a black market usually conjures up an image of small-time crooks and mafia-type organizations, several large multinationals have been accused of smuggling or abetting it. JTI-Macdonald, a Canadian tobacco manufacturer, and its four US-based affiliates were charged with fraud and evasion of hundreds of millions of dollars in duties and taxes. These companies were accused of supplying Canada's black market. The scheme involved exporting their Canadian-brand cigarettes, manufactured in Canada and Puerto Rico, to the USA, "knowing that these products were being smuggled back into Canada and onto the commercial market."[20]

GRAY MARKET

A gray market exists when a manufacturer ends up with an unintended channel of distribution that performs activities similar to the planned channel – hence the term **parallel distribution**. Gray market goods move through this extra channel, internationally as well as domestically. In an international context, a gray market product is one

MARKETING ETHICS 12.1 AMERICAN COKE VS. JAPANESE COKE

Japan is Coca-Cola's most lucrative market, earning the company $1 billion in profits before taxes. About 50 percent of Coca-Cola's products in Japan are sold through vending machines, resulting in a profit of $1.26 in profit per case – compared with 94 cents in Germany and only 28 cents in the USA. Some entrepreneurs want to share that profit. As a result, consumers in Japan can buy either Japan-made Coke or Coke that comes from the USA. The price of American Coke is about 40 percent lower, in spite of the shipping cost. Coca-Cola certainly does not like it and has gone after two small exporters – Omni Pacific and Dependable Vending. Coke's lawsuits state that sale of its products outside the specified regions raises quality control issues, infringes its trademark rights, and violates bottlers' contracts.

The exporters have fought back and filed a countersuit contending that Coca-Cola itself has provided some Japanese bottlers with the discounted American-made Coke so as to undercut the exporters. Coca-Cola is accused of unfairly trying to control prices worldwide by using such methods as threats of legal action,

requiring bottlers not to do business with suspected transshippers, and blacklists of certain companies that distributors cannot sell to. These methods violate foreign fair-trade laws and American antitrust statutes. Ironically, Dependable Vending gets its goods from Coca-Cola Enterprises, the biggest bottler, that eagerly sells to anyone in order to meet its numbers.

Coca-Cola also went after Mushi Pardhan, a Tanzanian immigrant in Canada. Pardhan bought Coke products wholesale in Canada and shipped the "gray goods" to Hong Kong and Japan for a 14 percent profit margin. He bought a case for $4.25 (plus transport cost) and resold it for more than $6. The sales reached $4.8 million on a weekly basis. Coke, suing for trademark infringement, shut Pardhan down in 1995. A federal judge subsequently ruled that Pardhan bought and sold the products legally, and the Canadian Supreme Court refused to accept Coke's appeal.

Sources: "Coke Flips Its Top over Japan Sales," *San José Mercury News*, January 26, 2000; and "Distributor Dilemmas," *PROMO*, August 2000, 20.

imported by an unauthorized party. Products notably affected by this method of operation include watches, cameras, automobiles, perfumes, and electronic goods. The problem is particularly acute for Seiko, because one out of every four Seiko watches imported into the US market is unauthorized.

A gray marketer can acquire goods in two principal ways (see It's the Law 12.1). One method is to place an order directly with a manufacturer by going through an intermediary in order to conceal identity and purpose. Another method is to buy the merchandise for immediate shipment on the open market overseas. Asian countries in general and Hong Kong in particular are favorite targets because the wholesale prices there are usually much lower than elsewhere. The importance of the gray market even persuades some countries to specialize in handling such goods for the third country, primarily the

USA. Germany stimulates the practice by rebating all import duties and local VAT for re-exports. Paris' Roissy Airport is popular with international brokers because of its duty-free warehouse space for transshipments, which are not taxed either. The airport also allows quick delivery because goods simply move through it without any intermediate delivery.

The existence of the gray market has stimulated a great deal of debate. Complaints are made, and responses to the charges are offered. At least four questions must be asked. First, why does the gray market exist? Second, are gray market goods illegal? Third, do gray marketers perform any useful functions? Fourth, are gray market goods inferior?

Causes

Gray marketing of a product within a market often takes place because of the channel structure and

IT'S THE LAW 12.1   BLACK MARKET

The European Union filed lawsuits against Philip Morris and R.J. Reynolds, accusing them of organizing and running a multibillion-dollar international cigarette smuggling operation. The federal civil racketeering lawsuits alleged a conspiracy that evaded billions of dollars in customs payments, duties, fees, and taxes from the EU. To facilitate smuggling, these tobacco giants knowingly mislabeled or did not label their cigarettes, and they arranged practically untraceable payments for smuggled cigarettes that included money rerouted to Swiss bank accounts. In the case of R.J. Reynolds, the smuggling trail started in its Miami office. Winstons were sold there to Copaco, a Panama company. Cigarettes were shipped from North Carolina to Panama and then to the Netherlands. Shippers in the Netherlands next attached documents to show that the cigarettes were sent to Canary Islands or Easter Europe. Actually, the shipment was trucked to be sold in Spain.

The European Union later filed another lawsuit in New York against R.J. Reynolds to seek compensation for money laundering. According to the EU's estimates, it lost several billion dollars in taxes every year due to smuggling cigarettes from Eastern Europe and the Middle East into the EU. American companies supposedly and intentionally oversupplied Eastern European countries and elsewhere so that the surplus could be smuggled into the EU.

Sources: "Two Tobacco Giants Accused of Smuggling in Europe," *San José Mercury News,* November 7, 2000; "EU Files New Suit Against R.J. Reynolds," *San José Mercury News,* November 1, 2002.

---

margins. A manufacturer who wants to eliminate the potentially profitable gray marketing activity should restructure its pricing and discount policies. Parallel importation of trademarked products occurs for several reasons: (1) gray marketers can easily locate sources of supply because many trademarked products are available in markets throughout the world, (2) price differences among these sources of supply are great enough, and (3) the legal and other barriers to moving goods are low.

Although there are several causes, price differential is the only true reason for the gray market to exist. There is no justification for the existence of the gray market unless prices in at least two domestic markets differ to the extent that, even with extra transportation costs, reasonable profits can be made. This is a good example of the economic force at work. Gray market goods may be purchased, imported, and resold by an unauthorized distributor at prices lower than those charged by manufacturer-authorized importers/distributors. As a result, identical items can carry two different retail prices.

Legal dimension

At one time, whether or not gray market goods are illegal could not be answered with a great degree of certainty. Unlike the black market, which is clearly illegal, the gray market, as its name implies, is neither black nor white – legality is in doubt. For the US market, all US-registered trademark owners are protected under the Tariff Act of 1930 and Section 42 of the Lanham Act. The law *protects an independent American trademark owner* who invests money in promoting a brand to the extent that the owner becomes identified with that brand in the USA. The protection is granted to protect the mark owner from unfair competition by those seeking to sell the same goods without authorization. If the owner of a US trademark bought distribution rights from an "unrelated" foreign manufacturer, that owner is thus able to obtain an exclusion order from the Customs Service to forbid entry of goods bearing his brand name. Thus, only *independent American firms* are entitled to seek this protection. An exclusion order is not granted to foreign companies, and this includes those using their own US subsidiaries to import their goods into the USA. As a result, Canon and Minolta were unable to register their trademarks with the US Customs for the purpose of banning entry of gray market goods.

At present, the law seems to be more on the side of parallel distributors. The US Court of Appeals ruled that a trademark owner receives no injury to its reputation because there is no confusion about the product's origin, and that a manufacturer is capable of labeling and advertising to inform the public of the lack of warranty of gray market merchandise. Courts in other countries often take the same position. Japanese judges rule repeatedly for gray market importers. The British Fair Trading Act allows wholesalers to sell to any retailers, who in turn can buy from any wholesalers. The Ninth US Circuit Court of Appeals held that "this country's trademark law does not offer [the manufacturer] a vehicle for establishing a discriminatory pricing scheme simply through the expedient of setting up an American subsidiary with nominal title to its mark."

The US Supreme Court's rulings on two separate cases, though somewhat contradictory, appear to endorse gray marketing. Sharp Electronics Corp. stopped selling calculators to Business Electronics Corp., a Houston discount retailer, after receiving a complaint from a full-price retailer. The Supreme Court rules that such a cut-off is not an automatic violation of federal antitrust law because Sharp did not explicitly set prices. The high court, arguing that higher prices lead to better service which benefits consumers, held that manufacturers can cut off "free riders" who take unfair advantage of the greater service provided by full-price firms. In a five-to-four vote in another case, however, the Supreme Court legitimized the gray market. The Tariff Act of 1930 allows imports to be blocked only when requested by a US firm that was authorized by an unaffiliated foreign trademark owner to distribute its products. Foreign goods may be imported when the foreign and domestic trademark holders are "subject to common ownership and control."

At one time, certain exclusive sales territories were supported by nontariff barriers between member states of the European Union. However, the EU's elimination of nontariff barriers and border controls has made it possible for parallel imports to move freely across the EU, resulting in price competition. Under the EU concept of parallel imports, suppliers and distributors of products in one member state cannot use exclusive sales arrangements to conspire to block parallel imports of identical products from dealers in other member states. Such actions are a violation of EU antitrust laws.

The only industry-specific exception to the EU's normal competition principles is the automobile industry. The rules governing new car sales, known as "block exemption," restrict car dealers' competition. Even then, the rules still require the car makers to sell their cars to any EU citizens regardless of where they live. Volkswagen was found to have prevented Germans and Austrians from buying Volkswagen and Audi cars in Italy where the prices were cheaper. The European Commission fined Volkswagen a massive amount of €102 million. The amount was later reduced to €90 million because the EU's Court of First Instance ruled that the European Commission did not prove that Volkswagen cancelled some dealer franchises so as to punish them for facilitating cross-border sales. In the end, the European Court of Justice, the EU's high court, upheld the ruling in 2003.

Ethical dimension

To manufacturers and authorized dealers, parallel distributors are nothing but freeloaders or parasites who take advantage of the legitimate owners' investment and goodwill. Manufacturers also feel that these discounters deceive buyers by implying that gray market goods have the same quality and warranties as items sold through authorized channels.

Gray marketers naturally see the situation differently. They feel that manufacturers try to have it both ways – tolerating gray marketing when they need to get rid of surplus merchandise and condemning gray marketers when that need subsides. Gray marketers also accuse manufacturers of not wanting to be price competitive, and view manufacturers' distribution restrictions as a smoke-screen for absolute price control. Parallel distributors claim to align themselves more with consumers by providing an alternative and legal means of distribution, a means capable of delivering the same goods to consumers at a lower but fair price under the free enterprise system. Some parallel distributors have even sued Mercedes-Benz for restraint of trade, which is a violation of the Sherman and Clayton Acts. As pointed out by them, trademarks are designed to counter fraud rather than limit distribution.

Product quality

With regard to the charge that gray market goods are inferior, manufacturers and authorized dealers refuse to service such goods by pointing out that gray market goods are not for US consumption. Therefore, such goods are adulterated, second-rate, or discontinued articles, and consumers may be misled into believing that they receive identical products with US warranties. Gray marketers, however, do not buy this argument. According to them, there is really no proof that the products they handle are inferior. It is inconceivable that a manufacturer would stop a production line just to make another product version for the non-US market. As such, gray market goods are genuine products subject to the same stringent product control. Concerning the inferior warranty and the manufacturer's refusal to service gray market goods under warranty terms, parallel distributors show no concern, since they have their own warranty service centers that can provide the same, if not better, service. Their service offers are often closer to the market being served. Gray marketers also point out that they would not survive in the long run if they did not provide service and quality assurance.

Manufacturers' marketing strategies

The arguments used by both sides are legitimate and have merits. Only one thing is certain: authorized distributors are adversely affected by parallel

distribution. They lose market share as well as control over price. They may have to service goods sold by parallel competitors, and the loss of good-will follows when consumers are unable to get proper repair.

Manufacturers and authorized distributors definitely see the need to discourage gray marketing. There are several strategies for this purpose, and each strategy has both merits and problems. Although tracking down offenders costs money, disenfranchisement of offenders is a stock response. This move sends loud signals of commitment to distributors who abide by the terms of the franchise agreement. A one-price-for-all policy can eliminate an important source of arbitrage, but it ignores transaction costs and forecloses valid price discrimination opportunities among classes of customers who are buying very different benefits in the same product. Another strategy is to add distributors (perhaps former gray market distributors) to the network, but this approach may create disputes among current distributors.

There are both reactive and proactive strategies that may be employed (See Tables 12.1 and 12.2).[21] Reactive strategies to combat gray market activity are strategic confrontation, participation, price cutting, supply interference, promotion of gray market product limitations, collaboration, and acquisition. Proactive strategies are product/service differentiation and availability, strategic pricing, dealer development, marketing information systems, long-term image reinforcement, establishing legal precedence, and lobbying.

Certain strategies warrant further attention. When they want to track the trail of gray market goods, manufacturers can use serial numbers on products and warranty cards to identify those who are involved in unauthorized distribution. There are two problems related to this strategy. First, using special model numbers or identifying special model numbers or identifying marks on products increases inventory cost and affects the manufacturer's flexibility in rerouting products quickly and cheaply to markets with a sudden surge in demand. Second, even when unauthorized dealers are identified,

375

Table 12.1 Reactive strategies to combat gray market activity

Type of strategy	Implemented by	Cost of implementation	Difficulty of implementation	Does it curtail gray market activity at source?	Does it provide immediate relief to authorized dealers?	Long-term effectiveness	Legal risks to manufacturers or dealers	Company examples
Strategic confrontation	Dealer with manufacturer support	Moderate	Requires planning	No	Relief in the medium term	Effective	Low risk	Creative merchandizing by Caterpillar and car dealers
Participation	Dealer	Low	Not difficult	No	Immediate relief	Potentially damaging reputation of manufacturer	Low risk	Dealers wishing to remain anonymous
Price cutting	Jointly by manufacturer and dealer	Costly	Not difficult	No, if price cutting is temporary	Immediate relief	Effective	Moderate to high risk	Dealers and manufacturers remain anonymous
Supply interference	Either party can engage	Moderate at the wholesale level; high at the retail level	Moderately difficult	No	Immediate relief or slightly delayed	Somewhat effective if at wholesale level; not effective at retail level	Moderate risk at wholesale level; low risk at retail level	IBM, Hewlett-Packard, Lotus Corp., Swatch Watch USA, Charles of the Ritz Group Ltd., Leitz, Inc., NEC Electronics
Promotion of gray market product limitations	Jointly, with manufacturer leadership	Moderate	Not difficult	No	Slightly delayed relief	Somewhat effective	Low risk	Komatsu, Seiko, Rolex, Mercedes-Benz, IBM
Collaboration	Dealer	Low	Requires careful negotiations	No	Immediate relief	Somewhat effective	Very high risk	Dealers wishing to remain anonymous
Acquisition	Dealer	Very costly	Difficult	No	Immediate relief	Effective if other gray market brokers don't creep up	Moderate to high risk	No publicized cases

Note
Company strategies include, but are not limited to, those mentioned here.

Source: S. Tamer Cavusgil and Ed Sikora, "How Multinationals can Counter Gray Market Imports," *Columbia Journal of World Business* 23 (winter 1988): 78.

Table 12.2 Proactive strategies to combat gray market activity

Type of strategy	Implemented by	Cost of implementation	Difficulty of implementation	Does it curtail gray market activity at source?	Does it provide immediate relief to authorized dealers?	Long-term effectiveness	Legal risks to manufacturers or dealers	Company examples
Product service differentiation and availability	Jointly, with manufacturer leadership	Moderate to high	Not difficult	Yes	No; impact felt in medium to long term	Very effective	Very low risk	General Motors Ford, Porsche Kodak
Strategic pricing	Manufacturer	Moderate to high	Complex; impact on overall profitability needs monitoring	Yes	Slightly delayed	Very effective	Low risk	Porsche
Dealer development	Jointly, with manufacturer leadership	Moderate to high	Not difficult; requires dealer participation	No	No; impact felt in long term	Very effective	No risk	Caterpillar, Canon
Marketing information system	Jointly, with manufacturer leadership	Moderate to high	Not difficult; requires dealer participation	No	No; impact felt after implementation	Effective	No risk	IBM, Caterpillar Yamaha, Hitachi, Komatsu, Lotus Development, insurance companies
Long-term image reinforcement	Jointly	Moderate	Not difficult	No	No; impact felt in long term	Effective	No risk	Most manufacturers with strong dealer networks
Establishing legal precedence	Manufacturer	High	Difficult	Yes, if fruitful	No	Uncertain	Low risk	COPIAT, Coleco, Charles of the Ritz Group, LTD.
Lobbying	Jointly	Moderate	Difficult	Yes, if fruitful	No	Uncertain	Low risk	COPIAT, Duracell, Porche

Note
Company strategies include, but are not limited to, those mentioned here.

Source: S. Tamer Cavusgil and Ed Sikora, "How Multinationals can Counter Gray Market Imports," *Columbia Journal of World Business* 23 (winter 1988): 82.

there is a question of whether anything can be done to rectify the situation. When Canon stopped shipments to the Netherlands, Dutch dealers simply imported Canon cameras from Germany instead. Furthermore, any overt and concerted action against gray market dealers may be construed as an illegal restraint of domestic and international commerce. Another strategy involves educating consumers. Minolta ran advertisements to inform consumers that gray market cameras have inferior warranty. This strategy is risky because the message implies that something is wrong with the manufacturer's own products.

The most effective way to eliminate the gray market is to eliminate the cause–price discrepancy between markets. Price matching can put gray retailers out of business overnight, but this method requires the manufacturer to reduce prices in the most profitable markets. Another problem with this strategy is that it adversely affects the product's prestige image and brand value. Certain brands are successful due to their snob and exclusivity appeal, and they have to be promoted as luxury articles that must be expensive. In the case of automobiles, price cutting would disrupt both insurance rates and resale values, creating a peculiar situation by making new cars less expensive than used ones.

To resolve some of the problems pointed out above, the strategy of product differentiation should be used. Porsche makes its cars for the US market more powerful and better equipped in order to reflect the higher price. The assumption here is that the differences in features are noticeable and justify the price differential. Multiple brands may also be employed for the same product, with each brand assigned to a certain market. Like other strategies, however, the use of multiple brands affects the economies of scale and increases the production, inventory, and marketing costs.

One study uses the gray market activity as an independent variable, and strategic export performance and economic export performance as the dependent variables. Gray marketing does not hurt exporters' economic performance much because it also generates sales of its own. However, gray marketing interferes with exporters' efforts to achieve their strategic goals. Contrary to traditional thinking, foreign currency and inflation rate fluctuations do not appear to spur gray marketing. Likewise, it is often assumed that a company's exposure to overseas markets should give it internal skills to create an organizational environment that is capable of combating gray marketing. However, according to the empirical evidence, a company's international experience and the number of its markets have insignificant relationships with unauthorized imports. On the other hand, the low level of gray marketing is associated with distribution control, integrated channels, centralization, and product standardization.[22]

DISTRIBUTION OF SERVICES

Services, like products, also need distribution. As such, service providers need to design their distribution channels. The various determinants and decisions discussed above should apply to the marketing of services as well.

In general, services can be exported through four distinct modes: cross-border, consumption abroad, commercial presence, and movement of personnel.[23] The first mode is *cross-border*. This mode occurs when neither the producer nor the consumer physically moves. Instead the services are provided through a common channel such as the Internet. Education and training (i.e. distance learning), and professional services such as accounting are typical cross-border supply services.

Consumption abroad is the second mode. It takes place when the consumer/buyer is in the supplier's country. Tourism is a good example of this mode of delivery.

Commercial presence, as the third mode, occurs when the supplier establishes a local office in the country where the service is to be provided. Typical services that employ this mode include financial and consulting services.

Finally, *movement of personnel* consists of staff of the service company moving to the country where the service export is provided. Temporary ventures, such as engineering or construction projects, are examples of this type of service delivery. Employees of the firm travel to and provide contracted services for the duration of the project.

Let us consider the case of the education and training sector (see Figure 12.7).[24] The sector includes services defined at the level of post-secondary education, and it includes education services ranging from diploma and certificate through doctoral and post-doctoral degrees. Regarding distribution, the four modes of supply mentioned above certainly apply to the export of post-secondary education and training. A US institution may deliver online courses to foreign students based in their home countries. A more familiar form is for foreign students to travel to an American or European university for consumption abroad. Several European and American universities have now established commercial presence by opening a branch campus/training facility in a foreign country

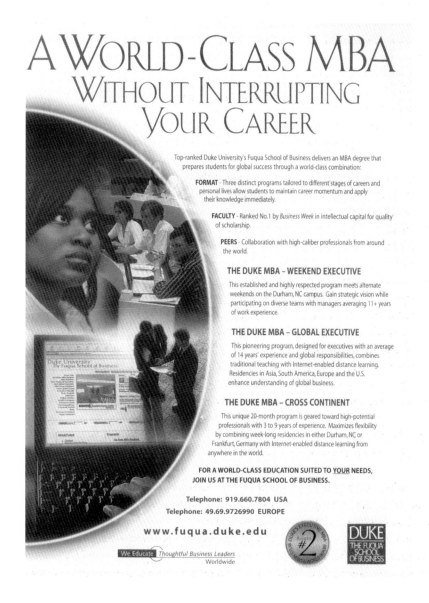

Figure 12.7
Distribution of education

379

through which they offer their courses and programs. Last but not least, Western institutions and corporations have also relied on movement of personnel in the sense that their faculty and trainers are sent abroad to deliver a course to consumers in another country.

CONCLUSION

A product, no matter how desirable, must be made accessible to buyers. A manufacturer may attempt to use a direct distribution channel by selling directly to end users abroad. The feasibility of this channel depends on the type of product involved. Generally, the sales opportunity created by direct selling is quite limited. Intermediaries are usually needed to move the product efficiently from the manufacturer to the foreign user.

This chapter has discussed the roles of domestic and overseas middlemen. The manufacturer has the option of selling or assigning sales responsibility to intermediaries in its own country and letting them decide about reselling the product elsewhere. Another option for the manufacturer involves bypassing intermediaries and dealing directly with foreign buyers, assuming that the manufacturer has enough expertise, market familiarity, resources, and commitment. With the myriad intermediaries available, it is impossible to prescribe a single distribution method that is ideal for all products and markets.

A number of factors – such as product type, regulations, customs, and intermediary loyalty – must be taken into account in designing and developing an international channel of distribution. These factors determine how long, how wide, and how many channels are appropriate. Ordinarily, those intermediaries that fail to add some value to the product as it moves through them are likely to be bypassed or dropped from the channel. But the manufacturer cannot afford to dictate terms, since an intermediary will carry a manufacturer's product only if the manufacturer minimizes channel conflict as well as providing some value to these sales intermediaries in return.

CASE 12.1   THE INTERNATIONAL RECORD INDUSTRY

Peter Spang Goodrich, Providence College

The international music recording industry is in a crisis. Internet piracy downloading of songs to MP3 format rampages. How can the industry recoup these lost revenues? Sales are off. There is ample evidence of fiscal difficulties among the major record labels.

The July 7, 2003 issue of *New Yorker* asked "Can the Record Business Survive?" Author John Seabrook notes:

"Sales of recorded music in the USA have dropped by more than a million units in the past few years, falling well below seven hundred million. . . .

"Around the globe, the record business is sixteen percent smaller than it was in 2000. Record labels blame the fans, for lacking the long-term loyalty to pop acts which record buyers used to have, and for engaging in wholesale 'piracy' of music, either by copying CDs or by downloading music illegally from the Internet. . . .

"Everything depends on getting people to pay for music that they now get for free."

Two opposing international marketing strategies with strong contrasts have been adopted to try to save the industry. Each uses a different promotional strategy to compete in a challenging legal environment. On the one hand, record executive Jason Flom advocates the continuation of the star system. Ninety-nine percent of the artists earn a pittance. Stars subsidize the major labels. Record companies thrive on the star system.

Flom is promoting his 17-year-old diva protégée Cherie. Flom presented Cherie to the Warner Brothers Group (WBG) in Barcelona. Normally, singers build a local base first before expanding their market nationally and globally. Flom reversed this. He wanted to market Cherie as an international star right away. At the WBG Barcelona meeting, Cherie was a big hit. The keen interest even among affiliates representing countries that Flom had assumed had no record market astounded him. So Cherie's first album will have French and Spanish tracks in addition to English.

Travel and relentless appearances are needed to sustain a hit record. Established stars do not appreciate these upheavals to their personal lives. Since Cherie is only 17 years old and craves stardom, she is eager to promote her record. The attitude of the major record labels is revealed at the November 2002 marketing meeting to "blow up Cherie." Aaron Simon is in charge of "product" management. It just so happens that the "product" is a human being.

On the other hand, many artists are hitting back against a perceived "plantation accounting" system. An increasing number of artists are going independent. Recording star Joni Mitchell said in *Rolling Stone*: "I would never take another deal in the record business . . . I'll be damned if I'll line their pockets . . . I hope it all goes down the crapper." In *W*, she called the recording industry a "corrupt cesspool" where "record companies are not looking for talent. They're looking for a look and a willingness to cooperate."

Consider the most striking case of folk-rock-country-blues-gospel singer-songwriter Michelle Shocked. She successfully sued Mercury Records on the grounds of violating the 13th Amendment to the US Constitution barring slavery or involuntary servitude. Mercury had turned down her proposed album because it did not fit their marketing model for her. In addition, it would not allow her to produce the album for another label. Effectively, her means of livelihood was stopped.

Shocked won the case in 1996 and is now the first major artist to own her entire body of work to market independently as she sees fit through Mighty Sound. Many other artists such as Jimmy Buffet (Mailboat Records), Ani Di Franco (Righteous Babe), and Joni Mitchell have rejected the major labels. They are marketing their own work through the Internet and direct marketing. In addition, these independents' work never goes "out of print." Of course, such independent production may be best suited to record sales runs of between 5000 and 10000. It will probably work best on niche markets such as jazz, folk, Latin, and world music.

Points to consider

1   How is the incredibly rapid growth of the Internet (which occupied but one paragraph in the 1997 edition of this text) helping the Shocked/Di Franco marketing method?

2   Is it the legal responsibility of the governments to control illegal music downloading over the Internet? What are the difficulties posed by the international nature of the internet? Consider one of the major downloading People-to-People (P2P) programs, KaZaA, commissioned by two Scandinavians and programmed by Estonians. How do governments shut down a P2P site which has no central location? How would the US government prosecute a downloader who lives in Canada? Can any one country effectively stop this practice? Would it help if prosecutions ceased but the government adopted an annual Internet use license of, say $5, to compensate the music industry for lost revenue?

3   Should the industry adopt Internet marketing such as the strategy of Apple Computer's iTunes Music Store which sells downloaded songs for 99 cents? An alternative might be selling MP3 players preloaded with an artists music together with cut-rate options to all future works. For example, Michelle Shocked might enter into a partnership with Apple to sell preloaded iPods for a premium of $50 over the costs of an empty iPod. Since Shocked has produced over 100 songs, the costs per track would be a nominal 50 cents. The rights to all future tracks could also be sold for the same 50 cents. Thus, if Shocked produced a CD with sixteen tracks that might sell for $15.99, those who bought the preloaded iPod could own the tracks from only $8. Would this scheme work? Would you consider it yourself?

4   What is the potential for self-promotion versus major record company sales? If one is entrepreneurial, what are the benefits and risks of this international marketing approach?

5   In 2002, the top ten bestselling albums accounted for 33.5 million copies. This was only half of the 2000 sales figures. These big sellers subsidize lesser selling albums and the development of new artists. The record industry cites this as proof that Internet piracy is killing the industry. Do you think that this is true or have sales merely diversified as a result of increased information about alternative artists provided by new technology?

6   Which of the two approaches – the star system or independent entrepreneurs – will provide the future for the international music industry?

CASE 12.2   SCHWARZKOPF, INC. DISTRIBUTION NETWORK

Daniel M. Evans, San José State University, and Heinz Bieler, Schwarzkopf Professional

Schwarzkopf is one of the leading hair care companies in the world. The "Professional Product" lines office is based in Hamburg, Germany. Professional Products are sold solely to beauty salons and beauty schools worldwide (see Figure 12.8).

An enterprising merchant named Hans Schwarzkopf established a chemist's shop on a bustling street in Berlin, Germany. He produced medicinals, perfumes, and the beauty care products favored by men and women of his day. In 1898, he compounded the world's first formula for shampooing hair. The news spread rapidly of the new Schwarzkopf powder shampoo, and the House of Schwarzkopf grew and became known throughout Europe as a maker of distinctive hair and beauty products.

Today, Schwarzkopf offers, worldwide, everything needed for beautiful hair, such as hair color, shampoos, conditioners, permanent waves, and styling products.

In 1978, Schwarzkopf was introduced into the USA for the first time. Schwarzkopf decided to follow tried and true European distribution methods. In Europe, especially in Germany, it is customary to offer products through direct sales to the clientele; in this case the beauty salons. Schwarzkopf has its own sales force which visits all the salons in Germany. Considering the size of Germany, the direct sales system works well. Furthermore, since the salon owners and workers are themselves products of the extensive German occupational training system, the direct sales force does not need to engage in fundamental training in the use of the hair care products.

Schwarzkopf established one warehouse in Los Angeles, and hired a few "educators" to call on prospective buyers. Schwarzkopf became an instant success in the Los Angeles area, but it proved difficult to service prospective customers in the rest of the USA. Schwarzkopf tried until 1993 to service customers directly as in Germany, but realized that the German distribution methods were not adequate for the USA market. Furthermore, sales personnel reported frustration in the ability of salons to use the professional products properly.

Points to consider

1   Why do you think it was difficult for Schwarzkopf to achieve satisfactory distribution throughout the USA?
2   In what other way did German assumptions about the USA market prove inadequate?
3   If you were responsible for Schwarzkopf in the USA, what changes in the distribution system would you recommend?

Figure 12.8 Schwarzkopf's product line

QUESTIONS

1   Distinguish between direct and indirect selling channels. What are the advantages and disadvantages of these channels?
2   Explain these types of direct channel intermediaries: foreign distributor and state-controlled trading company.
3   Explain these types of indirect channel agents: EMC, cooperative exporter, and purchasing agent.
4   Explain these types of indirect channel merchants: export merchant, export drop shipper, export distributor, and trading company.
5   Explain hot, moderate, and cold countries as classified by the country temperature gradient. What are the channel implications of this classification system?
6   What are the factors that affect the length, width, and number of marketing channels?
7   Why is it difficult – financially and legally – to terminate the relationship with overseas middlemen? What should be done to prevent or minimize such difficulties?
8   What are gray market products? Are they legal?

DISCUSSION ASSIGNMENTS AND MINICASES

1   Do you think that the US ETCs can compete effectively with Japanese trading companies?
2   How should Japan be classified: hot, moderate, or cold? Do you think this classification may change in the future?
3   Should the distribution channels of Volkswagen and Porsche be the same?
4   Honda created a separate dealer network for its Acura brand. Is there a need for this expensive strategy?
5   Sony Corp. of America, in an effort to include retailing in its operations, runs its own licensed stores in Japan and Europe. In the USA, Sony has opened the Sony Gallery of Consumer Electronics in Chicago. Inside the store, "boom boxes" and camcorders are displayed on pedestals as if they were art objects, and the Walkman is displayed on trendy mannequins. The gallery includes a life-size mock-up of an apartment with a built-in Sony home theater system. Some retailers are concerned that Sony might turn out to be both their supplier and competitor. How should Sony deal with this concern?
6   Do gray marketers serve useful marketing functions – for consumers and manufacturers?
7   US Customs regulations require watches to have a small inked stamp on the movement. Seiko thus charged that the gray market Seiko watches imported into the USA were unfit because the opening for marking harmed dust- and water-resistant seals and contaminated the watch movement.

   ■   Do you feel that gray marketers' marking to comply with customs regulations is harmful to the product?
   ■   Since Seiko is a popular brand and gray market Seiko watches are carried by a number of discounters and catalog showrooms, what should Seiko do to alleviate the problem of unauthorized imports?

NOTES

1   Mike W. Peng and Anne S. York, "Behind Intermediary Performance in Export Trade: Transactions, Agents and Resources," *Journal of International Business Studies* 32 (second quarter, 2001): 327–46.
2   Harald Trabold, "Export Intermediation: An Empirical Test of Peng and Ilinitch," *Journal of International Business Studies* 33 (second quarter, 2002): 327–44.

3   Kelly Hewett and William O. Bearden, "Dependence, Trust, and Relational Behavior on the Part of Foreign Subsidiary Marketing Operations: Implications for Managing Global Marketing Operations," *Journal of Marketing* 65 (October 2001): 51–66.

4   Richard Barovick and Patricia Anderson, "EMCs/ETCs: What They Are, How They Work," *Business America*, July 13, 1992, 2–5.

5   "Small Companies Look to Cultivate Foreign Business," *Wall Street Journal*, July 7, 1994.

6   Isaiah A. Litvak and Peter M. Banting, "A Conceptual Framework for International Business Arrangements," in *Marketing and the New Science of Planning*, ed. Robert L. King (Chicago, IL: American Marketing Association, 1968), 460–7.

7   "Carrefour Forced to Cut Stakes," *Bangkok Post*, June 13, 2002.

8   R. Scott Marshall and David M Boush, "Dynamic Decision-Making: A Cross-Cultural Comparison of US and Peruvian Export Managers," *Journal of International Business Studies* 32 (fourth quarter, 2001): 873–93.

9   Harry G. Broadman, "Competition and Business Entry in Russia," *Finance & Development*, June 2001, 22–5.

10   David A. Griffith and Michael G. Harvey, "A Resource Perspective of Global Dynamic Capabilities," *Journal of International Business Studies* 32 (third quarter, 2001): 597–606.

11   "Vin and Sprit Sets Venture for Absolut Distribution," *San José Mercury News*, March 21, 2001.

12   Daniel C. Bello and Ritu Lohtia, "Export Channel Design: The Use of Foreign Distributors and Agents," *Journal of the Academy of Marketing Science* 23 (spring 1995): 83–93.

13   Eric Michael Kennedy, "The Japanese Distribution System," *Business America*, May 17, 1993, 20–1.

14   Hesna Genay, "Japan's Corporate Groups," *Economic Perspectives* 15 (January/Febraury 1991): 20–30.

15   "Closing the Door on Malls," *San José Mercury News*, April 24, 2000.

16   "Warehouse Giant Costco Growing in Crowded Japan," *San José Mercury News*, September 22, 2002.

17   Vincenzo Sinisi and Thomas M. Federman, "Commercial Aspects of Italian Law," *Business America*, October 5, 1992, 12–14.

18   John T. Masterson, Jr., "Drafting International Distributorship and Sales Representative Agreements," *Business America*, November 21, 1988, 8–9.

19   "Dark Days for a Black Market," *Business Week*, October 15, 2001, 60–1.

20   "Canadian Maker Charged with Fraud," *San José Mercury News*, March 1, 2003.

21   S. Tamer Cavusgil and Ed Sikora, "How Multinationals Can Counter Gray Market Imports," *Columbia Journal of World Business* 23 (winter 1988): 75–85.

22   Matthew B. Myers, "Incidents of Gray Market Activity Among US Exporters: Occurrences, Characteristics, and Consequences," *Journal of International Business Studies* 30 (first quarter, 1999): 105–26.

23   Tony Michalski, "Going Global With Services Exports: A Guide to Available Support," *Export America* (May 2001): 17–19.

24   Jennifer R. Moll, Susan Gates, and Lesley Quigley, "International Education and Training Services: A Global Market of Opportunity for US Providers," *Export America*, May 2001, 19–21.

Chapter 13

Physical distribution and documentation

Imagine a world without lawyers, accountants, and insurance agents.

Murray L. Weidenbaum

CHAPTER OUTLINE

- ■ Modes of transportation
  - ☐ Land
  - ☐ Air
  - ☐ Water
- ■ Cargo or transportation insurance
- ■ Packing
  - ☐ Packing problems
  - ☐ Containers
- ■ Freight forwarder and customs broker
- ■ Documentation
  - ☐ Shipping documents
  - ☐ Collection documents
- ■ Conclusion

PURPOSE OF CHAPTER

Distribution is a necessary as well as a costly activity. According to one executive at Procter & Gamble, the average time required to move a typical product from "farm to shelf" is four to five months. Although it takes only about seventeen minutes to actually produce a product, the rest of the time is spent in logistical activities – storage, handling, transportation, packing, and so on.[1]

In the developed economies, the distribution sector typically accounts for one-third of the gross domestic product (GDP).[2] Furthermore, international logistics costs can account for 25 to 35 percent of the sales value of a product, a significant difference from the 8 to 10 percent for domestic shipment.[3]

Examples that could demonstrate some of the difficulty in physically moving products overseas are endless. Firms can become easily frustrated by the physical distribution problems overseas. Port congestion coupled with the lack of efficient materials handling equipment can cause long delays. Even inland movements can be a problem because some road networks cannot accommodate long containers and rail gauges vary across countries. China, for example, intentionally uses different rail gauges for security reasons (i.e., to prevent quick troop movement in the case of a foreign invasion). Not only must a company make arrangements for transportation, but it must also pay attention to how the product is packed for shipping. The process requires a great deal of paperwork throughout.

Paperwork is a global problem. It impedes trade, chokes a flow of trade, costs jobs, and loses government revenue. To move goods across borders worldwide, nine billion documents are required each year. According to the United nations Conference on Trade and Development, an average customs transaction involves twenty-seven parties, forty documents, 200 data elements (thirty of them are repeated at least thirty times), and the retyping of 70 percent of all data at least once. Of course, in many countries, the import-export paperwork is worse.[4]

This chapter examines the various issues related to the process of moving a product from one country to another, beginning by comparing and contrasting the major transportation modes. The discussion then focuses on insurance and packing for export. Next, the chapter examines two kinds of intermediaries that, in the area of physical distribution, are virtually indispensable – freight forwarders and customhouse brokers. Finally, a significant portion of the chapter is devoted to a discussion of documentation, including both shipping and collection documents.

MARKETING ILLUSTRATION   THE PAPER CHASE

Benetton's Sisley line of clothing contains microchip transmitters that make it possible for the Italian company to track its garments from the point of manufacture to the moment they are sold in any of its 5,000 stores. Philips Semiconductors has introduced the "smart tag" tracking technology. This technology employs a Philips Electronics radio frequency ID tag which replaces the traditional bar codes that have to be manually scanned. The ID is actually embedded in the clothes. This antenna-bearing chip is smaller than a grain of rice and is attached to clothes' labels. Any item returned to a store will automatically re-enter the inventory.

In many or perhaps most cases, marketers may find that it is much more practical to leave the physical distribution activities to specialists. Dell Computer Corp., for example, sells computers in 115 countries. It has arranged for Roadway Services Inc. to handle Dell's worldwide shipping. Earlier, Dell had to deal with dozens of carriers and found that it would have to hire 1000 to 2000 additional workers to meet the projected growth. Roadway, as a single-source provider, subcontracts and manages all customer shipments – both inbound and outbound.

MODES OF TRANSPORTATION

The availability of transportation is one important factor affecting a company's site selection, as noted in Figure 13.1. To move a product both between countries and within a country, there are three fundamental modes of transportation: air, water (ocean and inland), and land (rail and truck). Ocean and air shipments are appropriate for transportation between countries, especially when the distance is considerable and the boundaries are not joined. Inland water, rail, and highway are more suitable for inland and domestic transportation. When countries are connected by land (e.g., North America), it is possible to use rail and highway to move merchandise from locations, such as from the USA to Canada. In Europe, rail is an important mode due to the contiguity of land areas and the availability of a modern and efficient rail system.

The appropriate transportation mode depends on (1) market location, (2) speed, and (3) cost. A firm must first consider *market location*. Contiguous markets may be served by either rail or truck, and such is the case when goods are shipped from the USA to Canada or Mexico. To move goods between continents, ocean or air transportation is needed.

Speed is another consideration. When speed is essential, air transport is without question the preferred mode of distribution. Air transport is also necessary when the need is urgent or when delivery must be quickly completed as promised. For perishable items, a direct flight is preferable because a shorter period in transport reduces both spoilage and theft.

Finally, *cost* must be considered as well. Cost is directly related to speed – a quick delivery costs more. But there is a tradeoff between the two in terms of other kinds of savings. Packing costs for air freight are less than for ocean freight because for air freight the merchandise does not have to be in transit for a long period of time, and the hazards are relatively lower. For similar reasons, the air mode reduces the inventory in float (i.e., in the movement process). Thus, there is less investment cost because the overall inventory is minimized and inventory is turned over faster.

A firm must understand that there is no ideal transportation mode. Each mode has its own special kinds of hazards.[5] Hazards related to the ocean/water mode include wave impact, navigation exposures, water damage, and the various vessel motions (rolling, pitching, heaving, surging, swaying, and yawing). Hazard related to the air mode include ground handling and changes in atmospheric pressure and temperature. Hazards related to the rail and highway modes include acceleration/deceleration (braking), coupling impact, swaying on curves, and shock and vibration. Figure 13.2 describes the services of Yellow Freight System, an international carrier.

Land

Land transportation is an integral part of any shipment, whether locally or internationally. Some type of land transportation is necessary in moving goods to and from an airport or seaport. The land transportation mode involves rail and truck. When a large quantity of goods needs to be moved over a long distance by land, rail can prove to be quite economical. Europe and Japan have modern rail systems that are capable of moving merchandise efficiently.

On the other hand, trucks are capable of going to more places. In addition, trucks may be needed to take cargo to and from a railway station. When countries have joint boundaries, moving cargo by truck or train is often a practical solution. As a matter of fact, the US trucking industry is quite concerned about a NAFTA agreement which allows Mexican drivers to drive their trucks into the USA. It is debatable whether the real issue is a safety concern or a trade barrier.

Less developed countries generally rely on road transport. In Sub-Saharan Africa, road transport is the dominant form of transport.[6] This form of transport accounts for 80 to 90 percent of the region's passenger and freight movements. Unfortunately, the nearly two million kilometers of roads in Africa have been greatly damaged due to years of neglect. In any case, road transport may be the only access

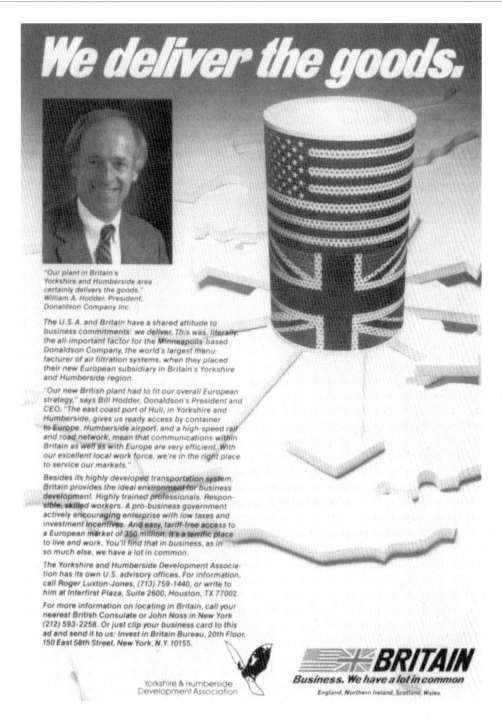

Figure 13.1 *Transportation and site selection*

Source: Reprinted with permission of Yorkshire and Humberside Development Association.

Figure 13.2 International carrier

to most rural communities – a situation common in Africa as well as in other developing economies.

Air

Of all the various transportation modes, air accounts for only about 1 percent of total international freight movement; yet it is the fastest-growing mode and is becoming less confined to expensive products. Air transport has the highest absolute rate, but exporters have discovered that there are many advantages associated with this mode. First, air transport speeds up delivery, minimizes the time the goods are in transit, and achieves greater flexibility in delivery schedules. Second, it delivers perishables in prime condition. Harris Ranch uses a 747 jumbo jet to fly live cattle from the USA to Japan. A premium price commanded by high-quality beef in Japan makes it possible to use air freight.

Third, it can respond rapidly to unpredictable and urgent demand. For instance, quick replacement of broken machinery, equipment, or a component part may be made by air. Fourth, it reduces to a minimum damage, packing, and insurance costs. Finally, it can help control costly inventory and other hidden costs, including warehousing, time in transit, inventory carrying cost, inventory losses, and the paperwork necessary to file claims for lost or damaged goods. These costs will increase as the time in transit increases. Furthermore, opportunity costs (e.g., lost sales and customer dissatisfaction) also adversely affect profit, especially in the long term. All of these costs can be minimized with air transport.

Traditionally, the appropriateness of air freight was determined solely by a value-to-weight equation, which dictated that air cargo should be confined to high-value products. One reason for that determination was that transport cost is a small proportion of such products' value. Another reason was that the amount of capital tied up with these products while in transit is high and should be released as soon as possible.

Recently, shippers have begun to shift their attention to the freight rates–density effect, which determines true costs rather than absolute costs of each transportation mode.[7] Air freight rates are usually quoted per unit of weight, and sea freight rates are usually quoted per unit of weight and volume (whichever yields more revenue for the steamship). For example, assume the freight rates are $350/ton by air and $60/ton and/or cubic ft by sea. At first, it would appear that surface (sea) transportation is a great deal cheaper, but for a product that is 1 ton and 7 cubic ft, the cost of sea freight ($420) is actually higher than that of air freight ($350). Therefore, sea freight is very cheap when goods are very dense (i.e., low volume per unit of weight). However, as density declines (i.e., the increase in bulk in relation to constant weight), the charge for sea freight rises rapidly. Consequently, air freight is quite competitive for such low-density goods as ladies' shoes, men's shoes, computers, color TV sets, refrigerators, and towels.

The dominant form of the international transportation of merchandise has always been ocean transport. Its main advantage is its low rate, though the savings achieved for many products are not necessarily greater than other transport modes on an overall basis. This helps explain why, when all the hidden costs related to ocean transportation are considered, air transportation is growing at a very rapid rate (see Figure 13.3).

Half a century ago, virtually all overseas trade went by ship. The use of air freight for high-value, time-sensitive products has jumped since then. The air mode has made it possible to outsource high-technology products (e.g., computers). A reduction in transit time by one day can reduce a product's price by 0.8 percent. Based on over $800 billion of manufactured imports per year, an extra day can add $7 billion to the costs. Because an ocean shipment, on average, takes twenty days, a shift from a twenty-day ocean shipment to a one-day air shipment can lower the price of a product by about 15 percent.[8]

Water

Bulk shipping is important in international trade because it is one of the most practical and efficient

Our international passengers start clearing customs before our planes even land.

While we're flying your packages overseas, detailed shipment information is flying ahead on UPSnet,™ our global data network.

That gives UPS customs brokers in destination countries a sizable head start: from 2 to 36 hours. And that gives us extra time to sort out potential clearance problems before the packages even arrive.

As a result, UPS international shipments are well on their way while other delivery companies are still getting their paperwork in order.

What's more, this technology doesn't just make us faster and more reliable. It makes us more efficient. So we can deliver to over 180 countries and territories, usually for a lot less than other companies charge.

So next time you have an international shipment to send, just send it UPS.

After all, many companies can fly your packages overseas.

It's what we're doing while they're flying that makes all the difference in the world.

We run the tightest ship in the shipping business.

Figure 13.3 *Air freight and customs*

means of transporting petroleum, industrial raw materials, and agricultural commodities over long distances. About 51 percent of the global bulk fleet consist of oil tankers, while dry bulk carriers account for 43 percent. The remainder of the fleet is made up of combination carriers which are capable of carrying either wet (crude oil and refined petroleum products) or dry (coal, iron ore, and gain) bulk cargoes. The bulk shipping industry, being highly fragmented, has no one organization which holds more than 2 percent of the total world fleet.[9]

Quotations for ocean shipping may be obtained from a shipping company or a freight forwarder. Steamship rates are commonly quoted on weight and measurement. Goods are both weighed and measured, and the ship will use the method that yields a higher freight charge. Less-than-container shipments carry a higher rate than full-container shipments.

There are three basic types of shipping company: (1) conference lines, (2) independent lines, and (3) tramp vessels. An ocean freight **conference line** is an association of ocean carriers that have joined together to establish common rules with regard to freight rates and shipping conditions. Consequently, the operators in the group charge identical rates. The steamship conference has also adopted a dual rate system, giving a preferential treatment to contract exporters. A contract exporter agrees to ship all or a large portion of its cargo on a regular basis on vessels of conference member lines – in exchange for a lower rate than that charged for a noncontract shipper. Nevertheless, the contract exporter is allowed to use another vessel, after obtaining the conference's permission, when no conference service is available within a reasonable period of time.

An **independent line**, as the name implies, is a line that operates and quotes freight rates individually and independently without the use of a dual-rate contract. Independent lines accept bookings from all shippers. When they compete with conference lines for noncontract shippers, they may lower their rates. In general, independent lines do not offer any special advantage for a contract shipper because they do not have a significant price advantage. Furthermore, their services are more limited and not as readily available.

Finally, a **tramp vessel** is a ship not operating on a regular route or schedule; that is, tramp steamers do not have the established schedules of the other two types of carriers. Tramp vessels operate on a charter basis whenever and wherever they can get cargo. They operate mainly in carrying bulk cargoes.

In some circumstances, a shipper may not have an option on the vessel to be used. Due to certain laws enacted to protect a country's interests, mandatory use of a particular vessel is not uncommon. Brazil's shipping restrictions require goods imported for use by public or public-supported enterprises to be transported aboard vessels with a Brazilian flag. All exported Japanese automobiles must be shipped on Japanese-owned ships, and the same restriction applies to all tobacco leaf imported to Japan.

The USA, while accusing other nations of erecting trade barriers, has the Federal Cargo Preference Act, which supports and favors US shipowners and maritime workers over foreign-flag vessels. Shipping between American coastal ports, including the movement of Alaskan oil, is legally reserved primarily for US flag vessels owned by American citizens, crewed by US seafarers, and built in the USA without construction subsidies and operated without using differential subsidies. Such vessels also receive preference in carrying US military and US government-sponsored shipments throughout the world.

In general, the rates charged by US conference lines are higher than the rates charged by lines of other nations. Foreign operators are able to charge lower rates because of the subsidies and support received from their governments. Soviet ships at one time were able to quote rates as much as two-thirds lower than US conference lines' published prices. Subsequently, conference lines (e.g., Seatrain) decided to give illegal rebates to major customers in order to win back cargo shipments lost to the Soviets.

393

CARGO OR TRANSPORTATION INSURANCE

Inland carriers generally bear the responsibility for any damage to goods while in their possession. The same thing cannot be said for ocean carriers. Their reluctance to accept responsibility is due to the numerous unavoidable perils found at sea. Such perils include severe weather, seawater damage, stranding, fire, collision, and sinking. As a result, ocean carriers refuse to accept any liability for loss or damage unless a shipper can prove that they were purposefully negligent – a difficult task indeed. To protect against loss or damage and to avoid disputes with overseas buyers, exporters should obtain marine insurance.

Marine cargo insurance is an insurance that covers loss or damage at sea, though in practice it also applies to shipments by mail, air, and ship (see Figure 13.4). It is similar to domestic cargo insurance but provides much broader coverage. The purpose of this insurance is to insure export shipments against loss or damage in transit. The insurance may be arranged by either a buyer or seller, depending on the terms of sale.

There are two basic forms of marine insurance: (1) special (one-time) coverage and (2) open (blanket) coverage. A **special policy** is a one-time policy that insures a single specific shipment. One-time insurance is relatively expensive because the risk cannot be spread over a number of shipments. Nevertheless, it is a practical insurance solution if a seller's export business is infrequent.

An **open policy** is an insurance contract issued to a firm in order to cover all its shipments as described in the policy within named geographic regions. The policy is open in the sense that it is continuous by automatically providing coverage on all cargo moving at the seller's risk. The policy is also open in the sense that the values of the individual shipments cannot be known in advance. Under this policy, no reports of individual shipments are required, although the insured must declare all shipments to the underwriter. The underwriter agrees to insure all shipments at the agreed rates within the terms and conditions of the policy. Open

marine cargo policies are written only for a specified time period. A single premium is charged for this time period, based on the insured's estimated total value of goods to be shipped under the policy during the term of the contract. The contract has no predetermined termination date, though it may be cancelled by either party at any time. A firm can also insure profit through a valuation clause in the cargo policy, which insures exports and contains a fixed basis of valuation. The following is an example of a typical valuation clause in a marine policy: "Valued at amount of invoice, plus 10 percent."

PACKING

Packaging may be viewed as consisting of two distinct types: industrial (exterior) and consumer (interior). Consumer packaging is designed for the purpose of affecting sales acceptance. The aim of industrial packaging is to prepare and protect merchandise for shipment and storage, and this type of packaging accounts for 7 cents of each retail dollar as well as 30 percent of total packaging costs.[10] Packing is even more crucial for overseas shipment than for domestic shipment because of the longer transit time and a greater number of hazards. Consumer packaging is covered extensively in Chapter 11; this section concentrates instead on industrial packaging.

Packing problems

There are four common packing problems, some of which are in direct conflict with one another: (1) weight, (2) breakage, (3) moisture and temperature, and (4) pilferage and theft.

Weight

Overpacking not only directly increases packing cost but also increases the weight and size of cargo. Any undue increase in weight or size only serves to raise freight charges. Moreover, import fees or customs duties may also rise when import duties are based on gross weight. Thus overprotection of the cargo can cost more than it is worth.

ONE THIRD IS COVERED BY LAND, TWO THIRDS BY WATER, AND ALL OF IT BY CIGNA.

The world's a big place. 27,459,880 square miles to be exact.

And if you're an international business buying insurance country by country, it can seem even bigger.

Dealing with other customs, policies and peculiarities can be more than just complicated. It can leave you unsure of your coverage. If not completely uncovered.

Thus the need for comprehensive global coverage. The kind of coverage that the CIGNA companies can provide.

As a truly global organization, CIGNA companies offer a wide range of property and casualty insurance all around the world. On both land and water. With local operations in nearly 80 countries, led by experienced representatives who know local customs inside and out.

Our global coverage can also help eliminate overlapping policies and gaps in protection.

What's more, we have a network of loss control specialists to help you prevent accidents.

As well as a worldwide claims-handling system that can process claims quickly should any accidents occur.

And with over 48,000 employees worldwide and almost 200 years of global experience, few companies can match our strength.

To learn more about our worldwide property and casualty coverages, write CIGNA Companies, Dept. R8, 1600 Arch Street, Philadelphia, PA 19103.

And find out just how small the world can be.

CIGNA

Figure 13.4 *Insurance*

Source: Courtesy of CIGNA Companies.

Breakage

Although overpacking is undesirable, so is underpacking, since the latter allows a product to be susceptible to breakage damage. The breakage problem is present in every step of ocean transport. In addition to normal domestic handling, ocean cargo is loaded aboard a vessel by use of a line (with several items together in a net), conveyor, chute, or other methods, all of which put added stress and strain on the package. Once the cargo is on the vessel, other cargo may be stacked on top of it, or packages may come into violent contact with each other during the course of the voyage. To complicate matters, handling facilities at an overseas port may be unsophisticated. The cargo may be dropped, dragged, pushed, and rolled during unloading, moving in and out of customs, or in transit to the final destination. In China, primitive methods (i.e., carts, sampans, junks, and so on) are used to move a great deal of cargo. Therefore, packing must be prepared to accommodate rough manual handling.

To guard against breakage, it may be desirable to use such package-testing equipment as vibration, drop, compression, incline-impact, and revolving drum. The cargo must not exceed the rated capacity of the box or crate. Attempts should be made to ensure that internal blocking and bracing will distribute the cargo's weight evenly. Cushioning may be needed to absorb the impact. Cautionary markings, in words and symbols, are necessary to reduce mishandling due to misunderstanding.

One universal packing rule is "Pack for the toughest leg of the journey." To accommodate this rule, cargo should be unitized or palletized whenever possible. **Palletizing** is the assembly of one or more packages on a pallet base and the securing of the load to the pallet. **Unitizing** is the assembly of one or more items into a compact load, secured together and provided with skids and cleats for ease of handling. These two packing methods force cargo handlers to use mechanical handling equipment to move cargo.

Moisture and temperature

Certain products can easily be damaged by moisture and temperature. Such products are subject to condensation even in the hold of a ship equipped with air-conditioning or dehumidifying equipment. Another problem is that the cargo may be unloaded in the rain. Many foreign ports do not have covered storage facilities, and the cargo may have to be left in the open subject to heat, rain, cold, and other adverse elements. In Morocco, bulk cargo and large items are stored in the open. Mozambique does the same with hazardous, bulk, and heavy items. Cargo thus needs extra strong packing, containerization, or unitization in order to afford some measure of protection under these conditions.

One very effective means of eliminating moisture is **shrink wrapping**, which involves sealing merchandise in a plastic film. Water proofing can also be provided by using waterproof inner lines or moisture-absorbing agents and by coating finished metal parts with a preservative or rust inhibitor. Desiccants (moisture-absorbing materials), moisture-barrier or vapor-barrier paper, or plastic wraps, sheets, and shrouds will also protect cargo from water leakage or condensate damage. Cargo can be kept away from water on the ground if placed on skids, pallets, or dunnage while having drain holes in crates.

There are several steps to ensure the proper way of packing to minimize moisture and breakage problems.[11] These steps are as follows:

1 Place water-barrier material on interior of sides and roof.
2 Use vertical sheathing.
3 Block, brace, and tie down heavy items.
4 Use new, clear, dry lumber and provide adequate diagonals.
5 Use multiple similar items.
6 Use waterproof tape to seal fiberboard boxes.
7 Palletize shipping bags.
8 Use proper gauge, type, and number of straps.

Pilferage and theft

Cargo should be adequately protected against theft. Studies have fixed such losses in all transportation modes in a range from $1 billion to in excess of $5 billion.[12] In the USA alone, the annual value of cargo stolen in transit exceeds $2.5 billion. Annual loss through theft is well over £100 million in Great Britain, with employees' criminal activity being the main contributing factor.[13] Pilferage levels are consistently high in Bangladesh and substantial in India. There are a few techniques that may be used as deterrents. One method of discouraging theft is to use shrink wrapping, seals, or strapping. Gummed sealing tapes with patterns, when used, will quickly reveal any sign of tampering. In addition, only well-constructed packing in good condition should be used.

Another area of concern is marking. The main purpose of marking is to identify shipments so that the carrier can forward the shipment to the designated consignee. Markings thus should not be used to advertise the contents, especially when they are valuable or highly desirable in nature. A firm is also wise to avoid mentioning the contents, trade names, consignees' names, or shippers' names on the package because these markings reveal the nature of the contents. Because markings are still a necessity, they should be permanent, though so-called blind marks should be used. To avoid handlers becoming familiar with the markings, blind marks should be changed periodically. Bright color coding helps in spotting the pieces.

Packing alone should not be expected to eliminate theft. Packing should be used in conjunction with other precautionary measures. One of the most effective means of reducing exposure to theft, pilferage, and hijacking is to insist on prompt pickup and delivery. Another good idea is to avoid shipping the cargo if it will arrive at its destination on a weekend or holiday. One Chicago importer of jewelry found, when he went to pick up his merchandise at the O'Hare airport on a Monday, that the cargo had already been claimed by someone else over the weekend.

Cargo theft is a significant concern everywhere, especially in developing countries. In Mexico, since the mid-1990s, truck hijackings have become an epidemic. Criminals prefer medicines, clothing, food, and consumer electronics because these items can be quickly sold. Because of the rising claims and losses, insurance companies have drastically increased the premiums on cargo insurance while requiring higher deductibles. As a result, some companies (e.g., Nestlé) no longer insure cargo, choosing to cover losses themselves. For protection, they have beefed up security. Trucks may travel in convoys, or they are accompanied by armed escorts. Global positioning systems are used to track trucks.[14]

Containers

An increasingly popular method of shipment is containerization. The growth of the use of containers has been explosive. About 90 percent of the world's cargo now travels via containers.

A container is a large box made of durable material such as steel, aluminum, plywood, and glass reinforced plastics. A container varies in size, materials, and construction. Its dimensions are typically 8 ft high and 8 ft wide, with lengths usually varying in multiples of 10 ft up to a maximum of 40 ft. A container can accommodate most cargo but is most suitable for packages of standard size and shape. Some containers are no more than truck bodies that have been lifted off their wheels and placed on a vessel at the port of export. These containers are then transferred to another set of wheels at the port of import for inland movement. This type of container may be loaded on to a ship, or may become a barcar when placed on a railway flatcar, or may be made into a trailer when provided with a chassis. Containers are ordinarily obtained from either carriers or private parties.

Containers can take care of most of the four main packing problems. Because of a container's construction, a product does not have to have heavy packing. The container by itself provides good protection for the product against breakage, moisture, and temperature. Because breaking into a container is difficult, this method of shipment discourages pilferage and theft as well. In addition, containers have substantially reduced the average transit time of ocean-shipped goods.

It is important to select the right container because containers come in varying sizes and types.

There are two basic types of container: (1) *dry cargo containers*, and (2) *special purpose containers*. Some of the various types of dry cargo containers are end loading, fully closed; side loading, fully enclosed; and open top, ventilated, insulated. Special purpose containers come in different types for refrigerated, liquid bulk, dry bulk, flat rack, auto, livestock, and sea shed.

Exporters may have to plan for the return of secondary packaging or the container, or both. Argentina's inefficient exports force those who do business with Argentina to ship most containers back empty.[15] One US car maker, after experimenting with containers, resumed shipping parts in wooden crates instead. Japanese firms have partially solved the Argentina problem by using collapsible racking and shipping systems so that items can be more densely packaged for return shipment.

Shipments by air do not usually require the heavy packaging that ocean shipments need. Standard domestic packing should prove sufficient in most cases. When in doubt, however, a company should consult the carrier or a marine insurance company for the best packing strategy. For a case in which a firm is not equipped to do its own packing, there are professional firms that package for export.

FREIGHT FORWARDER AND CUSTOMS BROKER

There are two intermediaries whose services are quite essential in moving cargo for their principals, across counties as well as within countries: freight forwarders and custom brokers. Their differing roles in the distribution process are shown in Figure 13.5. A freight forwarder generally works for exporters, whereas the customs broker generally works for importers. Because the functions are similar, freight forwarders sometimes act as customs brokers and vice versa.

A freight forwarder is responsible for the forwarding of freight locally as well as internationally. He or she is an independent businessperson who handles shipments for compensation. The kind of freight forwarder of concern here is the foreign or international freight forwarder who moves goods destined for overseas destinations.

A foreign freight forwarder is an exporter's agent (shipping agent) who performs virtually all aspects of physical distribution necessary to move cargo to overseas destinations in the most efficient and economic manner. To comply with export documentation and shipping requirements, the freight forwarder can take care of cargo from "dock to door." The services, when needed, include "the correct filing of export documentation, all arrangements with carriers, packing, crating and storage needs."[16] This freight forwarder can represent shippers in both air and ocean freight shipments because the procedures and documents required are very similar.

The freight forwarder's major contribution to the exporter is his or her ability to provide traffic and documentation responsibilities for international

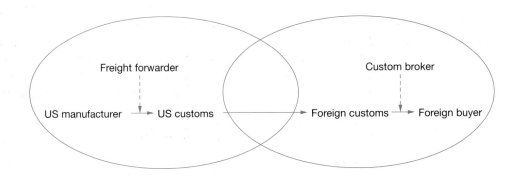

Figure 13.5 *Intermediaries that facilitate physical distribution*

freight movements. This middleman handles the voluminous paperwork required in international trade, and is highly specialized in (1) traffic operations (methods of shipping), (2) government export regulations, (3) overseas import regulations, and (4) documents connected with foreign trade and customs clearance. In brief, the freight forwarder arranges all necessary details for the proper shipping, insuring, and documenting of overseas shipments.

The freight forwarder can assist an exporter from the very beginning in preparing a shipment for overseas. Once the exporter receives an inquiry, it can turn to the freight forwarder for assistance in preparing its quotation. The freight forwarder can advise the exporter on freight costs, port charges, consular fees, cost of special documentation, insurance costs, and the forwarder's handling fees, as well as recommend the degree of packing needed, or arrange to have the merchandise packed or have it containerized.

The freight forwarder also prepares ocean bills of lading and any special consular documents, and reviews letters of credit, packing lists, and so on to ensure that all procedures are in order. After the shipment is made, the freight forwarder forwards all documents to the customer's paying bank with instructions to credit the exporter's account.

The freight forwarder can assist the exporter in other areas. This person can reserve space aboard an ocean vessel. He or she may consolidate small shipments into full container loads and, by so doing, can receive a lower rate from the carrier and pass on the savings to the shipper. The freight forwarder can arrange to clear goods through customs and to have the goods delivered to the pier in time for loading. This middleman then handles the goods from exit port to destination. If desired, the freight forwarder can further move goods inland in a foreign country through various affiliates. According to one study, freight forwarders feel that the United Kingdom is the easiest and China is the most difficult with regard to arranging international freight operations.[17]

The freight forwarder receives a fee from exporters. The service cost is a legitimate export cost and should be figured into the contract price charged to buyers. In addition, this person may receive a brokerage fee and/or rebates from shipping companies for booked space. In such cases, the freight forwarder's commission is paid by the ship lines. Because freight forwarders control most of the smaller shipments and because the less-than-container (LTC) traffic accounts for 17 to 18 percent of the business, carriers woo freight forwarders with extra rebates.

The counterpart of the freight forwarder for an exporter is the customs broker for an importer. As an individual or firm licensed to enter and clear goods through customs, a customs broker is a person or firm employed by an importer to take over the responsibility of clearing the importer's shipments through customs on a fee basis. A licensed customs broker named in a Customs Power of Attorney can effect entry. This broker is bonded, and the broker's bond provides the required coverage to carry on the responsibilities of the job. A customs broker may also act as a freight forwarder once the shipment is cleared. In the USA, a customs broker must be licensed by the Treasury Department in order to perform these services.

The customs broker is indispensable in the receipt of goods from overseas. The services are valuable because the requirements for customs clearance are complicated. To effect entry, a person must have evidence of right to entry (carrier's certificate), in addition to the commercial invoice, packing, and surety. Moreover, the person must fill out forms with regard to dutiable status and must also have the goods examined under conditions that safeguard the goods before they are released. Overall, entry is a two-step process – getting goods released and providing information for duty assessment and statistical purposes. The customs broker is in the best position to fulfill these requirements.

DOCUMENTATION

It is not an exaggeration to say that "paper moves cargo." To move cargo, documentation is a necessity. American firms used to complain about the cost of documentation and shipping in the EU. Documentation alone added 3 to 5 percent of the total cost of goods sold (see Marketing Strategy 13.1).

International direct marketers need to ensure that their delivery methods are convenient for their customers. As in the case of WearGuard Work Clothes, a US company, it has four options to fill orders for Canadian customers: US Postal Service parcel post, courier companies, bulk shipment, and local fulfillment. In the end, it chose TNT Mailfast to bring WearGuard's parcels into Canada, clear them at customs, and give them to Canada Post for local delivery. This method allows Canadian customers to receive the merchandise without having to pay duties or additional fees. The company also has a Canadian address so that Canadian customers can conveniently mail packages in case of customer returns.[18]

Product transportation in the European Union has become easier and more efficient. As of 1993, border controls were removed. Border stops are limited to checking on legal matters such as illegal immigration and drug trafficking. Since 1995, some EU states have allowed people to move freely within the EU without having to show their passports.

To facilitate cargo movement, nations have been working toward automated customs – paperless international customs procedures. The Customs Cooperation Council, representing more than 130 nations, has approved a plan whereby customs administrations around the world can work toward electronic data interchange. The main standards body for international electronic message is a United Nations-backed group called Edifact (Electronic Data Interchange for Administration, Commerce, and Transport). While Japanese companies do business with one another electronically, they use their own standards, which force outsiders wanting to establish computerized links to engage in expensive programming and translation efforts. Edifact, however, works everywhere. Japan has finally agreed to join with Singapore to create a regional Edifact board. By sending standardized digital messages at computer speeds, importers can bypass piles of bureaucratic paperwork. Use of paperless trading technology should significantly improve the speed and efficiency of data and global trade.

Exporters may want to consider purchasing an export-automation software package. Some of the export software incorporates the electronic data interchange (EDI) technology, making it possible for exporters to send computer-generated forms electronically rather than mailing the documents to freight forwarders, customers, banks, and government agencies.

To fill out the required documents, a company must insert the proper identification number for its product. All products must be "shoehorned" into some kind of category. If a product is constructed

MARKETING STRATEGY 13.1   LESS IS MORE

At one time, New Zealand Customs officials inspected every shipment as well as interacting with every person at the border. These practices are time-consuming and inefficient, so the country has begun to use risk-management strategies that allow the officials to focus on a truly suspicious activity while permitting legitimate goods and persons to quickly cross the border. Prior to customs reforms, for example, boat builders had to pay a duty on imported boat parts and later obtain a refund after the expor-

tation of a completed craft. The process necessitated a great deal of paperwork flowing back and forth. The reforms have made it possible for boat makers to merely register the parts with the Customs Service without having to tie up capital for months – not to mention less paperwork. New Zealand now collects relevant taxes and duties with a minimum of intervention.

Source: Mike Moore, "Tariff Reductions Aren't Enough," *Asian Wall Street Journal,* June 19, 2001.

out of several materials, it may be classified by the material that gives it its essential character. On January 1, 1989, the Harmonized Tariff System (HTS) went into effect. This system, designed to replace previous systems for classifying exports, contains logically structured nomenclature. There are twenty-one sections and ninety-nine chapters to arrange commodities according to general economic activity. The sections and chapters are arranged according to levels of processing, with primary commodities classified first, followed by the technically more complex products.

The HTS assigns a number to each product that is traded internationally to ensure that customs officers and statisticians around the world are referring to the same thing when they classify a particular product. Almost all countries now use the HTS. The HTS number refers to a six-digit product-specific code. To meet each country's statistical and tariff requirements, the remaining digits are country-specific. Certain countries also use either alphabetical subdivisions after the six digits or combined alphanumerical systems, making the entire number ten digits long. This is what the USA does with its Schedule B system when describing US imports.[19] As an example, the HS code for "widgets" is 12.34.56.78.90, the breakdowns are 12 (chapter), 12.34 (heading), 12.34.56 (subheading), 12.34.56.78 (tariff item), and 12.34.56.78.90 (HS classification number). When researching tariff rates for any region, it is important to first have the Harmonized System Number (HS) that corresponds to the product in question in order to obtain the exact rate.

Due to terrorist activities, security has assumed much greater prominence. The focus has shifted from drug smuggling to smuggling of biological, chemical, and nuclear weapons. In the aftermath of September 11, 2001 attacks on the USA, a more secure shipping network is a necessity. Some security measures that can be employed are: greater security at a plant or loading dock, greater security during transport, submitting information on cargo in advance, and using electronic seals for container shipments.[20]

Documentation now plays a significant role in combating terrorism. The twenty-four-hour rule requires a filing of detailed cargo information a full day before containers are loaded aboard US-bound vessels. In the past, it was hardly unusual for a container to be loaded at the last minute. Once on board, the cargo could still be sold, necessitating a change in destination. Freight forwarders could simply forward cargo information just five days before the cargo reached a US port. The cargo descriptions could be vague (e.g., "freight-any-kind" or "general freight"). These descriptions are no longer accepted. US Customs now requires shippers and freight forwarders to electronically submit a cargo manifest (a complete description of the cargo) to the National Targeting Center. Any suspicious or incomplete lists receive "no-load" messages. There are plans to require air, rail, and truck companies (just like their ocean counterparts) to list cargo manifests well in advance of arrival at airports, rail yards, and truck depots. Before the events of September 11, only 2 percent of cargo containers were inspected. The percentage has gone up to only 3 or 4 percent due to the sheer number of containers at US ports.[21]

There are many kinds of documents, and they can be grouped under two broad categories: (1) shipping documents, and (2) collection documents. Shipping documents are prepared to move shipment through customs, allowing the cargo to be loaded, shipped, and unloaded. Collection documents, in contrast, are submitted to a customer or the customer's bank for payment.

Shipping documents

There are several kinds of shipping documents. Such documents include export license and shipper's export declaration forms, among others.

Export license

An export license is a permit allowing merchandise to be exported, and virtually all countries require some form of export permit. In the case of the

USA, an export license is needed on all exports, except for shipments going to Canada and US territories and possessions. The USA has two broad categories of export licenses: general and validated. The difference between the two has to do with whether a particular license requires prior, written approval from the US Department of Commerce. The type of license required depends on the sophistication of the product, the destination country, the end use, and the enduser.

General license

A general license is a license for which no application is required and for which no document or written authorization is granted. It is a general authorization permitting the export of certain commodities and technical data without the necessity of applying for a license document. A general license allows the export through the Export Administration Regulations of all goods published in an authorization list and covers the export of nonstrategic goods (commodities not under restriction or control). Products that meet specific conditions may be shipped by merely inserting a correct general license symbol on the export control document known as a shipper's export declaration.

Validated export license

If an exporter does not qualify for a general license, the exporter may apply for a validated export license which, in effect, is a formal authorization document. The USA requires this kind of licensing for reasons of national security (strategic significance), short supply, or foreign policy. National security controls were necessary to prevent the export of strategic commodities and technical data to communist countries. Foreign policy controls, such as the restrictions placed on exports to South Africa and Namibia, are instituted by such licensing to promote US foreign policy. In the case of short-supply controls, the licenses are granted with an eye to preventing the depletion of scarce materials (e.g., Western red cedar and petroleum).

Many of the products shipped under individual validated licenses (IVLs) and special licenses need pre-export paperwork (e.g., a foreign consignee/purchaser statement or a government-issued import certificate) to obtain the necessary license. IVLs authorize individual sales of a certain product to a certain customer in a certain country. Special licenses (e.g., project and distribution licenses) authorize the sale of a range of products to many customers if exporters can show that they have implemented a strict control process.

For control purposes, the USA regulates computer exports by creating four tiers of countries. The Tier 1 countries are the closest allies. Tier 2, the largest group, has most of the rest of the world. Countries in Tier 3 are those that USA is wary of, and they include China, Israel, and Russia. The Tier 4 countries are American enemies and rogue states (Cuba, Iran, Iraq, Libya, North Korea, Sudan, and Syria), and computer exports to them are prohibited.[22]

Frequently, export controls are coordinated at the international level. Most of the export controls maintained by the USA are multilateral controls in the sense that they are maintained in cooperation with other countries. To coordinate export controls for security purposes, Western allies relied on an organization known as COCOM (Coordinating Committee on Multilateral Exports Control). COCOM, the most significant multilateral export control group, was created in 1949 to restrict the availability of strategic Western technology to controlled economies. In response to the rapidly changing international political and military environment, COCOM was disbanded in the 1990s.

For the USA, sensitive items continue to require an individual validated license (IVL) for export to the West. The sensitive items include advanced computer equipment, certain underwater detection equipment, and cryptographic equipment. Items that are controlled for foreign policy reasons continued to require an IVL. On the other hand, in 1989, the Commerce Department removed unilateral export restrictions on a broad group of goods and technology. The new rule makes it possible to ship without prior approval many commonly available items that were controlled for national security reasons for more than twenty-five years. Decontrolled items include general industrial equipment, photographic equipment, servo-mechanical units and synchronous motors, and a broad range of industrial chemicals.

The Export Administration of 1979 requires the Commerce Department to remove licensing requirements for US exports when items of comparable quality are freely available to Eastern Bloc countries in sufficient quantities to render US export controls ineffective. The 1988 Omnibus Trade Act also requires lifting export controls on high-technology products already available to former Eastern Bloc nations from other sources. Seagate Technology Inc. filed a petition in 1989 to remove small-capacity disk drives from long-standing export controls by demonstrating that a Bulgarian company, using its own technology, has been manufacturing comparable products.

Foreign and US firms that illegally export US products risk losing their export privileges. Exhibit 13.1 describes how business firms can watch out for illegal export schemes.

In spite of the export control, many US companies have been found to violate export laws. Hughes Electronics and Boeing Satellite Systems, the two top US aerospace companies, paid a record $32 million in fines in 2003 for unlawfully transferring rocket and satellite data to China in 1990s. The technology used to launch civilian rockets and satellites is similar to the technology for launching missiles. The companies "express regret for not having obtained licenses that should have been obtained" and "acknowledge the nature and seriousness of the offenses charged by the Department of State, including the harm such offenses could cause to the security and foreign policy interests of the USA."[23] To settle similar cases, Lockheed Martin and Loral Space and Communications paid fines of $13 million and $20 million. While regulations can be complex, it is difficult to understand how these large companies, with all their resources and export knowledge, have failed to understand the export regulations of the USA.

EXHIBIT 13.1   POSSIBLE INDICATORS OF ILLEGAL EXPORT SCHEMES

The following are some possible indicators that an illegal diversion might be planned by an export customer:

- The customer or purchasing agent is reluctant to offer information about the end use of a product.
- The product's capabilities do not fit the buyer's line of business: for example, an order for several sophisticated computers for a small bakery.
- The product ordered is incompatible with the technical level of the country to which the product is being shipped. Semiconductor manufacturing equipment would be of little use in a country without an electronics industry.
- The customer is willing to pay cash for a very expensive item when the terms of the sale call for financing.
- The customer has little or no business background.

- The customer is unfamiliar with the product's performance characteristics but still wants the product.
- Routine installation, training, or maintenance services are declined by the customer.
- Delivery dates are vague, or deliveries are planned for out-of-the-way destinations.
- A freight forwarding firm is listed as the product's final destination.
- The shipping route is abnormal for the product and destination.
- Packaging is inconsistent with the stated method of shipment or destination.
- When questioned, the buyer is evasive and especially unclear about whether the purchased product is for domestic use, export, or re-export.

Source: US Department of Commerce.

Shipper's export declaration (SED) form

In the majority of cases, exporters need to declare their shipments. American exporters, for example, are required to file SEDs for virtually all shipments, including hand-carried merchandise, and they must be deposited with an exporting carrier regardless of the type of export license. Exemptions apply to shipments to certain countries when the value is $2500 or less and when the shipment is not moving under a validated export license.

The SED is a multipurpose document. One of its purposes is to serve as an export control document. It declares the proper authorization for export by making reference to some type of export license. Another purpose of the SED is to compile basic statistical information on export shipments. These data are compiled and published to show the types of commodities exported and the countries that imported them.

Hazardous certificate

To export hazardous cargo, an exporter must use a shipper's certification or declaration of dangerous cargo. This document, required for all hazardous shipments, is used to describe the contents by providing the details and qualities of the items being shipped, their proper classification, required labels, and so on. This declaration must always be completed by the shipper (preferably on the shipper's letterhead) and signed by the shipper. There is no prescribed form for ocean shipments of hazardous materials at the present time. For all hazardous shipments moving via air freight, a shipper's declaration of dangerous cargo (air cargo) must be submitted to the airline.

Packing list

A packing list is a document that lists the type and number of pieces, the contents, weight, and measurement of each, as well as the marks and numbers. Its purpose is to facilitate customs clearance, keep track of inventory of goods, and assist in tracing lost goods. For insurance purposes, the packing list can be used in determining the contents of a lost piece. Furthermore, it is also useful in estimating shipping cost prior to export.

Shipper's letter of instructions

The shipper's letter of instructions is a form provided to the freight forwarder from the shipper giving all pertinent information and instruction regarding the shipment and how it is to be handled. When signed by the shipper, it also authorizes the forwarder to issue and sign documents on behalf of the shipper.

Dock receipt

A dock receipt is proof of delivery for goods received at the dock or warehouse of the steamship line. This document is required for shipments sailing from ports on the US East and Gulf coasts. Six copies of the dock receipt must be lodged at the receiving warehouse before freight can be accepted.

Collection documents

Before a seller can request payment, the seller must provide the buyer with a number of documents showing that the terms agreed upon have been fulfilled. The buyer requires such documents to protect itself and to satisfy its government's requirements.

Commercial invoice

To collect payment, an invoice is needed. There are two kinds of invoices: (1) *pro forma* and (2) *commercial*. A pro forma invoice is an invoice provided by a supplier prior to the shipment of merchandise. The purpose of this invoice is to inform the buyer of the kinds and quantities of goods to be sent, their value, and import specifications (weight, size, and so on). The buyer may also need the pro forma invoice in order to be able to apply for an import license and/or a letter of credit.

A commercial invoice is a document that provides an itemized list of goods shipped and other charges. As a complete record of the business transaction between two parties, it provides a complete description of merchandise, quantity, price, and shipping and payment terms. It is desirable that this invoice contains a breakdown of charges such as those related to inland transportation, loading, insurance, freight, handling, and certification. Because the invoice is required to clear goods through customs, all necessary information required by the buyer's government must be included.

The requirements of the exporter's country must be satisfied as well. The USA prohibits certain goods from being diverted to countries such as North Korea and Cuba. Therefore, the invoice may have to be prepared so that it includes an antidiversion clause or destination control statement. According to section 387.6 of the Export Administration Regulations, "No person may export, dispose of, divert, direct, mail or otherwise ship, transship, or re-export commodities or technical data to any person or destination or for any use in violation of or contrary to the terms, provisions, or conditions of any export control document, any prior representation, any form of notification of prohibition against such action, or any provision of the Export Administration Act or any regulation, order, or license issued under the Act."

Foreign customs invoice

A customs invoice is a special format invoice required by customs officials in some countries in lieu of the commercial invoice, as those officials may not recognize the commercial invoice for customs purposes. A foreign customs invoice is shown in Figure 13.6. This type of invoice generally contains the same information as the commercial invoice and may also contain certification with regard to value and origin of the shipment.

Consular invoice

In addition to the regular commercial invoice, several countries, notably those in Latin America, require legalized or visaed documents that often include a special kind of invoice known as a consular invoice. A consular invoice lists detailed comments prepared by a seller in the importing country's language on an official form supplied by the importer's government. Its purpose is to monitor merchandise and capital flows. Exhibit 13.2 lists those countries that require such documents.

A consular invoice must have an official stamp, seal, or signature affixed to it. This is the responsibility of the consulate general, who is a representative of the government of the importing country. The resident consul is supposed to verify the contents of the invoice (e.g., value, quantity, and nature of shipment) and to certify its authenticity and correctness. Usually, there is a fee for this service; Bolivia's consular fees for the notarization of invoices are 1 percent of the FOB value.

It is significant to keep in mind that the consulate is not obligated to facilitate imports by approving the submitted documents quickly. Because the consul may take his or her time in returning the visaed documents, an exporter should allow reasonable time for the processing of a consular invoice. It can be a frustrating experience to rush the consulate for the documents while the shipment is waiting.

Since a consular invoice is a legal document, any errors noted later require special consideration. An exporter cannot simply make corrections on a consular invoice that has been certified. Such corrections are considered forgery, and the criminal penalty can be quite severe.

Although a consular invoice usually contains the same information as a commercial invoice, the actual information required by the consulate depends on where the shipping is to be made. The best way to find out what is specifically required is to speak directly with the consulate or to consult one of the reference manuals available, such as *Dun and Bradstreet* or the *International Trade Reporter* of the Bureau of National Affairs (BNA).

Certificate of origin

A certificate of origin is a document prepared by the exporter and used to identify or declare that

COMMERCIAL INVOICE FOR THE CARIBBEAN COMMON MARKET

SELLER (Name, Full Address, Country)	INVOICE DATE AND NO.	CUSTOMER'S ORDER NO.
ABC COMPANY 84609 SOUTH LANE DETROIT, MICHIGAN 00000 U.S.A.	DATE: 10/1/87 NO: A495Z	PR8097

OTHER REFERENCES

CONSIGNEE (Name, Full Address, Country)	BUYER (If Other Than Consignee)
ANTIGUA WHITE SANDS MOTEL P.O. BOX 655 ST. JOHNS, ANTIGUA	

PRESENTING BANK

XYZ BANK, ST. JOHNS

COUNTRY OF ORIGIN OF GOODS

UNITED STATES OF AMERICA

PORT OF LADING	TERMS AND CONDITIONS OF DELIVERY AND PAYMENT
MIAMI	C AND F ST. JOHNS, ANTIGUA

COUNTRY OF FINAL DESTINATION	SHIP/AIR/ETC.
ANTIGUA	CARICOM V.109

SIGHT DRAFT, DOCUMENTS AGAINST PAYMENT

OTHER TRANSPORT INFORMATION	CURRENCY OF SALE
B/L NO. 185	U.S. DOLLARS

MARK AND NUMBERS	DESCRIPTION OF GOODS	GROSS WEIGHT(Kg.)	CUBIC METRES
A W S M ANTIGUA 1/2	RESTAURANT SUPPLIES	130 Kgs	1.354m3

NO. AND KIND OF PACKAGES	SPECIFICATION OF COMMODITIES (IN CODE AND/OR IN FULL)	NET WEIGHT (Kg.)	QUANTITY	UNIT PRICE	AMOUNT
2 CRATES	KITCHEN KNIFE A203	108 Kgs	50 DOZ	19.00/DZ	950.00

PACKING					25.00
FREIGHT	INLAND				35.00
	OCEAN				120.00
OTHER COSTS (Specify)	FORWARDING FEE				50.00
INSURANCE	N/A				

IT IS HEREBY CERTIFIED THAT THIS INVOICE SHOWS THE ACTUAL PRICE OF THE GOODS DESCRIBED, THAT NO OTHER INVOICE HAS BEEN OR WILL BE ISSUED AND THAT ALL PARTICULARS ARE TRUE AND CORRECT.

J. Doe

J. DOE, Clerk	10/9/87 DETROIT		
SIGNATURE AND STATUS OF AUTHORIZED PERSON	DATE PLACE		

TOTAL INVOICE AMOUNT

C&F ST. JOHNS	US$ 1,180.00

Figure 13.6 *Foreign customs invoice*

Source: Reprinted with permission of Radix Group International, Inc.

the merchandise originated in a certain country. It assures the buyer or importer of the country of manufacture. This document is necessary for tariff and control purposes. Some countries may require statements of origin to establish possible preferential rates of import duties under the Most Favored Nation arrangements. This certificate also prevents the inadvertent importation of goods from prohibited or unfriendly countries. The forms can vary, ranging from a shipper's own letterhead certificate to a countersigning by the Chamber of Commerce (see Figure 13.7). In some cases, such forms must be visaed by an importing country's resident consul. For international use, this document is generally notarized and chamberized.

EXHIBIT 13.2   COUNTRIES THAT REQUIRE A CONSULAR INVOICE

Near and Middle East
Saudi Arabia
Kuwait
Lebanon
Oman
Jordan
Bahrain
Syria
Yemen
Iraq
Iran
United Arab Emirates

South America
Colombia (by request)
Argentina
Uruguay
Paraguay

Central America
Panama
Nicaragua
Honduras
Guatemala

Far East
Philippines (by request)
Europe and Asia
Greece (by request)
Spain (by request)
Turkey

Africa
Libya

Caribbean
Dominican Republic

Source: Reprinted with permission of Radix Group International, Inc.

Inspection certificate

An inspection certificate is a document certifying that the merchandise was in good condition immediately prior to shipment. Many foreign buyers protect themselves by requiring a shipper's affidavit or an independent inspection firm to certify quality and quantity and conformity of goods in relation to the order, as well as to ensure that the goods contracted for have actually been shipped. This certificate is normally prepared by an independent firm other than the exporter, attesting to the quality or quantity of goods being shipped.

Special purpose documents

As in the case of an inspection certificate, an importer may request other special documents, such as a certificate of weight/measurement and a certificate of analysis in order to protect the importer's interests. A certificate of weight/mea-

surement is issued by an independent party attesting to the weight or measurement of the merchandise to be shipped. A certificate of analysis contains an expert's report on the findings or grading of the substance or composition of the product shipped. The document assures the buyer that the goods are those that an exporter contracted for shipment.

Insurance certificate

A certificate of insurance is a negotiable document issued to provide coverage for a specific shipment. It briefly describes the transaction and its coverage. Usually, an insurance certificate is issued as an open-coverage policy to protect any and all shipments and transportation as long as a certificate is filed for each shipment. Generally, the policy will cover most losses sustained during transit. Not restricted only to ocean shipments is a marine insurance policy, which covers all modes of transportation.

CERTIFICATE OF ORIGIN

2. EXPORTER (Principal or seller-licensee and address including ZIP Code)	**5. DOCUMENT NUMBER**	**5A. B/L OR AWB NUMBER**
SHIPPER OF AMERICA 1234 NORTH STREET CHICAGO, ILLINOIS U.S.A. ZIP CODE 60000	**6. EXPORT REFERENCES** 9246	

3. CONSIGNED TO
IMPORTER OF SAUDI ARABIA
P.O. BOX 740
JEDDAH, SAUDI ARABIA

7. FORWARDING AGENT (Name and address - references)
RADIX GROUP INTERNATIONAL
P.O. BOX 66213
CHICAGO, ILLINOIS 60666   FMC 232

8. POINT (STATE) OF ORIGIN OR FTZ NUMBER
IL

4. NOTIFY PARTY/INTERMEDIATE CONSIGNEE (Name and address)
GULF BROKERS LTD.
P.O. BOX 2009
JEDDAH, SAUDI ARABIA

9. DOMESTIC ROUTING/EXPORT INSTRUCTIONS

12. PRE-CARRIAGE BY	13. PLACE OF RECEIPT BY PRE-CARRIER	
14. EXPORTING CARRIER A VESSEL	15. PORT OF LOADING/EXPORT NEW YORK	10. LOADING PIER/TERMINAL
16. FOREIGN PORT OF UNLOADING (Vessel and air only) JEDDAH	17. PLACE OF DELIVERY BY ON-CARRIER	11. TYPE OF MOVE 11.a CONTAINERIZED (Vessel only) ☐ YES ☒ NO

MARKS AND NUMBERS (18)	NUMBER OF PACKAGES (19)	DESCRIPTION OF COMMODITIES in Schedule B detail (20)	GROSS WEIGHT (Pounds) (21)	MEASUREMENT (22)
I.S.A. JEDDAH MADE IN U.S.A. NO. 1/4	4	BOXES: POWER TOOLS MANUFACTURER: SHIPPER OF AMERICA 1234 NORTH STREET CHICAGO, ILLINOIS 60000 U.S.A.	843#	97'

The undersigned......JANE DOE..................(Owner or Agent), does hereby declare for the above named shipper, the goods as described above were shipped on the above date and consigned as indicated and are products of the United States of America Dated at.....CHICAGO, IL...................... on the..10th.. day of.....OCTOBER.......................19.87.

Sworn to before me this ..10th.. day OFFICIAL SEAL".......... 19.87.   *Jane Doe*
Debra Uvelli   DEBRA UVELLI   SIGNATURE OF OWNER OR AGENT
.....NOTARY PUBLIC.......... Notary Public, State of Illinois My Commission Expires 8/11/91.

The.....ANY TOWN ASSOCIATION OF COMMERCE AND INDUSTRY......................., a recognized Chamber of Commerce under the laws of the State of ....ILLINOIS....................., has examined the manufacturer's invoice or shipper's affidavit concerning the origin of the merchandise, and, according to the best of its knowledge and belief, finds that the products named originated in the United States of North America.

Secretary.........M. H. JONES.............................

Figure 13.7 *A certificate of origin*

Source: Reprinted with permission of Radix Group International, Inc.

Air waybill

An air waybill is basically a bill of lading issued by air carriers for air shipments. This transport instrument is not a negotiable document. As a result, a carrier will release goods to a designated consignee without the waybill.

Bill of lading

A bill of lading is a document issued to record shipment transportation (see Figure 13.8). Usually prepared by a shipper on the shipper's carrier's forms, this document serves three useful functions. First, as a document of title, it is a certificate of ownership that allows a holder or consignee to claim the merchandise described. Second, as a receipt of goods, it is issued by the carrier to the shipper for goods entrusted to the carrier's care for transportation. A bill of lading is thus proof of the carrier's possession of the freight. Third, as a contract of carriage, the bill of lading defines the contract terms between the shipper and his carrier. The conditions under which the goods are to be carried and the carrier's responsibility for the delivery are specified.

UNION STAR LINE

SAMPLE BILL OF LADING

SHIPPER/EXPORTER	DOCUMENT NO.
SHIPPER OF AMERICA INC. 1234 NORTH STREET CHICAGO, ILLINOIS 60000 U.S.A.	**EXPORT REFERENCES** 9876

CONSIGNEE	FORWARDING AGENT — REFERENCES
OVERSEAS IMPORTS LTD. 5678 JOHN AVENUE D-2000 HAMBURG, WEST GERMANY	RADIX GROUP INTERNATIONAL P.O. BOX 66213 CHICAGO, IL 60666 FMC 232

POINT AND COUNTRY OF ORIGIN

    IL

NOTIFY PARTY	DOMESTIC ROUTING/EXPORT INSTRUCTIONS
SAME	

PRECARRIAGE BY	PLACE OF RECEIPT
	CHICAGO

VESSEL	PORT OF LOADING	ONWARD INLAND ROUTING
DAS BOOT V.01	MONTREAL	

PORT OF DISCHARGE	PLACE OF DELIVERY
HAMBURG	

PARTICULARS FURNISHED BY SHIPPER

MARKS AND NUMBERS	NO. OF PKGS.	DESCRIPTION OF PACKAGES AND GOODS	GROSS WEIGHT	MEASUREMENT
OVERSEAS IMPORT 9876 MADE IN U.S.A. NOS. 1/5	5	SKIDS S.T.C. 10 CARTONS: BOOKS	2000#	100'
		FREIGHT COLLECT	LADEN ON BOARD OCT 10 1987	

These commodities licensed by U.S. for ultimate destination WEST GERMANY.
Diversion contrary to U.S. law prohibited.

FREIGHT CHARGES PAYABLE AT   DESTINATION

	PREPAID	COLLECT

Received from the aforenamed shipper the goods as described above by the shipper in apparent external good order and condition unless otherwise indicated herein or hereon to be transported in accordance with all of the terms printed, written, typed or stamped in or on this B/L of two (2) pages to which the merchant agrees by accepting this B/L any local privileges or customs notwithstanding.

In witness whereof, three (3) original BS/L have been signed, and if one (1) is accomplished by delivery of the Goods issuance of a delivery order or by some other means, the others shall be void if required by the carrier, one (1) original B/L must be surrendered, duly endorsed in exchange for the goods or a delivery order.

Dated at Port of Loading **UNION STAR LINE**   *J.W. Smith*

10	10	1987	By J.W. SMITH
MO	DAY	YEAR	FOR THE MASTER

B L No
911999-01

Figure 13.8 *A bill of lading*

Source: Reprinted with permission of Radix Group International, Inc.

Bills of lading can be issued for inland (overland), ocean, or air transport. An inland bill of lading is issued by railroad or truck lines. It authorizes movement of goods from the shipper's warehouse to the port or point of export. An ocean bill of lading, in contrast, applies to goods shipped by water and is issued by steamship lines. When the document is issued by an air carrier, it becomes an air waybill. In the case of a so-called **through bill of lading**, shipment is provided for two or more transportation modes for delivery to a final destination. Another kind of bill of lading is the NVOCC, which is issued by a "nonvessel operator common carrier" that consolidates freight into a container for shipping by regular liner vessels.

According to the International Chamber of Commerce, the bill of lading is acceptable only when it is marked **clean** and **on board**. The bill of lading is clean when the carrier sees no evidence of damage to the packing or condition of the cargo. The cargo thus must be received in good order and condition without exception or irregularity. A bill of lading is **foul** when there is indication of damage to the goods received. For an on-board bill of lading to be issued, the cargo must be loaded aboard the named vessel on the specified date of loading. In comparison, even though a received-for-shipment bill of lading also mentions a particular vessel, this document only implies that the goods have been received by the steamship company. In such a case, because the goods are not yet loaded on board a particular vessel, it is possible that the goods may end up on another vessel instead.

In addition to being classified as clean or foul and by types of transportation carriers, a bill of lading can be straight or negotiable. A **straight** bill of lading, under international law, is non-negotiable. It is consigned directly to a consignee rather than to order. As such, it allows delivery only to the consignee or party named on the bill. The carrier must be certain that the party receiving the goods is actually the named party. To obtain possession of the shipment, the foreign buyer simply shows one's proof of identity.

A shipper's **order** or **negotiable** bill of lading is a negotiable instrument that is consigned to order. When endorsed, it allows transfer of title to the holder of documents, and delivery can be made to a named party or anyone designated.

Both the straight and order bills of lading serve as collection documents. The buyer must pay for the goods, post bond, or meet other specified conditions before obtaining the bill of lading to claim the goods. The shipper endorses the bill and presents it to the bank for collection as evidence of satisfying the conditions stated in the letter of credit.

CONCLUSION

Moving cargo to an overseas destination is a much more complex task than transportation of freight locally. Other than the usual package designed to protect and/or promote a product while on display, packing (shipping package) is necessary if the merchandise is to be properly protected during shipment. Because of a greater number of hazards, the length of time during which the cargo is in transit, and a carrier's limited liability, the shipper should obtain marine insurance. In addition, the shipper should take necessary packing precautions to minimize any chance of damage. Containerization is one of several transportation modes that can achieve this goal.

Cargo cannot move without proper documentation. There are a huge number of documents that must be filed to satisfy an exporter's government requirements and an importer's legal requirements. To compound this problem, the document requirements of the various countries are far from being uniform. The shipper, however, does not have any option – the shipper simply must submit all required documents if a cargo is to be moved and if the shipper is going to collect payment from the buyer. There are specialists in cargo movement who can facilitate the process for a fee. Freight forwarders and customhouse brokers work for the shipper and the importer, respectively. They are capable of taking over all aspects of physical distribution and documentation. When the shipper wants to be relieved of these responsibilities, these intermediaries can help.

QUESTIONS

1 What are some of the hazards associated with the air, water, and land modes of transportation?
2 Explain how the freight rates–density effect can affect the choice of transportation.
3 Distinguish among conference lines, independent lines, and tramp vessels.
4 Distinguish between special coverage and blanket coverage.
5 When is an export license needed?
6 Explain the following documents: SED, dock receipt, invoice (commercial, foreign customs, and consular), certificate of origin, inspection certificate, air waybill, and bill of lading.
7 Distinguish among these types of bill of lading: clean, foul, straight, and negotiable.

DISCUSSION ASSIGNMENTS AND MINICASES

1 Is there an ideal mode of transportation based on market location, speed, cost, and hazard criteria?
2 What products are suitable for air shipping?
3 Explain how containerization can solve the four packing problems of weight, breakage, moisture, and temperature, and pilferage and theft.
4 What are the functions of a freight forwarder and a customhouse broker? Is it worthwhile to use these agents?

NOTES

1 Gene R. Tyndall, "We Must Manage Change Before It Manages Us," *Marketing News*, February 5, 1990, 14.
2 Martin Christopher, *The Strategy of Distribution Management* (Westport, CT: Quorum Books, 1985), 3.
3 John F. Magee, William C. Copacino, and Donald B. Rosenfield, *Modern Logistics Management* (New York, NY: Wiley, 1985), 193.
4 Mike Moore, "Tariff Reductions Aren't Enough," *Asian Wall Street Journal*, June 19, 2001.
5 Rupert Pennant-Rea and Ian G. Heggie, "Commercializing Africa's Roads," *Finance & Development* (December 1995): 30ff.
6 *Ports of the World: A Guide to Cargo Loss Control* (13th edn) (CIGNA), 46–7.
7 David Ross, "Air Freighting," in *Handbook of Physical Distribution Management* (3rd edn), ed. John Gattorna (Aldershot: Gower, 1983), 223–37.
8 "Security as a Trade Barrier," *Business Week*, December 31, 2001, 36.
9 Overseas Shipholding Group, Inc., *1993 Annual Report*, 13–14.
10 Charles A. Taff, *Management of Physical Distribution and Transportation* (7th edn) (Homewood, IL: Irwin, 1984), 261.
11 *Ports of the World*, 51.
12 *Ports of the World*, 52.
13 John Wilson, "Security in Distribution," in *Handbook of Physical Distribution Management* (3rd edn), ed. by John Gattorna (Aldershot: Gower, 1983).
14 "Sounding the Alarm in Mexico," *Business Week*, June 26, 2000, 74.

15 Magee, Copacino, and Rosenfield, *Modern Logistics Management*, 196.

16 Patterson Brown, "Freight Forwarders, Customs Brokers and Incoterms: Making Exporting Easier," *Export America* (November 2001).

17 Paul R. Murphy, James M. Daley, and Douglas R. Dalenberg, "Doing Business in Global Markets: Perspectives of International Freight Forwarders," *Journal of Global Marketing* 6 (No. 4, 1993): 53–68.

18 "WearGuard Does It Right in Canadian Launch," *DM News*, April 18, 1994, 22, 43.

19 Jim Robb, "Ask the TIC," *Export America* (January 2001): 14–15.

20 "US Customs Lays Stress on Secure Cargo," *Bangkok Post*, November 30, 2001.

21 "Anti-Terrorism Cargo Rules Please Nobody," *San José Mercury News*, February 19, 2003.

22 "Export Controls," *San José Mercury News*, February 2, 2000.

23 "Hughes, Boeing to Pay Fines," *San José Mercury News*, March 6, 2003.

Chapter 14

Promotion strategies

Personal selling, publicity, and sales promotion

Everyone lives by selling something.

Robert Louis Stevenson

CHAPTER OUTLINE

- Promotion and communication
- Promotion mix
- Personal selling
  - ☐ Personal selling vs. advertising
  - ☐ Varying quality and style of personal selling
  - ☐ Intercultural negotiation
  - ☐ Motivation
  - ☐ Telemarketing
  - ☐ Expatriate personnel
- Publicity
  - ☐ The nature of publicity
  - ☐ The management of publicity
  - ☐ Negative publicity
- Sales promotion
  - ☐ The nature of sales promotion
  - ☐ Restrictions
- Overseas product exhibitions
- Conclusion
- Case 14.1 Selling in the EU
- Case 14.2 AllWorld Corporation

PURPOSE OF CHAPTER

The Fiat example in the marketing illustration below provides clear evidence that a product must be promoted and that advertising is not the only means. A well-rounded marketing plan must include a proper promotion mix. This mix should not rely solely on advertising – personal selling, publicity, and sales promotion should also be included. This chapter examines the communication process in general as well as those promotional components other than advertising that are part of the process. Attention is given to the role of personal selling, both internationally and locally. The pros and cons of employing local nationals for selling are also discussed.

A section is devoted to the treatment of publicity, examining the principles related to a sound publicity campaign, with an emphasis on how to deal with negative publicity. A further section investigates the use of sales promotion and the influence of local regulations on the various sales promotion techniques.

MARKETING ILLUSTRATION   IMPECCABLE

Fiat Automotive S.A. needed a promotion campaign in Brazil for its redesigned Marea sedan and station wagon. The company told its agencies that a CD player was one Marea's top new features. As a result, the Impeccable campaign was born. The program focused on a giveaway of a premium CD containing music by well-known Brazilian singers (Milton Nascimento and Gilberto Gil). Direct mailings and consumer magazines' inserts were used to distribute the CDs. Recipients were urged to visit a Fiat dealership for a chance to win a Marea or concert tickets. They were required to bring a CD to be played during a test drive. When the drive was almost over, a salesperson would skip to the final track which gave an audio code that could be matched to a printed code located under the car's visor. Each person taking a test drive won concert tickets and could enter a secondary sweepstake for a second Marea. More than 22,100 CD recipients came in for a test drive, exceeding the campaign's goal by nearly 15 percent. More importantly, nearly 14 percent of them (about 3000 people) ended up buying a car. During the promotion period, the brand achieved an increase of 20 percent in sales.

The campaign also offered sales force incentives. Fiat aimed its motivation plans at individual salespeople as well as managers and dealerships as a whole, thus providing rewards to both an individual and a team.

Source: "A Real Gassser," *PROMO*, January 2002, 58.

PROMOTION AND COMMUNICATION

The purpose of promotion is both to communicate with buyers and to influence them. Effective promotion requires an understanding of the process of persuasion and how this process is affected by environmental factors. The potential buyer must not only receive the desired information but should also be able to comprehend that information.

Furthermore, the information must be sufficiently potent to motivate this buyer to react positively.

To communicate effectively with someone means that certain facts and information are shared in common with that person. **Communication** is basically a five-stage process consisting of source, encoding, information, decoding, and destination (see Figure 14.1). Encoding is a step that transforms the idea or information into a form that can

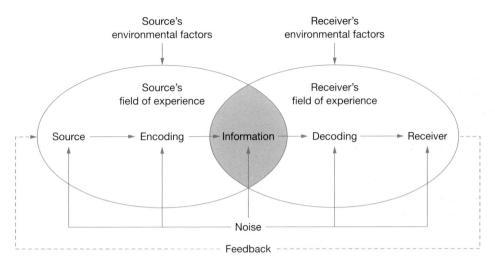

Figure 14.1 *The process of communication*

be transmitted (e.g., written or spoken words). For a receiver to understand the coded information, that person must be able to decode these words.

The source can encode and the receiver can decode only through the experience each has had. The two large circles in Figure 14.1 represent the **fields of experience** of each party. If the two circles have a large common area, communication is relatively easy because both individuals have similar psychological and social attributes. Communication is more difficult if the overlapping area is smaller. This is often the case with international communication. If the circles do not meet, communication is likely to be impossible; that is, the sender and the receiver have nothing in common, and they therefore have an extremely difficult time understanding each other. Moreover, **"noise"** (interference) can easily affect any one of the five stages, making the effect on the communication difficult to predict. Thus the sender must be receiver oriented. The message must consist of information that the receiver can relate to, and the information must be encoded with relevant images and words common to the receiver's experience and language.

It is not sufficient for the receiver to be informed only by the message; the receiver must also be persuaded to accept the information and to act as suggested. A promotional message thus must be designed in such a way that the purchaser reacts favorably. Effective motivation requires that the principles of mass persuasion be followed.[1]

The first principle is that the message must reach a person's sense organs. This may sound simplistic, yet frequently the message sent is not received by the intended audience. To ensure reception, the message must gain the attention of the receiver. If the right media are not available or if the wrong message channel is used, the message may never get to the intended receiver. Furthermore, if the cue is not appealing, the receiver may never open his or her senses to the message due to a lack of interest. Note that what is interesting in one culture may not be so in another. A message that refers to historical events in a home country (e.g., July 4) may have little meaning in a host country.

The second principle requires that the message should not contradict a person's cultural norms. It is possible, though not probable, that a message that is not consistent with the receiver's beliefs may sometimes be potent enough to make the buyer re-evaluate traditional beliefs. In most cases, such a message is likely to be rejected, discarded, or distorted. The effective promotional message is thus one that is accepted as part of the receiver's attitude and belief structure.

The third principle requires that the sender create a message that arouses the receiver's need and that suggests a particular action which will enable the receiver to achieve a desired goal. If the suggested action results in several goals being realized simultaneously, the potency of the message correspondingly increases. An advertiser should thus identify relevant needs and motives. Motives can differ greatly among countries, even when the same product is involved. Consider the automobile. American car buyers usually replace their automobiles every few years, and styling is important to them. A typical British car owner, however, is more likely to view the purchase as a long-term commitment, even though this perspective is also changing. For the Briton, the motive of functions in terms of durability outweighs the emotional appeal of styling.

The last principle suggests that the message must gain control of the receiver's behavior at the right place and time. The message should offer a well-defined path to reach the goal. If the purchaser is placed in a situation requiring action, the chances are increased that the buyer will take the suggested action. For example, Tokyo Toyopet, a division of Toyota, has done remarkably well by adhering to this principle. Its Toyota salesperson contacts a potential new car buyer immediately after the latter's car has completed its "shaken," a mandatory inspection in Japan for a three-year old automobile. The timing is effective because this is when the car owner is most likely to think about trading in the old vehicle for a new one.

Infiniti's communication campaign to introduce the brand seems to largely contradict the principles of mass persuasion. Although novel, the promotion campaign was severely criticized for failing to directly communicate the features and benefits of the Infiniti brand. The introductory TV spots and magazine advertisements did not show the product (i.e., the car). Instead, they showed pictures of rocks, trees, hay, and so on. The TV spots included "Distant Leaves," "Misty Tree," "Delicate Branches," "Flock of Geese," and "Summer Storm." Infiniti dealers were also upset.

PROMOTION MIX

To communicate with and influence customers, several promotional tools are available. Advertising is usually the most visible component of promotion, but it is not the only component. The promotion mix also consists of three other distinct but inter-related activities: personal selling, publicity, and sales promotion.

The four promotional components are not mutually exclusive, and it can be difficult at times to determine which one of the four activities a particular promotional tool may be. Consider the common trade fair. Promotion for a trade fair may be viewed as advertising because a fair sponsor, as well as participating companies, generally uses direct mail and newspapers to advertise the event. Since the media receive both advertising orders and news releases, they may be willing to provide free publicity for the fair as well. Furthermore, staffing at a display booth is necessary, and there will be plenty of opportunity for a company's representative to use personal selling to make sales. Finally, it is not uncommon for fair participants to offer free gifts and special prices during the display, and these techniques are classified as sales promotion tools. This chapter concentrates on personal selling, publicity, and sales promotion.

PERSONAL SELLING

According to the American Marketing Association, personal selling is an "oral presentation in a conversation with one or more prospective purchasers for the purpose of making sales." Personal selling, also commonly known as salesmanship, is used at every distribution level. The cost of personal selling is high. One extreme case is German software maker SAP, the world's leader in applications packages for client-server networks. In the USA, SAP America has removed the $140,000 annual limit on sales commissions, making it possible for a salesperson to earn as much as $2 million a year – more than what the company's top German executives make.[2]

In spite of the high cost, personal selling should be emphasized when certain conditions are met.

Industrial buying or large-volume purchases, characterized by a large amount of money being involved, justifies personal attention. Personal selling has also proven to be effective when the market is concentrated or when a salesperson must develop a measure of confidence in the customer for the purchase. The effectiveness of personal selling is also a function of product type. In general, personal selling works well with high-unit value and infrequently purchased products. Such products usually require a demonstration, are custom-made or fitted to an individual's needs, or involve trade-ins.

In the Far East, Asian businesspeople do not like to discuss business deals with a foreigner who does not come highly recommended by a mutual acquaintance. Personal contact is important to selling in South Korea, not only because of the value placed on personal relationships but also because such contact serves to bring the end user in touch with new processes and equipment. Because Japanese suppliers often visit their Korean customers, US suppliers need to visit Korea to augment the efforts of the local representative. At the same time, it is advisable to hold demonstrations, seminars, and exhibitions of their products in Korea.

Note that not all salespersons are directly involved in selling. So-called missionary salespersons, for example, have the task of educating potential buyers about product benefits and promotional campaigns in order to create the goodwill that may result in subsequent sales. When Foremost first introduced milk and ice cream products to the Thai market in 1956, the company sent sales representatives (missionary salespersons) to educate people by giving talks on sanitation and nutrition in schools and by providing free samples to students.

Personal selling vs. advertising

Personal selling is similar to advertising in the sense that both aim to create sales and that both must be understandable, interesting, believable, and persuasive. However, advertising differs from personal selling in several aspects. Advertising relies on a non-personal means of contact and sales presentation. When compared to advertising, personal selling commands a much larger share of aggregate promotional dollars and accounts for several times more in terms of the number of personnel. This relationship exists in all countries. In fact, the abundant labor supply in developing countries makes it easy and inexpensive to employ sales personnel. Shoplifting problems also necessitate the use of personal selling, making self-selection and self-service relatively rare.

The differences between advertising and personal selling may also be contrasted in terms of the communication process.[3] Advertising is a one-way communication process that has relatively more "noise," whereas personal selling is a two-way communication process with immediate feedback and relatively less "noise." Controlling the message is more difficult in personal selling than in advertising because salespersons may react to unforeseen situations in such a way that may differ from the company's policy. Yet advertising is usually less persuasive because advertisements are prepared in advance by those with minimal contact with customers and because the message must be kept simple to appeal to a large number of people. Personal selling, on the other hand, is more flexible, personal, and powerful. A salesperson can adapt the message to fit the client at the time of presentation, and stimuli can be presented to appeal to all five senses.

Varying quality and style of personal selling

The quality of personal selling varies widely from product to product, from employer to employer, and from one target group to another. In general, salespersons selling for manufacturers are better trained and more qualified than those working for wholesalers and retailers. In terms of the target market, salespersons who sell to industrial users are more likely to be "order getters" and are generally aggressive, well trained, and well informed. Industrial salespeople, receiving high compensation, must be capable of mixing easily with top management.

417

Those selling to wholesalers, retailers, and consumers have a more routine selling job, and these salespeople are "order takers" and generally less aggressive in securing new business. Expensive products require a higher quality of personal selling than do low-unit value, high-turnover products.

Personal selling is not viewed as a prestigious occupation in most countries. It is often taught in trade schools or vocational schools rather than in colleges, and thus the quality of personal selling outside the USA is far from exemplary. In Brazil, for example, salespeople are not very well trained by US standards.

Selling styles differ significantly. In Japan, employers are agreeable to the practice of having salespeople call on their employees at the workplace. Japanese salespeople sell cars door-to-door. Subaru went one step further. With its image as a vehicle for outdoor types, Subaru equipped its door-to-door salespeople with Sportsman's Guide catalogs. Sportsman's Guide, a US firm selling a proprietary line of sporting goods and accessories, was optimistic about this unique distribution channel.

In the USA, salespeople entertain clients at either breakfast or lunch. Overseas, it is much more common to meet for entertainment after business hours and to have sales discussions over dinner or in a nightclub. After-hours business contacts are much more important overseas than they are in the USA. Clients expect attention to be given to social functions in addition to business functions, including golf, drinking, dining, and so on. Potential customers expect to be wined and dined extensively. A salesperson commonly takes customers to bars and nightclubs for social contact with members of the opposite sex. Under such circumstances, salespeople must be prepared to be far more than order takers.

The personal selling tactic may have to be modified in some markets. Avon is able to use door-to-door selling in the USA and Latin America, but it found that the practice is an anathema in some cultures. Asians, for example, are wary of strangers; as a result, Avon's sales representatives stop only at the homes of friends and relatives. Neighborhood parties sponsored by Avon are a modified promotional technique that seems to work well in Asia, and the technique has been tested in Germany as well. In France, the prohibition of door-to-door selling has compelled Avon to shift to direct mail sales.

Personal selling must receive proper support in terms of training and information. It is difficult for salespeople to be effective without advertising support. Advertising creates awareness and helps make customers more receptive. Tokyo Toyopet's advertising, for instance, does not take the form of direct action advertising. Rather, it tells customers to be patient and to wait for one of the company's salespeople to call. Such advertisements are not product oriented since the intent is to sell a company image. These advertisements are employed not to attract customers to the showroom but to aid the salespeople's door-to-door sales activities.

Intercultural negotiation

Successful negotiations require some understanding of each party's culture and may also require adoption of a negotiation strategy that is consistent with the other party's cultural system. One strategy is to rely on stereotyping. It is possible, for example, to use stereotyped preconceptions to identify the personality traits of negotiators from different ethnic groups or countries. Although stereotyping allows an easy label, it is also risky because generalization may lead one to believe that members of the group must share the same traits. These prejudices, if believed, may affect business negotiations and their outcomes.

International marketers are interested in the effects of cultural adaptation on intercultural communication. Studies should be conducted to identify conditions that make it desirable for businesspeople to adapt their behavior in response to the culture of the other party.

Motivation

Like other employees, salespeople need to be motivated. In many countries, Western firms find it difficult to retain and motivate salespeople. The concept of individual recognition of sales representatives is at odds with Japan's team approach to business and its aversion to a compensation system that pays for performance. In Saudi Arabia, where selling is considered an undesirable occupation, qualified local sales representatives are hard to find due to a labor shortage. Because of India's various languages and social caste system, it is difficult for sales representatives to sell outside their own social level. In Brazil, the determination of sales force compensation and product pricing is affected by rampant inflation and national labor laws. It is thus a problem to pay someone less than the amount paid the previous year.

Based on a representative sample of the labor force in seven countries regarding what individuals seek from working, the two most dominant work goals are "interesting work" and "good pay," and these goals are consistent internationally, across different organizational levels, between the genders and among different age categories.[4] Although wage level has some explanatory value in predicting the compensation ratio, culture is a predominant factor that influences certain compensation patterns.[5] One study found that industrial salespeople's perceptions of organizational fairness varied across the USA, Japan, and Korea.[6]

Amway (Japan) Ltd., the subsidiary of privately held Amway Corp., is the corporation's top overseas affiliate as well as the ninth most profitable foreign company in Japan. Amway is able to bypass local retailers and wholesalers who often demand enormous markups. Amway does all its direct selling in homes through some 500,000 distributors (salespeople). Amway's cultlike corporate culture appeals to Japanese who prefer to identify strongly with their employers. As in the USA, Amway motivates salespeople by offering 30 percent commissions, bonuses, and trips abroad, and its pyramidal structure generously rewards distributors who bring new salespeople into their group. Distributors are attracted by the unusual brand of fraternal capitalism as much as by potential earnings.

Avon's joint venture with the Guangzhou Cosmetics Factory is the first foreign as well as Chinese company authorized to sell directly to Chinese consumers. Avon's concern about Chinese women's ability to understand the concept of direct sales disappeared rapidly when local representatives told Avon to double the prices and sold one month's allocation of cosmetics in five days. Most representatives like the self-esteem, independence, and extra income (commissions).

Certain factors may affect sales performance. Role conflict and role ambiguity have been found to have deleterious effects on sales personnel in the USA, Japan, and Korea. To reduce role conflict and ambiguity, a number of techniques may be used: sales training, training manuals, job descriptions, written company correspondence, lectures/discussions, case studies, role-playing exercises, training films, and so on.[7]

Telemarketing

Personal selling does not always require a face-to-face conversation. For instance, personal selling may be done over the telephone. Although telephone selling has been in existence for a considerable period of time, the growth of the direct marketing field has pushed this method of selling to the forefront. This marketing practice, now known as **telemarketing**, has become very popular among sellers – but not necessarily with consumers, who feel they are being inundated with such calls. Because of the effective lobbying of telemarketing firms, US lawmakers have been reluctant to pass laws restricting the use of telemarketing. As part of the lobbying effort, the firms pointed out that legislators' own fund-raising efforts would be impede by the proposed restrictions. However, the US and state governments finally implemented the do-not-call lists in 2003.

In overseas markets, telemarketing is not as far developed as it is in the USA. The limited availability of telephones for private households is one problem. The privacy laws are another obstacle. **Cold calling** (unsolicited sales calls) is receiving close scrutiny in the name of consumer protection and respect for privacy. A statutory cooling off

419

period may apply to sales closings over the telephone. Germany is even more restrictive. It prohibits cold calls on the grounds of privacy invasion, and this ban even applies to an insurance salesperson's announcement of a visit.

Expatriate personnel

One controversial subject for which there is no definite solution is the nationality of the salespeople to be used in a market abroad. Some marketers argue for the use in a foreign market of expatriate salespeople, or those from the home country. Others take the opposite point of view by contending that the best policy is to use local nationals or those salespeople who were born in the host country. According to one study, the higher the interdependence between a branch office and headquarters, the more US nationals are employed in overseas operations to manage the inherent uncertainty.[8] However, though managerial behaviors are related positively to job performance for managers in the USA, they were not related to job performance for American expatriate managers in Hong Kong or job performance for Hong Kong Chinese managers.[9]

Expatriate salespeople are viewed favorably because they are already familiar with their company's product, technology, history, and policies. Thus the only kind of preparation they would need is a knowledge of the foreign market. Yet this may be the greatest obstacle for the expatriate salesperson. Whereas some may enjoy the challenge and adjustment, other expatriate personnel find it difficult to cope with a new and unfamiliar business environment. The failure to understand a foreign culture and its customs without question will hinder the effectiveness of an expatriate sales force. British managers, for instance, have difficulty in running retail stores in the highly competitive US market, which is characterized by longer shopping hours and sizing differences.

Not only must an expatriate cope with new business conditions, but the expatriate's family must also share in the burden of making social adjustments. Life can be difficult both physically and

psychologically for those who are unable to make the necessary adjustments for an assignment that requires a lengthy relocation overseas. The expatriate may have second thoughts about accepting such an assignment, fearing that the distance from headquarters may eliminate chances for promotion or that the company may want to keep him or her abroad. Moreover, an overseas assignment may not be easy for American salespeople and their spouses because they may become frustrated with shopping for schooling, and the limited entertainment opportunities. Some may be driven by the boredom and frustration and may initiate an affair or begin to drink excessively. It is thus crucial that the personnel for overseas assignments be selected carefully. In fact, their families should also be interviewed to determine the suitability of their temperament for an overseas assignment.

An examination of "antecedents of spouse cross-cultural adjustment to interacting with host country nationals and to coping with general, foreign environment" found spouse interaction adjustment to be positively related with firms that sought the spouse's opinion about the international assignment, the spouse's self-initiated pre-departure training, and social support from family and host nations during the overseas assignment.[10]

Successful expatriates possess certain qualities that include cultural adaptability, patience, flexibility, and tolerance for others' beliefs. One study of network ties focuses on three characteristics of international managers – nationality, cultural distance, and expatriate status. Based on a network analysis of cross-subsidiary interactions among 457 managers in a multinational corporation, managers form strong, expressive ties with peers with a smaller cultural distance and from the same status group. But in the case of instrumental ties, they are stronger when peers differ in these background characteristics.[11]

Expatriates are likely to perform more effectively overseas if they are satisfied with their jobs. According to one study, job autonomy and material life satisfaction are key predictors for expatriate turnover tendencies.[12] According to another study, job characteristics as well as organization character- istics contribute significantly to expatriate satisfac- tion. In terms of job characteristics, an expatriate manager should be given more clarity and auton- omy. Regarding organization characteristics, it is important to involve expatriates in the decision- making process so that the adverse effect of geo- graphical isolation (and managerial isolation) can be minimized.[13] It is thus advisable for a company to design new job assignments based on past skills and experiences while opening up opportunities for future growth and development.[14]

An expatriate's commitment to the local opera- tion and the parent company is determined in part by one's satisfaction with the host culture. This sat- isfaction is in turn determined by one's consumer experiences. Market alienation, having a negative effect on satisfaction, can be reduced by participa- tion in the host marketplace. While cultural know- ledge is not directly related to one's satisfaction with the host culture, it has an indirect impact through its association with the participation in the host marketplace.[15]

Despite the problems associated with the use of expatriate personnel, local workers or the host country's own nationals may present another set of unique problems. Rather than having a multi- national perspective, they may be identified more closely with their home country. They may also not possess an understanding of the headquarters' busi- ness cultures and objectives. Furthermore, they may be geographically immobile in the sense that they may prefer staying in their own country rather than accepting a new position with more responsibilities abroad. Empirically, however, one study found no support for the widespread belief that expatriate personnel are more loyal to the company than host- country nationals.[16]

In all fairness, some disadvantages of using locals very likely apply to expatriates as well. More important is that these criticisms point out the prob- lem of ethnocentrism. Companies which are truly multinational realize that good foreign personnel, though somewhat different in their thinking and approach, can be valuable and effective employees.

Foreign personnel may also be able to provide knowledge and information that can be very valu- able to American companies. Hewlett Packard is one example of an American multinational company that owes its success to the use of foreign personnel. Its European operations are run autonomously by Europeans. Local pools of technical expertise are tapped to develop products for worldwide distribu- tion. New management ideas, such as flexible work- ing hours and a program to introduce the company to schoolchildren, were first developed in Germany before being adopted in the USA.

There are several advantages to be gained by an MNC in using foreign-born native personnel working in their own country. One advantage is that the company can avoid political, sensitive, or embar- rassing situations. Since the government and the local community undoubtedly prefer that their own nationals be hired instead of outsiders, the MNC can avoid charges of exploitation while gaining goodwill at the same time. Visa's European organization has been staffed and directed by Europeans in an effort to dilute its image as an American company.

Another advantage to be gained is that the company can compete quite strongly for high- quality local personnel. An MNC can offer above- market pay, which may likely be still lower than the pay scale in the MNC's home market. This situation applies to Japan as well. The stigma associated with the Japanese working for foreign companies has recently been crumbling. In the past, the Japanese were reluctant to work for US companies since they felt that it would be a barrier to promotion. They were also apprehensive about the role of politics within the organization. But younger Japanese are now more internationally oriented and are eager to join US companies, since these workers resent the Japanese system of seniority, dedication, and loyalty.

When the host country's people are employed locally, expatriate relocation and travel expenses can be avoided. The costs of keeping expatriates over- seas can be exorbitant. Cost-of-living adjustments may equal 80 percent of base salaries. In addition, a modest house in a Tokyo suburb may cost $11,000 a month. It is not unusual for GM to have to spend

421

$750,000 to $1 million on a manager and his or her family during a three-year stay overseas.[17]

The use of local personnel allows a company to proceed with its business more quickly since the adjustment period is eliminated. Language barriers and cultural difficulties are minimized. For example, it is difficult for an American salesperson to entertain foreign clients without an understanding of the local culture. Without a knowledge of the local language, even simple or casual interaction such as telling a joke is a struggle. In Japan, a majority of business is conducted verbally in face-to-face interaction, whereas in the USA much greater emphasis is placed on correspondence and report preparation. Realizing that the American business culture is different, Ricoh uses American personnel to run its US operations. Furthermore, Ricoh recognizes that local nationals, being identified as part of the local scene, can be both efficient and effective since they have business and government contacts.

One answer to the question of the nationalities of personnel is that suitability can be determined in part by the distribution level. Western salespeople can be used to contact overseas distributors, wholesalers, and large retailers. This international channel, however, is impractical at the consumer or local level. Most Japanese insurance companies and Avon, for example, use home makers as part-time salespeople for door-to-door sales. The American Family Life Assurance Company, likewise, uses no advertising in Japan but relies on a strong sales network and a full-time sales force selling group policies directly to companies.

When personnel are examined in key positions and at headquarters, usually most American companies have only Americans. In a way, this is understandable because of the vast supply of local talent available to fill such positions, but some American MNCs are now realizing that a well-trained American may not be so well trained to work on a worldwide basis. American Standard has instilled a stronger global orientation into its corporate decision-making process by using foreign managers to run many of its important US operations. Such

heterogeneity provides a company with linguistic capabilities, exporting know-how, skills in negotiating with foreign governments, and international flavor that many US managers lack.

When local personnel are employed, an MNC must pay attention to the host country's labor laws. Such laws can temper the firm's decisions with regard to hiring and firing. This is especially true in socialist countries. China, for example, has become a hybrid of capitalism and communism. The hiring rules there have been relaxed, making it possible for Chinese entrepreneurs to hire employees. MNCs, however, have to select employees from those sent to them by the state. The socialistic system, by guaranteeing jobs and security and by awarding bonuses equally among workers with no regard for performance, hampers efficient operations. As a result, workers are more concerned with a big bonus and not very interested in hard work. In any case, MNCs have recently gained more legal right to fire lazy or incompetent workers, though that right has not been extended to domestic enterprises. Nevertheless, MNCs should realize that a worker must be given many chances before that worker can be fired.

Women tend not to get international assignments. The reasons often offered range from the reluctance of women or their companies, to prejudice against women in foreign countries. One study found that women and their supervisors had different views on women's interest in pursuing international assignments as well as different expectations concerning the prejudice. Therefore, women and their supervisors should discuss the issues openly.[18]

PUBLICITY

The nature of publicity

Publicity is the nonpersonal stimulation of demand that is not paid for by a sponsor which has released news to the media. Advertising and publicity are quite similar in the sense that both require media for a nonpersonal presentation of the promotional message. One difference between the two is that, with publicity, a company has less control over how the message will be used by the media. Another difference is that publicity is presumed to be free in the sense that the media are not paid for presentation of the message to the public. In practice, a publicity campaign is not cost free because someone must be assigned to generate the publicity, and there are several direct and indirect costs. However, the cost of publicity is minimal when compared to the benefit.

Publicity offers several advantages. In addition to the low cost, the material presented is not recognized as paid advertising per se because it occurs in an editorial setting that makes it appear to have been generated by approval of the editorial staff. The material thus has more credibility, and consumers tend to accept it as news information rather than as advertising. This perception is particularly useful in countries where it is difficult to buy commercial time or advertising space.

Publicity should be used when a company advertises heavily, since advertising increases the likelihood that the media that have been used will reciprocate by using the company's news releases. Publicity is also effective when the editorial content can influence purchase, a point proven by Perrier. Publicity was an important part of Perrier's marketing program, since the company determined that it needed third-party endorsement by editors in news and lifestyle publications and broadcast media. Perrier therefore invited sixty editors and TV personnel to the mineral spring in France. The cost of $100,000 was more than offset by several positive articles that appeared later – which were worth several million dollars in publicity. Its other promotional vehicles were those associated with health and fitness, including marathons, road races, Perrier golf course openings attended by celebrities, and Louis Harris' *The Perrier Study: Fitness in America*.

There are several methods that may be used to gain publicity. Such methods include the following: contribution of prizes; sponsorship of civic activities; release of news about the company's product, plant, and personnel; and announcements of the company's promotional campaign, especially with regard to such sales promotion techniques as games and contests. Nike was able to overtake Adidas in the USA with effective publicity and sales promotion campaigns. In addition to asking athletes to help design shoes, Nike signed professional athletes to exclusive promotional contracts involving cash, free shoes, and promotion appearances. Shoes were given to top college teams, and the company gained additional exposure when these teams appeared on TV. Moreover, it sponsored running clinics, sporting events, and women's pro tennis events.

The management of publicity

Publicity is often viewed as a promotional component that is not possible to manage. News releases to the media may not be used by the media or, if used, not in the manner intended. In reality, the problem is not so much that publicity cannot be managed but that publicity is usually managed in a haphazard way.

Proper management is required for all publicity campaigns. Every campaign must first have a well-defined objective. Without a precise objective it is difficult to coordinate activities, and conflicting messages or items of little news value might be released. Confusion usually follows.

Much like the other three activities of promotion, the effectiveness of publicity must be measured. The effectiveness of publicity is not determined by the number of news releases or publication space and air time generated. Similar to advertising, personal selling, and sales promotion, the effectiveness of publicity should be measured by sales inquiries and changes in the attitude or response pattern of the public.

A person responsible for a publicity campaign should keep the needs of the media in mind. Any request for information should be handled promptly because any requested information is likely to be used. In most countries, magazines have small editorial budgets and are understaffed. A publicity placement is more likely to be accepted if it is submitted in the form that is ready to be used. For example, photos and materials that are camera-ready relieve the publication of budget and time constraints.

Negative publicity

Some publicity received can be far from favorable (see Cultural Dimension 14.1 and Marketing Ethics 14.1). R.J. Reynolds encountered this problem in Japan when it had to disclose that its 16,000 cases of Winston Lights, used as samples, contained illegally high levels of the dicamba herbicide, higher than permitted by US law. The poor publicity in quality-conscious Japan forced the company to call a press conference to allay fears of health hazards. Ajinomoto, a brand of monosodium glutamate, has been able throughout the company's history to dispel false rumors. In the 1910s a rumor was spread that Ajinomoto came from snakes. Another rumor, circulating in Islamic countries, was that Ajinomoto was processed from pig bones.

No company wants negative publicity. Without the proper handling of publicity, a situation may deteriorate. The adverse publicity generated by its powdered infant formula became a publicity night-mare for Nestlé. The company's idea of marketing a breast-milk substitute in developing countries to save babies from disease, malnutrition, and death backfired very badly. Church groups and consumer groups accused the company of promoting the product to those who could least afford it or who were unable to use it properly. The poor handling of the animosity that developed engaged the company in a long and costly conflict.

Ford and Firestone generated a great deal of negative publicity related to Ford Explorer and Firestone tires.[19] The Ford SUVs and Firestone tires were linked to more than 1400 accidents and other mishaps, and almost 100 people died as a result. Ford blamed the accidents on the Firestone tires and offered replacement tires to its customers, resulting in a recall of some 6.5 million tires. Firestone, on the other hand, put the blame in part on Ford's user instructions to underinflate the tires. Neither side appeared to handle the crisis well, and the termination of the partnership did not help matters.

Much has been learned from the Tylenol case, in which Johnson & Johnson was able to deal effectively with the contamination that occurred in its capsules. Marketers should carefully review how the

CULTURAL DIMENSION 14.1   A SINCERE APOLOGY

Snow Brand Milk Products Co. had serious publicity problems. Because of a dirty valve at its Osaka plant, its contaminated low-fat milk caused diarrhea and vomiting in thousands of residents in western Japan. The milk was recalled. More disclosures of contamination in other products followed. More people got sick, and there were more recalls. Soon the Osaka government alleged that Snow Brand recycled and resold milk products that were returned by stores. The company's senior officials were heavily criticized for responding slowly and inadequately to the health threat.

The Japanese way is for a company to apologize profusely. Even then, Snow Brand's scale of apology was extraordinary. The company sent 2000 employees to visit the more than 14,000 people who got sick from consuming the tainted milk. The workers bowed, apologized, and offered cash compensation. They were instructed not to talk back. They had to be quiet and take any insults, while telling the customers that the customers were absolutely right. Each of the contrition crews took as much as $2000 with them in a day and brought along gift certificates, apology letters, and customer complaint forms. Certainly, it was even painful for the victims to witness such acts. On the other hand, the food conglomerate, with $12.1 billion in annual sales, had plenty at stake.

Source: "Snow Brand Deploys Some 2,000 Staffers to Apologize Profusely," *Asian Wall Street Journal*, July 12, 2000.

MARKETING ETHICS 14.1   THE REAL THING AND THE REAL PROBLEMS

Product contamination in Belgium was one of the worst public relations nightmares in Coca-Cola's history. The Antwerp plant used substandard carbon dioxide, causing many Belgians to become sick from stomach upsets, nausea, and headaches. It was the first time that Coke had to remove its entire inventory in one country. Luxembourg and the Netherlands also ordered the recalls. In France, the government suspended sales of Coke from its Dunkirk plant because some cans were contaminated with a wood chip during shipping. Coca-Cola quickly sent a team of scientists to Europe to deal with the crisis.

Coca-Cola's attempt to acquire Cadbury Schweppes without seeking clearance from the European Union did not help the matter. European regulators were upset, and the deal failed. To improve its relationships with the EU governments, Coca-Cola's new CEO replaced almost all of its senior management team in Europe with local executives. Out of ten managers, only one American was retained as a division president in Europe.

Coca-Cola offered a set of plastic figurines that were derived from the Japanese TV series Robocon.

One robot figurine, Robowaru, had two swastika-like designs printed on its chest. This Buddhist symbol is common in Asia and is often confused with the Nazi swastika. Because of a local Jewish leader's criticism, Coca-Cola removed Robowaru.

Coca-Cola also has to contend with religions and rumors. In 2000, Egyptians received e-mail messages alleging that Coke's logo buried "No Mohammed, No Mecca" in Arabic in the script's curls. The company approached Egypt's mufti, the top religious authority. The mufti issued a religious edict which concluded that "there was no defamation to the religion of Islam for near or far." In addition, those who spread false claims "will be plunged into hell for 70 autumns."

Sources: "Things Aren't Going Better with Coke," *Business Week*, June 28, 1999, 49; "Coke's Hard Lesson in Crisis Management," *Business Week*, July 5, 1999, 102; "Coke Mending Fences in Europe," *The Nation*, June 24, 2000; "Is Douglas Daft the Real Thing?" *Business Week*, December 20, 1999, 44, 46; "Coke Survives Blasphemy Rumors," *San José Mercury News*, May 23, 2000; "Coke Pulls Toy with Swastika-Like Designs," *San José Mercury News*, May 1, 2003.

company was able to turn the negative publicity around and regain sympathy and trust. Based on these experiences, there are several "do's" and "don'ts" that should be kept in mind.

To begin with, it is not wise to criticize the media for reporting unfavorable news. The criticism serves to alienate the media by inflaming the issue and prolonging the attention being given to it. It is also not wise to ignore adverse publicity. This behavior may give the impression of arrogance, and it wastes crucial time that could be used to solve the problem if it is serious. A company should also avoid the "no comment" response because it conveys the impression of uncooperativeness and implies guilt. If a full disclosure is not possible for security reasons, the company's spokesperson should say so and ask for understanding from the media.

When preparing to respond to inquiries about a newsworthy event, it is crucial to review the facts, prepare news reports, and perhaps seek professional assistance. Personnel should be immediately organized to handle inquiries from consumers and reporters. Even when the problem is still unclear, contingency plans should be devised so that personnel can act quickly. In fact, there should be a contingency crisis management plan that forces executives to think in advance about how to deal with unforeseen crises.

Those companies facing the greatest levels of industrial and environmental risk are more likely than others to have crisis communication plans. Such companies include those in the extractive industries and food and drug manufacturers. It is thus surprising that, given the nature of the business, Union

Carbide failed to anticipate potential problems that could have occurred. As a result, the company was severely criticized for its handling of the devastating Bhopal (India) gas leak. Many inquiries in the early stages went unanswered, and at times the company appeared evasive when it did issue a response.

In dealing with the media, candor, preparedness, speed, and cooperation are all essential. If a company's guilt is undeniable, it is better to admit this at the outset so that attention can be shifted to the steps being taken to resolve the situation. Although a team effort is likely taking place, it is highly desirable that a top executive acts as the company's sole spokesperson so that inconsistencies can be minimized. The executive should be prepared to communicate quickly and professionally. He or she must possess accurate information and be ready to answer all questions. Since the media are eager to receive information, they can and should be accommodated, as well as exploited. The company can call news conferences that allow it to relay the information to the public through the media at no cost. At such conferences, the spokesperson can outline the steps being taken to protect the public interest. In effect, this tactic provides the company with free advertising and positive publicity.

If the product has serious potential ramifications, corporate image advertising may be used to reinforce the trustworthiness of the company and product. Market research can be valuable in tracking the public mood so that appropriate communication strategies may be adopted. Figure 14.2 shows how South Africa attempted to use advertising to deal with its country's negative image and bad publicity.

The company should also be decisive. Its decision should be based on the public good rather than cost as an overriding motive. If product recall is warranted because a situation is potentially dangerous to the public, the recall should proceed immediately. A company should avoid vacillation or hedging. Procter & Gamble poorly handled a problem of contaminated cake mixes in California by making contradictory announcements about the product's recall. A decisive response does not mean, however, that product recall is always the preferred

strategy. Gerber Foods took legal action against those states that wanted its baby food taken off the shelves because of broken glass found in some jars. The company's rationale was that the incident was an isolated one not related to its normal manufacturing process and that any recall would unduly alarm the public. Its position was subsequently supported by the results of an investigation.

SALES PROMOTION

The nature of sales promotion

Sales promotion consists of those promotional activities other than advertising, personal selling, and publicity. As such, any promotional activities that do not fall under the other three activities of the promotion mix are considered to be sales promotion. Qantas, for example, offers its passengers Connection Cards that may be used to purchase London Fog coats wholesale. The trade often uses the term indiscriminately. Businesspeople may use the term "promotion" when they actually mean "sales promotion." In this book, *promotion* is a broad term that encompasses sales promotion as well as the other three promotional activities.

The techniques of sales promotion are varied and numerous. The common ones used are coupons, sweepstakes, games, contests, price-offs, demonstrations, premiums, samples, money refund offers, and trading stamps. A combination of these may be used and is sometimes used in the same campaign. When Kelloggs expanded its business abroad, it had to enlighten consumers in South and Central America, the Middle East, and Asia about dry cereal and cold breakfasts. To instill this new eating habit, Kelloggs used samples and demonstrations in conjunction with a heavy advertising campaign. To regain market share in Japan, Procter & Gamble distributed 1.5 million diaper samples of improved Pampers. Each diaper box also carried a picture of a little bear. Parents could get baby items by saving the required number of bears.

Sales promotion is temporary in nature. Not being self-sustaining, its function is to supplement

South Africa

Houses for sale: $16 000 and less

Imagine buying a four-roomed, State-built house for as little as $880. Or a five-roomed house for between $2 331 and $16 000. It's happening right now – in South Africa.

SHARING A BETTER QUALITY OF LIFE

South Africa is involved in a remarkable process of providing fair opportunities for all its population groups. The South African Government is committed to ensure that each of South Africa's many nationalities have the ability and resources to realize their social, economic and political aspirations.

Housing is a leading example of South Africa's development process. And as an integrated part of its drive towards home ownership for everyone, the South African Government has given the go-ahead for the sale of 500 000 State-financed homes at discounts of up to 40 % of their market value.

MEETING THE HOUSING CHALLENGE

South Africa's urban Black population is expected to rise from 9 million currently to around 20 million by the turn of the century. It is estimated that an additional 4.9 million housing units will have to be provided to accommodate this phenomenal urbanisation.

The housing challenge is being met by both the Government and the private sector. Government initiatives are directed mainly towards providing the machinery and support for self-help building projects, while private enterprise provides loans, subsidies and guarantees.

THE FUTURE – BETTER PROSPECTS FOR ALL

A recent survey indicated that 82 % of all employers were prepared to provide their Black staff with assistance to buy their own homes.

The facts on housing present only part of the picture. Many aspects of South African life have changed – and are changing at an ever-increasing rate. The future is exciting because we have the people, the dedication and a buoyant economy to enable us to keep on providing opportunities and improving the quality of life of all our people.

Because South Africa is a microcosm of so many of the world's sensitivities, it is often a contentious subject. If you are faced with a decision regarding South Africa, make sure you have all the facts.

For more information, simply complete the coupon below.

To: The Minister (Information),
The South African Embassy,
3051 Massachusetts Avenue,
Washington D.C., 20008 N.W.
Please send me more information on socio-economic and political developments in South Africa.
Name ....
Address ....
....Code .....

We're looking forward to the future.

Figure 14.2
Management of negative publicity

Source: Reprinted with permission of the South African Consulate General, Washington, DC.

advertising, personal selling, and publicity. To launch Budweiser beer in Great Britain, Anheuser-Busch employed the "American" theme. Its TV commercials on the 4th of July and Thanksgiving Day were spots filmed in California with American actors. To supplement its advertising effort, the company used a variety of sales promotion techniques. It made posters, bunting, flags, pennants, T-shirts, and sweatshirts available to pubs and discos for promotional parties. Bud ashtrays, bar towels, coasters, football pennants, and similar items were offered for sale. Moreover, American disc jockeys were brought in to program American music nights.

Sales promotion is not restricted to the stimulation of demand at the consumer level; it may be used to gain middlemen's support as well. Moreover, the use of sales promotion is not limited to consumer products. It may be used with industrial selling too. Misawa Homes promoted its House 55 by sending samples to US Homes and Germany's

Okal. Pfizer, like other drug firms, attracts drug wholesalers by sponsoring trips and other events. Gifts are given to doctors, and doctors' wives are taken on shopping tours.

Sales promotion is effective when a product is first introduced to a market. It also works well with existing products that are highly competitive and standardized, especially when they are of low unit value and have a high turnover. Under such conditions, sales promotion is needed to gain that "extra" competitive advantage.

The effectiveness of sales promotion can be tempered by psychological barriers, and this fact is applicable to middlemen as well as to consumers. Some foreign retailers are reluctant to accept manufacturers' coupons because they fear that they will not be reimbursed. Consumers, on the other hand, may view rebates, mail-in coupons, and money-back guarantees with suspicion, thinking that something must be wrong with the product.

International marketers need to confirm the validity of a statement concerning the effectiveness of a sales promotion technique. Sometimes, casual observation and hearsay have a way of making a particular claim become a statement of fact without support of empirical evidence.

Restrictions

Although sales promotion is generally received enthusiastically in developing countries, the activity is still largely underused, which may be due more to legal barriers than psychological barriers. European countries have a larger number of restrictions than the USA in this area. The legal requirements are so diverse that the European Association of Advertising Agencies (EAAA) decided that the standardization of promotion regulations was very unlikely in the near future.

Since it would be impossible to know the specific laws of each and every country, marketers should consult local lawyers and authorities before launching a promotional campaign. For example, Belgium requires a government tax stamp on window signs. The purpose of this section is to show how certain sales promotional tools might be affected by local regulations.

Premiums and gifts

Most European countries have a limit on the value of the premium given. Colgate was sued by a local blade manufacturer in Greece for giving away razor-blades with shaving cream. Austria considered premiums to be a form of discriminatory treatment toward buyers. In France, it is illegal to offer premiums that are conditional on the purchase of another product. In Finland, premiums are allowed as long as the word *free* is not used with them. A gift is usually subject to the same restriction as a premium. Compared to the USA and the United Kingdom, which are very lenient, Belgium, Germany, and Scandinavia have strict laws concerning promotion owing to their desire to protect consumers from being distracted from the true value of a given product or service. Argentina, Austria, Norway, and Venezuela virtually ban the use of merchandise premiums. Other countries, being less restrictive, do not permit the value of the premiums to exceed more than a certain percent (e.g., 10 percent in Japan) of the value of a product that must be purchased so as to receive a premium.

Price reductions, discounts, and sales

Austria has a discount law prohibiting cash reductions that give preferential treatment to different groups of customers. Discounts in Scandinavia are also restricted. In France, it is illegal to sell a product for less than its cost. In Germany, marketers must notify authorities in advance if they plan to have a sale. Unlike in the USA, where there are all kinds of sales for all occasions (e.g., manager's sale, assistant manager's sale, buyer's sale), a sale in Germany is limited to such events as going out of business, giving up a particular product line, end of January (winter), end of July (summer), and a twenty-fifth anniversary. Both Austria and Germany are similar in the sense that special sales may be made only under certain circumstances or during

MARKETING STRATEGY 14.1 HELLO KITTY

Sometimes, it is difficult to tell whether McDonald's is in the food business or the toy business. Its Happy Meals contain toys for kids. In Hong Kong, the company offered cheap, limited-edition plastic Snoopy toys which, when resold, fetched as much as $40.

One of its most popular premiums centers on the Hello Kitty characters. This cute and stuffed feline toy by San Rio was designed in Japan for children a quarter of a century ago. While Hello Kitty appeals to the young in the USA, it has met with enthusiasm among adults in Hong Kong, resulting in a Hello Kitty café and a Hello Kitty credit card. When McDonald's

offer began, almost 1000 people lined up on the first morning. The promotion increased sales by 10 percent.

In Singapore, the Hello Kitty characters were dressed in various wedding outfits ranging from "romantic" to traditional Korean. Huge crowds gathered every Thursday when McDonald's released the next toy in the wedding series. In some instances the fight for toys became violent, while some people fainted.

Sources: "Hello Kitty Brings Chaos to McDonald's," *San José Mercury News,* January 29, 2000; "Hong Kong's Kitty Craze," *Business Week,* August 9, 1999, 8.

---

specified periods of time (seasonal sales). Moreover, discounts for payment on delivery may not exceed 3 percent, and any quantity discounts must be within the applicable industry's usual numerical range.

Samples

In Russia, tobacco firms freely distribute samples. The "Lucky Strike girls," for example, tour Moscow bars offering patrons a smoke and a light. Due to public criticism, Philip Morris has stopped the sampling practice in the USA. In addition, the USA does not allow alcoholic beer to be offered as a free sample, and this law also holds for taste tests. Germany restricts door-to-door free samples that limit population coverage as well as the size of the sample pack.

Sweepstakes, games, and contests

For a sweepstake to be legal in France, an entry form must be separate from an order form. Germany permits sweepstakes as long as they do not create psychological pressure on customers. In addition, they cannot be misleading, and they must not offer a prize of substantial value.

Lotteries that are not operated by governments tend to be illegal in many countries (e.g., France,

England, the USA). A lottery has three elements — chance, consideration, and price. For a sweepstake, game, or contest not to become an illegal lottery, a company must make certain that at least one of these three elements is missing (see It's the Law 14.1).

OVERSEAS PRODUCT EXHIBITIONS

One type of sales promotion that can be highly effective is the exhibition of a product overseas. This type of promotion may be very important because regular advertising and sales letters and brochures may not be adequate. For certain products, quality can be judged only by physical examination, and product exhibition can facilitate this process.

One very effective way to exhibit products abroad is to use trade fairs. Unlike trade shows in the USA, where the social or party atmosphere is prevalent, European trade fairs are an important part of the marketing mix that must be prepared with great care. These shows can account for one-third of a European firm's marketing budget. The state of Colorado helped Alpine Map Co. to pay for a booth at an international sporting goods show in Munich. The company has been going back ever since, and foreign sales now account for 40 percent of its total sales. In fact, the company is probably better known in Europe than at home.

IT'S THE LAW 14.1   ILLEGAL LOTTERY

Germany's national safety standards for consumer products are higher than those of the United Kingdom. While the USA, the United Kingdom, Poland, and Spain have by and large minimal regulations on promotional bonuses, it is not the case in Germany, Belgium, and the Scandinavian countries. In the latter group, retail sales that are combined with free mail-ins, cash off purchases, free drawings, free gifts with purchase, and so on are either forbidden or strictly regulated.

In Sweden, the authorities ordered TV4 to stop its broadcast of a Swedish version of a popular quiz show, *Who Wants to Be a Millionaire*. The government's Lottery Inspection Agency concluded that the program was not a real contest but more of a lottery. The TV station director begged to differ. He denied that contestants relied on guesses rather than knowledge.

There are two main types of trade shows: *horizontal* and *vertical*. At one end of the spectrum are broad, well-established, annual affairs (horizontal trade shows). The Hamburg Fair, for instance, exhibits almost everything in both consumer and industrial goods. At the other end of the spectrum are specialized types for products in specialized industries (vertical trade shows). Electronica, held annually in Munich, is a vertical trade show.

There are more than 800 international trade fairs each year. Trade fairs allow thousands of firms from many countries to set up "temporary stores or offices" in the marketplace to display their products. A strong feature of a trade fair is that prospects are in a buying mood. Another advantage is that buyers are seeking out sellers at a central location. Obviously, a trade show presents a much easier contact situation for a salesperson because there is no travel to many diverse locations to call on potential buyers.

An exhibitor should investigate whether it is worthwhile to use a carnet for products that will be shipped or taken to the exhibition. A **carnet** is an international customs document that facilitates the temporary duty-free importation of product samples in lieu of the usual customs documents required to bring merchandise into several major trading countries (see Figures 14.3 and 14.4). That is, a carnet is a series of vouchers listing the goods and countries involved where the product will be exhibited. For a fee based on the value of the goods to be covered, a carnet may be purchased in advance in the USA by American firms. Foreign firms can turn to their local carnet associations, which are members of the International Bureau of the Paris-based International Chamber of Commerce. By issuing carnets, these associations in effect guarantee the payment of duties that may become due on goods temporarily imported and not re-exported. A carnet holder is required to post security equal to 40 percent of the value of the goods to cover duties and taxes in cases where goods are not re-exported and duties not paid.

Because different national customs regulations can act as trade barriers, the World Customs Organization adopted the "Customs Convention on the ATA Carnet for the Temporary Admission of Goods" in 1961. The initials ATA are from the French and English words "Admission Temporaire/ Temporary Admission." A carnet offers a number of benefits: no temporary imports bonds, no registration of goods when leaving a country, unlimited reuse for all products listed on a carnet for one year, and coverage of most business-related items. The system is recognized by fifty-eight countries and twenty-seven territories worldwide.

In the USA, the US Council for International Business (USCIB), appointed by the US Treasury Department, is the sole issuer and guarantor of carnets. All carnet applicants submit a security deposit

INTERNATIONAL GUARANTEE CHAIN
CHAINE DE GARANTIE INTERNATIONALE

INTERNATIONAL GUARANTEE CHAIN
CHAINE DE GARANTIE INTERNATIONALE

GENERAL LIST / LISTE GENERALE
(May be used for Continuation Sheets / Feuille Supplémentaire)

X _Patricia Cohen_ X

Signature of Holder / Signature du titulaire

Signature of authorized official and stamp of the Issuing Association /
Signature du délégué et timbre de L'association émettrice

| VOUCHER No. | CONTINUATION SHEET No. | 0 | Carnet No. | 00-XXXXX |
| VOLET DE No. | FEUILLE SUPPLEMENTAIRE No. | | Carnet A.T. No. | |

Item No./ No. d'ordre	Trade description of goods and marks and numbers, if any/ Désignation commerciale des marchandises et, le cas échéant, marques et numéros	Number of Pieces/ Nombre de Pièces	Weight or Volume/ Poids ou Volume	Value/ Valeur	Country of origin/ Pays d'origine	For Customs Use/ Réservé à la douane
1	2	3	4	5	6	7
	TOTAL CARRIED OVER / REPORT					
1	P917 18KT CYNNABAR AND PLATINUM BRACELET	1	46DWT	$472	USA	
2	B251-22 18KT DIAMOND AND SABI BACELET	1	22DWT	$930	USA	
3	Z003 18 KT FACETED CUFFLINKS	2	19DWT	$157	USA	
4	BQ88CYN 18KT CYNNABAR AND PLATINUM BUCKLE AND TIP ON 1-1/4" BELT	1	55DWT	$456	USA	
5	G994RKT 18KT DIAMOND AND PEARL EARRINGS 8 DIA = 2.28CT 2 SOUTH SEA PEARLS	2	17DWT	$7425	USA	
6	Aubergine Satin Pants Sytle #D953321	1	1.5 lb	$100	EC	
7	Beige Brocade Dress Style #BOT22	1	2 lb	$75	DE	
8	Purple Sequin Long Dress Style #PT21	1	2 lb	$200	IT	
9	1998 Sony TCD Headphones, model TCD21, serial J712349985	1	1 lb	$225	JP	
10	Sony PVM 8041GT Monitor, Serial #2519587	1	8 lb	$840	JP	
11	Wireless Microphone System, Lectrosonics #1038	1	1 lb	$1600	US	
12	Fujinon Camera Lens, #060184	1	2 lb	$5000	JP	

NO CHANGES, OR ADDITIONS,
ABOVE OR BELOW THIS LINE.

General List includes ___0___ (number) "Continuation Sheets".

| TOTAL or CARRIED OVER / TOTAL ou A REPORTER | 14 | 60 lbs. | $17,480.- | | |

*Commercial value in country of issue and in the currency, unless stated differently. / Valeur commerciale dans le pays d'émission et dans sa monnaie sauf indication contraire.
**Show country of origin if different from country of issue of theCarnet, using ISO country codes. / Indiquer le pays d'origine s'il est différent du pays d'émission du Carnet en utilisant le code international des pays ISO.

Figure 14.3 Carnet

in the form of cash or a bond. The deposit is a collateral and will be drawn upon to reimburse the USCIB if it incurs a liability or loss in connection with the carnet. When the original carnet is returned, assuming no anticipation of claims, the cash deposits will be returned in full, and the bonds are terminated. The value of shipment and type of application (paper or electronic) determine the carnet fees.

For countries that do not accept carnets, a company has two other alternatives. It may apply for a Temporary Importation Under Bond (TIB). This is a document sold by a customs broker at the time of entry. Or it can rely on the duty drawback for temporary imports. This process requires an importer to register the goods at the time of entry into a foreign country and deposit the applicable

ATA Carnet Application

A. Holder Information:

1. Carnet Holder (Corporation or Individual):

Street Address (No P.O. Box):

City: **State:**   **Zip:**   **Phone:**   **Fax:**

2. IRS/SS No.:   **E-mail:**

3. Parent Company: **IRS No. of Parent Company:**
4. Person Duly Authorized & Title:

5. Authorized Representatives (individuals or agents) who will be shipping or hand-carrying the merchandise on the Carnet:

B. Carnet Preparation/Country Information:

6. Goods to be exported as: ☐ **Professional Equipment (PE)**   **7. Approximate Date of**
   (mark more than one if applicable) ☐ **Commercial Samples (CS)**   **Departure from U.S.:**
                              ☐ **Exhibitions and Fairs (EF)**   (enter date as "MM/DD/YY")

8. Type the NUMBER of visits in the space provided beside each country you expect to visit:

__ Andorra (AD)	__ Germany (DE)	__ Macedonia (MK)	__ South Africa (ZA)
__ Algeria (DZ)	__ Gibraltar (GI)	__ Malaysia (MY)	__ Spain (ES)
__ Australia (AU)	__ Greece (GR)	__ Malta (MT)	__ Sri Lanka (LK)
__ Austria (AT)	__ Hong Kong (HK)	__ Mauritius (MU)	__ Sweden (SE)
__ Belgium (BE)	__ Hungary (HU)	__ Morocco (MA)[2]	__ Switzerland (CH)
__ Bulgaria (BE)	__ Iceland (IS)	__ Netherlands (NL)	__ Taiwan (TW) - Call First
__ Canada (CA)[1]	__ India (IN)[2]	__ New Zealand (NZ)	__ Thailand (TH)
__ China (CN)[2] – Call First	__ Ireland (IE)	__ Norway (NO)	__ Tunisia (TN)[4]
__ Croatia (HR)	__ Israel (IL)[3]	__ Poland (PL)	__ Turkey (TR)
__ Cyprus (CY)	__ Italy (IT)	__ Portugal (PT)	__ United Kingdom (GB)
__ Czech Republic (CZ)	__ Ivory Coast (CI)	__ Romania (RO)	__ Other:
__ Denmark (DK)	__ Japan (JP)	__ Senegal (SN)	
__ Estonia (EE)	__ Korea (KR)[3]	__ Singapore (SG)	
__ Finland (FI)	__ Lebanon (LB)[4]	__ Slovakia (SK)	
__ France (FR)	__ Luxembourg (LU)	__ Slovenia (SI)	

 [1] certain PE items are admitted   [2] only EF items for certain events   [3] 100% security required   [4] CS items are not admitted

9. Number of times your merchandise will be leaving and re-entering the U.S.: _____

10. Number of countries transiting(s): _____ **List Countries to be transited:** _____

C. Delivery Instructions:

11. Courier Service	**12. Messenger Pick-up**	**13. Regular Mail**
(Include completed airway bill with your account number OR to use our courier service, include $20.00 for Shipping & Handling)		

D. Processing Fees:

14. Basic Processing Fee:	**Ship to:**
15. Expedited Service:	
16. Additional Certificate Sets Fee: ($5 each add'l set after 8)	
17. Continuation Sheet Fee: ($0 first sheet, $5 each add'l)	
18. Shipper's Export Declaration Fee: ($5 each)	
19. Refundable Claim Deposit:	
(for government agencies only; waiver must be download and submitted)	
20. Shipping and Handling:	
21. Country Surcharge:	
Total:	

Continue to next page for Security and Obligation.

Figure 14.4 *Carnet application*

duties and taxes. Later, at the time of departure, the foreign customs authority inspects and collects the appropriate paperwork for the product in question. A full refund follows.[20]

Overseas exhibits are a costly form of promotion. There are costs related to the design and construction of a booth. There are also the transportation costs of the booth and products for display. Labor is required to set up and dismantle the booth. In addition, there are the rental costs of space and furniture, other costs include staffing and transportation, and accommodation of representatives.

There are a few suggestions that exhibitors at trade fairs should keep in mind. Space cost is only a small portion of the total cost. Thus it is better to rent adequate space, since overcrowding discourages prospects from visiting the exhibit. Exhibit contents should be kept simple, and only the most important items are displayed. To avoid having to set up the booth late and dismantle it early, a company may want to locate its booth away from the freight entrance area. Mailing lists of prospects should be obtained, and letters are sent to them well before the opening day. It is also important to have a qualified representative at the booth who can make sales decisions. This representative should arrive early and leave late. Early arrival also gives the representative time to become acclimated. Plenty of business cards and brochures should be kept on hand. Finally, the local traffic patterns should be taken into account. Unlike in the USA, where people are used to turning right and walking on the right-hand side, some countries drive on the left-hand side of the street and people thus walk on the left-hand side of an aisle. An exhibitor may gain an advantage if it locates the exhibit on the left-hand side of an aisle, since visitors will walk on that side.

An exhibitor should notice and respect cultural differences in dress formality and the exchange of business cards. Overseas trade shows are serious affairs, and only businesspeople and buyers (not the general public) are admitted. Because most buyers want time to think about products, some serious follow-up after the show should be carried out. It may be worthwhile to spend a few extra days making calls to the most promising prospects. Later, the exhibitor should send letters with additional material or have a local representative call the visitors who stopped at the booth.

A trade show is not the only means of exhibiting products overseas. Companies may also rent space in trade centers to display merchandise on a more permanent basis. Vienna (Austria) and Taipei (Taiwan) are examples of two such trade centers located in two different parts of the world.

Because of the high cost of overseas exhibition, exporters should consult with their governments concerning their assistance and other related promotional activities. It is not unusual for govern-

ments to sponsor official participation in certain major international exhibitions. In the case of the USA, the Department of Commerce additionally organizes a *trade mission* from time to time. It may, for example, send a boat full of merchandise to an overseas port. Based on the belief that foreign sales of US consumer products are best developed through *in-store promotion*, its sponsored events are designed to promote sales of consumer merchandise directly to consumers in major department stores and mail order houses from Finland to Hong Kong.

CONCLUSION

A product, no matter how superior, should not be expected to sell itself. It must be promoted so that prospects can learn about the benefits provided by the product. The state of Pennsylvania, for example, had only one overseas office before 1980 but it now has several to promote its exports. The state of Ohio has determined that, for each $1 spent to promote its exports, it derives $260 in export sales.

A product may be promoted in several ways – advertising, personal selling, publicity, and sales promotion. Although advertising is the most prominent technique, the other three methods are no less important. For promotion to be most effective, however, all four of the promotional techniques should be used and coordinated. Two chapters are devoted to a discussion of the various aspects of promotion. This chapter has concentrated on the treatment of personal selling, publicity, and sales promotion. The next chapter is concerned primarily with international advertising.

Personal selling usually commands a major share of promotional expenditure. It is used internationally as well as locally at every distribution level and for all kinds of products. When expatriate sales personnel are to be employed, these personnel and their families should be screened for suitability before being given overseas assignments. For a variety of good reasons, qualified local nationals should be used whenever possible. If MNCs do not hire these qualified individuals, local progressive competitors are likely to employ them.

With limited media time and space available in many countries, it is necessary to develop some rapport with media people in order to try to gain free publicity. Finally, efforts in advertising, personal selling, and publicity activities should be supplemented and supported by sales promotion.

CASE 14.1 SELLING IN THE EU

Antonis C. Simintiras, University of Wales

It was a nice, warm, Sunday afternoon when Michael had to rethink his selling strategies for his region. Michael was born in England and after studying for four years at a major UK University he joined a leading British pharmaceutical company. Following a successful career in sales within the UK, he was promoted to sales representative for Southeast Europe. Based in Thessaloniki, Greece, he was made responsible for selling the entire range of products for the company's division to pharmacists, doctors and hospitals. Michael went through a rigorous and intensive training program for three months and learned a lot about cultural differences between the British and Southern Europeans. Although he was responsible for covering three countries in the Balkan region (Greece, Bulgaria, and Yugoslavia), Michael had recently come to the conclusion that his selling strategies in Greece were somewhat inappropriate.

After six months of hard work, Michael was happy with the progress that he made. He had managed to open several accounts with hospitals in all three countries and had built up a network of pharmacists and doctors, many of whom had either bought or agreed to buy his company's products. Recently, however, he noticed a change in the attitude of some of his most important customers, especially in Greece, which, in terms of priority, was the first market for development. Until a few months before, almost all of his customers showed a strong interest in his products and were happy to place orders. During the past two months, Michael noticed that the level of interest and willingness to buy deteriorated, to the extent that some of his customers were delaying reordering, despite the fact that their safety stocks were not allowing them such a relaxed attitude toward stock replenishment. Constant feedback from customers indicated that there was nothing wrong with either the products or his selling approach. Both his customers and their patients were very pleased with the products and a lot of positive publicity in the relevant press was generated throughout the region since Michael went there.

Sitting in his rocking-chair overlooking the Aegean Sea from his balcony, Michael was trying to find out what might have gone wrong. He thought he was consistent with his selling approach. He made professional presentations, used a problem-solving approach, followed up his sales, made sure that products were delivered on time. The service level that he offered was exceptional, and above all his strong interest in helping his customers by providing suggestions for growing their business was the best he could do to win the minds and hearts of all his customers. His selling experience in the UK helped him immensely with the above approach. He scrutinized his behavior but did not find any shortcomings or reasons for the apparent customer loyalty problem that he saw as forthcoming.

He played back mentally many of his encounters with his customers and was convinced that he always delivered a personalized and value-added solution to all of them. He could not recall any instance of not keeping his promises or not making an effort to see and discuss things from his customers' point of view. Being the only interface between the customers and the company in that region, his name became synonymous with the firm and this was something that his customers seemed to value. He believed that this approach was the most appropriate for establishing strong and lasting relationships with his customers that, in turn, could prove to be a significant barrier for competitors entering the market.

Michael remembered his training times and the interesting lectures about cultural differences between the North and South. He nodded his head in an affirmative way as if he wanted to say categorically that this was absolutely true. Then he recalled that profits come from repeat customers and customer retention can produce a disproportional return on his investment. He could afford no more time thinking! He had to take some sort of action. He realized that the solution (if there was one) to this problem was hidden somewhere in the cultural make-up of the customers with whom he was dealing. He decided to ring one of his customers (a Greek whom he had met in England during his university years) and invite him over to his house for dinner. This was the first time that Michael decided to socialize with a customer. His customer accepted the invitation and the following is an extract from their conversation after they had finished their dinner and Michael's problem had been discussed.

Customer   Michael, I do not think that you fully understand our culture.

Michael   I do not claim I do, but what do I miss or do wrong?

Customer   I think there is nothing that you do wrong. The issue perhaps is "what you do not do right."

Michael   What is it that I am not doing right then?

Customer   A salesperson interested in developing long-term relationships with his customers has to do certain things. Other than being professional in his dealings with the customers, a salesperson is expected to interact frequently with doctors, pharmacists and hospital officials in a social context in order to build trust. Frequent social interaction (i.e., in a non-stressful environment) indicates commitment over and above what is required by the protocol, enhances the feelings of trust, contributes to satisfaction of the customer and facilitates conditions for building attitudinal loyalty. This is something that we used to call "relationship selling" in England, as far as I remember.

Michael   I think I understand what you are trying to tell me. Much of the relationship-building activity takes place in social as opposed to work environments. Very much like the meeting we have here. I have got it, and I am ever so grateful to you for your help.

Customer   You are, as I remember you from the university years, "a fast learner"!

Points to consider

1   What is relationship selling and how does its application vary among different cultures?

2   Are business relationships that are enhanced by social interaction better for global selling?

3   Would you agree that commitment and trust are qualities that can be sold in a similar way to that of products and services? If so, is "relationship selling" a selling from a relationship-building point of view, or is it simply a traditional selling activity?

CASE 14.2   ALLWORLD CORPORATION

Ann-Marie Miller, Providence College

Introduction

Due to the events of September 11, 2001, the travel industry has experienced a major decline. In addition, the eagerness for and convenience of travel, especially foreign travel, has recently faded away. A potential corollary to this apprehension would be a reduced desire to engage in foreign business and foreign living. While many travel and business concerns are warranted, there still remains a world of endless possibilities, cultural interests and experiences in international living. It is imperative that Americans continue to live a life of freedom and resume their spending and working habits, especially where the exploration of new lands is key. Through these challenging times, it is necessary to continue to uphold the integrity of the economy in the public, producing, and service sectors. The following case examines the current role of the international human resources component and then introduces the AllWorld Corporation, an organization which provides a new outlook to overseas living and work.

HR's old ways

According to *Webster's Dictionary*, an expatriate is defined as "one who has taken up residence in a foreign country."

The human resources department (HR) of a given company is responsible for providing a wide array of administrative services to its expatriate employees through employee benefits, policies, and training programs. The expatriate population is often neglected in the world of HR. HR's lack of focus on overseas career needs often results in poor expatriate selection, management, and repatriation.

This, however, may be a line management problem and the re-education of executive management perhaps needs to be addressed. A key challenge for many companies involves attracting qualified employees to accept an overseas assignment. Reasons for transfer are career broadening, promotion, mergers and acquisitions, and untapped production possibilities within the markets of the world. Usually technical personnel or middle managers are selected for transfer and, during the selection process, priority is based on management or technical merit. Criteria in personnel such as personality, adaptability, and preference for independence are often completely overlooked.

A lack of HR involvement can lead to many problems regarding the assignment of expatriates overseas. As mentioned before, poor selection procedures tend to take place, leaving the decision up to senior management where HR skills are minimally understood. These unqualified decisions often prove very costly. Unclear goals pose another problem and may be attributed to poor planning. The logistics of the move becomes more important than the actual goal of the relocation. Once unrealistic goals are set, they will never be met. In addition, many line managers set their own goals once in-country. A major problem is insufficient cost predictions where costs are not properly projected. An overseas assignment may cost up to a million dollars. Other problems remain such as cultural issues, domestic and family concerns, political turmoil, economic instability, and complex labor laws. HR departments also continue to neglect another of the most important transitions: repatriation. An individual who has been overseas for a number of years may find that it is more difficult to move back to one's native country from having been overseas when compared to the initial transfer. Lastly, overseas assignment failure tends to be high due to a lack of employee preparation. Global Relocation Survey and Measuring Expatriate Success provides the following statistics, pinpointing HR's lack of involvement which can eventually lead to employee dissatisfaction:

- 34 percent of employees report that HR had little or no role in the selection process.
- 13 percent report that measurable goals are never set, while 22.5 percent set goals only 75 percent of the time.
- 75 percent report some failed assignments in their organizations, with 28 percent reporting a failure rate of 10–15 percent.
- Average size of responding organizations to the survey comprised 3200 employees with only twenty-four expatriates.
- Of transferred spouses, 49 percent were employed before assignment and only 11 percent found employment during an assignment.
- 70 percent of companies outsourced expatriate management.

AllWorld's first steps

AllWorld Corporation's mission statement states that the company "provides an overall expatriate relocation service designed to train, prepare and educate future expatriate employees for their overseas assignments. The service is based on international relocation."

AllWorld is a corporation in the introductory stage of its life cycle; the implementation of the marketing mix will produce the growth stage. As a new entrant in the consulting industry, this limited liability corporation (LLC) is attempting to redefine and reinforce the expatriate relocation experience. The purpose of the firm is to properly educate and acclimate soon-to-be expatriates to their new foreign home through cultural/language immersion, personal experience, and truthful testimony.

In regard to financial backing, AllWorld is currently deciding whether to rely on an IPO or to consider long-term capital markets for initial working capital. AllWorld intends to begin as a new independent business operation which will focus on expatriate relocation (headhunter). The growth opportunities for AllWorld are to ultimately replace corporate human resource departments for those similar services.

AllWorld provides a refreshing and informative insight through the education of its expatriate clients. The benefits of AllWorld's services can lead to corporate customer satisfaction, prolonged overseas assignments, and a willingness of employees to return overseas. AllWorld achieves what HR departments commonly overlook. Through a major focus on expatriate selection, management and repatriation, selection procedures, goals and cost projections will be accurate and well thought out. Cultural issues, domestic concerns, political turmoil, the causes of economic instability, and complex labor laws are all carefully examined. The location of AllWorld is built around its customer base. The majority of customers will be large international firms that wish to expand their number of overseas personnel but face complications due to lack of (or nonexistent) uninformed HR representatives when dealing with overseas expatriate assignments.

Employee selection at AllWorld makes the company unique. The company's employees are initially selected on their overseas experience. Selection is based solely on qualifications through and/or language/country experience. The provision of appropriate consulting and knowledgable personnel is based on regions of the world, with each region having its own well-versed set of representatives for that region. For instance, to be a country representative, you must be of that nationality, have lived overseas or have visited that country frequently to properly inform the client about a given assignment. This is not to say that every country will be represented. The projected goal of AllWorld in the future will be to represent every region or country that qualifies in the business model. In addition, each employee will establish contact with immigration attorneys in order to expedite work visas needed by our client base.

Marketing objectives

The marketing objectives of AllWorld are to persuade corporate clients to use AllWorld's services by attracting new clients, have existing customers specify the need for AllWorld's services, while reminding potential customers of the inadequacy of their own HR departments by showing how AllWorld can provide a global solution for expatriate employees. Its target market relies on employees accepting overseas assignments and deals only with the expatriation or repatriation process. In the company's marketing campaign, AllWorld will project various images to its clientele. Some examples include service, education, growth progression, potential market leadership, and dependability. The market position for AllWorld is yet to be established due to its recent inception. In the company's marketing campaign the need to experience AllWorld will stress its relocation services. AllWorld aims eventually to outperform existing HR departments. Promotion of AllWorld is based on personal contact through the prior experience of employees, with some emphasis on the company web page. Advertisements will be made in various international journals, newspapers, and magazines. Word-of-mouth and other recommendations are key promotional tools as well.

As services are based on the customer needs and wants, the pricing strategy will be competitive. Based on a commission strategy, AllWorld will be paid based on successful assignments of clients overseas. AllWorld's renumeration would be three to six months of employee salary, making it competitive to the industry standard.

To realize fully its place in the market, AllWorld must analyze the strengths and weaknesses of its competition. The competition includes any human resources department and other consulting agencies. For example, Prudential Relocation International has implemented a helpful way to deliver this service to new expatriates. Prudential's four main goals are: to meet the company's needs, prepare the assignee, maximize the investment, and reach and attain their goals. Prudential examines the company's policy statement which becomes the platform of the international assignment program. The firm is committed to help the transferred family prior to departure in order to gain the confidence to work in a new culture or environment. The firm's goal is to obtain a high return on the assignment while retaining and maintaining one's assets. In addition to offering international assignment reports, Prudential helps the employee's family acclimate while maintaining job productivity. Other competitors have similar goals. Again, as explained above, AllWorld wants to take this experience a step further.

Through this innovative strategy of preparing employees for overseas assignments, AllWorld hopes to become a market leader with a significant percentage of market share while maximizing profit and maintaining quality service leadership for its corporate clients.

Points to consider

1   If you were a corporate manager with overseas locations, would you consider AllWorld Corporation for your expatriate needs? Why or why not?
2   Where should AllWorld corporate headquarters be located, and why?
3   What elements of the marketing mix does AllWorld need to focus on in order to accomplish its goals, and why? How would it structure the marketing mix in order to accomplish these goals?

QUESTIONS

1   Explain how personal selling overseas may differ from how it is used in the USA.
2   What are the requirements of a good publicity program?
3   What is a carnet?
4   Explain why standard sales promotion tools (e.g., premium, coupon) may not be applicable or effective abroad.

DISCUSSION ASSIGNMENTS AND MINICASES

1   Compare domestic communication with international communication. Explain why "noise" is more likely to occur in the case of international communication process in all five stages (source, encoding, information, decoding, and receiver).
2   Why is telemarketing not as widely used outside of the USA?
3   Should expatriate personnel be used? What are some of the difficulties that they may encounter overseas? What can be done to minimize these problems?

NOTES

1   Wilbur Schramm (ed.), "How Communication Works," in *The Process and Effects of Mass Communication* (Urbana, IL: University of Illinois Press, 1961), 3–26.

2   "America's Latest Software Success Story Is German," *Business Week,* August 8, 1994, 46.

3   Harold C. Cash and W. J. E. Crissy, "Comparison of Advertising and Selling," in *The Psychology of Selling,* Vol. 12 (Personnel Development Associates, 1965).

4   Itzhak Harpaz, "The Importance of Work Goals: An International Perspective, " *Journal of International Business Studies* 21 (No. 1, 1990): 75–93.

5   Anthony M. Townsend, K. Dow Scott, and Steven E. Markham, "An Examination of Country and Culture-based Differences in Compensation Practices," *Journal of International Business Studies* 21 (No. 4, 1990): 667–78.

6   Masaaki Kotabe, Alan J. Dubinsky, and Chae Un Lim, "Perceptions of Organizational Fairness: A Cross-national Perspective," *International Marketing Review* 9 (No. 2, 1992): 41- 58.

7   Alan J. Dubinsky *et al.,* "Influence of Role Stress on Industrial Salespeople's Work Outcomes in the United States, Japan, and Korea, " *Journal of International Business Studies* 23 (No. 1, 1992): 77–99.

8   Nakíye Boyacigiller, "The Role of Expatriates in the Management of Interdependence, Complexity and Risk in Multinational Corporations," *Journal of International Business Studies* 21 (No. 3, 1990): 357–81.

9   J. Stewart Black and Lyman W. Porter, "Managerial Behaviors and Job Performance: A Successful Manager in Los Angeles May Not Succeed in Hong Kong," *Journal of International Business Studies* 22 (No. 1, 1991): 99–113.

10   J. Stewart Black and Hal B. Gregersen, "The Other Half of the Picture: Antecedents of Spouse Cross-cultural Adjustment," *Journal of International Business Studies* 22 (No. 3, 1991): 461–77.

11   Ivan M. Manev and William B. Stevenson, "Nationality, Cultural Distance, and Expatriate Status: Effects on the Managerial Network in a Multinational Enterprise," *Journal of International Business Studies* 32 (second quarter, 2001): 285–303.

12   Meg G. Birdseye and John S. Hill, "Individual, Organizational/Work and Environmental Influences on Expatriate Turnover Tendencies: An Empirical Study," *Journal of International Business Studies* 26 (No. 4, 1995): 787–13.

13   Earl Naumann, "Organizational Predictors of Expatriate Job Satisfaction," *Journal of International Business Studies* 24 (No. 1, 1993): 61–80.

14   Daniel C. Feldman and Holly B. Tompson, "Expatriation, Repatriation, and Domestic Geographical Relocation: An Empirical Investigation of Adjustment to New Job Assignments," *Journal of International Business Studies* 24 (No. 3, 1993): 507–29.

15   Sunkyu Jun, James W. Gentry, and Yong J. Hyun, "Cultural Adaptation of Business Expatriates in the Host Marketplace," *Journal of International Business Studies* 32 (second quarter, 2001): 369–77.

16   Moshe Banai and William D. Reisel, "Expatriate Managers' Loyalty to the MNC: Myth or Reality? An Exploratory Study," *Journal of International Business Studies* 25 (No. 2, 1994): 233- 48.

17   "The Fast Track Leads Overseas," *Business Week,* November 1, 1993, 64ff.

18   Linda K. Stroh, Arup Varma, and Stacey J. Valy-Durbin, "Why Are Women Left at Home: Are They Unwilling to Go on International Assignments?" *Journal of World Business* 30 (fall 2000): 241–55.

19   "A Crisis of Confidence," *Business Week,* September 18, 2000, 40–2; "Jac Nasser's Biggest Test," *Fortune,* September 18, 2000, 123ff.; "Ford vs. Firestone: A Corporate Whodunit," *Business Week,* June 11, 2001, 46–7.

20   "Ask the TIC: Temporary Imports, ATA Carnet," *Export America* (March 2001): 14–15.

Chapter 15

Promotion strategies

Advertising

Worldly wisdom teaches that it is better for reputation to fail conventionally than to succeed unconventionally.

John Maynard Keynes

CHAPTER OUTLINE

- The role of advertising
- Patterns of advertising expenditures
- Advertising and regulations
- Advertising media
  - ☐ Television
  - ☐ Radio
  - ☐ Newspapers
  - ☐ Magazines
  - ☐ Direct mail
  - ☐ Outdoor
  - ☐ Internet
  - ☐ Screen (cinema)
  - ☐ Directories
  - ☐ Rural media
  - ☐ Stadiums
  - ☐ Other media
  - ☐ Media mix
- Standardized international advertising
  - ☐ Three schools of thought
  - ☐ Feasibility and desirability
  - ☐ Research and empirical evidence
  - ☐ A decision-making framework
- Global advertising: true geocentricity
- Conclusion
- Case 15.1 The Marlboro Man: should we modify his image overseas?

PURPOSE OF CHAPTER

The examples in the marketing illustration below emphasize the need to communicate with buyers and to endow a product with a distinct image. A product must not only be physically superior but must also be psychologically desirable. Frequently, a product's psychological attributes are even more important than its physical characteristics. To convince consumers that a product is psychologically superior, a company uses advertising. A product has to be differentiated from competitive brands, and the differences can be either real or imagined.

The marketing of products overseas underscores the necessity for the adaptation of communication. To advertise internationally, a firm cannot simply repeat the same message indiscriminately in all markets. A message that elicits a favorable response in one country can easily fail to communicate with an audience in another country. To complicate the matter, there are constraints on advertising that preclude the use of certain kinds of media in certain countries.

The purpose of this chapter is to examine advertising practices in various countries. The variations in advertising practices are discussed, as well as particular problems associated with the use of advertising media abroad. Finally, the chapter closely analyzes the most controversial subject in international advertising – standardized advertising. Some practical guidelines are offered that may be useful in resolving the controversy.

MARKETING ILLUSTRATION   THUMB DOWN AND THUMB UP

Coca-Cola Co. acquired the Thums Up brand in India in 1993. Thums Up is a sweeter local cola that at one time commanded more than 60 percent of carbonated beverage sales. Because of Coca-Cola's neglect, Thums Up's market share plunged to just 15 percent by 1998. Finally, the chief of operations in India has managed to get an approval from Coca-Cola to push local brands as much as Coca Cola. Advertising and distribution have been strengthened. Within a year, Thums Up has made it back to become the No. 2 soda in India.

In the case of Coke itself, the operations chief has introduced a new advertising campaign that equates Coke with *thanda*, the Hindi word for "cold." He also uses Bollywood movie star Amir Khan as Coke's celebrity spokesman. The advertising campaign has been a big success.

Source: "Finally, Coke Gets It Right," *Business Week*, February 10, 2003, 47.

THE ROLE OF ADVERTISING

Developing and socialist/communist countries, emphasizing production and distribution efficiency, usually attack advertising as a wasteful practice whose primary purpose is to create unnecessary wants. Yet advertising serves a very useful purpose – consumers everywhere, irrespective of their countries' political systems and level of economic development, need useful product information.

Interestingly, Russian consumers were found to exhibit more favorable attitudes toward advertising in general, whereas American respondents felt that advertising resulted in greater negative social effects.[1]

Since the 1950s, China has prohibited foreigners from advertising there because advertising was considered politically inappropriate. In the 1980s, however, China changed its policy in order that the

441

Chinese population could be informed of products available, just as in a modern industrial society. Virtually all media are now available for advertising: billboards, department stores' display cases, telephone books, newspapers, magazines, and journals. Even radio and TV time is available and may be purchased. TV advertising is quite a bargain, since a sixty-second spot for the nationally broadcast China Central Television I network costs only $5000. Chinese viewers generally enjoy watching the commercials shown.

A correlation has been demonstrated to exist between advertising expenditures and a country's GNP and level of economic development. As a country becomes more industrialized, the level of advertising expenditure tends to increase as well. The USA is highest in per capita advertising at $499 per person. In the case of Japan, Canada, Germany, and France, the figures are $298, $266, $196, and $154 respectively.[2] Regarding the Commonwealth of Independent States (CIS), foreign companies are responsible for about half of the advertising done there. The advertising expenditures in the CIS are quite tiny and represent only the amount of a small advertising account in the USA.

Many of the largest advertisers in the USA also advertise heavily overseas. Procter & Gamble and General Motors, for example, are among the largest advertising spenders in France and Canada. Local firms in markets outside the USA often view this kind of expenditure as an unfair trade practice. They fear that American firms could easily overwhelm local firms in terms of advertising dollars.

PATTERNS OF ADVERTISING EXPENDITURES

In one study, advertising-to-sales ratios varied across fifteen countries, ranging from 0.95 for Yugoslavia to 7.62 for Australia. These ratios were not related to population size, number of directly competing brands within the firm, or number of directly competing brands outside the firm.[3]

Advertising expenditures vary widely from industry to industry. Mars allocates 5 percent of the company's total sales to advertising. Manufacturers of dolls and stuffed toys maintain an advertising-to-sales ratio of more than 15 percent. On the other hand, manufacturers of certain nonconsumer goods (e.g., industrial machinery and equipment and agricultural chemicals) do not advertise very much, spending perhaps less than 0.5 percent of their total sales.[4]

The relationship between advertising expenditure and sales generated has been well documented. Certain variables determine the size of the advertising budget as well as the size of the overall marketing budget. According to the well-publicized ADVISOR models, the size of an advertising budget is a function of: sales (+), number of users and other participants (+), customer concentration (−), fraction of sales made to order (−), stage in life cycle (−), and product plans (+). The size of a marketing budget is a function of: prospect–customer attitude differences (−), proportion of direct sales (+), and product complexity (−). It should be pointed out that the importance of particular predictor variables is not uniform across countries.

It is important to note variations in the different types of marketing expense – when expressed as a percentage of sales – across countries and product categories. The variations in the marketing expense ratios indicate that executives should be careful when they approach advertising budget decisions in other cultures.

ADVERTISING AND REGULATIONS

Advertising can be affected by local regulations in several ways. The availability of media (or the lack of it) is one example. When and how much media time and space are made available, if at all, is determined by local authorities. Belgium prohibits the use of electricity for advertising purposes between midnight and 8 a.m. German laws regulate TV advertising contents and limit advertising on the national TV channels to twenty minutes a day, forcing advertisers to switch from state-run TV to private channels. Greece and South Korea ban the erection of new signs. Furthermore, nationalism may intrude in the form of a ban on the use of foreign languages and materials in advertising.

The advertising industry may have a local self-regulatory organization which regulates the style and content of promotional activities. As in the case of England, the Committee of Advertising Practice has issued new codes which require all nonbroadcast advertisements to be "legal, decent, honest and truthful."[5] For instance, no medium may be used to advertise alcoholic drinks if more than 25 percent of the audience is aged under eighteen years. Children should not be encouraged to eat or drink at bedtime or to replace main meals with confectionery or snack foods. Regarding motor vehicles, speed or acceleration should not be the predominant message, and cars on public roads must not be shown to exceed speed limits. Those selling treatment of minor addictions and bad habits must acknowledge the vital role of willpower.

The legitimacy of comparative advertising has not been fully settled in many countries. Certain products are banned altogether from certain media, or from advertising in certain countries.

A number of countries have complete bans on cigarette advertising. Interpreting the law creatively, R.J. Reynolds attempted to circumvent Norway's ban on cigarette advertising by advertising "Camel boots" instead. The advertisement used the same model, trademark, and lettering in the word Camel as those used in Camel's cigarette advertisements. After a protest, the advertisement was eventually withdrawn. Advertisements in France are limited to a picture of a cigarette package with no "seductive imagery." To overcome this restriction, cigarette makers create products such as Marlboro cigarette lighters and Pall Mall matches that are purposefully made to resemble cigarette packages because there is no restriction on how such products may be advertised. In Sudan, Philip Morris advertised by having the Marlboro cowboy hold a Marlboro lighter.

ADVERTISING MEDIA

International advertising is the practice of advertising in foreign or international media when the advertising campaign is planned, directly or indirectly, by an advertiser from another country. To advertise overseas, a company must determine the availability (or unavailability) of advertising media. Media may not be readily available in all countries or in certain areas within the countries. Furthermore, the techniques used in media overseas can be vastly different from those employed in the USA.

Television

For Americans, television is taken for granted because it is available everywhere and in color. Outside of the USA, even in other advanced nations, it is a different story altogether. This difference may explain why US advertisers spend $20 billion each year on TV commercials, four times the amount European advertisers spend.

In most countries, television is not available on a nationwide basis due to the lack of TV stations, relay stations, and cable TV. Color television, for the poor, is a rarity. Nevertheless, the viewing habits of people on a lower income should not be underestimated because of the "group viewing" factor. For example, a TV set in a village hall can attract a large number of viewers, resulting in a great deal of interaction among the villagers in terms of conversation about the advertised products.

In many countries, TV stations are state controlled and government operated due to military requirements. As such, the stations are managed with the public welfare rather than a commercial objective in mind. The programming and advertising are thus closely controlled. The programs shown may vary widely and are usually dubbed in the local languages. European governments particularly abhor the US private broadcast model with its degenerate mass programming. More recently, however, European restrictions have been reduced on featuring films with frequent interruptions from advertisements. The reduction is due in part to an attempt by European countries such as France to end the government monopoly on media and to privatize the broadcast business by making available private broadcasting franchises.

Commercial TV time is usually extremely difficult to buy overseas. This is true even in Europe and Japan, where television is widespread. The usual practice in Tokyo is to use TV advertising to bombard the market, but the challenge for the marketer is to get air time. There are several reasons why television advertising time is severely limited. Many countries have only a few TV channels, which may not schedule daytime television or late-night programs. With less broadcast time comes less advertising time. Some countries do not allow program sponsorship other than spot announcements. Belgium, Denmark, Norway, and Sweden ban advertising on television altogether. Some governments permit advertising only during certain hours of operation. In Germany, advertising on television is permitted only between 6.15 and 8 p.m. (except for Sundays and holidays) for a total advertising time available of twenty minutes. That same number of commercial minutes also applies to Switzerland. The problem of getting a fraction of the available television time was so severe for Unilever that the firm had to make adjustments in media strategy by relying more on other media. In most countries, the situation is such that an advertiser is fortunate to get air time at all.

There are at least two tactics an advertiser can employ to overcome the problem of lack of broadcast time for advertising. One is to use shorter commercials. In the USA, 61 percent of TV spots are thirty-second commercials, and 35 percent are fifteen-second commercials. In Japan, 79 percent of TV spots are fifteen-second commercials. Not surprisingly, clutter is worse in Japan: there are sixteen commercials per hour in the USA but thirty commercials per hour in Japan.[6]

Although disputed in the USA, fifteen-second spots have become the norm in a number of countries. Spots shorter than thirty seconds are an overwhelming majority in France (71 percent), Japan (79 percent), and Spain (80 percent). In fact, the Japanese even have eight-second spots that function almost like billboards on TV and yet are graphically compelling.[7]

Another tactic is to purchase TV time well in advance. With a waiting list of 100 companies, TV advertising time in the Netherlands must be booked with a year's notice. Those advertisers able to get air time still face other advertising hurdles. For example, commercial interruptions may be long and frequent, creating a severe problem of clutter.

Advertisers sometimes use TV stations in one country to reach consumers in another country. Canada is a prime example. More than 75 percent of Canadians are clustered within 100 miles of the US border, and 95 percent are within 200 miles. Thus, nearly all Canadians are within the broadcast range of US stations. US advertisers often use US TV stations to communicate with Canadian consumers. In fact, Canadian advertisers themselves make it a practice to use US stations at the border (e.g., Detroit, Spokane, and Buffalo) to air commercials aimed primarily at the Canadian market. Reasons for this practice are that American TV stations have higher program ratings than do Canadian stations, and that the Canadian audience in total spends some twenty-six billion hours a week viewing US shows – the equivalent of 78 percent of the total hours spent watching Canadian English-language TV programs.

New technology may allow advertisers to solve some of the problems related to TV time and government regulation (e.g., a ban on the advertising of certain products or to certain groups). Cable TV is available in Western Europe. Commercial programs, for example, can be beamed from the United Kingdom to cable networks in Norway, Finland, and Switzerland. Retransmitting the signal, however, is still illegal in Norway.

Satellite TV may present another solution and is gaining wider acceptance. McDonald's and Mars have begun to funnel some advertising dollars to the Sky Channel satellite network. Cable TV and satellite TV are often international media in the sense that they reach multiple countries outside the country where the broadcast originates. Turner Broadcasting's Cable News Network has a global reach of more than sixty million households in more than 200 countries and territories. MTV's thirty-three channels across the world have access to almost 375 million households. MTV, VH1, and Nickelodeon altogether reach one billion people in eighteen languages in 164 countries.[8]

The two cable or satellite channels that are truly international are CNN and British Broadcasting Corp. Because of CNN's US-centric approach during the Iraq war in 2003, the BBC was able to attract new audiences all over the world with its authoritative coverage of the war. Its balanced coverage frustrated those from the Right as well as those from the Left. Those on the Right called the BBC the Baghdad Broadcasting Corp., while those on the Left dubbed it the Blair–Bush Corp. For those in the middle, the BBC stood for better, balanced coverage.[9] France has TV5 that broadcasts internationally, but this French-language channel primarily offers movies and general programming. France is in the process of creating a government-supported all-news channel to present its point of view that may counter those of CNN and the BBC.[10]

Regionally, Channel V is an Asian alternative to MTV. Channel V is 87.5 percent owned by Star Group, News Corp.'s wholly owned subsidiary. Both Channel V and Star Group have their headquarters in Hong Kong. In order to localize its operations, Channel V has moved the production of its Channel V International from Hong Kong to Malaysia. Its six other channels have local production teams that focus on China, Taiwan, Korea, India, Thailand, and Australia.[11]

One advertising problem with this new technology has been that, when an advertisement is aired, consumers in all countries are exposed to an identical message. But improved technology has now made it possible for advertisers to beam particular advertising versions to different countries.

Radio

Radio is no longer king of the media in the USA, but it retains its status in many countries as the only truly national medium. In Mexico, for example, radio provides coverage for 83 percent of the country. It is popular for several reasons. A radio set is inexpensive and affordable — even among poor people. It is virtually a free medium for listeners: the programs are free, and the costs of operating and maintaining a radio set are almost negligible. Furthermore, illiteracy poses no problem for this advertising medium. As a communication medium, radio is entertaining, up-to-date, and portable. The medium penetrates from the highest to the lowest socioeconomic levels, with FM stations being preferred by high-income and better-educated listeners. Not surprisingly, radio commands the largest portion of advertising expenditures in a great number of markets.

In order for radio stations in the USA to survive and counter the threat of television, they have adopted the "magazine" format by specializing in a particular type of programming. Advertisers must not assume that stations have adopted this same approach abroad. In many countries, radio stations have not become specialized in a particular program format and see no need to be selective in order to attract the listening audience. Radio stations commonly vary their programming format throughout the day, sometimes as often as every half hour. An audience shift should thus be expected, and a consequence of this practice is that it may not be easy to reach the target market effectively.

Unlike US stations, which do their own programming and hire their own announcers or disc jockeys, overseas stations are quite liberal in selling air time to outside operators. This is true in spite of the fact that for security reasons most overseas stations are owned, controlled, and operated by the government. Once the air time has been sold, the program format is determined by the sponsor or independent disc jockey. Thus listeners' loyalty is not so much to the station but to the disc jockey who may roam from one station to another throughout the day.

Newspapers

In virtually all urban areas of the world, the population has access to daily newspapers. In fact, the problem for the advertiser is not one of having too few newspapers but rather one of having too many.

445

In the USA, large cities can rarely support more than two dailies. In other countries, a city may have numerous newspapers dividing the readership market. Lebanon, with a population of 1.5 million, has some 200 daily and weekly newspapers, with an average circulation per paper of only 3500.

Newspapers in communist countries are controlled by the government and are thus used for propaganda purposes. China's newspapers, for example, tend to carry news items that the government deems to express some moral and social value.

Believing that sensational news attracts readership, most non-US newspapers in the free world are set up in a sensational news format. It is the rule rather than the exception for these newspapers to concentrate on murders, robberies, scandals, and rapes. Even the United Kingdom, where its citizens are known for their reserved manner, is not exempt from this practice. World news and nonscandalous political news often take a back seat to the more sensational news. As a result, non-US newspapers look more like such weekly US tabloids as the *National Enquirer* and *Star*. A newspaper that concentrates on news of substance and quality (i.e., unsensational news) must pay for this in terms of low readership.

Many countries have English-language newspapers in addition to the local-language newspapers. The English-language newspapers are patterned more like the traditional American paper, with an emphasis on world, government, and business news. This vehicle would be appropriate for an advertiser to reach government and business leaders, educated readers, upper-class people, and those with affluence and influence. The aim of the *Asian Wall Street Journal* is to supply economic information in English to influential businesspersons, politicians, top government officials, and intellectuals. It was not designed to be a newspaper for mass readers.

Many countries have nationally distributed newspapers, as shown in Figure 15.1. However, it is difficult to find a true national newspaper because almost every newspaper tries to be somewhat local

in nature. Even in the USA, before *USA Today*, the closest thing to a national newspaper was perhaps the *New York Times*, with the *Washington Post* in second place. Clearly, it is even more difficult to have an international newspaper. Those papers distributed internationally include the *International Herald Tribune* and such financial newspapers as the *Wall Street Journal* (with the *Asian Wall Street Journal* for Asian countries) and the United Kingdom's *Financial Times*. As might be expected, these newspapers are not available everywhere, and the circulation is low. *Financial Times*, a century-old daily covering British business, international business, and economic and political news, has a worldwide circulation of about 230,000, with only 6000 sold in the USA and Canada. Still, *Financial Times* offers US advertisers access to upscale readers in Europe and other parts of the world.

American advertisers are accustomed to having separate editorial sections in American newspapers and are often frustrated by foreign papers. A twenty-page newspaper may still have sections for sports, entertainment, fashion, business, and science, but each section may comprise only one page. Thus it becomes difficult for an advertiser to match the product to the proper section or environment (e.g., tire and automotive products in the sports section) in a local newspaper.

Furthermore, with so many newspapers dividing a small market, it is expensive to reach the entire market. There are some 380 and 800 newspapers in Turkey and Brazil, respectively. With advertisements in just one paper, the reach would be quite inadequate. Advertising in several papers, on the other hand, is also impractical. It is fortunate for advertisers that people often read or subscribe to two or more dailies and often share newspapers. Despite a small circulation, readership may still be high. Usually, the pass-along rate in foreign markets is much higher than that in the USA, but reliable estimates of circulation of overseas newspapers are difficult to obtain. The figure provided by the newspaper publisher may be highly inflated, and there is no meaningful way, at least for advertisers, to measure or audit the circulation figures.

Figure 15.1 *Japan's top English-language business newspaper*

Magazines

Nowhere in the world are there so many and varied types of consumer magazines as there are in the USA. Because US magazines segment the reading market in every conceivable manner, there are magazines for the masses as well as for the few and selected. This makes is possible for advertisers to direct their campaigns to obtain **reach** (the total number of unduplicated individuals exposed to a particular media vehicle at least once during a specified time period) or **frequency** (the intensity or the number of times within a specified period that a prospect is exposed to the message) or both. Foreign magazines are generally not highly developed in terms of a particular audience. They do not segment their readers as narrowly as do US magazines, and they do not have the same degree of accurate information about reader characteristics. In Brazil, there are very few magazines, and people read all three or four of them. This results in **duplication**, which can be a waste of promotional effort unless frequency is the objective.

Marketers of international products have the option of using international magazines that publish regional editions (e.g., *Time*, *BusinessWeek*, *Newsweek*, and *Life*). In the case of *Reader's Digest* and several other popular magazines, local-language editions are distributed (see Marketing Strategy 15.1). Allen-Edmonds, a shoe company, was able to increase its foreign sales by advertising its shoes in the international editions of such magazines. For technical and industrial products, magazines can be quite effective. Technical-business publications tend to be international in their coverage. These publications range from individual industries (e.g., construction, beverages, textiles) to worldwide industrial magazines covering many industries. A trade magazine about China, for example, is a suitable vehicle for all types of industrial products of interest to the Chinese government. In Europe, the number of business publications is seven times as high as that in the USA. There are more than 1000 technical and trade journals in Scandinavia. Canada, in contrast, usually has only one trade magazine for each market segment, making it easier to cover the entire Canadian market.

Local (i.e., national) business magazines are a good vehicle to reach well-defined target audiences. *Nikkei Business* is one such magazine in Japan (see Figure 15.2).

Unlike the US market, which has an organization such as the ABC (Audit Bureau of Circulations) to audit the circulation figures for most magazines, the circulation figures of overseas magazines are somewhat unreliable. Furthermore, overseas magazines

---

MARKETING STRATEGY 15.1   THE MAGAZINE AS A CULTURAL PRODUCT

Reader's Digest, publishing in forty-eight countries and nineteen languages, reaches some 100 million readers. The company, appreciating both universal and local appeals, exports a business strategy rather than a culture. "We understand that people the world over hunger for information that is relevant to their lives, in their . . . language, and form their own perspective. We produce magazines, books, and other products that meet that need. For all intents and purposes, each edition of *Reader's Digest* is a local product, with as much as 30% of the editorial content researched and written by local editors. It is the only American magazine with international editions that routinely imports overseas content for US edition."

For decades, men's magazines have been around in Japan and Australia. The region is now embracing a new experience: international titles with Asian editions. *Esquire*, *GQ*, and *FHM* have started up Asian editions that target young, active, urban men with high disposable income. South Korea is the biggest market in Asia for such products. Why do South Korean men read these international magazines? A good reason has to do with the fact that these magazines have adapted their editorial concepts and contents to fit the various readerships. The Asian editions, not merely publishing in local languages, cover local trends and personalities. A magazine is a cultural product. As such, it must reflect a local culture.

Thailand has 648 magazine titles, both local and international. Women's magazines, the most competitive segment, account for 60 percent of the market. In 2003 alone, five more Thai-language versions of foreign titles were announced. Among them are *Elle Girl* and *Marie Claire* from France and *Her World* from Singapore. A Thai version of *Madame Figaro* from France was just recently introduced. The Thai edition of *Lisa* (from Germany and sold in nineteen countries) is the ninth foreign-language title of the magazine.

Source: "Timing Concerns Don't Deter Launch of Men's Magazine," *Asian Wall Street Journal*, November 15, 2001; "Five Women's Magazines to Enter the Fray," *Bangkok Post*, September 16, 2003.

JAPAN'S BUSINESS LEADERS ALL LOOK ALIKE.

It's easy to spot business leaders in Japan. There's a Japanese business leader lurking behind every copy of NIKKEI BUSINESS.

NIKKEI BUSINESS is exclusively for Japan's corporate crème de la crème — a very choice body of 200,000 subscribers selected by NIKKEI BUSINESS' own publishers: Nikkei-McGraw-Hill.

To our readers, we're a valued cover-to-cover information source for international business, with a wealth of informed articles written exclusively by an in-house staff of experts.

To our advertisers, we're unparalleled advertising effectiveness. 100% on-target. With no spillover.

And no wastage.

So get behind NIKKEI BUSINESS and put NIKKEI BUSINESS behind you. And follow Japan's leaders right to the top.

Subscriptions: 202,677 (as of Aug. 5, 1985 issue)
Net paid circulation is regularly audited and certified by Japan ABC.
186,830 (1984)
For further information write to Yoshihiko Shimada, Advertising Manager, 1-14-6 Uchikanda, Chiyoda-ku, Tokyo 101, Japan. Tel. (03)233-8031 Telex: J29902 NKMCGRAW

日経ビジネス
NIKKEI BUSINESS
Nikkei-McGraw-Hill, Inc., Publishers of Nikkei Business

North American Sales Network: New York Tel. (212) 997-2806. Chicago Tel. (312) 751-3716. Los Angeles Tel. (213) 480-5221. Houston Tel. (713) 462-0757. Toronto Tel. (416) 259-9631

Figure 15.2 *A national business magazine*

Source: Reprinted with permission of Nikkei-McGraw Hill, Inc.

tend to depend more on news-stand sales than on subscription sales, making it difficult to calculate consistent volume or to predict the size of readership in advance. Because many magazines are unaudited, either by choice or by lack of an audit bureau, it is not sensible to exclude unaudited publications from the media schedule. Even when publications are audited, the information given may not be adequate. The English ABC provides minimum information, whereas the German IVW audit is very thorough.

Direct mail

Confusion usually arises when such terms as direct mail, direct advertising, direct marketing, and mail order are discussed. It is important to understand that direct marketing is a broad term that encompasses the other related terms. According to the Direct Marketing Association (DMA), **direct marketing** is "the total of activities by which products and services are offered to market segments in one or more media for informational purposes or to

449

solicit a direct response from a present or prospective customer or contributor by mail, telephone, or personal visit."This is a more than 1-billion business in the USA. As a system, direct marketing has two distinct components: (1) promotion, and (2) ordering/delivery (see Figure 15.3).

Direct marketers can promote their products through all **advertising media**. They can solicit orders by making announcements on television or in magazines (usually with coupons or order forms). Television home shopping is a form of direct marketing. Some cable TV channels (e.g., the Home Shopping Network in the USA and the Canadian Home Shopping Network) are designed specifically for this purpose. In any case, local regulations must be followed. In France, advertisers cannot show direct sales telephone numbers on screen. Viewers must call the number on screen to obtain a second number for placing orders.[12]

Frequently, marketers rely on **direct advertising** in media created for that purpose. These media consist of direct mailings and all forms of print advertisements distributed directly to prospects through a variety of methods (i.e., advertising materials distributed door-to-door, on the street, or inside the store or those placed inside shopping bags and on auto windshields). **Direct mail** is thus only one kind of direct advertising medium, which is in turn a part of general advertising media or the promotional methods of direct marketing. Of course, the use of direct mail is not limited only to direct marketing.

With regard to ordering, buyers can place orders by telephone (often with a toll-free number), through a personal visit, or by mail. An order that is sent in by mail and fulfilled by mail delivery is called a **mail order**. Thus mail order is not a medium; rather it is only one of several means that may be used to place and handle orders. An ordering method consists of one of the two components of the direct marketing system.

For this discussion, direct mail and direct marketing are considered together. There are several reasons for doing so. Direct mail generally accounts for a major portion of direct marketing advertising expenditures. In addition, many reports on direct marketing campaigns do not provide a detailed breakdown of the advertising dollar accounted for by media other than direct mail.

Direct mail is largely undeveloped in many countries. This is especially true where labor is cheap and abundant and where it is just as easy to use a salesperson to make sales calls. Furthermore, for countries with high illiteracy, this medium is not suitable for promoting consumer products.

Without doubt, the USA is the most developed market for the advertising medium of direct mail. Foreign marketers as well as American marketers have a wide selection of buyer lists that permit them to contact the intended target audience with minimum waste.

European marketers lag far behind the USA in exploiting the medium of direct mail. There are also more restrictions on collection of personal data (see It's the Law 15.1). In Germany, mail cannot be sent to those who have requested that their names be removed from mailing lists. If an addressee has a label on one's mailbox refusing direct mail, delivery cannot be made. Furthermore, although personal data may include year of birth, date of birth is not allowed.[13]

US practices in using direct mail require some modification when taken abroad. There is difficulty

Figure 15.3 Direct marketing

IT'S THE LAW 15.1 KEEP IT PRIVATE

Because there is no pan-European law, each country's law must be analyzed. In France, it is illegal to collect data having to do – directly or indirectly – with membership of trade unions. In Germany, as a consequence of the Nazis' use of personal information to identify enemies, the country's data-protection laws may be the most restrictive in the European Union. Germany prohibits virtually all activities regarding collecting, storing, and processing personal data. In general, all storage, communication, and erasure of personal data are not allowed unless expressly permitted by the data-protection act. Data processing is prohibited unless a person has given his or her written consent. In England, the Direct Marketing Association Code of Practice requires list owners to warrant that "the data have been fairly and lawfully obtained and all private individuals whose data are included have been given an opportunity to object to the use of their data by persons other than the list owner and that the data of those who have objected have either been deleted from or so marked in the list."

Unlike the USA which has relied on the industry's self-regulatory approach, the European Union has adopted the government-led approach. European privacy laws, based on Europe's history and legal traditions, are comprehensive and applicable to all industries. After all, protection of information privacy is regarded as a fundamental human right in Europe.

The European Directive on Data Protection, taking effect in 1998, requires the European Commission to determine the adequacy of data protection in third countries and to prohibit personal data flows to countries without adequate privacy regimes. Any organizations wanting to receive personally identifiable information from the European Union must provide adequate privacy protection. Electronic commerce certainly needs data transfers. Multinational corporations and their affiliates routinely exchange a huge amount of information. The information ranges from personnel phone directories to more sensitive information such as personnel records and credit-card bills. As a result, Microsoft and hundreds of American companies have agreed to comply with the European Union's Safe Harbor framework. Information may be collected for "specified, explicit and legitimate purposes, and to be held only if it is relevant, accurate and up to date."

Sources: James A. Reiman, "Understanding Variations in European Market Laws," *DM News*, July 25, 1994, 8–9; Jeff Rohlmeier and William Yue, "The Safe Harbor Privacy Framework," *Export America* (January 2001): 21–4; "Europe's Tough Privacy Rules Spill Over to US," *San José Mercury News*, August 30, 2002.

---

in making a direct transposure of a US mailing piece without change into a European mailing kit due to various weight rules and other unique regulations. Population direct mail lists are another serious problem since foreign list owners do not trust renters and brokers. List generation and management is still primitive abroad. American list owners enhance their lists with such information as buyer's frequency, recency, and dollar value, but direct marketers used to those practices can become frustrated with list brokers in Europe (except in Germany) because basic selection criteria are not even provided. In addition, privacy laws are more restrictive abroad than in the USA. For example, Germany allows only two unique selection criteria per order when renting a list.

US companies using direct mail to contact customers abroad may find **remailing** useful and economical. There are three basic ways to move a marketer's promotional material from the USA. First, the ISAL (International Surface Airlift) system was designed by the US Postal Service to use a combination of air and surface transportation. This is the least expensive way of moving materials for bulk mailers and publishers. After being received at ISAL's acceptance points, the material is airlifted to selected distribution points around the world where it merges with other surface-mail pieces. Second, mailers who do not want to bother with ISAL's requirements can pay a surcharge to ISAL consolidators, which are private companies that will sort, bag, and transport the material to an ISAL gateway city. Finally, remailers are private distribution services that provide a turnkey system and negotiate private rates with airline cargo divisions.[14]

Outdoor

Outdoor advertising includes posters, billboards, painted bulletins, roadside and store signs, and electric spectaculars (large illuminated electric signs with special lighting and animated effects). Given the huge impact and impressiveness of size and color, outdoor advertising serves well as reminder promotion for well-known products.

Outdoor advertising is frequently used overseas because of the low cost of labor in painting and erecting such displays. In addition, this is considered a free medium, because an advertiser can simplify place its posters on any available wall, bus-stop shelter, tree, or fence without paying for it. The practice also encourages one advertiser to replace other advertisers' posters with one of its own.

Unlike most media, outdoor advertising is one medium in which the USA seems to lag behind other countries in terms of per-capita advertising expenditures and sophistication. This is an advanced and dominant medium in Europe and Canada. Outdoor advertising is also very important in countries without commercial TV (e.g., Belgium). In Saudi Arabia, outdoor and transit posters account for more than a quarter of all media spending, about ten times the US percentage.

Outdoor advertising does not have to be uninteresting. One advertiser changes its outdoor illustration and message frequently – with the model removing an item of clothing each time the poster board is changed. Another advertiser made it appear that the billboard was gradually being eaten away by termites.

New technologies have added such design options as backlighting, projection, Day-Glo paints, three-dimensionals, extensions, reflective disks, bows, and cutouts. Fiber optics may eventually replace neon because fiber optics are much more energy efficient and weigh less than neon glass tubing. Some advertisers have turned to video billboards that can show a twenty-second commercial repeatedly.

When using outdoor advertising, certain rules should be followed. Illustrations should be large, and words should be kept to a minimum. A rule of thumb is to say "what must be said" and not "what can be said." Simple, contrasting colors should be used: white on black or red seems to work well. The right typeface is crucial; certain typefaces are difficult to read. Having all letters in capitals can be equally as difficult and should be avoided.

Internet

One recent medium that has gained worldwide attention is the Internet. Unlike other media, the Internet is global in nature, creating both worldwide opportunities and problems. It is unknown whether the law governing an Internet promotion should be the law of the upload site or that of the download site. Although all the other media allow marketers to a certain extent to restrict delivery of their messages, the Internet is an all-or-nothing proposition. Thus, it is so easy to violate many domestic laws. Also, given its international nature, the Internet requires global planning, and the cultural dimension must be considered. A successful website is the one that has been carefully planned, taking into account the various languages and cultures.

One significant development is that new software has allowed a multinational marketer to make users' locations dictate a particular website to which users will be exposed. For example, those in Western Europe trying to access the website of Coca-Cola may end up with a European site rather than the one seen by their American counterparts. In addition, owing to technological improvements coupled with marketing goals, the Internet has become a more selective medium. Yahoo has created regional portals. Many international marketers such as Coca-Cola have added local websites in local languages.

The Coca-Cola Company has stated that, in spite of the core brand being well recognized all over the world, it is still "very much a local operation, meeting the demands of local tastes and cultures in nearly 200 countries." Visitors to its website are encouraged to select the country of interest. At one time, Atlanta dictated everything, and the local divisions were not allowed to set up their own websites and instead had to show only the corporate home page. Coca-Cola's Belgian website now reflects the more international approach, and the trilingual (Dutch, French, and English) site draws more than three million hits per month.[15]

While Internet usage is a worldwide phenomenon, it does not mean that a marketer should standardize its Internet strategies on a worldwide basis. A study of advanced Internet users from twenty countries reveals differences in beliefs, attitudes, perceptions, and Internet buying behavior based on user experience and home country or region. Such differences remain even after controlling for social, cultural, and macroeconomic variables.[16]

In the case that an international marketer wants to offer only one website (unlike Coca-Cola's strategy), its website must be designed to accommodate global users. While graphics are appealing, they slow things down, especially when users in most countries have slower connections. Thus by limiting graphics and other high-bandwidth features, the site is faster and universally appealing. By adopting a global perspective for the website, a company can enhance its international opportunities. Global functionality and language concerns should be addressed.[17]

While shopping and Internet use are global behavior, shopping manner and the determinants of the Internet sites' attractiveness may be culture-bound. To determine the crucial characteristics of a website, one study investigated the shopping tasks of 299 respondents from twelve countries. In general, site quality, trust, and positive affect toward it are related to both purchase intentions and site visitors' loyalty. Because the impact of these factors varies across regions and product categories, a website probably should be tailored for each region as well as each product category.[18]

By 2005, 70 percent of the estimated one billion Internet users will be non-English speakers. The localization of websites, particularly transaction-based websites, requires native language capabilities. Research indicates that Web users are three times more likely to make purchases over the Internet if a site is in their native language. Some languages, particularly character-based ones such as Chinese or Japanese, have double-byte requirements, necessitating added memory, cost, and disk space.[19]

It is not a simple task to build a multilingual e-commerce site.[20] Other than the language that must be overhauled, a site must be able to handle different currencies, characters, and measurements. Some languages have words that must be read from right to left. Certain US Net icons such as shopping carts are alien in some countries. Therefore, a global website has to be culturally sensitive.

Screen (cinema)

In virtually all countries, the cinema is a favorite activity for a social gathering. People are avid moviegoers because of the limited television broadcasting and because of people's natural desire to go out to a place of social gathering. Cinemas (or theaters, as they are called in many parts of the world) are classified as first-class or second-class and sometimes even third-class, depending on how soon new films are shown there. Theaters usually operate on a reserved-seat basis, with advance reserve bookings being highly encouraged.

Similar to outdoor advertising, the cinema is a very popular advertising medium outside of the USA. Cinemas sell commercial time to agencies or advertisers. The usual practice is for a theater to begin its program with a showing of slides of advertised products, and this slide show is followed by commercials. The theater may then proceed to show newsreels and documentaries that may contain paid news items such as a store opening. Then, just before the showing of the main feature, there are short promotional films or teaser trailers of coming attractions. An intermission can present another opportunity for advertising.

Cinema advertising has several advantages. It has the impact of outdoor advertising without the drawback of being stationary. It has sight and sound like television but with better quality. Furthermore, cinema advertising has a true captive audience. A disadvantage is that some moviegoers may resent having to watch commercials, but such resentment is likely to be a minor problem, since moviegoers are usually in a positive and receptive mood. The more serious problem is that patrons, knowing that there will be some commercials shown first, take their time in showing up and may be wandering into and around the theater until the main feature begins.

Directories

Directories are books that provide listings of people, professions, and institutions. The yellow-page telephone directories, with a listing of various types of companies, are a prime example. Directories may be sold or given away free of charge. Since the telephone is not widely available in many areas and the information is not accurate, this medium has been underused outside of the USA. In some countries, governments and private entities publish trade directories of local exporters and their advertisements.

The popularity of cellular or mobile phones presents another unique problem. In Japan, the number of mobile phones has now exceeded the number of fixed telephones. Given the fact that cellular phone owners may switch the telephone services from one company to another, their telephone numbers are somewhat temporary. In addition, there is no compilation of cellular phone numbers so as to publish a directory.

Rural media

In marketing to developing countries, marketers must understand the use of rural media. Mobile units, for example, may be sent to areas lacking access to mass media. Such vehicles can play recorded music and advertising messages over amplifiers or loudspeakers attached to the vehicles' rooftops. A marketer can also attract an audience by arranging for some type of festival advertising held at a temple or school. A free outdoor movie may be shown during the festival while advertising is broadcast through loudspeakers to the captive audience. In a way, such rural media are not very different from the traveling "medicine" shows of the American past.

Stadiums

Stadium advertising is also appropriate, especially in soccer stadiums, because soccer (i.e., football) is the most popular and passionate sport in the world. Signs can be displayed on stadium walls, and the advertising rules for outdoor advertising should be applied. The objective of this advertising is not so much to communicate with those in a basketball or football stadium but rather to communicate with TV viewers. For nonstop games such as soccer and hockey, a broadcaster can show the entire game while including logos or brief advertising messages on the edges of the screen – at the top, bottom, side, or all around, with the game being shown in the middle part of the screen.

Cigarette marketers are major sponsors of sports and cultural events (e.g., billiards, horse-racing, rugby, and concerts) in England because these events receive extensive TV coverage. In effect, the prominent display of names and logos allows companies to associate their brands with glamour, health, vitality, and success.

Other media

There are several other advertising media that are traditional and common in developing countries and elsewhere. Some of these media are **advertising specialties**, a variety of inexpensive items (e.g., pens, calendars, letter openers) carrying the advertiser's name, address, and a short sales message. In spite of the cost, such items are relatively durable.

Because of their attractive appearance and low production cost, Ajinomoto's calendar-type products make an effective display in Japan and other Asian countries. A charming, attractive young girl (Miss Ajinomoto) serves as an "eye-catcher" to help advertise products. Ajinomoto provides three-ounce bottles to restaurants as toothpick holders or salt and pepper containers. In addition to using the traveling cinema, a popular form of entertainment, Ajinomoto also uses the traveling cooking school, which combines the expertise of a cook and a nutritionist, to provide instruction and education to many institutions such as schools. Moreover, the company uses "exhibitions," or public service advertising, to promote total company image and technical expertise, such as with the anti-cancer medicine Lentinan and the sugarless sweetener Aspartame.[21]

Media mix

There is no one single advertising medium that is suitable for all countries and products. The media mix has to vary from one target market to another.

The basis principles of media selection apply in all markets. In general, an advertising medium should be selective and cost-effective in reaching a large number of the intended audience. It should deliver the kind of reach, frequency, and impact desired, assuming that there are no particular legal restrictions.

Tokyo Toyopet provides a good illustration of how advertising media are selected to promote cars – in this case, Toyota cars. Newspapers and magazines, due to their national circulation in Japan, are unsuitable because this division of Toyota only concentrates on the Tokyo market. TV time is not readily available and much too expensive. As a result, radio advertising is the clear-cut choice.

STANDARDIZED INTERNATIONAL ADVERTISING

Standardized international advertising is the practice of advertising the same product in the same way everywhere in the world. The controversy of the standardization of global advertising centers on the appropriateness of the variation (or the lack of it) within advertising content from country to country. The technique has generated a heated and lively debate for four decades and has been both praised and condemned – passionately.

Doing research is difficult in this area due to the ambiguous *definition* of standardization itself. Strictly speaking, a standardized advertisement is an advertisement that is used internationally with virtually no change in its theme, copy, or illustration (other than translation). More recently, a new breed of advocates of standardization has claimed that an advertisement with changes in its copy or illustration (e.g., a foreign model used in an overseas version) is still a standardized advertisement as long as the same theme is maintained. This new and broadened definition can cloud the issue even more with the added element of subjectivity. Because standardization is a matter of degree rather than an all-or-nothing phenomenon, a more precise definition of standardized advertising, conceptually and operationally, would go a long way toward solving the confusion created by contradictory claims.

Dewar's advertising is a good example of how difficult it is to state with certainty whether or not a certain advertisement is a standardized advertisement. After twenty years, the highly regarded US "Profiles" campaign for Dewar's Scotch whisky was tailored to markets around the world. The format is the same in every country: it provides biographical information, hobbies, and philosophies to portray the successful lifestyle of an entrepreneurial "life-achiever" who also happens to be a typical and famous Dewar's drinker (see Figure 15.4). Previously, Dewar's overseas advertising used translations of American advertisements, but research revealed that the use of local personalities would communicate a stronger message. The localized profile advertisements used in Spain featured profiles of a Spanish author and a 29-year-old Spanish flight instructor and former hang-gliding champion. The Australian campaign gave Dewar's profiles of a 33-year-old Melbourne entrepreneur, a jewelry designer, and a photojournalist. In Thailand, the

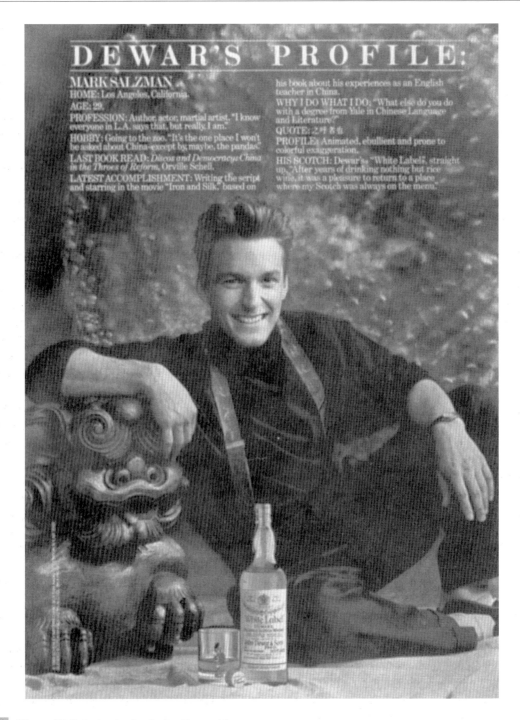

Figure 15.4 A standardized advertisement?

Source: Reprinted with permission of Schenley Industries, Inc.

advertisement featured a Bangkok architect. These campaigns were handled by the local Leo Burnett offices.[22] Because of the inclusion of both the standardization and localization elements, it is very difficult to determine whether these campaigns are more standardized than localized (or vice versa) — without a precise definition of the concept of standardization.

The issue of advertising standardization, without doubt, has far-reaching implications. If it is a valid strategy, international business managers should definitely take advantage of the accompanying benefits of decision simplification, cost reduction, and efficiency. On the other hand, if the premise of this approach is false, the indiscriminate application of standardized advertising in the marketplace will cause more harm than good since it may result in consumers misinterpreting the intended message. Consequently, the important function of advertising to facilitate a consumer's search process can be seriously impaired.

Three schools of thought

There are three schools of thought on the issue of standardized advertising: (1) standardization, (2) individualization, and (3) compromise.[23] The standardization school, also known as the *universal*, *internationalized*, *common*, or *uniform* approach, questions the traditional belief in the heterogeneity of the market and the importance of the localized approach. This school of thought assumes that better and faster communication has forged a convergence of art, literature, media availability, tastes, thoughts, religious beliefs, culture, living conditions, language, and therefore advertising. Even when people are different, their basic physiological and psychological needs are still presumed to remain the same. Therefore, success in advertising depends on motivation patterns rather than on geography. British Airways' image advertisements featuring movie stars, which were designed by Saatchi and Saatchi in the 1970s to trumpet the newly sleek British Airways, have been cited as an example of a successful standardized campaign.

The opposite views of the standardization school is the localization school, also known as the *non-standardization*, *specificity*, *individualization*, *adaptation*, or *customization* approach. This conventional school of thought holds that advertisers must particularly make note of the differences among countries (e.g., culture, taste, media, discretionary income). These differences make it necessary to develop specific advertising programs to achieve impact in the local markets. A good illustration of the importance of localization is the Shiseido case. The Japanese corporation, the world's third largest cosmetic company, did poorly in its first attempt to penetrate the US market because its advertisements featured only Japanese models.

Between these two extreme schools is the compromise school of thought. While recognizing local differences and cautioning against a wholesale or automatic use of standardization, this middle-of-the-road school holds that it may be possible, and in certain cases even desirable, to use US marketing techniques everywhere under some conditions.

Jain has proposed a framework for determining marketing program standardization. Standardization is more practical and effective under these conditons.[24]

1 Markets are economically alike.
2 Worldwide customers, not countries, are the basis for identifying the segments to serve.
3 Countries have similar customer behavior and lifestyle.
4 The product has cultural compatibility across countries.
5 There is a great degree of similarity in a firm's competitive position in different markets.
6 The firm competes against the same adversaries with similar share positions in different markets.
7 Product is industrial or high-tech (versus consumer product).
8 Home market-positioning strategy is meaningful in the host market.
9 Countries have similar physical, political, and legal environments.

457

10 There are similar marketing infrastructures in the home and host countries.

11 Firms possess key managers who share a common world view.

12 Strategic consensus exists among parent–subsidiary managers.

13 Authority for setting policies and allocating resources is centralized.

Keegan provides a set of guidelines that can help in determining when it is appropriate to use standardized advertising. According to Keegan, there are five international product and promotion strategies.[25] The choice of strategy depends on such factors as cost, need, and use conditions. A particular product may be extended (i.e., unchanged) if use conditions are uniform across markets. Likewise, a promotional campaign may be standardized or extended if consumer need for this particular product is universal. As a company moves from the first strategy toward the last, there is a corresponding increase in cost.

The first of the five strategies is *one product, one message, worldwide*. This strategy is feasible if both the need and use conditions are uniform across countries. Not many products satisfy these conditions, though Coke and Pepsi are often cited as examples. Other examples include diamonds, Chivas Regal Scotch, and BMW automobiles. Mentioned in jest by some authorities are products that may be even more truly global, such as Israeli Uzi submachine-guns, French Exocet missiles, Russian Kalashnikov rifles, and nuclear weapons.

The second of the five strategies is *product extension-communications adaptation*. A product may be extended to other countries because of uniform use conditions, but the promotional message will probably need to be changed since needs vary. Toothpaste is used in the same manner everywhere but often for different reasons. People in the north of England and the French-speaking areas of Canada use toothpaste primarily for breath control, making the appeal of fluoride toothpastes rather limited. Anheuser-Busch and its partners market the same beer in many countries but customize their advertisements (based on American themes) for each national market.

Product adaptation-communications extension is the third strategy. When use conditions differ but need remains constant across markets, modification of product but not promotion is necessary. Black and Decker, although wanting to globalize its power tools, must make several product adjustments to fit certain markets. The tools everywhere look the same on the outside, but inside it is another matter, especially for markets in which the variations in electrical outlets and voltages require different circuits and cords.

Dual adaptation is the fourth strategy. Both the product and the promotion have to be changed for a foreign market owing to variations in need as well as use conditions in different countries. Refrigerators made for the USA, for example, must be modified to accommodate 220-volt and 50-Hz electricity overseas. The large refrigerator and its spacious freezer compartment do not appeal to people in countries where shopping for fresh food is done daily and where a refrigerator is used mainly for short-term storage. In addition, with the high cost of electricity in virtually all markets outside the USA, the advertising appeal must be based on low electricity consumption, durability, reliability, and compactness.

Product invention is the last strategy. This strategy may have to be used if the existing product is too expensive for foreign consumers. A brand new product with different features may have to be designed in order to make it affordable. For generations, Indians have called *dhobis* to collect dirty laundry from middle-class neighborhoods and wash it upon the rocks in the rivers. Seeing this as an opportunity for product invention, Whirlpool Corp. has appealed to young professional Indian couples who want Western-style automatic washing machines by offering what it calls the World Washer. Whirlpool's compact washers have specially designed agitators that do not tangle saris, the flowing outfits worn by a large number of Indian women. Variations of the World Washer are also manufactured and sold in Brazil and Mexico, and there are plans to export them to other Asian and Latin American countries. Apart from minor variations in the controls, the three versions are nearly identical and sell for $270 to $650. The World Washer is a simple, affordable, bare-bones washer that does only eleven pounds of washing, or about half the capacity of the typical US model.[26]

Keegan's guidelines, although useful, are quite general. Thus one must consider other relevant factors and treat them explicitly.

Feasibility and desirability

For an international advertising manager, the decision is affected by his or her perception of whether it is "feasible" and "desirable" to implement standardization. In some cases it may be feasible but not desirable to use a standardized advertisement; in other cases it may be desirable but not feasible to do so. The applicability of advertising standardization is a function of these two conditions.

The *feasibility* issue has to do with whether environmental restrictions or difficulties may prohibit the use of a standardized campaign. Three common problems are *literacy* (for print advertisements), *local regulations*, and *media and agency availability*.

Because illiteracy adversely affects the comprehension of advertising copy, the text portion of an advertisement must frequently be minimized or replaced with pictures. Visual aspects influence perceived similarity of advertising.[27] Nevertheless, not all types of pictures are universal in their meanings, and some may not be an effective means of communicating with nonliterate market segments. Therefore, although pictures are more universal than words, international marketers should still research their markets before attempting to communicate with them through pictures.

Many countries have laws that place restrictions on the nature, content, and style of advertising messages. The Marlboro cowboy was banned in England on the grounds that cowboy worship among children might induce them to take up smoking. So the company had to use noncowboys driving around Marlboro country in a Jeep.

Germany's emphasis on fair competition results in the prohibition of slander against competitors. As a result, the advertiser must be wary of using comparatives (e.g., better, superior) and superlatives (e.g., best, most durable). In China, Duracell battery commercials were taken off the air because the drumming bunny's endurance claim violated the rules that prohibit superlative claims and comparative advertising. Likewise, Budweiser's "King of Beers" slogan was found to be unacceptable.

A multinational advertiser wishing to use a standardized advertising campaign needs to rely on an advertising agency with a worldwide network to coordinate the campaign across nations. Unfortunately, almost no agencies, regardless of size, are in a position to control local agencies overseas. In spite of this difficulty, a few multinationals (e.g., Bayer, Colgate-Palmolive) have decided to consolidate their global advertising at one agency. Ogilvy & Mather Worldwide, overseeing 272 offices, created "White on White" TV commercials to sell laundry detergent in France and was later used to replace twenty different local campaigns in thirty countries. Similarly, IBM's Personal Systems Group awarded its entire sales promotion business to Einson Freeman Promotional Campaigns, making it the first global brand to use a single agency.

It should be noted that the use of a single agency to handle worldwide advertising, while resembling the standardization approach, does not necessarily mean that the approach is purely standardization. While Colgate-Palmolive believes that there is no need to reinvent a winning formula, the directive of IBM's Personal Systems Group is "Do it once, replicate, and localize."

According to one study, advertising agency executives believe that client pressure will result in greater use of standardization. However, they also feel that client pressure and "saving money" are among the least important reasons for standardization because it makes no sense to use a bad or unproven campaign just to save money. Local agencies tend to think that they can produce better advertisements for their local markets and that creative impact should be the most important reason

459

as to whether an advertisement should be standardized or localized.[28]

A study of ethical perceptions provides another relevant perspective. Relative to the USA, hiring personnel from other advertising agencies was viewed more negatively in Korea. Also in Korea, clients' expectations for favors as well as social obligations arising from gifts received may require a different response.[29]

Degree of feasibility varies from country to country, facilitating the implementation of standardization in some countries while creating problems in others. Furthermore, an environment may change, permitting either more or less opportunity for standardization in the future. Therefore, feasibility is dependent on the situation and does not offer solid support for either of the two extreme schools of thought.

Three major criteria exist to judge the degree of *desirability* of a standardized advertisement. One of these is the amount of *cost savings* that may be achieved. Thus standardization is desirable only when the derived saving in production cost of this type of advertisement is significant.

Another criterion of desirability is *consumer homogeneity*, a major assumption of the uniform approach. If consumers were indeed homogeneous across countries, the debate would be resolved, since consumers could then be motivated in exactly the same way. Are consumers homogeneous? The proponents of each school of thought have offered

real-life examples that are subjective and highly judgmental. Consumers would be better served if the collection of empirical data were based on research designs that eliminate the effect of confounding factors. The results of the literature review of management responses, consumer characteristics, and consumer responses indicate that there is no theoretical or empirical evidence to support the standardization perspective in its present form.[30] As an example, a sample of Dutch respondents exhibited a somewhat negative attitude toward the use of the English language in TV commercials. When the English text was shown on the screen as well as spoken, about 50 percent of the subjects made a correct interpretation. Without the text being shown, the percentage dropped to just 22 percent. Therefore, the use of a foreign language (English in this case) made it more likely for a commercial to be misunderstood.[31] Language thus poses a challenge.

The third criterion of desirability has to do with the degree of *cooperation of an MNC's foreign subsidiaries and national managers*. Because of subsidiaries' involvement, it is a good idea to investigate the standardization decision-making process by studying two organizational factors (decision powers of subsidiaries and familiarity with foreign markets at headquarters) and two cultural factors (similarity in market position and country environmental conditions). MNCs are more likely to centralize control and adopt standardization when they understand similarities in market position, when

---

MARKETING ETHICS 15.1 NOT A LAUGHING MATTER

Cadbury ran an advertisement in a Mumbai newspaper. The advertisement featured a map highlighting the boundaries of India's Jammu–Kashmir state, the Indian-controlled part of a disputed region. The company compared the Kashmir region to a chocolate that was too good to share. The copy below the map read: "Issued in the spirit of Independence Day by Cadbury Temptations – International chocolates you'd love to share but won't." India and Pakistan have

fought two wars over the province. Cadbury was rebuked for using a highly sensitive issue as a topic for advertising. After all, the dispute has claimed the lives of thousands of people and soldiers. The company apologized. In hindsight, both Cadbury and its advertising agency should have known better.

Source: "Cadbury Apologizes for India Ad," *San José Mercury News*, August 23, 2002.

they are familiar with foreign contexts, and when they develop shared values and beliefs among subsidiary managers and headquarters managers. Otherwise, standardized decisions are likely to be challenged by local subsidiaries.[32] Similarly, another study confirmed that a global company's ability to foster successful relationships in terms of marketing operations between the headquarters and its foreign subsidiaries can enhance product performance across markets. As a firm tries to standardize its marketing programs, the subsidiaries' acquiescence becomes increasingly important.[33]

Research and empirical evidence

At present, the research focus has shifted toward a more limited level of *horizontal homogeneity*. Instead of showing that multiple countries are basically equivalent (when it is now quite clear that they are not), several researchers have moved away from the country as a unit of analysis. Instead, they focus on examining whether a subset of one national market is similar to another subset of another national market. This is what Hassan and Blackwell and Unnava *et al.* call a *global segment*.[34]

A recent study focused on "marketing universals" which are defined as "consumer behaviors within a segment and toward a particular product category that are invariant across cultures." The researchers used a sample representing thirty-eight nationalities and found that, while certain behaviors are likely to be universal, others are not. Therefore, marketing strategies should not be uniform across countries.[35]

At present, the available empirical data deal with the effectiveness of standardization only in an indirect manner. The available data are concerned primarily with showing how national markets differ in some ways without indicating whether such differences actually affect the effectiveness of international standardization. Most of the recent studies have shifted the emphasis to *national advertising practices*. The evidence is rather overwhelming that certain advertising methods (e.g., use of symbols, comparative advertising) may be the norm in some countries but the exception in others. The

researchers are virtually unanimous in cautioning against the automatic use of standardization. According to them, since consumers are used to a certain advertising method which is predominant in their country, these consumers may not be receptive to other advertising tactics.[36]

One group of researchers has focused on *corporate responses* by investigating whether multinational firms prefer to standardize or localize their campaigns. Overall, companies are more likely to employ localization rather than standardization, and advertising in particular is the component of the marketing mix that is most adapted. However, a recent interview with 150 Norwegian exporters, focusing on standardization and cooperative climate, found that companies with high local market knowledge had better performance. While the researcher believed that this relationship partially supported the standardization approach, it should be noted that standardization usually focuses on the home country while ignoring the preference of the host countries. As also noted by the author, standardization programs should not be initiated without a thorough understanding of local market conditions.[37]

Examinations of advertisement content have repeatedly found that, in practice, the content or message of advertisements varies significantly from one market to another. In the case of children's TV commercials from China and the USA, a content analysis found that Chinese commercials reflect China's traditional cultural values and its social and economic development level. However, there appears to be a shift in China from the elderly to the young, reflecting the country's one-child policy. There is also some evidence of Western values creeping in.[38] Another study compared the US and Chinese advertising appeals in terms of cultural values. The youth/modernity appeal, supposedly reflecting Westernization, is equally and prominently displayed in both sets of commercials. Yet the Chinese commercials emphasize the following cultural values more frequently: (1) the soft-sell appeal in seven product categories, (2) the veneration elderly/tradition appeal in six product categories, (3) the oneness with nature appeal in two product categories, and (4) the group consensus and status appeals each in one product category. In contrast, the US advertisements more frequently use the hard-sell appeal, the time-oriented and individual/independence appeals, and the product merit.[39]

Japanese advertisements are also distinct. A content analysis of how teenage girls and "girlish" images were portrayed in eight issues of *Seventeen* magazine (four being the US edition and four being the Japanese version) found culture-based differences. There is a higher frequency of verbal and visual girlish images in the Japanese issues.[40] An analysis of women's magazine advertisements in Germany and Japan focused on ad format, use of models, male and female role portrayal, and value appeals. While there are some similarities, there are also distinct cross-national differences in the way marketers adapt their strategies. The nontraditional approaches in targeting women are more culturally specific than the traditional approaches. Male role portrayal is an important element of the non-traditional approaches in women's magazines.[41] Similarly, a study of TV commercials from Japan, Russia, Sweden, and the USA in terms of the masculine–feminine continuum found that feminine countries show a higher degree of emphasis on relationships for male and female characters. Since not all cultures share the same values, advertising standardization appears to be strategically unwise.[42]

One content analysis examined advertisements from the USA, Egypt, Lebanon, and the United Arab Emirates. In Arabic magazine advertisements, people are depicted less frequently. When these advertisements show women, the women wear long dresses. The American advertisements, in contrast, provide more information content, price information, and comparative advertising.[43] Yet another content analysis found that standardization is a flexible policy that may be adapted to accommodate different market circumstances.[44]

While Hollywood movies are an international medium, the acceptance of these movies as well as products placed in them may vary from one country to another. Unlike commercials that can be adapted

for a particular country, product placement is not so adaptable because a movie shows a product being placed in the same way all over the world. Consumers in the USA, France, and Austria exhibited varying responses with regard to acceptability and purchase behavior. As an example, Americans were more likely to accept and purchase the products shown in the movies. However, there was also some degree of convergence. For example, women were less positive than men, and this less positive attitude was persistent across all three countries. In any case, one implication is that it is a good idea to identify specific segments in terms of country, product, and individual differences.[45]

In practice, the degree of standardization depends in part on corporate policy and strategic planning. At the same time, it depends on the importance of a particular overseas market and the insistence of the head of that subsidiary. As in the case of Harley-Davidson, the corporate headquarters had always required the Japanese to use the US print advertisements.[46] But the president of the Japanese unit felt that desolate scenes and the tag line "one steady constant in an increasingly screwed-up world" were not meaningful to Japanese buyers. He was finally able to obtain permission in to run a separate advertising campaign. The advertisements juxtaposed American images with traditional Japanese ones (e.g., American riders passing a geisha in a rickshaw). While it is difficult to determine the effect of the new campaign on sales, the waiting lists for Harley-Davidson motorcycles have grown longer.

After having seen or experienced difficulties in implementing the standardization concept, most international advertisers today have had second thoughts about standardization and have moved toward some degree of localization. Parker Pen Co. launched an ambitious "one world, one voice" program in 1984 to sell its writing instruments all over the world. The campaign was a big disappointment, and the company has once again tailored its advertisements to local markets. As Procter & Gamble's international chief has pointed out, although "technology" (e.g., gel toothpaste) is global, other aspects such as taste, coloring, packaging, and advertising of the technology are usually local.

In conclusion, an overwhelming number of studies does not show evidence that supports standardization. Instead, most studies have found consumer, market, and media differences. However, the empirical evidence that contradicts the use of standardization is indirect in nature. This is not surprising because it is very difficult to design a study that truly proves the validity (or lack of it) of advertising standardization. It is possible though to design a more rigorous study that will address the issue in terms of cause and effect.[47]

A decision-making framework

All forms of advertising standardization should not be ignored by the marketer. This technique may be appropriate on a modest scale, though definitely not on a worldwide basis. A limited homogeneity does existing in many cultures around the world. Thus it is a good idea to find out when and where this limited scale of homogeneity exists so that some level of standardization may be considered.

For decision-making purposes, market segmentation can provide a practical framework for standardizing advertising, as shown in Figure 15.5. If the world is treated as one whole market, a standardized advertisement may then be used. But if the world is divided into several segments (i.e., regions or countries), each segment probably requires its own custom-made marketing mix (i.e., a localized advertisement).

A market should be segmented when five requirements are met: identification, accessibility, differential response, segment size, and cost/profit. Each country (or region) should be considered as a distinct segment if the following conditions are met:

1 The marketer can identify the country's unique demographic characteristics.
2 The responses to a unique marketing mix of customers in the country will be appreciably different from those of other countries.
3 The country is accessible through available selective advertising media with minimum promotion waste.
4 The country's population size is large enough to justify the specially designed marketing campaign.
5 Incremental cost as a result of the segmentation is less than incremental profit.

When all these segmentation criteria are met, market segmentation is applicable but advertising standardization is not. There is no question that the USA is a market segment on its own due to its unique characteristics and responses, media availability, market size, and great profit potential. As such, Asian and European marketers generally design advertisements specifically for the US market. In contrast, these marketers are more likely to introduce in, say, Asian countries (except Japan) the advertisements that they have already used in their own countries. This action may be due to their belief that these other markets are either similar or are not economically significant enough to justify nonstandardized advertising.

In a number of cases, it may not be strategically sound to localize an advertisement for a particular market. Some countries are too small to warrant that kind of special attention and the associated cost. From 1870 to the 1920s, as tariff rates slowly rose, the number of nations remained stable or decreased. When trade barriers fell dramatically after World War II, the number of small countries soared from seventy-four in 1946 to 192 in 1995. At present, over half of all nations have smaller populations than the state of Massachusetts.[48] It is almost impossible to justify why an international firm should design an advertisement specifically for Tuvalu, whose economy relies on fishing and coconuts, and has a population of only 10,000.[49] Even on a bigger scale, it may be easier to justify why, in many instances, standardization should not be employed when marketing in the CIS countries. In spite of their new-found independence, they are still similar in many ways. Perhaps more importantly, their market sizes may not be adequate:

Figure 15.5 *A decision-making framework for advertising standardization*

Source: San Onkvisit and John J. Shaw, "Standard International Advertising: A Review and Critical Evaluation of the Theoretical and Empirical Evidence," *Columbia Journal of World Business* 22 (fall 1987): 53.

Armenia (3.8 million citizens), Azerbaijan (8.1 million), Georgia (5.4 million), Kazakhstan (14.9 million), Kyrgyzstan (4.7 million), Tajikistan (6.2 million), Turkmenistan (5.4 million), and Uzbekistan (25 million).[50]

Marketers should understand that standardization is not a universal tool that can be automatically used without proper consideration. It makes no sense to forge worldwide uniformity and conformity for management's convenience if consumers seek diversity and individuality. Standardization and advertising are not synonymous. Advertising is supposed to (1) inform and (2) persuade customers (3) effectively. Standardization may fail to perform any (or all) of these three objectives. Thus it is critical to pretest each advertisement in an international context to determine the effectiveness in terms of attention getting, comprehension, and persuasion.

It is probably a mistake to use either standardization or localization on a wholesale basis. Some degree of standardization or localization on an international or regional basis should be carefully considered. While a US campaign may not work well in Europe, some type of pan-European advertising may be possible. Yet even then, some country-specific information may still be required. It is important to realize that a well-thought-out advertising idea tends to perform reasonably well in multiple markets without a great deal of adjustment, but any flaws associated with a standardized advertisement will multiply in tandem with the number of countries. As advised by McCollum Spielman, Worldwide's chief executive officer, "the best precept to follow is to do your homework. When entering another country, make sure that your ad campaign meets the basic rules and preconditions of its targeted culture. Test it! And be sure to test through a researcher who is part of that culture."[51]

GLOBAL ADVERTISING: TRUE GEOCENTRICITY

Criticisms of myopic standardization should not be interpreted as an endorsement for a polycentric approach, which requires custom-made campaigns for each individual market. Localization, practiced for its own sake, can be just as myopic. What is desirable is a kind of geocentricity, which is not the same thing as standardization.

Standardization is basically a campaign designed for one market (home country) but exported to other markets regardless of justification. In contrast, a geocentric campaign requires an advertisement to be designed for the worldwide audience from the outset in order to appeal to shared common denominators while allowing for some modification to suit each market. The geocentric approach combines the best of both worlds (i.e., the cost-reduction advantage of standardization and the advantages of local relevance and effective appeal of individualization). For example, Levi Strauss has switched from all localized advertisements to a pattern advertising strategy that provides the broad outlines, but not the details, of the campaign.

Devising a global advertisement is anything but easy. However, with some planning, it is possible to create an advertisement which can maintain the main theme internationally while allowing necessary adaptation. A global advertisement should be adaptation-ready in the sense that necessary and desirable adaptation is planned at the time of conception rather than after the fact. Coca-Cola Co.'s "General Assembly" campaign is a good example. The campaign shows a thousand children singing the praises of Coke. Because each McCann office had permission to edit the film to include close-ups of a youngster from its market, at least twenty-one different versions of the spot existed.[52]

The success of IBM's Subtitles campaign has demonstrated that it is possible to integrate global and local action if the markets are similar and if the product/brand is perceived similarly in those markets. Previously, the company allowed each of its core thirteen semiautonomous business entities to develop its own independent business strategy. Seeing greatness in the sum of the parts, IBM's chairman reintegrated these units into a cohesive whole in 1993. One advertising agency was appointed in 1994 to have the prime responsibility for executing IBM's communication programs with a single voice worldwide.

The Subtitles campaign achieved global imagery through the use of the same footage in each country while employing local subtitles to translate the foreign language of the commercial. Local subtitling permits each country to retain its home cultural accent. The message of the campaign was that IBM could deliver simple and yet powerful solutions to manage information anywhere and any time for individuals and companies of all sizes. The company wanted to communicate that it was vigorous and innovative while maintaining the latent strengths of global scope, leadership, and reliability. Naturally, the international implementation encountered some local difficulties ranging from limited access to television commercials to the common practice of dubbing for foreign language films and commercials.

The campaign was run in forty-seven countries, and was pretested and/or tracked in over twenty markets worldwide. Although individual markets showed some response variation, the responses to the campaign were considerably consistent. Among those who were aware of the campaign, their responses showed that the company's key attribute dimensions improved significantly while measures of negative attribute dimensions declined. In comparison, the other brands tracked did not show positive movement. Thus the Subtitles campaign has proved to be one of IBM's longest and most successful runs of the company's image campaign in recent history.[53]

In designing a global advertisement, a marketer should take certain attributes into account.[54] The characteristics of a global advertisement are: (1) it should be visual, (2) it must have some universal appeal, (3) it must be adaptation-ready, (4) it combines both standardization and localization, (5) it assumes both homogeneity and heterogeneity, (6) it combines efficiency with effectiveness, and (7) it is simultaneously global and local. These characteristics are essential in meeting the needs of the marketer as well as the needs of worldwide consumers.

CONCLUSION

In developing countries, advertising is often viewed as something wasteful. In socialist/communist countries, it may be seen as incompatible with political objectives. It is undeniable that certain advertising practices are misleading, deceptive, and wasteful. Just as undeniable, however, is that advertising serves a useful function by providing customers with relevant information for intelligent decision making. Although the US style of advertising is not necessarily suitable for all other countries, it does make a significant contribution to the high standards of living in the USA.

US advertisers need to realize and understand that foreign media are not always readily available. Many of the media, especially the broadcast media, are government operated and controlled for security reasons. Broadcast media are considered sensitive instruments because the equipment may be used for espionage or for supporting a coup attempt. It is a common practice for revolutionaries staging a coup to seek control of radio and TV stations for psychological warfare.

Even when foreign media are available, American advertisers must appreciate their different style and approach. Such media as outdoor, cinema, and rural advertising are used extensively outside the USA. Moreover, advertisers in many parts of the world rely more on a repetitive effect than on sophistication within a message. Direct-action advertising and the hard-sell approach may have to give way to an indirect-action approach, emphasizing the reputation and image of a company or brand name even though this usually does not result in immediate sales.

Because of the variations found in advertising regulations, media availability, media approaches, and consumer characteristics, there is a high degree of risk in employing standardized advertising on a worldwide basis. Although a global advertisement may have the advantage of lower cost, cost reduction should not always be the overriding motive. Advertisers need to be less ethnocentric and to show more consideration and regard for foreign consumers. All advertisements, standardized or not, should be tested for suitability for the intended audience before being used in the marketplace.

CASE 15.1 THE MARLBORO MAN: SHOULD WE MODIFY HIS IMAGE OVERSEAS?

Jeffrey A Fadiman, San José State University

The downfall of Winston was due in part to the broadcast ban on cigarette advertising. R.J. Reynolds had a difficult time adapting Winston's appeal to the print media. In contrast, Marlboro did not have this problem, and Philip Morris was able to use magazines and other print media to promote its Marlboro brand effectively. Overtaking Winston in 1976, Marlboro is now the undisputed leader in both the USA and worldwide.

Marlboro's success was quite spectacular. It was responsible for the transformation of Philip Morris from a small tobacco company to the number-one cigarette company in the USA. But it was not an overnight success. Initially introduced in a soft box with, among other filters, a red-cork tip, Marlboro had a female image which made the brand unpopular among men. The company decided to make a few changes, which included the neutral-cork tip and the addition of a flip-top, crush-proof box. Perhaps the most important change was the advertising theme. Marlboro's advertisements featured the rugged-looking men, tattooed laborers, and cowboys "who came up the hard way." These virile men usually told something about their he-man lives and explained why they chose Marlboro. Philip Morris was extremely successful in creating a unique image that allowed a man to project himself through the cigarettes he smoked. Winston, on the other hand, could not acquire this distinct image.

The Marlboro cowboy is now a legend. Most US consumers (including many others in all parts of the world) are accustomed to seeing the Marlboro Man. All advertisements of the Marlboro line (full-flavored Marlboro, Marlboro Lights, and Marlboro 100s) have one thing in common – the cowboy. He may ride a horse or he may sit at a campfire. He may be alone or he may be with other cowboys. But he is always in the advertisements. The image is so strong that the copy needs only a few words, shown in Figure 15.7. It is the cowboy that does all the talking, though without actually speaking. Yet the message is readily understood.

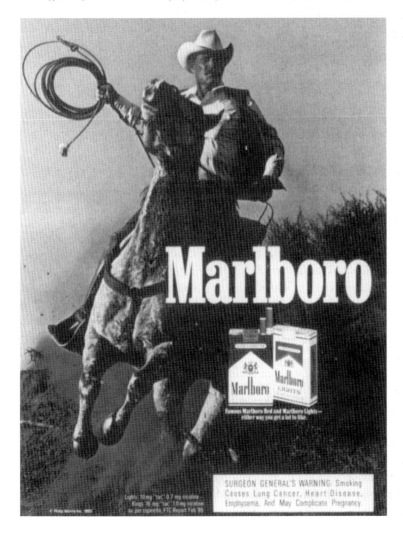

Figure 15.6
The Marlboro Man

Source: Reprinted by permission of Philip Morris USA.

Points to consider

Consider the Marlboro advertisement and select a certain country as your target market. Write a formal business memo to a chief executive officer of a small international advertising agency in which you submit suggestions about:

1 How would you modify the advertisement in order to make it more attractive to a selected target clientele (identify) within the country you have chosen?
2 Why would each change you suggest help the product image to conform more closely to their expectations?

Note: Rough sketches would be nice but are not necessary. Word-pictures can be drawn with equal skill. Simply show each change you are making. It is the originality, imagination, and effectiveness of each suggestion, not your artistic skill, that will count.

QUESTIONS

1 Cite some foreign regulations that restrict the use of either advertising in general or certain advertising practices in particular, and offer the rationale for these regulations.
2 Why is it difficult in most countries to buy (a) TV time and (b) newspaper space?
3 Outside of the USA, why is radio probably the closest thing to a national medium of communication?
4 Although the USA is well known for the creation of many new media, what media are more popular overseas than in the USA?
5 Offer the arguments for each of these three schools of thought: standardization, individualization, and compromise.
6 Is there any empirical evidence to support standardized advertising (or its homogeneity assumption)?
7 Are standardization and market segmentation compatible strategies?

DISCUSSION ASSIGNMENTS AND MINICASES

1 Does advertising serve any useful purpose in developing countries and socialist/communist countries?
2 Explain how the programming approach of the US television industry may differ from those used in other countries.
3 Do you think that there is a market for a world or international newspaper?
4 Many American consumers consider direct mail as junk mail, a term that is offensive to the direct marketing industry. At present, this medium is largely underdeveloped outside of the USA. What is your assessment of the future of direct mail overseas?
5 As an advertising manager, do you plan to use a standardized advertisement?
6 Harman Kardon audio and video products are aimed at the high-end segment of the market. The company has decided to advertise its products with the same graphic throughout the world. By producing basically one advertisement in six languages (English, Dutch, French, German, Italian, and Japanese), the company expected to save at least $200,000. The Zagoren Group was assigned the duty of coordinating the cooperative effort. The US full-page version appearing in *Audio* and *Stereo Review* showed a Harman Kardon amplifier on a grand piano with a black background and "The Components of High Performance" as the headline. For this advertisement to be used overseas, should any changes be necessitated by production and other requirements?

NOTES

1 J. Craig Andrews, Srinivas Durvasula, and Richard G. Netemeyer, "Testing the Cross-national Applicability of US and Russian Advertising Belief and Attitude Measures," *Journal of Advertising* 23 (March 1994): 71–82.

2 Johny K. Johansson, "The Sense of 'Nonsense'" Japanese TV Advertising," *Journal of Advertising* 23 (March 1994): 17–26.

3 Nicolaos E. Synodinos, Charles F. Keown, and Laurence W. Jacobs, "Transnational Advertising Practices: A Survey of Leading Brand Advertisers in Fifteen Countries," *Journal of Advertising Research* 29 (April/May 1989): 43–50.

4 "Advertising US-style Adapts to New Market," *We Mbi*, August 24 to September 6, 1992.

5 Alan K. Toulson, "British Ad Codes Set Hard Rules for Advertiers," *Global Direct Marketing*, February 20, 1995, 3.

6 Johansson, "Japanese TV Advertising."

7 Wayne Walley, "Have :15s Hit Their Peak?" *Advertising Age*, November 13, 1989, 16.

8 "MTV's World," *Business Week*, February 18, 2002, 81–4.

9 "Suddenly, the BBC is a World-Beater," *Business Week*, April 28, 2003, 98.

10 "France Plans an All-News Broadcast," *San José Mercury News*, May 13, 2003.

11 "Channel V Plans Move to Malaysia," *Bangkok Post*, June 11, 2002.

12 "Time Warner Bows 'Buns of Steel' in UK," *Global Direct Marketing*, March 13, 1995.

13 Han Jürgen Schaeffer, "Negotiating German Direct Marketing Laws," *Global Direct Marketing*, January 23, 1995, 14.

14 Richard Miller, "How to Get Your Mail Shipped to Europe," *DM News*, December 23, 1991, 26, 37.

15 "For Coke, Local Is It," *Business Week,* July 3, 2000, 122.

16 Patrick D. Lynch and John C. Beck, "Profiles of Internet Buyers in 20 Countries: Evidence for Region-Specific Strategies," *Journal of International Business Studies* 32 (fourth quarter, 2001): 725–48.

17 "Worldwide-Friendly Sites Draws Returns," *Marketing News*, September 2, 2002, 24.

18 Patrick D. Lynch, Robert J. Kent, and Srini S. Srinivasan, "The Global Internet Shopper: Evidence from Shopping Tasks in Twelve Countries," *Journal of Advertising Research* 41 (May to June 2001): 15–23.

19 Duaine Priestley, "E-Commerce: Challenges and Opportunities," *Export America*, 34–35.

20 R. Crockett, "Surfing in Tongues," *Business Week E.Biz*, December 11, 2000 EB 18.

21 Kelichi Koseki, "Marketing Strategies as Adopted by Ajinomoto in Southeast Asia," *Journal of Advertising Research* 30 (April/May 1990): 31–4.

22 "Dewar's Prifiles Travel Well," *Advertising Age*, August 14, 1989, 28.

23 For a comprehensive review of the theoretical issues and empirical evidence, see Sak Onkvisit and John J. Shaw, "Standardized International Advertising: A Review and Critical Evaluation of the Theoretical and Empirical Evidence," *Columbia Journal of World Business* 22 (fall 1987): 43–55.

24 Subhash C. Jain, "Standardization of International Marketing Strategy: Some Research Hypotheses," *Journal of Marketing* 53 (January 1989): 70–9.

25 Warren J. Keegan, "Multinational Product Planning: Strategic Alternatives," *Journal of Marketing* 33 (January 1969): 58–62.

26 "A Little Washing Machine That Won't Shred a Sari," *Business Week*, June 3, 1991, 100.

27 Klaus Backhaus, Katrin Muhlfeld, and Jenny Van Doorn, "Consumer Perspectives on Standardization in International Advertising: A Student Sample," *Journal of Advertising Research* 41 (September to October 2001): 53–61.

28 Tom Duncan and Jyotika Ramaprasad, "Standardized Multinational Advertising: The Influencing Factors," *Journal of Advertising*, 24 (fall 1995): 55–68.

29 Young Sook Moon and George R. Franke, "Cultural Influences on Agency Practitioners' Ethical Perceptions: A Comparison of Korea and the U.S.," *Journal of Advertising* 29 (spring 2000): 51–64.

30 Onkvisit and Shaw, "Standardized International Advertising."

31 Marinel Gerritsen *et al.*, "English in Dutch Commercials: Not Understood and Not Appreciated," *Journal of Advertising Research*, (July to August 2000): 17–000.

32 Michel Laroche *et al.*, "A Model of Advertising Standardization in Multinational Corporations," *Journal of International Business Studies* 32 (second quarter, 2001): 249–66.

33 Kelly Hewett and William O. Bearden, "Dependence, Trust, and Relational Behavior on the Part of Foreign Subsidiary Marketing Operations: Implications for Managing Global Marketing Operations," *Journal of Marketing* 65 (October 2001): 51–66.

34 Salah H. Hassan and Roger D. Blackwell, "Competitive Global Market Segmentation," in *Global Marketing: Perspectives and Cases*, ed. Salah S. Hassan and Roger D. Blackwell (Fort Worth, TX: Dryden Press, 1994), 53–75; H. Rao Unnava *et al.*, "Communications in Global Markets," in *Global Marketing: Perspectives and Cases*, ed. Salah S. Hassan and Roger D. Blackwell (Fort Worth, TX: Dryden Press, 1994), 253–71.

35 Niraj Dawar and Philip Parker, "Marketing Universals: Consumers' Use of Brand Name, Price, Physical Appearance, and Retailer Reputation as Signals of Product Quality," *Journal of Marketing* 58 (April 1994): 81–95.

36 For a list of these studies, see the 3rd Edition of this textbook.

37 Carl Arthur Solberg, "The Perennial Issue of Adaptation or Standardization of International Marketing Communication: Organizational Contingencies and Performance," *Journal of International Marketing* (September 2002): 1–21.

38 Mindy F. Ji and James U. McNeal, "How Chinese Children's Commercials Differ from Those of the USA: A Content Analysis," *Journal of Advertising* 30 (fall 2001): 79–92.

39 Carolyn A. Lin, "Cultural Values Reflected in Chinese and American Television Advertising," *Journal of Advertising* 30 (winter 2001): 83–94.

40 Michael L. Maynard and Charles R. Taylor, "Girlish Images Across Cultures: Analyzing Japanese Versus U.S. *Seventeen* Magazine Ads," *Journal of Advertising* 28 (spring 1999): 39–64.

41 Katharina M. Dallmann, "Targeting Women in German and Japanese Magazine Advertising: A Difference-in-differences Approach," *European Journal of Marketing* 35 (No. 11, 2001): 1320–41.

42 Laura M. Milner and James M. Collins, "Sex-role Portrayals and the Gender of Nations," *Journal of Advertising* 29 (spring 2000): 67–73.

43 Fahad S. Al-Olayan and Kiran Karande, "A Content Analysis of Magazine Advertisements from the United States and the Arab World," *Journal of Advertising* 29 (fall 2000): 69–82.

44 Greg Harris and Suleiman Attour, "The International Advertising Practices of Multinational Companies: A Content Analysis Study," *European Journal of Marketing* 37 (No. 1, 2003): 154–68.

45 Stephen J. Gould, Pola B. Gupta, and Sonja Grabner-Krauter, "Product Placements in Movies: A Cross-Cultural Analysis of Austrian, French and American Consumers' Attitudes toward This Emerging, International Promotional Medium," *Journal of Advertising* 29 (winter 2000): 41–58.

46 "The Rumble Heard Round the World: Harleys," *Business Week*, May 24, 1993, 58, 60.

47 Sak Onkvisit and John J. Shaw, "Standardized International Advertising: Some Research Issues and Implications," *Journal of Advertising Research* 39 (November/December 1999): 19–24.

48 "More Trade, More Nations," *Business Week*, March 19, 2001, 32.

49 "Up Front," *Business Week*, May 1, 2000.

50 "The Next Oil Frontier," *Business Week*, May 27, 2002, 52–4.

51 Harold M. Spielman, "Local Partnerships: The Strategic Asset in Multicultural Research," *Journal of Advertising Research* 35 (January/February 1995): RC8–15.

52 "Goodbye Global," *Advertising Age*, November 16, 1987, 22, 36.

53 Wayne R. McCullough, "Global Advertising Which Acts Locally: The IBM Subtitle Campaign," *Journal of Advertising Research* 36 (May/June 1996): 11–15.

54 Sak Onkvisit and John J. Shaw, "Marketing/Advertising Concepts and Principles in the International Context: Universal or Unique?" in *New Directions in International Advertising Research, Advances in International Marketing*, Vol. 12, ed. Charles R. Taylor (Amsterdam: JAI, 2002), 85–99.

Chapter 16

Pricing strategies

Basic decisions

> Overseas operations should be told never to forget three no's. Never get involved in legal issues, never allow the formation of labor unions, and never fail to collect accounts receivable.
>
> Takashi Kiuchi, General Manager of Planning and Administration,
> International Operations Group, Mitsubishi Electric Corporation

CHAPTER OUTLINE

PURPOSE OF CHAPTER

While price is important, it is not a wise strategy to sell on price as a continuing policy. A product's price must reflect its proper value in the eyes of the consumer. To demonstrate the complexity of pricing decisions, in the case of Japanese firms, the need to adjust their prices is derived from an attempt to neutralize any threat from newcomers. For the Korean manufacturers, the strategy of offering lower prices is to penetrate the advanced economies and to compensate for the unknown quality of their goods. The low prices, however, still allow the Korean manufacturers to make sufficient profit margins due to their lower labor costs. In both cases, the pricing strategies are somewhat constrained by host-country regulations, such as the antidumping laws.

This chapter examines pricing decision in an international context. The chapter begins with a discussion of the role of price in general. It proceeds to cover the various factors that can affect price, with special attention given to certain variables that are unique to the international market (e.g., foreign exchange rate, dumping, price control). Methods for dealing with a foreign country's hyperinflation and transfer prices will also receive some attention.

MARKETING ILLUSTRATION   THE PRICE IS RIGHT

Coca-Cola, with a market share of 16.5 percent, is the No. 3 Cola brand in India. It trails far behind Pepsi-Cola, which commands 23.5 percent. To bring Coke back to life, the operations chief persuaded the headquarters in Atlanta to revamp pricing and advertising. In 2001, a new size (a 6.8-oz. bottle) was introduced for 10 cents, targeting rural areas and lower income urban markets. In 2003, the price of a 10.1-oz. bottle was reduced from 24 cents to 17 cents. Both the little bottle and price cuts were a big success. In addition, to save 57 percent on import duties, Coca-Cola is now using more local raw materials.

India is a paradox. On the one hand, with soft-drink consumption of just seven 8-oz. servings per capita annually, the market is small. On the other hand, because of that per capita consumption, India has the world's greatest growth potential. After all, in comparison, neighboring Pakistan claims an average of fourteen servings. Mexico, at present, is the world's hottest soda market, accounting for 1500 servings.

Source: "Finally, Coke Gets It Right," *Business Week,* February 10, 2003, 47.

THE ROLE OF PRICE

Price is an integral part of a product — a product cannot exist without a price. It is difficult to think or talk about a product without considering its price. Price is important because it affects demand, and an inverse relationship between the two usually prevails. Price also affects the larger economy because inflation is caused by rapid price increases. Yet among the marketing decision variables, price has received the least attention. "The export-pricing literature is characterized by a distinct lack of sound theoretical and empirical works."[1]

Price, however, is no more important than the other three Ps. One should not forget that price should never be isolated from the other parts of the marketing mix. Price should never be treated as an isolated factor.

Price is often misunderstood, especially by many executives. Consumers do not object to price. What they object to is the lack of a relationship between the perceived value of the product and the price being charged. They want a fair price, and a fair price can be either high or low as long as it reflects the perceived value of the product in question. Too high a price causes consumers to resist making a purchase because the value is not there.

Price can be absolutely high from a cost standpoint yet relatively low from a demand standpoint, in relation to its value and other features. Therefore, price must be lower than the perceived value or exactly reflect the perceived value. For example, a markdown may be needed for damaged or obsolete goods, but a "high" price may appear to be quite reasonable when extra value is added to a product. Consumers around the world do not mind a high price if they indeed "get what they pay for." However, this is often not the case.

PRICE STANDARDIZATION

One area of pricing that has received some attention is the issue of pricing standardization. A study of the marketing mix by large US-based industrial firms in their Latin American businesses found that the degree of standardization varied across individual elements, with branding and product being least adapted. Perhaps because of government regulations, price and advertising elements were most adapted. In comparison with the same firms' European and Latin American strategies, price was similarly adapted in both regions.[2]

According to one study, most American multinational firms standardize their prices in most world markets because they are probably cost driven.[3] Due to market variations, one has to wonder why these firms are inflexible and whether they have been successful overseas. Perhaps these firms have been able to be rigid due to the fact that they do not rely on foreign sales very much and that they do business primarily with industrialized countries. In contrast, those companies that are more committed to international business localize their prices and are more successful overseas.

Whether price should be uniform worldwide is a subject of much debate. One school of thought holds that, from the management's viewpoint, there is no reason for an export price to differ from the home price. In addition, economists believe that arbitrage will eliminate any price differential between markets. This is especially the case with the European Union due to the free movement of goods, the elimination of customs barriers, and the harmonization of VAT rates. In addition, the free movement of people will enable them to easily observe prices of the same products in neighboring countries. As a result, internationally recognized consumer goods with wide European distribution are likely to have a more uniform pricing system.

A multinational corporation needs to coordinate prices across its multiple markets – without violating national laws. A study of South Korean, Taiwanese, Hong Kong, and Singaporean firms operating in Europe found that they had closer relationships with their parent firms and that they had greater autonomy in strategy and pricing decisions.[4] In the case of Nintendo, it was fined $147 million by the European Commission for price collusion with seven European distributors. The company organized a cartel that operated from 1991 to 1998, and it allowed companies to keep prices for its games and game consoles artificially high in certain countries. These distributors agreed to refuse to sell to buyers from the other European countries, resulting in extraordinarily wide differences in prices among countries.[5]

PRICING DECISIONS

Pricing is one area of marketing that has been largely overlooked. Of the four Ps of marketing, pricing is probably the one that receives the least attention, especially in an international context.

One problem with an investigation of pricing decisions is that theories are few and vague. Most of the theories that do exist reduce the large number of pricing variables to a discussion of demand and supply. Because the few theories are inadequate, many pricing decisions are based on intuition, trial and error, or routine procedures (e.g., cost-plus or imitative pricing).

When pricing a product, a company must consider a number of factors. The factors of cost and supply are always relevant – domestically and internationally. Other factors such as exchange rate, tariffs, and culture are more applicable in the case of international marketing.

Supply and demand

The law of supply and demand is a sound starting point in explaining companies' price behavior. A common practice is to reduce the large number of pricing factors to two basic variables: demand and supply. In an efficient, market-oriented economy, demand is affected by competitive activity, and consumers are able to make informed decisions. Price, as a measure of product benefit, acts as the equilibrator of supply and demand. On the supply side, suppliers compete for consumers' limited funds by constantly cutting costs and enhancing product value. On the demand side, any increase in demand is followed by a higher price, and the higher price should in turn moderate demand. The higher price, however, usually induces manufacturers to increase the supply, and more supply should lead to a reduction in price which will then stimulate demand once again.

The demand–supply model of pricing seems to work best with commodities under a monopoly situation. OPEC, an oil cartel, once controlled the supply of oil so tightly that the cartel was able to push oil prices up sharply. The demand remained high for a period of time because consumers were unable to adjust their driving habits immediately. In the long run, however, high prices curbed excessive demand, and oil prices tumbled during the mid-1980s. The law of supply and demand, in this circumstance, operated in the predicted manner. The moral could be that even a monopolist cannot keep on increasing prices without eventually reducing demand. Unfortunately, consumers have also adjusted their behavior when prices improve by embracing SUVs and fuel-inefficient vehicles, thus

allowing OPEC's control on supply to boost price in the early part of the twenty-first century.

However, this pricing model based strictly on demand and supply is oversimplified. The straightforward relationship between supply and price can be affected by several factors. Numerous products have been so differentiated that supply alone as a factor is essentially irrelevant. If a product has a distinct, prestigious image, price may become secondary in importance to image. For such a product, supply can be reduced and price increased without curtailing demand. Waterford Glass became the bestselling fine crystal in the USA by carefully nurturing its "posh image" as well as by controlling the supply. Waterford held down volume while maintaining premium prices. According to the company, there is no advantage in owning a product that anyone can buy.

Because demand-and-supply analysis can only broadly explain companies' price behavior, it is necessary to consider other relevant factors that affect demand or supply or both, and that ultimately influence pricing decisions.

Cost

In pricing a product, it is inevitable that cost must be taken into account. British Airways at one time blindly matched the competition's prices without carefully considering its cost structure. By instituting carefully considered restrictions on discount seats, the company was able to increase its yield significantly.

The essential question is not whether cost is considered but rather what kind of cost is considered and to what extent. The typical costs associated with international marketing include: market research; credit checks; business travel; international postage, cable, and telephone rates; translation costs; commissions, training charges, and other costs involving foreign representatives; consultants and freight forwarders; product modification; and special packaging.

For one school of thought, the thinking is that export price should be lower than home price because the home market actually gains in its

MARKETING STRATEGY 16.1   REAL INDIAN SOAPS

While consumers in affluent countries often view developing countries' products with distrust, their counterparts in developing countries may often share the same view. When multinationals begin to do manufacturing in Nepal, they have to contend with consumers' bias against the made-in-Nepal products. Many are upset that they can no longer get real Indian soaps and that instead they have to buy Lux soaps that are made by Nepal Lever. Unilever has launched a campaign to educate consumers in Nepal. The company wants to change consumers' beliefs that Nepalese-made goods are inferior. The campaign seems to be working. Prior to the campaign, the Indian version of the company's Fair & Lovely skin cream beat the local version by a margin of three to one while commanding a price premium of 10 to 20 percent. The price premium has narrowed significantly.

Source: "Battle for Dominance in the Soap Market Washes over Nepal," *Asian Wall Street Journal*, June 28, 2001.

overhead expenses by spreading these costs over an expanded production volume. Furthermore, a low price may be necessary, at least at the beginning, to penetrate a foreign market.

The second school of thought, however, argues that the **cost-plus method** (i.e., **full cost**) should be used in pricing a product for the overseas market. All costs – including domestic marketing costs (e.g., sales and advertising expenses, marketing research costs) and fixed costs (e.g., research, development, and engineering) – must be paid for by all other countries. As such, the company begins with a domestic price and then adds to its various overseas costs (e.g., freight, packing, insurance, customs duties). This pricing practice, with its high degree of centralization, is also ethnocentric. In effect, with an allowance for transportation costs and tariffs, the same price prevails everywhere in the world. Although the method is simple and straightforward, it is far from being ideal, because it is easy for the price to end up being too high.

Traditionally, Mercedes-Benz used the cost-plus method when pricing its cars, making engineers insensitive to costs. The company found that its costs were 30 percent above Lexus. Now the company has shifted toward setting prices according to the competition. Engineers and plant managers are required to meet the market-driven target price.

A number of international marketers use **marginal-cost pricing**, which is more polycentric and decentralized. This pricing method is oriented more toward incremental costs. An implicit assumption is that some of the product costs, such as administration costs and advertising at home, are irrelevant overseas. In addition, it is likely that research-and-development costs and engineering costs have already been accounted for in the home market and thus should not be factored in again by extending them to other countries. The actual production costs plus foreign marketing costs are therefore used as the floor price below which prices cannot be set without incurring a loss. Japanese companies often rely on this type of pricing strategy to penetrate foreign markets, as well as to maintain market share. For the Japanese, breaking even is regarded as a success. The Japanese are thus willing to sacrifice profit in order to keep their factories going.

The incremental cost method has the advantage of being sensitive to local conditions. Subsidiary or affiliate companies are allowed to set their own prices. A potential shortcoming in using this method is that, because research-and-development costs and the costs of running the headquarters' operation must be borne solely by the home-country market, full cost may not be adequately taken into account by overseas subsidiaries.

In the long run, it is dangerous to be price competitive without being cost competitive. Grundig, for example, tried to gain market share in the VCR market by lowering its higher priced product model, only to realize that it was losing $40 for every unit sold. There is, however, a possible solution for firms with high costs resulting from high tariffs, transportation costs, and high manufacturing costs at home. They have a choice of either producing their products in the overseas market or granting licenses to local producing firms there.

If a company is unable to control costs or to price its product sufficiently high to cover costs, sooner or later the company will be forced to leave the market.

Elasticity and cross-elasticity of demand

Because of the elasticity and cross-elasticity of demand, a company does not usually have the option of changing or holding its price steady, independent of action taken by its competitors. Ford, thinking that its number-one position in England was insurmountable, moved unilaterally to end price wars by eliminating discounts and incentives. This action proved to be a strategic error because competitors did not follow suit, and Ford's dominant market share dropped from 32 percent to 27 percent. Always remember that it takes only one company to start or continue a price war.

To be competitive does not mean that a company's price must be at or below the market. A superior or unique product can command a higher price. US beef, generally from grain-fed cattle, sells better in Japan than does low-priced Australian and New Zealand beef because cattle in those countries are raised on grass and yield leaner meat. A product with a desirable image can also hold its price above the market. This has always been Sony's strategy, and Sony has stayed away from price wars that may damage its image. But Sony has on occasion been forced to lower prices when, as a result of competitors' price cuts, the price gap between it and other competitors has widened too far.

A company can insulate itself against cutthroat pricing to a certain extent by cultivating a unique and desirable image. A prestigious image allows a firm to act more or less as a monopolist and to gain additional pricing freedom. Cartier takes full advantage of its reputation. A watch made by its subcontractor for $125, for example, was sold by Cartier for almost five times that amount. More than two-thirds of BMW owners are repeat buyers. Because of their brand loyalty, BMW is able to price its cars 10 to 30 percent above its competitors' comparable models.[6]

For most consumer goods, a country's per capita income is a good indicator of a market's ability to pay which may indirectly determine a product's elasticity of demand. However, some chic products have a strong demand, and low per capita income is not a deterrent. As in the case of Levi's 501 jeans, the product's worldwide success indicates that a high price can succeed in countries with low per capita income. In fact, it is possible that, for such products, a higher price may even propel the rise in demand.

Exchange rate

One pricing problem involves the currency to be used for billing purposes. As a rule, a seller should negotiate to bill in a strong currency, and a buyer should try to gain acceptance in a weak currency. European firms can also minimize exchange risk by using euros in place of an individual currency for quotation and billing.

The exchange rate is one factor that generally has no impact in domestic marketing but is quite crucial in international marketing. Since March 1985, a sharp drop in the dollar value against other major currencies caused the earnings of US MNCs to jump because their overseas profits when repatriated brought in extra dollars after exchange. In contrast, the devalued dollar brought nothing but displeasure to Japanese exporters. Because of the upward spiral of the yen, Komatsu was forced to raise its prices three times in 1985 and 1986. Komatsu's loss of price advantage forced the company to open a plant in the USA in 1986. Other companies such as Nissan, Honda, and Toyota also had to increase their prices several times. The largest price increase was in a market virtually controlled by the Japanese (e.g., expensive consumer electronics such as CD players and fancy VCRs). Their ability to increase price was, however, more limited at the low end of the market, where the Koreans were right on their heels.

Domestic manufacturers cannot expect to gain competitive advantage solely because of the drop in their home currency. Since its peak in 1985, the foreign exchange value of the US dollar had dropped by more than 50 percent by 1987. In 1994, the US dollar lost more than 10 percent in value against the Japanese yen. In the first three months of 1995, the dollar dropped about 20 percent more in rapid succession to hit one new all-time low after another again and again against the Japanese yen. Japanese car makers had to increase their US prices repeatedly in the 1990s. According to Nissan Motor Co., for each single yen increase against the German mark, Nissan's revenue and net income were reduced by six billion yen.[7] For each one-yen increase against the dollar, the company lost six billion yen annually in sales and profits. For every one-yen drop in the value of the US dollar, the losses for these Japanese firms are as follows: Toyota Motor Co. (ten billion yen), Sony Corp. (five billion yen), and NEC Corp. (two billion yen).[8]

The significant decline of the US dollar should have dramatically reduced – but did not – the deficit in US international trade. Instead, the deficit in US merchandise trade rose. Explanations ranged from the J-curve to the dollar's strengths against the currencies of Canada and many newly industrialized countries.

Even though dollar prices of imports to the USA indeed increased substantially, a depreciating dollar by itself cannot close the trade gap. A falling dollar, although making imports more expensive, has little meaning if prices for domestic substitutes increase to allow imports to maintain a price advantage. The potential price effects on trade resulting from an exchange rate change require taking into account the domestic price developments for competing goods. One must examine how importers, exporters, and domestic producers price their products in terms of the falling dollar.

The real issue is the relationship between import prices and prices for domestically produced com-petitive goods. These exchange rate/price relation-ships are basic in measuring the impact of an exchange rate change on countries' actual trade balances.

Market share

A high market share provides pricing flexibility because the company has the advantage of being above the market if it so chooses. The company can also choose to lower its price because of the better economies of scale derived from lower production and marketing costs. Market share is even more crucial for late entrants because market share acts as an entry barrier. That is, without market share, a company cannot achieve the high volume necessary to improve its efficiency.

Market share can be bought with a very low price at the expense of profit. Compaq shocked the Japanese market in 1992 by selling desktop PCs for less than half the price of Japanese manufacturers. Other US firms soon joined in and grabbed one-third of the market. Fujitsu, Japan's biggest computer company, then started dumping in its home market and lost $300 on each $2000 machine that it sold, amounting to more than $1 million each day.

Various hypotheses explain the differences in pricing behavior between US and Japanese firms, and they range from the dollar's dominant international role and the substantial market power of US goods to the large size of the US domestic market, which permits insensitivity to exchange rate fluctuations. Another explanation is a model based on differences in planning horizons and hystereses.[9]

Hysteresis is a type of market inertia that says that the relationship between two or more variables depends crucially on past history. Hysteresis can occur when a firm has increasing returns to scale or when consumers are loyal to particular brands, making it very difficult for new entrants to sell their products at the same level of profit as established firms. In a hysteretic environment, when there is a differentiated shock (i.e., something that temporarily changes costs for some but not other producers), those firms facing higher costs must either raise prices to maintain profits in the short term and risk losing market share in the long run or raise prices less sharply to keep market share in the long run and maximize long-term profits. Japanese price behavior may thus be a rational strategy for long-run profit maximization rather than a predatory, singled-minded obsession with market share.

Because US manufacturers usually do not practice price discrimination between domestic and foreign customers, a change in the value of the dollar appears to be reflected entirely in the foreign currency price of US exports (i.e., complete pass-through of the exchange rate change). Japanese manufacturers, on the other hand, have a tendency to maintain stable yen prices domestically while keeping their export prices fairly stable by absorbing a significant part of yen fluctuation in the form of flexible profit margins. This pricing behavior, reflecting incomplete pass-through, generates "dumping" when the yen appreciates and lower prices domestically than abroad when the yen depreciates.

Tariffs and distribution costs

As a rule, when dumping and subsidies are not involved, a product sold in a host country should cost more than an identical item sold in a manufacturer's home market. This is the case because the overseas price must be increased to cover tariffs and extra distribution costs. In Japan, both tariffs and quotas combine to restrain imports and force the prices of imported goods upward. In addition, the long distribution channel (i.e., many middlemen) common in many countries around the world is responsible for price escalation, often without any corresponding increase in distribution efficiency. Foreigners in Japan may be shocked to find that an order of plain toast (without coffee) can cost a few dollars.

Culture

US manufacturers should keep in mind that neither the one-price policy nor the suggested list price will be effective in a number of countries. In the USA, a common practice is for retailers to charge all buyers the same price under similar buying conditions. In most other countries, a flexible or negotiated price is common practice, and buyers and sellers often spend hours haggling about price. Thus, price haggling is an art, and the buyer with the superior negotiating skills is expected to

CULTURAL DIMENSION 16.1   RICE: A SACRED CROP

Rice is a very emotional issue among the Japanese and Filipinos. For decades, the Japanese have been told that rice grown in foreign countries is unsuitable for their palates as well as possibly unhealthy. Japan's tariff rate on rice is 580 percent. In the Philippines, rice is an integral part of the country's culture and history, and rice imports are a national shame.

When Thai rice was first imported into Japan, there was a great deal of controversy and ongoing media hysteria. *Weekly Gendai*, a Japanese magazine, ran a headline reading "Can You Still Trust Foreign Rice?" next to a photo of a dead mouse, cigarette butts, and liquor bottle caps atop a basket of Thai rice. American rice faces the same problem. Japanese

media have used scare campaigns and alleged that pesticides used on California rice have caused unwanted abortions and cancer.

Because of government controls on rice imports, the prices of rice are substantially higher in the Philippines when compared to its Asian neighbors at the comparable levels of economic development. Filipino farmers are able to get 28 US cents per kilogram of rice, even though Indonesian, Thai, Vietnamese, Indian, and Chinese farmers are paid only 12 to 18 cents.

Source: "The Philippines' Iron Rice Bowl," *Asian Wall Street Journal*, June 19, 2001.

do better on price than those unfamiliar with the practice.

ALTERNATIVE PRICING STRATEGIES

Pricing involves more than simply marking up or down, and a price that can change in terms of an increase or decrease is not the only answer to moving a product. There are several other alternatives available for making price changes that should be considered. These strategies include the timing of the price change, number of price changes, time interval to which price change applies, number of items to change, use of discount and credit, and bundling and unbundling. US car makers have become rather ingenious in employing these strategies. They change the price by small amounts a number of times over the year. By increasing price significantly at the end of the current model year and then doing so again for the new model year one month later, the company can claim that the price increase for the new model is small because the calculation of the increase is based on the last price of the current year's model. Not surprisingly, GM saves the heftiest price increase for the end of the year in order to facilitate high sticker prices on the new models that are shortly introduced.

The effect of price can be masked and greatly moderated by *financing* or *credit terms*. Airbus, a European consortium owned jointly by four companies from France, Germany, the United Kingdom, and Spain, assembles and markets airplanes as an alternative to carriers that prefer not to buy American. In its eagerness to penetrate the US market, the consortium provided export financing that subsidized Eastern Air Lines by more than $100 million. For Boeing, the consortium engaged in predatory export financing just to get sales.

Discounts (cash, quantity, functional, and so on) may be used to adjust prices indirectly. Large buyers are in a position to command a higher discount if it can be granted legally. Although a quantity discount may provide an incentive for dealers to work harder, it often discriminates against smaller middlemen. Ricoh, concluding that it was not a sound practice

to compete on price, decided to ignore tiered pricing that rewarded dealers with large orders. Ricoh uses only flat-rate prices, and small dealers pay the same price as large dealers.

Another method used to moderate the price effect is to *bundle* or *unbundle* the product. The price reflects the bundling or unbundling of the product. Bundling adds value and increases prices a little or not at all for added value. This is the strategy used by Japanese car makers, who increase the base price of their cars just enough to cover actual costs. The Japanese also sell cars in the USA with more standard equipment and fewer options. The strategy makes sense because their vehicles must be shipped from overseas factories, and any custom orders would only serve to delay production and shipment. Moreover, the price charged covers a "bundle" of standard equipment and represents good value for buyers.

Detroit takes the opposite route. US car makers keep prices low by offering a base price for a barebones product. Any other equipment is optional and at an added cost. US car makers thus offer a car with several hundred options. By allowing a buyer to choose any equipment combination at extra cost for each option, a fully equipped US car can become quite expensive, as Detroit charges and seeks to make a profit from each additional item in the option combination.

Ford has begun to experiment with the bundling approach by making available three levels of trim (bundling), each containing many items as standard equipment. The approach provides several benefits. It simplifies the production-and-assembly system while cutting costs and speeding up delivery time. Without having to stock a large and confusing number of options, better inventory control is achieved. With fewer combinations available, quality control should also be improved. In addition, the method provides a clearer market image for the brand.

It cannot be said that a bundling strategy is always superior or inferior to an unbundling strategy. Bundling offers a buyer more product for less money while simplifying production and marketing activities. The overall bundle, of course, is not likely to match the buyer's need completely. On the other hand, a product can be unbundled so that the buyer does not have to pay for any extras not wanted. In effect, the price can be made more affordable by unbundling the product.

When a company faces escalating export prices due to the addition of transportation charges, customs duties, extra packing costs, and so on, it should consider strategies to moderate the impact of price escalation.

Foreigners usually regard US and German goods as being of good quality and performance but also as being too expensive. Because they are price-conscious, exporters should consider means to keep prices reasonable. They may want to adapt their products by taking out those features that are attractive but not crucial. Larger shipments will lower freight costs, or they may want to consider local manufacturing so as to eliminate expensive freight altogether. On the other hand, exporters should realize that affordable prices will result in repeat business. Furthermore, an initial order for a piece of equipment will lead to demand for spare parts and components and auxiliary equipment. Finally, they should stress that the superior quality of their products ultimately results in lower production costs.

DUMPING

Dumping, a form of price discrimination, is the practice of charging different prices for the same product in similar markets. As a result, imported goods are sold at prices so low as to be detrimental to local producers of the same kind of merchandise. Boeing and McDonnell Douglas, for example, accused Airbus of receiving $9 billion in subsidies from the government consortium, enabling the company to price each airplane at some $15 to 20 million less than the true cost. Dumping also applies to services. Japanese banks in California were accused of dumping money in the US market by pricing their loans at an interest rate lower than that charged by US banks.

Types of dumping

There are several types of dumping: sporadic, predatory, persistent, and reverse. **Sporadic dumping** occurs when a manufacturer with unsold inventories wants to get rid of distressed and excess merchandise. To preserve its competitive position at home, the manufacturer must avoid starting a price war that could harm its home market. One way to find a solution involves destroying excess supplies,

IT'S THE LAW 16.1 FISH AND CHIPS

In 2003, the US Department of Commerce made a final determination in two cases. It ruled that South Korea's Hynix Semiconductor received unfair subsidies for its DRAMS from 2001 to mid-2002. If the US International Trade Commission decides that these imports harm or threaten American industries, the USA could impose countervailing duties of 44.71 percent against Hynix.

In another case, the final determination was that Vietnam was dumping its products on the US catfish market. If confirmed by the US International Trade Commission, antidumping tariffs of up to 64 percent could be imposed. Vietnam strongly denied the dumping charges and accused the USA of protectionism.

It claimed that its low-priced exports were due to the ability of Vietnamese producers to breed whiskered fish far more cheaply than American farmers. The USA countered by saying that, due to Vietnam's "non-market economy," its supposedly low labor costs could not be measured properly against those of a free market. In addition, US farmers were successful in persuading the US Congress to force Vietnam to change the name of its catfish to the Vietnamese terms "tra" and "basa."

Sources: "US May Slap Big Tariffs on Two Imports," *Bangkok Post*, June 19, 2003; "Vietnam Fears Tariffs on Shrimp," *San José Mercury News*, July 26, 2003.

as in the example of Asian farmers dumping small chickens in the sea or burning them. Another way to solve the problem is to cut losses by selling for any price that can be realized. The excess supply is dumped abroad in a market where the product is normally not sold.

Predatory dumping is more permanent than sporadic dumping. This strategy involves selling at a loss to gain access to a market and perhaps to drive out competition. Once the competition is gone or the market established, the company uses its monopoly position to increase price. Some critics question the allegation that predatory dumping is harmful by pointing out that if price is subsequently raised by the firm that does the dumping, former competitors can rejoin the market when it becomes more profitable again.

Hitachi was accused of employing predatory pricing for its EPROM (electrically programmable read-only memory) chips. A memo prepared by the company urged US distributors to "quote 10 percent below competition (until) the bidding stops, when Hitachi wins." The Justice Department, after a year-long investigation, dropped the probe because it found that there was insufficient evidence to prosecute.

Zenith has long accused Japanese television manufacturers of using predatory dumping. It charged in its antitrust suit that major Japanese manufacturers, through false billing and secret rebates, conspired to set low, predatory prices on TV sets in the US market with the purpose of driving US firms out of business in order to gain a monopoly. Both the Japanese and US governments defended the Japanese firms' cooperation on the grounds of "sovereign compulsion." In other words, the defendants' cooperation was the result of compliance with the Japanese government's export policy. After sixteen years of legal maneuvering, the US Supreme Court dismissed the conspiracy theory but ordered a trial concerning the dumping charge.

Persistent dumping is the most permanent type of dumping, requiring consistent selling at lower prices in one market than in others. This practice may be the result of a firm's recognition that

markets are different in terms of overhead costs and demand characteristics. For example, a firm may assume that demand abroad is more elastic than it is at home. Based on this perception, the firm may decide to use incremental or marginal-cost pricing abroad while using full-cost pricing to cover fixed costs at home. This practice benefits foreign consumers, but it works to the disadvantage of local consumers. Japan, for example, is able to keep prices high at home, especially for consumer electronics, because it has no foreign competition there, but it is more than willing to lower prices in the US market in order to gain or maintain market share. Japanese consumers, as a result, suffer by paying higher prices for Japanese products that are priced much lower in other markets.

The three kinds of dumping discussed above have one characteristic in common: each involves charging lower prices abroad than at home. It is possible, however, to have the opposite tactic – reverse dumping. In order to have such a case, the overseas demand must be less elastic and the market will tolerate a higher price. Any dumping will thus be done in the manufacturer's home market by selling locally at a lower price.

Legal aspect of dumping

Whether or not dumping is illegal depends on whether the practice is tolerated in a particular country. Switzerland has no specific antidumping laws. Most countries, however, have dumping laws that set a minimum price or a floor on prices that can be charged in the market.

Illegal dumping occurs when the price charged drops below a specified level. What is the unfair or illegal price level, and what kind of evidence is needed to substantiate a charge of dumping? The case of Melex golf carts from Poland illustrates the difficulty in determining a fair price. The success of Melex in the USA led to an accusation of dumping. The US Treasury Department was unable to ascertain whether Melex's US price was lower than prices at home in Poland because Poland has no golf-courses and no demand for such a product. The cost of production was unsuitable for determining its fair price. Poland, as a socialist economy, does not allow market forces fully to dictate the costs of factors of production. For this reason, the 1974 Trade Act does not allow production costs in a communist/socialist country to be used for comparison purposes.

To determine fair costs, the Treasury began to use a small Canadian manufacturer's costs as reference prices, only to see the Canadian firm stop making golf carts. In addition, Poland protested that the Canadian firm's production costs were too high and unsuitable for comparison. The Treasury's next step was to rely on reference prices of a comparable product from free-market countries. Mexico and Spain were chosen because they were considered to be similar to Poland in terms of their level of economic development. Even though Mexico and Spain do not produce golf carts, they were used anyway to determine what their production costs would be if they produced such a product. After much review and discussion, the ruling was that the "constructed" value did not differ appreciably from Melex's actual price.

The 1980 ruling did not end the matter. The American producers still wanted Melex to pay the dumping charges for the years 1979 to 1980, and the Commerce Department's 1992 review imposed a duty of $599,053.51 plus interest. Melex has continued to fight the case which has outlasted five US administrations, Poland's martial law, and the Soviet Union empire.[10]

One item of evidence of dumping occurs when a product is sold at less than fair value. The Commerce Department, for example, made a final determination that imports of certain small business telephone systems and subassemblies from Japan and Taiwan were being sold in America at less than fair value. Subsequently, the US International Trade Commission made final determinations and found injury to industries in the USA from such imports. The Commission's injury finding led to antidumping duties being placed on imported products to offset their price advantage.

Another example of dumping evidence is a product sold at a price below its home market price or production cost. The USA relies on the official US trigger price, which is designed to curb dumping by giving an early signal of an unacceptable import price. In the case of steel, the trigger price sets a minimum price on imported steel that is pegged to the cost of producing steel in Japan. According to the General Accounting Office, some 40 percent of all imports at one time were priced below the trigger price.

To provide relief, the Antidumping Act requires the US Department of Commerce to impose duties equal to the dumping margin. The antidumping duty is based on the amount by which the foreign market value or constructed value exceeds the purchase price or an exporter's sale price.

Petitioning or threatening to petition can create harassment effects by forcing foreign firms to restrain sales. Due to investigations and the threat of duties, importers frequently reduce shipments, increase prices, or both.

It is understandable why domestic firms want antidumping policies. However, whether such policies benefit the economy is another issue altogether. As concluded by an economist of the International Monetary Fund, "antidumping, as currently practiced, is anticompetitive, threatens to further distort trade patterns, and undercuts the benefits of multilateral liberalization efforts."[11] Indeed, the US International Trade Commission's study ("The Economic Effects of Antidumping and Countervailing Duty Orders and Suspension Agreements") has come to the conclusion that the overall effect of antidumping duties is negative.

The USA deems dumping to be illegal if: (1) the Department of Commerce makes a final determination that dumping has taken place, and (2) the International Trade Commission rules that such imports harm or threaten the US industries. In the case of dynamic random access microchips (DRAMs), most American producers ceased production under pressure of low-price imports, primarily those from South Korea. Micron Technologies, the only significant remaining producer, suspected Taiwanese and Korean manufacturers of unfair trade practices. In the end, the US

483

International Trade Commission ruled that the US computer chip industry was not harmed or threatened with injury by Taiwan imports that were sold for less than fair value, thus ending Micron's complaint.[12] However, with regard to Korea, the Import Administration ruled that Korean manufacturers sold DRAMs in the USA at prices below their cost of production, and duties were imposed at the border.[13]

Dumping is a controversial practice. Just as controversial are the antidumping laws, especially those of the USA. The 1916 Antidumping Act of the USA has infuriated trading partners. As may be expected, these partners asked the WTO to intervene. The WTO ruled that the ancient US law violated international trade rules. The USA appealed, arguing that the law was not about dumping but about antitrust instead. The WTO appeals panel confirmed the lower court ruling, explaining that the penalties were too severe and that the standards for applying them were too weak.[14]

Economists generally argue that the widely used antidumping measures have been abused for protectionist purposes. Over 1800 antidumping investigations have been initiated since 1995. While industrial countries have traditionally been the main users of such measures, developing countries have been more active in recent years; between 1994 and 2001, they initiated almost two-thirds of all investigations. Most antidumping actions have been concentrated in a small number of sectors, especially steel, chemicals, textiles, and consumer electronics, often at the low-tech end of a product range.[15] For the USA, import-sensitive companies (especially steel makers) are responsible for filing nearly half of all dumping petitions.[16]

How to dump (legally and illegally)

Dumping is a widespread practice. Exporters and their importers insist on its use, when necessary, and will find ways to cancel the practice. One can learn from the Mitsui case. Mitsui was responsible for generating the largest dumping case and pleaded guilty to all twenty-one counts involving kickbacks

and the falsifying of documents to customs officials in order to sell steel below trigger prices. Mitsui attempted to conceal its dumping activities through several means. It hid the origin of the Japanese steel products by disguising them as US made (e.g., wire rope imported to Houston). It submitted false documents to conceal the true merchandise value and backdated invoiced to avoid trigger prices. Furthermore, it gave its US customers a rebate equal to the difference between the nominal exchange rate and the actual exchange rate, and the calculations were made after product entry. These illegal rebates totaled $1.3 million between 1978 and 1981. Another deceptive method involved the use of damage claims. Mitsui honored false claims that goods were damaged during shipment and granted credits of $22,676 for damaged Korean wire nails without investigating or reporting these losses to its insurance company. In spite of these ingenious methods, Mitsui was exposed and paid heavy fines for dumping and fraud.

Without doubt, dumping is a risky practice that can cause a great deal of embarrassment, in addition to the payment of large financial penalties. Thus a preferable strategy is to use other means to legally overcome dumping laws. One method that can help avoid charges of dumping is to differentiate the exported item from the item being sold in the home market. By deliberately making the home product and its overseas version incomparable, there is no home market price that can be used as a basis for price comparison. This may be one reason why Japanese car makers market their automobiles under new or different names in the USA. Another method used to circumvent dumping laws is to provide financing terms that can have the same effect as price reduction.

The dumping problem may also be overcome if the production of a product, rather than its importation, is carried out in the host country. This option has become necessary for Japanese manufacturers, who have no desire to lower prices in Japan because they do not have to contend with foreign competitors. The high prices at home, however, work to the disadvantage of Japanese manufacturers because it is easy to prove that they are engaged in dumping in the US market. For Japanese VCR manufacturers there is a dilemma: they cannot make their US prices too low without violating dumping laws, and yet the prices charged cannot be so high as to encourage Korean firms to move in and take market share away. One solution may be to manufacture the sets in the USA. To minimize the higher costs prevailing in the USA, Japanese firms could import as many components and parts from Japan as practical. As in the case of Japanese forklift makers, they were accused of dumping by the Hyster-Yale unit of NACCO Industries Inc. When the International Trade Commission ruled in Hyster's favor and when the US government imposed import duties of up to 51.3 percent on Japanese models, the Japanese firms quickly set up US assembly plants and were able to avoid paying the duties. By doing so, they held their US market share at about 50 percent.

PRICE DISTORTION

Dumping laws are not the only cause of price variations. The power of the market force in setting prices can be moderated by a government's price policy. Few governments allow the market to set prices completely of its own accord. When a government is actively involved in buying and selling local and foreign goods, price deviations usually and readily follow. Because of the political influence of the agricultural sector in Japan, Japanese rice farmers are able to price their rice at several times more than US prices, resulting in Japanese consumers paying double or triple the world price.

On most occasions, a government sets the price artificially high in order to discourage the domestic consumption of imported products. Generally, however, government policy is to keep prices artificially low in the case of necessities that are essentially for public welfare. A government's licensing policy and patent enforcement can affect market prices indirectly as well.

Inflation is often the primary cause of price controls. Inflation affects public welfare and encourages workers to demand higher wages. In addition, inflation increases the pressure of currency devaluation which will affect prices of virtually all products and services.

When a situation of price distortion exists, a company must devise a strategy to deal with it. In 1985, Argentina was experiencing an inflation rate of 1000 percent. Merchants knew that price controls were inevitable, and they increased their prices rapidly and drastically in order to circumvent the restrictions when price controls were implemented. Another method of dealing with price controls involves the creation of a "new" product that is not subject to old or existing prices. A new brand name or a new package may or may not be adequate for this purpose.

Companies themselves are sometimes responsible for price distortion. The European Union has initiated an investigation to determine whether major film companies may have deliberately introduced mechanical differences in their products so as to enforce price differences across markets. The investigation centers on whether Disney and six other major film companies may have made their DVDs incompatible in different regions so as to prevent a disc bought in one country (e.g., the USA) from being played in Europe or elsewhere.[17]

For a long time, Europe tolerates or encourages corporate cooperation. Some governments have supported price-fixing to protect small shops. Germany does not permit retailers to reduce more than 3 percent off manufacturers' suggested prices, and books cannot be discounted. Cartels were legal in the Netherlands until 1996. The beer industry does not seem to have vigorous competition. Big brewers enjoy huge market shares in their home markets. Interbrew, the owner of brands Stella Artois and Abbaye de Leffe, makes almost 60 percent of beer consumed in Belgium. Heineken's market share in the Netherlands is about the same. These brewers own a large number of bars and often use exclusive deals that last for up to ten years, shutting out new entrants. Because of almost non-existent price competition, critics believe that the brewers have a long history of collusion. Breweries naturally deny any price fixing or market conspiracy.

A new EU law has taken effect, and it prohibits brewers dominant in their home markets from owning restaurants or cafés.[18]

The EU has begun to aggressively pursue antitrust cases. European car makers have long kept domestic prices 30 percent or more higher than they are abroad. When Volkswagen tried in 1998 to prevent German dealers from importing cheaper cars from Italy, the European Commission fined it more than $100 million. In addition, fifteen shippers, including Britain's P&O Nedlloyd, Denmark's Maersk Line, and the US's Sea-Land Service, were fined a record $314 million. Furthermore, eight steel producers were fined $95 million for conspiring to fix prices of seamless steel tubes.[19]

Many former communist and socialist countries have now moved in the direction of market-oriented prices. Since the start of the reforms in 1992, Russia has lifted price controls on more than 90 percent of wholesale and retail goods and has privatized most state-owned enterprises to varying degrees.[20]

Table 16.1 shows how prices in general differ greatly from country to country. Table 16.2, in contrast, shows prices of automobiles in particular.

INFLATION

Once the price is set, it must still be adjusted periodically because of the impact of inflation. During 1985, the runaway inflation in Argentina made it easy to see that prices had to be adjusted upward on a sharp and continuous basis. Supermarkets there adjusted prices twice each day, and restaurants marked their prices in pencil to make easy daily changes. Argentine consumers rushed out to purchase goods as soon as they were paid, as a one-day delay could cost them dearly in terms of higher prices.

An inflationary environment creates numerous problems. A firm's price may be constrained by government price controls. It is also difficult to guarantee prices over an extended period of time. Catalog houses, for example, face a dilemma because they can neither maintain the prices printed in their catalogs nor print new catalogs

frequently. Any installment payment plan adds to the complexity.

Domestically and internationally, marketers must take time lag in receiving payment into account. A country's inefficient banking system may be a cause of the delay. For example, Gosbank was once the central bank for all the states within the Soviet Union. The bank's dissolution drastically reduced the efficiency of the interstate banking system. Exporters and importers had to wait two or three months to clear payment orders, and the risk was too great at the time when inflation was high.

When a marketer operates within a highly inflationary environment, it must think like its customers in order to protect itself. There are several strategies that may be devised for this purpose. First, merchants must collect their accounts receivable quickly. To protect itself, American Express requires its Argentine cardholders to pay their charge account purchases even before the bills are sent. Second, a product may be modified by reducing the quantity or eliminating extra frills so that an affordable price can be achieved. Third, sometimes it may be better not to make a sale. Some Argentine retailers and distributors felt that they would come out ahead by closing their stores for a month instead of making sales because their inventories would greatly appreciate in value over the interval. Fourth, the marketer can insulate itself against the declining value of a depreciating local currency by posting its prices in terms of an appreciating hard currency.

Another means of protection is through the accounting system. A company has the option of valuing its inventory and costs of goods sold based on either the **FIFO** (first in, first out) or **LIFO** (last in, first out) basis. During a period of stable prices, it may not matter very much which method is used, but in a country experiencing high inflation, it may turn out to be a matter of survival for a marginal company as to which accounting inventory valuation method is used.

The FIFO method will understate the cost of goods sold during a period of high inflation, and this will result in excessive paper profits that are subject to the payment of higher taxes and dividends. The

Table 16.1 *Prices around the globe*

City	Excl. rent Zurich = 100	Incl. rent Zurich = 100	City	Excl. rent Zurich = 100	Incl. rent Zurich = 100
Oslo	117.8	111.3	Lisbon	65.1	68.5
Hong Kong	108.1	122.5	Dubai	65.1	73.6
Tokyo	106.7	110.3	Barcelona	63.0	61.8
New York	104.5	120.2	Auckland	62.1	63.9
Zurich	100.0	100.0	Mexico City	61.1	62.5
Copenhagen	98.9	97.9	Lagos	59.4	50.9
London	97.6	111.4	Budapest	55.9	57.3
Basel	97.5	92.6	Ljubljana	55.0	59.1
Chicago	97.2	101.4	Istanbul	54.9	65.6
Geneva	95.6	98.3	Moscow	53.6	56.2
Lugano	93.9	90.2	Nairobi	53.6	51.8
Stockholm	91.1	88.1	Warsaw	50.7	51.8
Paris	89.3	92.4	Jakarta	50.4	59.7
Helsinki	86.1	84.5	Tallinn	50.0	46.1
Los Angeles	84.3	87.5	Vilnius	48.8	46.1
Vienna	84.2	85.2	Caracas	47.6	57.8
Dublin	82.8	89.2	Bangkok	45.8	44.3
Brussels	79.2	75.7	Lima	45.4	48.8
Frankfurt	78.5	78.0	Johannesburg	44.9	48.3
Amsterdam	77.3	81.0	Riga	43.4	39.9
Seoul	76.5	77.6	Kuala Lumpur	42.9	42.5
Berlin	75.4	71.9	São Paulo	41.7	41.5
Miami	74.6	74.2	Santiago de Chile	41.5	42.2
Milan	74.4	82.9	Prague	40.5	41.8
Athens	73.8	72.0	Bratislava	38.3	38.9
Rome	73.4	79.7	Rio de Janeiro	38.2	38.4
Taipei	73.1	84.3	Bogotá	38.0	34.4
Singapore	72.1	79.1	Manila	36.8	42.6
Tel Aviv	70.2	70.3	Sofia	35.4	33.3
Shanghai	69.7	71.9	Bucharest	33.2	29.9
Madrid	68.4	67.5	Karachi	32.7	33.3
Toronto	66.6	67.9	Kiev	32.5	34.3
Manama	66.1	68.3	Buenos Aires	30.6	27.8
Sydney	66.1	68.3	Mumbai	28.7	28.3
Montreal	65.6	60.7			

Source: Prices and Earnings (Zurich: UBS AG, 2003), 6.

problem is made more difficult because there is less cash available for the replenishment of inventory, which when purchased is acquired at much higher prices. Thus, a firm is wise to adopt the LIFO system, which will improve the amount of cash flow.

By assuming that the last item bought at a higher price will be the first item to be sold, the cost of goods sold is overstated, resulting in less profit being generated. Subsequently, less tax and dividend will be paid, and there are more funds remaining for

Table 16.2 *Car prices and maintenance costs*

City	Mid-price car	Price USD	City	Mid-price car	Price USD
Amsterdam	Peugeot 307	23,500	Madrid	Ibiza 1.9 SDI Stella	13,300
Athens	Peugeot 607	37,300	Manama	Toyota Corolla 1.8	27,300
Auckland	Holden Astra City Sedan 1.8	17,400	Manila	Toyota Corolla GLi 1.6	14,600
Bangkok	Toyota Alfis 1.8	18,700	Mexico City	VW Jetta Europe Austero	13,000
Barcelona	Citroën Xsara 1.6i	16,500	Miami	Hyundai Sonata 2002	14,200
Basel	VW Golf 2.0	22,300	Milan	VW Golf 1.8 GTi	18,000
Berlin	VW Golf IV	20,300	Montreal	Mazda Protegé E5	15,900
Bogotá	Peugeot 306	11,900	Moscow	Vaz 2112 1.5	6,000
Bratislava	Skoda Octavia Classic	11,900	Mumbai	Maruti Zen LX	7,900
Brussels	VW Golf 2.0 Highline	23,300	Nairobi	Toyota Corolla 1.8	26,000
Bucharest	Dacia 1310	25,800	New York	Ford Taurus	23,900
Budapest	Ford Mondeo Ambiente 2.0 TDC	8,800	Oslo	Toyota rav4	39,200
Buenos Aires	Peugeot 206	4,000	Paris	Renault Laguna 1.8	23,200
Caracas	Chevrolet Astra 1.9	18,200	Prague	Skoda Octavia 1.9	14,700
Chicago	Nissan Maxima 2.0	29,400	Riga	Ford Mondeo 1.8i	16,700
Copenhagen	Peugeot 307 2.0 SE	13,100	Rio de Janeiro	VW Golf City 1.6	5,800
Dubai	Mitsubishi Galant 2.0	31,500	Rome	Fiat Punto 1.9	16,300
Dublin	VW Passat SAL 1.8T	19,800	Santiago de Chile	Toyota Yaris	8,100
Frankfurt	VW Golf 1.8	23,800			
Geneva	Opel Zafira 1.8i	25,700	São Paulo	Opel Vectra 2.2	10,200
Helsinki	Toyota Avensis 1.8 VTTi	24,200	Seoul	Hyundai New EF Sonanta 2.0	36,200
Hong Kong	Nissan Primera 2.0	27,400	Shanghai	Buick 25G	14,100
Istanbul	VW Passat 1.8	26,600	Singapore	Korea Optima 2.0 DOHC	44,900
Jakarta	Toyota Corolla Altis	19,100	Sofia	Seat Cordoba 1.4	10,500
Johannesburg	Toyota Corolla 160i	11,300	Stockholm	Volvo V70	29,200
Karachi	Suzuki Baleno 2003	6,900	Sydney	Holden Commodore	16,600
Kiev	VAZ-21102 1.5	37,700	Taipei	Honda 2000C	18,100
Kuala Lumpur	Proton Wira 1.8	17,000	Tallinn	Mazda 6 2.0	18,600
Lagos	Peugeot 505	23,300	Tel Aviv	Mazda 6 2.0	28,500
Lima	Toyota Yaris 1.5	13,500	Tokyo	Honda Accord 2.0E	17,600
Lisbon	VW Golf 1.9 TDI	29,100	Toronto	Toyota Corolla CE	14,800
Ljubljana	VW Golf IV 1.9 SDI	15,900	Vienna	VW Golf TDi	19,000
London	Vauxhall Astra GSI 2.0i	26,400	Vilnius	Mazda 6	15,100
Los Angeles	Honda Civic DX	15,500	Warsaw	Toyota Corolla Sedan 2.0f	24,500
Lugano	Honda CR-V 2.0	26,300	Zurich	Ford Focus 2.0	20,100
Luxembourg	VW Golf 1.9 TDI	20,400			

Source: Prices and Earnings (Zurich: UBS AG, 2003), 17.

the purchase of new inventory. Anderson Clayton, for example, uses the LIFO method to reduce its tax liability in Mexico. The improvement in cash flow reduces the need to borrow funds in that uncertain monetary environment.

After World War I, several European economies experienced hyperinflation. Unbelievably, Germany recorded an astronomical 3.25 million percent in a single month in 1923. Thus modern hyperinflation is quite mild by comparison. The recent episodes of modern hyperinflation include Argentina (with a peak twelve-month inflation rate of 20,266 percent in 1990), Bolivia (23,447 percent in 1985), Brazil (6821 percent in 1990), Peru (12,378 percent in 1990), and Ukraine (10,155 percent in 1993).[21]

Table 16.3 *Stabilization programs and inflation performance, 1989–99*

	Maximum annual inflation	Year in which inflation was highest (%)
Albania	237	1992
Armenia	10896	1993
Azerbaijan	1787	1994
Belarus	1997	1993
Bulgaria	579	1997
Croatia	2585	1989
Czech Republic	52	1991
Estonia	947	1992
Georgia	7486	1993
Hungary	35	1990
Kazakhstan	2961	1992
Kyrgvz Republic	958	1992
Latvia	1162	1992
Lithuania	1162	1992
Macedonia, former Yugoslav Republic of	1780	1992
Moldova	2198	1992
Poland	640	1989
Romania	295	1993
Russia	2510	1992
Slovak Republic	58	1991
Slovenia	247	1991
Tajikistan	7344	1993
Turkmenistan	9743	1993
Ukraine	10155	1993
Uzbekistan	1281	1994
CEE	651	1991
Baltics	1091	1992
Other former Soviet Union	4943	1993

Source: Adapted from *Finance & Development*, September 2000, 4.

TRANSFER PRICING

A common practice is for an MNC's many subsidiaries to trade among themselves or with the parent firm. For example, almost one-third of all US exports go to US subsidiaries and business affiliates overseas. According to the United Nations World Investment Report, intrafirm trading of goods and services among multinational corporations has soared, amounting to about one-third of total world trade.

Initially, it may seem that any price charged should be acceptable because the sales are among subsidiaries. If the selling price is relatively low, the profit is made by the buying unit. If the price is relatively high, the profit is made by the selling subsidiary. In the final analysis, the same amount of profit is still made by the parent firm which ever is the case. This situation, however, is complicated by taxation. The transfer prices used, therefore, must be carefully considered (see Figure 16.1). To comply with the complicated tax laws, the 500 biggest US companies spend more than $1 billion a year, with half of the cost attributed to international tax rules.[22]

There are four basic methods used to determine transfer prices. The first method involves transfers at *direct manufacturing costs*. The problem with this method is that when a buying subsidiary acquires merchandise at a very low price it has no incentive to hold down expenses or to maximize profits. The selling unit is also likely to be unhappy for not showing profit, feeling that it is subsidizing an affiliate of the firm's operations.

The second technique involves a transfer at *direct manufacturing cost plus a predetermined markup* to cover additional expenses. Profit is produced and added at every stage. The disadvantage of this method is that the price generated may be too high because market conditions are given secondary consideration to the markups taken.

The third course of action involves the use of a *market-based transfer price*. The price, though competitive, may end up being too low for the selling subsidiary because production cost may not be considered.

489

Figure 16.1 Tax laws and transfer pricing

The fourth and final process employs an *arm's length price* as a basis for determining transfer price. This price would be the price that unaffiliated traders would agree on for a particular transaction. The problem with using this method occurs when the product has no external buyers or is sold at different prices in different markets.

Cost-plus and market-based pricing were the most popular methods used both in more developed and less developed countries. The findings show that size and legal considerations (e.g., compliance with tax and custom regulations, antidumping and antitrust legislations, and financial reporting rules of host countries) are influential in the use of market-based transfer pricing. However, the extent of economic development in host countries and economic restrictions (e.g., exchange controls, price controls, restrictions on imports, and political and social conditions) are either unimportant or secondary determinants of a market-based transfer pricing strategy. US Treasury Regulation 1.482 prescribes the following transfer pricing methods: the uncontrolled price method, the resale method, the cost-plus method, and some other appropriate method when none of the methods described above is applicable.[23]

Ordinarily, the parent firm should attempt to maximize its income in low-tax countries and minimize profit in high-tax markets. To minimize the income of a buying subsidiary in a high-tax country, use of the arm's length price is appropriate. In fact, any permissible costs should be added so that the price charged will be so high that it leaves the buyer with only a small profit subject to tax.

On the other hand, if the buying subsidiary is located in a low-tax country, its income should be maximized. This may be achieved by using a transfer price based on only direct production costs. In this case, the buyer will acquire the product for resale or use at a very low price. Its high profit is, however, subject only to low tax rates in this market. Although Cartier's corporate home is in low-tax Luxembourg, it wisely prices its watches so that most of the markup is collected by its lower taxed Swiss subsidiary.

Section 482 of the US Internal Revenue Code requires arm's length dealing between related parties. An arm's length price or charge is defined as the amount or price that would be charged or would have been charged for the same product or service if independent transactions with unrelated parties under similar conditions were carried out. This requirement applies to (1) loans; (2) both goods and services (e.g., performance of marketing, managerial, technical, or other services for an affiliated party); and (3) possession, use, occupancy, loan, and assignment of tangible and intangible property.

If the IRS finds that adjustments are needed to correctly reflect a company's income, it is empowered to distribute, allocate, or apportion gross income, deductions, credits, or allowances among related organizations regardless of whether they are organized in the USA. The purpose of the Internal Revenue code is to prevent a low intercompany transfer price that shifts income away from the USA. At the same time, the application of the code is intended to ensure that the transfer price of a sale from a foreign company to a related US company is not so high as to result in a small income being realized in the USA. The US Customs Service, however, has a different perspective – it keeps an eye out for low transfer prices, which in turn reduce customs duties and which may result in dumping.

The IRS employs several methods to determine an arm's length price. When available, comparable uncontrolled sales must be used. When such sales do not exist, the resale price method is the next alternative to be used. When the first two methods are not applicable, it is permissible to use the cost-plus method. Any other appropriate pricing method may be used only when it is reasonable to do so and when the first three methods are not relevant.

In general, US firms with foreign subsidiaries can minimize their US taxes by overpaying the foreign subsidiaries for goods and services received or undercharging them for goods and services rendered. In the case of DHL Corp., the world's largest international air express network which links more than 80,000 cities in more than 200 countries, it was ordered by the IRS to pay $194 million in back income taxes and $75 million in penalties. The IRS determined that DHL and its subsidiaries shifted taxable income to a Hong Kong subsidiary.[24] The IRS has also determined that, between 1966 and 1988, the various Hyatt companies under-reported income by $100 million because they paid too little for the Hyatt brand and other services provided by the US parent. A 1999 ruling has determined that the $10,000 one-time fee that Hyatt International paid for each hotel bearing the Hyatt name was much too low.[25]

According to President Clinton, the USA could bring in $45 billion in four years by taking care of the transfer pricing problem. The new US regulations allow companies to use greater flexibility, judgment, and subjectivity in determining what they charge foreign operations for certain services. At first, it seems that the new regulations may encourage firms to be even more aggressive in their transfer pricing schemes to maximize profits. The IRS, however, feels that firms will have to be more careful because the "best method rule" requires them to identify the best way to determine the prices that they charge their other operations.[26]

When possible and applicable, a US company should try to maximize foreign tax credits since they may be used to reduce US income tax. Moreover, it should consider locating a tax haven to shelter and maximize its income by using the tax haven to collect royalties, fees, dividends, and so on.

The OECD has published guidelines on transfer pricing. Most countries use the OECD guidelines to determine an arm's length price.

CONCLUSION

To set price, the concerns of all affected parties must be addressed. A manufacturer needs to make a profit. So do resellers, who demand adequate margins for their services. Moreover, competitors' reactions in terms of their price responses must be anticipated. Finally, it is necessary to take into account both consumers and the value they place on the product.

Several factors must be taken into consideration in setting price, including cost, elasticity of demand, supply, product image (prestige), turnover, market share/volume, product life cycle, and the number of products involved. The optimum mix of these ingredients varies by product, market, and corporate objectives.

Price setting in the international context is complicated further by such factors as foreign exchange rates, relative labor costs, and relative inflation rates in various countries. Other important considerations are export packing costs and charges, transportation costs, tariffs, tax laws, and profit remittance restrictions.

CASE 16.1 BLOOD DIAMONDS

De Beers maintains its power by using a system that sells exclusively to 125 "sightholders" (diamond merchants from the world's leading diamond-cutting centers). These sightholders gather ten times a year in London to buy stones from De Beers' exclusive sales unit, the Central Selling Organization. They are a crucial link in the supply chain of brokers, cutters, and wholesalers that produces engagement rings and other jewelry of the world's fragmented $56 billion diamond retail trade. Sightholders do not have to buy what DeBeers offers, but they will not be invited back for another "sight."

De Beers has two big problems. On the one hand, human rights groups accuse it of buying illicit (blood or conflict) diamonds from African rebels and rulers who use the proceeds to finance their wars. On the other hand, the company's usual strategy of hoarding diamonds is becoming more and more expensive. For a very long time, De Beers has accumulated raw gems so as to control the supply made available to the world as well as to control the world diamond prices. However, the strategy has become an expensive proposition since there are so many diamond producers, making it difficult for the company to keep absorbing the ever-increasing supply on its own.

De Beers has found a way to kill two birds with one stone. It uses the social problem (the controversy over blood diamonds) to address its commercial problems. The company has suspended all buying of diamonds outside of its own proprietary stones and its contractual purchases. It has announced plans to certify all diamonds sold to sightholders as nonconflict stones. It has told 125 sightholders that they will lose access to De Beers stones if they deal in blood diamonds.

The plan is to use its refusal to handle conflict diamonds to re-invent De Beers as a socially responsible crusader. To improve its image, De Beers has positioned itself as a "supplier of choice." While still wanting to maintain its global leadership for uncut diamonds worth $7 billion to $8 billion a year, it aims to become a branded, high-value diamond trader.

De Beers, also known as the syndicate, has another motive. It wants the world in general and the US government in particular to forgive and forget its monopoly or cartel status. It is hopeful that the new image will help to convince American antitrust regulators that it is no longer a monopolist that fixes prices of industrial diamonds. With the antitrust problems being unresolved, De Beers cannot set up operations in the USA which is the world's largest retail market for polished stones. Half of the world's retail sales takes place in American jewelry stores. As part of its rebranding campaign, the Central Selling Organization has become the Diamond Trading Co.

Diamonds have traditionally been graded and valued based on the four Cs – cut, color, clarity, and carat. Is it possible to make "country of origin" the fifth C in the grading system? Canada is doing just that by touting its diamonds as politically correct.

Skeptics dismiss the idea as a gimmick. Some players, however, are counting on it, claiming that the fifth C is not any country of origin but Canada. Boasting Canada's reputation as a peaceful, socially progressive country, and stressing that Canadian diamonds are mined under ethical, environmentally friendly conditions, these organizations are striving to distinguish Canadian diamonds from blood diamonds. Since country of origin has always played a part in defining the quality of a product (e.g., Swiss watches, Italian leather, French wines), it is conceivable that it may work for Canadian diamonds.

Sirius Diamonds Inc. laser-engraves a polar bear on its Canadian stones. Henry Birks & Sons Inc. engraves its Canadian diamonds with a maple leaf and serial number. The government of the Northwest Territories provides a certificate for each diamond that is mined, cut, and polished there. Each certificate has a serial number that is engraved by laser on to the diamond, but some retailers complain that wholesalers are charging as much as 20 percent more for Canadian diamonds.

Points to consider

1   Evaluate DeBeers' pricing practice.
2   Evaluate DeBeers' attempt to promote a new image.
3   Will consumers care where a diamond comes from?

Sources: "Why De Beers Washed Its Hands of Blood Diamonds," *San José Mercury News*, August 27, 2000; "Political Correctness by the Carat," *Wall Street Journal*, April 17, 20, 2003.

QUESTIONS

1   Explain how exchange rate and inflation affect the way you price your product.
2   What is dumping? When does it become illegal? What can a seller do to circumvent antidumping regulations?
3   What methods can be used to compute a transfer price (for transactions between affiliated companies)?

DISCUSSION ASSIGNMENTS AND MINICASES

1   How should US farmers price their products?
2   To protect itself, how should a marketer price its product in a country with high inflation?
3   Price haggling is an art. Discuss how you can haggle effectively.
4   Explain why US car makers prefer to use the "unbundling" approach in pricing their cars while their foreign competitors tend to use the "bundling" pricing approach.

NOTES

1   Matthew B. Myers, S. Tamer Cavusgil, and Adamantios Diamantopoulos, "Antecedents and Actions of Export Pricing Strategy: A Conceptual Framework and Research Propositions," *European Journal of Marketing* 36 (No. 1, 2002): 159–88.

2   Robert Grosse and Walter Zinn, "Standardization in International Marketing: The Latin American Case," *Journal of Global Marketing* 4 (No. 1, 1990): 53–78.

3   A. Coskun Samli and Laurence Jacobs, "Pricing Practices of American Multinational Firms: Standardization vs. Localization Dichotomy," *Journal of Global Marketing* 8 (No. 2, 1994): 51–73.

4   Ivy S.N. Chen and Veronica Wong, "Successful Strategies of Newly Industrialised East Asian Firms in Europe," *European Journal of Marketing* 37 (No. 1, 2003): 275–97.

5   "Nintendo Fined $147 Million in Europe," *San José Mercury News*, October 31, 2002.

6   *Business Week*, November 5, 2001, 55.

7   "Nissan Motor Co. to Accelerate Plan for Cutting Costs," *Wall Street Journal*, June 28, 1994.

8   "Japanese Firms Struggle to Survive the Weak Dollar," *San José Mercury News*, April 9, 1995.

9   Jack L. Hervey, "Dollar Drop Helps Those Who Help Themselves," *Chicago Fed Letter* (March 1988).

10 "Legal Charges Keep Electric Golf Cart Going – to Court," *Wall Street Journal*, May 24, 1995.

11 Michael Leidy, "Antidumping: Unfair Trade or Unfair Remedy?" *Finance & Development* (March 1995): 27–9.

12 "Micron Loses Ruling on Taiwan Chip Sales," *San José Mercury News*, November 20, 1999.

13 "Import Administration," *Export America* (August 2001): 10–12.

14 "WTO Panel Dumps on the US," *Business Week*, September 11, 2000, 53.

15 Hans Peter Lankes, "Market Access for Developing Countries," *Finance & Development* (September 2002): 8–13.

16 "A US Trade Ploy That Is Starting to Boomerang," *Business Week*, July 29, 2002, 64–5.

17 "EU Launches DVD Price Probe," *The Nation*, June 13, 2001.

18 "Invasion of the Cartel Cops," *Business Week*, May 8, 2000, 130.

19 "Cartel Cops."

20 Harry G. Broadman, "Competition and Business Entry in Russia," *Finance & Development* (June 2001): 22–5.

21 Carmen M. Reinhart and Miguel A. Savastano, "The Realities of Modern Hyperinflation," *Finance & Development* (June 2003): 20–1.

22 "Taxing Multinationals: The Donnybrook Ahead," *Business Week*, September 9, 2002, 86–7.

23 Mohammad F. Al-Eryani, Pervaiz Alam, and Syed H. Akhter, "Transfer Pricing Determinants of US Multinationals," *Journal of International Business Studies* 21 (No. 3, 1990): 490.

24 "DHL Owes $269 Million, IRS Claims," *San José Mercury News*, October 12, 1995.

25 *Business Week*, March 31, 2003, 81–2.

26 "New Tax Rules Expand Multinationals' Flexibility in Dealings with US Units," *Wall Street Journal*, July 6, 1994.

Chapter 17

Pricing strategies

Countertrade and terms of sale/payment

Money often costs too much.

Ralph Waldo Emerson

CHAPTER OUTLINE

PURPOSE OF CHAPTER

The trade practices of Asian countries (e.g., Malaysia, Indonesia) and Eastern/Central European countries illustrate the fact that money is not the only means of payment. Due to the fact that many Eastern European countries and less developed nations often lack hard currency, they resort to alternative pricing mechanisms. International marketers may thus be forced to enter into some kind of countertrade scheme so as to do business with those countries. Although countertrade may be complex and time-consuming, it is manageable. A section of this chapter is devoted to the examination of countertrade as an alternative method of trading. The various types of countertrade are discussed.

Another section of this chapter deals with pricing terms used in international quotations. To be competitive, it is the job of a responsible exporter to provide a quotation that is complete and meaningful. It is important for both the buyer and the seller to specify and know the point of delivery where risk shifts from one party to another. A poorly prepared quotation results in confusion and possibly a loss of sale.

Finally, the chapter ends with a review of payment methods. The different payment methods involve a certain degree of financing and risk. It is thus critical to specify the timing and means of payment that are satisfactory to both parties. A misunderstanding regarding delivery terms may cause an exporter to become responsible for unintended shipping costs. To make the matter worse, by unknowingly failing to meet contractual obligations, the exporter may not be able to collect payment. While certain safeguards are necessary, they should not be so cumbersome or costly as to deter business.

MARKETING ILLUSTRATION   NONCASH TRADE

Malaysia's 15 billion ringgit ($3.95 billion) plan aims to expand and electrify 635 kilometers of railway that runs down the spine of Malaysia Peninsular. Most of the project will be financed by barter trade. The country will use palm oil to pay Indian and Chinese state-owned railway companies for more than 10 billion ringgit in construction contracts. Funds from palm oil sales are put in a special account and will be paid out to Indian and Chinese contractors as progress payments on the railway job. In the 1990s, Malaysia also used palm oil to buy Russian-built combat planes. Just like Malaysia, many Asian and Eastern and Central European countries have done countertrade deals. Thailand, for example, has exchanged 200,000 tons of 15-percent broken rice for such Indonesian goods as aircraft, freight-train carriages, and ammonia. Indonesia, being cash-strapped, set up a countertrade agreement with Russia in 2003. In order to get four Sukhoi Su-30 fighter jets, four helicopters, and spare parts, Indonesia agreed to trade palm oil, tea, coffee, and fifteen other commodities. The deal was worth $150 million to $175 million.

Sources: "Indonesia Reportedly to Deal Goods for Arms," *San José Mercury News,* April 11, 2003.

COUNTERTRADE

Countertrade, one of the oldest forms of trade, is a government mandate to pay for goods and services with something other than cash. It is a practice which requires a seller, as a condition of sale, to commit contractually to reciprocate and undertake certain business initiatives that compensate and benefit the buyer. In short, a goods-for-goods deal is countertrade.

Unlike monetary trade, suppliers are required to take customers' products for their use or for resale. In most cases these are multiple deals that are separate yet related, and a contract links these separable transactions. Countertrade may involve several products, and such products may move at different points in time while involving several countries. Monetary payments may or may not be part of the deal.

There are three primary reasons for countertrade: (1) countertrade provides a trade financing alternative to those countries that have international debt and liquidity problems, (2) countertrade relationships may provide developing countries and MNCs with access to new markets, and (3) countertrade fits well conceptually with the resurgence of bilateral trade agreements between governments.[1] The advantages of countertrade cluster around three subjects: market access, foreign exchange, and pricing. Table 17.1 lists potential motives for countertrade.

Countertrade offers several advantages. It moves inventory for both a buyer and a seller. The seller gains other benefits, too. Other than the tax advantage, the seller is able to sell the product at full price and can convert the inventory to an account receivable. The cash-tight buyer that lacks hard currency is able to use any cash received for other operating purposes.

Countertrade constitutes an estimated 5 to 30 percent of total world trade. Countertrade greatly proliferated in the 1980s. Perhaps the single most important contributing factor is LDCs' decreasing ability to finance their import needs through bank loans.

Regarding Russia, its officials have estimated that 90 percent or more of the transactions having to do with "critical imports" involve reciprocal trade exchanges. Countertrade in Russia may proliferate because, with the Russian banking system in disarray, it is difficult to arrange traditional export financing (e.g., letter of credit). Noncash forms of payment may account for as much as two-thirds of all transactions in Russia. There are thousands of intermediaries acting as barter specialists. One deal involves a governor paying for a $17 million airplane by trading gas paid to his government in lieu of energy royalties, giving a middleman commission of 10 percent. Velta Co., once one of the Soviet Union's biggest bicycle makers, stays in business by swapping its bicycles for raw materials and electric power. The company's 4000 employees have to accept one bicycle a month in lieu of a paycheck.[2]

Table 17.1 Potential motives for countertrade

	Types of countertrade				
	BT[1]	CA/ST[2]	CP[3]	BB[4]	OF[5]
Avoids using foreign exchange	Yes	Yes	No	Rarely	No
Avoids repayment of external debt	Yes	Yes	No	No	No
Hides price discounts	Yes	Yes	No	No	No
Shifts risk	Yes	Yes	Yes	Yes	Sometimes
Substitute for foreign direct investment	No	No	Yes	Yes	Yes
Political factors dominant	No	Yes	No	No	Yes

Notes
1 BT   Barter
2 CA/ST   Clearing arrangement/switch trading
3 CP   Counterpurchase
4 BB   Buyback
5 OF   Offset

Source: Jean-François Hennart, "Some Empirical Dimensions of Countertrade," Journal of International Business Studies 21 (No. 2, 1990): 248.

Russia is a virtual economy dominated by barter, mutual nonpayment, and money surrogates, such as promissory notes (veksel), and tax authorities have been forced to collect in-kind tax payments. Countertrade is a consequence of failures in corporate governance. In this regard, countertrade is both a means of avoiding payment of private or public debts in cash and a way of concealing the real state of affairs — not only from tax authorities but also from minority shareholders and employees. Noncash settlements make it possible for owner-managers to degrade assets and divert cash flows in a less transparent way.[3]

Countertrade is pervasive in Russia for a number of reasons. Direct subsidies to enterprises were cut and demand for many industrial products fell after price and trade liberalization. The ensuring credit crunch could not be solved by banks because bank lending to enterprises is very limited. As a result, the enterprises ran up arrears to suppliers and finally used offsets to settle these arrears. The state itself also fostered the noncash economy by allowing tax offsets. The federal and local governments accepted goods in lieu of tax payments, and state utilities also accepted most of their receipts in kind.[4]

Noncash transactions, by substituting for trade and bank credit, help firms to survive in a credit-constrained environment. In the case of time-lagged nonmonetary deals, an enterprise essentially enjoys a credit from its partner because a payment does not have to be made until later. Even in the case of a spot barter, a seller is forced to accept either goods now or money later, being mindful of the fact that "later" may turn out to be "never." This artificial demand allows goods to be produced by the old-style, inefficient enterprises that should have gone out of business.[5]

Because of the nontransparent nature of countertrade, there are implicit subsidies from the state in the form of tax offsets which amount to tax discounts. Because barter prices are arbitrary, tax evasion is facilitated. In addition, by allowing inefficient enterprises to remain, countertrade acts as an entry barrier for new firms. There is a vicious cycle: barter makes it harder to screen firms and monitor

their performance. As their access to bank credit is further reduced, they have to barter even more.

Types of countertrade

There are several types of countertrade, including barter, counterpurchase, compensation trade, switch trading, offsets, and clearing agreements. Figure 17.1 provides a classification of countertrade.

Barter

Barter, possibly the simplest of the many types of countertrade, is a one-time direct and simultaneous exchange of products of equal value (i.e., one product for another). By removing money as a medium of exchange, barter makes it possible for cash-tight countries to buy and sell. Although price must be considered in any countertrade, price is only implicit at best in the case of barter. For example, Chinese coal was exchanged for the construction of a seaport by the Dutch, and Polish coal was exchanged for concerts given by a Swedish band in Poland. In these cases, the agreement dealt with how many tons of coal were to be given by China and Poland rather than the actual monetary value of the construction project or concerts. It is estimated that about half of US corporations engage in some form of barter, primarily within the local markets of the USA.

Counterpurchase (parallel barter)

Counterpurchase occurs when there are two contracts or a set of parallel cash sales agreements, each paid in cash. Unlike barter, which is a single transaction with an exchange price only implied, a counterpurchase involves two separate transactions — each with its own cash value. A supplier sells a facility or product at a set price and orders unrelated on nonresultant products to offset the cost to the initial buyer. Thus the buyer pays with hard currency, whereas the supplier agrees to buy certain products within a specified period. Therefore, money does not need to change hands. In effect, the practice

Figure 17.1 *Classification of forms of countertrade*

Source: Jean-François Hennart, "Empirical Dimensions," 245.

allows the original buyer to earn back the currency. GE won a contract worth $300 million to build aircraft engines for Sweden's JAS fighters for cash only after agreeing to buy Swedish industrial products over a period of time in the same amount through a counterpurchase deal. Iraq persuaded the New Zealand Meat Board to sell $200 million worth of frozen lamb for a purchase of the same value of crude oil. Brazil exports vehicles, steel, and farm products to oil-producing countries from whom it buys oil in return.

Compensation trade (buyback)

A compensation trade requires a company to provide machinery, factories, or technology and to buy products made from this machinery over an agreed period. Unlike counterpurchase, which involves two unrelated products, the two contracts in a compensation trade are highly related. Under a separate agreement to the sale of plant or equipment, a supplier agrees to buy part of the plant's output for a number of years. For example, a Japanese company sold sewing machines to China and received payment in the form of 300,000 pairs of pajamas. Russia welcomes buyback.

Switch trading

Switch trading involves a triangular rather than bilateral trade agreement. When goods, all or part, from the buying country are not easily usable or saleable, it may be necessary to bring in a third party to dispose of the merchandise. The third party pays hard currency for the unwanted merchandise at a considerable discount. A hypothetical example could involve Italy having a credit of $4 million for Austria's hams, which Italy cannot use. A third-party company may decide to sell Italy some desired merchandise worth $3 million for a claim on the Austrian hams. The price differential or margin is accepted as being necessary to cover the costs of doing business this way. The company can then sell the acquired hams to Switzerland for Swiss francs, which are freely convertible to dollars.

Offset

In an offset, a foreign supplier is required to manufacture/assemble the product locally and/or purchase local components as an exchange for the right to sell its products locally. In effect, the supplier has to manufacture at a location that may not be optimal from an economic standpoint. Offsets are often found in purchases of aircraft and military equipment. One study found that more than half of the companies countertrading with the Middle East were in the defense industry and that the most common type of countertrade was offset.[6] These companies felt that countertrade was a required element in order to enter these markets.

Clearing agreement

A clearing agreement is a clearing account barter with no currency transaction required. With a line of credit being established in the central banks of the two countries, the trade in this case is continuous, and the exchange of products between two governments is designed to achieve an agreed value or volume of trade tabulated or calculated in nonconvertible "clearing account units." For example, the former Soviet Union's rationing of hard currency limited imports and payment of copiers. Rank Xerox decided to circumvent the problem by making copiers in India for sale to the Soviets under the country's "clearing" agreement with India. The contract set forth goods, ratio of exchange, and time length for completion. Any imbalances after the end of the year were settled by credit into the next year, acceptance of unwanted goods, payment of penalty, or hard currency payment. Although nonconvertible in theory, clearing units in practice may be sold at a discount to trading specialists who use them to buy saleable products.

Problems and opportunities

Although countertrade is a common and growing practice, it has been criticized on several fronts. First, countertrade is considered by some to be a form of protectionism that poses a new threat to world trade. Such countries as Sweden, Australia, Spain, Brazil, Indonesia, and much of Eastern Europe demand reciprocity in order to impose a discipline on their balance of payments. In other words, imports must be offset by exports. Indonesia links government import requirements in contracts worth more than Rp. 500 million to the export of Indonesia products, other than oil and natural gas, in an equivalent amount to the foreign-exchange value of the contract.

Second, countertrade is alleged to be nothing but "covert dumping." To compensate any supplying partners for the nuisance of taking another product as payment, a countertrading country frequently trades its products away at a discount. If the countertrading country discounts directly by selling its goods itself in another market instead of through a foreign firm, dumping would clearly occur, but, according to an International Trade Commission study, the practice does not seem to be harmful to the USA. Countertrade activity actually results in US exports always greatly exceeding the value of imports. Thus it would appear that many products which US firms agree to take from their customers for overseas marketing are not dumped back on the US market.

Third, countertrade is alleged to increase overhead costs and ultimately the price of a product. Countertrade involves time, personnel, and expense in selling a customer's product – often at a discount. If another middleman is used to dispose of the product, a commission must also be paid. Because of these expenses, a selling company has to raise the price of the original order to compensate for such expenses as well as for the risk of taking another product in return as payment. The fact that the goods are saleable – either for other goods or, in the end, for cash somewhere else – means that additional and probably unnecessary costs will be incurred. As explained by Fitzgerald, "Countertrade requirements, like any trade restrictions, increase the cost of doing business. These costs cannot be passed into the international market but must be borne within the country imposing the requirements."[7] It is believed that barter transactions are

responsible for reducing Russia's revenues by 500 billion rubles.[8]

Related to this charge of increasing costs is the problem of marketing unwanted merchandise that may remain unsold. A company may have to take on the added job of marketing its customer's goods if it does not want to lose business to rivals who are willing to do so. McDonnell Douglas was able to secure a contract to sell 250 planes to former Yugoslavia only after agreeing to market such Yugoslav goods as hams and other foods, textiles, leather goods, wine, beer, mineral water, and tours. The company had a difficult time selling the $5 million worth of hams and finally did so to its own employees and suppliers. With regard to the Yugoslavian tours, the best the company could do was to offer the trips as incentives to employees.

Financing, essential in virtually all types of conventional transactions, becomes more complicated in the case of countertrade. This is especially true when the sale of one product is contingent on the purchase of an unrelated product in return. Understandably, banks may hesitate to provide credit for such a deal because of their concern that the exporter may not be able to profitably dispose of the product given to the exporter as payment.

When a company is unable or does not want to be concerned with disposing of the product taken from its customer, it can turn to companies that act as intermediaries. The intermediaries may agree to dispose of the merchandise for a commission or they may agree to buy the goods outright. The Mediators is one such middleman organization which operates a $500 million a year business globally.

An examination of countertrade literature found that an overwhelming number of the published articles were theoretical rather than empirical.[9] There are a few empirical studies, however, that have shed some light on the practice of countertrade. According to one model, developing countries which impose countertrade have the following characteristics: declining foreign exchange reserves, commodity terms of trade, balance of trade, and increasing debt service ratios. There is some evidence that these

501

variables can help exporters identify those countries which are likely to be countertraders.[10]

The results of one study dispel some widely held views about countertrade. First, the relationship between a country's credit rating and its propensity to countertrade is not as strong as commonly believed. Second, buyback and counterpurchase are substitutes for foreign direct investment. Third, there is a surprisingly large volume of countertrade between developing countries themselves. Fourth, each countertrade type seems to have its own separate motivation (see Table 17.1). Barter allows exchange without the use of money and explicit prices. Barter is therefore useful in order to bypass: (1) exchange controls, (2) public or private price controls, and (3) a creditor's monitoring of imports.[11]

Those firms that tend to benefit from countertrade are the following: (1) large firms that have extensive trade operations from large, complex products; (2) vertically integrated firms that can accommodate countertrade takebacks; and (3) firms which trade with countries that have inappropriate exchange rates, rationed foreign exchange, import restrictions, and importers inexperienced in assessing technology or in export marketing. In contrast, firms whose characteristics are the opposite of those enumerated above are likely to encounter significant barriers to countertrade operations and to receive few benefits.[12]

In general, the US government is opposed to government-mandated countertrade. However, recognizing that countertrade is a fact of life, the US government has maintained a hands-off policy toward countertrade arrangements that do not have government intervention or that American exporters choose to pursue. It does not oppose participation by American firms in countertrade transactions when they do not have a negative impact on national security, but the US policy prohibits federal agencies from promoting countertrade in their business and official contacts.[13]

Interestingly, the US government itself has published a guide on countertrade practices so that US firms may take advantage of marketing opportunities in the former Soviet Union.[14] The irony is that the Russian government, seeking hard currency earnings, now appears to prefer cash transactions and has begun to discourage countertrade transactions of marketable commodities. However, those Russian products that do not have a ready market will probably still require some form of countertrade.

There is no question that countertrade is a cumbersome process: yet a firm is unwise not to consider it. Similar to other trade practices, countertrade presents both problems and opportunities. More often than not, problems of countertrade are psychological rather than real obstacles. Problems may be overcome. One need only remember that in the final analysis all goods can be converted into cash.

PRICE QUOTATON

A quotation describes a specific product, states the price for that product as well as a specified delivery location, sets the time of shipment, and specifies payment terms. When a company receives an inquiry from abroad, the quotation must be very detailed in terms of weight, volume, and so on because of the customer's unfamiliarity with foreign products, places, and terms. Since the time of shipment is crucial, the prepared quotation should specify whether the time mentioned is from the factory or the port of export and whether it includes the estimated inland transit time. Furthermore, price quotations should state explicitly that they are subject to change without notice. It is a good idea to specify the precise period during which a specific price or offer remains valid.

Because it is often requested by a buyer, a **pro forma invoice** may have to be prepared and supplied with or instead of the quotation. Even when it is not requested, it is still good business practice to include it with any international quotation. This type of invoice is not for payment purposes; it is essentially a quotation in an invoice format. The buyer uses it to apply for an import license or to arrange for funds. A pro forma invoice should be conspicuously marked "pro forma invoice," and it should include a statement certifying that the pro forma invoice is true and correct as well as a statement describing the country of origin of the products.

TERMS OF SALE

Trade terms

The quotation must include terms of sale. In the USA, it is customary to ship FOB factory, freight collect, or COD. Such terms, however, are inappropriate for international business, and other terms such as EXW, FAS, FOB, CFR, CIF, DEQ, and DDP should be used instead.

All companies should use Incoterms which are a set of international rules used to interpret the most common terms in foreign trade. Developed under the auspices of the International Chamber of Commerce, Incoterms are recognized by the United Nations Commission on International Trade Law as a global standard. By defining the responsibilities of buyers and sellers for delivery of goods under sales contracts, the use of Incoterms reduces uncertainties by eliminating varying interpretations of foreign trade terms. Because there are several versions of Incoterms, the seller should clearly refer to Incoterms 2000 whenever the terms are used (e.g., FOB London Incoterms 2000).[15]

Incoterms have four basic categories. The E terms are used when seller will make goods available to the buyer on the seller's own premises. F terms are used when the seller will be required to deliver goods to a carrier appointed by the buyer. C terms are used

when the seller will be required to contract for carriage, but will not assume risk of loss or damage to goods, or of additional costs that may occur after shipment and dispatch. Finally, D terms require the seller to bear all costs and risks needed to bring goods to the place of destination. In general, Incoterms base the interpretations on the party who is best equipped to handle the task. For example, loading and unloading obligations have been shifted to the seller under the free carrier seller's place term because this shipment is being unloaded at the seller's place and because the seller will have personnel and equipment available to load.

Table 17.2 describes the point of delivery and risk shift for these different terms of sale. These terms are discussed next.

Ex works (EXW) or ex – named point of origin

Ex means *from*, and the price quoted is calculated from the point of origin. There are several variations of this term, and they include *ex factory*, *ex warehouse*, *ex mill*, *ex plantation*, and *ex mine*. Under these terms, the seller makes goods available to the buyer at a specific time and place, usually at the seller's place of business or warehouse. The buyer takes delivery at the seller's premises and bears all risks and expenses from that point on.

FAS – named port of shipment

FAS stands for *free alongside ship*. Under this term, the price includes delivery of goods along side the

Table 17.2 Point of delivery and where risk shifts from seller to buyer

	EXW	FAS	FOB	CFR	CIF	DEQ	DDP
Supplier's warehouse	X						
Export dock		X					
On board vessel			X	X	X		
Import dock						X	
Buyer's warehouse							X
Main transit insurance risk on	Buyer	Buyer	Buyer	Buyer	Seller	Seller	Seller

vessel or other mode of transportation, and the seller pays all charges up to that point. This term does not include the cost of loading. It is customary to use the port of export as the point of origin for this transaction. The seller's legal responsibility ends once it has obtained a clear wharfage receipt. A significant change should be noted. Under Incoterms 2000, the seller is required to clear the goods for export. Previous Incoterms versions required the buyer to arrange for export clearance.

FOB – named point

FOB stands for *free on board*. Like the other terms within the quotation, the point where the price is applicable must be mentioned. There are a number of classes, and the point in question may be any one of these: the named inland carrier at the named inland point of departure, the named inland carrier at the named point of exportation, the named port of shipment, and the named inland point in the country of importation.

Nevertheless, the point used for quotation is usually the port of export. In such a case, the price includes local delivery and loading. The seller's responsibility does not end until goods have actually been placed aboard the ship and a bill of lading issued. The buyer arranges for overseas transportation and bears all costs and risks from the time the goods are placed on board (i.e., passes the ship's rail).

CFR – to named point of destination

CFR stands for *cost and freight*. Usually, this term will name the overseas port of import as the point in question. The price generally includes the cost of transportation to the named point of debarkation. The buyer, in turn, is expected to pay for insurance. Like FOB, the risk of loss or damage to the goods is transferred from the seller to the buyer when the goods pass the ship's rail.

CIF – to named point of destination

CIF stands for *cost, insurance, and freight*. Again, the point used for quotation may be any location, but

the International Chamber of Commerce recommends that this point should be the destination. The CIF price includes the cost of goods, insurance, and all transportation charges to the point of debarkation (destination). The delivery costs are thus extended beyond the country of export. Although the price covers more items or activities than FOB, the seller's obligations still end at the same stage (i.e., when goods are aboard or loaded). The seller pays for insurance, and the seller's insurance company assumes responsibility once the goods are loaded. Firms exporting to the EU should note that duties are imposed on the CIF value of the shipment.

Delivered ex quay (DEQ) – named port of destination

The seller is required to deliver the goods to the quay at the predefined port of destination and clear them for importation. The seller must also take on all risks and costs including duties, taxes, and any other charges. To avoid confusion, the term should mention either "duty paid" or "duty unpaid."

DDP – delivered duty paid

An example of this kind of quotation is "duty paid landed US." With the payment of this price, the seller undertakes the delivery of goods to the place named in the country of import, generally the buyer's warehouse, with all costs and duties paid. The seller obtains an import license if required and arranges for an overseas customhouse broker to clear the merchandise through customs and to act as a freight forwarder by forwarding the goods locally to the final destination.

The terms of sale mentioned above also have some variations. For example, **CPT** (carriage paid to) and **CIP** (carriage and insurance paid to) – to a named place of destination – are used in place of CFR and CIF respectively for shipment by modes other than water.[16] In the case of **FCA** (free carrier) to a named place, the term replaces "FOB named inland port" and may be used for multimodal transport, container stations, and any mode of transport (including air).

Quotation guidelines

Although the potential buyer will probably specify the terms to be used, the seller should make certain that the quotation or price is meaningful when specific terms are not requested. It is unwise for a company in a suburb of Chicago to quote a price as "FOB Evanston, not export packed." The buyer may have no way of knowing that Evanston is a suburb of Chicago. Even if the buyer does know where Evanston is, that firm would have difficulty determining how much the local transportation or freight charges would be to move the goods from Evanston to the Chicago port. Moreover, the buyer would surely be interested in knowing what the packing costs for export are, since the merchandise would have to be packed for export. Without a meaningful quote, it is difficult to receive serous consideration from a potential buyer.

Whenever possible, the exporter should quote CIF. Better still, the quote should include a breakdown for the C(ost), I(nsurance), and F(reight). The buyer is then aware of all the relevant costs needed to get the product to the port in its country, and the buyer can decide whether it should arrange for the insurance and/or freight. If the seller needs assistance, a freight forwarder would be helpful in determining the CIF price.

Although the CIF price yields the greatest amount of information for the buyer, terms other than CIF may prove more appropriate under certain circumstances. If the exporter needs to conserve cash, the exporter should not quote CIF or any terms beyond it (e.g., delivered duty paid). If currency convertibility is a problem, FOB terms may be more desirable for both parties; that is, the buyer pays freight in its own currency or arranges to use a ship from its own country. China, for example, controls shipping arrangements for imports and exports in order to preserve foreign exchange and retain the insurance business. The country's foreign trade corporations (FTCs), responsible for most foreign trade, prefer selling on CIF terms while buying FOB in order to underwrite all freight charges and insurance themselves. One potential problem encountered in this case is that ships arranged for the Chinese FTCs have been known to arrive considerably late, incurring high interest and warehousing costs for American firms. Moreover, delays at Chinese ports are another problem, and that can hold up the payment even more.

METHODS OF FINANCING AND MEANS OF PAYMENT

There are several payment methods. It should be noted that how buyers handle payments can vary

---

MARKETING STRATEGY 17.1   QUOTATION

A quotation describes the product, its price, time of shipment, terms of sale, and terms of payment. A good quotation should include the following:

1 buyer's name and address
2 buyer's reference number and date of inquiry
3 brief description of requested products
4 price of each item
5 gross and net shipping weight
6 total cubic volume and dimensions packed for export
7 trade discount

8 delivery point
9 terms of sale
10 terms of payment
11 insurance and shipping costs
12 validity period for quotation
13 total charges to be paid by customer
14 estimated shipping date to factory or US port
15 estimated date of shipment arrival.

Source: "Price, Quotations, and Terms of Sale Are Key to Successful Exporting," *Business America,* October 4, 1993, 12–15.

from one part of the world to another. In Asia, the typical payment terms of sixty to ninety days are common and considerably longer than those in the USA. Credit cards and checks are pretty much a US phenomenon. In Europe and elsewhere, credit cards are mainly used by the affluent. For online purchases beyond the US border, account-to-account (A2A) payments seriously challenge credit and debit cards. A2A payments make it possible for consumers to move money between their own accounts, send cash to a friend or relative, or pay a merchant or utility. Not requiring a plastic card, paper checks, or cash handling, the transfer of funds takes place via a direct electronic link between a user's bank and a recipient's bank. A2A transfers are not only easy to use, but they also enable merchants to receive a payment more quickly without having to wait for a check in the mail. "There are cultural differences between the US and other countries that extend to the way consumers pay for a purchase. Not only are there still a lot of cash-oriented societies, but a lot of countries don't have the same approach to card acquiring and processing as the US."

Some methods provide financing to buyers, whereas other methods assure sellers of prompt payment.[17] Table 17.3 compares these payment methods. Figure 17.2 shows payment terms risk/ cost tradeoff.

Consignment

When a consignment is used, goods are shipped but ownership is retained by the seller. This means that the product is furnished on a deferred-payment basis, and once the product is sold the seller is reimbursed by the consignee. In effect, the seller is providing full financing for the consignee. The problem with consignment sales is that a high degree of risk prevails. First of all, it is costly to arrange for the return of merchandise that is unsold. In addition, due to the distance involved, the seller has difficulty keeping track of the inventory and its condition. Certain safeguards are thus necessary. For example, the contract should specify the party responsible for property insurance in the event that there is damage to the merchandise while in the possession of the consignee. Because of these problems and difficulties, the method is not used widely by American exporters. Consignment, however, can be a satisfactory arrangement when the sale involves an affiliated firm or the seller's own sales representative or dealer.

Open account

With an open account, goods are shipped without documents calling for payment, other than the invoice. The buyer can pick up goods without having to make payment first. The advantage with the open account is simplicity and assistance to the buyer, who does not have to pay credit charges to banks. In return the seller expects that the invoice will be paid at the agreed time. A major weakness of this method is that there is no safeguard against default, since a tangible payment instrument does not exist. The lack of payment instrument also

Figure 17.2 *Export payment terms risk/cost tradeoff*

Source: *Business America*, February 1995, 6.

Table 17.3 *Methods of payment*

American firms involved in international trade face a unique set of problems. Ultimately, the goal of any exporter is to make a sale and be paid. In return, the importer wants to receive the agreed upon goods. Factors such as distance, time, language, culture and country regulations must be taken into consideration by the prospective parties, if their needs are to be satisfied. The importer or exporter should ask himself some of the following questions before selecting the most appropriate method of payment.

- How reliable is the exporter?
- How long has the exporter been shipping?
- Is the exporter's product subject to inspection?
- How creditworthy is the importer?
- Has the importer demonstrated the ability to pay promptly?
- Can the importer count on getting the goods on time?
- What credit terms are offered by the competition?
- What are the political and economic conditions within the importer's and exporter's countries?
- What is the value of the goods?
- Is this a one-time shipment or does the possibility exist for additional orders?
- Is the product standardized or specialized, and is it resaleable?

After carefully evaluating the previous questions the importer or exporter is now prepared to select the proper payment method.

Method	Payment	Goods available to buyer	Risk to exporter	Risk to importer
Cash in advance	Before shipment	After payment	None	Relies on exporter to ship goods as ordered
Letter of credit	When goods shipped and documents comply, with L/C*	After payment	Little or none depending on L/C*	Relies on exporter to ship goods described in documents
Sight draft, documents against payment	On presentation of draft to buyer	After payment	Buyer can refuse goods	Same as L/C* unless he can inspect goods before payment
Time draft, documents against acceptance	On maturity of draft	Before payment	Relies on buyer to pay draft	Same as above
Open account	As agreed	Before payment	Relies completely on buyer to pay his account	None

Note
*L/C denotes letter of credit. The terms "exporter," "beneficiary" and "seller" are used interchangeably throughout the workbook unless otherwise noted. The terms "importer," "applicant" and "buyer" are also interchangeable.

Source: International Workbook (Chicago: Unibanc Trust, 1985), 1. Reprinted with permission of Unibanc Trust.

makes it difficult to sell the account receivable. To compound the problem, the buyer often delays payment until the merchandise is received – a standard practice in many countries.

Because of the inherent risks of an open account, precautions should be taken. The seller must deter-mine the integrity of the buyer by relying on prior experience, or through a credit investigation. Toward this end there are several organizations that can provide some assistance in terms of credit information. First, there are commercial credit agencies such as the International Dun and Bradstreet's

American Foreign Credit Underwriters Corp. Second, such organizations as chambers of commerce and trade associations may be contacted. In addition, commercial banks and their overseas branches or correspondent banks usually have some useful credit information. Finally, government sources can also be valuable. World Traders Data Reports, for example, has a great deal of information on foreign firms. In any case, a prudent credit decision should take into account an importing country's political risk and economic conditions.

Before granting credits, an exporter needs to assess a buyer's creditworthiness. Credit bureaus overseas should be consulted. In addition, credit scoring is another useful technique. Credit scoring is a process that converts customer credit and financial information into a numerical format that is then combined to create a score. The scores will represent the levels of risk. There is a general consensus that international business involves many risks that include customer credit worthiness, country (economic and political), bank (transactional and portfolio), transitional market, currency, legal (contract), regulatory and systematic failure. But credit executives do not agree on whether it is possible to construct an automated scoring model that is robust enough to address all the risks simultaneously without requiring a judgmental factor.

Credit insurance is another useful tool to mitigate risks. This is a standard practice in European business-to-business transactions. The advantages are protection against buyer insolvency, greater borrowing power, and higher sales. However, the insurance, while covering a buyer's inability to pay, does not cover the buyer's unwillingness to pay. As such, disputes related to a buyer's dissatisfaction with the goods are not covered. Some sellers are hesitant to pay the cost of insurance, typically between 0.1 and 0.4 percent of sales for domestic accounts and between 0.25 to 1 percent of covered sales for export accounts. They do not realize that their own bad debt reserves are actually a form of credit insurance.[18]

Cash in advance

The seller may want to demand cash in advance when:

1 The buyer is financially weak or an unknown credit risk.
2 The economic/political conditions in the buyer's country are unstable.
3 The seller is not interested in assuming credit risk, as in the case of consignment and open account sales.

Because of the immediate uses of money and the maximum protection, sellers naturally prefer cash in advance. The problem, of course, is that the buyer is not eager to tie up its money, especially if the buyer has some doubt about whether it will receive the goods as ordered. By insisting on cash in advance, the seller shifts the risk completely to the buyer, but the seller may end up losing the sale by this insistence.

Bill of exchange (draft)

A means of financing international transactions is through a bill of exchange or draft, which is a request for payment (see Figure 17.3). The request is an unconditional order in writing from one person (drawer) requiring the person to whom it is addressed (drawee) to pay the payee or bearer on demand or at a fixed or determinable time. The drawer, usually the exporter, is the maker or originator of the draft requesting payment. The drawee, usually the buyer, is the party responsible for honoring or paying the draft. The payee may be the exporter, the exporter's bank, the bearer, or any specified person. In short, a draft is a request for payment. It is a negotiable instrument that contains an order to pay a payee. As noted by John Stuart Mill many years ago, the purpose is to save expense and minimize the risk of transporting precious metals from place to place as payment of imports. The bill of exchange simply allows banks to make adjustments by debiting or crediting accounts maintained in buyer or seller names with other banks.

IT'S THE LAW 17.1   NIGERIAN SCAMS

Nigerian scam artists have made headlines in the USA. The *Wall Street Journal*, for example, has published lengthy articles describing how they have defrauded American firms and citizens. Crooks have gone high-tech. Instead of using mailing or faxing their scam letters, they now rely on e-mail. In one year alone, Americans fell for the scam and lost $100 million after giving out their account numbers. If unreported losses can be accounted for, the total should be much higher. The Nigerian scams have been so successful to the point that they are Nigeria's No. 3 or No. 4 export.

The most prevalent method involves money transfer schemes. Claiming to try to defraud the Nigerian government, the scam artists typically propose to transfer millions of US dollars to an overseas bank account owned by a foreign firm which is promised a percentage of the transferred funds as "commission." The funds are alleged to be overpayments from previous government contracts. The crooks then request information about the company's bank, as well as blank, signed company letterhead and pro forma invoices. The firm owning the account is told it will receive a percentage of the transferred funds as "commission." The American firm may also be solicited for a "transaction fee" to enable the supposed transfer of funds. Invariably, American firms, instead of receiving any money for their assistance, find that the Nigerian fraud artists have used the letterhead and bank information to withdraw money from their US accounts.

The following is a scam letter.

NIGERIA NATIONAL PETROLEUM CORPORATION(NNPC) PLOT 19, FALOMO ROAD. IKOYI-LAGOS, NIGERIA.

ATTN: Managing Director/CEO

I am Dr Buba Onuwu director of procurement and contracts with Nigeria National Petroleum Corporation (NNPC). I have decided with my director general

in office to contact you quickly on this business of transferring the sum of USD$30,000,000.00 (Thirty million United States dollars only) into a foreign bank account. The need is very urgent. I got your contact from Nigerian chambers of commerce and it is with business trust that made me to contact you in this matter. I write to solicit for the transfer of this money into your account. This money was generated from an over-invoiced contract sum in my corporation (NNPC). We have generally agreed that 20 percent of this said fund is for you as compensation for using your bank account in transferring this money. Ten percent should be for all expenses made for this business, while 70 percent is for us. Please note that we will arrange to meet you immediately after successful conclusion of this transfer. The 70 percent share of ours will be used for investment overseas. Your assistance and cooperation is highly needed. I assure you that this business is 100 percent risk free and as such you should not entertain any fear in dealing with us.

Should this interest you, we will require your banking information as mentioned below: 1. YOUR BANK NAME AND ADDRESS 2. YOUR ACCOUNT NUMBER WITH THE BANK 3. NAME TO BE USED AS BENEFICIARY 4. YOUR BANK TELEPHONE AND FAX NUMBER. Contact me on the above e-mail address and we hope to conclude this business within 14 working days. Please while writing to me don't forget to include your personal telephone and fax numbers, for easy and quicker communication. I anticipate your urgent positive reply.

Best Regards, Dr Buba Onuwu

Sources: "Doing Business in Nigeria: Distinguishing Between the Profitable and the Questionable," *Business America* (December 1997): 30–2; "Nigerian Financial Scam Generating Reader Responses," *San José Mercury News*, April 17, 2003; "The List: Gotcha!" *Business Week*, July 16, 2001, 10; "Ask the TIC," *Export America* (July 2001): 16–17.

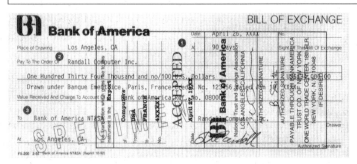

BILL OF EXCHANGE

1. A bill of exchange or draft is an instrument, much like an ordinary check in appearance, which is used as a formal demand for payment in a business transaction.
2. This bill of exchange is a sight draft and is drawn in accordance with both the application for the commercial latter of credit on page 12 and the irrevocable documentary letter of credit on page 16.
3. XYZ Toys Export Ltd., the beneficiary, is the payee, or recipient of funds.

4. As established by the irrevocable letter of credit on page 16, all drafts must be marked with Bank of America's credit number for identification purposes.
5. Bank of America, Los Angeles, is the drawee, or bank to which this bill of exchange is presented for payment.
6. The drawer is the party who signs an order directing the drawee, Bank of America, Los Angeles, to pay a specified sum of money to the payee. In this situation, XYZ Toys Export Ltd. is both the drawer and the payee.

BILL OF EXCHANGE—BANKERS' ACCEPTANCE

1. This "usance" bill of exchange or time draft is Randall Computer Inc.'s demand for payment at 90 days sight, under Banque Emmettrice Internationale's irrevocable usance letter of credit. Randall Computer Inc. would endorse the draft on the reverse side at the time they present it to Bank of America, Los Angeles with their documents.
2. Bank of America, Los Angeles, is the drawee and accepts the draft on April 27, XXXX. The draft will mature on July 26, XXXX, 90 days from the acceptance date. Randall

Computer can either retain the acceptance until maturity or discount the draft through Bank of America, Los Angeles, and receive an amount less than its full face value.
3. On the maturity date of the acceptance, July 26, XXXX, Bank of America, Los Angeles, will pay Randall Computer Inc., or the presenter of the draft if it was discounted and sold in the secondary market, and charge the account of Banque Emettrice Internationale. Unless the acceptance was discounted, Randall Computer Inc. will receive payment for the goods sold to Produits Electroniques S.A. 90 days after sight, in accordance with their agreement.

Figure 17.3 *A bill of exchange*

Source: Trade Banking Services (Bank of America Corporation, 1994), 24–5. Reprinted with permission of Bank of America.

The transaction process occurs in this way. The drawee accepts the draft by signing an acceptance on the face of the instrument. If the buyer does not accept (sign) the bill, the buyer is not given the attached documents to obtain goods from the steamship company, since the shipment is made on the negotiable order bill of lading. In practice, banks are responsible for payment collection. The original order bill of lading is endorsed by the shipper and sent to the buyer's bank along with the bill of exchange, invoices, and other required documents (e.g., consular invoice, insurance certificate, inspection certificate). Once notified by the bank, the buyer pays the amount on the draft and is given the bill of lading, which allows the buyer to obtain the shipment.

There are two principal types of bill of exchange: sight and time. A **sight draft**, as the name implies, is drawn at sight, meaning that it is paid when it is first seen by the drawee. A sight draft is commonly used for either credit reasons or for the purpose of title retention. A **time (usance** or **date) draft** is drawn for the purpose of financing the sale or temporary storage of specified goods for a specified number of days after sight (e.g., thirty, sixty, ninety days, or longer). It specifies payment of a stated amount at maturity. As such, it offers less security than a sight draft since the sight draft demands payment prior to the release of shipping documents. The time draft, on the other hand, allows the buyer to obtain shipping documents to draw up merchandise when accepting the draft, even though the buyer can actually defer payment.

At first sight, it may seem that a time draft is not really different from an open account, since the goods may be obtained or picked up by the buyer before making payment. There is one crucial difference, however. In the case of the time draft, there is a negotiable instrument evidencing the obligation. Since this document may be sold to factors and discounted immediately, the seller can obtain cash before maturity. In the USA, factors are financial institutions that buy accounts receivable from manufacturers.

There are other variations of this kind of draft. If bills of lading, invoices, and the like accompany the draft, this is known as **documents against payment (D/P)**. If financial documents are omitted to avoid stamp tax charges against such documents or if bills of lading come from countries where drafts are not used, this type of collection is known as **cash against documents**. Frequently, the draft terms may read "90 days sight D/A" or **documents against acceptance**. Upon accepting this draft, the buyer is permitted to obtain the documents and the merchandise while not being obliged to make payment until the draft matures.

Bankers' acceptance

A bankers' acceptance assists in the expansion of credit financing. A bankers' acceptance is a time draft whose maturity is usually less than six months. The draft becomes a bankers' acceptance when the bank accepts it; that is, the bank on which the draft is drawn stamps and endorses it as "accepted." Drafts drawn on and accepted by nonbank entities are called **trade acceptances**. US dollar bankers' acceptances are negotiable instruments and may be used in conjunction with letters of credit.[19]

An acceptance becomes the accepting bank's obligation, and once accepted it becomes a negotiable instrument that may be bought or sold in the market like a certificate of deposit (CD) or commercial paper. Daily newspapers usually list the daily prices of bankers' acceptances in the financial section. The acceptance commission is the reason that a bank lends its name, integrity, and credit rating to the instrument. The discount charge is computed at the current prime bankers' acceptance rate from date of purchase to maturity. The bank has primary responsibility for payment to the acceptance holder at maturity, but the draft originator still has secondary liability in case the accepting bank does not honor the claim.

Letter of credit (L/C)

An alternative to the sight draft is a sight letter of credit (L/C). As a legal instrument, it is a written undertaking by a bank through prior agreement with its client to honor a withdrawal by a third party for goods and services rendered (see Figure 17.4). The document, issued by the bank at the buyer's request in favor of the seller, is the bank's promise to pay an agreed amount of money on its receipt of certain documents within the specified time period. Usually, the required documents are the same as those used with the sight draft. In effect, the bank is being asked to substitute its credit for that of the buyer. The bank agrees to allow one party to the transaction (the seller, creditor, or exporter) to collect payment from that party's correspondent

511

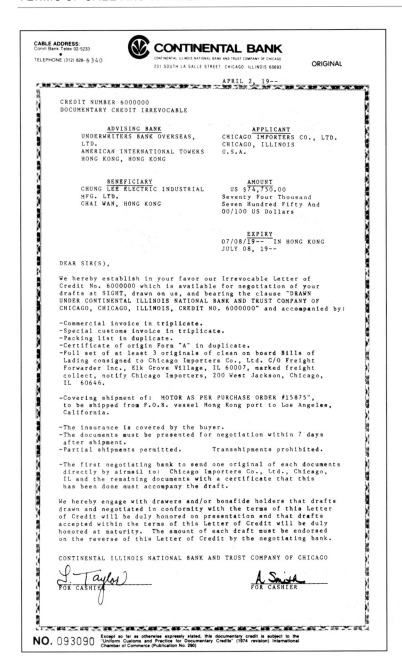

Figure 17.4 *Import commercial letter of credit*

Source: Reprinted with permission of Continental Illinois National Bank and Trust Company of Chicago.

bank or branch abroad. Drafts presented for payment under the L/C are thus drawn on the bank. The importer can repay the bank by either making an appropriate deposit in cash or borrowing all or part of the money from the bank. The drawee (buyer) is usually responsible for the collection

charges by banks at home and overseas. Figure 17.5 examines the process involved in a letter of credit.

Several banks may be involved in the process. The *issuing bank*, as a rule, issues letters of credit for its current customers only, even if collateral is offered by someone else. In contrast, the *advising bank* is the

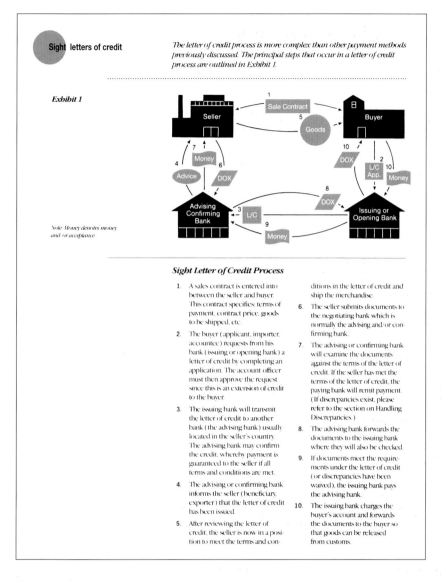

The letter of credit process is more complex than other payment methods previously discussed. The principal steps that occur in a letter of credit process are outlined in Exhibit 1.

Sight Letter of Credit Process

1. A sales contract is entered into between the seller and buyer. This contract specifies terms of payment, contract price, goods to be shipped, etc.

2. The buyer (applicant, importer, accountee) requests from his bank (issuing or opening bank) a letter of credit by completing an application. The account officer must then approve the request since this is an extension of credit to the buyer.

3. The issuing bank will transmit the letter of credit to another bank (the advising bank) usually located in the seller's country. The advising bank may confirm the credit, whereby payment is guaranteed to the seller if all terms and conditions are met.

4. The advising or confirming bank informs the seller (beneficiary, exporter) that the letter of credit has been issued.

5. After reviewing the letter of credit, the seller is now in a position to meet the terms and con-

ditions in the letter of credit and ship the merchandise.

6. The seller submits documents to the negotiating bank which is normally the advising and/or confirming bank.

7. The advising or confirming bank will examine the documents against the terms of the letter of credit. If the seller has met the terms of the letter of credit, the paying bank will remit payment. (If discrepancies exist, please refer to the section on Handling Discrepancies.)

8. The advising bank forwards the documents to the issuing bank where they will also be checked.

9. If documents meet the requirements under the letter of credit (or discrepancies have been waived), the issuing bank pays the advising bank.

10. The issuing bank charges the buyer's account and forwards the documents to the buyer so that goods can be released from customs.

Figure 17.5 *Process involved in a sight letter of credit*

Source: International Workbook (Chicago: UnibancTrust, 1985), 3. Reprinted with permission of UnibancTrust.

bank which notifies the exporter that an L/C has been issued. The issuing bank forwards the L/C to the advising bank (its foreign correspondent), which is usually selected for its proximity to the beneficiary. In the case of a *confirming bank* the same services are performed as the advising bank but also the confirming bank becomes liable for payment.

There are several types of letters of credit, including revocable, irrevocable, confirmed, unconfirmed, standby, back-to-back, and transferable.

Revocable letter of credit

With a revocable L/C, the issuing bank has the right to revoke its commitment to honor the draft drawn on it. Without prior warning or notification to the seller, the bank can cancel or modify its obligation at any time before payment – even after shipment has already been made. Since the bank's commitment is not legally binding, the protection to the seller is minimal. Exporters generally do not want to accept a revocable L/C.

Irrevocable letter of credit

This type of L/C is much preferred to the revocable letter of credit. In this case, once the L/C is accepted by the seller, it cannot be amended in any way or cancelled by the buyer or the buyer's bank without all parties' approval. It is possible, however, for the buyer who receives proper documents but unsuitable goods because of fraud to obtain an injunction preventing the banker from paying the fraudster. When Worlds of Wonder, a US toy company, filed for bankruptcy protection, four Hong Kong creditors/suppliers were able to use irrevocable letters of credit to collect $16.5 million from an undisclosed bank. Another Hong Kong manufacturer, Applied Electronics, could not recover any of its debt since it held no outstanding letters of credit.

Confirmed letter of credit

For the exporter, it is highly desirable for the L/C to be confirmed through a bank in the exporter's country because the exporter then receives an additional guarantee of payment from a second bank (i.e., the confirming bank). The advising bank sends a cover letter along with the original L/C to the exporter, stating that the L/C has been confirmed. A US exporter is in a much better position if there is a US bank that accepts the responsibilty of paying the letter of credit in case of refusal to do so by the buyer and/or the buyer's bank (i.e., issuing bank in a foreign country). In the early 1980s, the political crisis in Iran, for example, made it impossible for many American sellers to enforce the payment terms specified in unconfirmed letters of credit. Naturally, a confirmed L/C is more desirable when

payment is guaranteed by two banks instead of one, especially if there is some doubt about the issuing foreign bank's ability to pay. Moreover, since the confirming bank is located in the same country as the exporter, the exporter is able to receive payment more readily by presenting documents to the confirming bank (rather than the issuing bank abroad) to show that all obligations have been completed.

Honesty is a virtue that cannot be taken for granted in international trade. A seller may, for example, ship unordered or inferior goods while collecting payment. A buyer may refuse to pay for goods received. It must be emphasized that a marketer can never be too cautious or careful when dealing in international trade. In the case of a confirmed letter of credit, the seller should not accept a statement from a bank that "confirms the existence of an L/C" because to confirm the existence of something is not the same thing as to confirm an L/C. A confirmed L/C requires the bank's engagement (i.e., taking obligation). In addition, the bank that confirms the L/C must be financially sound, and the exporter should specify that "the confirming bank must be acceptable to the seller."

Unconfirmed letter of credit

When the L/C is not confirmed by a bank in the seller's country, the certainty is less and payment slower. An unconfirmed letter of credit may still be acceptable as long as the foreign bank that issues it is financially strong. In fact, some multinational banks are so well known that they prohibit letters of credit issued by them to be confirmed because confirmation would tarnish their prestige. However, letters of credit can still be confirmed confidentially.

It is possible to combine the several types of L/C. A letter of credit can be revocable and confirmed, irrevocable and unconfirmed, and so on. For maximum security and earliest payment, the seller should ask for an irrevocable and confirmed L/C. Japan's MITI, for example, requires irrevocable letters of credit before it will issue insurance coverage for exporters to Brazil.

Standby letter of credit (bid or performance L/C)

Unlike the purpose of a commercial L/C, which is trade-related, the purpose of a standby L/C (special purpose or bid or performance L/C) is to guarantee a seller's obligation under a contract or agreement. It is used for such purposes as a performance bond, bid bond, surety bond, and loan agreement (see Figure 17.6). In this case, it is the buyer that requires the seller to open an L/C naming the buyer as a beneficiary, instead of the other way around. The reason for this arrangement is that the subsequent failure of the seller to fulfill the agreement can be

quite damaging to the buyer, since a period of time has elapsed and the buyer has to seek a new supplier all over again. Because of the possibility of a loss of profit as a result of a delay or failure of the seller, the buyer needs to be assured that the seller is indeed capable of delivering goods or completing the project as promised. A standby L/C is thus a bank's guarantee to the beneficiary that a specific sum of money will be received by the beneficiary under certain conditions. If the beneficiary is the buyer, the firm can draw under the standby L/C only when the applicant (seller) fails to meet its obligations. On the other hand, the beneficiary can

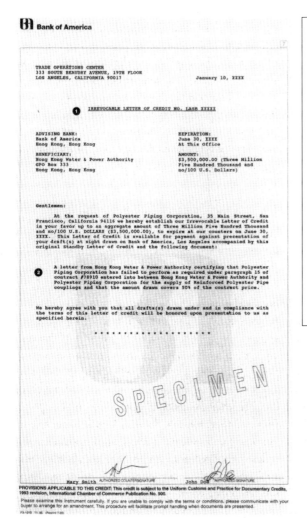

> IRREVOCABLE STANDBY LETTER OF CREDIT
> 1. An irrevocable letter of credit is a letter of credit that cannot be changed or modified without the consent of all parties involved: the applicant, the issuing bank, and the beneficiary. An irrevocable standby letter of credit is issued by a bank, at the request of its customer, to support a contract between the bank's customer and other parties.
> 2. These are the particular terms and conditions of the credit, as outlined in the application for the standby letter of credit. Hong Kong Water & Power Authority, the beneficiary, can draw under the letter of credit only when they can certify that Polyester Piping Corporation has failed to perform according to the terms of the contract. In order for Hong Kong Water & Power Authority to effect a drawing under the credit, they would have to present their draft on Bank of America, Los Angeles, accompanied by the original letter of credit and the required letter of certification.

Figure 17.6
Standby letter of credit

Source: Trade Banking Services (BankAmerica Corporation), 30–1. Reprinted with permission of Bank of America.

515

also be the exporter, which can ask for full or partial payment as the project progresses. Thus the seller is assured of payment for sales made on open account. The buyer draws by presenting the seller's draft with unpaid invoices, and the bank then releases all or part of the money to the seller.

Back-to-back letter of credit

When the seller is a trading firm or middleman who must pay a supplier before asking the supplier to deliver goods to a foreign customer, the middleman may have to obtain an L/C naming the supplier as the beneficiary. This can become a problem if the middleman has inadequate resources to obtain a loan or an L/C from a bank. What the intermediary can do is to use the commitment of the customer's issuing bank (i.e., the customer's L/C) to collateralize issuance of the second L/C by the intermediary's bank in favor of, say, the supplier. This is an entirely separate transaction from the original or master L/C. The intermediary (seller) assigns the proceeds of the original L/C to its bank, which in turn issues the bank's own L/C in favor of the supplier for an amount not exceeding the original L/C.

Because a back-to-back L/C is a transaction entirely separate from the original or master L/C, the bank issuing back-to-back credit is liable for payment to the supplier even if there is a failure to complete the requirements of the original credit. Not surprisingly, many banks are reluctant to be involved in back-to-back transactions, preferring to handle the transferable credit option instead.

Transferable letter of credit

Again, when the seller is an agent or broker for the supplier of the goods, it is difficult for the agent to have an L/C issued to the supplier if the agent's credit standing is weak or unknown. To solve the problem, the agent or broker may request a transferable L/C from the buyer. This type of L/C allows the beneficiary (i.e., agent) to transfer *once* rights in part or in full to another party. The agent as the first beneficiary requests the issuing or advising bank to

transfer the L/C to its supplier (second beneficiary). The transferring bank receives a commission for doing so. A reduction in the amount, unit price, shipment period, and validity period are allowed. Since the agent receives a fee or commission for the selling effort, the bank will pay the supplier based on the supplier's invoices for the transferred (lesser) amount. The agent then receives the difference between the full price (the agent's own invoice) and the lesser amount (the supplier's invoice). The transferee (supplier), after making the shipment, submits documentation to receive payment. After this is completed, the original beneficiary (agent) obtains a commission by substituting its invoice with any other documents evidencing price for the total value of the sale. The beneficiary presents a draft for the difference between the supplier's draft and sales value covered under the credit.

The dilemma for the agent is that, unlike a back-to-back L/C, there is a possibility that the transferable L/C may reveal the identity of the supplier to the agent's customer and vice versa. Once the buyer learns of this identity, the buyer may elect to contact the supplier directly in the future to avoid paying a commission to the agent.

If the original beneficiary (agent) does not want the buyer to be identified, the beneficiary's name or a neutral forwarder's name may be substituted for the buyer's name. The failure of the agent to provide the bank with substitute documents immediately will defeat the whole purpose, since the bank has the right to deliver the transferee's documents to the issuing bank.

Advantages and disadvantages of letters of credit

The L/C offers several advantages. First, it offers security while minimizing risk. The bank's acceptance of the payment obligation is a better credit instrument than a bill of exchange that has been accepted by the buyer. An L/C creates a better relationship with the buyer since all terms are specified and both parties are protected. In addition, the exporter can receive payment before maturity by discounting the L/C. An L/C can be discounted at a lower rate because it offers greater security than a bill of exchange. The discount charge is usually computed at the current prime bankers' acceptance rate from date of purchase to maturity.

For the buyer, the L/C also offers several benefits even though the buyer may have to bear the burden of financing. First, the buyer can buy now and pay later. Second, the L/C offers the assurance of prompt delivery. There is also an expired date for credit, and no payment is made until the goods are placed in the possession of a transport carrier for shipment. In addition, the seller must complete the terms specified in the L/C before payment is released. Third, the buyer may receive a better price since the seller does not have to adopt unnecessary safeguards or to sell the L/C at deep discount. The buyer, as a result, may even qualify for the seller's cash discount.

It is imperative that the seller carefully examine the L/C terms to make certain that he or she understands them and can meet the requirements. The seller must examine such items as the description of the merchandise, trade terms, price, delivery date, required documents, the party responsible for insurance, departure and entry points, and so on. The seller must also determine whether the L/C received is confirmed and irrevocable if requested as such. The seller should not accept an L/C requiring that the inspection certificate be signed by a particular individual because if that individual, due to death or other reasons, cannot sign the certificate, the exporter is unable to fulfill all the requirements and cannot collect payment. A precautionary measure may be to insist that the certificate be issued by a particular inspection company rather than a specific person associated with the company.

In spite of the many advantages, the L/C does have disadvantages as well. The instrument lacks flexibility, is cumbersome, and is the most complex method of obtaining payment. Any changes in the terms require an amendment to the L/C. Although suitable for a routine transaction, the L/C does not work well when the transaction is unusual and requires flexibility. It can also be expensive for the buyer if the government requires a prior deposit before establishing the L/C. For example, Lebanon requires banks to have their customers make a 15 percent deposit on documentary letters of credit on goods to be sold in Lebanon.

Another reason why the L/C can be a burden to the buyer is that it entails credit exposure. As such, the buyer's credit must be approved in advance by the buyer's bank. This is understandable because the L/C is issued on an unsecured basis, and the buyer-applicant only pays when the issuing bank is called on to make payment. Without a satisfactory credit standing, the bank may require cash or other collateral for its own protection. In fact, a cash deposit may not even be acceptable if the importer has financial difficulties or an unknown credit reputation, since prior creditors may later lay claim to that amount of money in the event of the importer's bankruptcy. As a result, the bank will treat a request for an L/C as a request for a loan or line of credit. As such, the practice will tie up a portion of the buyer's available line of credit. Furthermore, L/C fees may range from 1 to 3 percent or perhaps even higher of the L/C amount.[20] These fees, of course, add to the importer's costs.[21]

It should be pointed out that an L/C is not a foolproof document. Guria, a private company based in the Republic of Georgia, was persuaded by an American businessman to relax the terms under which he could collect on an L/C for his handling of the purchase of 2900 metric tons of sugar on behalf of Guria. The businessman then withdrew $768,500, but the sugar was never delivered. In another case, National Westminster Bank PLC paid out $1.8 million on an L/C to an Italian businessman who forged documents to show the bank that 5000 metric tons of sugar were on the way to a buyer in Saudi Arabia. The Saudis found out that the shipment never occurred, and the Czechoslovakian bank that issued the L/C refused to pay the British bank.[22] Certainly, the existence of an L/C is not a substitution for proper business investigation.

The most significant portion of the cost for an L/C is confirmation. The confirmation cost, being variable, may range from about 1 percent for a low-risk country to 6 percent or more for a high risk country (e.g., Russia). The instrument, because of its relative greater degree of safety, has a much lower incidence of losses, reschedulings, or restructurings than the other normal term international loans. For almost two decades, there appear to have been no losses on the confirmed letters of credit, except for the Dominican Republic, Nigeria, and Iraq – countries that after all failed to meet the minimum country risk standards at the time.[23]

CONCLUSION

The exporter must make an effort to quote a meaningful price by using proper international trade terms. When there is doubt about how to prepare a quotation, freight forwarders should be consulted. These specialists can provide valuable information with regard to documentation (e.g., invoice, bill of lading), and the costs relevant to the movement of goods. Special financial documents such as letters of credit, however, require a bank's assistance. International banks have international departments that can facilitate payment and advise clients regarding pitfalls in preparing and accepting documents.

Even when an exporting firm is assured of payment, it still needs to consider the source of payment and to determine whether it is legitimate. The company should adopt money-laundering prevention rules. It is important to know one's client and exercise due diligence so as to avoid undue scrutiny from law enforcement agencies.

CASE 17.1 COUNTERTRADE: COUNTERPRODUCTIVE?

In modern times barter and its numerous derivations, which have conceptually been gathered together under the rubric "countertrade," have gained renewed stature in international trade. This has occurred despite the fact that international money and credit markets have attained unparalleled levels of sophistication.

Where readily acceptable forms of money exchange and viable credit facilities are available, markets shun cumbersome and inefficient barter-type transactions. But, international liquidity problems and government restrictions on the operation of markets have prompted many less-developed countries (LDCs) and nonmarket economies (NMEs), as well as industrial countries, to promote "creative" trade transactions that circumvent the normal exchange medium of modern markets.

The *shortcomings* of countertrade include the following:

1   Countertrade has a high inherent transaction cost.
2   Countertrade limits competitive markets.
3   Countertrade contributes to market distortions that lead to inappropriate economic planning.

Inefficiency in transactions costs

The underlying weakness of countertrade as a mechanism of trade and exchange is its inefficiency. The indivisibility of goods made barter inefficient, for example, and forced those involved with such trade to search for a better way. Barter gave way to goods/services-for-money exchange, which permitted transactions to incorporate divisibility as well as time shifting. The opportunity for more convenient (i.e., efficient), multiparty trade became a reality.

A major factor in the expansion of world trade during the last half of the twentieth century has been the emergence of a few widely accepted currencies, especially the US dollar, as settlement currencies for international transactions. The development of international credit markets to support trade depended on the fact that transactions could be entered into without undue concern by the parties involved as to the delivery of the specific quantity and quality of goods and the timeliness of payment. A key characteristic of this type of market is that the channels of communication and exchange are well defined and relatively simple.

As a consequence of this clarity and simplicity, such markets are efficient. Specifically, the direct and indirect costs involved in the process of exchange account for a relatively small portion of the total cost of the transaction.

Such efficiency is not present in the conditional transactions that make up countertrade. The inefficiency cost must be borne by one or more of the parties involved.

Many countertrade transactions are entered into because the importing country is unable to obtain financing in the international markets and is short of hard-currency reserves. The lack of access, or limited access, to the credit markets may be due to restrictions on the country, placed as a condition for specific new lending by the International Monetary Fund (IMF) or foreign commercial banks. In this environment countertrade is sometimes viewed by an LDC government as a means of engaging in trade without the cost of entering the international finance markets.

Whereas it is correct that countertrade may mean that the international financial markets may not have to be tapped, it is not correct to assume that there are no financing costs associated with a countertrade transaction. In fact, because of the complexity associated with carrying out a countertrade transaction, the cost is higher than if the LDC has had access to those credit markets. Moreover, countertrade may end up subverting the capital and austerity restrictions that in some cases are a part of an IMF/LDC lending agreement.

In countertrade the costs of financing are shifted. They become implicit rather than explicit. The seller may absorb this cost in the form of accepting the obligation to buy or use or resell goods it otherwise would not accept (thus reducing its return on the transaction). Alternatively, the seller may build the transaction's finance costs into the price the buyer must pay. The finance costs are there, though hidden.

Limiting competition

There is another implicit cost when countertrade is required by the LDC or nonmarket economy (NME) buyer as a condition of the transaction. Countertrade limits the potential number of sellers in the market. Not every seller firm is willing or able to engage in countertrade; thus, an LDC or NME buyer that insists on countertrade as part of a trade package limits its potential for obtaining a competitive product, service, or price. The fact is that engaging in countertrade costs the LDC or NME economy more in terms of real resources than a straight commercial transaction.

Market distortions and false signals

Developing countries may not have well-developed international marketing facilities. As a result they often find it difficult to break into international markets with goods and services that are nontraditional for their economy.

In other cases an LDC or NME may choose to develop a new domestic industry by buying the technology and plant from abroad. Domestic demand may not be adequate for an efficient plant size. In response, they may opt for a larger, more efficient (but possibly from a world supply view, redundant) plant with the expectation of placing the marginal production on the international market.

Under such conditions counterpurchase or buyback agreements may be sought by the LDC or NME to finance the importation of plant and equipment for a new industry (as in a buyback agreement) or general imports (as in a counterpurchase agreement). The LDC or NME also may be seeking a more knowledgeable partner to handle the international marketing of goods for which it does not have the expertise.

The difficulty with this approach is that countertrade may be used to get goods onto the international market that would not "make it" under usual conditions and will not be competitive once the buyback agreement expires.

Further, the industrial country firm that accepted the counter-traded goods may dump them, which would be disruptive to international markets. The result may be that the LDC or NME producer may falsely interpret the signals and overestimate the real market demand for the dumped goods as being stronger than a longer-term, unsubsidized, market can bear.

Moreover, the secondary consequences of countertrade transactions are not benign. The inefficiencies of countertrade – the false-price signals that result in the building of redundant plant and equipment – tend to promote the establishment of bureaucracies within governments and private firms that have "bought into" countertrade. In turn, these bureaucracies have a vested interest in maintaining the economic distortions that undergird the growth in countertrade.

Summing up

Countertrade is a significant factor in modern international trade. In its different forms it is used as a marketing tool, as a competitive tool, as a tool to restrict trade alternatives, and as a tool to tie the trade of one country to another country. Countertrade in a modern world economy with highly developed goods, capital, and financial markets appears on its face to be an incongruous development. Countertrade is a costly, inefficient, and disruptive anomaly. Yet observers of international trade suggest that the volume of countertrade is growing.

Countertrade takes place in a world of imperfection where the political and economic policies of government and industry distort the relationships between and within the goods, capital, and financial markets.

Points to consider

1   Discuss the pros and cons of countertrade as a form of trade.
2   As a manufacturing firm located in a developed country, you are interested in taking advantage of the Eastern European markets' movement toward market-oriented economies. However, your potential customers lack hard currency and have asked you to consider countertrade. Are you willing to engage in countertrade? Why or why not?

Source: Abbreviated and adapted from Jack L. Hervey, "Countertrade – Counterproductive?" *Economic Perspectives* (January/February 1989): 17–24.

QUESTIONS

1   Explain these terms of countertrade: barter, counterpurchase, buyback, offsets, clearing agreement, and switch trading.
2   Explain these terms of sale: EXW, FAS, FOB, CFR, CIF, DEQ, and DDP.
3   Explain: (a) bill of exchange, and (b) bankers' acceptance.
4   Explain these types of letter of credit: revocable, irrevocable, confirmed, unconfirmed, back-to-back, and transferable.

DISCUSSION ASSIGNMENTS AND MINICASES

1   Given that countertrade is a fact of life which is not going to go away, is there any valid argument from a *theoretical* standpoint for this method of doing business?

2 Assume that you are a manufacturer being asked to submit a quotation to a potential buyer. How are you going to prepare your quotation in terms of (a) terms of sale and (b) terms of payment?

NOTES

1 Jack L. Hervey, "Countertrade – Counterproductive?" *Economic Perspectives* (January/February 1989): 17–24.

2 "Russia: What Happens When Markets Fail," *Business Week*, April 26, 1999, 50–2.

3 Raj Desai and Itzhak Goldberg, "Stakeholders, Governance, and the Russian Enterprise Dilemma," *Finance & Development* (June 2000): 14–18.

4 "Noncash Transactions Increase in Russia after Transition to Market Economy," *IMF Survey*, November 20, 2000, 381–82.

5 "Noncash Transactions."

6 John A. Angelidis and Nabil A. Ibrahim, "Countertrading with the Middle East: An Empirical Investigation of Challenges and Opportunities," *Journal of Global Marketing* 8 (No. 2, 1994): 97–114.

7 Bruce Fitzgerald, "Countertrade Reconsidered," *Finance & Development* (June 1987): 46–9.

8 Ann Ring, "Countertrade Business Opportunities in Russia," *Business America*, January 11, 1993, 15–16.

9 Sam C. Okoroafo, "An Integration of Countertrade Research and Practice," *Journal of Global Marketing* 6 (No. 4, 1993): 113–27.

10 Sam C. Okoroafo, "A Managerial Approach to Predicting Countertrade Demands by Developing Countries," *Journal of Global Marketing* 6 (No. 1/2, 1992): 171–83.

11 Jean-Francois Hennart, "Some Empirical Dimensions of Countertrade," *Journal of International Business Studies* 21 (No. 2, 1990): 243–70.

12 Donald J. Lecraw, "The Management of Countertrade: Factors Influencing Success," *Journal of International Business Studies* 20 (spring 1989): 41–59.

13 Pompiliu Verzariu, "Trends and Developments in International Countertrade," *Business America*, November 2, 1992, 2–6.

14 *A Guide on Countertrade Practices in the Newly Independent States of the Former Soviet Union* (Washington, DC: US Department of Commerce, 1995).

15 "Incoterms 2000," *Export America*, 11–12. See also the website of the International Chamber of Commerce for Incoterms 2000. Also see www.look4logistics.com.

16 "Price, Quotations, and Terms of Sale Are Key to Successful Exporting," *Business America*, October 4, 1993, 12–15.

17 Banks with international departments have publications that explain the various types of collection methods and documents. For example, see *Trade Banking Services* (BankAmerica Corporation, 1994).

18 "What's This Credit Worth?" *Collections and Credit Risk* (November 2000): 43ff.

19 *Trade Banking Services*, 5.

20 D. Grant McKinnon, "Export Sales – the Importance of Setting Competitive Payment Terms," *Business America* (February 1995): 6–7.

21 For an in-depth discussion see John F. Dolan, *The Law of Letters of Credit: Commercial and Standby Credits*, 2nd edn (Boston, MA: Warren Gorham Lamont, 1991).

22 "Deals Too Sweet to Be True," *Business Week*, July 10, 1995, 122.

23 "Export Payment Terms Adjust the Risk to Exporters and the Cost to Importers," *Business America*, 26–8.

Chapter 18

Sources of financing and international money markets

Owe your banker a thousand pounds, and you are at his mercy. Owe him a million, and the position is reversed.

John Maynard Keynes

CHAPTER OUTLINE

■ Nonfinancial institutions
  ☐ Self-financing and debt financing
  ☐ Equity financing
■ Financial institutions
■ Government agencies
■ International financial institutions/development banks
  ☐ World Bank
  ☐ International Development Association (IDA)
  ☐ International Finance Corporation (IFC)
  ☐ Multilateral Investment Guarantee Agency (MIGA)
  ☐ International Centre for Settlement of Investment Disputes (ICSID)
■ International Monetary Fund (IMF)
  ☐ Special drawing right (SDR)
  ☐ Functions
■ Financial centers
  ☐ Euromarket
  ☐ Asian Dollar Market
■ Conclusion
■ Case 18.1 Too close for comfort

PURPOSE OF CHAPTER

The examples in the marketing illustration below demonstrate the crucial role that financing plays in securing overseas projects. Financing is important to the operations of both importers and exporters. Importers seek financing for the purchase of merchandise. Exporters likewise need financing to manufacture their products and maintain their inventories. Furthermore, overseas buyers attempt to shift the financing function to their suppliers. If an exporter agrees to extend credit, the exporter must in turn obtain financing for this purpose. Financing is not a problem only for small firms. In fact, in the case of international multi-million-dollar projects, sellers' financing is usually expected, and financing terms often separate winners from losers.

Trade finance arises from the export of goods and services, when the buyer and seller negotiate the amount, time, and terms of payment. The financing needs of the seller and buyer are almost always not compatible, and sometimes they may even be in conflict. Naturally, the buyer desires a competitive price and a payment arrangement that does not tie up one's credit line, whereas the seller wants a financing arrangement that offers quick payment and protection against default. The method of trade finance attempts to accommodate these differences. Trade finance can be supplied by parties in the private sector (e.g., the buyer's cash in advance payment) or by parties in the public sector (e.g., a bank's financing of the sale).

The purpose of this chapter is to discuss the various aspects of financing. The chapter covers both the local and international sources of financing that are available to public and private buyers, including the various private and nonprofit financial institutions. The chapter also examines such offshore financial centers as the Euromarket and the Asian Dollar Market.

Any business, no matter how large or small, domestic or international, always requires some kind of financing for its operations. Because international financing must deal with financial and economic conditions in more than one country, this activity involves more uncertainty and complexity than does domestic financing. The greater complexity of international financing, however, is accompanied by a greater number of financing options. In addition to the standard channels, there are also other sources available almost exclusively for international business. These sources include:

1   Nonfinancial institutions
2   Private financial institutions
3   International agencies
4   The International Monetary Fund (IMF)
5   The Euromarket.

MARKETING ILLUSTRATION   MONEY IS AN EMOTIONAL SUBJECT

According to the former chairman of the New York Stock Exchange, "growth in global investing will not allow markets to be competitive if they constrain themselves to a time clock."

Aegon, a Dutch insurer, listed its shares in New York in 1985. At the time, nobody understood the full implications of the listing. By allowing its shares to be traded in the USA, Aegon was able to raise capital. The stock price fourteen years later made it possible for Aegon to use its stock as money to buy Transamerica Corp. The $10.8 billion takeover was financed mainly with stock. In effect, the company became the third largest insurer in the world in terms of market capitalization.

Likewise, DaimlerChrysler, Vodafone Group PLC, and a growing number of competitive European companies have used their soaring stock prices to finance their acquisitions. Daimler was the first of Germany's DAX 30 companies to seek a listing in the USA in 1993. The company's US shares were instrumental in a $335 billion merger with Chrysler Corp. Had the US tax laws been comparable to those of Germany, it might have been Chrysler that acquired Daimler instead.

Amway Asia Pacific Ltd., a Hong Kong-based company, is the exclusive distributor for about 175 products of its parent firm, Amway Corp (see Figure 18.1). Amway Asia Pacific distributes the products in Australia, Hong Kong, Macau, Malaysia, New Zealand, Taiwan, and Thailand. To raise capital to finance its operations, Amway Asia Pacific made an initial public offering in late 1993. Its stock was valued at $18 a share but actually opened on the New York Stock Exchange at $26.50. One reason why the company's stock is attractive is that it gives investors an opportunity to profit from the burgeoning market in China.

Sources: "A Graveyard Shift for the NYSE?" *Business Week,* March 8, 1999, 44; "Memo to Europe's CEOs: Try Listing on Wall Street," *Business Week,* March 8, 1999, 54; "Amway Japan Gears Up for Stock Issue; Analysts Differ on Company's Outlook," *Wall Street Journal,* June 24, 1994.

Building a worldwide business... from Michigan.

Amway's world headquarters in Ada, Michigan, putting the final touches on the metal globe sculpture situated among 60 national flags representing Amway's worldwide presence.

Amway Corporation is proud to be one of the many worldwide operations that got its start in Michigan. In 35 years, Amway has grown from a neighborhood business to a world leader in the direct sales of diverse, high-quality consumer products. Independent Amway distributors are the heart of this company... but Michigan will always be our home.

And you thought you knew us.

If you'd like more information on Amway and its international operations, call 1-800-544-7167
Amway Corporation, 7575 Fulton St. East, Ada, Michigan 49355-0001

Figure 18.1 *Amway and world business*

Source: Reprinted with permission of Amway Corp.

NONFINANCIAL INSTITUTIONS

Self-financing and debt financing

There are several nonfinancial institutions that can provide financing. First, there is self-financing because a business can use its own *capital* or can withhold *dividends* so that profits can be plowed back into the organization for further business expansion. Second, retailers and manufacturers alike may be able to seek *trade credit* and financial assistance from certain middlemen, such as export merchants and trading companies. Third, when joint ventures are formed, *foreign partners* can also lend a helping hand. Fourth, subsidiaries of MNCs may borrow from *affiliated firms* as well as from the *employee retirement fund*.

Finally, the business may decide to raise equity capital by selling *stocks*, or it may depend on debt financing by selling *commercial paper* or *bonds*. Bond buyers or holders are the firm's creditors rather than its owners. US firms may sell bonds in either the USA or foreign countries, with Eurobonds as a prime example. Treasurers of US firms must decide whether their bonds to be sold abroad are to be denominated in the dollar or in foreign currencies. In any case, it should be noted that debt financing requires the services of investment banks. Virtually every multinational bank or multinational brokerage house has a division that acts as an investment bank.

Another source of financing is **venture capital**. Venture capitalists invest funds in a firm in exchange for a share of ownership. Although known for their investments in high-technology firms, venture capitalists have diversified their portfolios. There are about 600 venture capital firms in the USA. Private investors, however, fund most ventures. Venture Capital Network in Durham, New Hampshire, is a nonprofit service affiliated with the University of New Hampshire. Attempting to match entrepreneurs with investors, the Network charges investors $200 a year and those seeking capital $500 annually for registration.

When self-financing is used, a company should take advantage of a tax shelter for its export profit.

Because the EU's exports are exempt from value-added taxes, the US Congress gave a tax break to American firms by creating a **foreign sales corporation** (FSC, pronounced "fisk"). A FSC is a special kind of corporation, making its possible for it to gain a corporate tax exemption from 15 to 32 percent of the earnings generated by the sale or lease of exported goods (i.e., extraterritorial income derived from goods for sale or use abroad). Some 6000 US companies took advantage of it, resulting in a $4 billion tax break. In particular, Boeing Co. was the biggest user of this scheme in 2001, avoiding $222 million in US taxes or 12 percent of its entire earnings that year. Acting on the EU's complaint, the WTO ruled in 1999 that the FSC program was an illegal export subsidy that gave American companies unfair trade advantages. The USA appealed and lost again. The WTO told the USA to change its law or risk paying a penalty that could reach $4 billion in damages. The USA did indeed rewrite its tax law, creating another tax break that was even more lucrative and that could result in $6 billion of tax break.

The rationale or excuse of the USA was that this tax shelter prevented US companies from being taxed twice on income from foreign sources. The WTO panel, however, ruled that the law was an illegal export subsidy because the US government offered a lower tax rate on export profits than on import and domestic profits. The US Treasury Department was forgoing income related only to goods being sent abroad. In addition, the said income had no link to a foreign state and would therefore not be taxed anywhere else. The EU complained that the new US legislation made only cosmetic changes. The WTO later ruled in 2002 against the USA for the third time, stating that the US tax provisions were in violation of the WTO's rules on subsidies.[1] The EU imposed sanctions in 2004.

Based on a survey of private firms in China, 80 percent feel that their lack of access to finance is a serious constraint. These Chinese companies rely heavily on self-financing for both start-up and expansion. The principal owners, start-up teams, and their families provide more than 90 percent of their initial capital. In the case of post-start-up

525

investments, the firms still depend overwhelmingly on internal sources, coming from the principal owners or out of retained earnings. Among the external funding sources, informal channels, credit unions, and commercial banks are about equally represented. Outside equity (including public equity) and public debt markets do not play a significant role. Regarding firm size, internal sources become less important as firms grow larger. For smaller firms, share of commercial bank loans increases with firm size. For the largest firms, commercial banks are the second most important source of funds, after retained earnings. Apparently, banks provide more support for larger and more successful private firms. However, Chinese banks play a relatively small role in financing private firms, with 29 percent of the firms securing loans in the previous five years.[2]

There is conflicting evidence on the relationship between corporate international activity and cost and level of debt financing. To gain a better understanding of the relationship, one study explored the impact of firm internationalization on debt financing by using a market-based sample of American firms. The findings show a nonmonotonic relation between firm international activity and both the cost and level of debt financing. Contrary to prior research, firm international activity is associated with a 13 percent reduction in the cost of debt financing and a 30 percent increase in firm leverage.[3]

A company's nationality may be useful in predicting its financial leverage. *National culture* appears to affect corporate capital structures. According to a sample of 5591 firms across twenty-two countries, countries with high scores on cultural dimensions of "conservatism" and "mastery" tend to have lower corporate debt ratios. Such effects are strong and remain significant even after consideration is given to differences in economic performance, legal systems, financial institutions, and some other well-known determinants of debt ratios.[4]

Equity financing

With regard to the other means of self-financing, it is a common practice for MNCs to use both equity and debt financing. As an example, Munich Re, the world's largest reinsurer, announced in 2003 that it would sell new shares worth $4.4 billion to shore up its capital base.

A company can raise equity capital by selling stock, both in its own country and in foreign markets. American stocks are traded in London, and European stocks are traded in New York. Israel has sixty-two companies quoted on US exchanges, second only to Canada.[5]

It is not surprising that international exchanges like to attract new listings. The New York Stock Exchange, with 234 foreign firms, has been trying to get newly privatized companies in Europe to list in New York.[6] Japanese companies have been paying more attention to this strategy. Toyota first listed its shares on the New York Stock Exchange in 1999, allowing its three long-time shareholders (a bank and two casualty insurers) to sell their holdings for $1.5 billion. NEC Corp., a Japanese computer and communications equipment maker, has also planned to list its existing shares on the New York Stock Exchange. Foreign investors already own about 30 percent of NEC. The listing should enable NEC to later issue new shares to pursue mergers and acquisitions in the USA.[7]

The London Stock Exchange has 524 foreign companies. It claims that it is less expensive to list in London than in New York because its regulatory branch is not as strict as the Securities & Exchange Commission. In addition, a European Union rule allows brokers licensed in one country to deal directly on other European Union exchanges.

American investors interested in buying foreign securities, instead of working through foreign securities firms and exchange currencies, should consider American Depository Receipts (ADRs). Issued by US banks, ADRs represent ownership of a set amount of the respective security on deposit in a foreign branch. Benetton, for example, offers 8 to 9 million (ADRs) worth approximately $150 million on the New York Stock Exchange. For those wanting to own foreign securities when ADRs are not available, they may find it easier to deal with mutual funds that invest in a particular country or region.

Although many firms limit the listing of their securities to their domestic exchanges, the growing internationalization of capital markets suggests that more and more firms perceive that the benefits of listing their stocks on foreign exchanges outweigh the related costs. A study of 459 internationally traded MNCs, with at least one foreign listing on one of nine major stock exchanges, found strong evidence that financial disclosure levels and the level of exports to a given foreign country significantly influenced foreign listing locations.[8]

Another investigation of the motives for listing abroad analyzed data on 481 multinationals. There is a significant correlation between the likelihood of listing abroad and a firm's relative size in its domestic capital market as well as its ratio of foreign to total sales. In general, the absolute size of firms (and their relative size), their main line of business, and their nationality affect the decision to list on foreign stock exchanges. Firms that are larger within their domestic capital markets appear more likely to list abroad. Regarding the extent of a firm's dependence on foreign consumer and product markets, firms that generate a greater portion of their revenues abroad are more likely to list on a foreign stock exchange. Firms are willing to list on stock exchanges located in capital markets that are smaller than their own because of the positive relationship between foreign sales and listing abroad. Furthermore, listing abroad increases visibility in that country and provides free advertising.[9]

Equity markets appear to have a life cycle consisting of four distinct stages. As an equity market becomes more developed and has some degree of credibility, market liquidity increases. In the final (mature) stage, the most active stocks are just as liquid as those listed on industrial country exchanges.[10] There is strong evidence that greater stock market liquidity supports (or precedes) economic growth.[11]

Emerging stock markets vary greatly in terms of the number of firms listed, the number of new listings per year, market capitalization, and so on (see Marketing Strategy 18.1). Naturally, such markets carry significant risk, but emerging stock markets are likely to play an increasingly important role in financing companies' growth. The share of total world capitalization represented by the emerging markets has soared.[12] It goes without saying that the emerging stock markets can be very volatile. Take the case of Turkey. This stock market has alternated between being one of the world's best performing markets and one of the worst. In 1992, the market's

MARKETING STRATEGY 18.1 EMERGING STOCK MARKETS

Emerging economies should create an effective framework for the development of private equity markets. Private equity markets in China are at an embryonic stage of development. In fact, offshore venture funds seem to be a far more important source of capital for start-ups in China than domestic funds. Chinese firms rely more on internal sources of financing than do their counterparts in transition and developed economies.

In transition economies, the share of internal funding is significantly lower in advanced reformers such as Estonia (33 percent), Poland (34 percent), and Lithuania (37 percent). In the USA, a far smaller share of financing is internal. Even for small and medium-sized enterprises under two years old, internal financing reached a maximum of 54 percent of total financing.

Vietnam has a brand new and fledgling stock exchange. The market capitalization is about $48 million, and the average daily turnover is a mere $70,000. Only four companies have listed so far, and all of them happen to be formerly state-owned enterprises. The market is open two hours a day, three days a week.

Sources: Neil Gregory and Stoyan Tenev, "The Financing of Private Enterprise in China," *Finance & Development,* March 2001, 14–17; "Never Mind the Snail's Pace. This Is Capitalism," *Business Week,* November 20, 2000, 57.

loss of 53 percent of its market capitalization was among the worst in the world. The market bounced back the following year, gaining 111 percent and becoming the top performing stock market. Then, in 2001, due to the economic and political crises, the stock market lost 15 percent of its value in one day and promptly lost another 18 percent, the largest drop ever, two days later.[13]

Because of various regulatory and traditional barriers to entry, stocks have historically played a relatively minor role in corporate financing in many European countries. In the case of German equity markets, for example, until recently, the largest banks that had a monopoly on brokerage effectively controlled access to the stock exchange. Small firms, being kept from issuing equity, remained captive loan clients. In addition, the integration of banking and commerce in Germany has contributed to large German firms' traditional reliance more on bank credit and bonds than on equity to finance growth. German firms use their equity holdings to exert ownership control over industrial firms. As may be expected, stock exchanges were small, inefficient, and illiquid.[14]

One study examined a relationship between market valuation and geographic scope of US MNCs' foreign operations. According to the evidence, based on the importance of location of MNC operations, MNCs with presence in developing economies have significantly higher market values than MNCs that operate only in advanced economies. Also the market value impact of intangible assets increases with the degree of an MNC's expansion into developing locations only.[15]

FINANCIAL INSTITUTIONS

International companies have several options in financial institutions that have the capability of dealing in international finance (see Figure 18.2). The most common alternative are banks (and nonbank banks), both domestic and overseas. In addition to the well-known giant banks that operate globally, there are many medium-sized banks that have international banking departments. The multi-

national banks can make arrangements to satisfy all kinds of financing needs.

Other than making loans, banks are also involved in financing indirectly by discounting (i.e., factoring) letters of credit and time drafts. Some **factoring houses** buy accounts receivable with or without recourse at face value and then provide loans at competitive rates on 90 percent of the factors' acquired but not yet collected receivables. In general, factors help clients eliminate several internal credit costs by providing credit guarantee of receivables, by managing and collecting accounts receivable, and by performing related bookkeeping functions. The industry average factoring commission for these services is 1 percent. Factoring is a substantial part of business for a company such as Heller International (see Figure 18.3).

An exporter usually initiates a factoring arrangement by contacting a factor offering export services. This factor then requests a credit undertaking on the importer from an affiliate (import) factor, through an international correspondent factor network. After local approval of credit, the exporter ships the goods on open account and submits the invoice to the export factor. The export factor then sends it to the import factor for credit risk assumption and administration and collection of the receivables. Typically, the exporter does not deal with the import factor. In any case, factoring export receivables allows small and medium-sized exporters to be competitive as it is a hassle-free method of financing export sales and collecting payment from buyers.

Another familiar financing tool for European exporters but rather an unknown tool for American firms is forfaiting which finances about 2 percent of all world trade. **Forfaiting** originates from the French term "a forfait" which means to surrender or relinquish rights to something. When used, an exporter surrenders possession of export receivables by selling them at a discount. The cost depends on country risk. For sales to Japan and France the discount rate may be 6.75 percent, and terms may reach five years, whereas sales to Pakistan may boost the discount rate to 7.75 percent with a one-year term limit. Generally, an exporter consults with a

Figure 18.2
Financial services

forfaiter before incorporating the discount rate into the final selling price.

Export factoring and forfaiting are similar since both involve selling export receivables to a third party at a discount. There are a few differences, however, between the two parties. First, factors like a large percentage of an exporter's business, but forfait houses do not mind working on a one-off basis. Second, while factors specialize in short-term receivables (up to 180 days), forfaiters tend to work with medium-term receivables. Finally, forfaiters

are more willing to deal with high-risk countries. To protect themselves, forfait houses require a guarantee from a reputable commercial bank in the importer's country. The guarantee is in the form of an **aval** (bank guarantee). An endorsement with the words "PER AVAL" or "GUARANTEED PER AVAL" is stamped directly on to the notes or bills by the guarantor bank.[16]

Banks may provide **equipment leasing** as another alternative form of financing. The most attractive benefit of leasing is its low cost while

529

For a total perspective to serve your financial world best... Heller is the one.

The one that zeros in on creative solutions that answer all your needs. Get the Heller point of view for any or all of your financing needs, which include:

Asset-Based financing expertise to assist you in major acquisitions or mergers, meeting working capital needs or other types of financing. Professionals with the deal structuring expertise, funding capacity and service capabilities to serve your industry and market.

Factoring to provide specialized credit and collection expertise and working capital funds in marketing your products throughout the U.S. and around the world.

Equipment financing programs to facilitate the sale of equipment from the manufacturer to the end user. An integrated multi-service offering which satisfies financing requirements for each step in your distribution process.

Commercial Real Estate financing to support you in every phase of your project's development—from site development to permanent financing.

Heller wants to be involved in your financial planning process. As part of Heller International, there are 72 offices worldwide, staffed with professionals dedicated to a high level of performance. We've recently changed our name to Heller Financial emphasizing our commitment to set standards of excellence no one in the industry can match. We welcome you to test our commitment.

For more information and a copy of our 1984 Annual Review call: **1-800-458-4924.** (In Illinois, call: 1-800-621-2429. In Canada, call: 1-416-482-4012.)

Heller Financial

Asset-Based Financing · Factoring · Equipment Financing · Real Estate Financing
105 West Adams Street, Chicago, Illinois 60603.

Heller Financial, Inc. is an operating subsidiary of Heller International Corporation.
© Heller Financial, Inc. 1985.

Figure 18.3 Factoring

Source: Reprinted with permission of Heller Financial.

allowing an exporter to conserve capital and improve cash flow. Leasing may involve 100 percent financing with no down payment (see Figure 18.4). It may be used in conjunction with conventional lending sources.[17]

In the United Kingdom, companies have a number of financial institutions to contact for loans. These institutions include foreign banks, British clearing banks, merchant banks (factor houses), finance houses, investment trust companies, pension funds and insurance companies, leasing firms, and development capital and other specialist venture-capital organizations. In Germany, companies may be able to obtain short-term loans for German and foreign banks, usually by overdraft.

At present, among the world's largest banks, Japanese banks dominate the top ten positions. Figures 18.5 and 18.6 show two international banks with a strong presence in the world's financial markets.

Figure 18.4 Lease financing

Source: Reprinted with permission of Bank of America.

SANWA BANK INTRODUCES *GLOCAL BANKING.* THERE IS NO ALTERNATIVE.

In the world of financial services, most banks are following one of two courses.

Global banking. And local banking.

But global banking often loses sight of local conditions, local needs.

While local banking lacks the reach and the perspective to serve your needs around the world.

Which is why the introduction of *glocal banking* — from Sanwa Bank — is important news.

Sanwa provides a full range of financial services tailored to meet *local* needs in every city where Sanwa does business.

And, beyond that, access to the Sanwa *global* network; a formidable resource only a bank that ranks among the four largest in the world* could provide.

Local needs. Global strength.

For corporate finance. For public projects. To meet your every financial need. From rapid fund access to swift financing to M&A services to credit analysis. And etc., etc., etc.

So see Sanwa.

And see what a difference *glocal banking* can make.

Sanwa Bank

Capital strength. Capital ideas.

*FORTUNE, August 22, 1994

The Sanwa Bank U.S.A. & Canada Network

U.S.A.
Branches: New York:212-339-6300 Chicago:312-368-3000 San Francisco:415-597-5200 Los Angeles:213-896-7407
Agencies: Atlanta:404-586-6880 Dallas:214-744-5555
Loan Production Office: Boston:617-654-2930
Rep. Offices: Houston:713-654-9970 Cleveland:216-736-3380
Subsidiaries: Sanwa Bank California:213-896-7000 Sanwa Business Credit Corporation:312-782-8080 Sanwa Leasing Corporation: 810-637-4100
Sanwa General Equipment Leasing:410-821-7200 Sanwa Securities (U.S.A.) Co., L.P.:212-527-2500
Sanwa Futures L.L.C.:312-341-6530 Sanwa Financial Products Co., L.P.:212-407-3500 Sanwa Bank Trust Company of New York:212-361-2111

Canada
Rep. Offices: Toronto:416-366-2583
Subsidiaries: Sanwa Bank Canada
Toronto Head Office:
416-366-2583
Sanwa McCarthy Securities Limited
Toronto Head Office:
416-862-9160

Figure 18.5 *An international bank and financial services: Sanwa Bank*

Source: Reprinted with permission of Sanwa Bank.

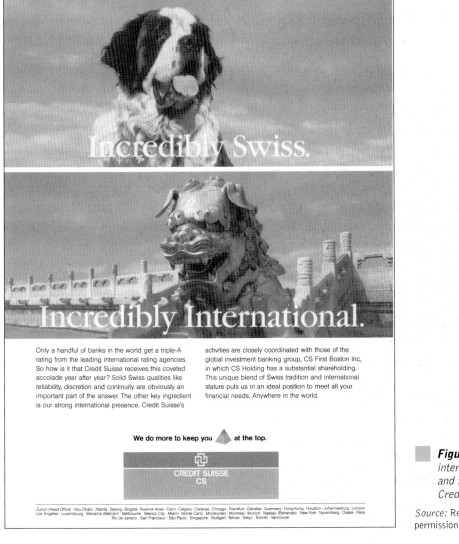

Incredibly Swiss.

Incredibly International.

Only a handful of banks in the world get a triple-A rating from the leading international rating agencies. So how is it that Credit Suisse receives this coveted accolade year after year? Solid Swiss qualities like reliability, discretion and continuity are obviously an important part of the answer. The other key ingredient is our strong international presence. Credit Suisse's activities are closely coordinated with those of the global investment banking group, CS First Boston Inc, in which CS Holding has a substantial shareholding. This unique blend of Swiss tradition and international stature puts us in an ideal position to meet all your financial needs. Anywhere in the world.

We do more to keep you at the top.

CREDIT SUISSE
CS

Zurich (Head Office) · Abu Dhabi · Atlanta · Beijing · Bogotá · Buenos Aires · Cairo · Calgary · Caracas · Chicago · Frankfurt · Gibraltar · Guernsey · Hong Kong · Houston · Johannesburg · London · Los Angeles · Luxembourg · Manama (Bahrain) · Melbourne · Mexico City · Miami · Monte Carlo · Montevideo · Montreal · Munich · Nassau (Bahamas) · New York · Nuremberg · Osaka · Paris · Rio de Janeiro · San Francisco · São Paulo · Singapore · Stuttgart · Tehran · Tokyo · Toronto · Vancouver

Figure 18.6 *An international bank and financial services: Credit Suisse*

Source: Reprinted with permission of Credit Suisse.

GOVERNMENT AGENCIES

It is not unusual for governments to provide **concessionary financing**. Such public loans, as a rule, carry lower than market interest rates, and their terms are more favorable than those of private financial institutions. Governments' role in financing can also be indirect but significant. Japan, for example, uses qualification for public loans as an inducement for private banks to co-finance. The qualification carries this significance by implying that any investment would be in the national interest and that the firm in question is financially sound.

To win a project in a developing nation, an exporting country may provide **tied aid** which is concessionary financing terms conditioned on the purchase of the equipment and services from the donor country. Trade-motivated tied aid may thus persuade a buyer to lean in the direction of the donor — not necessarily on the merit of product quality and true price. Ellicott Machine Corp. International, a small US company, lost market share in Indonesia where the Indonesian

533

government has been the company's largest single customer for dredging equipment for over 100 years. The market share loss was due to European competitors' use of tied aid soft loans.

To win back market share, a team of trade promotion agencies – Export-Import Bank, the Department of Commerce, the Department of Transportation, the US Embassy, and TDA – joined forces. Export-Import Bank approved a $22 million direct loan to Ellicott. The Secretary of the Department of Transportation wrote a letter to the Indonesian Minister of Communications. Furthermore, TDA hosted a reverse trade mission which allowed Indonesian officials to visit the USA to learn about American-made equipment. As a result, Ellicott was able to sell five split barges, one tug boat, and spare parts to P.T. Runkindo, Indonesia's state-owned dredging company.[18]

The USA has several government agencies that provide financial assistance. One is the Small Business Administration (SBA). In addition to its regular SBA loans, this agency can assist small firms in their export activities through its Export Revolving Line of Credit Loan (ERLC) which is under the SBA's guarantee plan. Another agency is the Overseas Private Investment Corporation (OPIC). Although best known for its Insurance Department's political risk insurance programs, OPIC also makes direct loans and works with private capital to provide OPIC-supported funds.[19]

A major source of funding for US firms is the US Export-Import Bank (Eximbank), which is responsible for the promotion of exports through financial assistance. Among its activities are direct loans, protective guarantees for banks' loans, and export credit insurance. Eximbank has several financial assistance programs. Its working Capital Guarantee program allows exporters to obtain pre-export financing by providing repayment protection for US bank loans. Another kind of payment protection is through the Foreign Credit Insurance Association (FCIA) Export Credit Insurance policy, which protects those exporters that extend credit to foreign customers. The policy covers political and commercial risk.[20]

In addition to providing direct loans, Eximbank may induce commercial banks to make loans by guaranteeing payment in case of default. The process is simple. An exporter applies to a bank for the financing of export sales, and the bank then applies to Eximbank for guaranteed coverage of both commercial and political risks. Furthermore, Eximbank may buy the bank's export loans at a discount through its Discount Loan Program so that banks can acquire funds for further lending.

European governments have been offering **mixed** or **blended credit**. This type of financing package combines an official, conventional loan with either outright grants or foreign aid grants at below market rates, in effect reducing the actual interest rate based on the condition that donor countries' products are bought. France, the heaviest user of this technique, won Malaysia's contract for a $200 million turnkey power plant by disguising its thirty-year loan at a 4.5 percent rate as an aid grant, which made up almost half of the financing package. Mixed credit is particularly important in the sale of high-technology capital goods, and the indiscriminate use of this technique in foreign aid/export financing packages has fostered a built-in expectation for it on the part of buyers.

The USA, considering the use of mixed credit as unfair export credit subsidies, has fought back by making financing more costly for OECD members. The new OECD guidelines require mixed credit to include at least 50 percent grants, up from the internationally agreed 25 percent. Furthermore, the USA has begun to play the same game by offering some unusually low-interest loans. For example, it assisted General Electric with a $30 million gas-turbine project in India with a 32.5 percent aid grant. GE had the lower bid, but credit assistance from Eximbank was nevertheless crucial in securing the project. In another case, the Eximbank offered a $100 million mixed credit line to Thailand for the purchase of US high-technology products. Another technique used to create a built-in disincentive for cheap credit is for the USA to retaliate against its European competitors with longer payback terms.

This discussion should illustrate to international marketers that a low price by itself does not necessarily provide advantages, especially in the case of expensive projects. Government financing is a necessity, and this involves more than just a low interest rate. The effective rate can be greatly moderated by the amount to be financed, outright grants, varying maturity dates, and other financing techniques.

INTERNATIONAL FINANCIAL INSTITUTIONS/DEVELOPMENT BANKS

One major source of financing is international nonprofit agencies. There are several regional development banks, such as the Asian Development Bank, the African Development Bank and Fund, and the Caribbean Development Bank. The primary purpose of these agencies is to finance productive development projects or to promote economic development in a particular region. The Inter-American Development Bank, for example, has as its principal purpose the acceleration of the economic development of its Latin American member countries. The European Bank for Reconstruction and Development (EBRD), located in London, is funded by thirty-nine countries and two European Union organizations. The USA, with a 10 percent share, is the largest single shareholder. The bank targets 60 percent of its loans for the private sector in Central and Eastern Europe. The five multilateral development banks (World Bank, Inter-American Development Bank, Asian Development Bank, African Development Bank, and the European Bank for Reconstruction and Development) have annual commitments topping $45 billion. They are active in all major economic sectors and offer good long-term export opportunities for equipment suppliers, contractors, and consultants. Therefore, they are an important financing source.

In general, both public and private entities are eligible to borrow money from such agencies as long as private funds are not available at reasonable rates and terms. Although the interest rate can vary from agency to agency, these loan rates are very attractive and very much in demand.

Of all the international financial organizations, the most familiar is the World Bank, formally known as the International Bank for Reconstruction and Development (IBRD). The World Bank Group consists of five associated institutions. They are: (1) IBRD, (2) IDA, (3) IFC, (4) MIGA, and (5) ICSID. Each institution has a distinct role in the mission to fight poverty and improve living standards.

The World Bank has two affiliates that are legally and financially distinct entities, the International Development Association (IDA) and the International Finance Corporation (IFC). All three organizations have the same central goal: to promote economic and social progress in poor or developing countries by helping to raise standards of living and productivity to the point at which development becomes self-sustaining.

Toward this common objective, the Bank, IDA, and IFC have three interrelated functions, and these are to lend funds, to provide advice, and to serve as a catalyst in stimulating investments by others. In the process, financial resources are channeled from developed countries to the developing world. The hope is that developing countries, through this assistance, will progress to a level that will permit them, in turn, to contribute to the development process in other, less fortunate countries. Japan is a prime example of a country that has come full circle. From being a borrower, Japan is now a major lender to these three organizations. South Korea is moving in a direction similar to that of Japan nearly a quarter century ago.

World Bank

The World Bank is owned by the governments of the 184 countries that have subscribed to providing its capital. Only countries that are members of the International Monetary Fund can qualify for World Bank membership. The USA, with 22.4 percent of the subscribed capital and 20.6 percent of the voting power, is the Bank's largest shareholder. By tradition, the World Bank's president is an American.

535

Members are quite diverse in their characteristics, ranging from China, the most populous, to Vanuatu, which has population of slightly more than 100,000, and from the United Arab Emirates, with a per capita GNP of more than $30,000, to Bhutan, which has a $180 per capita GNP.

The IBRD obtains most of its funds through borrowing in the capital markets of the USA, Europe, Japan, and the Middle East. The process is not unlike a private firm's seeking debt financing through the sale of securities. Such funds, in turn, are made available only to creditworthy borrowers, mainly for those projects that have high real rates of economic return. The Bank's decisions are based on economic considerations only, and the political character of a member country is irrelevant. As a result, the World Bank does not make loans in support of military or political goals. Financial assistance is otherwise restricted in the sense that it may be used to purchase goods and services from any member country as well as from Switzerland, which is not a member.

IBRD loans are usually repayable over fifteen to twenty years, with a grace period of three to five years. Each loan must be made to, or be guaranteed by, the government concerned. The interest rate that IBRD loans carry depends on the cost at which the Bank raises funds in capital markets.

In order not to expose the World Bank to excessive interest rate risk, a pool-based variable rate lending system was initiated in 1982. Interest charges applicable to the outstanding balance on all loans are uniformly adjusted every six months, up or down, in accord with the average cost of the pool of IBRD borrowings. A spread of fifty basis points is added to the World Bank's own cost of borrowings. Because the new lending system has added a potential element of volatility to borrowers' costs, the Bank strives to find a point at which there is a balance between the susceptibility of the lending rate to change and the pursuit of the Bank's other important objectives. In any case, a degree of volatility is inevitable, though the World Bank attempts to reduce the impact of these variations through its policies.

International Development Association (IDA)

Because very poor countries may have difficulty in borrowing on IBRD terms, the IDA was established specifically to assist such countries. The IDA has 164 nations as members. By definition, a very poor country is generally one with an annual per capita GNP of $696 or less (in 1993 dollars), and approximately fifty countries fall under this classification. In practice, most of the IDA loans go to those countries that barely exceed half of the specified annual per capita GNP, and most of these countries are located in Africa south of the Sahara and in South Asia. These countries, though very poor, must still have sufficient economic, financial, and political stability to qualify for IDA loans.

Whereas the World Bank makes "loans," the IDA provides "credits." These credits are made only to governments, even though these governments routinely relend funds to their private and public enterprises. The credits must be repaid over fifty years, and there is a ten-year grace period before the beginning of the repayment of the principal. IDA credits carry no interest, but there is an annual commitment charge of 0.5 percent on the undisbursed portion and a service charge of 0.75 percent on the disbursed amount of each credit. These charges are intended to cover the administrative costs of running the IDA program.

International Finance Corporation (IFC)

Although the IDA shares the World Bank's staff, the IFC has its own operating and legal staff. Unlike the Bank and the IDA, which have many operating aspects in common, the IFC works closely with private investors. In addition to providing convertible debentures, underwriting, and standby commitments, the IFC invests in commercial enterprises within developing countries and is able to take equity positions. By functioning in this area, the IFC complements the work of the World Bank by providing assistance in business areas that are impractical for the bank to operate. The IFC's total membership has become 175 countries.

The IFC's main function is to assist in the economic advancement of developing countries by promoting growth in the private sector of their economies, and by helping to mobilize domestic and foreign capital for this purpose. The IFC provides financial, legal, and technical advice, and contributes an element of confidence to the venture of the parties. Its special role is to mobilize resources on commercial terms for business ventures and financial institutions where a market-oriented approach is both applicable and preferable. It will not, however, provide financing if sufficient capital can be obtained on reasonable terms from other sources. Its lending criteria include foreign exchange earnings, increased employment skill improvement and acquisition, higher productivity, and development of a country's natural resources on reasonable terms. The IFC has become more active in helping companies in developing countries raise financing through international offerings of investment funds and individual corporate securities.

Multilateral Investment Guarantee Agency (MIGA)

The activities of the World Bank, IDA, and IFC are supplemented by those of a new affiliated international organization – the Multilateral Investment Guarantee Agency (MIGA). Established in 1988, MIGA has a specialized mandate: to encourage equity investment and other direct investment flows to developing countries through the mitigation of noncommercial investment barriers. To encourage international corporate investment so that developing countries can attract qualified investors, MIGA offers investors guarantees against noncommercial risks (especially risk of war or repatriation); advises developing member governments on the design and implementation of policies, programs, and procedures related to foreign investments; and sponsors a dialog between the international business community and host governments on investment issues. Industrialized countries should also benefit from MIGA's augmentation of the existing capacity to insure their overseas investors, from its innovative

types of guarantees, and from the efficiency derived from the free flow of investment resources. MIGA has 163 members.

International Centre for Settlement of Investment Disputes (ICSID)

ICSID has 139 members. It encourages foreign investment by providing international facilities for conciliation and arbitration of investment disputes. Many international agreements concerning investment refer to ICSID's arbitration facilities.

INTERNATIONAL MONETARY FUND (IMF)

During the Great Depression of the 1930s, many countries resorted to competitive currency devaluation and trade restrictions to maintain domestic income, resulting in lower trade and employment for everyone. Concern over these "beggar-thy-neighbor" policies led to a conference at Bretton Woods, New Hampshire, in July 1944, attended by delegates from forty-four countries. The IMF was born there on December 27, 1945, to institute an open and stable monetary system. Through consultation, collaboration, and financing members with balance-of-payments problems, the IMF facilitates the growth of international trade, raises levels of income and employment, and develops the productive resources of all its members.

The IMF is a cooperative apolitical intergovernmental monetary and financial institution. It began financial operations on March 1, 1947. The IMF has 184 countries as members. There are 2650 staff from 140 countries. Its total resources are SDR 21.7 billion.

As a "pluralist" international monetary organization, its multiple activities encompass financing, regulatory, and promotional purposes. It acts as a source of balance-of-payments assistance-*cum*-adjustment to members, as a source and creator of international liquidity, as a reserve depository and intermediary for members, as a trustee, and as a catalyst. The use of the IMF's resources is based on balance-of-payments need, on equal and on discriminatory treatment of members, and on due regard for members' domestic, social, and political systems and policies.

Guided by its charter (Articles of Agreement), the IMF has six prescribed objectives:

1   To promote international cooperation among members on international monetary issues.
2   To facilitate the balanced growth of international trade and to contribute to high levels of employment, real incentive, and productive capacity.
3   To promote exchange stability and orderly exchange arrangements while avoiding competitive currency devaluation.
4   To foster a multilateral system of payments and transfers while eliminating exchange restrictions.
5   To make financial resources available to members.
6   To seek reduction of payment imbalances.

Membership in the IMF is open to any nation that controls its own foreign relations and is willing and able to fulfill the obligations of membership. Each member has a quota based on its subscription contribution to the fund. This quota determines the member's voting power and access to the IMF's financial resources. The IMF employs a system of weighted voting power that combines a basic allotment with a variable allotment. To recognize the sovereign equality of nations, each member has a basic allotment of 250 votes. To protect the interest of members with a greater magnitude of international trade and financial transactions as well as to account for the differences in subscriptions, variable allotment is used as well, resulting in one vote for each part of the member's quota that is equivalent to a special drawing right (SDR) of 100,000. The USA accounts for some 19 percent of the total.

Special drawing right (SDR)

In former times, gold and foreign exchange were the major reserve assets, and there was some concern that an increase in the rate of such assets might not be adequate to sustain trade and maintain full employment. Furthermore, deficits in the balance of payments of reserve-currency countries could interfere with the confidence in the reserve currencies. In response to this apprehension, the First Amendment to the Articles of Agreement was created and took effect on July 28, 1969, and the special drawing right (SDR) was established.

Created by the IMF as a new asset, SDR is a composite fiduciary reserve asset to supplement existing reserve assets (see Exhibit 18.1). It is the unit of account in which the fund expresses the value of its assets (see Table 18.1). The value of the

Table 18.1 *SDR valuation*

Currency	Currency amount	Exchange rate[1]	US dollar equivalent
Euro	0.4260	0.98060	0.417736
Japanese yen	21.0000	118.67000	0.176961
Pound sterling	0.0984	1.53800	0.151339
US dollar	0.5770	1.00000	0.577000
Total			1.323036

Notes
SDR 1 = US$1.32304
US$1 = SDR 0.755837
1   Exchange rates in terms of US dollars per currency unit, except for the yen, which is expressed as currency unit per US dollar.
Source: "What Is the SDR?" *IMF Survey*, September 2002, 28.

EXHIBIT 18.1   SDR

In 1969, the IMF created the SDR as an international reserve asset to supplement members' existing reserve assets. It is the unit of account of the IMF and some international and regional organizations. The SDR is a purely official asset, held by member countries, the IMF, and certain other international institutions. It is used primarily in transactions with the IMF, either by members settling obligations to the IMF, some of which must be paid in SDRs, or by the IMF making interest payments and loan disbursements to members.

The IMF allocates SDRs to its members in proportion to their IMF quotas. SDR allocations are not loans; members may use them to meet a balance of payments financing need without undertaking economic policy measures or repayment obligations.

The SDR's value is based on the value of a basket of currencies. Movements in the exchange rate of any one component currency will tend to be partly or fully offset by movements in the exchange rates of the other currencies. Thus the value of the SDR tends to be more stable than that of any single currency in the basket, which makes the SDR a useful unit of account.

The basket is reviewed every five years to ensure that the currencies included in it are representative of those used in international transactions, and that the weights assigned to the currencies reflect their relative importance in the world's trading and financial system.

The latest change in the valuation basket was in 2001 and took account of the introduction of the euro. The new valuation basket includes the US dollar, the euro, the Japanese yen, and the pound sterling. Its value is determined daily based on exchange rates quoted at noon in the London market.

Source: Abridged from "What Is the SDR?" *IMF Survey,* September 2002, 28.

SDR is generally more stable than that of any single currency in the basket because movement in the exchange rate of one of the component currencies tends to be partly or fully offset by movements in the exchange rates of the other currencies. The SDR basket comprises the five members with the largest exports.

The term "special drawing rights" partly emphasizes the similarity with members' drawing rights on the General Resources Account, whereas special conveys the notion of SDR's uniqueness and difference from other existing drawing rights in the IMF. From a historical perspective, SDR is the first kind of an interest-bearing reserve asset created by international consensus. Unlike commodity money, the value of SDR as an asset is derived from the commitments of voluntary participants to hold and accept SDRs rather than from any intrinsic properties. SDR has been allocated to its members since 1970 in proportion to their respective quotas.

Functions

Among intergovernmental organizations, the IMF is unique in its combination of regulatory, consultative, and financial functions.

Regulatory function

Reflecting its objective of avoiding disruptive fluctuations and the rigidity of rates, the IMF administers a code of conduct with respect to exchange rate policies and restrictions on payments. Having the authority to influence some of its members' practices, the IMF must exercise firm surveillance over their policies. Toward this end, the Fund has adopted three principles, spelled out in the document entitled *Surveillance Over Exchange Rate Policies,* to guide members in their conduct and to specify their rights and obligations. First, members are obligated to refrain from manipulating exchange rates to gain an unfair competitive advantage. Second, members must intervene if necessary to counter disorderly conditions that disrupt short-term movements in the exchange rates of their currencies. Last but not least, members should consider the interests of other members in their intervention policies.

Consultative function

A number of countries are handicapped in the effort to design suitable foreign exchange programs by the scarcity of reliable statistical data and of personnel with suitable skills in economic analysis and management. This is the area in which the IMF can be of assistance to such members. Due to the nature of the work, the IMF has built up a body of practical knowledge of balance-of-payments statistics, analysis, and policy, and of associated fields. The IMF's research in these topics makes it well qualified to offer advice.

Financial function

The IMF's primary financial purpose, as set out in Article I, sections v and vi, is "to give confidence to members by making the general resources of the Fund temporarily available to them under adequate safeguards, thus providing them with opportunity to correct maladjustments in their balance of payments without resorting to measures destructive of national or international prosperity," and "to shorten the duration and lessen the degree of disequilibrium in the international balances of payments of members."

The IMF's financial resources are made available under a spectrum of policies and facilities that differ mainly in the type of balance-of-payments need and in the degree of conditionality. Access to resources is open to members in amounts related to their quotas, and the rules governing access apply uniformly to all members. Based on guidelines related to the economic indicators of the external position of a country, the Fund assesses both a member's balance-of-payments need (the magnitude of financing) and the adequacy of measures to correct the underlying balance-of-payments disequilibrium (adjustment program). "Need" is a function of the member's balance-of-payments position, its foreign reserve position, and the developments in its reserve position. Even though the three elements are considered distinct and separate and each one alone can represent the member's need, it is the IMF's judgmental consideration of all three in combination with which it justifies that need.

FINANCIAL CENTERS

MNCs have made it an increasingly common practice to raise capital offshore. There are four broad types of offshore financial centers: primary, booking, funding, and collection. A **primary center** (e.g., London, New York) is an international financial center located in a highly developed industrial country. With financial systems highly developed, these centers serve worldwide clients by offering all kinds of financial services.

A primary center is at one extreme; a **booking center** (e.g., Nassau) is at the other. International banks may wish to take advantage of a country's highly favorable tax regulatory system by opening a "shell branch" there which may be nothing more than one small room or a post office box. The purpose is to serve the financial needs of those outside the country by booking Eurocurrency deposits and international loans. The OECD has accused thirty-five jurisdictions of engaging in "harmful tax practices" by encouraging foreign companies to set up tax shelters in their territories (see It's the Law 18.1). Tyco International Ltd., for example, has set up 150 subsidiaries abroad and has reduced its tax obligations by $600 million a year (see Marketing Ethics 18.1).

A **funding center** (e.g., Singapore) collects funds from outside a region for that region's internal use. A funding center may thus be characterized by inward intermediation of offshore funds. In contrast, outward financial intermediation is a characteristic of a **collection center** (e.g., Bahrain). This type of center has low absorptive capacity of the region's economies, resulting in excess savings

IT'S THE LAW 18.1   TAX HAVENS

Tourism accounts for 40 percent of the $4.5 billion economy of the Bahamas. Financial services, accounting for almost 20 percent of the economic activity, are an increasingly important factor. More than 400 banks and trust companies and 600 mutual funds have offices there. These entities manage nearly $600 billion in assets.

Nassau, the tiny capital of the Bahamas, has liberal trust laws and no income tax to go with its balmy weather. There are no taxes on corporate profits, retail sales, capital gains, or income from inheritances. Another attraction is that Nassau promises inviolable secrecy because only signatories on an account can access bank records.

In 2000, OECD accused thirty-five jurisdictions of engaging in "harmful tax practices." These jurisdictions include the Bahamas, Barbados, the US Virgin Islands, and twelve other Caribbean regimes. The Bahamas fought back by stating that OECD's action was a retribution against the smaller countries' competitive tax regimes.

It is an irony that the US tax laws are so complicated and inefficient to the point that the US Treasury may be better off by simply exempting overseas income from taxes. This will encourage American companies to bring their profits home, and the USA may end up collecting $7 billion more. The nation's 500 biggest companies are forced to spend more than $1 billion a year in their effort to comply with tax laws. Half of these costs are probably linked to international tax rules.

Source: "Taxing Times for Tax Havens," *Business Week,* October 30, 2000, 96ff; "Taxing Multinationals: The Donnybrook Ahead," *Business Week,* September 9, 2002, 86–7.

MARKETING ETHICS 18.1   BEING UNAMERICAN

Companies will go anywhere in their pursuit of profits (or avoidance of taxes). They are not bashful in exploiting low tax rates abroad. The idea is to maximize income in low-tax countries while shifting expenses to high-tax nations. Perhaps the most aggressive scheme is to incorporate in a country that is a tax haven. While the tactic usually creates an uproar in the home country, these companies feel that it does not pay to be nationalistic.

As in the case of Tyco International Ltd., it followed the moves of Cooper Industries, Ingersoll-Rand Co., and others. By moving to Bermuda, it has managed to cut its effective tax rate from 36 percent to 23 percent. The company is now saving $600 million a year. Tyco has since set up 150 subsidiaries in Barbados, the Cayman Islands, and Jersey.

Source: "Taxing Multinationals: The Donnybrook Ahead," *Business Week,* September 9, 2002, 86–7; "The Corporate Tax Game," *Business Week,* March 31, 2003, 79–83.

accumulated in the collection center for international banks to invest.

The globalization of finance has been driven by: (1) advances in information and computer technologies, (2) the globalization of national economies, (3) the liberalization of national financial and capital markets, and (4) competition among the providers of intermediary services. Global capital flows in 2000 totaled $7.5 trillion, a fourfold increase over 1990. Because of this growth in cross-border capital movements, net capital flows rose from $500 billion in 1990 to nearly $1.2 trillion in 2000.[21]

Euromarket

One place where governments and businesses can go to borrow money of a desired currency at a competitive rate is the Euromarket. This international market of foreign currency deposits in Europe has no fixed physical boundary, though London, as a hub, is its main location. Actually, the Euromarket is simply a telephone and telex network run by a few dozen international giant banks. Citicorp, for example, operates through its foreign branches in dozens of countries to provide global banking services to MNCs in any type of currency.

Unlike American banks, which accept nothing but US dollars for deposit, European banks are relatively liberal and routinely accept all types of money, which do not have to be converted into any specific local currency. When a depositor needs funds and must withdraw them, no conversion is required, and the depositor will get back the same currency as deposited earlier.

Traded on the Euromarket are Eurocurrencies, which the world's major banks bid for and employ. **Eurocurrencies** are monies traded outside of the country of their origin. A Swiss franc becomes a Eurocurrency (i.e., Euro-Swiss franc) when it is traded anywhere outside Switzerland. Despite the *Euro* prefix, a Eurocurrency is not necessarily restricted to denominations of European and American currencies. Representing a claim against North American, Asian, and Caribbean banks, the currency can be a Euroyen, for example, held by a Hong Kong bank in the Caribbean.

The Eurodollar, just one of many Eurocurrencies, is simply US dollars deposited in banks outside of the USA (e.g., in Europe, Canada, and Japan). When Hong Kong or Singapore banks accept deposits and make loans in US dollars, such dollars become Asian dollars. The Eurodollar once commanded more than 90 percent of the Euromarket, with the German mark in second place, holding about 10 percent of the Euromarket.

Eurocurrency deposits have continued to grow rapidly. Because it is easier and cheaper than issuing corporate bonds in Japan, the Japanese are the biggest issuers of Eurobonds.

One unique feature of the Euromarket is its stateless financial system. Although governments place restrictions on the operations of their national money markets, such restrictive measures do not apply to the Euromarket in spite of the fact that it shares the same locations and facilities as do the national markets. There is no central bank or control, and the Euromarket has no international authority to which it must answer. As an independent market of its own, it has its own interest rate structure, and anyone can invest or trade in it. Because it has no reserve requirements, it is able to offer high rates on deposits and also to make loans at lower rates.

Asian Dollar Market

Since its inception in 1968, the Asian Dollar Market has grown at a rapid rate. The need for this offshore financial market in Asia is the result of the time zone differences among East Asia, Europe, and the USA, making it difficult for Asian bankers to complete transactions within the same day. The growth was aided by the liberalization of regulations in Singapore.

The Asian Dollar Market is a group of banks in Singapore and Hong Kong that accept deposits and make loans in US dollars. Their deposits are time, rather than checking accounts. The two major centers, though different, complement each other. Hong Kong serves as the major center for syndicated loans in the Far East, whereas Singapore dominates the funding side of the market. Put simply, Singapore gathers deposits from various sources while Hong Kong deploys them.

CONCLUSION

Any businessperson can surely appreciate the necessity of having adequate financing and cash flow. It is not uncommon for an importer to turn to its supplier for financial assistance. For the exporter to insist on cash in advance or the equivalent (such as a letter of credit), the sale may be jeopardized.

To finance operations, a company, in addition to selling securities, can turn to middlemen and various financial institutions for loans. Over and above the US market, there are other important capital markets, such as the Euromarket and the Asian Dollar Market, in which financial resources can be secured. For a financial arrangement of significant value, government assistance can be requested from the US Export-Import Bank, which has a variety of programs ranging from direct loans to participation arrangements with private lenders. It is unfortunate that the US government is not as aggressive in this respect as are other governments.

As for the government itself, borrowing can occur with the IMF to support its currency and to finance temporary trade deficits, or borrowing can be initiated with the World Bank and its affiliates (IDA and IFC) to finance development projects. Private enterprises can benefit indirectly from the funds made available by the World Bank and IDA, as they can contact the IFC directly.

CASE 18.1   TOO CLOSE FOR COMFORT

Because of the technology that allows international trading hookups and because of the existence of multinational investment banks, it is quite easy to trade stocks, bonds, currencies, futures, and options on a twenty-four-hour basis and move money across the world in minutes. Because of the industrialized world's *laissez-faire* approach, there is virtually no authority to control the flow of capital. As a result, for better or worse, some $2 trillion move around among securities markets every day. Although some people applaud the liberalization of world capital markets, just as many people would like to have more government supervision and control.

Bad news travels fast. In the case of financial markets, it may be a matter of seconds. The speed of information transmission was most evident on Black Monday of October 19, 1987. It was a day of financial meltdown. In two sessions during the week preceding Black Monday, the Dow Jones Industrial Average (DJIA) stock index dropped 95 points and 108 points. When world trading resumed on Monday, Hong Kong recorded a 420-point drop. When the New York market opened, waves of selling began. At the end of the day, the DJIA had a record one-day decline of 508 points, which wiped out 23 percent of the index's value or the equivalent of $1.1 trillion. The plunge, when compared to the 1929 stock market crash, was worse in terms of percentage and speed.

Other markets soon followed the New York Stock Exchange – down. There were sell signals everywhere. Tokyo, the world's largest capitalized market, saw a drop in stock value of 14 percent of $400 billion in capital. The decline there of 3836 points was four times the previous single-day drop of 831 points. Sydney lost 25 percent, or $39 billion of the value of Australian stocks. London followed suit, with a plunge of 250 points, or 12 percent of the Financial Times Index of 100 stocks, bringing the two-day loss to 500 points, or 22 percent. Sharp declines were recorded on exchanges in Taiwan, South Korea, Malaysia, Thailand, and Singapore. The same thing happened in Frankfurt and Dusseldorf, Amsterdam, Toronto, and Mexico City. The Hong Kong market was closed for the rest of the week.

The panic repeated itself the following week. On October 26, the Hong Kong market reopened and promptly lost 33 percent of the stock value. The losses elsewhere were as follows: Tokyo (5 percent), London (6 percent), and Frankfurt (6 percent). Then it was New York's turn – a loss of 8 percent. The problem seemed to go round and round like an echo. In all, the world witnessed a loss of $1.6 trillion in global stock market value within days.

There is no question of the chain reaction, akin to knocking over domino pieces. Not so clear, however, were the causes of the panic. The various explanations were the Reagan administration's apparent willingness to allow the dollar to fall, the US trade deficits, fear of global economic recession, mutual funds' massive selling, and computerized program trading.

Also unclear was whether the financial markets in the USA led the declines of the others or whether it was the other way around. Did New York lead Hong Kong, or did Asian markets influence European markets before affecting the New York and Chicago markets that would open later on the same day? At one time, the dominance of the USA was obvious. When the USA sneezed, others caught the cold. However, today, Japan dominates the list of the world's ten leading banks, and its own financial force allows it to act on its own. What is obvious is the interrelatedness of the various markets. They can all quickly act and react to the developments in other markets.

Another piece of the puzzle is the reactions of consumers and investors in the short and long run. Consumers who lost their wealth on the stock markets may decide to curb their spending. The decline in consumption may then lead to a cut in production and employee layoffs. The group that took the immediate brunt, ironically, were the people employed in the securities industry.

In some ways, the Asian economic crisis of 1997 was a repeat of Black Monday. It all started with the Thai baht. Thailand's central bank spent tens of billions of dollars to defend its flawed exchange rate system and insisted that the baht would not be devalued. Then, without any warning, the baht was allowed to float in July, essentially being devalued. The loss of confidence immediately spread to the other financial and asset markets throughout the region. The values of the currencies of Thailand, Indonesia, the Philippines, and South Korea fell sharply, accompanied by the huge losses in the regional stock and property markets. The crisis culminated in the collapse of the Korean won and the Indonesian rupiah in late 1997. The economies that were adversely affected included Hong Kong, Indonesia, South Korea, Malaysia, the Philippines, Singapore, Taiwan, and Thailand. These economies saw their output drop by more than 6 percent the following year. The declines of real GDP were: Indonesia (15.3 percent), Thailand (8 percent), Malaysia (7.5 percent), and South Korea (7.0 percent).

Some experts believe that the globalization of financial markets is inevitable due to the common denominator – money. The global economy has already been closely linked with the aid of technology. Consequently, each financial market is not and cannot be independent. In reality, it is more like a single, global securities exchange with branches in other countries. This reality provides investors and MNCs with more flexibility – so much flexibility that any individual country will find it exceedingly difficult to impose capital controls. The price of this flexibility is a greater degree of market volatility and perhaps chaos in global equities.

Points to consider

1   Black Monday and the Asian economic crisis were about ten years apart. Can an event like that of Black Monday happen again – perhaps in three to five years' time?

2   At the time of those difficult weeks in October 1987, Germany was in better economic shape than the USA, which had record trade deficits and budget deficits. Germany planned just before Black Monday to sell its 16-percent stake in Volkswagen. Should the crash of the US markets have had any impact on West Germany's plan?

3   Because of the globalization of the financial market, some financial experts predict that the international stock indices (based on stock prices of companies worldwide) may eventually replace such national indices as the DJIA and S&P 500 in representing the equity investment sentiment. The Salomon-Russell Global Equity Index and the Salomon-Russell Non-US Equity Index are examples of this development (see Figure 18.7). Do you agree with the prediction? Why or why not?

4   Stock indices are like brand names, with the world's most well-known stock index being the Dow Jones Industrial Average (DJIA). All stock indices have one thing in common: they are supposed to gauge the interests of investors in their respective markets. Unlike the S&P 500 index used by serious investors to determine the strength of the US stock market, S&P Japan and S&P Europe represent the investors' sentiments in Japan and Europe respectively (see Figures 18.8 and 18.9). Do you feel that these national and regional indices serve a useful function in helping investors analyze their international investment opportunities?

Figure 18.7 *Global equity indices*

Source: Reprinted with permission of Salomon Brothers, Inc.

QUESTIONS

1 Name some of the financing sources for exporters.
2 Is it possible to raise capital by issuing stocks in a foreign country?
3 What are the functions (or services) of a factor?
4 What is mixed or blended credit?
5 What are the goals and functions of the World Bank, IDA, and IFC?
6 What are the role and functions of the IMF?
7 What is SDR?
8 What are the Euromarket and Eurocurrencies?

Figure 18.8 *S&P Japan*

Figure 18.9 *S&P Europe*

DISCUSSION ASSIGNMENTS AND MINICASES

1   The WTO has ruled against the USA three times that a FSC is an illegal subsidy. Should the USA reformulate the program to conform to the WTO's trade rules?

2   Given that foreign competitors through their governments' assistance are able to offer below-market interest rates or financing, how can US firms fight back to remain competitive?

3   Since New York is the financial center of the world, is there any need for US multinationals to use the Euromarket and/or the Asian Dollar Market?

4   The Hawley Group has plans to widen its shareholder base: "In addition to common share lists in the U.K. and Bermuda, and its sponsored American Depository Receipt (ADR) facility in the US, Hawley has recently obtained share listings in both Australia and New Zealand, imminently expects listing on the international Division of Montreal Stock Exchange, and is holding active discussion in Frankfurt and Tokyo." Is there any need for Hawley to be listed in so many markets?

5   The worldwide demand of many financial products results in the mutual offset link by the Singapore International Monetary Exchange (SIMEX) to the Chicago Mercantile Exchange (CME), which allows a contract bought on one exchange to be sold on another. On the Chicago Mercantile Exchange (CME) floor, the most popular stock index traded is the S&P 500. The interest in overseas stocks explains why the CME

holds the exclusive rights outside Japan to create, market, and trade the Nikkei 225 Stock Average futures contract. The Nikkei Averages are a Japanese stock index based on stocks of all the major publicly held Japanese corporations. The averages are developed by NKS (Nihon Keizai Shimbun), which publishes the world's largest circulation daily business newspaper. The CME has sublicensed its rights for the Nikkei 225 to the SIMEX for trading in the Asian time zone because too few Japanese stocks are traded on US security exchanges.

Some believe that, in the future, that which is traded will be the averages based on stock prices of companies worldwide. One development in this direction is Morgan Stanley's granting the CME a license to trade futures based on the Morgan Stanley Capital International Europe, Australia, and Far East (EAFE) stock index. The EAFE index is a diversified portfolio on non-US stocks that cover thirty-eight industries and represents 63 percent of the total market value of these countries' stock exchanges. It is considered the performance benchmark of international market activity.

Do you think that the day may come when US stock indices (e.g., Dow-Jones Industrial Averages, S&P 500) may be overshadowed or even replaced by a world or global stock index that represents the movement of stock prices worldwide?

NOTES

1 "Foreign Sales Corporations," *Export America*, December 2000, 32–3; "Trading Volleys," *Offshore Finance USA.* (September/October 2001): 12–13; "Taxing Multinationals: The Donnybrook Ahead," *Business Week*, September 9, 2002, 86–7.

2 Neil Gregory and Stoyan Tenev, "The Financing of Private Enterprise in China," *Finance & Development* (March 2001): 14–17.

3 Sattar A. Mansi and David M. Reeb, "Corporate International Activity and Debt Financing," *Journal of International Business Studies* 33 (first quarter, 2002): 129–47.

4 Andy C.W. Chui, Alison E. Lloyd, and Chuck C.Y. Kwok, "The Determination of Capital Structure: Is National Culture a Missing Piece to the Puzzle?" *Journal of International Business Studies* 33 (first quarter, 2002): 99–127.

5 "Out of the Desert, into the Future," *Business Week*, August 21, 1995, 78–79.

6 "Modernize This Old-Boy Club? Rubbish!" *Business Week*, January 22, 1996, 39.

7 "NEC Expects to List Shares in the USA," *Asian Wall Street Journal*, June 26, 2001.

8 Shahrokh M. Saudagaran and Gary C. Biddle, "Foreign Listing Location: A Study of MNCs and Stock Exchanges in Eight Countries," *Journal of International Business Studies* 26 (No. 2, 1995): 319–41.

9 Shahrokh M. Saudagaran, "An Empirical Study of Selected Factors Influencing the Decision to List on Foreign Stock Exchanges," *Journal of International Business Studies* 19 (spring 1988): 101–27.

10 Michael G. Papaioannou and Lawrence K. Duke, "The Internationalization of Emerging Equity Markets," *Finance & Development*, September 1993, 36–9; "Emerging Stock Markets: What Benefits and Policy Concerns Are Involved?" *IMF Survey*, June 27, 1994, 201, 203.

11 Ross Levine, "Stock Markets: A Spur to Economic Growth," *Finance & Development* (March 1996): 7–10.

12 Levine, "Stock Markets," 7.

13 "Turkish Bourse Falls 18% in Midst of Political Crisis," *San José Mercury News*, February 22, 2001; "Turkish Lira Plummets in Economic Crisis," *San José Mercury News*, February 23, 2001.

14 Christine Pavel and John N. McElravey, "Globalization in the Financial Services Industry," *Economic Perspectives* (May/June 1990): 3–18.

15 Christos Pantzalis, "Does Location Matter? An Empirical Analysis of Geographic Scope and MNC Market Valuation," *Journal of International Business Studies* 32 (first quarter, 2001): 133–55.

16 Mary Ann Ring, "Innovative Export Financing: Factoring and Forfaiting," *Business America*, January 11, 1993, 12–14; Elnora Uzzelle, "Forfaiting Should Not Be Overlooked as an Innovative Means of Export Finance," *Business America* (February 1995): 20.

17 *Trade Bank Services* (BankAmerica Corporation, 1994), 5.

18 "The National Export Strategy," *Business America*, 1995, 37.

19 "Ask the TIC: Export Financing Programs," *Export America* (August 2000): 14–15.

20 "US Government Financing for Service Exports," *Export America* (May 2001): 32–3.

21 Gerd Hausler, "The Globalization of Finance," *Finance & Development* (March 2002): 10–12.

Chapter 19

Currencies and foreign exchange

I don't distinguish between national and foreign capital. There is no flag on capital.

President Carlos Menem, Argentina

CHAPTER OUTLINE

PURPOSE OF CHAPTER

George Soros and his Quantum Group serve as an introduction to the value of money as well as the impact of foreign exchange. It is clear that even a highly regarded professional trader could be wrong. All currency traders, international bankers, exporters, and multinational corporations realize that volatility exists in the international financial markets. For example, foreign exchange fluctuations probably cost Lufthansa AG 200 million marks in 1995. Therefore, for firms with international activities, foreign exchange risk is inevitable and must be managed to keep it at a minimum.

The purpose of this chapter is to discuss the various issues related to international finance. First, it examines the meaning of money as a medium of exchange. Second, it examines the role of foreign exchange in international trade while discussing the functions of foreign exchange markets. Third, it focuses on the effect of currency devaluation and appreciation. There is also an evaluation of the various systems of foreign exchange and their implications. Finally, some practical guidelines are offered about hedging options used to reduce foreign exchange risk.

MARKETING ILLUSTRATION   THE MAN WHO COULD MOVE MARKETS

George Soros is perhaps the world's most powerful and successful investor. To communicate his views he uses articles in newspapers, statements to wire services, and letters to the editor. His actions and words have rocked the world financial markets and angered the countries' central banks. He played a major role in derailing the European currency system. When central banks were on the opposing side of Soros' trades, they often lost.

He went against the British pound in 1992 and won. In 1993, he made an announcement on German TV that he was selling the German mark while buying US dollars. According to his letter to *The Times* of London, the Bundesbank had kept interest rates high for too long and had to reduce short-term rates sharply. The mark did indeed decline, while the US dollar climbed. His opinions, being so respected, have become self-fulfilling in several instances.

He shorted the Thai baht in early 1997, forcing the economies of Thailand and several other countries to collapse, so when it was time for Soros to attend Thailand in 2001 to promote his new book, the Thai people certainly did not forget. Some promised to throw eggs and excrement at him. Others wanted to file criminal charges against Soros for his role in starting the Asian economic crisis. Thailand's senior police officers warned that they could not guarantee his safety. Logic prevailed, and Soros cancelled his trip.

In defense of Soros, the collapses of the Asian currencies and economies could not have happened without the systems' flawed fundamentals. It was the Bank of Thailand that chose to gamble tens of billions of dollars to defend its indefensible exchange rate system. It was the Thai government leaders who funneled billions of baht into various pockets and who spent lavishly on mega-projects without addressing the social, educational, and health needs. Soros certainly did not urge Thai banks to lend recklessly to those who speculated on real estate or stocks.

From time to time, even George Soros could be wrong. In 1994, he believed that Japan would lower interest rates and that the Japanese yen would fall in value against the US dollar. However, trade talks between Japan and the USA broke down. When markets reopened, traders concluded that the USA would try to push up the yen in order to narrow the US trade deficit. The yen surged by nearly 5 percent. As a result, the $12 billion of assets held by Soros's Quantum Group lost nearly 5 percent. He suffered a loss of $600 million in a single day on February 14, 1994.

Sources: "The Man Who Moves Markets," *Business Week*, August 23, 1993, 50ff.; "A $600 Million Valentine's Day Massacre," *San José Mercury News*, February 26, 1994; "Editorial: Soros Alone Cannot Be Blamed for Crisis," *Bangkok Post*, February 1, 2001.

MARKETING ETHICS 19.1 A LOOSE CANNON VS. A MORON

There is no love lost between the billionaire hedge fund financier George Soros and Malaysian Prime Minister Mahathir Mohammed. Soros sees nothing wrong with shorting certain currencies while offering advice to treasury officials around the world about how to avert financial disasters. Among his victims are the British pound, German mark, and Thai baht. In 1997, it started with the devaluation of the Thai baht that instantly spread to many other countries in Asia. The Malaysian ringgit was not spared.

Mahathir declared that all currency trading should

be illegal. He was certainly upset with Soros, calling him "a moron" who set Malaysia back twenty years.

Soros countered by saying that Mahathir's proposal was a "recipe for disaster." He added that Mahathir was "a loose cannon" who was "a menace to his own country." Explained Soros: "Markets cannot be left to correct their own mistakes because they are liable to overreact and to behave in an indiscriminate fashion."

Source: "Asia Official, Financier Face Off over Free Trade," *San José Mercury News,* September 22, 1997.

MONEY

Money is so simple that most users take it for granted. Actually, it is one of the great innovations in history.[1] Being so simple, useful, and common, money facilitates the exchange of goods and services. In the USA, numerous currencies circulated during the late 1700s and throughout most of the 1800s. It took nearly 140 years after becoming one nation for the USA to have a successful central bank in 1914.[2]

A **hard currency** is hard because of the solid trust that people have in the currency and not

because of its gold backing. Businesspeople must have faith that the country issuing the currency will fulfill its obligations. For money to function as a store of value, there must exist something of value to store. Even though Russia has gold and oil, people still have doubts about the ruble as a store of value.

An Act of Parliament does not make a currency hard or international. Currencies become internationalized only because they meet the needs of official institutions and private parties more effectively than do other financial assets. According to the Federal Reserve Board, nearly two-thirds of the $300 billion of US currency in circulation is outside

CULTURAL DIMENSION 19.1 PAPER MONEY

Due to the existence of credit cards, debit cards, online banking, and so on, it is reasonable to expect paper and metal currency to have already become obsolete. But that is not the case in the USA where the currency per capita (held by the public) exceeds $620 billion, basically $2200 for every man, woman, and child. Per capita holdings of currency in Europe are lower but still significant, exceeding $1000 in most countries, with Germans and Austrians having over $1800 per person. Japan, however, leads them all with more than $4000 for every living person.

One advantage of cash over electronic money is that it promises anonymity to the holder. For criminals and money launderers, cash is a currency of choice. In fact, the euro, because of its 500 euro notes, should be more popular than the US dollar whose largest notes are $100 bills. However, if cash facilitates illegal activities and tax evasion, should governments then not try to outlaw paper money?

Source: Kenneth S. Rogoff, "The Surprising Popularity of Paper Currency," *Finance & Development* (March 2002): 56–7.

of the USA. Ex-communist economies and South America's inflation-wracked countries demand US dollars in their attempt to seek economic stability. Panama and Liberia have long used the US dollar as their official currencies. Honduras, Hong Kong, and several Asian countries have pegged their money to the dollar. While it is true that the US dollar now comprises only half of official foreign exchange reserves, the dollar is still the world's most instantly and easily recognized international currency. Due to historical reasons, the former Soviet economies were hesitant to accept the German mark. Japan, on the other hand, is reluctant to allow the yen to become an international transaction currency.

An international currency fulfills three basic functions in the global monetary system: it serves as a medium of exchange, a unit of account, and a store of value. As a *medium of exchange*, private parties use an international currency in foreign trade and international capital transactions, whereas official agents use it for balance-of-payments financing and to intervene in foreign exchange markets. As a *unit of account*, private parties use an international currency for invoicing merchandise trade and for denominating financial transactions, whereas official agents use it to define exchange rate parities. As a *store of value*, international currencies are held by private agents as financial assets (e.g., in the form of bonds held by nonresidents) and by official agents (such as central banks) as reserve assets.

For a currency to be used internationally, two sets of factors are essential. First, there must be confidence in the value of the currency and in the political stability of the issuing country. Second, a country should possess financial markets that are substantially free of controls. These markets should be broad (i.e., contain a large assortment of financial instruments) and deep (i.e., have well-developed secondary markets). The country should also possess financial institutions that are sophisticated and competitive in overseas financial centers.

FOREIGN EXCHANGE

Foreign exchange transactions involve the purchase or sale of one national currency against another. The easiest way to understand this type of transaction is to view money as just another product that customers are willing to buy and sell. Like other products, money can be branded, and the US dollar, Swiss franc, Japanese yen, and so on are simply some of the brand names for a money "product." Some of these brand names carry more prestige and are more desirable than others, much like brand names of consumer products.

People often wonder why it is necessary to have so many different currencies (see It's the Law 19.1). Obviously, it would be preferable to have only one worldwide currency that could be used anywhere on Earth, similar to the US dollar's being used and accepted in all fifty states. But a global currency is currently impossible due to two uncontrollable factors – national sovereignty and inflation.

Under normal circumstances, it is very rare for a country to adopt another country's currency as its own. One exception is Liechtenstein, which signed a customs treaty with Switzerland in 1923, making the Swiss franc its official currency. Moreover, Liechtenstein's customs affairs are administered by Switzerland.

Many Americans, knowing that the dollar is widely accepted, do not understand why the US dollar cannot become a global currency and why other nations resist replacing their national currencies with the US dollar. The resistance may perhaps be better understood if one imagines the tables being turned. Would the American public be willing to abandon the dollar and replace it with a new global currency? The fact that the USA is so unwilling to embrace the metric system in spite of its demonstrated superiority underscores this point clearly. Because of *national pride*, no nation wants to give up its identity and sovereignty, and this includes its national currency. National pride may also explain Great Britain's reluctance to allow the pound to join the European Monetary System (EMS), especially since the British believe that the pound has a more important role in the international financial world. Great Britain withdrew the pound from the EMS in 1992 and has so far refused to switch to the euro.

IT'S THE LAW 19.1   CURRENCY QUOTIENT

Match the country with the currency:

Elementary level

1	France	A	dollar
2	Hong Kong	B	euro
3	Japan	C	dollar
4	United Kingdom	D	pound
5	USA	E	yen

Intermediate level

1	Australia	A	dollar
2	Mexico	B	won
3	Russia	C	peso
4	South Africa	D	rand
5	South Korea	E	ruble

Advanced level

1	Bangladesh	A	tugrik
2	Burma	B	pataca
3	Cambodia	C	riel
4	Macau	D	kyat
5	Mongolia	E	taka

A less emotional but often uncontrollable issue is *inflation*, which reduces the value of money (i.e., purchasing power). Since it is impossible for all nations to have an identical inflation rate, the effect of inflation on the value of various currencies is uneven. In Argentina, the inflation rate was greater than 400 percent in 1984, and it subsequently accelerated to more than 800 percent, forcing the government to adopt the austral as its new currency in 1985. Inflation in the USA at the same time was running in single digits. In China during the 1940s, the currency had so little value that the Chinese had to cart their money around in wheelbarrows. After World War I, the value of the German mark stood at 4 trillion marks to a dollar.

These examples should make clear that it is impractical for any single currency to be used on a worldwide basis while maintaining constant value in all countries.

FOREIGN EXCHANGE MARKET

Firms needing to make payment for foreign business transactions never seem to have enough currency on hand, and it is cumbersome for them to seek out those with adequate amounts to sell. There is thus a need for a foreign exchange market to suit all individuals and institutions in order that they may contact one another for this purpose. The foreign exchange market as it exists has no central trading floor where buyers and sellers meet. Most trades are completed by banks and foreign exchange dealers using telephones, cables, and mail. As a worldwide market, the foreign exchange market operates twenty-four hours a day.

The foreign exchange market facilitates financial transactions in three different ways. First, it provides *credit* or *financing* for firms engaged in international business. This can be achieved through a variety of means, such as letter of credit, time draft, forward contract, and so on. Second, it performs a *clearing* function similar to a domestic bank's clearing process for checking-account customers. Clearing is a process by which a financial transaction between two parties involving intermediation between banks is "settled." In the case of international clearing, the funds are transferred on paper from a commercial customer to its local bank, from there to a New York bank, and finally to a foreign bank abroad. The process allows payments to be made for foreign goods without a physical transfer or movement of money across countries.

Third, the market furnishes facilities for *hedging* so that businesses can cover or reduce their foreign exchange risks. **Hedging** is an activity that is used as a temporary substitute purchase or sale for the actual currency. This temporary transaction allows users to protect the price they secure from fluctuations because it establishes equal and opposite positions in the market.

The rationale for hedging lies in the exchange rate fluctuation, which can move significantly and erratically, even within a short time. For example, due to inflation and instability, the Russian ruble lost 27 percent of its value against the US dollar in a single day in 1994. The panic started when the central bank stopped supporting the declining ruble. The ruble tumbled from 3081 to the dollar to 3926, and it was a record fall. In just three months, the ruble lost half its value. Consumers, to hedge against price increases, bought merchandise as much as they could, while merchants sharply marked up prices.

Figure 19.1 provides a good illustration of the high degree of volatility in the foreign exchange market. Since it is common for a customer to take some time in accepting the quoted price, placing an order, and making payments, financial loss caused by exchange rate movement can easily occur. Without a hedge, an American exporter selling to an Italian customer will suffer financially when the euro declines in value (or the dollar increases in value) because the euros paid, after conversion, will yield fewer dollars than first expected.

Some observers may conclude that, though the danger of the falling euro to the US exporter is real and serious, there is an equal opportunity for the euro to gain in value instead. Under this scenario, the exporter can increase the expected profit – once from the sale of the goods and again from the exchange gain. Based on this contention, the exporter would miss the windfall profit if the exporter had hedged. The problem with this idea, however, is that the exporter is in reality a mere amateur as far as the speculation game is concerned. He or she may be an expert in and have wide knowledge of the manufacturing and selling of products. However, the exporter is not in the business of making windfall profits and should concentrate on familiar trading operations rather than attempting to be a gambler in the unfamiliar and risky game of currency speculation. The caution applies to the Italian importer as well, especially when payment is to be made in dollars instead of euro. As demonstrated by Shell Sekiyu, a Japanese-Dutch oil refiner and distributor, its finance department lost more than $1 billion by making a bad bet in the futures market that the dollar would rise in 1993.

The foreign exchange market provides a hedging mechanism needed to protect corporate profits against undesirable changes in the exchange rate that may occur in the future. For this purpose, the market has two submarkets – spot and forward. The two differ with respect to the time of currency delivery. The **spot market** is a *cash* market where foreign exchange is available for immediate delivery. In practice, delivery of major currencies occurs within one or two business days of the transaction, whereas other currencies may take slightly longer. A US firm holding foreign currency can go to its bank for immediate conversion into dollars based on the spot rate for that day.

Exporters should also consider doing some hedging well before the arrival of foreign funds, and this is where the **forward market** becomes significant. Companies can protect themselves by selling their expected foreign exchange forward. A forward contract is a commitment to buy or sell currencies at some specified time in the future at a specified rate. By signing a forward contract of, say, forty-five days, a company has locked in a certain rate of exchange and knows precisely how many dollars, after conversion, it will get – even though payment, conversion, and delivery will not be made until later (i.e., forty-five days after).

It should be understood that the exchange rate specified in the forty-five-day forward contract is not necessarily the same rate as the forward rate of

Figure 19.1 *Volatility of the foreign exchange rate*

Source: Reprinted with permission of Daiwa Securities Company Limited.

the next day or the spot rate of forty-five days later. Both rates change constantly, fluctuating from day to day and even from minute to minute. The only rate that will stay unchanged is the one agreed on by the bank and the hedger as stipulated in the signed forward contract, even though subsequent forward and spot rates may move drastically the day after the signing of that contract.

An exporter should realize that, in most cases, the spot rate is irrelevant for the preparation of price quotations and the determination of operational costs, since foreign currency as payment is not received until a later date. Since there is no immediate conversion, the forward rate is the more appropriate one. The expectation in terms of interest rate inflation has already been factored into the agreed-on forward rate.

It is not uncommon for companies to limit their exposure to foreign currency fluctuations by requiring payments in US dollars or other currencies corresponding to the currency in which costs are incurred. They may use forward exchange contracts to hedge foreign currency transactions. These contracts allow the companies to exchange, say, US dollars for foreign currencies at maturity at rates agreed to at inception of the contracts.

FOREIGN EXCHANGE RATE

The foreign exchange rate is simply a *price* – the price of one national currency as expressed by the value of another. This exchange price, once established, allows currencies to be exchanged one for another. The exchange rate, however, is more than just a price of a currency. It affects the cost of imported goods and exported goods; the country's rate of inflation; and a firm's profit, output, and employment.

Much like the price of any other product, the price of a currency is determined by the demand and supply of that currency. When the currency is in demand, its price increases, but if a currency's supply increases without any corresponding increase in demand, its value declines.

With excess imports comes an excess supply of money because a large volume of money must be generated to pay for all the imports. With excess money in circulation, the business community, as well as the general population, begins having doubts about its value, making the currency appear over-valued. In contrast, excess export results in too much demand for the exporting nation's currency, since foreign buyers require large amounts to pay for goods. The currency then becomes expensive due to its scarcity, and its real value increases.

The demand of a currency is determined by several factors. Some of these include the following:

1 Domestic and foreign prices of goods and services.
2 Trading opportunities within a country.
3 International capital movement as affected by the country's stability, inflation, money supply, and interest, as well as by speculators' perceptions and anticipations of such conditions.
4 The country's export and import performance.

During the first term of the Reagan administration, the demand for dollars was extraordinarily strong because of cheap land, huge markets, economic growth, low inflation, and a relatively high interest rate in the US market. The perception that the USA was the most stable country was bolstered further by investors' confidence in former President Reagan. These favorable factors, operating in conjunction, were more than enough to push the dollar sky-high despite the huge trade deficits of the USA at the time.

Inflation discourages lending but encourages borrowing, because a loan when due can be repaid with less expensive money. A country with high inflation tends to have a weak currency, which is usually accompanied by high interest rates. The higher interest costs do not necessarily make it an undesirable place to take out loans.

Currency equilibrium

A nation's currency is in equilibrium when its rate creates no net change in the country's reserve of international means of payment. The equilibrium rate operates to keep the nation's balance of payments in proper perspective over an interval of time by making imports equal to exports. When in equilibrium, the foreign exchange rate is stable, perhaps fluctuating slightly before returning to its parity position.

Despite most nations' desire to maintain currency equilibrium, currency has a tendency to get out of balance. The equilibrium is affected by the intensity of such fundamental problems as inflation and excess import. Both inflation and excess import are negatively related to the subsequent price of the currency. In theory, neither persistent trade surpluses nor deficits are desirable. Persistent trade surpluses are unwelcome because they make the surplus nation's currency too cheap and imported products too expensive, resulting in a loss of local consumers' buying power.

More serious than the surplus problem is the problem of persistent trade deficits. When this occurs, an adjustment of the disequilibrium is necessary to restore the equality of demand and supply. The adjustment may be achieved through several techniques. For instance, the disequilibrium within limits can be temporarily financed while waiting for the disequilibrium to reverse itself. Persistent deficits cannot be financed for long periods because the country would soon exhaust its reserves and credits in the effort to pay for imports. The country may opt to choose to control its money supply in order to correct the situation. Trade deficits eventually cause a country to take steps to tighten its money supply. By buying up excess supplies of money, the government makes money less available for imports, and the economy ultimately slows down.

There are other methods that can help in restoring equilibrium by shifting demand away from foreign goods. Trade restrictions such as tariffs and foreign exchange controls achieve this purpose by making imports more expensive. If all else fails, the government may resort to changing its exchange rate in order to alter the price relationship of goods traded between two countries. The new rate would reflect a new equilibrium, which would be reinforced by an increase in the cost of imported goods.

Effect of devaluation

Devaluation is a reduction in the price of one currency in terms of other currencies. As in the case of Russia before its economic crisis in August 1999, it gave up 6.7 rubles for each dollar. Then the crisis hit, and the exchange rate jumped to about 23 rubles per dollar by the end of the year. Turkey did not fare any better. In early 2001, the country's currency lost 28 percent of its value in a single day. Turkey was forced to let its currency float freely to prevent capital flight and stabilize its stock market.[3]

To the layperson, devaluation carries negative connotations, but countries that wish to stimulate exports normally want to devalue their own currency. To understand the effect of devaluation, one might consider two possible exchange rates: assume that the Japanese yen is going to be devalued from 110 yen to the dollar to 120 yen to the dollar.

A question one might then ask is whether the new rate (i.e., 120 yen) is better than the old rate as far as Japanese exporters are concerned. The answer is a definite yes. One dollar now receives 10 more yen, meaning that a dollar spent in US currency will purchase 120 yen-worth of Japanese goods rather than 110-yen worth. In effect, it becomes attractive for others to buy from Japan because they essentially get 10 extra yen worth of merchandise for free. This effect helps to explain why Komatsu had a $20,000 price advantage at one time over Caterpillar on a $100,000 tractor. The explanation for the differential is that the dollar was too expensive in relation to the yen.

Another question one might ask is what effect devaluation will have on Japanese importers. This time, the effect is unfavorable because Japanese importers are required to spend 10 more yen to get the same amount of goods for each dollar as before. The yen devaluation has therefore made imported goods more expensive for Japanese importers and consumers.

Likewise, if the USA elects to pursue the goal of full employment, the 110-yen rate is preferred because this rate makes it easier for Japan to import more American goods without having to spend a relatively larger amount of yen. This increase in demand in Japan is accompanied by a rise in employment in the USA.

However, if the US goal is to maximize consumer welfare, the 120-yen rate is better because American consumers can get more of the relatively inexpensive imported products without having to spend relatively more dollars for them. Yet this positive effect is countered by a negative one – the demand for imported goods reduces the demand for domestic products, and unemployment increases in the USA.

How well does devaluation really work? Although devaluation is supposed to expand exports and reduce imports, in practice the actual impact is often not as great as one might expect, especially in the short term. There are several reasons for this. Initially, the trade balance may worsen instead of improve. The country in difficulty often has a low marginal propensity to save, and buying habits and long-term contracts make it difficult in the short run to alter the physical trade volume.

Devaluation, instead of correcting the problem, can aggravate inflation – the very thing it is intended to control. Workers, seeing imported goods are more expensive than before, often demand wage increases to compensate for their loss of buying power. To compound the problem, domestic industries usually take advantage of the situation by boosting their own domestic prices. This is the route frequently taken by the US steel and automobile industries whenever import prices are driven up by devaluation or other restrictive measures. Therefore, devaluation cannot work in the long run because if these effects continue to cycle and recycle, a collapse of the economy is the result. In order to be effective, devaluation must be accompanied by a program to urge local firms to exercise self-restraint and to encourage people to consume less and save more. In February 1989, the Sandinista government of Nicaragua devalued its currency (cordoba) and raised prices for petroleum products for the third time that year. The devaluation was designed to contain hyperinflation that had reached 20,000 percent in 1988.

One must also keep in mind that a substantial time lag occurs between the change in currency value and its impact on the physical flow of trade. The lag occurs because suppliers and buyers need time to adjust their habits and decisions before they start getting used to the new exchange rates. Furthermore, although devaluation makes imports more expensive, consumers may fail to curtail their purchases of those imports. This phenomenon is known as the **J curve** because it takes quite a while for the economy to round the turn of the J. One should then expect a modest swelling of the trade deficit to occur after devaluation, before a sharp recovery can follow if the right steps have been taken. In general, economists believe that it takes about eighteen months before an increase in import prices can have significant impact on the volume of trade adjustment.

If the economy is successful in expanding exports and reducing imports as intended, devaluation should increase the national income, which in turn will stimulate the volume of imports once again. Thus the initial effect of devaluation can be reversed in the long run. Moreover, any deliberate devaluation carried on will result in a beggar-my-neighbor policy, which will export domestic unemployment to other countries. The deliberate practice of devaluation can easily provoke other trading partners to retaliate by lowering their own money value. Because of these consequences, the net gain from devaluation in the longer run is not going to be as large as its initial gain.

EXCHANGE RATE SYSTEMS

There should be no doubt that an exchange rate can be quite volatile and that anyone who is unfortunate enough to make an incorrect decision about the rate's direction will pay for it dearly. Anyone having any doubts about the validity of this statement need only consider Argentina. In 1981, the Argentine peso plunged to only one-seventh of the value of what it had been at the beginning of the same year.

The concern over such a severe reduction in value has led economists and government officials into a heated and continuing debate over the best exchange rate system. All existing systems have strengths as well as weaknesses, and there is probably no such thing as a perfect exchange rate system. The major exchange rate systems may be ranked in terms of increasing flexibility: fixed rate (gold standard and adjustable peg), semifixed (wide band and crawling peg), and flexible or floating rate.

Gold standard

The gold standard was the start of modern exchange rate systems. Gold was first developed as the standard of international exchange in the United Kingdom in the late 1700s, and many other nations had followed suit by the mid-1800s. In the case of the USA, the US Coinage Act placed the dollar on the gold standard in 1873.

Each country was required to link its currency value to gold by legally defining a *par value* based on a specified quantity of gold for its standard monetary unit. Thus, exchange rates had fixed par values as determined by the gold content of the national monetary links. A modification of this system occurred at a later date, and it became known as the gold exchange standard. Created in 1922, the modified system allowed countries to use both gold and the US dollar for international settlement because the USA stood ready to redeem dollars in gold on demand.

In 1930, a dollar was defined as containing 23.22 grains of fine gold (with 480 grains in a troy ounce), whereas a British pound had 113 grains. In 1971, the gold content of the dollar was redefined from 0.888671 grams of gold to 0.73666 grams. The price of gold, being $20.67 per fine troy ounce in 1879, was later changed to $35 in 1933. The increase in gold price in effect devalued the dollar. Because each national currency had to be backed by gold, each country's money supply, in turn, was determined by its gold holdings.

Because of this common denominator (i.e., gold), all currencies' values were rigidly fixed. Although the values were fixed by law, that does not mean that these exchange rates could not fluctuate to some small degree in accordance with the demand and supply of a currency. The fluctuation had to be within the limits set by the costs of interest, transport, insurance, and handling of gold from one country to another.

The gold standard functioned to maintain equilibrium through the so-called *price-specie-flow mechanism* (or, more appropriately, the *specie-flow-price mechanism*) with specie meaning gold. The mechanism was intended to restore the equilibrium automatically. When a country's currency inflated too fast, the currency lost competitiveness in the world market. The deteriorating trade balance resulting from imports being greater than exports led to a decline in the confidence of the currency. As the exchange rate approached the gold export point, gold was withdrawn from reserves and shipped abroad to pay for imports. With less gold at home, the country was forced to reduce its money supply, a reduction accompanied by a slow-down in

economic activity, high interest rates, recession, reduced national income, and increased unemployment. The onset of hard times would pressure inflation to be reduced. As domestic prices declined, demand for domestic products increased, and demand for imports declined. Price deflation thus made domestic products attractive both at home and abroad. The country's balance of payments improved, and gold started to flow into the country once again. The price-specie-flow mechanism also restored order in the case of trade surpluses by working in the opposite manner.

There are several reasons why the gold standard could not function well over the long term. Because gold is a scarce commodity, gold volume could not grow fast enough to allow adequate amounts of money to be created (printed) to finance the growth of world trade. The problem was aggravated further by gold being taken out of reserve for art and industrial consumption, not to mention the desire of many people to own gold. The banning of gold hoarding and public exporting of gold bullion by President Franklin Roosevelt was not sufficient to remedy the problem.

Another problem of the system was the unrealistic expectation that countries would subordinate their national economies to the dictates of gold as well as to external and monetary conditions. In other worlds, a country with high inflation and/or trade deficit was required to reduce its money supply and consumption, resulting in recession and unemployment. This was a strict discipline that many nations could not force upon themselves or their population. Instead of having sufficient courage to use unemployment to discourage imports, importing countries simply insisted on intervention through tariffs and devaluations instead. Nations insisted on their rights to intervene and devalue domestic currencies in order to meet nationwide employment objectives. Because of the rigidity of the system, it was only a matter of time before major countries decided to abandon the gold standard, starting with the United Kingdom in 1931 in the midst of a worldwide recession. With a 12 percent unemployment rate at the time, the United

559

Kingdom chose to leave the gold standard rather than exacerbate the unemployment problem. Monetary chaos followed in many countries.

Par value (adjustable peg)

The need to restructure the international monetary system after World War II was the incentive for the delegates of forty-four countries to meet at Bretton Woods, New Hampshire, in 1994. The result of the meeting was the creation of the World Bank to finance development projects and the International Monetary Fund to promote monetary stability while facilitating world trade expansion. The IMF system, also known as the par value, adjustable, or Bretton Woods system, was created to overcome the problems associated with the gold standard. The inadequacy of gold as an international currency was overcome by turning to the US dollar. As the other international currency, the dollar provides added reserves for stability as well as liquidity for gold and currencies.

The IMF required a fixed exchange ratio or par value. The agreement fixed the world's paper currencies in relation to the US dollar, which was fully convertible into gold. Regarding the dollar as the acceptable store of value, countries were willing to receive it in settlement for international balances. Based on policies designed to avoid disruptive fluctuations and rate rigidity, members had to establish a par value for their currency, either directly in terms of gold, or indirectly by relating the par value to the gold content of the US dollar (within a margin of 1 percent on either side of parity). The IMF prohibits any unauthorized use of multiple exchange rates.

A correction of the par of exchange was possible in the case of a fundamental disequilibrium. The IMF was required to concur with a change from the initial par value through a cumulative amount of up to 10 percent. Any change in par value beyond this amount required the IMF's approval. However, there was difficulty in determining (1) when a fundamental disequilibrium existed, (2) whether the currency was overvalued or undervalued, and (3) the extent of the overvaluation or undervaluation.

To discourage speculation, the change in par value was kept infrequent, resulting in a late adjustment. Further, during a crisis, there was no time for mutual consultations as called for by the IMF's Articles of Agreement. In fact, mere rumors of pending consultations would probably be more than enough to encourage intense speculation. For instance, if the dollar sank in value to its lower limit but was not allowed to go further, no one would want to buy it at that point because its value was being kept artificially high. Its high price did not reflect its actual lower value. Speculators, knowing that devaluation had to follow soon and that the dollar had nowhere to go but down once devaluation took effect, would sell dollars first before buying them back at a new lower rate or price. With only sellers and no buyers, the resulting panic could force the financial markets to close.

One more problem with the par value system was the burden it placed on the dollar. The constant requirements for more and more dollars to finance the ever-expanding trade volume made foreign central banks and private holders nervous, weakening their confidence in the dollar and heightening speculation. After starting strong, the dollar ended up being weak and unwanted, just as predicted by Gresham's law: Bad money drives out good money.

An analogy may be used to explain this problem. A man of wealth and reputation is able to obtain credit to buy anything he desires, but as he begins to overextend himself or as he prints his own money, the confidence of creditors in him and his money would severely erode. This analogy may serve to explain why Japan does not want its yen to become a reserve currency.

The consequent lack of confidence in the US dollar drove creditors to turn to gold once again as an alternative. As the gold price rose, a gold pool was created in 1961 to stabilize its market price. When the pool sold gold to bring its price down, it had a negative impact on the dollar because 59 percent of the pool was a contribution from the USA. As the US gold reserve shrank from $24 billion to $12 billion in 1970, the gold price remained stubbornly high, and confidence in the dollar eroded further. The pool was finally dissolved, and a two-tier gold price came into being; that is, central banks agreed to continue to buy and sell gold at the official price of $35 an ounce, but the free market price was allowed to seek its own level.

To many people, the adjustable peg lacks the certainty of the gold system as well as the flexibility of the floating system. In spite of the periodic growth in world trade, low inflation, and low interest rates under the IMF system, the problems created for the dollar were so great that President Richard Nixon finally severed the link between the dollar and gold in August 1971, thus ending the Bretton Woods international monetary system. Citizens of the USA were once again allowed to own or trade gold on 31 December 1974, and the dollar was permitted to float to seek its own value.

Crawling peg (sliding or gliding parity)

A cross between a fixed rate system and a fully flexible system are the semifixed systems such as the crawling peg and the wide band. They differ from fixed rates because of their greater flexibility in terms of the exchange rate movement. However, they are not a floating system either because there is still a limit with regard to how far the exchange rate can move.

Because the infrequent adjustment of the IMF's par value system necessitated a large devaluation at a later date, the crawling peg rate was developed. The idea is to adjust the rate slowly by small amounts at any point in time on a continuous basis to correct for any overvaluation and undervaluation. The continuous but small adjustment mechanism (e.g., as little as 0.5 percent a month or 6 percent for the whole year) was designed to discourage speculation by setting an upper limit that speculators could gain from devaluation in one year.

The crawling peg system requires countries to have ample reserves for the prolonged process of adjustment. In addition, the minor adjustments may not correct the currency's overvaluation or undervaluation. Consider the case of Brazil, which has employed a form of a crawling peg to remedy its

hyperinflation problem by devaluing its currency (cruzeiro) by a few percentage points each month. Usually, the devaluation of 2 percent each week takes place on Thursdays, as if it were some kind of a supermarket special. However, even this annual adjustment total of more than 100 percent is not enough, and from time to time the 2 percent mini-devaluations must be supplemented by a maxidevaluation. In December 1979 and February 1983, for example, Brazil suddenly chopped the value of the cruzerio by 30 percent and 24 percent, respectively.

Similarly, Mexico has devalued the peso at a controlled rate that proved too small to reflect the peso's proper value. In the first part of 1985, the peso lost more than 85 percent of its value against the dollar on the free market. In contrast to the official rate of 24 pesos to the dollar, the free market exchange houses charged 325 pesos, and the rates at the border were even higher. Considering that only a few years earlier the exchange rate was less than 100 pesos to the dollar, it may at first seem that the extent of the devaluation was dramatic. However, it was not enough. In mid-1986, the peso plunged a great deal more, resulting in each US dollar fetching more than 700 pesos. Near the end of 1987, the peso lost as much as 59 percent in value in only a few days and ended the year at the rate of 2200 pesos to a US dollar. Such large devaluations are exactly what speculators wait for.

In late 1994, *Business Week* magazine mentioned that Mexico's use of crawling peg to systematically devalue the peso had worked well in controlling inflation while boosting exports.[4] Yet only a month later the peso was in full crisis. The collapse of the Mexican peso at the end of 1994 as well as the economic crisis which ensued in 1995 was a result of Mexico's attempt to keep the value of the peso artificially high, but when the government ran out of reserves to support the currency, the peso collapsed and savagely hit Mexican citizens.

Wide band

The purpose of the wide band is to compensate for the rigidity of the fixed rate systems. Similar to and yet different from the adjustable peg system, the wide band allows the currency value to fluctuate, say, 5 percent on each side of the par. Not being dedicated primarily to exchange rate changes, this system uses the more flexible movement to warn speculators of the adverse consequences when their guess about the direction of the exchange rate proves to be wrong.

To pursue the elusive goal of exchange rate stability, the European Monetary system (EMS) incorporated certain features in order to force member countries to make adjustments to correct their divergent economic conditions. As a miniature Bretton Woods system, the EMS employed the so-called grid-parity system to link the members' currencies so tightly that they became almost a single currency. The EMS had a fixed exchange rate among members, and the participating currencies could fluctuate by up to 2.25 percent on either side of their bilateral "central rates" against other members, with the exception of the volatile lira's 6 percent fluctuation on either side.

The EMS created a currency bloc known as the European Currency Unit (ECU) to provide a substitute as well as a complement to the US dollar. The ECU was a composite of several national currencies. The weights for each currency were based on the relative GNP of each country and each country's share in intra-European trade. The weights were examined every five years or if the relative value of any currency changed by 25 percent.

Under the wide band scheme, a country pursuing more inflationary policies will find the prices of its international goods going up, necessitating a depreciation program to correct the country's balance of payments in order to slow growth and curb inflation, while eventually risking recession. The country's exchange rate would then sink toward the floor under its par value. Once the fixed limit is reached (i.e., after hitting either the floor or the ceiling), the country is back to the rigidity of the fixed rate all over gain. Moreover, if a wide band is desirable due to the increase in flexibility, a country may be better off with no limit for movement at all.

Floating (flexible) system

Under the fixed systems, excessive demand for gold developed and the USA was forced to suspend the sale of gold in 1968, except to official parties. However, taking this action did not help, and by the late 1960s the dollar came under increasing pressure due to the prolonged and steep deterioration in the balance of payments. A crisis of confidence developed and foreigners' reluctance to hold dollars resulted in a change in the dollar's historic value. On August 15, 1971, the USA suspended the convertibility of the dollar into gold and other reserve assets altogether, and it floated the dollar to force a change in the parity as well as a review of the IMF. The subsequent Smithsonian Agreement resulted in a revaluation of other currencies and the devaluation of the dollar by 10.35 percent. In February 1973, following a great deal of speculation against the dollar, the crisis renewed, and a second 10 percent devaluation followed. The crisis forced the official foreign exchange markets to close in Europe and Japan for about two and a half weeks. When these markets reopened, all major currencies were allowed to float.

After an initial period of remarkable stability, the dollar sank rapidly for seven weeks because of balance-of-payments deficits, Watergate revelations, renewed inflation in the USA, and a tightening of money abroad. Had the fixed systems been in effect, a traditional crisis would have resulted. Foreign exchange markets would have been closed, and large-scale adjustment of parities would have been necessary. With the dollar free to float, however, the beneficial effect was that speculative pressures were reflected in a sharp drop in the exchange value of the dollar without a closing of the market. The resultant devaluation, in turn, helped the USA to improve its trade performance.

In October 1978, another crisis came along for the US dollar. Concerns over inflation in the USA prompted a panic selling of the dollar, and the stock market plunged. In spite of the risk of recession, the Carter administration was forced to take drastic measures. Among the measures taken were an increase in the Federal Reserve's discount rate, gold sale, and dollar buying. Initially, the magnitude of the action took the market by surprise. Gold prices dropped, and the bond market, stock market, and dollar all rose significantly. Yet by the end of the month, the strong anti-inflation policies themselves weakened confidence in the government, and chaos ensued. Additional panic selling drove the dollar to record lows. Once again, by allowing the dollar to float, the traditional adverse consequences of market closings and official devaluation were averted.

Under a flexible or floating system, the market force, based on demand and supply, determines a currency's value. A surplus in a country results in an appreciation of its currency, immediate higher prices, mass reserve, and opportunity costs. In addition, too much money on reserve leads to a loss of investment opportunities. On the other hand, a country's deficit will lower its currency value, making it easier to export more later.

In the absence of government intervention, the float is said to be *clean*. It becomes *dirty* (i.e., managed) when there is central bank intervention to influence exchange rates, which is a common action, especially by those with inflation and trade problems. A country experiencing inflation must reduce public spending and the money supply to cool its economy. However, due to the delayed impact of devaluation on trade improvement, such restrictive measures need time to achieve their intended purpose before inflationary pressures work themselves back into the economy through higher import prices. Therefore, the country must continuously monitor and defend its currency over the time that the changes are taking effect.

Interventions are unlikely to change a market trend. Central banks' combined resources are not adequate to reverse a fundamental trend in the foreign exchange market. The foreign exchange reserves held by central banks total only $1 trillion, about the average daily volume of currency trading. On June 24, 1994, the Federal Reserve Board and sixteen other central banks spent more than $3 billion to support the US dollar. Market forces,

determined to send the dollar the other way, fought back. By the end of the day, the dollar was even worse off than it was before the intervention, proving an old rule in currency intervention (i.e., "Do not try to row upstream").[5] However, one recent study of the Institute for International Economics broke with the conventional wisdom by stating that intervention could serve an effective policy tool. The published study maintained that intervention on the foreign exchange market is useful to determine how the market perceives a country's macroeconomic policy.[6]

OFFICIAL CLASSIFICATION OF EXCHANGE RATE REGIMES

The IMF has identified eight types of exchange rate regimes.[7] These regimes may be divided into three broad groups: floating, intermediate, and hard peg.

Floating exchange rate regimes include independently floating regimes (in which the exchange rate is market determined, with intervention only to moderate exchange rate fluctuations) and managed floating regimes with no predetermined path for the exchange rate.

Intermediate exchange rate regimes include soft pegs (conventional pegs to a single currency or a basket of currencies, horizontal bands, and crawling pegs with and without bands) and tightly managed floating regimes (under which authorities attempt to keep the exchange rate stable without any commitment to a predetermined path).

Hard peg regimes include currency boards and exchange rate regimes with no separate legal tender (such as formal dollarization and currency unions like the CFA franc zone and the euro area).

It should be noted that a country's official classification of its exchange rate regimes may be more fiction than fact. The declared regime often differs from actual country practices. A study of 153 countries dating back to 1946 found that, in the 1950s, 1960s, and early 1970s, 45 percent of the countries that officially claimed a pegged exchange rate actually had some variant of a float. In the 1980s and

563

1990s a new type of misclassification emerged: 53 percent of the official "managed floats" turned out to be de facto pegs or crawling pegs. These misclassifications may have led to a false conclusion that a freely floating exchange rate might be an unwise choice for policy makers. The countries with official floating exchange rates experienced an average annual inflation rate of 174 percent while achieving a meager annual per capita growth rate of 0.5 percent. However, after weeding out countries with de facto pegs or "freely falling" episodes (cases where the twelve-month inflation rate was 40 percent or more), countries with true floats actually had annual inflation rates below 10 percent and an annual per capita growth of 2.3 percent.[8]

In practice, exchange rate regimes vary along a continuum. There is also evidence that countries have moved away from intermediate exchange rate regimes toward floating and, to a lesser extent, hard pegs.[9] For countries that have integrated themselves closely with global capital markets, they need to choose between the two extremes – either a floating currency or a hard peg. Some economies (e.g., Hong Kong and Argentina) have hardened their pegs by introducing currency boards. A monetary union provides even harder pegs.[10]

EVALUATION OF FLOATING RATES

Given that a perfect system does not exist, how does one go about evaluating existing systems? A system is acceptable when, given a certain rate of inflation in a country, the value of that country's currency is reduced in the international exchange markets by the same extent, while the value of the currency in a country with no inflation holds steady or moves up accordingly. The system being used should not allow countries to manipulate their rates to gain an unfair advantage over rival trading partners. In essence, a good system promotes stability, certainty, and inflation control.

The fixed rate and floating rate systems have diverse natures and characteristics. Therefore, both of the systems cannot meet the same goals of certainty, stability, and inflation control. Advocates of the fixed rate plan believe that the certainty and rigidity of exchange rates can promote economic efficiency, public confidence, and inflation control. In recent years, several US public officials have been encouraging the return of some kind of gold standard. If this system could indeed work as intended, there would probably be no need to have more than one world currency.

One book published in 1994 generated some interest by claiming that floating exchange rates would create catastrophes (e.g., the hyperinflation which gave fuel to fascism and World War II).[11] The author advocated a return to the classical gold standard. However, the book provided little empirical evidence that the floating system has impeded economic growth, and the author's analysis was heavily criticized.[12]

Experience has shown that fixed rates do not work well for a prolonged period. For fixed rates to work, the gold price must remain fixed to control inflation – a difficult if not impossible requirement. In addition, making fiat money convertible into gold cannot guarantee the willingness to achieve long-term stability in the purchasing power of money. Furthermore, while gold prices and general prices tend to move together over long periods of time, short-term movements of gold prices have been much more erratic than movements in general prices. Other commodity indices provide better early warnings of fluctuations in inflation than gold. Therefore, there are better alternatives than a gold standard on which to base monetary policy.[13]

Other problems associated with fixed rates include massive capital flows during a crisis and the closing of financial markets. According to Morgan Guaranty, between 1976 and 1985, citizens of Mexico and Venezuela sent $53 billion and $30 billion, respectively, out of their countries. It is also unrealistic to believe that the USA wants its money supply to be backed by gold and to be at the mercy of major gold producers such as South Africa.

Critics of floating exchange rates contend that the system causes uncertainty, which discourages trade while promoting speculation. In fact, world exports climbed steadily for eight years after the float was put in place, and it is apparent that the system does not interfere with world exports.

The claim that uncertainty encourages investors to speculate and destabilize exchange rates is probably invalid. The fixed rate system is more likely to encourage speculation by giving speculators a one-way, no-lose bet to make money, as the exchange rate can move in only one direction once the upper limit is reached. Whatever the fault of the floating rates, the fixed rate regime is subject to the same fault, probably to a greater magnitude.

Because of a lack of the inherent discipline imposed by fixed rates, floating currencies are said to encourage inflation. In reality, the flexible rate system makes the consequences of inflationary policies more readily apparent to the general public, labor, and employers in the form of a declining foreign value of the currency and an upward trend in domestic prices. This public awareness makes it easier to implement proper policies to correct the situation without reacting in a crisis atmosphere, as might otherwise occur. These countries are then able to pursue the mixture of unemployment and price objectives that they prefer and that are consistent with international equilibrium.

The floating system should be accepted with reservation. One problem occurs due to a high degree of short-term volatility and the large medium-term swings in exchange rates. In addition, floating rates do not work well during recessions or through a faltering economic recovery. The float may exacerbate inflationary problems by quickly feeding higher import costs into local wages and prices. When Mexico devalued its peso in 1976, labor unions won a 23 percent wage increase, which served only to force the government to make a second devaluation just two months later. The plunging value of the peso in late 1994 and 1995, on the other hand, created a great deal of unemployment and hardship in Mexico.

A decade of floating exchange rates has shown that developing countries have realized more benefits than problems. Floating rates do not necessarily result in a currency's free fall, and they do not imply higher inflation or lower output. Of the twelve

countries surveyed for the period 1985 to 1992, inflation declined in six countries following floating and accelerated in only one (Nigeria). Regarding output, of the eleven countries surveyed, six experienced faster GDP growth; only Brazil and Paraguay showed decline in growth after floating.[14]

The financial crises experienced by many emerging market economies appeared to have one thing in common. These economies maintained soft pegs by pegging their exchange rates in value to either a particular currency or a basket of currencies. As in the case of the Asian economic crisis, the five Asian economies (Thailand, Indonesia, Malaysia, the Philippines, and Korea) were actively managing their exchange rates, partly to promote their competitiveness.

To maintain soft pegs, the authorities were committed to defend it but would allow rate changes under a significant attack. However, the increased integration of their national capital markets and the international capital markets makes it almost impossible to sustain soft pegs over extended periods. The international capital markets simply will not allow domestic policy mistakes to go unnoticed and unpunished.[15]

In spite of some limitations, the floating system was able to carry the world through a number of economic crises quite smoothly. The floating system has proven itself through several periods of raging inflation, deep recession, and massive money movements. Many observers continue to find fault with it, but other systems have just as much, if not more, of the same flaws. At present, there does not appear to be a superior alternative that can be used.

FINANCIAL IMPLICATIONS AND STRATEGIES

It is extremely difficult to predict the movement of a currency. As an example, the US dollar depreciated by about 10 percent against the German mark and the Japanese yen during the first half of 1994, even though the Federal Reserve Board pushed up the federal funds rate while the Bundesbank lowered its rates and the Japanese prime minister resigned.

During the first few months of 1995, the dollar dropped by about 20 percent more against the Japanese yen before beginning a surge of 25 percent. The euro was introduced at $1.18 to the dollar on 1 January 1999, floated to below 83 cents in October 2000, and soared to a record high of $1.29 in early 2004; that is, down 31 percent and back up more than 50 percent in four years with no obvious economic fundamentals to explain gyrations.

Early warning systems

While exchange rate movements are predictable at longer horizons based on the countries' varying interest rates, business firms have to find some practical ways to deal with short-term volatility. It may be worthwhile to consider some early warning systems.

While some models have as many as twenty indicators, the IMF researchers have developed a simple five-variable macroeconomic model for an after-the-event analysis. The indicators are: degree of real exchange rate overvaluation, size of current account deficit as a share of GDP, growth rate of exports, rate of growth of reserves, and ratio of short-term external debt to reserves. The model worked reasonably well, producing results with relatively high warning signals for Korea, Thailand, Indonesia, and Malaysia, but not for the Philippines.[16]

Investment banks have been developing their own in-house models to predict currency crises. One such economic model is Deutsche Bank's Alarm Clock (DBAC). While these models are certainly not perfect, they seem to be far superior to some of the alternative indicators often used by the markets and analysts. Even though there were many false alarms, the models were able to anticipate potentially dangerous pressures at work in foreign exchange markets.[17] In addition, they are objective and mechanical, thus minimizing analysts' biases.

Hedging

"Hedges protect yards from dogs and businesses from financial exposure."[18] One study found a firm's size (as measured by foreign exchange turnover) to have the most important effect on its risk management practices. The effect of size is in terms of the use of computer technology, the use of both physical and synthetic products, and the number of both short-term and long-term foreign funding activities employed.[19]

In practice, size is irrelevant because any prudent firm must manage foreign exchange risks. One study focused on the extent to which industry actively manages rather than hedges foreign exchange risk. According to the results, 70 percent of firms trade their foreign exchange exposures, and some traders do so without internal foreign exchange dealing limits or controls on their position taking. The favored techniques of risk management are demonstrated by the extensive use of synthetic products (options and swaps) in addition to the more usual physical products such as spot and forward transactions.[20]

There are a number of hedging methods, and they include forward contracts, swaps, or options. One method involves the interbank market, which offers both spot and forward transactions. An importer or buyer may purchase foreign currency immediately on the **spot** (or *cash*) **market** for future use. When the foreign exchange is not needed until sometime in the future, the seller (or buyer) can turn to the **forward market**, usually entering into a forward contract with a bank agreeing on the purchase and sale of currencies at a certain price at some future time. Smaller companies often have trouble obtaining forward contracts from their banks for two reasons. First, they are not well known. Second, their transaction sizes are too small to attract banks' interest.

Regardless of size, any company may use the **futures market** for hedging. The main difference between forward and futures contracts is the "standardized" sizes and delivery dates of the futures transactions. The standardization feature provides market liquidity, making it easy to enter and exit the market at any time, but this same feature excludes the likelihood of meeting individual needs exactly.

MARKETING STRATEGY 19.1   THE BIG MAC INDEX

The Economist charts the cost of a Big Mac at McDonald's restaurants around the world. The Big Mac Index is a measure of what it costs to buy a Big Mac in the various parts of the world. Some people use the Big Mac Index as a convenient substitute for the purchasing power parity theory, which states that, although short-term factors may unduly affect exchange rates once in a while, purchasing power should be the same all over the world. The Big Mac Index simply looks at how much a Big Mac sandwich costs at McDonald's restaurants in different countries. For example, if a Big Mac costs $2.19 in New York City, but costs $2.78 (or 27 percent more), in Tokyo, then the interpretation is that the Japanese yen is 27 percent overvalued compared to the US dollar. Similarly, if a Big Mac costs $4.21 in Norway and 74 cents in Hungary, the krona is 92 percent overvalued, and the forint is 66 percent undervalued.

The Big Mac Index is a surprisingly accurate comparative of international currency. It found in 1994, for example, that the Japanese yen was overvalued by more than 60 percent. While it is true that short-term factors (e.g., politics, trade deficits, and interest rates) can greatly affect currency valuations, economic fundamentals tend to assert themselves over the long term. Therefore, in the case of Japan, according to the purchasing–power–parity theory, it is only a matter of time before the dollar would rise and the yen would fall.

The Big Mac Index's greatest triumph has to do with the euro. When it was launched in January 1999, virtually all economists predicted the euro's rise against the dollar. The Big Mac Index suggested instead that the euro started off significantly overvalued. One of the best-known hedge funds, Soros Fund Management, considered but disregarded the sell signal given by the Big Mac Index. When the euro tumbled, Soros was not happy.

In 2002, while the US dollar was riding high, the Big Mac Index determined that the dollar was more overvalued than at any time in the measure's sixteen-year history. Not long after, the dollar began its decline, and the weakness persisted throughout 2003.

One problem with the Big Mac Index is that it is unable to predict when the change in currency value will take place. In 1995, in spite of the acknowledgment that the dollar was greatly undervalued against the yen, the dollar kept sinking and hitting new record lows. However, there was some evidence of the validity of the index. In March 1995, McDonald's Co. Japan Ltd., the largest restaurant chain in Japan, announced that it would cut the prices on its hamburgers by about 30 percent. The price cut was attributed to the rising value of the yen against the dollar and lower operating expenses, since McDonald's imports many of its supplies. In April 1995, while the US price for a hamburger was about 59 cents, McDonald's cut its price again in Tokyo by 38 percent from $2.53 to the unheard price of $1.56 in Japan.

Sources: George Anders, "What Price Lunch?" *Wall Street Journal*, September 23, 1988; "Shorting the Yen," *Worth*, September 1994, 61; "Big Mac Currencies," *The Economist*, April 21, 2001, 74; "Hamburger Helper," *CBSMarketWatch.com*, April 29, 2003.

The most dominant futures market for foreign currencies is the International Monetary Market (IMM) division of Chicago Mercantile Exchange (CME) in Chicago (see Figure 19.2). These global commodities demand twenty-four-hour attention. To meet this need, the LIFFE (London International Financial Futures Exchange) and the SIMEX (Singapore International Monetary Exchange), both patterned after the IMM, make twenty-four-hour trading a reality. SIMEX is examined in Figure 19.3.

Currency options, once illegal in the USA, provide another hedging alternative. The most important characteristic of options is an option buyer's ability to limit the loss, if the buyer's guess is wrong, to the premium paid. A buyer of a currency option acquires the right either to buy or sell

Figure 19.2 *Chicago Mercantile Exchange*

Source: Courtesy of Chicago Mercantile Exchange.

The Exchange with foresight

SIMEX, the Singapore International Monetary Exchange, is an innovator in the financial futures market. As Asia's first international financial futures exchange, SIMEX has grown rapidly by developing new ways to meet the changing needs of participants around the world.

SIMEX was the first to introduce an unprecedented mutual-offset system with the Chicago Mercantile Exchange (CME); this allows investors to establish a position on one exchange and transfer it to or liquidate it on the other. Equally important, SIMEX has similar rules and trading systems as the CME's for safeguarding its market participants.

In response to the need for a way to hedge Japanese equities, SIMEX launched trading in Nikkei Stock Average Futures, the first exchange to offer a

futures contract on what is now the largest stock market in the world. This offers more efficient and economical participation in the Japanese stock market together with greater flexibility.

It is innovations such as these and the efficient, well-regulated trading that keep SIMEX in the vanguard of futures trading.

Futures contracts currently traded on SIMEX include Eurodollars, Nikkei Stock Average, Deutschmark, Japanese Yen, British Pound, US Treasury Bond and Gold.

It's not surprising, therefore, that participants from all over the world have discovered the benefits of using SIMEX and have recognised its foresight in futures trading.

The Singapore International Monetary Exchange Limited
1 Maritime Square, #09-39 World Trade Centre, Singapore 0409. Tel: (65) 278 6363. Telex: RS 3800. Cable: SINMEX. Fax: 2730241

Call us today to discuss how SIMEX can play a part in your financial plans.

Figure 19.3 *SIMEX*

Source: Reprinted with permission of Singapore International Monetary Exchange Limited.

a fixed amount of foreign currency at a set price within a specified time period, and the buyer may exercise this right when it is profitable to do so.

Both *futures* and *options on futures* significantly reduce risk. However, there are two key advantages of options on futures over futures. First, since a trader is able to take positions smaller than standard futures contracts, options on futures allow small businesses to hedge more effectively. Second, compared to futures, options on futures provide greater flexibility by allowing hedgers to cap their exposure.

Although banks have been and still are the first choice of corporations seeking to manage foreign exchange risk, exchanges have devised new ways to attract firms or to get banks to work through exchanges. Coca-Cola Co. hedges its foreign earnings by buying options. GAF Corp., a New Jersey specialty chemicals and building materials conglomerate with $1 billion in sales, works with either a bank or an exchange, depending on the dollar volume. It uses exchanges for most of its options transactions when they fall in the range of $5 million to $25 million because exchanges are more competitive in transactions of that size. When the amounts exceed $25 million, GAF uses banks instead.[21]

Table 19.1 provides a comparison of a variety of hedging methods. One study found that it is not a common practice to adopt innovative foreign exchange risk management products. In fact, the simple, first-generation product (i.e., forward contracts) is still more popular among American corporations than the second-generation (e.g., swaps, futures contracts, and options) and third-generation products (e.g., cylinder options, synthetic home-made forwards/options, foreign currency warrants).[22]

Hedging, like buying insurance, can be expensive. It costs about $26 million to hedge $500 million worth of earnings. A forward contract costs half a percentage point per year of the revenue being hedged.[23] This explains why Eastman Kodak Co. has decided to abandon hedging, believing that the ups and downs of currencies would simply even out in the long run.

Multinationals, due to the nature of their operations, may be able to employ a natural hedge. The technique involves matching revenues and costs in the same currency. One variation of the technique is to manufacture and buy supplies locally. By using locally earned revenues to pay for production of local goods, a company can minimize the earnings that must be translated or repatriated. Another variation of the method is to look at the net exposure. Coca-Cola manages most of its foreign currency exposures on a consolidated basis by using natural offsets to determine the net exposure. In addition, the weakness in one currency is often offset by the strengths in others over time.

It should be noted that a firm's ability to construct operational hedges has an impact on its exchange rate risk exposure. Those multinationals with greater breadth are less exposed to currency risk. In contrast, those with more highly concentrated networks (greater depth) are more exposed.[24]

Leading and lagging

In order to deal with the complexity of international trade, two strategies should be considered: leading and lagging. For an MNC with a network of subsidiaries, several techniques may be used to reduce foreign exchange. Subsidiaries with strong currencies could delay or lag the remittances of dividends, royalties, and fees. Those in weak currency countries could try to lead, or pay promptly, their liabilities. It is important to recognize, however, that these strategies involve speculation since no one really knows the timing and extent of the movement of a currency.

Invoicing

The currency to be used for the purpose of invoicing should be considered carefully. Toyota Motor Corp. operates two factories in England. Since the United Kingdom has so far refused to give up the pound sterling for the euro, Toyota faces a risk of losing money when it converts its euro revenues into pounds to pay for British-made components. To solve the problem, Toyota has told its local suppliers to set prices in euros for any new business. Ideally, Toyota wants to eventually pay bills in Europe in euros as it expands operations in the region.[25]

When the buyer is in a soft currency but the seller is in a hard currency, the invoice should use the seller's currency. However, the buyer's currency (or that of another selected third country) should be used for invoicing when the buyer is in a hard currency but the seller is in a soft currency. When both the buyer and the seller are in soft currencies, they should consider a third currency as an alternative, but if both are in hard currencies, it may not matter much whether the buyer's currency or the seller's currency is employed. Note that these invoicing strategies apply also to an MNC's subsidiaries that trade with one another. Furthermore, when the volume justifies the cost, the MNC should coordinate the invoicing activities by setting up a reinvoicing center.

Pass-through costs

Domestic firms should not expect to improve their performance solely on the basis of foreign competitors' misfortunes (i.e., appreciation of foreign

Table 19.1 How foreign exchange products compare

Product	Who arranges	Credit line required	Margin required	Front-end premium	When valuation occurs	Extent of limitation of risk	Type of taxation	Minimum size	Ease of offset	Need for in-house supervision
Borrow the foreign currency	Bank	Yes	No	No	Periodic	Both directions (upside and downside)	Ordinary	Effectively none[1]	Easy	Yes
Foreign exchange forward	Bank	Yes	No	No	Maturity	Both directions	Capital gains	Effectively none[1]	Difficult	No
Swap	Bank	Yes	No	No	Periodic (settlement)	Both directions	Ordinary	Effectively none[1]	Difficult	No
Over-the-counter (OTC) option	Bank	No	No	Yes	Maturity	One direction	(Review)	Effectively none[1]	Easy	No
Hybrid: Buy one OTC option, sell another	Bank	Yes	No	No	Maturity	Within a range only, then unlimited	(Review)	Effectively none[1]	Easy	No
Hybrid: Collar	Bank	Yes	No	No	Maturity	Risk, within a range, then	Capital gains	Effectively none[1]	Difficulty or easy	No
Exchange options: on physicals	Exchange	No	No	Yes	Maturity	One direction	(Review)	Fixed by exchange	Easy	Possibly
on futures	Exchange	No	No	Yes	Maturity	One direction	Capital gains	Fixed by exchange	Easy	Possibly
Futures	Exchange	No	Yes	No	Daily	Both directions	Capital gains	Fixed by exchange	Easy	Yes

Note
1 Although less than $1 million is rare.

Source: Joe stein, "Forex Products Treasures Like," Futures (December 1988): 35. Reprinted from Futures magazine, 219 Parkade, P.O. Box 6, Cedar Falls, Iowa 50613.

competitors' currency). After all, foreign firms are still in a position to decide how much of the cost increase to pass on to buyers. Regarding the gap in percentage terms between the appreciation in the value of each country's currency measured in dollars and the price of its exports measured in dollars, Japan passed on far less of its currency-induced cost increases. Specifically, Japan passed on only 53 percent of its currency-induced price increases and left a large 47 percent gap between the increase in its dollar-measured costs and the dollar price of its exports. In the case of the United Kingdom, it passed on more than the currency appreciation by 10 percent and almost exactly its labor cost increases. Germany, in contract, passed on 100 percent of its currency increases, resulting in a 0 percent gap. However, Germany passed on 83 percent of its labor cost increases, leaving a 17 percent labor cost gap.[26]

Other strategies

Hedging techniques are not adequate in managing long-term exposure for foreign exchange risk. Other production and marketing strategies should be considered. This is exactly what Oki Electric Industry Co. Ltd. did to cope with the yen's rapid appreciation in 1993. The company shifted production of high-export-ratio products overseas. It built another production plant in Thailand for printer components and also planned to increase overseas procurement.

Renault, a French car maker, believes that geographic diversification is a natural hedge. The assumption is that the many currencies will balance each other out. This assumption, however, may be occasionally debatable. Renault itself lost $108 million in one quarter in 1992 due partly to the sharp devaluations of the British and Italian currencies.[27]

Globalization offers protection from currency fluctuations. One study confirmed that exchange rate uncertainty, while having a negative effect on capacity expansions by domestic companies, has no effect on investment by multinational firms. Evidently, multinational corporations can manage exchange rate uncertainty better than domestic firms because they are able to shift their production among different countries to minimize the effects of uncertainty.[28]

In the late 1980s, Komatsu was hit hard by the strong yen. To solve this problem, this Japanese firm established strategic alliances overseas to shift production abroad. Komatsu has a joint venture with Dresser Industries in the USA while being linked in Europe with Hanomag, which has 20 percent of the German wheel-loader and bulldozer market. In addition to its ties with Korea's Samsung Shipbuilding and Heavy Industries, Komatsu imports sheet metal parts from its Indonesian joint venture and has a long-standing agreement with Robbins, a US firm, on underground machinery.

Japanese multinationals have demonstrated how they have been able to cope – painfully but successfully – with the strong yen. In the early 1980s, Japan's net foreign assets were only $25 billion. The overseas stake should exceed $1 trillion at the end of the century. These assets should earn Japan a large amount of profits, dividends, and interest.

Japanese exporters have responded to the surging yen by sacrificing profit margins in order to hold the line on export prices in real terms. They have accelerated their direct investment in nearby Asia to capitalize on low cost labor. At the same time they have shifted production at home from commodity-type products to high-value quality products. In addition, geographic diversification has allowed Japanese firms to soften losses due to yen appreciations.

Finally, it should be pointed out that an exporter's overvalued currency may still have some unintended benefits. Japanese firms have been able to use their overvalued yen to buy raw materials from abroad at a lower cost, thus reducing their manufacturing costs. Furthermore, the adverse currency movement may allow a company to show market commitment while gaining market share.

CONCLUSION

This chapter, although somewhat technical in nature, has covered various financial circumstances related to international marketing. Borrowing money is one thing, but exchanging money is another matter altogether. There have been, there are, and there always will be dreadful accounts about how companies were caught short by the devaluation of a currency. For decades, authorities have debated the merits of the various competing currency exchange systems. Although no single system is able to eliminate completely the volatility of rate movements, there is at present no superior alternative to the system of managed floating rates.

Regardless of the exchange rate system used, rate changes are almost always a certainty, and thus some degree of risk is inevitable. Because MNCs have no determination with regard to the exchange systems – fixed or floating rates – they must attempt to reduce their foreign exchange exposure. To hedge, multinationals may consider any one of the following markets: spot, forward, futures, options, and brokers' services. Other alternatives may include using adjustable prices and billing in strong currencies.

Due to the varying rates of inflation among countries, the impact of inflation on the value of the currency cannot be overlooked. For companies with assets in a high-inflation country, the value of their assets can be substantially and adversely affected. Yet MNCs can benefit from inflation if they know how to borrow money wisely. With regard to the timing of payment, money managers should lead in soft currencies and lag in stronger currencies. For an MNC with subsidiaries in many countries, reinvoicing is a well-advised strategy.

In spite of an increasing number of techniques believed to minimize foreign exchange exposure, it is premature to expect that the methods discussed here are all the techniques that corporate managers can employ. With trends indicating movement toward further deregulation in an increasingly complex world of financial activities, it is just a matter of time before new strategies are created to manage exchange risks.

CASE 19.1 UPS AND DOWNS: A FOREIGN EXCHANGE SIMULATION GAME

What goes up must come down. This applies to most currencies as well. The up and down movements greatly and eventually affect what consumers have to pay or are willing to pay for imported products.

For an international marketer, the effect of foreign exchange rate changes on operations and pricing is unavoidable. The marketer must estimate *how much* the value of a currency will go up or down and predict *when* the movement will occur. This, to say the least, is not an easy task, and it perplexes even the most experienced money manager. The marketer may be wrong about the direction of the move. Even if the guess is right, the timing may be off. The marketer may thus initiate a move too soon or too late. Without the right timing, the marketer may begin to question the decision concerning the direction.

Assuming that the marketer made the right decisions on the direction and timing, he or she still has to consider the *magnitude of change*. Or the marketer may think that the currency has moved enough and then begins to hedge or remove the hedge. In other words, there are short-term and long-term trends. They may move together or move in the opposite direction. In effect, it is more than just making one basic decision. Every day (or even every minute) poses a new situation requiring a decision about whether the action is necessary.

Assume you are going to export your products to both Japan and Germany, and assume that the value of the merchandise is $100,000 for each country. You will receive payments in Japanese yen and euro respectively in three months. Your net profit margin is 5 percent. Consult the exchange rates for today by looking up the information in a daily newspaper. One convenient method is to consider the currency futures tables that may be found in the the *Wall Street Journal* and many daily newspapers. The *Wall Street Journal* and *New York Times* also provide options information (simply consider the nearby month as a benchmark). It should be noted that the sizes of the currency contracts are the same for both futures and options.

Points to consider

1 Since you will receive payments in three months, do you think that there is any need to hedge your exposure?

2 Assuming that hedging is desirable, what is your hedging preference: cash, forward, futures, or options?

3 Do you want to hedge both the Japanese yen and euro?

4 When do you want to hedge? (NB: You can hedge at any time within three months.)

5 Consider the exchange rates at the end of the three-month period and see how the profit from the sale of your products is affected by the rate changes as determined by your decisions.

QUESTIONS

1 Explain how inflation and nationalism make it impossible for a single global currency to exist.

2 Why do companies involved in international trade have to hedge their foreign exchange exposure?

3 Distinguish between the spot market and the forward market.

4 Should an exporter use the spot rate or forward rate for quotation?

5 Is devaluation good for exports and imports? Why is the impact of devaluation usually not immediate?

6 Explain how these exchange rate systems function: (1) gold standard, (b) par value, (c) crawling peg, (d) wide band, and (e) floating.

7 How does a clean float differ from a dirty float?

8 How can an MNC hedge or cover its foreign exchange exposure?

9 How does the forward market differ from the futures and options markets?

10 How does inflation affect a country's currency value? Is it a good idea to borrow or obtain financing in a country with high inflation?

11 What are leading and lagging, and how should they be employed with regard to payment and collection?

DISCUSSION ASSIGNMENTS AND MINICASES

1 Should the world abolish all local currencies except the US dollar, which would function as a global currency?

2 Should the world adopt a basket of the five or ten leading currencies (e.g., US dollar, Japanese yen, Swiss franc) as a global currency for international trade?

3 Should European firms insist on the euro for all buying as well as selling transactions?

4 Japan has aggressively pursued the lower yen value. Is this strategy good for Japan?

5 Should the USA abandon the float in favor of the gold standard or some other type of fixed or semifixed system?

6 Both fixed and floating rates claim to promote exchange rate stability while controlling inflation. Is it possible for these two divergent systems to achieve the same goals?

7 How should an MNC reduce its foreign exchange risks?

8 Honda was the first of the Japanese car makers to manufacture its cars in Ohio for the US market. The success of its assembly plant in Marysville (Ohio) led to a second Ohio plant. Honda also began exporting its cars from the American plant to Japan. Mazda and Mitsubishi followed suit. Other Japanese companies that export or plan to export products or components made in the USA to Japan include Hitachi, Yamaha, Fujitsu, and Sony. Politically and financially, what are the benefits of (a) manufacturing cars in the USA for US consumption, and (b) exporting cars to Japan?

9   International travelers often wonder why it is necessary to have so many different currencies. Obviously it would be preferable to have just one worldwide currency that could be used anywhere on Earth. After all, the fifty states of the USA use the US dollar, and most members of the European Union use the euro. If the euro can replace the mark, franc, and others, it should also be theoretically possible to have a single world currency. If not, at the least, the big three currencies (the US dollar, euro, and yen) should fix the exchange rates among themselves, preferably at the rates of $1, €1, and ¥100. These currencies could form a common monetary policy that serves as the anchor for the world price level.

Nobel Prize economist Robert Mundell has been advocating a new world currency that merges the dollar, euro, and yen. All currencies will then be converted into this international money. The supply of this currency will be supervised by an international board, and monetary gains from its issue will be split along the IMF quotas. As suggested by Mundell, the name of the world currency should be the *dey* (dollar, euro, yen) or perhaps the *intor*.

Is it practical to create and introduce the world currency as envisioned? Assess the likelihood of success of this universal currency.

NOTES

1   Robert D. Laurent, "Is There a Role for Gold in Monetary Policy?" *Economic Perspectives* (March/April 1994): 2–14.

2   Jack L. Hervey, "Europe at the Crossroads," *Chicago Fed Letter*, August 1993, 1–3.

3   "Turkish Lira Plummets in Economic Crisis," *San José Mercury News*, February 22, 2001.

4   "A New Stability in Mexico's Economy," *Business Week*, November 7, 1994, 26.

5   "Dollar Doldrums Alone Won't Force the Fed to Tighten," *Business Week*, July 11, 1994; "The Unloved Buck," *Wall Street Journal*, June 27, 1994.

6   "Study Examines Effectiveness of Foreign Exchange Market Intervention," *IMF Survey*, March 22, 1993, 82–3.

7   "A New Way of Looking at Exchange Rate Regimes," *IMF Survey*, November 4, 2002, 344–5.

8   "In Brief," *Finance & Development* (September 2002): 3.

9   "A New Way."

10 "Alan Blinder Draws Seven Key Lessons for International Finance from Tumultuous 1990s," *IMF Survey*, November 20, 2000, 383–4.

11 Judy Shelton, *Money Meltdown: Restoring Order to the Global Currency System* (New York, NY: Free Press, 1994).

12 Michael Spencer, "Book Review," *Finance & Development* (March 1995): 53.

13 Laurent, "Role for Gold."

14 Peter J. Quirk and Hernan Cortes-Douglas, "The Experience with Floating Rates," *Finance & Development* (June 1993): 28–31.

15 "Have Asian Crisis Countries Reverted to Precrisis Exchange Rate Practices?" *IMF Survey*, February 25, 2002, 56–9.

16 Andrew Berg and Catherine Pattillo, *The Challenge of Predicting Economic Crises, Economic Issues No. 22* (International Monetary Fund), 2000.

17 "Early Warning Systems: Fad or Reality?" *IMF Survey*, November 12, 2001, 347–8.

18 James T. Moser, "A Good Hedge Keeps Dogs Off the Yard," *Chicago Fed Letter* (November 1989).

19 Jonathan Batten, Robert Mellor, and Victor Wan, "Foreign Exchange Risk Management Practices and

Products Used by Australian Firms," *Journal of International Business Studies* 24 (No. 3, 1993): 557–73.

20 Batten *et al.*, "Foreign Exchange Risk Management."

21 Jon Stein, "Forex Products Treasurers Like," *Futures* (December 1988): 34–6.

22 Kurt R. Jesswein, Chuck C.Y. Kwok, and William R. Folks, Jr., "Corporate Use of Innovative Foreign Exchange Risk Management Products," *Columbia Journal of World Business* 30 (fall 1995): 70- 82.

23 "Perils of the Hedge Highwire," *Business Week*, October 26, 1998, 74ff.; "Business Won't Hedge the Euro Way," *Business Week*, December 4, 2000, 157.

24 Christos Pantzalis, Betty J. Simkins, and Paul A. Laux, "Operational Hedges and the Foreign Exchange Exposure of US Multinational Corporations," *Journal of International Business Studies* 32 (fourth quarter, 2001): 793–812.

25 "Toyota Tells U.K. Suppliers to Use Euros," *San José Mercury News*, August 11, 2000.

26 Steven Strongin and Jack L. Hervey, "The Dollar Can Only Do so Much," *Chicago Fed Letter* (October 1989).

27 "A Garden of Hedges," *Business Week*, April 19, 1993, 96–7.

28 Jose Manuel Campa, "Multinational Investment under Uncertainty in the Chemical Processing Industries," *Journal of International Business Studies* 25 (No. 3, 1994): 557–78.

Index

COUNTRY/CITY INDEX

NAME INDEX

SUBJECT INDEX